By the same author

DE GAULLE
THE RULER 1945–1970

DE GAULLE
THE REBEL 1890–1944

JEAN LACOUTURE was Foreign Editor of *Le Monde* (1957–75) and a Director of the Parisian publishing house, Le Seuil (1961–81). His many books include biographies of André Malraux (1971), Léon Blum (1977), François Mauriac (1980) and Pierre Mendès France (1981).

PATRICK O'BRIAN has translated works by Simone de Beauvoir, André Maurois and Jacques Soustelle. He is the distinguished novelist and is also the author of biographies of Picasso and Sir Joseph Banks.

DE GAULLE

THE REBEL
1890–1944

Jean Lacouture

Translated from the French
by Patrick O'Brian

HARVILL
An Imprint of HarperCollins*Publishers*

First published in France 1984 as
De Gaulle: Le Rebelle 1890–1944 by
Editions du Seuil

This abridged version first published in English 1990 by
Collins Harvill

This paperback edition first published 1993 by
Harvill
An Imprint of HarperCollins*Publishers*,
77–85 Fulham Palace Road,
Hammersmith, London W6 8JB

2 4 6 8 9 7 5 3 1

ISBN 0-00-271288-1

Printed and bound in Great Britain by
Hartnolls Limited, Bodmin, Cornwall

Contents

*PUBLISHER'S NOTE: Sources are given in the notes at the back of the book; footnotes are the author's unless supplied by the translator, when they are indicated thus: (trs.).

Preface

The Rebel, the first of three volumes of biography which I have devoted to General de Gaulle, appears here in its English edition with light cuts that disturb neither the balance nor the spirit of the original.

Much to my regret the publishers have found it necessary to condense the subsequent volumes, *The Politician* and *The Sovereign*, into a single volume, *The Ruler*. This cannot but affect the sense, in view of the fact that the book concerns a personality as complex and "controversial" as Charles de Gaulle.

JEAN LACOUTURE
June 1990

Acknowledgements

With the publication of the second volume, *The Ruler*, the author will acknowledge his debt of thanks to all those who have consented to meet him or who have helped him. In the meantime, he expresses his gratitude to those who have helped him with his researches or who have very kindly read or clarified the manuscript: Catherine Grünblatt, Marie-Christine Gerber, Dominique Miollan, Martine Tardieu, Paul Flamand, Georges Bris, Jacques Nobécourt and Jean-Claude Guillebaud.

The author and publishers are grateful to the copyright holders for permission to reprint the following copyright material:*

from *The Second World War*, Vol. II, *Their Finest Hour* by Sir Winston Churchill. Copyright 1949 by Houghton Mifflin Company. Copyright © renewed 1976 by Lady Spencer Churchill, The Honourable Lady Sarah Audley, The Honourable Lady Soames. Reprinted by permission of Curtis Brown, London, and Houghton Mifflin Company, Boston, MA, on behalf of the Estate of Sir Winston Churchill.

from *The Second World War*, Vol. III, *The Grand Alliance* by Sir Winston Churchill. Copyright 1950 by Houghton Mifflin Company. Copyright © renewed 1977 by Lady Spencer Churchill, The Honourable Lady Sarah Audley, The Honourable Lady Soames. Reprinted by permission of Curtis Brown, London, and Houghton Mifflin Company, Boston, MA, on behalf of the Estate of Sir Winston Churchill.

from *The Second World War*, Vol. IV, *The Hinge of Fate*, by Sir Winston Churchill. Copyright 1950 by Houghton Mifflin Company. Copyright © renewed 1977 by Lady Spencer Churchill, The Honourable Lady Sarah Audley, The Honourable Lady Soames. Reprinted by permission of Curtis Brown, London, and Houghton Mifflin Company, Boston, MA, on behalf of the Estate of Sir Winston Churchill.

from *The Blast of War* by Harold Macmillan. Copyright © 1967, 1968, by Thomson Newspapers Ltd. Reprinted by permission of Macmillan, London, and Harper & Row, Publishers, Inc., New York.

from *Roosevelt and Hopkins: an Intimate History* by Robert E. Sherwood. Copyright 1948, 1950, by Robert E. Sherwood. Reprinted by permission of Harper & Row, Publishers, Inc., New York.

from *Diplomat among Warriors* by R. Murphy. Copyright © R. Murphy, 1964. Reprinted by Permission of Brandt & Brandt, Literary Agents, Inc., New York.

from *Crusade in Europe* by D. Eisenhower. Copyright © D. Eisenhower 1949. Reprinted by permission of Doubleday, a division of Bantam, Doubleday, Dell Publishing Group Inc., New York.

from *Churchill and De Gaulle* by Dr F. Kersaudy. Copyright © Dr F. Kersaudy 1981. Reprinted by permission of HarperCollins Publishers Ltd., London.

from *Footprints in Time* by J. Colville. Copyright © J. Colville 1976. Reprinted by permission of HarperCollins Publishers Ltd, London.

from *The Times*, 8 June 1940. Copyright Times Newspapers Limited, 1940. Reprinted by permission of Times Newspapers Limited, London.

from the *Sunday Times*, July 1940. Copyright © Times Newspapers Limited, London, 1940. Reprinted by permission of Times Newspapers Limited, London.

*A full bibliography will be given in volume two, *The Ruler*.

I

THE IDEA

CHAPTER ONE

The Star

The year was 1905. Kaiser William II's landing at Tangier had made Europe shudder; and as Charles Péguy wrote, it opened "a new epoch in the history of my life, in the history of this country, and undoubtedly in the history of the world." In Paris, at the Jesuit college of the Immaculée-Conception, a fifteen-year-old boy named Charles de Gaulle, inspired perhaps by this event but without mentioning it, wrote this unusual account in a small brown notebook:

> In 1930 Europe, angered by the government's ill will and insolence, declared war on France. Three German armies crossed the Vosges. The command of the strongest army was entrusted to General von Manteuffel. The Field-Marshal Prince Frederick Charles [of Prussia] took the head of the second. In France everything was very rapidly organized.
>
> General de Gaulle was placed at the head of 200 000 men and 518 guns; General de Boisdeffre commanded an army of 150 000 men and 510 guns. On 10 February the armies took the field. De Gaulle quickly fixed upon his plan: he was first to save Nancy, then join hands with Boisdeffre and crush the Germans before they could unite, which would certainly have been disastrous for us.[1]

And so on for twenty pages. This schoolboy in a general's hat described the conflict with astonishing exactness and authority – a conflict that he had taken care to place at a time when he would be the age of Napoleon at Wagram.

Even in the middle of his adolescence Charles de Gaulle saw himself at the head of the armies of France. Taking precedence over a Boisdeffre, the inheritor of one of the most considerable names in French military history, he defied Manteuffel and Frederick Charles, manoeuvring regiments and batteries with the skill of a second Maurice de Saxe. It could be said that in these days there were thousands of boys of fifteen who knew the order of battle at Austerlitz by heart who at some time or another took themselves for Turenne or Chanzy.* But what boy among them all, in an educational system which stressed the graduations of rank more than any other and in which humility was looked upon as a virtue of the strong, would have dared to offer his Jesuit schoolmasters so very striking a self-portrait?

At fifteen Charles de Gaulle already saw himself, already knew himself, as General de Gaulle. He saved Nancy, marched upon Strasburg, besieged Metz,

*Two legendary French generals: Turenne of the seventeenth century, Chanzy of the nineteenth. (trs.)

preserved the unfortunate Boisdeffre from disaster, bullied the government and drove it on, addressed Europe. Already he possessed that sense of symbol and gesture which was to make him the most dramatic of all public men in French history.

Just what did these premonitions amount to? Twenty-five years later, writing his *Le Fil de l'épée*,* Charles de Gaulle took care to let us know: "Is not that which Alexander called his 'hope', Caesar 'his fortune' and Napoleon 'his star' simply the certainty that a particular gift placed them in such close relations with reality that they could always master it?" Reality, or what strength of mind turns it into? In any event the "certainty" was emphatically there, and the "gift". One never becomes anything other than what one is. Imagination, energy, circumstances, do the rest.

Charles-André-Joseph-Marie de Gaulle was born between three and four o'clock in the morning of 22 November 1890 at his grandmother's house in Lille. He was the third child and the second son of Henri de Gaulle and Jeanne Maillot.** The child was christened two days later in the nearby parish church of Saint-André, a rather fine Carmelite building in the baroque style. The godmother was his aunt Lucie Maillot and the godfather his uncle Gustave de Corbie, a teacher at the Institut Catholique.

We must pause for a moment to consider these geographical facts rather than the particular middle-class aspects of the matter such as the highly respectable district in which the rue Princesse lay, the "good form" of the house, the beauty of the garden behind it, and the statuette of Notre-Dame-de-la-Foi in a niche on the façade of the courtyard.

But how far should one emphasize Lille, this place of his birth? In his *Mémoires de guerre* de Gaulle describes himself as "a little Lillois in Paris", a statement that draws him more distinctly towards the Nord than if he had written "a little Parisian from Lille".*** When they are asked today, Charles de Gaulle's relatives usually minimize the General's bonds with the Nord, and it is easy for them to do so by pointing out that the de Gaulles had been Parisians for four generations, whereas the General spent only the first weeks of his life at Lille.

But the Maillots, for their part, were most emphatically Lillois, and although one may be a de Gaulle one is nevertheless primarily one's mother's son. Lille was not only his cradle. It was also the capital of a region whose threatened frontier became a life-long obsession, a region in which he passed his holidays either in the rue Princesse, where the children came back for Easter and at the end of the summer, or at Wimereux, where their grandmother took a villa for them and their Corbie and Droulers cousins in August; a region in which he chose to begin his military career, at Arras; and finally a region in which he found a wife, at Calais.

This indwelling influence of the Nord was one of the essential factors in the General's being. As Paul-Marie de La Gorce expresses it so well, "All his life

Le Fil de l'épée was de Gaulle's book on military thought. See Chapter Seven. (trs.)
**The elder brother was Xavier; then came Marie-Agnès. (trs.)
***Lille is the capital of the department of the Nord. (trs.)

long, when he called to mind the French nation it was the people of the north of the country that he saw. When he spoke to the French, it was the French of the Nord that he had in mind."[2] That is to say, when he was thinking kindly of his countrymen. When he growled, "The French are clods,"* he was thinking more of those south of the Loire.** When, between June 1940 and April 1969, he called them to resistance or to reason, it was above all the others he was speaking to, the France of coffee rather than the France of wine. And this in spite of the strongly unified sense he had of the French community – from an historical point of view more than a geographical, perhaps.

A man of the Nord, then, who would be happy only in squalls; who would choose his house on the road by which the Frankish warriors came, blown by the wind of the great plains; who loathed the "gentle hills", what was called "la douce France", the self-indulgent living, the snug side of the southerners and their too-easy cordiality. A man of heavy weather, like that which he had known on the strand at Wimereux, when Henri de Gaulle, looking for his children, had to hold his top-hat with both hands. A man of storms, who as a writer continually turned to nautical metaphors, and who, on the eve of the great Algerian convulsion, with a kind of voracious laugh cried out to his ministers, "Hang on tight to the mast: she's going to roll!"

A Parisian too, however, like all those de Gaulles since that Jean-Baptiste who was an attorney in the court of parliament in the days of Maupeou.*** A Parisian of the seventh arrondissement, that capital of warriors, priests and jurists which stretches from the Champ-de-Mars to the Invalides and from Saint-François-Xavier to Sainte-Clotilde, the citadel of virtue and study, of arms and of the law – where Rodin rose up to add the arts. In these streets, these avenues, there is not a shop, not a bank, not a place of trade, except for a few cafés which allowed retired soldiers to confront one another in learned retrospective battles and colonels' sons to meet generals' daughters over a glass of lime-blossom tea.

De Gaulle's Paris was like Peking, or the Berlin of the beginning of the century or the Washington of the mid-nineteenth century – a city entirely given over to administration and to learning, a mandarin's city in which of the Three Estates only two were busy: the clergy and the nobilities of the legal robe, of science and of the sword. A community of churches, hospitals and barracks, of splendid gardens and hidden convents, where on the occasion of an election, that ultimate extravagance of the republican regime, the polling-booths saw the arrival, after High Mass, of long lines of monks and friars and cohorts of grizzled warriors in dark suits.

Paris, yes. But a Paris that was neither "gay" nor of commerce; not Zola's Paris, nor Offenbach's, nor even the Paris of Baron Haussmann. A Paris which, to paraphrase Pascal, was "only the capital of France", of a certain spiritual, organizing and military France that sprang fully armed from the brain of Henri de Gaulle's second son.

*The original is *veaux*. (trs.)
**As we shall see, he made some harsh remarks about towns in the south.
***Maupeou (1714–92) was made Chancellor of France in 1768 by Louis XV. (trs.)

When he came to write about this country of his birth de Gaulle said that in those days "France cultivated its melancholy, while at the same time it relished its wealth". Wealth and melancholy were certainly there. But France was nevertheless the centre of immense expectation. As the sociologist, Gustave Le Bon, one of the real masters of the day, said in his *Evolution des peuples*, "We are in one of those periods of history in which for a moment the heavens remain empty. From this fact alone, the world must change."

An age comparable to that of the Enlightenment? Yes, by antithesis: individualism, democracy and positivism, about to reach their highest point during the Dreyfus case, were already being undermined by those currents that Zeev Sternhell describes so powerfully in *La Droite révolutionnaire*[3]: the cult of violence, the mobilization of crowds, the decay of intellectualism, the upwelling of the subconscious. Of course the parts the actors had to play was not yet decided. The man who meant to defend the individual and the law called them both subtly in question; the man who worked for the overthrow of the radical republic was undermining the foundations of the positive intelligence upon which he claimed to build the future; the man who aimed at placing socialism at the service of nationalism only obscured the one by the other. It was a general confusion, this first rehearsal, in a still dark theatre, of an enormous tragedy of which the rise of European socialism and the opposition of the imperialisms in their various national forms were no more than the preludes.

A feverish time, a fertile time. Cézanne, Debussy and Claudel were on the threshold. Marx and Nietzsche were knocking at the door; but so were Drumont and Sorel,* the militants of the "cercle Proudhon". That tragic couple who were to ferment antisemitism in its modern form and to unleash a workers' populism so scornful of the law. And already Georges Vacher de Lapouge, the ideologist of naked ferocity, the true forerunner of Nazism, was pouring out his doctrine at the university of Montpellier.

The child Charles de Gaulle was not, as Flaubert said of Hannibal, "clothed with the indefinable splendour of those who are destined for great undertakings". But the outlines of his character stood out very soon. Marie-Agnès, his very attentive elder sister, knew him perhaps better than anyone else, and with whom he had to take less care of what he said than in the presence of his parents:

> Charles was rather a difficult child. My father had a great deal of authority over him but my mother, on the other hand, had none whatsoever. He never obeyed her at any time. I remember a scene of his one day at Wimereux, at the house of an uncle. He must have been about seven. Charles said to our mother, "Maman, I should like to ride the pony." "No, you rode yesterday." "Then I'm going to be naughty." And straight away he threw his toys on the ground, shouted, cried, stamped.

*Edouard Drumont (1844–1917), was an anti-semitic writer and journalist; Georges Sorel (1847–1922) was the author of *Reflections on Violence* (1908), a widely read anarcho-syndicalist manifesto. (trs.)

Another time Charles was flinging books at Pierre's head.* The bedroom door was locked and he would not open it for our mother, who wanted to come in, being anxious about Pierre's crying. He was pugnacious, unruly and much given to teasing. When I was ten I was the big sister** who defended the little ones against Charles: Jacques was three years younger than he and Pierre six. One day when Charles was playing with us my father called him. "Charles, are you being good?" "Yes, Papa." "You are not bullying Jacques?" "No, Papa." "Nor Pierre?" "No, Papa." "Well then, here are two sous so that you will go on being kind to your brothers."[4]

Charles liked every kind of game – diabolo, croquet, flying a kite, playing ball, blind-man's buff. And he very often played with tin soldiers with his brothers. Xavier was the King of England and commanded the English forces; Jean de Corbie, our cousin, was Emperor of Russia, Charles was always the King of France and he always had the French army under his orders. There was never any question that it should be otherwise. He would summon Jacques: "You're the King of the Mysterious Island", and Pierre, "You're the Pope and you're in command of the Papal Guard!"

My father always made the five of us work during the holidays. Charles did fairly well. It was at school that he did no work (though from time to time he would be first in French and history). He didn't learn his German and he didn't always hand in his homework. What he really liked was writing poems and reading. When we were little we used to look at the Epinal pictures of *La Vie des saints* and *L'Histoire sainte*; we would gaze at them for hours on end – the martyrs delivered up to wild beasts, Jonah who had spent three days in the belly of a whale, Joseph sold by his brothers, the tower of Babel, Noah's ark.

The de Gaulle children, who had a subscription to the *Journal des voyages*, also read, like everyone else of their age, *Sans famille*, *Robinson Crusoe* and *The Swiss Family Robinson*, *The Last of the Mohicans*, *La Prairie*, *Le Trappeur de l'Arkansas* and *L'Héritier de Charlemagne*.

Oh, what a man our father was! Witty, charming, wonderful. He knew how to talk to children on their own level. He used to sing rounds with us, and he taught us traditional songs. During the holidays, in the Nord, he often took us to the pastry-cook's and there we ate quantities of cakes. Then he would say "Confess", and we would admit the number we had taken. He also used to say, "Every time you take a cake, you save a sou." (Because cakes cost three sous each in Paris and only two in the Nord.) We were not very fond of going for walks, except with him. He would say "Fall in by the door", and we would set out happily, gathered round him. During our walk we would stop at the country ale-houses to eat cheese and drink cider or beer.

Henri de Gaulle's grandchildren still remember his very great kindness, his lively

*The youngest of the brothers.
**Two years older than Charles.

good nature and his gift for teaching, particularly the children of Marie-Agnès, with whom he spent the last years of his life at Le Havre, in the thirties, always benign, ready for anything, full of consideration, highly cultured, amusing himself by solving problems in mathematics as though they were crossword puzzles.

Although memories of Wimereux and Lille recur so often in Marie-Agnès' reminiscences, the de Gaulle children were not systematically confined to the Nord. In the last days of the century their father had bought a house near Nontron in the Dordogne for a song; it was called La Ligerie and it was an old place built for some rural notability, and its solid rounded masonry dovecote gave it something of the look of a turreted manor buried among its trees. They set off for La Ligerie in the middle of July, to stay a full month. And there, under the great trees and in the coppices, "King Charles" did not confine himself to making his brothers carry out manoeuvres: he called up the children of the neighbourhood, to form the perfect infantrymen for the great plans of the twelve-year-old strategist.

In Paris Henri de Gaulle liked taking his children to the Arc de Triomphe or to Napoleon's tomb in the Invalides, and sometimes, on a Sunday, as far as Le Bourget or Stains, where he had fought during the last months of 1870. By way of celebrating Charles's birthday, he took him to see one of the first performances of *L'Aiglon*.* The confrontation of Sarah Bernhardt and Lucien Guitry left an indelible impression on Charles's adolescent mind.

The few cuffs exchanged between the brothers and the demands of this imperious little boy had practically no effect on the affectionate, equable atmosphere in which Charles passed his childhood. He was not the cleverest of Henri de Gaulle's children. Xavier, the oldest boy, seemed much more gifted. He became, it may be added, an engineer in the government Department of Mines before being Consul-General at Geneva.

Jacques, the third son, was also an engineer: but this was before he fell victim to a sleeping sickness epidemic that entirely paralysed him at the age of thirty. He was bed-ridden, dumb and racked with pain for twenty years; and perhaps he was the brother most loved by Charles, who seems to have suffered almost as much from Jacques' infirmity as from that which some years later was to strike his own child, the third. As for Pierre, he was to be found at the General's side in 1944, the president of the Paris municipal council, senator for the Seine, and lastly Deputy for Paris.

No one could bear witness to the efficacity of the various forms of Catholic education in France at the turn of the century more than Charles de Gaulle: he was taught first by the Christian Brothers, then by the Jesuits of the Collège de l'Immaculée Conception, then by those of Antoing in Belgium, and finally by the masters of the Collège Stanislas.

In October 1900 Charles de Gaulle went on to the college where his father was to become prefect of studies, to work in the sixth form, the form in which the boys began to learn Latin. In the photograph taken before the school broke up for the winter holidays he is to be seen in the third row, looking somewhat retiring,

**L'Aiglon* and *Cyrano de Bergerac* are the two celebrated plays of Edmond Rostand (1868–1914). (trs.)

obviously intimidated, his neck rising from a kind of Claudine collar. And he was not yet very tall for his age.

Yet a photograph taken eighteen months later shows that Charles de Gaulle did possess a certain character. On 31 May 1902, to celebrate the head-master's birthday, the boys put on a little musical comedy written by one Auguste Thibault and called *Pages et Ménestrels*. The main character was Philip Augustus, King of France: it was agreed that the part should be given to the young de Gaulle, who did not have to be asked twice – he was used to the role, from Wimereux to La Ligerie. This was his first referendum. Charles, crowned, wrapped in a velvet cloak and with an imposing Maltese cross on his chest, had a not inconsiderable air.

The painter Roger Wild, a contemporary, speaks of him in the playground, unmoved by the hail of various objects that the little boys threw at any of the seniors who passed within range. Another of his companions states that he was quite good at football: "He shot really very well. It was always de Gaulle who took the penalty-kicks. But he often used to carry the whistle, too. He was already fond of being the referee."[5]

Until he reached the second form, which he did at fourteen, Charles de Gaulle was only an average pupil – so much so that his father threatened him with a wide variety of punishments if he did not follow his elder brother's example – but a year later he asserted himself as the top boy of the class. The prize-list of July 1906 has been preserved, and in it he is mentioned ten times; with six first prizes (particularly in French composition, mathematics, history and geography) one second and three *proxime accessits*: he was far and away the most outstanding pupil in that year.

Why this sudden change? Because from that time onwards he had formed a very specific ambition: he was determined to sit the examination for Saint-Cyr.* His father reminded him that for success it was not enough to recite the set pieces from French History. He acknowledged the truth of this and set about preparing himself for the future trial with the energy which from this time onwards he showed in everything he undertook. "Suddenly he became another boy," his sister remembered. "Easy to get along with and reasonable. Yes, everything was different." It was at this time that Charles de Gaulle wrote "a summit is not a crowded place".

In October 1907, three years after the law curtailing the influence of the Church in Education had been passed, Henri de Gaulle sent his second son to carry on with his schooling at the Collège du Sacré-Coeur at Antoing in Belgium, quite close to the French frontier. Charles, whose mind was already bent solely on preparing for the Saint-Cyr examination, chose the study of elementary mathematics. On 30 November he wrote to his father:[6]

> I have had a great misfortune this week. In the mathematics examination we had on the twentieth, I was twelfth. Then, since luck is not with me this month, I have just been marked second in physics and chemistry. I still read a great deal of history and natural history, and above all a great deal of German. They read us an account of the latest fighting on the Algerian

*The Ecole Speciale Militaire, the French Military Academy, was founded by Napoleon in 1808. (trs.)

> frontier. Lieutenant de Saint-Hilaire of the Tirailleurs,* who was killed in action, is the cousin of one of the boys here and it seems that he was an old boy of the rue des Postes.**

This is the letter of an ambitious, exacting, very hard-working pupil, ending with an interesting reference to the calling of arms, which obsessed him even in this Belgian retreat. The machinery was in place. It is also worth observing that the young man, when writing to his father, signed not only his Christian name but his surname as well, as though "Charles de Gaulle" was already something of a reference, a seal that had to be kept entire.

At the same time an eloquence asserted itself. Some of the words uttered by Charles de Gaulle in the name of his fellows on the occasion of a retreat organized by the Jesuit fathers at Notre-Dame-du-Haut-Mont have often been quoted: "The Jesuits' pupils are often reproached with having no character: we shall be able to prove that the reproach is unfounded. The future will have greatness, for it will be moulded by our deeds."

Charles spent the summer of 1908 in Germany, going from Baden to the Black Forest. He proved an enquiring, interested observer. He noted the number of killed in the 1870 war on the memorials: forty-one out of about one hundred men who had fought in one Baden village. He read the papers, observing that "the newspapers are quite hostile to us". And he ended, "Something has changed in Europe these last three years, and as I observe it I think of the unrest that comes before a great war." Not badly observed and stated for a seventeen-year-old schoolboy.

In October 1908 Charles de Gaulle went to the Collège Stanislas and there he was to prepare himself for the Saint-Cyr examination. In the rue Notre-Dame-des-Champs I found the "marks obtained by the pupil de Gaulle, Charles" from October 1908 to July 1909. Curiously enough they are higher when they refer to the daily lessons rather than to the examinations, in which the young man seems to lose his powers: in the first term he contrived to be no more than eighteenth out of twenty-nine, but in April he is to be seen in the third place and at the end of the year he was second. Let us quote from his masters' end of year report observations: "Charles is an excellent pupil, but he is becoming rather talkative and if this goes on it will lose him time. That would be a pity, because if he wishes, he is capable of brilliant success."

Several of his history papers for this year have been kept: history was his strong point. The most striking aspect of a seven-page essay on the 1871 Frankfurt Treaty is its remarkable evenness of tone. Even when he is speaking of the fate of the eastern provinces the young man does not think proper to raise his voice. He prefers to point out – not unjustifiably – that:

> The annexation of Alsace and Lorraine, apart from the fact that henceforward it created a cause of permanent hostility with France, compelled the Empire to engage in huge expenses and huge military sacrifices. Fur-

*The Tirailleurs were a reconnaissance regiment. (trs.)

**The school where de Gaulle's father was a teacher was in this street. (trs.)

thermore, the fifteen hundred thousand new German subjects in no way increased the power of their masters but on the other hand obliged them to make political and financial efforts whose end is still not in view.

It might have been an old Quai d'Orsay* hand speaking – if not one from the English Foreign Office. But this equanimity has its other side. It is paid for by an obvious flatness. The spirited writer who two years earlier spoke of the "next European war" in so breathless a style, is now satisfied with setting down observations based on reliable sources. Did he need the spur of imagination to shine?

He is more promising, more "himself" already (and in any case he was not yet eighteen), at least for the ideas if not for the style, in an exercise written on the subject of France at the time of the Consulate, an exercise that is a strong condemnation of Bonaparte's "absolute power". "The right of choosing the civil servants and deputies out of the list of notables entirely did away with the effects of universal suffrage." And the young de Gaulle was a supporter of the First Republic's foreign policy: "The revolutionary wars," he wrote in the same exercise, "had placed France in the first rank of European powers once more and had to a great extent repaired the disasters of Louis XV's reign."

Obsessed though he was at that time by an army career, Charles de Gaulle also believed that he was a poet and he endlessly wrote verse. His sister bears witness to this. At thirteen, she heard her mother threaten Charles with "tearing up his poems" if he were not less unbearable. Was she obliged to do so? None of these childhood rhymes have survived.

The first "work" of Charles de Gaulle is a piece that its author's subsequent fame has provided with an obviously excessive reputation. All those who pride themselves upon writing about de Gaulle feel obliged to deal with his "comic playlet", *Une mauvaise rencontre*. This rhyming fable written at fourteen was sent (by the boy himself?) to the jury of a literary competition; having singled it out, the jury offered the author either twenty-five francs or publication. Naturally de Gaulle chose fame over fortune and for a quarter of a century it was the sole entry of Charles de Gaulle in the catalogue of the Bibliothèque Nationale.

In the family it is said that Mme de Gaulle happened to chance upon the copies in her son's drawer: in any event, Charles and his cousin Jean de Corbie had acted *Une mauvaise rencontre* at home as early as the summer of 1905. Everything seems to show that it gave great pleasure. The sketch brings a jovial brigand on to the stage, and he, brandishing his pistols, robs a traveller.

> Some are born kings, others princes,
> Officers, judges, governors of provinces,
> This one will be born a carter, that a manufacturer,
> Still another a mason: I was born a brigand.

Une mauvaise rencontre reveals not so much character as an environment, a cultural climate and a fashion. This comic fable shows us less Charles than one of the

*The French Foreign Office, which is on the Quai d'Orsay in Paris, is usually referred to in this way. (trs.)

literary landscapes that he had to travel through, one of the stages in a journey of initiation that was soon to assume a more painful form.

From his days at the Collège Stanislas, we have a poem and a short story. Charles de Gaulle's personality scarcely shows through, but for all that the young man thought them important enough to sign, for an eventual publication, with a pseudonym, Charles de Lugale – transparent enough, however, for the authorship to be attributed to him.

The poem belongs to what might be called the literature of Saint-Cyr:

> Quand je devrai mourir, j'aimerais que ce soit
> Sur un champ de bataille.
> J'aimerais que ce soit le soir. Le jour mourant
> Donne à celui qui part un regret moins pesant
> Et lui fait un linceul de voiles
> Le soir! . . . Avec la nuit, la paix viendrait des cieux
> Et j'aurais en mourant dans le coeur et les yeux
> Le calme apaisant des étoiles.*

The influence of *Cyrano* and *l'Aiglon* are obvious here, but it is pleasant to see that this warrior enamoured of Rostand also yearned for a little sweetness. The sigh of a flute answers these trumpet-blasts.

"Charles de Lugale's" first story, called *Zalaina*, also belongs to this literature in uniform. A young officer of the colonial army meets a Melanesian beauty, Zalaina, in New Caledonia; she loves him enough to try to kill him, together with herself, when she thinks he has abandoned her. The arms of the crime are exotic flowers.

This young man of eighteen had not yet fashioned his style. Let us hear this account of his hero's awakening:

> . . . Beside my bed, Zalaina's naked corpse. Death had at least respected her features and her shape. I burst into tears, and this completed my recovery. The physician listened to the story of Zalaina, and nodding he said "She knew the extremely poisonous nature of these flowers. She thought that if she were to put you to death at the same time as herself, your two souls would join their ancestors and live together forever."

For the man to evolve from this adolescence, torn as he was between a showy cynicism and a very bookish kind of emotion, the upheavals of the era were demanded. Did the evacuation of Fashoda strike him very hard, as early as the age of eight?** Henri de Gaulle can be trusted to have tried even then to inspire his

*When I have to die, I should like it to be/On a battlefield./I should like it to be in the evening. The dying of the day/Gives the one who is leaving a less poignant sorrow/And makes him a shroud of mists/The evening! With the night peace would come from the sky/And in dying I should have in my heart and my eyes/The soothing calm of the stars. (trs.)

**In 1898 a group of French explorers claimed the village of Fashoda on the Upper Nile for France. Surrounded by British territory, their action provoked an Anglo-French crisis. Following British pressure and the intervention of Declassé, the French foreign minister, the explorers withdrew in 1899 to the consternation of the French public. (trs.)

elder son's indignation. It is also reasonable to suppose that in the following year the head of the family would have given his opinion about the second trial of Dreyfus: we know that Henri de Gaulle gradually came to doubt the condemned man's guilt, and that he did not keep his convictions to himself.

Who can doubt that in 1904 the conversation at the family meals touched upon the Entente Cordiale?* But quite certainly less than upon the law forbidding the Church to teach. In 1905 military service was reduced to two years and above all there was the landing of Kaiser William at Tangier. But the law dealing with the separation of the Church and the State must also have come like a thunder-clap. What could the de Gaulles have said when Georges Clemenceau came to power in 1906 except that the "trollop" of a Republic had lacked nothing but this savage anticlerical.

It is all there in his *Mémoires de guerre*:

> When I was an adolescent, what happened to France interested me beyond anything else, whether it was a matter of history or the struggle of public life. I therefore watched the drama that was, without a pause, being acted in the forum, with pleasure but also with severity. All the more so since at the beginning of the century there appeared the premonitory symptoms of the war. I must admit that in my first youth I imagined this unknown adventure without horror and glorified it in advance. In short, I did not doubt that France would have to go through enormous trials, that the whole point of life consisted of one day rendering her some conspicuous service, and that I should have the opportunity of doing so.

This was written, it is true, many, many years later by a General de Gaulle in retirement at Colombey, worn with glory and bitterness. But how does it come about that one never for a moment doubts the exactness of the recollection? If, forty years later, de Gaulle stated young Charles's hopes and motives in such a way, it is quite obviously because that was what they were. He was not trying (in this place at all events) to embellish his account and he was too much an historian to trifle with ideas and words or to fabricate a self other than it was.

That Charles who was so impatient to taste the "point" of life on a higher plane and to render France a "conspicuous" service was indeed the tall thin young man with a prodigious memory, a notebook crammed with aphorisms and quotations, and a habit of producing disconcerting outbursts and peremptory remarks who at the end of the summer of 1909 was feverishly waiting for the results of the entrance examination for Saint-Cyr.

*The term used to describe the improved relations between France and Britain. (trs.)

CHAPTER TWO

The Red

"When I joined the army it was one of the greatest things in the world." Here the author of the *Mémoires de guerre* seems to force his legendary memory a little. In 1909? This was only three years after the rehabilitation of Dreyfus, when Zola's words were still ringing in all ears:

> I accuse General Mercier of one of the greatest iniquities of the century. I accuse General Billot of having had the certain proofs of Dreyfus' innocence in his hands and of having suppressed them. I accuse General de Boisdeffre and General Gonse of having made themselves guilty of the same crime! And these men can sleep! They have wives and children whom they love!*

1909 was only ten years after Fashoda; four years after the blow of Tangier – a blow which remained unanswered, and this when the Russian ally's disastrous war in the Far East made the future look very dark; four years after the reduction of military service to two years, and at a time when Jaurès' pacifism was in full flow, though even that was being outflanked on the left by the violent antimilitarism of Gustave Hervé and the anarcho-syndicalists of the Conféderation Générale du Travail (CGT).

It is true that at the same period Foch was teaching at the Ecole Supérieure de Guerre, thus proving that the military body was not without a brain; General Lyautey was preparing his proconsular rule in Morocco; and that the General Staff had finally equipped the soldiers with Lebel rifles and the 75 millimetre gun. But at Saint-Cyr, where there had been two thousand candidates at the end of the century, there were no more than seven hundred in 1908. The troops rarely left their gloomy barracks except to deal with the great strikes of the beginning of the century, a task they found repellent; and the High Command, utterly set in its ways (apart from three or four exceptions) did almost nothing to satisfy the desire for renovation made evident by the work of the military intelligentsia.

One of the greatest things in the world? If, in about 1904, Henri de Gaulle's son had wanted to build his future on a sure foundation, he should have turned to the University.** It then held sway; and he would have been well advised to teach that history which he had in his blood and which he never wrote without a capital H; in this way he would have made use of that didactic instinct which he had from his father and from his own nature, and he would have done so at a time when the

*Zola's famous attack on the anti-Dreyfusards, *J'accuse*, was published in 1898. (trs.)
**The University in the French sense, covering the whole field of teaching. (trs.)

French school of history had a splendid reputation inherited from illustrious masters – Renan, Taine, Fustel de Coulanges, Camille Jullian, Albert Sorel – and being in the act of passing on from the positivism whose last fires had been lit by Lavisse to that social history which the group of the *Annales* was to bring to the front rank of contemporary science: for were not Lucien Febvre and Marc Bloch contemporaries of Charles de Gaulle?

Yet it was towards the army that he directed his steps. Because it is natural for sons to fulfil their father's dreams? There was something of that in his decision. As soon as Henri de Gaulle told him of his success in the examination he wrote: "You have been the first to add the title of Saint-Cyrien to my name. This is in the order of things, for is it not to you in the first place that for a whole mass of reasons I owe my success in this examination?"[1] The relation is emphasized, the debt acknowledged, the relay is taken on. But we must also take into account what Charles de Gaulle later called "the circumstances". First and foremost, the chance of "revenge". The share that the loss of Alsace-Lorraine played in the cultural and emotional formation of the de Gaulle children – as of many other French children of the time – has already been noted.

But pending the time of the revenge (which the French army at the beginning of the century "felt coming with equanimity and even with a secret hope" as General de Gaulle was to write) there was an atmosphere forming that contributed a great deal to the young man's commitment. It was an atmosphere of uncertainty and division, and it is called up for us by a letter from General Béthouart, who made the same choice as de Gaulle, at the same time, and who was with him at Saint-Cyr. "It was the state of affairs prevailing in France that induced both the one and the other of us – neither from a family with military traditions – to go into the army." It was a state of affairs no longer caused by the storms of the Dreyfus affair and not yet by the imminence of the war: it was a troubled atmosphere, a confusion, an incoherence that urged these young men to look for an order, a structure, a solid mass of certainties.

The search for an order, a "church"? Still better, the search for a synthesis and a unity. The de Gaulle of 1909, that young Frenchman desperately eager to render a "conspicuous" service, would have found an opportunity of doing so in the University. But the intellectual and political arguments in which French society was involved, were too confused for him to venture to assume a leading role, as he was discovering.

Though it was challenged, weakened and embittered, the French army, it is true, did remain one of the "great things" of France. And the order it offered was, from a certain point of view, the freest that could be imagined. Standing to attention is an admirable posture, and one that allows the stander to think at his leisure and to resist in silence, until better times should come. The army of the Republic was perhaps the only State corporation in which there was expressed that unanimity which Charles de Gaulle dreamt of, and expressed in a style marked with its fundamental conviction of being the pick of the nation. It was a focal point of synthesis, a crossroads of unification. That was why he was going to dig himself in there.

* * *

On 30 September 1909 Charles de Gaulle, on holiday at Wimereux, heard from his father that he had passed the Saint-Cyr entrance examination. Of the 800 candidates 221 were selected and he was 119th. It was not brilliant, but he was not yet nineteen and this was the first time he had sat for it. The outlook was good. That was what the delighted father and son told one another. On 7 October Charles undertook a voluntary enlistment for four years. But before crossing the threshold of the Saint-Cyr the new officer-cadet, like all his comrades, was to serve for a year in the ranks; this had been laid down by the law of 21 March 1905 which, in the full flow of the democratization of the army, meant to subject the future leaders to the common soldiers' harsh and disagreeable experiences, on the basis of the somewhat empty rule that one cannot command without having first obeyed.

Following the advice of his father, who was quite happy to see him as a private soldier so long as it was in an historic place, apt to foster exalting memories, he chose for this purpose the 33rd Infantry Regiment of Arras, an army town haunted by the memory both of Condé and Turenne – and of *Cyrano de Bergerac*.* The 33rd Infantry Regiment was one of the most famous in France: it had won glory at Austerlitz, Wagram and Moscow. A Colonel Schwartz commanded the regiment, a Captain de Tugny Charles de Gaulle's company, the fifth.

Charles did not care for this trial at all and he took exception to its methods. Much later he told his friend Colonel Lucien Nachin that "he remembered his makeshift instructors with little enthusiasm"; "but for all that," adds Nachin, "his deeply-rooted vocation overcame all these involuntary attempts at making him detest the soldier's trade." And he did draw this conclusion from his course, that "by taking the measures directly opposed to those [he had] been victim of, reasonably satisfactory results might be counted upon".[2]

Excellent: these "directly opposed measures"! Already, and as early as the first cook-house fatigues, there could be seen that rebellious temperament which was to carry him far. Yet it would be a mistake to suppose that this irritation made him adopt the attitude of a misunderstood martyr for the benefit of his own family. In January 1910 for example he wrote this fairly cheerful letter to his father:

> We have just come back from a twenty-four kilometre march which was quite tiring because of the rain and the muddy roads. It is good training for the trial-marches. Up until now marching has never seemed to me hard, even with our present load, which is very like the full load; it was in fact from the pack that I had expected difficulties. They did not happen. Tomorrow, at the café des Voyageurs, I am standing the dinner laid on for the Parisians.

And private de Gaulle added a piece of information which proves that this "trial" was not solely directed at putting young men of his kind through the humiliations and labours that leaders should undergo before handing them out: "It is next

*The fourth act of Rostand's play takes place there. [Marshal Turenne defended Arras from Condé and the Spanish in 1654. (trs.)]

Saturday that I give my lecture to the entire third batallion: I have a vague idea that the major will be there, if not the colonel. I shall not be able to say until after whether the presence of such important people is desirable from my point of view or not." In April 1910 private de Gaulle was promoted to corporal. Would it not be possible to move him on to the higher rank straight away, a promotion justified by the personality of this conscript, exceptional enough to be thought fit to hold forth before his colonel? To the person who made the remark, Captain de Tugny, replied, "Why do you think I should make a sergeant of a young fellow who would not feel he had had his due unless he were made Constable?" (Under the French monarchy the Constable was, after God and the King, the supreme commander of the armies. He was the sovereign's sword-bearing arm.)

Was it because of the tone he adopted when he was speaking to his superiors? The style he assumed when addressing an audience of officers? Or his way of recovering after he had been plunging through the mud of the Pas-de-Calais? The fact is that this simple private did not pass unnoticed. "Constable". The witticism lived on, taken up as the years went on by jealous comrades, irritated instructors, short-sighted generals and above all in the decisive hours of June 1940 by Winston Churchill.

It was to this period before Saint-Cyr that there belongs the second tale from the imagination of "Charles de Lugale", one that he called *Le Secret du spahi* with the sub-title *La Fille de l'agha*. The editor of the *Lettres, Notes et Carnets* says, "Its author preserved the printed version of this piece of fiction in a folder marked 'Short story published by me in 1910 in *Le Journal des voyages*'."

It is easy to picture Corporal de Gaulle sitting in the barracks canteen from which he dated his letters to the family, wearing his ill-fitting fatigue-dress, sucking the end of his pen, and, to escape from the dreary horizon streaked with the rain of Artois, inventing the story of Lieutenant Meillan, a Spahi officer in the south of Algeria who, having been given the task of dealing with the abuses of an agha addicted to pillage, falls in love with Medella, his daughter, and decides to kill himself in order to prevent her capture by his unit. Let us listen to Charles de Lugale, the teller of this desert tragedy:

> Without waiting another second I set off with all my men at full gallop and I was lucky enough to catch up with the agha and the greater part of his tribe. Medella had managed to escape. When we returned that evening I had the body of my unfortunate comrade brought in. The men and I agreed to say nothing about what had happened. At Mahroum Meillan was buried with the ceremonies due to any officer killed in action. But as it always happens in this world, the truth was known later, and that is why I tell this tale. I had looked through Meillan's pockets to send his family whatever I should find. In his dolman there was one of those short blue bodices worn by the Arab girls in the nomadic desert tribes.
>
> A few weeks after this there was a singer in the streets of Mahroum chanting the legend of the agha's daughter whose eyes killed her father's enemies.
>
> CHARLES DE LUGALE

Whether he was dreaming of the Sahara or not, it was "in pouring rain" that on 14 October 1910 Charles-André-Marie-Joseph de Gaulle entered the famous gateway of Saint-Cyr a few weeks before his twentieth birthday as an officer-cadet in the "Fez term" – so called because of the operations which the army was carrying out in Morocco and which led to the signature of the treaty a year and a half later that was to bind Morocco to France for so many years and to open a splendid field of action for young officers.

Here are the first reactions of the new boy (at Saint-Cyr they are called "bazars"), from a letter to his father written the next day: "I had reckoned on being able to write you a note after dinner, but the seniors who have been here these four days past spent that time in giving us lectures, and in persecuting us too, though not viciously."[3] Let us in any event refrain from seeing him as a wonderful youth at Saint-Cyr, a military Rimbaud. He was above all a good student, though somewhat imperious with his masters on occasion.

Charles de Gaulle summed up the basic facts about his position at the school for his family: the complement of Saint-Cyr was divided into four groups, "two for the seniors and two for us. I belong to the third, commanded by Captain Mellier". Each group had its dormitory and its class-room. The refectory was common to them all. Obeying the rules they rose at 5.30 a.m., breakfasted at 6 and then had a period of preparation; at 7 this was followed by physical training, fencing, riding or German (the only obligatory language); at 9 "cleaning up"; 9.30 lectures. Lunch at noon. From 1 to 4 p.m., military instruction in the strict sense; from 4.30 onwards oral tests and preparation; at 7.30 dinner, followed by free time; at 9 roll-call; at 10 "lights out".

A week after he had joined Charles wrote to his mother:

> With our lectures, our preparation, our drill and training, fencing, riding, polishing,* gymnastics, etc. our days are more than filled, and in spite of a year's regimental service we are rather worn by the very sudden beginning of a variety of occupations. The weather here has been vile for the last two days and it has turned the plateau de Satory into a sewer in which we wade about, drilling from one till four. Our going out on Sunday depends on two questions, that of the strikes,** which seems to me to be settled, and that of clothes, which is not quite resolved. Your very affectionate and respectful son,
>
> CHARLES DE GAULLE[4]

The first thing that was noticed about Charles de Gaulle at the military school as elsewhere was his unusual height (the school's descriptive list only set him down at six foot one-and-a-half inches, whereas he was two-and-a-half inches taller). This earned him a string of nicknames that ran from "the huge asparagus" to "turkey-cock", and from "fool at length"*** to "double yard-stick". On the evening of his

*The cleaning of weapons and shoes.
**The railwaymen's general strike which lasted from 10 to 17 October 1910.
***The original is *sot-en-hauteur*, which sounds very like the French for high jump. (trs.)

arrival, de Gaulle appeared and was ordered to get up on the table, one of his seniors crying "This is just how I had imagined him!"

Saint-Cyr had two parallel hierarchies; the "strass", and the "fines". The first was made up of hard workers, swots or grinds; the second of freakish, spirited creatures. The first aimed at succeeding in their career according to the acknowledged rules; the second at establishing their reputation as dashing characters very successful with women (a classification that history often upset, de Gaulle having been an "oil" and Pétain a "fine"). The first earnestly absorbed the subjects on the theoretical side (*la pompe*), history, administration and topography, and they were promoted sooner; the others gave the appearance of being interested only in the "mill" – shooting, physical education, manoeuvres and sense of command.

Although Charles de Gaulle arrived with only a modest rating – 119th – he straight away asserted himself as a "Strass". He was intensely keen to "learn in order to conquer" (Saint-Cyr's motto), attentive at lectures, eager to listen to the instructors but also to put them right – so much so that the school's magazine published a drawing with the legend, "The Saint-Syrien de Gaulle undergoing an oral in history: the examiner is in a tight corner." Although he may have irritated a number of people but he did so well that he raised himself to the 45th place in the first-year classification.

Although he snored loudly by night, the officer-cadet de Gaulle was quite unobtrusive by day. He had some friends at the school; Jacques de Sieyès (whom we shall find again in New York in 1940) and Gustave Ditte, a general's son, who was to be the best man at his wedding. He went for long walks with them, talking about service matters as well as the future of the army and the prospect of the coming war.

It is a strange thing, but de Gaulle, a student so eager for self-improvement, does not appear to have had anything like close relations – relations of the kind that ensure success through rivalry – with the man who very soon made it evident that he was the outstanding officer-cadet of the year: Alphonse Juin, a gendarme's son from Algeria, a keenly intelligent man who in spite of the fact of passing out head of his term, with remarkable examination-results, chose the modest infantry, as did de Gaulle.

It was only at the end of the first year that the officer-cadets made their choice between the infantry and the cavalry, between the *biffe* and the *basane*, the second more attractive and readily accessible to those with a "de" to their name. Charles de Gaulle nevertheless chose foot-slogging. Not, as we have seen, because he had particularly enjoyed his time in the Arras infantry regiment but, according to the remark he uttered later when speaking to his colleague Pierre Billotte, "Because it is more military!"

It was also at the end of the first year that those who had still been no more than "other ranks" up until this time became real officer-cadets and formed the term whose name they would continue to bear. Thus the "Fez term" was baptized on 12 July 1911. A term's baptism does not occur without some play, review or pantomime. The person who was most in view that year was Charles de Gaulle, first dressed up as a village bridegroom, made all the more gigantic by a vast top-hat and then appeared in a review called *En voyant l'astique* where he had two parts to play, that of "Salhuile" (a direct allusion to his "pumping brute" inclinations).

And a year later he was to be seen once more on the occasion of the next "triumph" as a traditional clown in a pointed hat. Under the direction of a ring-master who was his friend Jacques de Sieyès he did a turn of trick-riding together with a horsewoman who was none other than the future General Herreman. A jovial soul then, the lofty Charles? In any case this "pumping brute" was capable of "playing the game" with an unexpected liveliness and spirit, as he was to show on other occasions.

But he had not come to this school solely to be applauded as a clown. He worked hard and steadily; he marched, ran, carried, held forth, recited, raised objections – and carefully copied into his notebook a piece that he had taken from Victor Hugo and that he then adopted as a rule for living: "Concise in style. Precise in thought. Decisive in life." And all things being considered he was to practice these precepts better than his master.

A glance at the reports when he left the school on 1 September 1912 with the rank of second lieutenant will show that he had not wasted his time at Saint-Cyr. Let us look at his record:

CAPTAIN'S REPORT

Conduct	Faultless
Manners	Very good
Intelligence	Very lively and quick
Upbringing	Carefully attended to
Character	Upright
Attitude	Very fine
Zeal	Very sustained
Military spirit	Highly developed
Physical appearance	Agreeable
Power of marching	Very good
Resistance to fatigue	Great

General estimate
A very highly gifted cadet. Conscientious and earnest worker. Excellent state of mind. Calm and energetic nature. Will make an excellent officer.

Report of the major in command of infantry exercises
A thorough soldier, much attached to the service, very conscientious.
Calm and forceful in command.
Will make an excellent officer.

General appreciation by the officer commanding the school
Has made continual progress since his joining the school, has a great deal in the way of abilities, energy, zeal, enthusiasm, and power of command and decision. Cannot fail to make an excellent officer.

The following figures show that this remarkable eulogy has its quantitative basis. The only subject in which the cadet de Gaulle did not reach the average mark was musketry: 8.6 out of 20. He just managed to average in horsemanship and fencing; but he had 17.7 in military history, 18.5 in geography, 19 in fortification and map exercises, and several 20's – in field-service, dealing with manoeuvres, and psychological training. Here was an "oil" who had done his utmost to shine in the "mili" too.

In the final results he was thirteenth – another thirty-two places gained during his second year – but he was still far behind Juin, the head of the list. A position which in any event gave him the choice not of his branch – he had already chosen the infantry – but of the kind of regiment he would serve in. Generally the most highly esteemed were the rifle regiments, the Foreign Legion and the overseas units then engaged in the glamorous operations in Morocco. The postings least in request were those affecting the *biffe inté*, the infantry regiments in the home garrisons which were the destination of those at the bottom of the list.

Yet that was what the Constable chose: Second Lieutenant de Gaulle decided to go back to the 33rd Infantry Regiment at Arras in which Corporal de Gaulle had served with so little pleasure. Masochism? Or determination in this young man with so many desires, and with perhaps contradictory impulses, to go deep into austerity and renunciation, taking firm root there. But, although he never confided this to anyone, perhaps he already knew that he was going to encounter a far from usual chief: since June 1911 33rd Infantry Regiment had been commanded by Colonel Pétain.

Philippe Pétain, the son of a Picardian peasant, had taught at the Ecole de Guerre, and he had made himself a double legend: that of an outstanding teacher with a mind independent enough to advocate, against the General Staff's official doctrine, the superiority of fire over the offensive, and that of a chief with a character strong enough to reply to a man sent from the ministry to ask the names of the officers in his regiment who went to Mass: "Since I am in the front rank, it is not my custom to look behind me." This stroke went the round of the messes, where people often spoke of this "well-built, imposing, enigmatic colonel, then filled with a cold energy, an unrivalled vitality and drive, and an already legendary originality of mind, of very high standing, authoritarian, haughty."[5]

The Pétain–de Gaulle encounter (in so far as the regimental relations between a second lieutenant and the colonel with nineteen captains and thirty-two lieutenants and second lieutenants under his orders can be called as such) is one of the inevitable virtuoso chapters in Gaullography. The encounter so marked de Gaulle that forty years later, and in spite of everything, he wrote in his *Mémoires de guerre*, "My first colonel, Pétain, showed me the real value of the gift and the art of commanding."[6]

As soon as he received the official notification of his posting to the 33rd Infantry Regiment (RI), on 10 October 1912, Second Lieutenant de Gaulle wrote his chief the letter which began with the time-honoured formula, "Called to the honour of serving under your orders." To which the colonel replied in a no less conventional manner.[7] At the Schramm barracks a few days later the second lieutenant reported to Colonel Pétain, about whom he now knew enough to be impressed.

He saw a very handsome man rise to his feet, a man of fifty-six, practically bald, with a pepper-and-salt moustache, an ivory-coloured face and periwinkle-blue eyes that still charmed women and those who heard him. The peasant from Picardy had the air of a king in classical tragedy. A true Gallic chief painted by Gérôme. De Gaulle knew that he would not learn much more that first day. His comrades might call him the Constable, but Pétain's colleagues called their man *Précis-le-sec* ("dry and exact"). Sixteen words were enough: "You are posted to the sixth company, Captain Saliceti's. I bid you welcome to the army."

It is strange, but no letter from the second lieutenant to his parents about this exceptional event has come down to us. Yet everything leads one to suppose that Charles could not have avoided telling his father with many eloquent comments about his good fortune in serving under a chief of such calibre, and one who was all the more engaging because the firmness of his mind and of his convictions, both in the field of theory and in that of day-by-day relations with the ministry and the staff seemed to have broken his career. Although he was marked as a republican, here he was, in a fair way to ending his army days three or four years later as a colonel in the fogs of Arras – Pétain, the outstanding teacher at the Ecole de Guerre whose term-fellows were all generals.

De Gaulle, endowed with a prodigious memory and driven by General Lyautey's notion of the "officer's social rote" and an "apostolic zeal",[8] knew the record-sheet of all his recruits by heart. He did not confine himself to the supervision of the polishing and cleaning and the exact folding of blankets or to helping them with their letters and their family problems. He also took it upon himself to address them as an instructor in the duties of citizenship and in military ethics. At some unknown date he drew up notes for a talk to the recruits and in a way they amount to the first "speech" of Charles de Gaulle.

> You are now no longer ordinary men: you have become soldiers. Have you already wondered why? France is a nation. But is she the only nation in the world? No! There are other nations that ask nothing better than to conquer us, to stop us speaking French and to take away our freedom. So France has provided herself with an army; she has decided that each of her sons should come and serve her in his turn, and here you are! It is forty-two years now that France has been at peace and if foreigners choose to declare war on her, they will find someone to answer them, I can tell you. From now on our land, our houses and our children shall remain ours. And then France has not only enemies abroad to fear. At home there are often people who look for an opportunity to foster trouble and prevent the good citizens from living in peace.
>
> And who can tell whether this very year may not be decisive for the country's future? I do not have to tell you that the situation abroad looks more threatening than ever. Let us reflect that tomorrow's victory may depend on each one of us.[9]

The conscripts of 1913, from Nancy to Rennes and from Grenoble to Bordeaux, must have heard a great many pep-talks of this kind. But what gives Charles de Gaulle's example a particular interest is this passage, not at all in agreement with Pétain's ideas:

> One must have the offensive spirit. This means that one must in all places and at all times have one single idea, that of advancing. As soon as the fighting begins everybody in the French army, the commanding general, the chiefs and the soldiers have only one idea left – advancing, advancing to the attack, reaching the Germans so as to spit them or make them run away.

The least that can be said is that these words do not express Philippe Pétain's fundamental notions. To be sure, it may be observed that promoting the recruits' "offensive" spirit does not imply that one wholly adopts the General Staff's theory of attack whatever the cost. Yet here de Gaulle does allow himself to state that the "commanding general" as well as the basic infantryman should have only one idea in his head – the offensive.

In the great argument which at that time divides the strategists who were to lead the French forces in the coming war, there was on the one hand Lt-Col. de Grandmaison, head of the army's 3rd Bureau* and the General Staff's soothsayer, and on the other, General Lanrezac. Grandmaison based himself on France's mission of regaining the lost provinces to advocate an offensive that must be prepared "with passion, with exaggeration and based on the finest details of training".[10] Grandmaison could claim at least the moral support of General Foch, the most highly considered of military theorists. Lanrezac summed up this fashionable doctrine in these words: "Are we to attack? Then let us attack the moon!" That was certainly the opinion of Pétain, for whom gunfire was the decisive factor and who justified the offensive only as an advance of the line of fire. Attack must follow the gunfire, never precede it.

Whether it gave rise to a private disavowal of the colonel by the second lieutenant or not, and whether it was the cause of a direct statement to the second lieutenant on the part of the colonel or not, the argument was there, a reflection in the shadows of a provincial barracks of the argument that was then deciding the country's fortunes for the first months of the war. Pétain was often to make the young de Gaulle's mind accept his arguments, though by temperament and in his heart de Gaulle was a passionate believer in the offensive, which, by the way, he called "movement".

If Pétain did mark points against him, the 1913 manoeuvres in the region of Arras is a case in point. They were conducted by General Le Gallet, who was in command of the division to which the 33rd RI belonged: it was a bayonet attack carried to its utmost extreme with bugles sounding the charge and scarlet trousers well exposed to the enemies' fire. When the time came for criticism in the town hall, all the officers being present, Colonel Pétain was asked for his opinion. "Gentlemen, in order to strike your minds with greater force, General Le Gallet has displayed a synthesis of all the errors that a modern army should no longer commit." It is easy to imagine the heaviness of the silence that fell upon the meeting and the intensity of the glances that were exchanged. One can also imagine how deeply this example of clear-minded fearlessness impressed a non-conformist mind like that of Charles de Gaulle.

*The 3rd Bureau dealt with operations and training. (trs.)

When, fifteen years later,* he came to draw a portrait of Pétain, de Gaulle described a man of strong character and an untrammelled mind, not that of a fertile thinker: "A master known to have scorned the good fortune of a humble follower. Power of criticism preserved from commonplace favours. Majesty of independence. Glamour of the secrecy provided by a deliberate remoteness; the watchful irony and even the pride in which this loneliness wraps itself." Yet the lieutenant stood out, if not from the strength of such arguments as "gunfire kills", then at least from the general philosophy that Pétain drew from them. The remarks that he made in his private notebook bear witness to this: they almost all call his chief's ideas in question:

> *Arras, October 1913:*
> Variations in the relative importance attributed to gunfire and movement during the course of history. Fighting in the middle ages. Essentially offensive. The Commons take up arms. Gunpowder makes its appearance. The intervention of fire-arms. Decay of the offensive spirit. Marshal de Saxe does not allow fire by mass formation and by salvo. As for the onslaught, it was carried out by a deep column; deep order** was suitable for the Revolution and the Empire. But the Restoration brought back the former king's officers and the mistaken ideas of fire prevailed over movement. The study of 1866 gave the French army false notions.
>
> The Russian–Japanese war. The Japanese always pushed their attacks home against both the front and the flanks. At no point did gunfire alone settle the question. "The bayonet was at work all the time," says Solovieff. The advance was carried out by successive dashes making wonderful use of the terrain.[11]

Nothing could be clearer. The "false notions" and the "wrong ideas" come from the superiority attributed to fire. Salvation is to be found in the offensive, the dash ahead and the bayonet. Colonel Pétain could not have dreamt of a more stubborn, faithless disciple.

Certainly Charles de Gaulle had a lively admiration – lasting a dozen years longer – for his colonel at Arras, for his rigorous character, his very high professional qualities as a commanding officer, his style and his influence. But in the depths of his heart and mind the disagreement remained. It is not absurd to see here, as early as 1913 and on the subject of the fighting spirit, the origin of the worm that was to eat the fruit: in de Gaulle's idea of Pétain from those days onwards there was always something of that intellectual refusal of 1913, a conviction that the "great man" had a limited mind.

Whether or not Pétain observed these reserves in his young subordinate, he took no notice of them. They did not make him any the less kindly in his report of him or the comments that went with them. Although his congratulations on the occasion of de Gaulle's promotion to lieutenant in October 1913 were merely conven-

*In *Le Fil de l'épée*: we shall see that this "portrait" is not only that of the Marshal.

**This was invented by the Comte de Guibert: it was the origin of the Napoleonic "shock-effect" strategy.

tional, his earlier observations bore witness to a most emphatically favourable opinion.

> *Memorandum for the first quarter, 1913:*
> Left Saint-Cyr 13th out of 211: from the beginning has asserted himself as an officer of real worth who promises very well indeed for the future. Devotes himself wholeheartedly to his duties as an instructor. Has given a brilliant lecture on the causes of the conflict in the Balkan peninsula.
>
> *Memorandum for the second quarter, 1913:*
> Very intelligent, passionately attached to his profession. Led his platoon perfectly during the manoeuvres. Worthy of all praise.[12]

At the end of 1913 Colonel Pétain left Arras to take command of a brigade. But there is still something to be said about the relations of the two men at that time. Legend has it that these relations were not confined to the strictly professional sphere and that Pétain, a tireless womanizer, entered into competition with Lieutenant de Gaulle on manoeuvring-grounds other than those which General Le Gallet had chosen.[13] One day when he was talking to me about de Gaulle with that high-strung sarcastic tone which was peculiar to him, François Mauriac said with a half-laugh, obviously speaking from sound information, 'De Gaulle's women? The same as Pétain's."

We may nevertheless trust de Gaulle to have focused his passion on another object. Witness this lecture delivered before the fifty-odd junior officers of the 33rd RI and entitled simply "On Patriotism".[14]

> I do not think that any human love has inspired more numerous and also more arduous devotions. All we want to fight against is chauvinism, that cast of mind which induces some people to give a blind and unvarying approval to whatever their country does abroad, good or bad. On the other hand it must be said that although chauvinism is excessive, it is a hundred times, a thousand times better than a patriotism that argues too much. Vercingetorix and Jeanne d'Arc quite certainly had to be chauvinistic to accomplish the deeds that history has handed down to us. As I was told six months ago by Déroulède, whom M. de Freycinet has called "the greatest patriot of the century", the man who does not love his own mother more than other mothers and his own country more than other countries loves neither his mother nor his country![15]

Is it possible to be very understanding towards chauvinism and at the same time preserve one's clear-mindedness with regard to the enemy? On 1 April 1914 Lieutenant de Gaulle lectured the officers of the third battalion of his regiment on the German army: only his notes have been preserved. The speaker pointed out the "recent formidable increase in effectives and equipment" of the Kaiser's forces, the youth of the German field officers and generals in comparison with their French opposite numbers, the relative strength of the armies (60 000 more men on the other side of the Rhine), and the excellence of the enemy's communications. He said that the German rifle (the Mannlicher) was "faster and easier to manage" than the Lebel but that its bullet had less power of penetration; that "the German artillery is thought to be inferior to ours", but that the German army's training was "good", adding that "like us, the Germans advocate the attack at all costs". And he ended with a complacent observation that contrasts with the restrained, moderate words that went before: "France has therefore nothing to worry about. It is up to us, the officers, to create this strength."

Lieutenant de Gaulle felt the coming of the "unknown adventure" which he foresaw "without horror" and "glorified in advance". Now, in the early summer of 1914, neither the reading of the papers nor the arguments in the messes could take him by surprise. Whether or not there was Sarajevo, whether or not an Archduke, had not the time come for throwing the dice?

He would be twenty-four in three months. From his pale face, which exercise had made lean and effort made tense, his nose stood out more and more. His eyes were very close together giving him the look of a mountain bird. A short lock of hair hung over his forehead. A slight moustache made a circumflex accent over his upper lip, and his chin retreated somewhat into a very high collar. His outline was still somewhat frail but long marches had strengthened it and a still occasionally uncertain voice had already acquired its trumpet-tone.

In these months of impending war how could he have failed to read the great military writers? This statement of Clausewitz's must at that time have struck him more than any other: "Since all wars have their own character, and since in their evolution they all display a great many special features, each one of them may be looked upon as a sea unknown to the commanding general." How the young de Gaulle would have liked to discover that "unknown sea"! And he believed in the truth of the matter. What was really known of the coming war? This de Gaulle must have dreamt of that particular uncharted voyage.

Although his notes of this time, unlike those of the years to come, make no mention of any "civilian" reading, it is known that the de Gaulle of 1914 devoured quantities of books unrelated to military questions. At that time who ruled over the intellectual landscape of a young man shaped by a Catholic education, intensely interested in history, permeated with nationalism and curious about everything? Barrès, the founders of *L'Action française*, the renewers of Catholic thought and above all Péguy and Bergson.

Barrès had just published *La Colline inspirée*. He was a prince for the young people of the time and his pitiful slip into the anti-Dreyfus camp was not enough to degrade him in the eyes of a patriot like the lieutenant of the 33rd RI. Charles de Gaulle rarely quotes him and there is nothing to tell us that he placed him in the first rank as a writer. But what a proponent of French continuity he was, a man for whom "any period in which French energy blazes out is a good period", from the Capetian monarchy to the Revolution and the Empire.

Which was why Charles de Gaulle always had reserves about the fire-eaters of *l'Action française* who wanted to erase from history both Carnot the regicide and Gambetta the republic-founder. But when one was eighteen when the daily *AF* was launched how could one avoid being dazzled by the intellectual pugnacity of Charles Maurras and by the anti-Germanism of the historian, Jacques Bainville?

It was in 1914 that two young writers who looked upon Maurras as their chief, Henri Massis and Alfred de Tarde, and who adopted the pseudonym of Agathon, published an enquiry which has remained famous and from which it appeared that the young people of France were in agreement upon ideas concerning the nation, revenge (for Alsace-Lorraine), order and spirituality which did not seem to be those which inspired the left-wing majority in the chamber of deputies that had been elected in the spring of 1914. What capital ammunition this was for Lieutenant de Gaulle, that fighter for "moral strength"!

He also found it in René de La Tour du Pin and Albert de Mun, those masters of the Catholic renewal; to be sure, de Mun, who twenty years earlier had gone a long way in the direction of the "social Catholicism" inspired by the Leo XIII of *Rerum Novarum*, had recently made a prudent retreat to the bases of his family traditions. A deeper influence was that of the Marquis de La Tour du Pin, whom Henri de Gaulle looked upon as a master and whose works he made his son read.

René de La Tour du Pin joined the *l'Action française* very early and with de Mun he began a scheme for working men's clubs. He wrote *Vers un ordre social chrétien* (1907) and *Aphorismes de politique social* (1909), and he advocated "the harmony of the social body", which implied a break with "the liberalism and individualism of 1789, which were responsible for the class-struggle", and a reconstitution of the trade corporations, those king-pins of the social structure.

But the masters of the young man in uniform were Péguy and Bergson. At this time Péguy was leading the charge against Jaurès and all forms of pacifism. De Gaulle was enchanted by the polemical dash and spirit of *Notre jeunesse* and by the historical mystique of *Le Mystère de la Charité de Jeanne d'Arc* and *Les Tapisseries*. How exactly that France peopled by patriotic monks, egalitarian knights and Christian artisans corresponded with his dream!

What Lieutenant de Gaulle liked more than anything else was the fact that this socialist and Dreyfusist should have become the most fearless celebrator of French nationalism. To hear that France was a whole which had spoken with a single voice these last thirteen centuries, that "the choice was not between the Ancien Régime and the Revolution. It was between the whole of the ancient France, both pagan and Christian, traditional and revolutionary, monarchist, royalist and republican – and on the other hand, on the other side and on the contrary a certain primitive domination that corrupts the Republic."

Henri Bergson was then looked upon as a kind of prophetic witness of the return to things of the spirit, a pioneer of the mystical renaissance. His *Evolution créatrice* (1907), was held to be a manifestation of the rediscovery of God by intuition, by the *élan vital*. And French Catholicism rejoiced at the thought that the greatest philosopher of the time, coming from Judaism, should travel towards Christianity by such light-strewn paths. Later, in *La France et son armée*,* de Gaulle spoke of how much the "renewal" of French spirituality owed to Henri Bergson at the beginning of the century.

What the young officer setting off for unknown shores found in Bergson was a distrust in categories and systems. It was the living thinker who said to the men of

**France and her Army.* (trs.)

his time, discover yourselves, have a fresh intuition of the world, "time is not a path you travel over twice". From Bergson de Gaulle learnt that when the moment for action has come everything will have to be worked out anew and that the most experienced of captains will plunge into "an unknown sea".

Europe's convulsions from the end of June 1914 onwards were certainly of a kind to strengthen Charles de Gaulle's most deeply held convictions. From one chancellery to another and in every General Staff a momentous tragedy was enacted, just as it might have been described in the oldest works on diplomatic history. It was a fascinating spectacle, he said later, to watch the masses urged on towards the catastrophe all through July 1914: a "conspiracy of those dark forces that the ancients would have called fate, Bossuet a divine decree, and Darwin the law of the species."

It was not without an inward jubilation that he observed the disappearance of the "theories that might have been expected to hinder the movement".

> Not a single body or association rose up to condemn the mobilization. Not a single vote was lacking in parliament to pass the bill providing money for the war. The official forecast had been that 13 per cent of those called up for service would be either conscientious objectors or absentees; in fact the proportion did not reach 1.5 per cent. Three hundred and fifty thousand volunteers besieged the recruiting offices. Frenchmen living abroad took trains and ships by storm to get back to the mother-country. Three thousand men who had deserted in time of peace came hurrying to the frontiers asking for the honour of being allowed to fight.[16]

The *Union sacrée* proclaimed by Poincaré the day after the assassination of Jaurès confirmed Lieutenant de Gaulle in his certainties: that the motherland was a single whole and that ideologies were of little consequence when the fate of the nation was at stake. It was the socialist Viviani who took the country into the war. It was the Dreyfusist Péguy who urged it on to battle. And in Germany the same phenomenon was observed: apart from Karl Liebknecht, the leaders of the powerful Social-Democrat party, Bebel and Ebert, scarcely thought of discouraging the wave of popular feeling that flung workers and peasants in the direction of the border. It was quite certainly towards the service of the motherland that the vital impulse carried people, whether it was to be called nationalism or chauvinism. De Gaulle, all his convictions verified, was ready.

Charles de Gaulle had been exercised in the art of command during peacetime. He had absorbed as much history as one can know at the age of twenty; he knew his geography so well that "the tributaries of the Seine were like the lines in the palm of his hand". Moreover, he had established a personal code of ethics based upon these principles: France's exceptional mission in the world; the certainty of the outstanding part that a man of character such as himself would at some time be called upon to play; the primacy given to intuition and inventiveness; a nationalism that integrated classes and periods.

CHAPTER THREE

The Fire

On 1 August 1914 Lieutenant Charles de Gaulle wrote in his private notebook, "Everybody expects the mobilization-order for this evening." At four-thirty that afternoon, Lieutenant-Colonel Stirn, Colonel Pétain's successor at the head of the 33rd RI of Arras, was informed of the news. The die was cast. He added: "Absolute calm on the part of the troops and the population. But uneasiness on many faces. What important men the officers are now." He was posted to the 1st Battalion; and in the 11th company, commanded by Captain Maes, he was to be responsible for the 1st platoon.

The next day was given over to the preparation of those already enlisted. On 3 August – the day Germany declared war – the reservists were incorporated. On the fourth, "a great number of deserters came in, and invalided men asked to be allowed to serve." And on the fifth he wrote, "Goodbye, my rooms, my books, my familiar objects. How much more intense life does seem, and how the smallest trifles stand out in relief when perhaps everything may be coming to an end."[1]

The 33rd RI steered for the Ardennes: their mission would therefore be to defend the Meuse. On the seventh, at Bourg-Fidèle, Charles at last found time to write to his mother: "My very dear Mama, here we are in the open country, full of spirits and confidence. The troops are absolutely admirable. I have not had a single letter from you or anyone else since 1 August."[2]

Next day the regiment's journal recorded among other things that "during the days of the sixth and the seventh the 33rd covered seventy kilometres without leaving a single straggler, marching with reservists out of training, most of whom were wearing new boots." But although Lieutenant de Gaulle had shown that he was a good marcher, on this occasion he rode a mare.

As the Germans had invaded Belgium, Lanrezac's army and especially its first corps under Franchet d'Esperey – to which the 33rd RI belonged – advanced to meet them. Great things were in preparation: "Now one has the feeling that the army is concentrated and that we are going to march to some purpose," noted de Gaulle calmly on the eleventh.[3]

On 13 August, watched by a German plane overhead, they entered Belgium. Charles de Gaulle's notes concerning 14 and 15 August:*

> Night march. Everyone feels we are going into battle, but everyone is determined and in high spirits. The enemy no longer occupies Dinant. We therefore enter the town. The men, all in, sleep lying in the street. Captain Bosquet and I sitting on chairs.

*Written two weeks later, in hospital after his wound.

> At six in the morning, boom! boom! the music begins. The enemy shells Dinant furiously. These are the first shots of the campaign we have received. What was my impression? Why not say? Two seconds of physical emotion, a tightening of my throat. Then that was all. The men began by looking serious, then banter came to the top again.

There was the eleventh company taking shelter in a railway trench on either side of a level-crossing. De Gaulle: "I sat on a bench in the street and stayed there out of bravado. There was in fact no merit about it since I was not in any way alarmed." The first wounded came in. Then the flood increased, pitifully. Several officers of the 33rd were said to have been killed. Now, from the height of the citadel, the enemy opened very heavy rifle-fire on them.

Still no sound from the French artillery: "It was not fear that seized us but fury." And now here was the 11th company called upon to go in with the bayonet to prevent the enemy from crossing the bridge.

> To reach my platoon I had to go over the level-crossing. I decided to cross at a walk. Lord, what a tingling in my legs! I shouted "First platoon, advance with me!" and I raced forward, knowing that our only chance of success was acting very fast. I had the feeling that at that moment my self split in two, the one running like an automaton and the other anxiously watching him. I had scarcely crossed the twenty yards that separated us from the beginning of the bridge when something struck my knee like a whip-lash, making me trip. I fell and Sergeant Debout fell on top of me, killed outright. Then there was an appalling hail of bullets all round me. I could hear the muffled sound of them hitting the dead and wounded scattered over the ground. I extricated myself from my neighbours, corpses or little better, and there I was crawling along the street under the same hail of bullets. How it came about that I was not riddled like a sieve during the passage will always be one of the great problems of my life.
>
> Limping and in a bad way, I dragged myself to the Meuse bridge. Our artillery was firing at a tremendous rate. It was high time! I busied myself by gathering together what was left of the regiment in Dinant. Night fell; my task was over. The peasants organized the transport of the wounded in carts. I got into one of them.

The regiment's journal records the affair of the Dinant bridge in these words: "before the enemy attempted to cross the bridge, Major Bertrand launched the 11th company in a counter-attack. This company was decimated. It attempted its counter-attack twice without success. Lieutenant de Gaulle was wounded, and the company was forced to withdraw and take shelter in the houses of Dinant."

Lieutenant de Gaulle was evacuated first to Charleroi, where he was received by his utterly amazed sister, Marie-Agnès, who was at that time living there with her husband, Alfred Cailliau, then to Arras; he was suffering from "a bullet-wound in the right fibula with paralysis of the sciatic nerve". He was operated on at the

Saint-Joseph hospital in Paris, with later treatment at the Desgenettes hospital at Lyons. It was there that he wrote his account of the fighting adding that his "wound had not hurt him at any time" but that his right foot was paralysed. In any event, this baptism of fire had allowed him to make certain clarifications. In the first place he had found that after "two seconds of physical emotion" the pain had not affected him. Those close to him have often observed that Charles de Gaulle never seemed to be incommoded by any illness whatsoever, treating his body with a total indifference, whatever the circumstances.

But although his frame neither trembled nor suffered, the lieutenant of the 33rd was led, at least in his innermost heart, to another equally important observation: "The first clash is an immense surprise. In a moment it is clear that all the courage and valour in the world cannot prevail against gunfire."[4]

On 12 September he wrote to his mother; he spoke of himself only to say that he was being made to follow "an electrical treatment to bring the damaged nerve back to life", but he surveyed the battle of the Marne, which was then being fought, with the eye of a chief of staff and he stated, "it was going to be a plain, thorough-going victory, the deserved revenge for our first set-backs in Belgium. After that it will be a matter of winning the decisive game and the question will be settled". He uses the same tone in a letter to his father two days later:

> Our dead must have quivered in their graves when they heard the victorious steps of our soldiers and the terrible rumbling of our guns. France is coming to herself again. The generalissimo has at once cut the losses by not persisting in the decisive battle on the Meuse. He has chosen a new terrain, escaping from the enemy's grip without a check and completely modifying the faulty disposition of his forces. On the Marne the fighting was much better coordinated. The enemy will not be able to halt our pursuit before the Meuse and Luxembourg, and we shall have all the glory of having beaten the army that thought itself the finest in the world in a great and decisive battle – and that without the Russians having been absolutely necessary to us.

This survey certainly has style. But what is surprising in these two letters is the analysis of the first set-backs, which are attributed to "over-rapid offensives", and the "inadequacy" of many generals and to the "slowness of the English troops". But the emphasis is not upon the essential lesson, the supremacy of fire over attack. Still he is markedly resistant to Pétain's lessons, which experience had verified so strikingly before his very eyes!

It was probably during his convalescence at Lyons that de Gaulle wrote a still-unpublished story called *Le Baptême* whose autobiographical nature is disturbing, to say the least. It is about a Lieutenant Langel (an anagram if not of Gaulle then at least of Ganlle) aged twenty-three who at the beginning of August 1914 leaves "a small town" at the head of his platoon and almost at once enters "the inferno of fire". Straight away he is wounded in exactly the same circumstances as those of the battle at Dinant and then evacuated to Lyons, where he writes this account.

Now Lieutenant Langel is the lover of his captain's wife. The captain tells Langel that as he is sure of being killed in the first engagement he will hand him his pocket-book so that he may give it to his wife. The captain is indeed killed and the lieutenant wounded. The widow visits Langel in his hospital bed at Lyons.

> She took the pocket-book and looked at it through her tears for a long while. Her husband had had it delivered to her by her lover. What had happened between them before the trial, at the time when they were both no more than poor open-hearted men? In her lover's eyes she read the irreparable. She moved to take the young man's hand, but he grasped both of hers and kissed them with the tenderness of a farewell.[5]

A few weeks later de Gaulle wrote to his mother from Cognac where he finished his physiotherapy. He foresees "a return to the front quite soon; it will be at the best moment". As early as 15 October he took the train to rejoin the 33rd RI in Champagne where the two opposing armies had been dug in for some weeks past and where he found his men wearing the horizon-blue which made them less of a mark for the enemy's fire. He returned to the writing of his private notes:

> *19 October:* awoke to gunfire. Then all the trenches to see my comrades. Some places only 50 yards from the enemy, who still holds the village of La Ville-au-Bois and its surroundings.
> *22 October:* quite heavy shelling during the day and brisk rifle-fire. Champagne for lunch; the company cyclist had just brought it from Rheims.
> *1 November:* quiet night. The news from the Nord is still good. But how slowly it goes, upon my word! Sauternes and champagne for lunch. Very cheerful. Some guests. We drank to the offensive. The Germans could be heard singing in their trenches. Hymns, no doubt. What strange people!

Writing to his father on 15 November (he now addressed his letters to "Major de Gaulle"), he once again spoke of his confidence in victory, because of "the certainty that time is on our side". He was more specific when he wrote to his mother two days later: "December will no doubt see the supreme battle between the Russians and the reinforced Germans and the reorganized Austrians. It is certain that this will be a third victory for our allies followed by what will now be a rapid invasion." On 7 December, still to his mother: "What is this war but a war of extermination? A war of this kind, which in its range, significance and fury goes beyond anything that Europe has ever known, cannot be waged without enormous sacrifices. It *has* to be won. The winner will be the side that desires it most ardently."

At this time there occurred two highly significant incidents in which de Gaulle can already be seen whole and entire, both in his character and in his relations with his surroundings. He had observed that by night in the neighbourhood of a little wood called the Bonnet Persan, the Germans were digging a new trench towards the French positions. He sent a platoon to do the same thing in reverse and cut off the enemy's advance.

> With this approach-trench finished, a hearty burst of fire would have sick-

> ened the *Boches** working at the Bonnet Persan. But my report to Major Batdebat produced this reply: "Very well. But do not undertake anything like this in our sector. You will cause fireworks. Leave the enemy in peace at the Bonnet Persan, since he leaves us in peace in our part of the world!" I felt like saying, "But the Bonnet Persan is in our part of the world, and far beyond the Bonnet Persan too!" Trench-warfare has a serious drawback: it exaggerates this feeling in everyone – if I leave the enemy alone he will not bother me. One is very weak against this notion in wartime. It is lamentable.

A few days later the colonel sent to tell him that he had received two mortars and that he did not know what to do with them. De Gaulle asked for the mortars, set them up and prepared for firing.

> While this was going on X came to see me, and speaking in the name of the third battalion he said roughly this: "These mortars are only a joke, aren't they? If they are fired the German artillery will reply and we shall get the backlash. You only have to report that they have been fired and then not fire them." I turned X out. The next day my mortar fired. But the day after that I was relieved. The company that replaced me did not fire. Major M did not come to see me for a week, and the whole 3rd Battalion looked upon me with an evil eye.[6]

Charles de Gaulle was way ahead of the others, frothing with eager impatience, despising the prudent and the pliable, unbearable and unborne, wholly taken up with his vision of greatness, of outstanding action and of "conspicuous service". Isolated? Not entirely. Two days later Colonel Claudel, the new commanding officer of the 33rd RI, offered him the post of adjutant. A complex, difficult part to play and one that would arouse jealousy. Lieutenant de Gaulle replied, "It is of great consequence to a young lieutenant like myself certain of learning a great deal at this job if God grant me life." God and the colonel: for the adjutant was from now on at the regimental staff's quarters, fifty yards behind the trenches: "the breadth of the Styx", as Jean Pouget remarks.

On 18 December the regiment set off from Fère-en-Tardenois for the region of Châlons-sur-Marne. The soil of Champagne was thick mud. A dismal Christmas with rain "in the middle of very violent shelling", he told his mother before going on to describe his new position as the colonel's adjutant in these words:

> These new duties please me very much, first because of their importance and then because they are interesting, for one sees much more than if one were commanding a company. Yet it was something of a wrench to leave my 7th company. I had only commanded it in the trenches but it had satisfied me entirely. In these two months under my orders it had lost 27 killed and wounded, which is in no way excessive.

On 11 January 1915, he wrote to her again:

*French slang for Germans, the equivalent of "Krauts". (trs.)

My very dear Mama,
We are in an ocean of mud here, so there are quite a lot of sick (five officers and 300 men). The Germans are well dug-in, but we shall get them for all that. Colonel Claudel has left the command of the regiment in order to have a brigade. We are under Colonel Boud'hors, and I remain his adjutant. Apart from that all goes well. This war *has* to end in our favour. A thousand affectionate wishes to Papa and Pierre,

Your very affectionate and respectful son,
C. de Gaulle[7]

A week later he was mentioned in despatches and decorated with the Croix de Guerre, and on 10 February he was promoted captain (temporary rank*). He was still adjutant and he showered the officers of the regiment with notes, instructions, remonstrances and incitements. On 20 February, for example: "the first duty of company-commanders is to raise their men's morale to the highest pitch. The First Corps has the honour of beginning the great effort of liberating the territory of France. Losses are of small importance so long as the result is achieved."

The date of his second wound is difficult to determine, for the regiment's journal only shows the losses "from 10 February to 10 March" – among them four officers killed, two missing, 13 wounded (including Captain de Gaulle) and nearly 700 men out of action.

According to the notes that he left at that time, it seems that this wound in the Argonne – his left hand pierced right-through by a shell-splinter – must be placed in March (the tenth, says Philippe de Gaulle).[8] It was not until mid-April that he was evacuated to a hospital, for at first he thought the wound of no consequence. But it became infected, causing a swelling of his forearm, the paralysis of his hand and a violent fever. This time he was taken to Le Mont-Dore, until June 1915, when he was sent to the trenches of the Aisne.

It is then that he wrote a vitriolic little piece entitled *L'Artilleur*, the gunner, from which it appears that he had still not forgotten those minutes spent on the Dinant bridge waiting in vain for the heavy French guns to open fire. As he is described by the infantry-captain de Gaulle, the gunner is a shrewd, cunning fellow who lacks nothing, lives well in sheltered, comfortable quarters and "concerns himself primarily with eating, drinking and sleeping".

When the weather is fine and everything is quiet, the gunner sometimes comes into the front line. On these occasions he has the look of an elegant lady who is visiting the poor. The infantrymen crowd round, welcoming him, because infantrymen are humble and they are almost ashamed that anyone should think of them and come to see them; they do their best not to look too dirty, too stupid, too dismal. Besides, the gunner is a good fellow, and he even swaggers about the trench. He makes jokes about the Germans, who in fact have never done him much harm. Sometimes he accepts an invitation to dine in an infantry mess. He criticizes the operations. Then he goes quietly away, full of compassion, indulgence and pride.[9]

*Promoted but on probation. (trs.)

And two months later he found time to write this to a fellow-officer:

> This morning, in the Desaix trench, I met your cyclist B: he went past without taking any notice in an unbelievably offhand way and of course without saluting. On my direct order he was good enough to salute, though very sloppily even then. Leaving you to follow this up.[10]

And still the same martinet of a captain: "Not enough use is made of rifles. Blazing away with neither aim nor care is useless but the enemy finds a frequent and tenacious shot unbearable. That is quite enough reason to fire at him."

What a "tenacious" warrior he was, this de Gaulle. As eager to do the enemy harm as to look after the health of his men, giving exact details of all the ways of protecting oneself from gas: there are continual references to it from this autumn of 1915 onwards. For some weeks in November he had the interim command of the third battalion, and he increased both reproofs and requests for reward and promotion, drawing them up in the commander-in-chief's style that he already possessed.

Let us also record this characteristic stroke of de Gaulle at the front, told by Etienne Répessé, then a lieutenant in the 33rd RI and later his publisher and friend. The captain (he assumed the full rank on 3 September) was inspecting the firing-line together with two lieutenants. A shell exploded near at hand. The two young officers threw themselves flat. De Gaulle remained standing. "Were you frightened, gentlemen?" he said. An impressive gesture. But where would the French army have been in 1918 if all the officers had remained standing under the shrapnel for four years?

In a letter to his mother of 18 November he rejoices because,

> The force of circumstances is going to compel us to give up the eastern expedition. A mistake that might have been fatal to us. And now that our minds are free from this error let us make ready with all our might for the coming decisive victory, the victory that will free our own territory, that will expel the enemy from Belgium and that will allow us, if we have a certain amount of boldness, to settle ourselves there in his place, which, if we are capable of desiring it, will give us our natural frontier, the Rhine. Briand* is in a terribly difficult position. Yet I have not the least wish to see him go. What would be the good of it?

A month later it was the expected outburst of anger against the political authorities:

> Parliament grows more and more odious and stupid. The ministers have literally all their time taken up by the sittings of the chamber, the reading of petitions or the most absurd injunctions uttered by any odd tradesman that politics has made a deputy. Even if they wanted to, they absolutely could not

*Prime minister at that time.

> find the time to run their departments. We shall be the conquerors as soon as we have swept this riff-raff out of the way, and there is not a Frenchman who will not shout for joy, especially the soldiers. Besides, the idea is on the move, and I shall be very much surprised if this regime outlives the war.[11]

Yet five years later this despiser of the parliamentary system published a book explaining the "discord in the enemy's camp" and the collapse of the German State in 1918. The German imperial regime was caused by the German High Command's control of political decisions.

On 1 January 1916 Captain de Gaulle, wishing his 10th company a happy new year, allowed himself an expression of emotion that cannot, to judge by the first words, have been at all usual: "I needed an occasion like this to tell you that although the harsh necessities of war and the calls of discipline require your captain to be severe, he is nevertheless very fond of you."

In January a violent fever pinned him to his dug-out for ten days, but he managed to avoid being sent to the rear. On 14 February he told his mother that it was likely that the regiment would be withdrawn from the front line "to re-equip us and to set us up from the point of view of morale, so that when better days come we shall be in very good form for the great efforts called for by the command."

Yet in wartime some people propose and others dispose. Verdun was coming closer. By 24 February everything had changed: "So the enemy has decided to make one last attack," he wrote to Mme de Gaulle.

> At the start of the furious battle that is now beginning, I am sure that the enemy is about to experience a sounding, ruinous defeat. No doubt he will take some trenches more or less all along the line even though he may lose them later; no doubt he will hit hard, and we shall have to call upon all our armies' moral and material resources to bear it without weakening. Do not be frightened if in the days and weeks to come news reaches you only irregularly.

An astonishing foretelling of what the battle of Verdun was to be and, indeed, of his own fate. As early as the end of February this prophet of victory, always harping on the same string, knew and said that the coming months would be terrible. The first phase of the German attack began on 21 February. The news travelled fast from one trench to another and it was known that this time the German empire was throwing enormous forces into the battle. Furthermore, as early as the twenty-fifth, General Joffre, taken by surprise, summoned Pétain, whom he loathed, and as a desperate measure entrusted him with the defense of Verdun.

This appears to be the time when a photograph was taken showing Charles de Gaulle, rather badly dressed in the horizon-blue then worn by the fighting part of the nation, his dark-gloved hands holding a swagger-stick as a fencer holds his sword between two bouts, the peak of his soft képi shading his almost unbearably grave eyes, his very long neck muffled in a kind of scarf, and a thick moustache under a nose less provocative than usual.

As he stands there, on his powerful gaitered legs, leaning a little back as though to survey the surroundings with greater advantage, he looks more determined than arrogant, more solid than bellicose. It is a mature Charles de Gaulle, serene and given balance by his terrible contact with the facts of war and humanized by the ordeal, who faces the lens.

Is this still the tireless pursuer of soup-eating sentinels, the giver of dictatorial lessons, the captain-who-remains-standing-under-the-shrapnel, the mixture of Cyrano and Horatius who always seemed to want to make poor mortals ashamed of being merely men? Perhaps not. It looks as though something more human and more natural had taken possession of him shortly before he went into the hell of Verdun.

By 25 February 1916 the 33rd RI had completed a movement that in one week carried it from Nanteuil-la-Fosse in the Aisne to the outskirts of Verdun. Everything goes to show that the 1st Army Corps to which it belonged was one of the active forces that the High Command was throwing into the cauldron to stop the first gaps caused by the German onslaught. At dawn on the twenty-sixth the regiment entered Verdun, where it took up quarters in the Petit-Miribel barracks.

The next day the regiment was given an extremely dangerous sector to the north of Douaumont. On 1 March it moved to its positions between the locality called Le Calvaire and the fort of Douaumont, which had just fallen into the hands of the Germans.

At noon on this same 1 March Colonel Boud'hors gave Captain de Gaulle a task of the first importance, that of reconnoitring the regiment's position and above all its liaisons to the right and the left. De Gaulle went to see the colonel in command of the 110th RI, which the 33rd had just relieved, and he was told that the German offensive was over. Yet on pushing his reconnaisance farther over this shell-swept terrain Captain de Gaulle saw the enemy was obviously preparing a second attack and that this attack was imminent.[12]

When this mission had been carried out, Captain de Gaulle recorded in the regimental journal that "there was no front-line trench, no communication-trench, no wire, no sketch-map". Everything had been wiped out by the terrible shelling that the sector had been subjected to for the last five days. Furthermore, when de Gaulle had pointed this out an hour earlier to the officers of the 110th whose relief he was preparing one of them, Captain Destouches, called him an "energumen" – an enthusiast, a fanatic.[13] When one has just spent days under heavy fire one does not much care for being given lessons by fresh troops.

Colonel Boud'hors – who relied more and more on the opinion of the learned and energetic captain – at once told the staff of the "precariousness" of his position under the direct threat of the Douaumont fort, where the enemy was beginning to set up machine-guns and artillery which, as he wrote in the journal, would do immense damage unless "our heavies* can overwhelm the fort".

Next we must read the staggering account of that 2 March 1916 between Le Calvaire and Douaumont church – the sector held by the 3rd Battalion under

*Heavy artillery being understood.

Major Cordonnier, to which Captain de Gaulle's 10th company belonged – in the 33rd RI's journal, almost certainly written by Colonel Boud'hors himself:

> From six thirty in the morning, terrible shelling by heavy artillery over the whole breadth of the sector and to a depth of three kilometers. The earth trembled without a pause; the noise was unbelievable. No liaison,* either forward or to the rear, was possible; all telephone-wires had been cut and any messenger sent out was a dead man. [The] last came back to me wounded and said "The Germans are twenty yards away.", on the road from Douaumont to Fleury. Guns at the ready, we prepared to defend this approach-road whatever the cost.
>
> At about one fifteen in the afternoon, after a bombardment that had already cut the lines to pieces, the Germans launched their advance to encircle the 3rd Battalion. It was the 12th company, on the left of the 10th, that bore the brunt of their attack. The first who were seen were Germans rushing down from the fort *wearing French helmets*. Major Cordonnier, who was behind the centre of the 11th company, cried "Do not fire: they are French!" and almost at once he fell wounded or killed by a bullet in the throat,** while Sergeant-Major Bacro shouted "Fire away; they are Germans", himself shooting furiously. Soon the Germans were in the rear of the 10th company.
>
> It was then that this magnificent feat was performed. The 10th company was seen to charge straight forward at the massed enemy reaching the village, engaging them in a terrible hand-to-hand struggle in which these brave men received blows from rifle-butts and bayonets from every side until they were overpowered. Seeing itself completely surrounded, the 10th company launched itself in a furious attack led by its commanding officer, Captain de Gaulle, charging close-packed bodies of men, selling its life dearly and falling gloriously.

From that moment, therefore, Colonel Boud'hors assumed that de Gaulle had been killed among his men; and it was for that reason that some days later he put him forward for the Légion d'Honneur, with this draft of a mention in dispatches:

> Although he had been badly wounded by a bayonet-thrust [de Gaulle] after a furious hand-to-hand engagement, organized a knot of resistance in which his men fought until all the ammunition was gone, the rifles were shattered and the unarmed defenders had fallen. Although he had been badly wounded by a bayonet-thrust [de Gaulle] continued to be the heart of the defence until he fell senseless from the effects of poison-gas.

At Verdun, General Pétain received the draft concerning his former subordinate; he took it over, making the captain's role even more exalted and turning it into a

*Communication. (trs.)

**Charles de Gaulle gave an account of his death in a letter to his family. (*Lettres, Notes* . . . 1, p. 312–13.)

mention in his own despatches, published in the *Journal officiel* of 7 May 1916:

> When his battalion, having undergone extremely heavy shelling, was decimated and when the Germans were reaching his company on all sides, Captain de Gaulle, a company-commander well known for his great intellectual and moral value, led his men in a furious charge and a fierce hand-to-hand engagement, the only solution he thought compatible with military honour. Fell in the fighting. An incomparable officer in all respects.

This famous text cannot be used as an historical reference for General Pétain was even farther from the action than Colonel Boud'hors, to whom he owed what he knew. This second mention is no closer to reality than the first, in so far as "fell in the fighting" led the reader to suppose that the captain had not survived. Furthermore, some days later Henri de Gaulle, having learnt that his son was "missing", went to see the colonel of the 33rd, now resting, to know what to think about Charles's conduct and his fate. Boud'hors told him that the captain "had done his duty to the end".

When he returned from captivity thirty months later, Charles de Gaulle wrote Colonel Boud'hors a letter in which he said, "As it usually happens after unfortunate events, you have no doubt only been able to gather contradictory pieces of information about the engagement, more or less marked with the boastfulness of some, the disparagement of others and the defeatism of others again."[14]

To know what happened on 2 March 1916 north-west of Douaumont, between the shell-battered church and the ploughed-up road from Tavannes, one would like to refer to other witnesses of Charles de Gaulle's conduct on that tragic occasion.

On 16 April 1966 Samson Delpech, a farmer of the Haute-Garonne, wrote this account:

> I was transferred to the 33rd RI, 10th company, 2nd platoon, 7th squad, which had been decimated a few days earlier; and about ten days later I saw a new captain arrive, a very young man of 24 – Charles de Gaulle. He called us together and talked to us, thoroughly raising our morale by telling us that if ever there was anything rough to go through, he would be the first; and indeed our brave captain kept his word and we followed with enthusiasm.
>
> Then on the evening of 1 March we went to take up our positions in the village of Douaumont, where all that was left was a few bits of wall. To get there we went through the redoubts of the Douaumont fort in single file, because there were so many corpses piled up on either side it was horrible. When we reached our trench, Captain de Gaulle ordered us to dig it deeper; but alas every stroke of the pick uncovered dead bodies and we had to give it up and be satisfied with a depth of no more than two and a half feet.
>
> It was eleven in the evening. The night was quiet but about six o'clock in the morning the shelling began, mildly until eight, but from eight until twelve-thirty it became an absolute hell, a never-ending thunder, so that crouching in my trench I had to make a little hole in the ground with the

> front of my helmet to protect my head from splinters of every kind: so did my comrades.
>
> Then there was the attack. The Germans came in waves; we stopped five, but they broke through on our flank. We were surrounded, and under the orders of our Captain de Gaulle we were forced to surrender.

It will be observed that M. Delpech does not speak of the captain's wound. But who could see and remember everything in that hell paved with corpses?

De Gaulle's version of the facts is convincing. On 12 March 1916 he wrote to Marie-Agnès from the camp at Osnabrück where he was interned: "I fell into the enemy's hands in the fighting near Douaumont on March 2; I was wounded there by a bayonet-thrust in the thigh but not badly, and I have now recovered entirely."

Lastly, General Perré, whose hatred pursued de Gaulle for half a century,* stated that "according to one of his friends" who had been a prisoner with Charles de Gaulle, the Germans, who used to return the sword surrendered by officers distinguished for their courage, did not do so for de Gaulle.

With the passage of years, Charles de Gaulle reassembled the sequence of events on that terrible day; and his son Philippe, Admiral de Gaulle, echoes it faithfully in an article in *En ce temps-là, de Gaulle* (No. 6, p.96).

Having spoken of the extraordinary violence of the shelling of the 10th company's positions since dawn and the fury of the attack launched by the enemy, he describes the fighting in these words:

> From their shattered positions, the surviving defenders (37 for the 10th company) opened fire with their few undamaged weapons. A second bombardment, as violent as the first, completed the destruction of the battalion while the Germans outflanked it and carried on in its rear. The subsequent attack entirely isolated what was left of the 10th company ... From that time on there was only one chance of escaping annihilation which was to re-establish contact with the nearest friendly unit on the right.
>
> My father tried to lead his last able-bodied men in that direction but presently the handful of French soldiers was overwhelmed. My father, having flung a grenade at hazard, leapt into a shell-hole at the same time as several Germans. In the rush one of them gave him a thrust with his bayonet: the blade went in at the upper third of his left thigh and emerged in the middle third of the other side. He at once lost consciousness from the very severe pain.
>
> When the wounded man came to himself again, he found himself among a group of haggard young German soldiers belonging to the Prussian Guard. My father was given a first dressing by Dr François Lepennetier, the battalion medical officer, and the assistant-surgeon Gaston Detrahem, both of whom had just been captured as well, together with about sixty survivors, all that was left of the 3rd Battalion of the 33rd. In three days the regiment had lost 32 officers and 1443 non-commissioned officers and men.**

*The reason is shown in Chapter 15.

**At least 60 per cent of the strength.

Why does one, with but little hesitation, find this version more believable than the others? Not only because it is surrounded by sound guarantees but also because it agrees infinitely better with everything we know about Captain de Gaulle from other sources. Certainly, the bravest may no longer be himself after hours of enormously heavy shelling; nerves may give way, and a man may be shaken and half stunned.

Yet all those who saw anything of de Gaulle at that time observed in him an almost inhuman want of emotion in circumstances of this kind – a magnificent indifference to both terror and pain (though not, as we have seen, claiming any merit for it) and in addition an exceptional pride and sense of duty. If he can be reproached for anything at that time it is for "overdoing things". But whether it was excessive or not, everything leads one to believe that on that particular day he did what was required of him by his temperament and his mission.

CHAPTER FOUR

The Get-Away

"You can imagine how sad I am, finishing the campaign like this," wrote Charles de Gaulle to his sister Marie-Agnès[1] on 12 May 1916 from the camp at Osnabrück,* where he had been interned for some weeks. At first he was taken from Douaumont to Pierrepont, then to the hospital in the citadel at Mainz; and soon after that, "completely recovered" from his wound, he was transferred to the transit-camp at Neisse.

"Finishing the campaign like this." Was it being taken prisoner or was it being wounded that reduced his spirits to such an extent that he could write these words? Or was it not rather because he knew that from now on his letters were read by the German censors and that he had to conceal his intentions? The fact is that the apparent resignation did not last long and he did not spend much time thinking of himself as out of action: the history of Captain de Gaulle's thirty-two months of captivity, from March 1916 to November 1918 is primarily that of his attempts at rejoining his comrades in the firing-line.

Almost all his letters show his disgust for his condition as a prisoner, his extreme frustration at being unable to take part in the effort of the war, and sometimes even a kind of shame. Writing to his father on 15 July 1916 he speaks of his "lamentable exile" from those historic moments in which he "no longer counts for anything". And to his mother in September: "For a French officer, the state of being a prisoner is the worst of all."[2]

The captive's opinion of the German nation did not improve on closer acquaintance. Admittedly, on one occasion he did observe that it was not the people "who had fought at Douaumont or Belloy" who inflicted "vexations" upon his comrades and himself, because "they knew what we are worth and are often polite enough to tell us so"; it was the non-combatants.

So much resentment mounted up in his mind that he expressed the wish to see "hundreds of German officers made prisoner and quietly sent off to Dahomey".** And, no prophet for once, he added: "You will laugh when I tell you that among the Germans around us there are numbers – educated men for the most part – who have the audacity to come from time to time and talk to us about an alliance between their race and ours after the peace!!!"[3] This feeling of unbearable exile from history and this loathing of the people whose captive he was were not enough to plunge the captain of the 33rd RI in total despair for long. Although it is certain that when he told his family about his situation his

*Near Münster.

**In Benin, part of the French Empire. (trs.)

words were affected by his wish not to add to their sorrow, these remarks ring true:

> We are all in very good humour here and for each one of us our comradeship is the greatest comfort.
>
> As for myself, this way of life suits me very well. Since we are not allowed out I have decided to work at my German and to read Greek and Roman history, pen in hand.

In terms of Charles de Gaulle's cultural formation and training and of his intellectual evolution, we probably do not possess a more interesting document – before the beginning of his career as a writer in any case – than the extracts from his private notebook, as they are published in the first volume of *Lettres, Notes et Carnets*. Greek and Roman history were not his only basis. Exercises for the memory and quick summaries mingle with personal notes of the liveliest interest; we have the feeling that Charles de Gaulle's culture is being built up and moulded before our eyes.

Many of the statements and aphorisms that he put down in this notebook attracted his attention only because he was in a state of vacuity and isolation. But is not this openness, this availability, this kind of intellectual virginity more revealing than any other condition of mind and body?

Whether it was a period of burial or of continuation of his culture, his life was haunted, one might say justified, by an obsession – that of the escape which all prisoners in the world, their eyes filled with longing, call the "get-away".* A fighting-man could not bear being kept away from the battle and a patriot of his kind cursed himself for not serving his country in danger. In this environment the preparations for the get-away were the most absorbing distraction. Escape thus combined these two factors of the Gaullian dynamism as he defined them himself in the early pages of his *Mémoires de guerre* and which have already been discussed: the "conspicuous service" and the "whole point of life".

Reading Stendhal may have interested Captain de Gaulle, but not nearly so much as this form of action in which boldness was combined with guile. Risks taken, cleverness proved and a nasty trick played on the hated gaolers: every man, and especially a young officer, sighs for the days when he might play cops and robbers.

In April 1916, Captain de Gaulle, transferred from Osnabrück eastwards to the transit-camp of Neisse, drew up a scheme for escaping in a boat on the Danube. The scheme must have been detected by the authorities because at the end of April we find him in what was called a "reprisal" camp, a former saw-mill at Szuczyn in Lithuania.

The fifty-odd French officers sent to Szuczyn – where they lived together with some hundred Russians – had a far from ordinary leader in the person of Lt-Col. Tardiù, a Marine who had passed his career in Tonkin, a little crooked man with a chin like a shoe, whose insolence towards his keepers was so great that he was

*The French is *la belle*, which makes rather better sense of the text. (trs.)

court-martialled thirty-seven times, and by the time of the armistice he had been given about a hundred years of detention (in return for which he played a part in the German revolution of November 1918, crying "I am organizing chaos!").

Under the aegis of this steel-hard character, who was sufficiently impressed to grant him the rank of major on his own authority, Charles de Gaulle made friends with Lieutenant Roederer who slept on the straw mattress next to his. Roederer had been at the famous Ecole Polytechnique and he was an engineer in the Department of Mines; furthermore he spoke Russian, which was why he had the nickname of Gospodin.* Could one dream of a better escape-companion that this specialist in tunnels who spoke the language of the country that one would necessarily have to aim for, starting from a place so far to the east as Lithuania?

De Gaulle and Roederer decided to escape in August but the hole dug in the corner of the barn where they slept was soon detected by guards and this earned the entire body of French officers a variety of punishments, including that of being deprived of their Russian batmen. Tardiù had insisted upon their assuming responsibility as a whole. A few weeks later, in September, the Szuczyn camp was done away with and the three "awkward customers" Tardiù, de Gaulle and Roederer were transferred to a prison of quite a different nature, Fort IX at Ingolstadt in Bavaria, which its builders had described as a "high security camp".

Fort IX already had its legend, and one of its inmates, Lieutenant A.J. Evans, a British pilot captured on the Somme in 1916, recounts it in his book *The Escaping Club*. Between 100 and 150 officers, Russian as well as English or French, known for their tendency to escape, were concentrated there. The fiery Colonel Tardiù found himself perfectly at home in this band of unruly characters, and he and de Gaulle soon took particular notice of a Russian officer named Mikhaïl Tukhachevsky, the journalist Rémy Roure, the publisher Berger-Levrault (who was to bring out *le Fil de l'épée* ten years later), the very aristocratic Major Catroux, Captain Lelong and the already famous airman Roland Garros.

It was a curious atmosphere, that of the Ingolstadt fort, perched on the bank of a Danube that still foamed like a mountain torrent. "They are all criminals here", roared General Peter, the commander of the camp. Did the prisoners hope to repeat the operation? Straw mattresses were set fire to all the time; water bombs, concerts on mess-tins conducted by Colonel Tardiù and carried on late into the night were a permanent feature; and wandering among the continuous tumult there might be seen a tall, mocking fellow, blowing his cold-reddened nose, who answered to the name of Charles de Gaulle.

De Gaulle soon reached his conclusion: the lay-out of the fort, the barbed wire all round it and the surveillance from outside made a direct escape extremely doubtful. But the little town's garrison had its own hospital, to which there was attached a building reserved for prisoners of war. He was determined to get himself sent to it and swallowed the picric acid that his mother had sent him for his chilblains: the next day this produced the symptoms of a severe jaundice – yellow eyes, blotched complexion and cloudy urine.

The camp medical officer thought the case serious enough to send the tall

*The Russian for sir or mister. (trs.)

captain to the hospital, where he met Captain Ducret, also planning an escape. But the two officers observed that the prisoners' annexe was almost as closely guarded as the fortress itself: high palisades and sentries on the watch.

The hospital reserved for the Germans – most of them casualties from Verdun – was not guarded; the problem therefore consisted of passing from the annexe to the main building, which in any case was where the prisoners were taken for treatment every day. While a French workman, an electrician, did them the kindness to pile up their food and civilian clothes day-after-day in the hut he lived in close to the hospital courtyard, they bribed the German who took them to the main building and succeeded in getting him to buy them a map of the surrounding countryside. "From that moment on," wrote de Gaulle in 1927 "the man was at our mercy. Being told that if he did not obey we should report him at once and he would be court-martialled, he bought us a military cap in the town, and after a last and very strong resistance he let us have his trousers." This was 29 October. It was a Sunday, when there was a great deal more coming and going at the hospital than at other times. Ducret put on the male nurse's left-off coat, and once night had fallen it was under his guard that de Gaulle walked into the hospital and thence to the electrician's hut, where the food and the civilian clothes were hidden.

There they were, their rucksacks on their backs, on their way to Switzerland: Schaffhausen was about two hundred miles away. They travelled only at night and the continual rain slowed them down. Seven days had already passed since they had set off.

> At about 21 hours 30 on Sunday 5 November, the eighth day of our escape, we reached Pfaffenhoffen, a small town 30 kilometres south-west of Ulm, having travelled two thirds of our journey. We thought we should pass through without trouble. But it was Sunday. When we reached the central square, which was very well lit, we suddenly found ourselves in a crowd of young people of the town, who were fooling about in the streets. A week of living rough had given us the look of gallows-birds and we were noticed at once. We were arrested and taken to the town lock-up.

Charles de Gaulle was brought back to Fort IX. He decided to keep quiet for a while, hoping that a display of "good conduct" would get him transferred to a camp less unsuitable for carrying out his plans. From November 1916 to July 1917 he led a new kind of life at Ingolstadt, writing and reading and organizing lectures whose aim was not only to do away with boredom, to improve the prison community's level of general culture, to avoid intellectual rustiness and to maintain the collective morale – starting with his own – but also to hide his various preparations for escape behind a veil of serious study. His companion Rémy Roure, himself a journalist, told me how de Gaulle was "often alone, plunged in the reading of the German papers, jotting down his impressions, searching with extreme eagerness in the enemy's bulletins of victory for the still barely-perceptible signs of the turning tide, and very attentively studying the characters of the military and civilian leaders, searching for the gaps in their armour".[4]

During the last days of 1916 Charles de Gaulle considered that he had done enough research to be able to offer his companions – many of whom were of higher rank than himself and could not fail to be surprised by his boldness – a very broad picture of the war in progress. His accounts were spread over six months, from December 1916 to June 1917 and they have come down to us (reworked later?) in the form of four chapters. Two are joined under the general title "Concerning the war" and the two others are called "Concerning the higher direction of the war".[5] What Charles de Gaulle produced here was the beginning of a treatise on modern warfare in the light of what could be learnt from the first two years of the fighting.

These four lectures, read several decades later, still compel recognition for the solidity of their information, the discernment of their opinions, the breadth of the syntheses and the boldness of the criticism. Here everything foretells the great military historian; and it is by no means sure that his *La Discorde chez l'ennemi* or even *la France et son armée* quite fulfilled the promise contained in the lectures given by this twenty-seven-year-old prisoner-of-war captain to about a hundred of his companions, probable divided between irony and admiration.

Speaking of the offensives in Champagne during 1915 in which he was engaged before being wounded at Mesnil-lès-Hurlus, the captain of the 33rd RI said this:

> The infantrymen who took part in them, and who survived them, have a sad and bitter memory of those disastrous areas of attack where every day fresh corpses were piled up in the filthy mud; of those orders to attack whatever the cost, given over the telephone by such a distant command after a trifling artillery preparation, scarcely ranged or not ranged at all; of those assaults carried out with no illusions against deep and undamaged networks of barbed wire into which the best officers and the best men advanced, to be caught and killed like flies in a spider's web. In my humble opinion the later shortcomings of certain units that you have all heard about had no other cause than the demoralization arising from these pitiful experiments in which the infantry, the instrument that was used, reached as I can assure you the very depths of despair. Every time they were caught between the certainty of pointless death within ten yards of the trench they started from and the accusations of cowardice that the command – too much on edge and in any case devoid of illusions itself – was so generous with if the losses were not thought heavy enough for the command to be able to shelter itself behind.[6]

What more terrible words were ever written about that war? Here Captain de Gaulle lets his memory and his heart speak out – he lets their pity and their anger overflow. When one remembers that these "lectures" were primarily organized to "maintain the morale" of the captive officers, one can gauge the strength of the emotion that filled this twenty-seven-year-old officer at the recollection of those butcheries in which the mind of the command was so taken up with "sheltering behind the dead against those on higher levels still".

Charles de Gaulle was not much more backward in his criticism of the general conduct of the war. Here for example are some extracts from his Fort IX lectures:

> Gentlemen, it seems probably that History will state that the first phase of the war came to an end in October 1915. Up until that time France and her allies had not lost hope that the war might be brought to an end in the near future and at one blow. During that first period it must be admitted that in France the management of the war was by no means satisfactory. On the one hand the concept of the government's part in the higher direction was only slowly acknowledged; and on the other the organization set up before the war did not correspond to the needs that arose. I say nothing about the crisis that lasted from 15 August to 15 October, those tragic days when France, gasping with the effort, saw nothing but her armies in the fiery furnace and thought of nothing but halting the hideous invasion and then thrusting it back – those days when it seemed that there no longer existed anything except the battle itself.
>
> A decree of November 1915 appointed General Joffre commander-in-chief of the French armies and gave him authority over all our troops in all theatres of operations ... Then again the allied war councils laid down a good over-all strategy ... Thus, gentlemen, you had the general running of the war in the hands of the government, but now advised and helped as far as action was concerned by specialists, the ministers of war and of the navy. This system was incomparably better than that which went before, and the outcome proved it [but] we also have to observe that it bore within itself a considerable number of disadvantages. The third period of the campaign began with the winter of 1916 to 1917 and we are still in it at present. But in the meanwhile, gentlemen, Truth was beginning to become apparent, and very early in 1917 a decree set up a new organisation for the higher direction of the war. General Lyautey became war minister. Gentlemen, soldiers are made to act, to serve, and to command; parliamentary discussion is rarely their strong point. Passion and changeability mingle with arguments of this kind, which confuses them. In such a context discontent assumes by definition the character of bitter, violent criticism, which usually offends the attitudes of mind and the ways of thinking which soldiers possess and which they ought to possess by reason of their profession.

In that spring of 1917, as things were in the act of happening, de Gaulle explained and judged with a surprising clarity. His geographical isolation preserved him, perhaps, from the effects of the extreme proximity of the facts in time, and his different sources of information saved him from an excessive partiality. To be sure, the picture of the military situation in 1917 took little account of the entry of the Americans into the war. Some historians endowed with a depth of perspective would carry the description of the great arguments of 1914–1917 much farther. But let us admit that this prisoner's outlines already suggest a great deal.

Another point to observe in these commentaries on the Gallic wars is the discretion with which the former lieutenant of Arras speaks of the part played by General Pétain,* Charles de Gaulle's first commanding officer, the man who

*Who had just been promoted on 17 May to Commander-in-Chief of the French forces.

beyond all others had been revealed by the war, and who beyond all others was shown to have been right by the frightful disasters of 1914 and 1915. The general whose fame was now equal to that of the rivals: Joffre and Foch, Lyautey, Gallieni, Castelnau, Sarrail. De Gaulle only speaks of this officer, whose teaching in the matter of the "fire that kills" had proved to be one of the golden rules of this war, rules whose non-observance had led to the horrors which the prisoner-captain described with such a splendid indignation only as any other observer of the time might have spoken. Certainly he describes him as "exceptional"; but he attributes less praise to him than he does to Joffre or Foch.

What is so admirable (if one may say so) is that all the lessons learnt during the last three years, all the proofs drawn from the progress of the war, and all the very great fame and standing achieved by Pétain had been unable to make the captain give way. He acknowledged the facts, he admited the success and he counted the dead, respecting the commander who had spared the greater number of lives. But he did not join the other man's side. He might spend years in the "Pétain household", observe its rites, obey the master's directions, serve him diligently and agree with his views for a while, but he did not do so without applying the mental reservation taught by his Jesuit masters.

Once his lectures were done with, Charles de Gaulle felt that his time of "good behaviour" was over, and in June he set about looking for a prison from which it would be easier to escape. His request for a transfer was granted.

In July 1917 the Ingolstadt lecturer, accompanied by three of his comrades from Fort IX, Pruvost, Tristani and Angot (an airman and formerly one of his father's pupils in the rue des Postes), reached an old fortress, somewhat more agreeable than the one they had just left, at Rosenberg, near Kronach in Franconia (Bayreuth was not far off). It was a very handsome sixteenth-century building, bristling with lofty towers and perched on a steep rocky peak.

The French officers, numbering about fifty, were held in the central and highest part of this old Franconian fortress, where the ghosts of Wallenstein or Gustavus Adolphus might have appeared at any moment. They were guarded by comfortingly stout territorials. They got along together reasonably well, and they appeared to be waiting for the war to come to an end: newcomers had the appearance of intruders.

All the more reason to decide upon their plans without delay. The prisoners' part of the building was surrounded by two walls and two moats: the inner moat was their place for walking and the outer was adorned with a tennis-court that lay about twenty feet below the top of the rampart upon which the sentries made their rounds. So far, there was nothing that could not be crossed. The real problem lay with the sheer wall of rock upon which the castle was built and down which they would have to make a perpendicular descent. The four men did not know how high it was. Thirty feet? Or one hundred and twenty? The opinions of those who spoke to them about it varied as widely as that. So how long were they to make their rope? They plaited a ninety-foot length, using strips of sheet. They made an eighteen-foot ladder that could be taken to pieces.

On the evening of 15 October 1917 the rain was coming down very hard. This was to their advantage: the sentries would sit tight in their boxes and the sound of the rain would muffle the footsteps of the escaping prisoners. At the last moment another travelling-companion appeared, Captain de Montéty, who had reached Rosenberg that very day: they took him with them.

At about ten o'clock de Gaulle and his squad, who had crossed all the obstacles without much difficulty, were at the top of the cliff. They lowered Tristani on the end of the rope: he did not reach the bottom but remained swinging in the air. They hauled him up again and looked for a better lowering-place. A little farther on a fortification, some thirty feet high at the foot of the cliff might allow them to land. But only in two stages. One of the escapers would therefore have to stay up there to throw the rope down to those who had reached the top of the redan. Montéty, the newcomer, said he would do it.

It was then (according to Jean Pouget) that de Gaulle warned his companions: "Gentlemen, since I am physically incapable of climbing down a smooth rope more than a few yards, I beg you will lower me by hand." This they did.[7] Towards midnight, at the foot of the cliff, the four acrobats could set their course for the Swiss frontier. Schaffhausen was once more their destination, but this time it was not two hundred miles that lay between them and it, as had been the case at Ingolstadt, but nearly three hundred.

> After ten days march in the direction of Schaffhausen we were worn out with cold and fatigue and we had the unfortunate idea of sheltering for the day in a pigeon-house that stood by itself in the middle of the fields. Peasants working nearby heard us and warned a soldier who was guarding the Russian prisoners employed at a neighbouring farm. At nightfall the soldier and some civilians surrounded the pigeon-house and called upon us to come down. We were obliged to obey.[8]

De Gaulle and Tristani quickly decided to stake everything on one throw, because they knew that their escapade would result in their being sent straight back to Ingolstadt. On 30 October they sawed through a bar in their window; then, when a sentry's back was turned, they reached the courtyard while a friend put the bar back and hauled up the line by which they had climbed down. Dressed in civilian clothes and wearing false moustaches and spectacles they mingled with the German employees coming and going by the postern-gate and walked off. But they had been seen climbing down from the window; the alarm was given, their absence was established and the neighbouring gendarme posts were told to be on the alert.

This time, still in a hurry, they had decided to take the train at Lichtenfels (fifteen miles from Rosenberg) and go to Aix-la-Chapelle, where they would be in sight of the Dutch frontier. They reached the station at midnight. But the first train did not leave until five in the morning. Their stratagem had been observed, and the moment they stepped into their compartment the military police seized them by the collar.

They were sent back to Ingolstadt with all the unruly prisoners, the unrepentant members of the escaping club. He was not at all surprised, but even so, he was depressed for a while. This can be seen from a letter of 19 December 1917, that for once he addressed to both his father and his mother. It was the bitterest he wrote in the whole of the war. The most poignant, too:

> At the present moment a sorrow that will end only with my life, a sorrow more bitter than any I think I shall meet with at any time, is wringing me more severely than ever. When one is wholly formed for action, being so totally and irremediably useless during the hours we are now passing through; and being useless furthermore in my present position, which is the cruellest for a man and a soldier that can be imagined! Forgive me for showing this weakness and for complaining.[9]

The best written portrait we have of Charles de Gaulle as a prisoner dates from this period, when he rejoined his companions in Fort IX. We owe it to Ferdinand Plessy who published this recollection of the Constable as a prisoner at Ingolstadt and then Wülzburg.

> My first impression was that of a tall form, talking eagerly and at the same time sweeping a close-packed group of attentive listeners along with him almost at the double. He seemed to me unapproachable. I saw him closer when he came to visit Captain Brillat-Savarin in casemate 16, to which I had been assigned when I first came. It was obvious that de Gaulle thought very highly of this handsome soldier. When he addressed him his voice was warm with affectionate respect. De Gaulle had an unquestionable ascendency over those around him. Although his manners were unaffected and sometimes even familiar, he knew how to keep people at a distance. All the other young captains called one another *tu*. No one ever said *tu* to de Gaulle.[10]

The punishment for his two attempts at escape from Rosenberg was inflicted "during the winter of 1917–1918 in the usual conditions, shuttered windows, no light, special diet, nothing to read, no writing materials, half an hour's exercise a day in a court measuring a hundred square yards".

While Charles de Gaulle was lying in this kind of tomb at least one of his companions in Fort IX, Tukhachevsky, succeeded in making his get-away. "If you go back to Russia now [this was in December 1917]," his French friends said, in the hope of keeping him back, "they will shoot you, since you are the son of a noble family." "Shot? I shall be a general at twenty-five!" He was a marshal at forty. And he was shot at forty-three.

In May 1918, the members of the escaping club were transferred to the fortress of Wülzburg, a splendid military building in the Vauban manner,* three miles from Weissenburg.

In spite of its failure de Gaulle thought of repeating the operation he and Captain Ducret had tried at Ingolstadt – that of being escorted out of the camp by a comrade wearing a German uniform. Here indeed the conditions were more

*See footnote to page 79. (trs.)

favourable: the tailor of the *Landsturm* that provided their guards was installed on the ground floor of the building in which de Gaulle and his companions were detained. All that had to be done to obtain a non-commissioned officer's uniform was to break into the shop with the help of a few accomplices.

The idea was to behave as though the prisoner de Gaulle was to be transferred to another camp and escorted out of the fortress by a sentry. To make the operation more convincing the chaplain of Wülzburg, known to be one of de Gaulle's particular friends, along with Lieutenant Meyer, an infantryman like himself, went with him. They bade one another a most affectionate farewell. A civil orderly opened the door of the gateway. A few hundred yards away in the countryside, de Gaulle and Meyer came out of a thicket wearing civilian clothes. They laid their course for Nuremberg, there to take a train for Frankfurt.

They walked one day and one whole night and they had covered about half the distance (37 miles) when a patrol of military police asked them for their papers. It was all over. That same evening they were taken back to the fort at Wülzburg, where Charles de Gaulle once again found his friends Major Catroux, Captain Brillat-Savarin (who was soon transferred to Switzerland) and Lieutenant Plessy who now occupied the bed next to his in room 4.

They talked of nothing but escape, of course. Plessy, younger and lighter, thought of climbing the ramparts. De Gaulle, who knew his limits in this respect, preferred guile. He had noticed that every Monday morning the fort's dirty linen, heaped up in an enormous basket by orderlies, was taken to Weissenburg. Why not take all or part of the space in the basket and get oneself carried out between the moment the quartermaster checked the contents of the basket and the moment it was sent off, padlocked – the quartermaster and the laundress each had a key, no one else. But coping with the hinges was child's play for the "canaries", the team of evasion-specialists and technicians who were very well equipped at Wülzburg.

It was during the morning of Monday 7 July that Captain de Gaulle and his companions executed the plan. Having padlocked the basket, the quarter-master walked off to find the sentries who were to go with it. He would probably be away five or ten minutes. The moment he was out of sight, de Gaulle and two canary specialists went into the room, where two fatigue-men were waiting by the basket. With two strokes of a punch the canaries opened the basket; it was quickly emptied of its linen, which the fatigue-men carried back to the wash-house. While they were doing so, de Gaulle fitted himself as well as he could into the basket. The canaries closed the lid again, replaced the pivots of the hinges by a supple steel cable painted the colour of the wickerwork, and passed the ends of the cable through the side of the basket so that de Gaulle, inside, could grasp and hold them in his hand.

The loading of the basket and its carriage to Weissenberg took place without a hitch. When everything was quiet again de Gaulle pulled the cable-end to free the hinges. He raised the lid without difficulty and managed to get out of the basket unseen. Wearing civilian clothes, he mingled with the passers-by, walked out of Weissenberg, hid in the neighbouring forest, and then made for Nuremberg, which he reached on the morning of the third day.

But bad luck dogged him. He was suddenly struck down with a violent intestinal flu and by the time he came to Nuremberg he was trembling with fever. His plan had been to take a night train (they were the least strictly watched) from Nuremberg to Frankfurt and then the next day another to Aix-la-Chapelle; but in his then state, he thought it better to get into the first train that was leaving rather than be immobilized by his illness.

At the Nuremberg station he had no difficulty in buying a ticket and he got into the crowded Frankfurt express. He stood in the corridor, holding a handkerchief over his mouth and behaving as though he had a violent cold, so as to avoid having to talk to his neighbours. But he once again chanced upon the military police: both ends of the corridor were guarded and there was nothing for it but surrender.

In July 1918 the news from the front was not good: it was the second battle of the Marne, into which Ludendorff was throwing all the imperial forces set free by the German-Soviet agreement of Brest-Litovsk in March 1918; a battle whose outcome, until the check at Villers-Cotterêt on 19 July, was as uncertain as that of the hand-to-hand struggle of 1914. Although he now believed that the war would last a long while, Charles de Gaulle refused to lose confidence. In a letter to his father on 16 July he spoke of his "rational pride in belonging to the admirable French army, against which nothing can prevail, an imperishable model of courage, of fighting science, and of the will to conquer".

He said the same to the others in the barrack-room, particularly to Plessy.

> Looking at the map with the German lines along the Marne between Epernay and Château-Thierry, he thundered out, "He thinks he is in a winning position; but he is really only sinking himself a little deeper!" "He" was Ludendorff: De Gaulle loathed him.
>
> When he had finished studying the map he went down into the courtyard, where he found his usual group of listeners. During his circular walk he set forth his ideas on the position and on the developments that were to be foreseen. Then, physically relaxed, he would come back to room 4, where he would often lie on his bed and meditate in silence, lighting a cigarette from time to time. When his meditation was over he would leap up and put his thoughts in writing.
>
> Next to the study of the front, his greatest interest was that of the newspapers. He loved following the development of public opinion now that the initiative had returned to the Allies. He watched for the slightest display of Bavarian separatism, which was always ready to start up once things began to go badly. He wrote his own communiqué on the home situation and pinned it up on the door of our building. He was positively delighted when he saw the interpreter-sergeant reading it at length.
>
> He very rarely spoke about himself, so I was surprised when one evening he made this unexpected confidential remark, "Did you know that fundamentally I am a shy man?" I protested vigorously. The statement was in absolute contradiction with the ease of his natural ascendency and with his outstanding eloquence, helped by a prodigious memory.

At the time I thought that what de Gaulle called his shyness was nothing but an extreme modesty. The primitive arrangements of Wülzburg obliged the prisoners to live in complete openness. The room with the showers, in particular, was equipped with no more than benches against the walls and with a duckboard in the middle and the sprinklers over it. No partitions to hide one's nakedness from the others. Thus I became acquainted with the anatomy of all my companions from Major Catroux, the most senior, to the Abbé Michel, our chaplain.

All except one: de Gaulle. What time did he choose to wash by himself? I never thought about it, but the fact is there – I never saw de Gaulle naked.

Meanwhile the process of liberation was moving fast; Foch, now reinforced by the Americans, drove a sword-point at Ludendorff's retreating army, back from Château-Thierry in July to Douai in October. It was now, when everything told the national community that the darkness was ending, that in a fairly predictable psychological reversal the individual Charles de Gaulle plunged into a heartbroken melancholy. On 1 September 1918, when the enemy fronts were beginning to crack everywhere, he wrote to his mother:

> I am buried alive. The other day I read in some paper that prisoners returning to France were called "ghosts". What aim can I have? My career, you say? But if I cannot get into the fighting again between now and the end of the war, shall I stay in the army? And what commonplace kind of a future would I have there? Three years, four years of war in which I have not taken part: perhaps more!* The first, the essential condition for a future in the army, as far as officers of my age with some degree of ambition are concerned, will be to have gone through a campaign, to have learnt how to judge it,** to have moulded one's reasoning, and to have tempered one's character and one's authority. From the military point of view I have no illusions; I too shall be no more than a "ghost".[11]

How could so flamboyant a character, moved by such a noble ambition, avoid feeling that at the moment of the great liberation fortune had betrayed him? Shut out from history, rejected by fame, a "ghost".

Even at that time, and without looking at the lost, troubled officer of 1918 in the light of the prodigious future that we all know about, one could easily have objected that a miracle would be required to make a "ghost" of a man who had begun the war in August 1914 at the head of a platoon of front-line troops in the 33rd RI, and that the army which he so astonishingly thought of leaving could not fail to need men such as himself.

Charles de Gaulle served his sentence between 15 September and 10 October 1918:

*Up until that time, taking his wounds and his captivity into consideration, he had missed two years and ten months.

**It is known that he was not behind-hand in this respect.

> I was first sent to the military prison at Passau, mingled promiscuously with the German convicts – murderers, deserters, thieves, etc. Then, three days later, after my vigorous protests and the threat of a hunger-strike, I was taken to Magdeburg where I finished the three weeks at the same time as the other sentenced officers.

From his confinement at Magdeburg, that place so loaded with warlike memories that it could not leave a French historian unmoved, standing there in the shadow of the fort of Scharnhorst. On 15 October and from Wülzburg, to which he had been returned, he spoke of his total participation in the general happiness – Berlin had asked for an Armistice on 4 October. Yet on 1 November, having paid a tribute to our "beloved dead", he let a gust of his "ghost's" resentment come to the surface.

> It is true that for me the immense joy I share with you is mingled with the indescribable and even more bitter regret at not having played a better part in it. I feel that this regret will never leave me all my life long, whether it be short or long.[12]

Just where he was when the Armistice was signed is hard to say. We know that at this period he made a short stay at the Ludwigshaven Anilinfabrik. On 1 December we find him at Romanshorn on the Swiss frontier, at Geneva the next day, and on 3 December at Lyons. Then after a fleeting visit to Paris here he was with his family at La Ligerie, where Henri de Gaulle had particularly wished to gather them all, far from the ruins and the wounds of war.

It is from those days, when a wonderstruck French family saw all four of the young men who had set out come home alive, that there dates a photograph taken in front of the old house in Périgord. It shows the four de Gaulle brothers, two captains (Xavier and Charles), one lieutenant (Jacques), and one officer-cadet (Pierre) buttoned up in their identical uniforms – Charles's brothers had exchanged their black gunner's jackets for horizon-blue like his. The sombre "ghost", somewhat to the rear by way of symbolizing his state during these last years and set in the rigidity of one who had been excluded, nevertheless stands there without any obvious complex. He knew that for those who can look it in the face, history is never finished and closed.

Besides, he was far from supposing that the French army was so sure of its definitive victory that it could turn up its nose at energy and gifts like his. Far from it, as may be seen from the end of his last lecture to his companions at Wülzburg at a date that is not exactly known:

> The nations of old Europe will end by signing a peace that their statesmen will call a peace of mutual understanding and which in fact will be a peace of exhaustion. But everyone knows, everyone feels, that this peace is only a shabby cloak thrown over unsatisfied ambitions, hatred more inveterate than ever and unextinguished national anger.[13]

CHAPTER FIVE

The School

The Armistice was not peace, and the peace was not to be serenity. In the opinion of men like Captain de Gaulle, who in this field was fully representative of the majority of French public opinion, France had had one enemy in 1914 and now she had two. The crushed German was still the Boche who was responsible for the murder of millions of soldiers. For his part the Russian was now no more than "the Bolshevik", the still more hateful traitor who had stabbed his allies in the back at Brest-Litovsk. So in the West all that mattered now was keeping the vanquished nation down, and in the East liquidating the Red Revolution.

Who could cherish these plans and these dreams more intensely than a nationalist officer quivering with the frustrations of captivity. "I finish the war," he wrote to his mother "overflowing with a general xenophobia and wholly convinced that to make ourselves respected we must come back to the rational use of our military strength, now the greatest in the world".

Now, at the dawn of 1919, when the victors were gathering at Versailles, Captain de Gaulle above all expected of Clemenceau and Foch that they should brandish the "flaming sword" in order to "impose upon the odious loser, a defeat totally crushing politically, militarily and economically", and he openly rejoiced that "a great expedition to Russia was being prepared". For the moment he was only the "ghost" intensely eager to get back into the struggle.

But Charles de Gaulle had enough intelligent ambition to wish this struggle to be primarily studious. He knew perfectly well that what he had lost during this two-and-a-half years was not the chance of fighting and of proving his courage – that was already done – but experience of the new techniques and of the new developments in combat. As far as general strategy was concerned he knew pretty well all that could be known by an officer of his time. But what had escaped him after 1916 was the field tactics, the use of weapons and the methods of organization that must have changed the face of battle between Verdun and Rethondes.* So he went to school.

This whole period from the beginning of 1919 to the end of 1924 was his time of readaptation. With a certain time-lag he absorbed the lessons of the war: he learnt. But we know that de Gaulle, unlike the British who have different words for learn and teach, tended to make the process a single operation, and on occasion he did not scorn improving the knowledge or the powers of reflection of the person charged with instructing him.

* * *

*Rethondes was where the Armistice was signed. (trs.)

The weeks of leave at La Ligerie passed quickly. While he was there he learnt that a refresher course for company-commanders returned from captivity was about to start at Saint-Maixent. He hurried there, and five days after his arrival he wrote to his mother, "From the psychological point of view I am as it were reborn, finding myself back in military life". He thought the teaching, given by officers coming directly from the front, was well done, and he observed that as his studies were concerned with "whatever has appeared in the way of new weapons or equipment and their use" he would soon be "perfectly fitted for taking command". Furthermore, the colonel in charge of the course told him confidentially that with his service-record he could, if he wanted to, "make himself a very fine career".[1] If he wanted to!

But he was already thinking of something else. "I am on tenterhooks," he wrote to his family on 21 January. He had not yet had any answer from the War Ministry, to which, just before going to Saint-Maixent, he had sent a request to be seconded to the Polish army. What was all this about? The great expedition against the Soviets, seen as starting from Warsaw or Bucharest or even Odessa, where a Franco-Greek expeditionary force was being gathered under the orders of General d'Anselme? Or more simply the training of the army of an allied country, thousands of whose subjects were then assembled in the Seine-et-Marne under the orders of General Joseph Haller (a Pole who had deserted from the Austrian army and had reached France by way of Russia) in order to form the framework (four divisions) of the Warsaw government's army?

Here do not let us fall into Polish romanticism. Charles de Gaulle was not setting out in order to pay France's debut to Poniatowski or Dombrowski.* Nor should we see him as a crusader armed for the battle against the Red Antichrist. On 11 February he wrote to tell his father that he had heard that volunteers were being recruited for the "Eastern army" and that he had at once sent in his name "with joy".[2] He did not exclude the Polish mission. But if he had the chance of "going through a campaign in an equally active fashion with French troops" he would "eagerly" choose the second hypothesis.

In a letter to his father he regretted that France "was sinking in an ocean of stupidity, idleness and official insolence. Whatever may be his position in the hierarchy, no one does his job. How very much we need a Richelieu or a Louvois!"**

At the beginning of April he was at Lorrez-le-Bocage, just about to leave for Warsaw, where he would be engaged in instructing the officers. He was already provided with a batman who, as he told his mother, had served in the German army during the war, and had fired on him at Berry-au-Bac in 1915. The French mission had its quarters at Mödlin, some twenty miles from Warsaw, a huge military base where the instruction was to be carried out.

The first impressions were not very good. The officers, who had been trained by the Austrians, the Germans or the Russians as the case might be, did not welcome the French instructors without reservation. Around Pilsudski*** the rivalries and

*The former was one of Napoleon's marshals, the latter a Republican general. (trs.)
**The Marquis de Louvois (1639–91) was Louis XIV's War Minister. (trs.)
***The new master of Poland, a general trained in the Austrian army.

the intrigues increased in number. After a month in Poland the new instructor wrote, "Left to themselves these people are good for nothing, and the worst of it is that they believe themselves to excel in everything." No one is more blindly contemptuous than an inexperienced traveller.

As we have seen, he did not mind displaying his xenophobia at this time; and it was capable of taking the form of antisemitism. He included this remark in a description of the troubled state of Polish society in 1919:

> In the midst of all this, countless . . .,* utterly loathed by all classes of society and all of them enriched by the war, during which they profited at the expense of the Russians, the Boches and the Poles; and they are quite favourable to a social revolution in which they would gather in a great deal of money in exchange for a few dirty tricks.

Was it the Poles' good nature? The Polish women's charm? The Légion d'honneur which he was awarded in July? The fact that he was promoted major "on the score of being in Poland"? Or the pleasure he took, and was always to take, in teaching? In a letter to his mother written in August 1919 he described himself as being "pretty well as I remember myself before that vile captivity. I have recovered confidence in myself and in the future". "The Polish army will have been what I meant it to be, a military restoration for me. Afterwards, I shall work on my own behalf."[3]

The best account of Major de Gaulle's teaching in Poland is quite certainly that of the officer who was then his assistant and interpreter, Lieutenant de Medvecki.[4]

> At Rembertow, some ten miles from Warsaw, we had the advantage of a huge camp, rather like that at Mailly, for the officer-pupils, with the offices and all the administrative services. Since Poland had decided to follow the French tactics of movement on the battle-field, the greatest possible number of officers** had to be taught as quickly as it could be done, so that the necessary uniformity of doctrine should be achieved. Everything concerned with the advance of troops and fighting was strictly reserved for Major de Gaulle, the head of the course. He was a brilliant lecturer, listened to with the keenest attention; and he already knew how to entertain an audience with an unexpected, trenchant witticism.
>
> The relations between de Gaulle and the other French instructors were extremely reserved. They were young officers and took advantage of their position as conquerors to give themselves a good time and go to Warsaw, where they were cherished and adored. De Gaulle rarely went to Warsaw, and when he came back from it he used to talk philosophy to me. I remember

*The shamefaced points of suspension inserted here (by the author or by the editor?) cannot hide the fact that Jews are meant. It may be added that the remark tells us more about the circles in which Charles de Gaulle then moved (the drawing-rooms of Warsaw and the Polish officers' messes) than about his inmost feelings, which were later seen to be quite different.

**Among whom were a good many who had fought in the German army, "De Gaulle's most attentive listeners", observes Medvecki.

> an occasion when he was wishing me good night at his cottage door just as one in the morning was striking and he said, "You know, Medvecki, we belong to the generation of catastrophes".

In May 1920, allied to Petliura, the Ukrainian hetman, the Poles flung themselves upon the Ukraine and seized Kiev. That was carrying the challenge to Russian power too far; two months later the Red army, trained by Budienny and Tukhachevsky who was de Gaulle's friend at Ingolstadt (already a general at twenty four) hustled the Polish divisions back to within forty miles of Warsaw.

Tukhachevsky, who was accompanied by a political commissar named Stalin, proclaimed, "The road to the world-wide blaze lies across Poland's dead body!" And at the same time a revolutionary "government" was set up at Bialystok under the presidence of Julian Marchnowski, who called upon the Polish workers to rise. Charles de Gaulle, watching these earthquakes, told his family that now, at the beginning of July 1920, the most disturbing factor "was not so much the retreat of the Polish troops as the unhappy confusion of the public mind".

On 3 July, just as Tukhachevsky's threat to Warsaw became quite clear, he wrote to his mother, "Are we going to be brought to armed intervention against the Russians here? It is very risky."[5] All the more risky since the German Social Democratic government baulked against any "violation of its neutrality" and even spoke of an alliance with Moscow.

In any case, France, which claimed to be actively helping the Polish ally, sent General Weygand at the head of a "diplomatic" mission on 21 July, a mission charged with finding a political solution. But Foch's confidential agent also had the mission of "advising" Pilsudski, whom he saw as "the rampart of Christian civilization in the West". At the beginning of August the Red army was held on the Bug. A fortnight later Pilsudski launched a counter-attack and thrust the enemy back towards East Prussia. Weygand, whose part in the "miracle of the Vistula" has never been made quite clear, was back in Paris at the end of August.

Charles de Gaulle gave an account of his mission with the Polish General Staff during those dramatic days of July and August 1920 in an article that retained the form of the notes he made in the field and that was published (without signature) as early as 1 November of the same year in *La Revue de Paris* under the title of *La Bataille de la Vistule*. In comparison with his lectures as a prisoner it is a little disappointing. It does nevertheless contain some moving observations on the extreme poverty of the Polish people: "To measure the depth of wretchedness that human beings can reach, one must have seen the horrible crowds in the Praga or Wola suburbs. Our civilization is very fragile. All the wealth it is so proud of would soon vanish under the furious assault of the desperate masses."

On 5 August Major de Gaulle once again beheld "noble Warsaw quite silent: the city felt the Russians at its gates". On the fourteenth, when the counter-attack had been launched, he took part in the recapture of Hrubischow by the Poles. And on the seventeenth, there was Pilsudski thrusting his northward movement home:

> The enemy, taken completely by surprise at finding his left flank attacked by the Poles, whom he had supposed to be in a desperate state, offered no

> serious resistance at any point but either broke and fled in every direction or surrendered, whole regiments at a time. Ah, what an elegant manoeuvre we saw here! Our Poles had wings to carry it out, and the very soldiers who a week ago were physically and psychologically exhausted now hurried forward, accomplishing marches of twenty five miles a day.

On the road back to Warsaw:

> the peasants took off their hats to us. Here was the Praga bridge, and this time we should not have to blow it up! And here at last was the capital. A deep sound of restrained joy arose from the crowd, and in the people's eyes could be seen their proper pride in the reborn Poland's first great victory.

It is easy to imagine how the officers who had taken any part at all in this victorious campaign were welcomed in this capital, where it was usual for war, music and love to take the form of a trio. And it was now that de Gaulle, who mixed so little with his young colleagues, decided to indulge himself a little. He had been appointed chief personal assistant to General Niessel, head of the French mission, and he was at the centre of that French "court" which the victory had hung about with glory.

The recollections of the inhabitants of the Nowy-Swiat, Warsaw's rue Royale, date from this short period from August to October 1920: they readily speak of a French officer, built like a light horseman, who was often to be seen at the famous café Blikle, where he ate *ponskis** in the company of an exceptionally small person said to be the Countess Czetwertinska. A legend? For his part, Jean Pouget, quoting from a Polish memoir, speaks of parties at which Charles de Gaulle, together with his friends Laperche and Touzet du Vigier** was the cynosure of all eyes – evening parties in those drawing-rooms which were never unwilling to look upon uniformed Frenchmen with particular favour.[6]

It was not the ladies of Warsaw alone who favoured him: his superiors, both Polish and French, did the same. His conduct in Poland considered as a whole – his lectures at Rambertow until July, his taking part in the Vistula operations together with General Bernard during the summer, and his time on General Niessel's personal staff – earned him a crop of reports and mentions in dispatches which amply justified his foray to the East. His personal file was studded with eulogies: thus, on 20 December, when his mission came to an end, we find:

> An officer of the very first rank; has somewhat lofty airs however which may harm him with his comrades. A great loss for the infantry instruction school, where it will be exceptionally hard to replace him. Furthermore, the Polish authorities made a most flattering request that he should remain as an instructor in the battalion-commanders' course.

*Something like doughnuts, but very much lighter.
**Who was to command the 1st Armoured Division in 1944.

A few days later came a fresh bow in his direction:

> An officer whose qualities destine him for a very fine military future – a collection of qualities rarely combined in the same degree: a bearing that inspires respect, a strong personality, firm character, active and cool in the presence of danger, wide culture, great intellectual value. Suitable for employment as instructor in military school. Also seems an obvious candidate for the Ecole Supérieure de Guerre.

The next day this drum-roll was completed by a note, also written by General Bernard, in which there is a word that may cause some surprise: "Modest". Modest? The reader will have raised his eyebrows. Perhaps Charles de Gaulle did the same.

From the Poland that he was leaving he did not bring back only praise; the discovery of wretchedness on a huge scale and the strengthening of his powers as a teacher. Poland was also the most striking confirmation of an idea that he had faintly discerned as early as 1914 and that was to be at the heart of his political, diplomatic and military doctrine as long as he lived, to wit, that men are actuated above all by national solidarity.

The Russians, confronted with the Polish invaders of the Ukraine, had reacted as Russian patriots; the Poles, confronted with the Bolsheviks calling for a people's rising and for the brotherhood of the poor, had reacted as Poles. Tukhachevsky, the young comrade of Ingolstadt, had not been able to enter Warsaw as Bonaparte had entered Milan. In the course of a century, had "national anger" taken precedence over collective ideology?

The Polish experience was also fruitful as far as his calling was concerned. In the report on the Polish army that he wrote for the General Staff at the end of his mission there is a remark that rings out like a warning – it is a flashing signal in Charles de Gaulle's thought and his deeds: "Tanks should be brought into the field in a body, not separately."[7] These few words brought back from Warsaw were to be at the origin of a great many more. If it were only for this single observation, the Polish campaign would have been worthwhile.

But why shorten this mission that was so rich in both instruction and laurels? Among the notes concerning his chief personal assistant towards the end of 1920, General Niessel wrote this short but eloquent remark: "Captain de Gaulle wishes to return to France in order to marry."

The notion of marriage had been in his mind for some time, encouraged by his mother. It was in reply to a suggestion of Mme de Gaulle's that he first spoke of this hypothesis in July 1919, confessing that his cousin Thérèse Kolb had made a "vivid impression" upon him and that he had been "very deeply struck" by her charm and her intelligence. "But," he added, "it is years now since I saw her and I cannot believe that she remembers my commonplace being."[8] What happened to Thérèse Kolb? When Charles brought the subject up again in November 1919 there was no longer any question of her. Replying to his mother, who had written to him about the marriage of his brother Xavier, he said, "You know what I hope this year will bring me myself – a family, and, in the peaceful quietness of a deep and sanctified love, the power of giving someone else all the happiness that a man can give." That is how, in that milieu and in that era, one spoke to one's mother.

Major de Gaulle left for Paris on leave at the beginning of October 1920. On the Vistula he had just thrown back one hundred million Bolsheviks. But in Paris he was about to fall into a family ambush. He had not been back in France a week before Mme Denquin-Ferrand, a friend of his parents (and his father's god-daughter) gave a party to which de Gaulle was invited. Among the other guests there were the Vendroux, distinguished people from Calais, together with their twenty-year-old daughter Yvonne. This was the first phase of a conspiracy which no one has ever described in so pure a contemporary style nor with greater accuracy than the girl's brother Jacques, who was, if not the prime mover, then at least one of the main performers.

The family tree of the Vendroux published by Yvonne's elder brother at the beginning of this book shows them as being descended from a Pope, which is not usual among good Catholics; nor, it must be added, among others.[9] Yet it does appear that Julius III had a natural daughter, Mme de Monti, who, having married a Caffieri (the grandfather of the sculptor Mazarin brought to France who had a son whose godfather was Louis XIV) became the ancestress of a young lady who married Jacques Leveux, the mayor of Calais just before the Revolution. Under the Empire a Leveux daughter married a certain Jacques-Philippe Vendroux.

The Vendroux, whose name was originally Van Droog, had been obliged to leave the Low Countries by the flood that enabled William of Orange to repel Louis XIV. Since the beginning of the eighteenth century they had been inhabitants of Calais, and good, solid middle-class inhabitants of Calais. They were ship-owners, town councillors, members of the chamber of commerce and consuls for various powers. Jacques-Philippe IV (numbers were used, as at Versailles or Schönbrunn), Yvonne's father, was also the chairman of the board of directors of a biscuit factory, so that since the beginning of the century the name had been connected more with food than shipping.

His wife, Marguerite Forest, was from the Ardennes. Photographs show her as very fair and very good-looking with a slightly pointed, tip-tilted nose, a brilliant complexion and a slim figure. She was the sixth woman in France to pass her driving-test; and during the war she was matron of the Calais hospital, where she made such use of her authority that she was awarded the Croix de Guerre. She was a distinguished woman from a well-to-do family: they possessed an old family house in Calais, land in the nearby village of Coulogne, a flat in Paris, and above all the Château de Sept-Fontaines near Charleville, a splendid Premonstratensian abbey that had become the Forests' house. People of real weight.

From Jacques Vendroux's portrait of his sister we see that Yvonne had spirit and a straightforward character. Here is one example. The nuns of the Visitation convent at Périgeux, where she had been sent during the war had no baths, so they took their girls once a week to the municipal bath-house. Although the girls had separate cubicles the nuns insisted that they must keep on their slips while they bathed. She, at the risk of causing a scandal, just left hers beside the bath. At the same period, as we have seen, Charles de Gaulle's companions wondered how he managed never to be seen naked under the shower at Wülzburg.

A family photograph shows Yvonne Vendroux among her people in 1920. She is sitting upright in her chair, wearing a severe white blouse and an even more severe black skirt; she has a tennis-racket on her knee; her pale face, with its regular features, is good-looking; her brilliant eyes under a high forehead framed by a mass of black hair look straight forward. One can imagine Major de Gaulle receiving this photograph in his warriors' monastery of Rambertow: he took the train immediately afterwards.

We left them in Mme Denquin-Ferrand's drawing-room. Speaking of these moments, which seem to have been decisive, Jacques Vendroux merely tells us that the conversation turned upon a picture in the Salon d'Automne which was then much discussed – Van Dongen's *la Femme en bleu*. "Why don't we go and look at it together?" suggested the mistress of the house, a subtle character. "Then afterwards we can have tea there, at the Grand Palais." So there they were in front of Van Dongen's canvas ("How daring!"). Out of the corner of their eyes the conspirators observed two or three private remarks between the young lady and the major. The party had tea, an occasion that the chronicle makes almost as famous as the encounter of Jupiter and Alcmene: did he or did he not spill his cup of tea on Yvonne's dress? "No!" replies the horrified chorus of family piety. "Oh yes I did," states Charles. Let us be satisfied with that highly authorized version.

The Vendroux, as we have seen, had a small flat in Paris, in the boulevard Victor, and some days later an invitation to a ball at Saint-Cyr, addressed to Yvonne and her brother Jacques, was delivered there. The conspirators exulted. And yet the Vendroux wondered: Yvonne remained silent. Her brother was asked to sound her: "It's for him to say what he feels," she replied. "And he is nearly a foot and a half taller than I am." But for all that she did ask some questions about this awkward giant's past and future.

A tall blue figure came forward in the hall of the Hôtel des Réservoirs at Versailles, where the Saint-Cyr ball was being held. Would they dance? Jacques Vendroux saw nothing of the kind, but he did observe a long conversation carried out from "two armchairs with a proper space between them". The brother-chaperon treated them to orangeade: the major replied with a glass of champagne. "Your sister has just told me that she is very fond of mountains, and above all the alpine flora that can be seen when one is high up." And Yvonne Vendroux carried on with great spirit about Wimereux and the beaches of the Nord, where the two families must often have rubbed shoulders.

Back in Paris. "Well?" said Jacques. Yvonne: "I was not bored at all." A telephone-call from the Vendroux parents to their son: "The other side has expressed favourable feelings." Three days later Yvonne gave way: "It will be him or no one!" But Charles' leave came to an end on 20 November: the teas, suppers and family dinners therefore increased in number. They became engaged on 11 November. Champagne, a diamond ring and "the first kiss in public" as Jacques Vendroux specifically states. Charles had been obliged to promise General Niessel that he would return and spend two months with him in Warsaw. The marriage was fixed for April. Before then it was hoped that the Polish major, changed back into a French captain, would have obtained the appointment he was aiming at, that of professor of history at Saint-Cyr.

Back in Warsaw, Charles de Gaulle learnt that General Niessel was willing to set him free as early as 10 January. Writing to M. and Mme Vendroux at Christmas, he said, "When I think of the treasure that you have agreed to give me, I am filled with an immense gratitude towards you." Assuring them that "exile had never seemed to him so sad, and that for the dearest of reasons," he added, "Poor Poland is still thoroughly unsettled and very much to be pitied. When I leave it for good I shall take with me, as a summing-up of my impressions, the thought that keeping the country alive will be very difficult".[10]

Armed with a mention in dispatches for his conduct in Poland*, de Gaulle came back to Paris at the end of January. His posting as assistant-professor of history at Saint-Cyr was confirmed, and on 6 February the Vendroux made him welcome at Calais. The civil marriage was fixed for 6 April.

The mayor of Calais, M. Duquenoy-Martel, talked to the young couple about "the beautiful smooth path that an open-handed life has so generously laid out for you", and, referring to the bride's mother, he spoke of the ceremony in which "General Ditte, then military governor of the town, pinned the Croix de Guerre both on the maternal bosom and on that of her son, a son who had respected the virtues sucked in with his mother's milk".

They met again the next day for the "real" marriage in the church of Notre-Dame-de-Calais, a curious fortified building in Tudor style: a "three-horse Mass", says Jacques Vendroux, with an air by Bach, a sermon by the Abbé Baheux, a family friend, Mendelssohn's March, with all the middle class of Calais crowded into the vestry. Then an eleven-course dinner and a waltz executed by the captain ("I do not think life will provide me with any other chance of seeing my brother-in-law dancing"). At seven in the evening the pair took the train for Paris and then on to Lake Maggiore, "where", observes Jacques Vendroux, "they alone know what happened at Pallanza, in the scent of the Borromean isles".

Captain Charles de Gaulle was becoming more and more intimate with the military order: how could this be bettered than by teaching the young men of Saint-Cyr the history of battles? Perhaps he was never happier than during this year of 1921; at a time when the wife he loved told him that she expected a child at the end of the year, and when he was displaying the knowledge and the talent which he had already shown in Ingolstadt and Rambertow, and of which he was justly proud, before the audiences of the Saint-Cyr.

It was by no means easy. To lecture and to convince without becoming the target for commonplace mockery, this white-gloved, throttle-necked, black-booted speaker had to control his great semaphore-like frame and its over-wide gestures that swept away both objections and cups of tea, and that chest-voice that would suddenly rise into his throat and produce an untimely and involuntarily bantering quaver. He had to tame his body, that paradox, and turn his awkward-

*Three months later he was given the Polish order Virtuti Militari.

ness into an advantage. The evidence collected today leads one to suppose that he was already succeeding.

The son of the schoolmaster, de Gaulle was a teacher people listened to. He was already mastering that sometimes abrupt and sometimes flowing eloquence as well as those highly-skilled gestures and the virtuoso mimicry that were to earn the founder of the Fifth Republic some millions of votes at each election.

"At Saint-Cyr in 1921," says General Nérot,

> we had three history professors: Captain Morel, whose subject was the soldier in antiquity; Major Desmazes, who spoke about the French armies under the Ancien Régime; and Captain de Gaulle, who described their history from the beginning of the Revolution to the armistice of 1918. Morel was a first-rate teacher: people compared him to Ardant du Picq. But it was de Gaulle who impressed us the most. Each one of his lectures was literally an event.
>
> He was not the only one to walk into the great amphitheatre in boots and with a sword at his side. But with him it all took on a solemn and impressive air. He would take off his képi, unbuckle his sword which he would put next to his hat on the desk, and then, keeping his gloves on, he would gaze at the audience in a way peculiar to himself. Immensely tall, upright, with his stiff collar tight round his over-long neck, he would talk for two solid hours without looking at his notes. He quite overcame us. He made such an impression on his audiences that presently the cadres of the school came and sat on the front benches, field officers and then generals!
>
> The culminating point of these lectures – there were a dozen altogether – was when, dealing with the fighting-men at Verdun, he paused at length, then roared "Gentlemen, stand up!" and you would see the generals present rise just as we did, the ordinary students, while he paid homage to those who died at Douaumont. This tells one something about the captain's extraordinary ascendency over men of all ages and all ranks.

These lectures, published in *Lettres, Notes et Carnets*, do not show the movement, the skill and the surprising power of setting the matter in immediate perspective that made the prisoner of 1917 an unrivalled speaker. It may be said that striking the imagination by speaking of the arguments of the High Command at the time of Verdun is more suitable than giving still another account of Austerlitz. Then again the master of 1921 was addressing less experienced minds than was the speaker of 1917. It was proper to initiate them before urging them to reflect.

Nevertheless there were some fine passages, used later as drafts for *La France et son armée*. For example this reflection dealing with the question of Sedan and the beaten French army of 1870:

> The best instrument possesses no value in itself. Its value arises solely from the use to which it is put. But the leaders of this army had not earlier brought their minds to bear on the problems they would have to resolve; they had not done their work. What is more, their characters were influenced by the

> consequences of that psychological depression that had affected the whole French nation.

A passage in the same spirit links perfectly with this other reflection concerning 1916:

> It is no longer so much a question of knowing which is the better army as of knowing where the most staunch, reliable nation is to be found. More clearly than ever, though transposed from the purely military field to that of the nation, there appears this truth that is as old as war itself, that is to say as old as mankind: victory is a psychological question.

Many of the quotations or remarks to do with the French character in these lectures are taken from Caesar, concerning the Gauls' "weakness" of "nervous instability", or the "sudden and unexpected" nature of their decisions. But Charles de Gaulle does not confine himself to quoting Caesar; he moves steadily on to more and more personal remarks. "One single pupil of the Ecole Normale Supérieure killed in 1870. How many in 1914–1918?" And again: "The liking for criticism in the French soldier" who "frequently tries to get away from authority and who despises [his leaders] the more, the more they allow themselves to be made game of". Or this: "From the Dreyfus affair on, a weakening of the military ideal. A so-called social ideal takes its place. Pacifism wreaks havoc, too."

Thus, during 1921, Captain de Gaulle meditated, pen in hand; and this year, while he was teaching the officer-cadets of Saint-Cyr military history from Carnot to Foch, he also prepared most actively for the entrance to the Ecole Supérieure de Guerre, an aim that he had spoken of in his letters to his parents since the end of the war, and an aim to which his chiefs in the French military mission to Poland had also directed him. Until the end of the year he lived in a flat in the boulevard de Grenelle from which could be seen (and heard) the trains of the elevated railway running between the Nation and Etoile stations.

On 28 December a boy was born in the de Gaulles' home. And here we must deal with the persistent legend about Marshal Pétain being his godfather. The name Philippe was traditional in both the Vendroux and the de Gaulle families, the Vendroux boys being called Jacques-Philippe even more often than the de Gaulles were called Julien-Philippe. Furthermore, the fact that the Marshal was living outside religious marriage – he had not been married in church – would, in a family of this kind, have been enough to make it impossible for him to be the godfather of a child of Yvonne and Charles de Gaulle.

In short the captain was the father of a boy, a strongly-constituted boy, as Dr Levy-Solal the obstetrician affirmed. They had moved from Grenelle to 14 square Desaix in the fifteenth arrondissement, a fine flat with five rooms, much less noisy than the last. And then on 2 May 1922 the *Journal officiel* announced that Captain de Gaulle had been admitted to the Ecole de Guerre.

In the military world the Ecole de Guerre was the equivalent of the Ecole Normale Supérieure or the Conseil d'Etat in the civilian "meritocracy". The students came out with a *brevet*, a certificate, which meant that they were fit for the important posts. Walking in under the porch of the huge building in the Champ-de-Mars where Bonaparte used to work was the same as proclaiming an ambition to become one of those few men upon whom, three times in a century, the survival of the country depends. Can it be doubted that the assistant-professor of history at Saint-Cyr entered in that frame of mind? He desired to be, and to be as soon as possible, the successor of those men whose great achievements he had lectured upon at the military school.

The Ecole de Guerre was then commanded by General Debeney, a disciple of Pétain; and his assistants were the Generals Dufieux and Bineau. Among the professors are to be found Colonels Moyrand and Lemoine for general tactics, Etienne and Touchon for Infantry, Prioux for cavalry, Chauvineau for fortification and Duffour for history. These probably made up the jury which considered the candidate de Gaulle worthy of being admitted, particularly as his candidature had been preceded by this report from Colonel Gombeaud, the second in command at Saint-Cyr:

> Wide-ranging and well-based attainments, great capacity for grasping a problem quickly and setting it out brilliantly. Much followed and much appreciated as a lecturer by the students: has a great deal of influence over them.
>
> Is a candidate for the Ecole de Guerre; he will certainly be admitted and he will be a success there.

He passed, taking the thirty-third place, which was surprisingly modest. The first shadow in a picture that was to contain others. The great establishment of the Champ-de-Mars was one of the few in which Charles de Gaulle was not "fortunate" in Napoleon's sense of the word. Neither on the level of strictly professional success, since having entered in the 33rd place he passed out 52nd out of 129, after some serious differences with his instructors; nor on the human level, since he made friends with none of those who were his contemporaries there – Couquet, who passed out at the head of the list, Loustaunau-Lacau (that d'Artagnan without a Dumas), Laffargue, Chauvin, Georges-Picot, Bridoux – although with the last three he did maintain relations that were rather more than social and professional. And these companions were brilliant characters in various ways; yet twenty years later they were all far from London – indeed, some belonged wholly to Vichy.

When Charles de Gaulle went to Saint-Cyr in 1910, obsession with revenge dictated the line of conduct they were to follow to many people: in order to reconquer Alsace, one had to go and take it – one therefore had to attack. When he went to the Ecole de Guerre twelve years later France had won back Alsace and the control of the whole of the Rhine. The obsessions now worked in the opposite direction and had become defensive. On the tactical level this fundamental notion was strengthened by that of the "dividing of the terrain". Since one was lucky enough to fight only in an area that was already well known and under one's control, the right course was carefully to organize one's manoeuvres in relation to the given data.

Here is Georges Loustaunau-Lacau's spirited denunciation of "the mistake which consisted of looking upon what was in fact an art, as an exact science, a series of theorems":

> An art whose certainties are but fragile, since it is carried on by two parties, and of these two, the other seeks to deceive, producing his effort in the contrary direction. Lemoine, the champion of this stone-mason's strategy, worked out the terrain by the kilometer-man, the kilometer-gun, the kilometer-shell. When you listened to his battering-ram lectures you felt like calling out "But what if the enemy is not there? And what if there are other ways of destroying him with less ironmongery? And what about the third dimension? And surprise? And speed?" Having followed his line one ended up by wondering whether there were still men who were making war, friends or enemies. His victories arrived ready-cooked from the rear in lorries and by rail, like a cake coming from the kitchen to the pantry.[11]

Captain de Gaulle also thought this automatization of war, like the spatial fixation, harmful in so far as there was the danger that they might beget an intellectual fixity, a tactical anchylosis and a strategical paralysis. As we shall see, he expressed these disagreements and his resistance to anything that had a tendency to promote the defensive, the wait-and-see attitude and a belief in the supremacy of gunfire – the doctrine of the school's commander, Debeney: that is to say, of Pétain.

His school-fellows have drawn good pictures of this teacher reduced to the state of a pupil. Forty years later André Laffargue, now a general, devoted a few pages to him in his *Fantassin de Gascogne*.[12] The irony is obvious; so is the admiration:

> At the beginning-of-term meeting in the lecture theatre I saw a tall, very tall captain in horizon-blue make his way down the tiers to take his place again. He walked very straight, stiff and solemn, strutting as though he were moving his own statue. His face struck me and I could not help saying to myself "Well, there's someone who thinks no small beer of himself!"
>
> The two years that I spent with Charles de Gaulle at the Ecole de Guerre did away with this first somewhat unfavourable impression and made me ashamed of having had it. For the stranger was to become my closest neighbour in the little group that we were both posted to.
>
> I have retained the happiest memory of this association. De Gaulle never gave the appearance of setting himself apart from us, either by self-assertion or by a scornful remoteness. To be sure he was more silent and less exuberant than most, but he was always with us, taking his part and putting in his word with humour and originality. He was not unreserved, yet even so he had a fund of gaiety and he did not refrain from joining his rather sepulchral voice to ours when we sang in chorus during a journey.

Yet although General Laffargue takes great care to do his comrade of 1922 justice, he nevertheless remains reserved as far as the essence was concerned:

> His was one of those minds that begin by building up a solution, a system, in

their own heads. Once this is done they then apply their solution, their system, to the reality. If the reality accepts the solution, all is well. But if it does not, then there is trouble, because for a mind of this sort it is the reality that is mistaken. And it so happens that as early as the Ecole de Guerre I perceived that de Gaulle was one of those who begin by looking into their own heads.

General Chauvin was also one of his companions and he has left an excellent portrait of de Gaulle at the Ecole de Guerre:

> Although his gaze was firmly fixed on the outer world – and more on things than on people – he seemed above all to live an intense inner life; yet his taste for action prevented him from drifting into a sterile introspection. He was better equipped for deduction than for analysis, which is certainly the mark of a fighter, and he seemed rather disposed to build up systems.[13]

Charles de Gaulle, who had been very careful not to put a foot wrong during the first year, restrained himself less now that he was faced with the corpus of official doctrines embodied by General Debeney, and to be more specific – for it was at this level that the arguments took place – with what was called the "a priori doctrine", whose official expounder was here Colonel Moyrand, the professor of tactics. This officer, who had a great deal of talent and a strong character, had belonged to the 3rd Bureau of the General Staff during the war, and he taught that the action of war was carried on in a framework and with means that were known a priori and that they were usable as such, the commander looking upon his field of action as a chess-player looks upon his board. This infuriated de Gaulle, who, as we have seen from his earliest writings, was convinced that apart from a few simple principles the military art was a matter of circumstances.

At the end of this second and last year of teaching a trial was to take place at Bar-sur-Aube, the terrain picked for the "tactical journey" which traditionally formed the end of the cycle of studies and the fundamental test for those who aspired to high command. Colonel Moyrand was in charge of the manoeuvres. Feeling de Gaulle's intellectual resistance he tried to set a trap for him, giving him the command of the army corps, the biggest unit concerned; his comrades were entrusted with the various subsidiary units and Captain de Chateauvieux was his chief of staff.*

The whole day long, say both Laffargue and Chauvin, Colonel Moyrand faced de Gaulle with various situations, each time forcing him to counteract unlucky strokes, to foresee fresh measures and to take sudden decisions. "Our comrade," says Chauvin, "behaved perfectly, giving evidence of his clarity of mind and at the same time of his keen sense of action." And of his "firmness of spirit", says Laffargue.

*This account is based upon those of Generals Laffargue and Chauvin, which differ but which are complementary.

For the criticism in the evening they met in a class-room at the college of Bar-sur-Aube. Colonel Moyrand presided at the master's rostrum while de Gaulle sat opposite him, his long legs tucked, not without difficulty, under his schoolboy's desk: Chateauvieux was at his side. "It became obvious from the questions asked and the colonel's tone, strongly tinged with sarcasm and aggression, that this was no longer an examination but a trial," says General Chauvin.

> De Gaulle was even more aware of this than we were, but nothing in his behaviour showed it. He retained all his calmness, all his self-control, giving temperate replies and methodical explanations. But the more collected de Gaulle appeared the more the colonel showed his irritation. It was then that Moyrand had the idea of this last shaft, which was in fact a confession of defeat, so out of place was the question and so absurd: "Where is the transport belonging to the left-hand regiment of your division on the right?"
>
> "Chateauvieux," said de Gaulle, "be so good as to reply."
>
> "But it is you I am asking, de Gaulle!"
>
> "Colonel, you gave me the responsibility of commanding an army corps. If in addition to that I had to take upon myself those belonging to my subordinates I should no longer have a mind free enough to carry out my mission adequately: *de minimis non curat praetor*. Chateauvieux, be so good as to answer the colonel."
>
> "Very well. We knew that you looked upon many tasks as being beneath you. Now I am clear in my mind."

De Gaulle's mind was no less clear. A few weeks later the 44th term met in the great amphitheatre of the Ecole de Guerre for the last time; the meeting was presided over by General Dufieux, who had succeeded Debeney and who had the same attitude of mind.* The list of the newly certificated officers was read out in three sections, the first consisting of some fifty names qualified as *très bien*,** a section that was thought to be made up of the leaders of tomorrow. De Gaulle was not mentioned even in the second group. He was given no more than the qualification *assez bien*, deeply humiliating for one who from the beginning had set himself at such a height. Loustaunau-Lacau[14] wrote: "De Gaulle was very badly treated for having spoken so highly of the importance of circumstances in battle, and it was because of his courage that he passed out in the last section."

Yet his marks, except for riding and for infantry, were good, including those given by Colonel Moyrand for the notorious "journey", which amounted to 15.5.*** He had 15 for "general tactics and staff-work", which was low for a character of such size and such ambition. Is this to be looked upon merely as the price paid for the crime of having an independent mind and for having defied and

*He was a determined opponent of de Gaulle's campaign for an armoured army. Later he presided over Vichy's military court.

**In many French examinations there are four levels of success, *avec mention très bien*, *bien*, *assez bien* and no *mention* at all; at university level they correspond roughly to the first class honours, second, third, and pass. (trs.)

***The usual mark in French examinations is so many out of 20. (trs.)

humiliated Colonel Moyrand at Bar-sur-Aube? Yet that officer's reports[15] do not show a vengeful spirit. Moyrand, Joffre's former colleague, pointed out that during the "tactical journey" de Gaulle having displayed "resolution, calmness and power of command", then "adopted solutions that had little bearing on the position", but "frankly acknowledged" his mistake: Colonel Moyrand went on to write this passage which, like Pétain's mention in dispatches at Verdun, has rightly remained one of the classics of Gaullology:

> An intelligent, cultured and serious-minded officer; has brilliance and talent; very highly gifted; plenty of character. Unfortunately he spoils his undoubted qualities by his excessive self-confidence, his severity towards the opinions of others and his attitude of a king in exile. Besides, he seems more gifted for the synthetic and general study of a problem than for the thorough-going and practical examination of its execution.

De Gaulle had not come into conflict with a commonplace man; he only made the mistake of defying an establishment. And this echo is to be found even more clearly in the final report written by General Dufieux, the commander of the Ecole de Guerre:

> Strongly marked personality. Undeniable qualities which he unfortunately spoils by a somewhat detached [the general first put "remote" and then wrote over it] attitude and a certain amount of self-satisfaction. Has not paid as much attention to the school's work as he should have done. At all events, qualified to be very useful indeed on a staff.

Three months before this dismal prize-giving Charles de Gaulle had published *La Discorde chez l'ennemi*.[16] This captain who busied himself with the publication of a work in which he uttered decisive opinions on war and peace before he was even "certificated" irritated many of these not very highly literate generals.

The qualification *assez bien* that had been inflicted upon Captain de Gaulle did not pass unnoticed. Although Marshal Pétain's links with de Gaulle at that time were by no means what legend would have us believe, he was among the first to be roused by it. He had never hidden his esteem for his brilliantly gifted former subordinate. He had invited him to his house and he had gone so far as to say that de Gaulle was one of the very few officers who could claim him as a patron and that he would willingly appoint him to his personal staff, even if it were only for his qualities as a writer. In short, there was a danger that a humiliation inflicted upon the former lieutenant of Arras might reflect upon the Pétain "household", that Ark of the Covenant. The old leader, well known for reserve and indeed coldness, spoke of "scandal" and even "monstrous judicial error".

Jean Pouget gives a lively account of the curious steps taken by the Marshal. General de Lannurien, the very virtuous chief of the army's department of higher education, was summoned to the office of the head of the French army and there he was called upon to see that the marks given to Captain de Gaulle in June were rectified. Lannurien was dumbfounded; however highly placed at the peak of military hierarchy the Marshal was, Pétain could not be ignorant of the fact that no intervention "even on the part of a deputy or senator" was taken into account at the Ecole de Guerre!

The Marshal so imperatively insisted upon the necessity of placing no obstacles in the way of an officer destined for the highest responsibilities that Lannurien, having given way, persuaded Dufieux and Moyrand: some of the marks were touched up and in the end de Gaulle found himself provided with the qualification *bien*. It was a tolerably absurd operation, making nonsense of an institution without doing justice to an exceptional character.

The final remark of the person chiefly concerned was, "I shall never set foot in that hole again unless I go there as commanding officer." But in the meantime Captain de Gaulle was posted to Mainz where he was attached, for instruction, to the staff of the army of the Rhine, in the 4th Bureau, the least glamorous of them all, the one that dealt with accounts for rice, bread, salt and axle-grease. It was a peacetime Limoges.*

But what do these mishaps matter when one is the man General Chauvin speaks of in this way? After a field-day during their second year at the Ecole de Guerre Chauvin and de Gaulle were talking as they sat under a tree, and after a silence, Chauvin, rather surprised at his own words, said, "My dear fellow, I am going to say something that I dare say will amuse you, but I have a curious feeling that you are intended for a very great destiny."

In reply he expected a derisive laugh or de Gaulle's elbow in his ribs. For some moments there was no reply at all. At last he heard these words, which de Gaulle uttered slowly, in a toneless voice, his eyes gazing into the distance, "Yes, so have I."

It was in March 1924 however that Charles de Gaulle's first book, *La Discorde chez l'ennemi*, was published by Berger-Levrault, once a fellow-prisoner at Ingolstadt. The first drafts had been written in captivity and others in Poland. Charles de Gaulle was to publish more ambitious, more worked-over or more decorative books. But this one, written more simply than the brilliant essays of his forties or the majestic memoirs, has a special place on the Gaullologist's shelves. Very few of his works tell us so much about Charles de Gaulle's personality, his ideas and his conception of history than this work of his youth.

Let us note the lessons that he obviously meant to draw from this German tragedy. The first is a summing-up of his teaching at Saint-Cyr and of his resistance to the lessons of the Ecole de Guerre. "In war, apart from a few essential principles, there is no universal system, but only circumstances and personalities." Bugeaud** had said this before him: "In war, there are principles; but there are few of them." Yet who does not see that Captain de Gaulle's manner of putting it has quite another ring?

*In the 1914–1918 war unsatisfactory generals and other officers were posted to Limoges, far from the battle, where they could do no harm. (trs.)
**A Marshal of France who conquered Algeria in 1844. (trs.)

The second arises of its own accord from the masterly narrative of Ludendorff's attempt to bring down Chancellor Bethmann-Hollweg's civilian power in 1917 and impose his own de facto military dictatorship: the lesson is the necessity for maintaining the supremacy of the political over the military power, for if the military authority destroys the institutional framework and blows up its own legal basis, it commits suicide.

In one of his lectures at Saint-Cyr Captain de Gaulle had strongly condemned the imperial government's interference with the operations in August 1870. The principles of balance must necessarily work in both directions. But the golden rule that emerges from *La Discorde chez l'ennemi* is the necessity for placing the "management of the war" entirely in the hands of the political power; and by "management" or "direction of the war" is meant a whole body of data far more complex and manifold than what is meant by "the operations". And, as de Gaulle maintained with an irresistible conviction, it was because Tirpitz and Ludendorff tried to impose their own "direction of the war" on the civil power that they doomed the Empire to ruin.

The fact that a nationalist and conservative officer of thirty-three should so authoritatively lay down one of the essential precepts for the direction of the State, a principle so eagerly attacked by the most illustrious of his leaders, and that he should analyze the behaviour of the enemy whose prisons he had quite recently left with such almost scientific equanimity comes at just the right moment to demonstrate the minor nature of the disagreements with Dufieux and Moyrand. The man who wrote *La Discorde chez l'ennemi* was perhaps "in exile". He was not in bed and asleep.

And he was about to remind people of this with even more sharpness in March 1925 by publishing an article that was a mocking reply to the marks awarded by the gentlemen of the Champ-de-Mars; it was called "Doctrine a priori ou doctrine des circonstances", a systematic refutation of the teaching at the school he had just left, having though not without difficulty obtained his certificate.

> The French military mind is reluctant to acknowledge the essentially empirical nature that the action of war must assume. The French military mind perpetually endeavours to build up a doctrine that will a priori enable it at least to orientate the action and to conceive its form, without taking the circumstances that ought to be its basis into account. This mind continually tries to deduce the conception from constant factors known beforehand, whereas what ought to be done in each particular case is to infer this conception from contingent and variable facts.

Let there be no mistake: this was a manifesto. But was Charles de Gaulle fully aware of the degree to which his article criticized an unchanging aspect of the French mind? What he here called in question with such firmness was not merely an eccentricity in the leaders of a certain school of thought; it was also an entire French tradition, that stretched back to the age of Louis XIV.

It so happened that Pétain did not take offence. He first heard of the article through his confidential adviser Colonel Laure, who wrote a most appreciative report upon it. And Pétain was sufficiently intelligent and self-assured to prefer admiring those parts of de Gaulle's brilliant discussion that paid him homage rather than feeling uneasy about those that questioned his legend and his teachings. The same day he told one of his staff-officers to suggest that he should work for him in the drawing up of an historical work. De Gaulle, exiled in the 4th Bureau of the staff at Mainz, hastened to reply to so flattering an invitation. And a month later the Pétain, having read the first pages written by the Constable, congratulated him, adding that he was about to ask General Guillaumat, commanding the French forces in Germany, to place de Gaulle at his disposal, and ending "I shall summon you to Paris".

CHAPTER SIX

The Imperator

In our day it is difficult to grasp just how popular Pétain was in the years after 1918. He was the least disputed of all the marshals. Joffre had the priority – but malicious rumour tended to say that it was not he who had brought about the "miracle" of the Marne. Foch sat enthroned in a kind of empyrean traversed by lightning-flashes – but there was a smell of brimstone about him, for it was said that he had not been sparing of men's lives and that he had even less respect for the supremacy of civilian power. Lyautey, a disappointing war minister in 1916, had gone back to Morocco.

But as for Pétain, every French schoolboy knew that he was the "victor of Verdun". When Poincaré gave him the marshal's baton at Metz on 8 December 1918 he praised, among other merits, Pétain's "steadiness", a prime virtue now that peace had returned. It was known that the greatest military critic of the time, the Englishman Liddell Hart, thought him the only military chief whom France could not have done without between 1914 and 1918.

There was not a single political leader who did not praise him. The Left congratulated itself upon him. In Edouard Herriot's opinion he was a "real republican": in Blum's "the most humane of the commanders". Foch, Lyautey, Mangin and Castelnau worried the republicans in varying degrees. Pétain much less, although Poincaré had prevented him from succeeding Joffre, looking upon him as a candidate for dictatorship (this, according to his friend Fayolle, made Pétain say, "The Republic is afraid of me!". But was he not the friend of Paul Painlevé, the archetype of the progressive democrat and of Paul Valéry, the official poet of the republican régime? And who could be less suspected of clericalism than he? Yet even the Right saw him as a possible "resort" against the miseries of democracy.

His career, so slow until 1914, was so extraordinarily rapid during the war (an additional general's star every year). He had outlived the fighting and was given control of the whole body of the country's armed forces, whereas his rivals were mummified in honorific posts or sent off on remote missions. He was vice-president of the Conseil Supérieur de la Guerre and inspector-general of the army. He was in complete command of the General Staff, which he entrusted to his faithful followers Buat and Debeney in succession. He shaped France's military policy and he made or unmade careers.

During the early 1920s Pétain was a kind of military god. He was at one and the same time the chief and the father, loaded with all glory and the possessor of all power, the man who had been sparing of the soldiers' lives but who had not been listened to when he wanted to inflict a "German Sedan" upon the enemy. His marmoreal good looks, his grave bearing (worthy of a cardinal) and the brevity of his speech all combined to make him much more than a generalissimo or a victorious leader: he was a sort of tutelary figure in which not only an army but also a nation bled white by its victory acknowledged itself. No one lived, gained promotion or made a name except through Pétain, who in military circles was called the Imperator.

It is therefore hardly surprising that a man like de Gaulle, whose "star" had not spared him the handicap of being a prisoner of war while history was being made and while those characters that were to shape it after the victory were being formed, should have staked everything upon this omnipotent figure, to whom he was already linked by his service in the regiment at Arras, by a most cordial mention in dispatches, by a few meetings after the war and lastly and above all by the unusual intervention with the heads of the Ecole de Guerre on his behalf.

For the last quarter of a century a great deal of writing has been devoted to the establishment of a direct affiliation (complicated by sponsorship) between the stiff-necked innovating leader of 1914 and the man who on the eve of the next war was in his turn to try to overturn doctrines and prejudices – an affiliation that cruel history is supposed to have broken so tragically. A very literary opinion that seems to me to be based upon a series of misapprehensions.

A close study of the actions and public documents and a critical reading of the letters between them show not only a profound disagreement on the essential but also a most surprising ratio of emotional strength between the famous old man and the impatient captain. At the cost of gross simplification it could be said that Pétain, even after he had received challenges and rebuffs of a kind by no means usual in the army, entertained an affection for Charles de Gaulle, the affection of an old man without children and of a leader hitherto deprived of disciples worthy of himself. De Gaulle, though at first moved by these marks of esteem and like everyone else impressed by Pétain's historic stature, presently came to see him as no more than a figure-head, glamorous and efficient to be sure but sinking deeper and deeper into vanity and honours, the prisoner of a mediocre set of associates, astray in all ill-timed mission to Morocco, and covering the most baleful of military doctrines with his glory.

What a mass of contradictions! While for de Gaulle every day that took him farther from the war (in which he had been forced to realize the absurdity of the offensive at all costs) brought him more firmly back to the notion of movement, of mobility and of manoeuvre, Pétain on the other hand continued year after year to assert himself as a symbol of a military policy which was later to be summarized by the building of the Maginot Line. In 1927 he sponsored the law which baldly proclaimed that "the object of our military organization is to ensure the protection of our frontiers and the defence of our overseas territories". Is it surprising, then, that the first rifts in the relations between the Marshal and the major should have appeared towards the end of this same year of 1927? Yet in 1924, when the Marshal called him, how could de Gaulle have refused such an opportunity? He knew what part he had to play. The army was bogged down in the paralysing "a priori doctrine" and inhibiting prejudices, fossilized in the self-satisfaction and conservatism of its leaders.

What finer task was there than rousing this great dormant body? And where could it be struck better than at the head, the centre of decision, the personal staff of the man on whom everything depended, even if for a while de Gaulle had to put up with the atmosphere of servile flattery and with the ideas Pétain insisted upon. Who would deny that de Gaulle was ambitious? Not de Gaulle, in any event. He did not only have a clear idea of France. He also had a clear idea of the role that was destined for him. It comes back to the "conspicuous service" that he knew he was capable of rendering and that he wished to render, for the greater glory of the country and of himself.

Nor should the importance of the bonds already formed between the Imperator and his former lieutenant be forgotten. In giving his allegiance to Pétain for a while, de Gaulle had the exceedingly interesting experience of living close to a legend, the best "professional" of his time, a model of command and (to use a later expression) a holy cow. Since de Gaulle had so strong a passion for history, how could he fail to dream of studying, close at hand, one of those who had made it and who continued to direct it? A fine subject for research.

And this is without counting the fact that at the time the great man sent for him, exiled as he was in a remote garrison where he was condemned to uninteresting duties, de Gaulle knew himself to be in debt to Pétain. The affair of the Ecole de Guerre passing-out list had shown that the hard-hearted old leader possessed a treasure of such lively sympathy that although he was of a character entirely opposed to cliques and intrigues it led him to disobey the sacred laws of a jury's independence. When Pétain asked de Gaulle to help him, everything – gratitude, interest, curiosity, sense of history, ambition and patriotism – combined to urge him to come running.

Pétain did not lose any opportunity of showing his good-will towards de Gaulle, a kindness all the more remarkable in that he was by no means lavish with it: Weygand is not the only one who bears witness to this. And twenty-five years later the old Marshal, imprisoned in the fort of Montrouge before his trial, said to the chaplain who attended him, "Never did I take so much care of any young officer. It did not turn out well for me."

The reason that de Gaulle took such an important place in Pétain's views from 1921 onwards was that the Marshal was then concerned with two projects of great consequence, projects that might be realized with the assistance of a man of talent. The first was the drawing up of a very substantial document setting out the lessons to be drawn from the war which should form the preamble of a basic law on the reorganization of the army; the second, the production of a book that would give the head of the French army's academic ambitions a sound foundation. It was generally known, from the Académie Française to the corridors of the General Staff, that he would succeed Foch when Foch had the good taste to vacate his seat. But Pétain was not satisfied with this assurance; he disliked his predecessor sufficiently to wish to outdo him at least in the volume of his literary achievement.

The Imperator, who wrote virtually nothing whatsoever himself at any time, gathered a remarkable team of ghosts at 4b, boulevard des Invalides. The team, under the rule of Colonel Laure,* Pétain's principal private secretary, and Colonel Duchêne, his chief of staff, consisted of a number of colonels, majors and captains well known for their nimble pens. But although the Marshal was a very poor writer he was a pitiless editor, a great hunter of unnecessary adjectives, mistaken adverbs and improper expletives, and he did not think any of them able enough for his great plan.

There was one single man who was called for, and Pétain had read his finest pieces, from *La Discorde chez l'ennemi* to "Doctrine a priori et doctrine de circonstances". It was probably at the beginning of 1924 that Pétain first thought of publishing an important work on the army – a tribute to the past and programme for the future: historical portrait of the soldier, with the emphasis on the fighting-men of 1914–1918, above all those of Verdun. The idea can be seen taking shape in a letter he wrote to Colonel Bouvard on 27 September 1924: "I should very much like to go back to my first draft, the one in which the events of 1917 form part of the narrative and which could be called 'the soldier through the ages' or something of that kind."

It was then that the Marshal turned to de Gaulle. The text the Mainz captain presently sent was so satisfactory that on 20 March 1925 Pétain wrote, "I am much pleased with the first section of your work, which you call 'the fundamentals', and as to the form, I scarcely find more than a few words to change. The substance is faultless and it is sound doctrine. I shall only ask you to alter the title of the first section and put 'introduction' instead of 'fundamentals'." And in a postscript he added, "It is agreed, is it not, that you do not tell anyone of this work, which is to remain between ourselves alone." Nothing could have been plainer.

A fortnight later, when Captain de Gaulle was told by the Marshal of his approaching summons to Paris and posting to the boulevard des Invalides, he knew that he was being called in as a ghost, as the great leader's pen-holder. Philippe Pétain certainly had a liking for fine writing but not to the extent of putting literature above the requirements of the hierarchy. It was a question of "serving", and it has been known since Vigny's day that in this field *grandeur militaire* easily merges with servitude, or rather with self-effacement. At least so long as one is a subordinate.

Things were clear from the beginning. De Gaulle had accepted the terms of a tacit agreement which, for an officer like him, left no room for doubt: although it was of such a kind as to arouse rebellion in the writer that he was more and more definitely becoming. The germ of the entire crisis was there in that duality of natures which Pétain himself was too intelligent to be unaware of or to underestimate.

Pétain had secured the assistance of the man who was said to be the best writer in the army. Still, it is worth taking notice of Pétain's most surprising notion of collaboration. Loustaunau-Lacau became in his turn the Marshal's "pen-officer" and he tells how he wrote him a piece on "The peasant and the soldier" for the

*Pétain's secretary-general in the days of Vichy.

Revue des deux mondes.[1] The magazine sent him a cheque. He asked the Imperator what charity he was to send the money to. "Oh no," said the Marshal. "You wrote it and I accepted it. A thousand francs for you, a thousand francs for me!"

Here are two recollections of Captain Charles de Gaulle as the Marshal's pen-holder at the Invalides. The first is by Mlle Lucet, who was the Marshal's secretary for more than a quarter of a century, who told Jean Pouget about the gigantic Captain de Gaulle's daily arrival through the walks of the Champ-de-Mars at exactly two o'clock in the afternoon: "He wore a bowler hat and he carried a stick and he always looked preoccupied. As he walked he looked up into the sky and waved his stick as though he were writing in the air." And speaking of his work she said, "The Marshal was very hard to please; he often used to cross out and correct. But I remember Captain de Gaulle's pieces very well; they were always perfectly legible, and the Marshal made few corrections."[2]

Captain de Gaulle, received into the Pétain establishment on 1 July 1925, was given preferential treatment and this was not confined to the fact that the Marshal corrected his papers less severely than those of his colleagues. For whereas colonels crowded together three in a room, he was allowed an office to himself on the second floor. One of his visitors describes it as "low-ceilinged and full of smoke". But what office would not look low-ceilinged with de Gaulle sitting in it? And what room would not be full of smoke when for eight hours a day a smoker like him worked in it?

The Conseil Supérieur de la Guerre, that is to say Pétain, was then contemplating the construction of an immense series of fortifications on the north-east frontier: ten years later it was to become the Maginot Line. De Gaulle was required to write an article, drawn from many sources, that would give an account of the part played by permanent fortifications in the history of national defence. This he did in a few weeks and the article appeared in the *Revue militaire française* on 1 December 1925 under the title of "Rôle historique des places françaises".

There have been ironic remarks about the ease with which the prophet of movement lent himself to the glorification of fixed defence, and the ease with which de Gaulle, having become "pen-officer" turned out so much pseudo-Pétain. People often set the general body of his military writings against the dogmatic conclusion of the article in question: "For France the fortification of her territory is a permanent national necessity." Yet the "pen-officer's" argument is very intelligently shaded. He makes it perfectly clear that Napoleon suffered much, particularly in 1814, for having paid little attention to the fortified places that Carnot had restored. He points out how useful the fortifications had been to the strategists of the last war. But each time it is in order to emphasize that the primary function of these strong-points was to serve as a base for a manoeuvre. Far from maintaining that the continuous defensive line would ensure any sort of tranquillity, he recalled that a certain number of fortified entities would in no way do away with the necessity for manoeuvring; they would act as pivots for these movements and constitute their base. The aim of strong-points was to hamper the enemy's manoeuvres, not to economize those of our own army. We are far away from the idea of the Maginot Line.

But as it often happens, the readers of this article remembered only those parts of it that suited them. Since the notion that everything should "protect the national territory" was now prevalent, the great majority of people reading this delicately-shaded argument saw no more than that which agreed with this current of thought. On this point Nachin says, "This article carried public opinion with it and the plan for the fortification of the north-eastern frontier was completely successful. Perhaps too successful. Indeed, was it not reasonable to be uneasy at the excessive confidence that this armoured protection, said to be impregnable, would arouse in the country?"

De Gaulle very soon became aware of the harm done by a certain interpretation of his text. He wrote to Nachin:

> Bar the way: that was what Vauban wanted to do, and I still think that this state of affairs, which he carried into effect in the Nord, was a great deterrent to our enemies' mobility at the end of Louis XIV's time and in 1792–1793. I read the remark of Vauban's that you quote about the number of fortified places with great satisfaction.* Yes, few are needed; but those few must be good.[3]

Thus the pen-officer succeeded in preserving his freedom of manoeuvre and his dignity while at the same time he fairly and honestly furthered the projects of his chief. But it was on the neighbouring terrain, that of the famous *Soldat*, that the decisive match was to be played out between them.

In his smoke-filled office Captain de Gaulle was covering the pages that were to become the first draft of *Le Soldat*. From Meknès (the reasons for his presence there will be given later) the Marshal wrote to him on 20 November 1925 "I have just read 'Le soldat de l'Ancien Régime' with the liveliest interest. This chapter is completely successful. Your work as a whole, it must be added, pleases me very much and provides an excellent basis for the definitive book. When you reach the modern soldier, there will be a special chapter to be devoted to the colonial soldier. Perhaps a chapter would be too much; let us say a paragraph." (This "paragraph" kept for the soldiers of the colonial army is surprising from a leader who must have known how many Africans had left their bones between the Marne and Verdun.)

So between the Marshal and the captain, relations remained excellent. Yet something had happened a very few weeks after Charles de Gaulle's arrival at the Invalides that had not improved his opinion of his chief: on de Gaulle's side the euphoria of this glamorous collaboration lasted only a single summer. At the end of August 1925 Pétain agreed to take Lyautey's place to put down Abd el Krim's rebellion in Morocco.**

There was an epigram about Pétain that Charles de Gaulle often repeated,

*Sebastian Vauban, the seventeenth-century marshal who constructed a series of fortifications on the frontiers of France. (trs.)

**Abd el Krim's unsuccessful rebellion was launched against the French and Spanish. (trs.)

having said it for the first time on 11 July 1941 at Damascus, at General Catroux's table in the presence of several young Free French officers. "Marshal Pétain was a great man: he died in 1925." The General clarified and expanded this remark on various occasions, particularly during a talk he had in September 1968 with his then publisher, Marcel Jullian.

> He was an exceptional man. He was an exceptional leader; I have not changed my opinion. Unfortunately for France and for himself he died in 1925 and he did not know it. I was present at this death, and since I was fond of him it made me very unhappy. It happened like this: in 1925 he let Painlevé and Briand outwit him and induce him to go to Morocco and execute poor Lyautey. He went. When he came back he was not pleased with himself. He wanted to be an academician, he who had scarcely written anything in his life. Then a minister. Minister under M. Doumergue – can you imagine that? He was minister. He ran after honours, and the Maréchale [Madame Pétain] ran in front of him, even faster!

For de Gaulle, then, there was no doubt about the matter. He justified this much-discussed image of Pétain's "death" by the foul blow dealt to Lyautey, in which he saw less the assertion of a talent than the decay of a character and the deterioration of a sense of honour. In agreeing to go and "help" Lyautey, the founder of the protectorate, Pétain not only screened and guaranteed what Loustaunau-Lacau, de Gaulle's companion at the Ecole de Guerre, called "a baseness without a name" with his glory, but he also gave substance to the legend that Lyautey had collapsed when faced with the challenge of Abd el Krim.

When the infuriated Lyautey denounced the way his rival, loaded with honours, had "stabbed him in the back", a friend of Pétain's replied, "He obeyed orders". The man of Rabat roared "A maréchal-des-logis* obeys orders. A Marshal of France does not obey when they try to make him do dirty work!"

The Republic had never been very fond of Lyautey, the Marshal of Rabat. When it saw him weakened by age and staggering under the blows of a rebellious rustic, it seized the opportunity of dealing with his replacement by sending the "help" of a rival to whom he was totally opposed, a rival who was at once granted the reinforcements denied to Lyautey for months, so that he was able to restore the position in four weeks.

So from that time on, although he continued his work on *Le Soldat*, Charles de Gaulle did not allow himself to be shut up in complete subjection and he stepped aside from his role as a ghost as often as he could.

Was it because he already felt detached from his dependence on Pétain that Charles de Gaulle began to make contacts with the political world at this period? It is in 1925 that we find the first of the countless letters that he wrote to parliamentary figures, thereby breaking with a well-established tradition in his world. Furthermore the man to whom he sent it, Joseph Paul-Boncour, was a Socialist deputy for Paris. Later he was to be Minister of War, then of Foreign Affairs and for a very short time premier.

*A sergeant in a cavalry regiment. (trs.)

The deputy for Paris told de Gaulle that he had read his essay on the fortified places with the utmost interest. The Captain replied:

> It is my opinion that you personally are called upon to play the most important part in the building up of the new system of French defence. You zealously urge the changing of the present state of affairs and you have a sense of France's continuity, essential qualities in a statesman who is to play a great national role.

And he earnestly advised him to read "Doctrine a priori ou doctrine des circonstances".[4]

Whether de Gaulle was tending to break free or not, the Marshal's influence continued to work in his favour. It was quite certainly that influence which was responsible for his then being appointed instructor (though not professor) at the Ecole de Guerre. This new experience enabled him to put forward a curious plan of teaching for the use of the school, which he had found closed to the world and to the prospects of a new kind of fighting.

The plan tells one a great deal about the evolution of Captain de Gaulle's mind at the beginning of 1926: he paid the closest attention to those disciplines which up to then had not been admitted into the barracks and military schools. High on the list of subjects that he wanted to put on the syllabus was sociology. He suggested that the teaching of it should be entrusted to M. Fauconnet, the editor of the *Revue sociologique*, to Charles Gide (André's uncle), André Siegfried, Jacques Bardoux, René Pinon, etc. – which would have turned the Ecole de Guerre into a branch of the Ecole des Sciences Politiques, of which his teachers were the leading lights. Questions of military technique would be dealt with by Colonel Doumenc.

As for the philosophy of command, he thought it quite natural to claim the subject for himself. And in his view, this was not a question of handling a variety of abstract principles. He proposed dealing with the most urgent problems of the army. This is what may be called an absence of timidity.

The journey Pétain and de Gaulle made together in the Verdun region in 1926 provided the opportunity for the Marshal and the captain to work out the Ecole de Guerre "plot". Just before leaving for the east, Philippe Pétain told friends that, "I am going to travel over the front with the most intelligent officer in the French army and find out what he would have done if he had been on the [German] side."[5]

The Ecole de Guerre had not seen fit to pass de Gaulle at a level that would eventually allow him to teach there: the Marshal was going to oblige the school to accept his protégé as a lecturer, an unprecedented act in the history of the French Army. General Hering, the commander of the school and one of the Marshal's most faithful followers,* was simply told that in the next few months he would have

*And who was so to remain until his death, presiding over the Association for the Defence of the memory of Pétain and taking many steps to obtain his rehabilitation.

to arrange a series of three lectures to be given by Captain de Gaulle. The Marshal told Hering that he had read the texts and that they were of outstanding quality, originality and grandeur. There was nothing left for the head of the school but to obey.

Philippe Pétain even took the trouble of settling the details. The lectures would be given on three successive Tuesdays, at 10.30 a.m., in the "amphi-Louis", the lecture hall in which only the great men appeared, and in the presence of both terms together and the whole teaching body of the school and of the army. He himself would preside over these lectures on the nature of command given by a captain to an audience including many generals.

It was not possible to go farther in the desire "to teach a lesson", to enforce the acceptance of an individual, and to cause exasperation. What in fact did Pétain want? Was it a question of advancing de Gaulle? Of making him the instrument of revenge? Of gauging his resistance to hatred? Or of confronting two schools of thought at the risk of destroying that which was the richer in promise? At all events the business has a look of provocation.

On 7 April 1927* the Marshal, the captain and the staff of the school gathered in the professors' room of the Ecole de Guerre. As they went into the great amphitheatre the Marshal made a point of standing aside for de Gaulle: "Professor's privilege". And turning to the teaching body he said, "From this rostrum the professor has a right to teach whatever he chooses. I have done so myself!" This was treating his protégé as though he were already appointed and confirmed.

Captain de Gaulle, in full regimentals, white gloves, sword at his side, text in his hand – he never looked at it – stood facing an amphitheatre that was all the more tense since Pétain, before handing over to him, had deliberately said "Gentlemen, I ask you to listen attentively to the ideas that Captain de Gaulle is going to speak to you about!"** To appreciate the full piquancy of the situation one should bear in mind the snub inflicted upon de Gaulle three years before, his fury, the Marshal's anger, and the dubious manoeuvres that ensued.

The subject of the first lecture was "Warlike action and the leader". It began with the striking words which are used as the exordium of *Le Fil de l'épée* and which amount to a declaration of war against the "a priori doctrine", the dogma of the Ecole de Guerre: "Warlike action essentially assumes the nature of contingency." With a few slight changes, this lecture, like the two subsequent lectures "On character" and "On prestige", formed the basis of three articles published under the same titles in the *Revue militaire française* in 1930 and 1931 and reassembled after very careful rewriting and the addition of two chapters as *Le Fil de l'épée*, which appeared in 1932.***

These pieces of flamboyant eloquence, recited by heart in that rasping, grandiloquent tone which so struck Captain de Gaulle's hearers in those days,

*This is the date given by all the historians. Yet Charles de Gaulle tells his father about it in a letter dated 3 March 1927 (see p. 83). Was it a slip of the copyist's pen?

**Basing ourselves upon the upright Lucien Nachin's account, many of us have given these words as having been uttered by the Marshal on this occasion: "Listen attentively to Captain de Gaulle: the day will come when a grateful France will call upon him."

***See p. 101.

could not fail to impress some and exasperate others. The speaker seemed to delight in defying his former masters:

> It sometimes happens that soldiers, exaggerating the relative powerlessness of intelligence, neglect to make use of it.
>
> Our days are not very favourable for the education of military leaders, [for] as Scharnhorst says, in time of peace mechanically formed minds triumph over those that possess feeling and outstanding gifts. The recruitment of really able leaders becomes difficult when peace lasts a long time. The selection governing careers turns more readily to that which is pleasing than to that which is deserving.

Here was a great deal of wit, erudition (some thirty philosophers, statesmen, strategists and historians were quoted, from Socrates to Pasteur) and self-confidence in an officer who had not yet attained the rank of major but confronted by the army's "intellectual elite".

General Hering told J.-R. Tournoux about the explosion of rage in his office after the first lecture: "What arrogance! What insolence! It is unbelievable that the Old Man should patronize such an exhibition! He takes us all for fools!" The calmer Lucien Nachin gives this description of the audience: "The officers who composed it grasped only part of what he said. They may have been overcome by his extraordinary brilliance, but the impression they received, the state of mind that permeated them and the atmosphere that surrounded them maintained not only a positive want of understanding but even a kind of latent hostility to his teaching, a spirit of resistance and inhibition."

As for Charles de Gaulle himself, he does not seem to have been aware of the full malignity of the "resistance" aroused in the greater part of his hearers. It was in quite a satisfied tone that he wrote to his father: "The first [lecture], presided over by the Marshal, made a very great impression. Those on my side are delighted, the neutrals smile, and the sharks who swim round the ship waiting for me to fall in so that they may devour me have moved off to a considerable distance."[6]

De Gaulle, as a dramatist, made up his character by a process of superimposition. There are some of Pétain's features – the attitude and the behaviour, the brevity and the method. But starting with this tangible basis of acquired rank and fame, the brilliant captain breathed his own spirit into the pale, handsome, polished, formal marble statue whose limits he had measured, at least since the Moroccan affair. The rite was celebrated before the star-studded marble figure; but it was the celebrant who counted and who asserted himself.

Charles de Gaulle was able to make his way round the wall of mistrust that any fine speaker naturally comes up against in the silent service, though not without increasing its solidarity. Henri Boegner, the organizer of the Fustel de Coulanges Association, invited him to repeat his three lectures, which had not failed to arouse a certain amount of comment in Paris, at the Sorbonne.

What in fact was this association that took the name of the great historian of the ancient world? It was quite simply a satellite of the Action Française. Among the more zealous members therefore were some of the best-known intellectuals of the extreme Right: Charles Maurras, Maurice Pujo, Louis Bertrand, André Bellesort and Charles Benoist.

This does not mean that Charles de Gaulle agreed with their opinions. In order to get him to come they used Lyautey's name, which did not fail to impress the captain.* Furthermore he found the setting of the Sorbonne, which they offered, irresistibly attractive. Here was a first sketch of that amalgam of the university man and the soldier suggested by his plan of reform for the Ecole de Guerre some months before.

So he agreed to go to the Fustel de Coulanges Association's meeting, which would give him access to an amphitheatre crowded with an audience similar to that which went to hear Bergson at the neighbouring Collège de France: professors, intellectuals and fashionable women.

Little is known about the evolution of Pétain and de Gaulle's relationship as everything happened in private interviews, the only witness being the discreet Mlle Lucet. Yet even so one incident, the forerunner of many others, is spoken of. According to Colonel Bouvard, Captain de Gaulle's predecessor and still very close to the old leader's familiars, towards the end of 1926 "there was what seemed to be a stormy argument between the Marshal and de Gaulle, who came out of Pétain's office obviously tense and in a state of cold fury."[7]

The crisis became more "legible" from the moment when de Gaulle moved to a distance: from November 1927, two months after he had been promoted to major, he was required to do a stint in Germany. After this their letters allow one to measure the rift that was opening between two characters, two temperaments and two different conceptions of literary creation.

On 5 December 1927 the Marshal shows a certain sharpness with regard to the major: "Time is getting on and I receive no news of your work." Yet the book must have been well advanced, since Pétain speaks of the conclusion, which he intends to give the form of "scattered thoughts".[8]

On 13 January 1928 de Gaulle was stupified to read a letter from Colonel Audet who, like him, was one of Pétain's team of ghosts.

> The Marshal sent for me and told me of his wish that the research for the famous book should not be entirely interrupted by your departure. I protested that I had no aptitude whatsoever for the work he had in mind. I have been hesitating whether to speak to you of all this, fearing that you would be understandably displeased. I cannot collaborate on a piece of work that was dear to you without letting you know, although it is not a task I like at all.

Charles de Gaulle's reaction could not but be vigorous. It was that of a writer, not of a soldier. It took the form of two letters, one to Colonel Audet, the other to the Marshal.[9] The first is dated 16 January 1928:

*But de Gaulle refused to attend a dinner organized by the same people at which Lyautey, exiled from Morocco, was to make a speech hostile to the Republic.

Dear Colonel,
I am touched by the frank and open confidence that you show me and I thank you for it. You already know my opinion. A book is a man. Until now that man has been myself. If some other person, even if he were a Monstesquieu – even if he were you yourself, Colonel – takes a hand in it then one or two things must come about: either he writes a different book or he destroys mine, which will no longer have any character and will therefore be worthless. If the Marshal wishes you to write another book, I have no sort of objection to offer. I shall purely and simply take my book back. But if it is a question of mangling my ideas, my philosophy and my style I do object and I am going to tell the Marshal so.

The Marshal has never been willing to acknowledge the difference that exists between a book and a piece of writing for the General Staff. That is why I have often thought that this business would end badly.

This was indeed plain speaking. He could not have been firmer, whether he was dealing with "my property" or with the old chief's views of the calling of letters. The letter to Philippe Pétain was written in an even higher tone, even more stinging under the smoothness of its style:

Monsieur le Maréchal,
In 1925, when you did me the great honour of asking me to collaborate with you on *Le Soldat*, you were good enough to tell me that it would be a question of personal collaboration, that the work would be done between the two of us and that you would publicly acknowledge the part I had taken in it. It was in these conditions that I agreed to work with you. Besides I had too entire a confidence in your very superior judgment to imagine that you could look upon such a work as a "general staff" task. This book in which philosophy, history and style are concerned stands quite apart from anything written in the line of service.

It is for this reason that with a respectful insistence I ask you, Monsieur le Maréchal, not to hand over to any other pen that which I delivered to you alone. Although, out of my very great esteem for you and a desire to give certain ideas all the authority of your name for the public good I am perfectly happy to see you alone sign the book, I cannot give up that part of myself which I have put into it. In any event, even if I were to give it up, the future would inevitably take care to put things right.

Some people are already acquainted with the manner of thinking and the style that are to be seen in *Le Soldat*. In the nature of things, others will discover them later. Then again, although the entire world knows Marshal Pétain's value in action and reflexion, a thousand well-informed persons are aware of his dislike for writing. To answer questions before they are asked, to shut ill-natured mouths, and above all to be just, it is essential, Monsieur le Maréchal, that in a preface or foreword you should directly and clearly acknowledge your fellow-worker. This intelligent generosity will ensure the entirety of your fame, undamaged, in the literary as well as in other domains.

Firmness, lack of constraint, irony, high-mindedness: Major de Gaulle said what he had to say to the leader upon whom his military career depended. Nothing that etiquette and tradition require to be concealed on such occasions was concealed. The old chief's immediate followers therefore reacted with great bitterness. Colonel Laure, the Imperator's right-hand man, wrote sharply to de Gaulle: "Withdraw your letter to the Marshal. Do not lay down conditions: conduct yourself like a loyal follower – a conduct that is the pride of us who are soldiers." And all this was preceded by an open, direct threat in which de Gaulle's advantage and career were spoken of: the possibility of Major de Gaulle's being "struck off the list for the two years during which [he] had been entirely taken up by this work" and placed "on leave or unattached".

Marshal Pétain himself was intelligent enough not to let himself go to such extremes. He reacted to de Gaulle's peremptory lecture with a moderation in which more confusion than anger can be detected.

> My dear de Gaulle,
> I quite understand that Audet's letter should have disturbed you. What I am trying to do is not to provide my army comrades with a plain historical survey, however brilliant it may be. This survey must also give rise to certain principles of organization and employment that will be summed up in a final chapter to be drawn up under my supervision. As far as your share in the work as a whole is concerned, it will appear, as I have already told you, in the preface that we shall write together when the time comes.

Was this an armistice between de Gaulle and Pétain? Various witnesses, including Loustaunau-Lacau, state that towards the middle of 1928 the Marshal, in order to avoid having to make a public acknowledgement that the text of *Le Soldat* was written by de Gaulle, preferred putting the manuscript away in his safe, saying "It will never come out of here again!"

Yet in January 1929, answering the New Year's wishes of the major, who exhorted him to "finish off *Le Soldat*", the Imperator wrote to de Gaulle telling him that "*Le Soldat* is not dead . . . if you would like to carry on with your collaboration". What is more, fresh opportunities for "collaboration" were to arise: Foch's death in 1929 made it possible for Pétain to join the Academy. In June Colonel Laure told de Gaulle that the Marshal meant to sound him on the question of the "perfecting of the academic oration". Upon this de Gaulle wrote to Nachin, "We are busy with the speech the Marshal has to make when he is received into the Academy. It is for later – as late as possible. There has to be a eulogium of Foch, whom he could not bear – the feeling was mutual." From now on, sarcasm was never far from the surface when de Gaulle wrote about the old leader.

There was a danger that the tone might become positively sardonic when on 25 July, at Trèves, the major received a letter in which the Imperator did not hesitate to draw a parallel between himself as a writer and Paul Valéry, who was to receive him under the cupola of the Academy: "I am going to set myself to writing again. I used to do it fairly well in former days. As it is Paul Valéry who will answer my speech I shall not dislike comparing my style, stripped to the bone, with his, in which the thought vanishes beneath a piling-up of ornament."

Was de Gaulle to write this famous speech of the successful candidate for the Academy? He might laugh to himself but there was no doubt that he wished to be given the task. Putting the eulogy of Foch into Pétain's mouth with enough conviction for it to be acceptable to the vanished chief yet with enough treachery for the survivor to hear nothing but the false notes – here was the most fascinating of exercises for the moving orator and virtuoso politician that he had already become.

On 2 February 1930 the Imperator returned to the subject, suggesting an outline for de Gaulle and reminding him that he "did not mean to spare the criticism of his late colleague (in dealing with the operations directed by Foch, Pétain intended to devote only one paragraph out of five to the victorious offensive of 1918!). And Pétain made it quite clear: "If your work reaches me in time, that is to say about 15 March, I shall take great pleasure in using those parts which enter into the framework that I have drawn up for myself."

The piece he wrote for this occasion is magnificent.[10] So magnificent that Pétain did not want it, not only because the reservations with regard to Foch were swept away by the writer's enthusiasm for the strategist, the man of fire, faith and imagination, but also because the "manner of thinking and style" that de Gaulle had spoken of in his letter to Pétain in January 1928 were so apparent here, the direction of the argument so much in favour of the offensive and the spirit of imaginative manoeuvre that for Pétain it would have been an out and out denial of himself to take responsibility for this panegyric of his opposite.

It was not Charles de Gaulle who, under Pétain's academic cocked hat, paid homage to Foch that afternoon on 1931 but another, who put more measure into the praise and more weight into the refusal of what was due, thus giving a better rendering of the survivor's wishes.

Not all the pieces of these days were as fine as the Ecole de Guerre lectures or the eulogium of Foch.

Le Flambeau, a historico-heroic dialogue, was published in two issues of the *Revue militaire* (March and April 1928). Here we have four military men – passing on the flambeau, the torch of national defence from one to another between 1793 and 1826. It is like a sketch written for the end of year entertainment at Saint-Cyr. The machinery is artificial, the tone fit for a school, and the transitions are laborious: we are far from the author of "Doctrine a priori".

It is not surprising to see that the *Carnets*, the notebooks that the captain kept at this period, contain quotations from most of the authors the Constable liked best – Tacitus, Bossuet, La Bruyère, Vauvenargues, Goethe, Barrès, Psichari. But there is also to be found a most unusual commentary on Raymond Poincaré's *L'Invasion*, an account of the beginnings of the war of 1914. Charles de Gaulle, who did not think very much of the book, made fun of the former president of the Republic: "As he candidly says himself, he had had not the slightest contact with the people."

* * *

On 25 September 1927, then, having served as a captain for twelve years,* he was promoted major. He had been on the promotion roster for eight months. Every officer, whether he belonged to the "Pétain establishment" or not, had to serve for a "period of command" after each promotion, and de Gaulle felt called upon to give this period an exceptional brilliance. After his time with the Marshal and his sensational lectures at the Ecole de Guerre, what could be found that would keep him at the same miraculous level? He was sent to Germany, to command a battalion of light infantry, the 19th Chasseurs à pied (the 19th BCP), one of those that had suffered most in the recent war. It was stationed at Trèves, on the banks of the Moselle, a little town of Roman origins that had provided the world with an unusual citizen: Karl Marx.

The light infantry units were the preserves of those who had served in them from the beginning; they were "élite" bodies in which French narcissism claims to see the incarnation of the race, symbolized by the wearing of a beret and a brisker rate of marching than other units (120 paces a minute), and they were never made accessible to intruders like this de Gaulle, who had never served in anything but ordinary infantry regiments.

Was it the protection of the Marshal once more that brought him this favour? There is no document to support the hypothesis. But de Gaulle's reputation was beginning to precede him wherever he went. And the work impressed everybody, even the terrible General Matter, the director of infantry renowned for the harshness of his character. When Lucien Nachin, once his subordinate, told Matter of his pleasure and at the same time of his astonishment at seeing his friend Charles de Gaulle profiting from the suspension of a tradition so firmly established and maintained by those concerned, Matter, in his abrupt way, retorted, "I am appointing a future generalissimo of the French army!"[11]

*A perfectly usual period.

CHAPTER SEVEN

The Edge of the Sword

On 11 October 1927, when Charles de Gaulle reached Trèves and the 19th BCP which had been given to him so that his powers as a leader destined for the highest post might be measured, it was almost twelve years since he had had any command.* This proponent of authority who had just proclaimed its lofty philosophy to an audience of the army's intelligentsia was now called upon to produce his proofs once more. But how would it be now, after these long interludes in teaching, in the Marshal's establishment and in literature? The light-infantrymen of Trèves were going to learn what an intellectual was capable of when he was asked to show what he could do in the realm of facts.

These soldiers with whose command he had been honoured, this battalion that had suffered more tragically than any other in the war (its effectives renewed from top to bottom four times over) – just what did they amount to? Three months after his arrival on the banks of the Moselle he wrote to a friend in Paris:

> A light-infantry battalion in the army of the Rhine is still a fine body of men: I mean if it is at strength (721 men) and has fairly good conditions for instruction. In the 19th battalion there are even some good officers, particularly the young who had left the schools after the armistice and whose undiminished fervour is worth much more than their elders' experience: "Experience," said von der Goltz, "is disastrous for the soldier". We still have all the elements needed to remake an army for ourselves; but we no longer possess an army. Who will provide the Republic with a Louvois? Intelligent life is at a very low ebb in the army of the Rhine. In any case it is better so, for what can one "do" with intelligence, that impotent and pretentious quality? Mars was strong, handsome and brave, but he had little in the way of wits.[1]

A contemporary photograph shows him in the midst of the battalion's officers who were grouped on either side of his towering form: it must be admitted that these moustached, broad-shouldered captains around him, their badges of rank won in the firing-line, did not seem personally threatened by any excess of intellectualism. Was it out of an *esprit de corps* that from now on Charles de Gaulle would sometimes jeer at intelligence?

The country to which the Republic had sent him in order to see whether a "pen-officer" might become a man of the sword once more, is exceptionally

*He had been in the firing-line in Poland, but without exercising any authority.

beautiful. From the hillsides along the Moselle, bordered with vineyards, to the slopes of the Kyll valley and of the Kokelsberg and to the wooded foothills of the Eifel, this fearless walker must have found a landscape worthy of his meditations. But Trèves was no longer anything but a little town dominated by a gigantic statue of Our Lady, the Mariensaüle, and by the famous Porta Nigra, a majestic remnant of the days of the Antonines, blackened by the smoke of a barbarian fire – hence its name.

But it was by furious activity that he chose to assert himself, stirring up his men, and himself with them, with a kind of wild enthusiasm. The programme of his first ten months of command provided for a month's intensive training at the camp at Bitche, and ten days of exercises at the camp at Drose, without counting the garrison manoeuvres and those on a greater scale performed by the army of the Rhine. This did not satisfy him: he spurred his men on to even greater activity. It was nothing but forced marches, prolonged rifle exercises, competitions at various sports, a crossing of the frozen Moselle at the dead of night (stopped by the general in command before it could be carried out). Were the light infantry crack regiments or not? It was not under de Gaulle that they were going to lose their reputation.

He carried on to such an extent that some of his men, less anxious than he to belong to a crack regiment, asked to be transferred to France. "Every request of this kind will be punished with prison!" he thundered. One of "his" men nevertheless induced his member of parliament to ask the ministry to send an order for his transfer. Major de Gaulle kept his word: to the cells! Protests from the member, intervention by a higher command, threat of very serious penalties, a dart to Paris on the part of the Constable ("I belong to the Pétain establishment," he said to those in charge of the enquiry), interview with the Marshal, who obtained de Gaulle's absolution from the minister.

He lived in a small house on the bank of the Moselle opposite to that upon which there stood the 19th BCP's Sidi Brahim barracks, which he reached every morning by foot. At midday he lunched alone, usually in the room of the casino occupied by the garrison mess; but in the evening he used often to invite some of the young officers to his table around a bottle of Graves costing six francs, as might be seen from the label. There was no talking shop: he eagerly discussed Napoleon's campaigns, the prince-bishops of the seventeenth century or the medieval poets.

The future Mgr Rupp, who was a reserve-lieutenant in the 19th BCP under the orders of this unusual chief, drew a lively portrait of Major de Gaulle for André Frossard:

> De Gaulle attracted our attention immediately. He stood out not so much because of his size but because of his ego, which glowed from far off. We gauged his extraordinary loneliness by the measure of ordinary life. We said: pride, coldness, ambition, taking off into space. My friends and I had some understanding of his silence. What could he say? Who could he talk to? What about? He liked the young. But at that time what had he to ask of them? His battalion, the 19th, was under strict control. But intelligently, of course.

> Elsewhere there was mere strictness alone. We did not complain of excessive or unfair severity. We needed this drill.[2]

It was noticed that on 24 January 1929 he gave the third of seven talks provided for their members by the Trèves lecture society, "The rout of the German nation". One cannot say that this title was in the best of taste at a time when relations between Berlin and Paris had become cordial once more and at a moment when the French cabinet was making up its mind to bring the occupation to an earlier end than had been laid down. A Parthian shot?

Jean-François Duflos was only a lieutenant in the reserve when he found himself under the Constable's orders at Trèves. On the evening of a field-day in which he had made a number of blunders, shortly after he had joined the battalion, he was summoned by the commanding officer. De Gaulle, telling him of the frightful losses suffered in the course of history by the battalion which he commanded, spoke of Captain Duflos, who had been killed at the attack on Navarin: "It is three months now that you have been with us, and I did not know that you were his son. I ought to have known."

A few days later the lieutenant's mother came to see him. They lunched in the casino mess. De Gaulle, alone at his table, asked about the lady who was having her meal with one of his officers; he came over, bowed to Captain Duflos' widow and said, "Madame, you must see Trèves. I shall cancel all my afternoon engagements and act as your guide." For two hours on end, in his best uniform, the Constable led his guest from the Porta Nigra to the basilica and from the Moselüfer to the cathedral, describing everything in detail like an experienced specialist.[3]

The major's relations with his superiors on the other hand remained invariably tense. When General Putois, the garrison commander, publicly criticized the chasseurs' conduct during a manoeuvre, he at once heard de Gaulle, before the assembled troops, proclaim: "The 19th has behaved well: a day off." And when General Debeney, the former chief of the Ecole de Guerre and now at the head of the General Staff, sent a note telling him of the death of a former commanding officer of the battalion, he received a cutting reply to the effect that they had not waited for a message from the General Staff in Paris to pay their respects to the dead man. It looked as though he were deliberately trying to come into conflict with the hierarchy. The only one he looked upon with favour was General Guillaumat,* the commander of the occupation troops in Germany, and avowed disciple of Foch (and therefore on bad terms with Pétain).

Although he was not averse to conflict, he did not like "complications". The winter of 1928–1929 was terribly cold in the valley of the Moselle. An epidemic of influenza broke out, and the French papers at once described it as "German 'flu". The disease wrought havoc among the Trèves garrison: thirty dead, it was stated, "without counting the Annamese", seven of them in the 19th BCP alone. The government, then headed by Poincaré, was obliged to deal with scores of questions in parliament: what were the living conditions of our soldiers in peace-time?

*Whose son became Minister of Defence in 1959. (trs.)

A commission of enquiry was appointed and its chairman, Colonel Picot, addressing the Chamber, relieved the commanding officer of the 19th BCP, among others, of any responsibility: in this battalion "the large number of deaths was not owing to the way in which the men were treated: it is very well commanded indeed". And the speaker went on, "Since Private Gouraud died an orphan, the major [de Gaulle] decided to wear mourning for him. There is a leader for you!" (Loud applause.) From the government benches the prime minister cried, "Very good!", and this, coming from him, was worth a prominent mention in dispatches.[4]

This was a period heavy with bitter feelings, both private (we shall return to them) and public as well as professional. In the days of Locarno and the Kellog-Briand pact the Rhineland was an unrivalled observation-post, and from it de Gaulle saw the wasting away of France's ascendency over Europe, the diminution, month by month, of the formidable instrument that the French army had been, and the change in the ratio of power between Paris and Berlin. Before his eyes there stirred a Germany determined to rise again. How could he doubt the tragic nature of the future when he read Arthur Moeller van den Brück's most important book, *The Third Reich*?*

This strongly prophetic essay described a supranational Reich directed by Prussia, gathering together this "people that lacked space" and going beyond the limits of Bismarck's empire to dominate the whole of central Europe. "We Germans are destined never to leave others in peace," ended Moeller, who, horrified by the outlook revealed by his severe and exacting imagination, killed himself in 1924, a year after the publication of his book.

At the end of 1928 he wrote to Nachin in a tone as prophetic as Moeller:

> The army of the Rhine will not last much longer. The force of circumstances is destroying what Europe still possesses in the way of agreed and precious barriers. One must see that the Anschluss and then Germany's recovery, by fair means or foul, of what was taken from her for the benefit of Poland are close at hand. After that we shall be asked to return Alsace. To me this seems written in the heavens.[5]

This breaking up of the army of the Rhine which he watched with such anger was to take the most wounding possible aspect for him: he was told his battalion, the famous 19th BCP, was to be disbanded. On 9 October 1929, addressing the men of the demi-brigade to which the battalion he had commanded for two years belonged, he spoke of this "funeral" with the utmost bitterness:

> Like Oedipus at Colonus we should readily say, "Accept fate, but have the strength to curse it!" Seeing the treasures of zeal, courage and strength we represent together thrown to the four winds wounds us deeply. But it is also a fruitful wound and one that we shall allow to spread because it marks us and makes us resolved. I am thinking of you particularly, you young officers, because every day your enthusiasm comes up against painful realities. The

*Which dates from 1923, the year of the Nazi putsch at Munich.

> French army is wholly ready to start a fresh youth again the moment some powerful will meets and grasps its fate![6]

The disbanding of his battalion* was neither a punishment – the general commanding at Trèves did not allow the funeral to be performed without making a powerful speech in praise of the battalion's chief – nor the reason for Major de Gaulle's departure from Germany. He had "done" his two years of command there and now his mind was wholly taken up with the appointment he had long dreamt of – a teaching post at the Ecole de Guerre.

But other people were making other plans for him. Marshal Pétain, for example, to whom he had obviously suggested a recall to his personal staff at the Invalides, advised him to go and serve in Syria: General du Granrut, in command there, would welcome him. "It would go against my conscience to take you away from him," said the Marshal. "To move up the stages of the hierarchy in time of peace, one has to distinguish oneself by outstanding services. You are being given a chance; do not neglect it. That is my advice to you and it is quite disinterested." "Disinterested" or not, the advice gave de Gaulle no pleasure. What was evident was that the Imperator was in no hurry to see him at the Invalides again, and that he would not help him on towards the Ecole de Guerre, at least not this time. So he would have to shift for himself. Whatever the steps he took, he soon thought that he had been accepted if we are to believe General Laffargue's account in his *Fantassin de Gascogne*:

> One day I met my former comrade de Gaulle in the courtyard of the Ecole Militaire. He told me he had just been appointed professor at the Ecole supérieure de Guerre. I congratulated him and told him how happy I should be in that case to meet him more often.
>
> Yet a few days later I opened the *Journal officiel* and there I saw de Gaulle's posting to the army of the Levant. I was much astonished. What had happened?
>
> This is what I was told. When the professors learnt of his appointment they went to see the general commanding the school and said roughly this: "If de Gaulle comes here, we shall all leave!" The authorities did not persist, and the posting was altered.

Laffargue, though he was never a "Gaullist", felt no animosity against the Constable. His account is therefore to be accepted: it is cruel only for the fools who combined against the innovator. It also serves as a timely reminder that it was not his personal choice that took de Gaulle to the Near East in the autumn of 1929. His reasons for preferring to be in Paris once more were his fondness for the metropolis and then again his wish to remain close to the "centres of decision". Moreover, any posting overseas was made difficult by the care required for a handicapped child.

*A decision that was withdrawn three months later, after he had left for the Near East.

But he had to go. With all precautions taken and all the baggage gathered together, on 30 October 1929 Charles de Gaulle and his family went aboard the *Lamartine*, bound for Beirut. Was he going to find himself quite disorientated by this Near East that he did not yet call "complicated" but about which his would not have been merely simple notions? Between the news of his posting on 18 October and his embarcation at the end of the month, he had not had time to read much. But he must have looked over what had been written about the Levant since the beginning of the last century, from Chateaubriand, Lamartine and Renan to Barrès, Loti and Pierre Benoit.

And in any case Charles de Gaulle's interest in the Near East did not date from his posting there. Five years before this, Marshal Pétain had intended to inspect the French positions in the Levant. To prepare for the journey, Lieutenant-Colonel Catroux, said to be the most competent in this field, was summoned to Paris, and the Marshal told de Gaulle to collect his opinions. Catroux, meeting his fellow-captive of Fort IX at Ingolstadt once more, was struck by his young comrade's interest in Syrian and Lebanese affairs.

General Catroux, speaking to me in 1965 about these conversations, explained Charles de Gaulle's eagerness to understand matters of this kind: "There is nothing surprising about it: de Gaulle is an ardent Christian, and what could be more intensely interesting for a believer than this country where the great monotheistic religions were born and where they still confront one another with all their original fervour?" Unfortunately, de Gaulle did not have this incomparable guide to the complexities of Levantine politics, for a few months earlier Catroux had been posted to Morocco.

For a French officer was the Levant of 1929 a "sunny Rhineland" as Jacques Nobécourt so agreeably puts it[7] – which would both comfort a newcomer in the short-term and worry him in the long? General Gouraud, the one-armed, bearded and paternal founder of the "Great Lebanon", imposed by force upon Arab nationalism and English strategy, had left six years before this, and since then contradictory policies and personalities complicated a hopelessly entangled situation with private quarrels and intrigues.

No one knew exactly what the mandate over Syria and the Lebanon granted to France by the League of Nations amounted to. Furthermore, very few knew what these two countries were, or even whether they were separated by a frontier. The only things that were certain were the chaotic, vigorous Arab nationalism, the Maronites' awareness of their special status, the Druzes' awareness of their difference, and the activity of some thirty religious communities from Tyre to Aleppo and from Tripoli to Damascus – and lastly the passionate rivalry between French and English. And at the heart of this perilous jigsaw was Beirut.

At that time who could tell the exact nature of French eastern policy, based as it was on an obsessive urge to counter the moves of the British rivals. On the spot each man acted as he saw fit: and whereas in the Alaouites General Billotte imposed something very like a direct administration, at Damascus Catroux had set up the most flexible of protectorates. As soon as de Gaulle arrived, General de Bigault du Granrut, commanding the troops in the Levant where he had been waging war these last ten years, made de Gaulle responsible for both the second and third bureau (intelligence and operations: everything that mattered) – a very early mark of confidence to a newcomer.

Charles de Gaulle and his family settled in the Druze quarter, a good way from the Grand Sérail where the General Staff had its offices. A letter to his father of 21 November gives the first description of his position: "Roomy, new and well-placed house. Philippe [is] with the Jesuit fathers. Elizabeth* with the dames de Nazareth. Little Anne is well and she is making some progress. Yvonne is full of spirit and she is happy with the general situation."

In an article written many years later for the *Revue du Liban*, Mme Wéhbé, their landlord, spoke of the life of the de Gaulles in the Druze quarter: "De Gaulle was an early riser and he went to the Grand Sérail on foot. He was kind and most open-handed. The de Gaulles went out very little and rarely entertained. Mme de Gaulle was scarcely to be seen at all (too busy looking after her handicapped daughter Anne). She only appeared on Sundays. At eleven she and her husband went to the Capuchins' Mass at the church of St Louis." "As far as I am concerned," wrote de Gaulle to his father,

> I have taken up my duties as head of the 2nd and 3rd Bureaux. I think everything will go on very well. As early as next Monday I am leaving for Aleppo, from where I shall go to the Euphrates and beyond, to inspect our posts on the Turkish frontier. Then I shall go to Damascus and after that into the Jebel Druse. The country is quiet for the moment. Good impression from the military point of view. Not so good from the political, the high commissioner, M. Parisot** seeming undecided what course to follow: badly informed, too, and not backed up at all by Paris.

Five days later he wrote to his wife from Aleppo, telling her of the places he passed through on his journey (Deir-ez-Zor, Hassetché, Kamechlie, Ras-el-Aīn, Latakia, Tripoli). And he took advantage of this somewhat adventurous trip to the frontiers to unbosom himself with a delightful spontaneity:

> I love you with all my heart. Everyone here asks me, "And was not Mme de Gaulle much disturbed by your taking the field?" I answer with the truth, that is to say "No", and inwardly I think that perhaps she was but she is so good and so courageous that she pretended to be happy. I shall never forget how you supported me, and that at a time which was after all difficult.

His new and widespread duties made him the man who was supposed to know everything about the socio-political movements that kept the Lebanon, and above all Syria, in a state of perpetual agitation and the officer responsible for all military exercises and manoeuvres between the Euphrates and the Litani;*** yet the Constable still found time to put his eloquence to the proof. His Saint-Cyr

*The elder daughter of Yvonne and Charles. (trs.)

**This is of course M. Henri Ponsot, whose fellow-workers state that he was an able man both at Rabat and Beirut.

***The Lebanese river. (trs.)

comrade André Berlon, whom he found here at the head of the staff at Latakia, speaks with undiminished admiration of the three lectures he gave at the officers' club at Beirut, the subjects being the French army under the Monarchy, the Revolution and the Empire. "It was magnificent. How do you manage it, I asked him, talking like that without notes, so clearly and with such authority? It is very easy, he told me: I learn it by heart and then I repeat it to my wife. When she understands, I feel it is as it should be."

At Tripoli he met another Saint-Cyr companion, Emile Petit (who joined him in London and who ended up in the French Communist Party), who persuaded him to repeat his lectures in this northern capital. Colonel Massiet, the local commander, had not been consulted. He was vexed and protested to General du Granrut; Granrut ventured to give the over-eloquent Constable a mild rebuke. The matter went no farther: de Gaulle had perhaps done too much, but what he had to do, he did very well.

In those days, on the highlands that command the Beka Valley there was an active and dangerous band of robbers called the Dandaches. Major Berlon, in charge of the sector, informed the Lebanese Government, which was responsible for maintaining order so long as the matter did not affect the security of the country as a whole. But the Lebanese Government held back, for want of means. Berlon thereupon took it upon himself to mount an operation removing all the people living on the mountain and rehousing them in the Beka; he then seized some of the brigands.

The General Staff at Beirut – the High Commissioner was absent – took it badly. Was this not encroaching upon the Lebanese authorities' powers? But one officer stood up and spoke in favour of the major responsible for the operation. De Gaulle stressed that in these circumstances the public interest had been safeguarded, and he carried the High Command with him. A few days later the high commissioner, Ponsot, back in Beirut, decided in favour of Berlon and de Gaulle: action had been necessary.

It was at this time (June 1930) that he wrote one of his faithful Paris correspondents (Mayer or Nachin) this equivocal letter, full of contradictory remarks about his notions of the mandate:

> The Lebanon is a junction where everything crosses – religions, armies, empires, merchandise – yet where nothing changes. It is ten years now since we have been here. It is my impression that we shall scarcely get any deeper into the country and that the people are as foreign to us (and the other way about) as ever they were. It is true that for accomplishing anything we have adopted the worst system for this country, that is to say urging the people to improve themselves, even if we have to reward them to do so, whereas nothing has ever been carried out here, neither the canals of the Nile nor the aqueduct of Palmyra, nor a Roman road nor an olive-grove, without compulsion.
>
> In my opinion we are doomed either to reach that point or to leave the place. Sceptics would add a third solution, to wit: let today's fumblings go on since time does not count and systems, like bridges and houses, easily manage to stand for centuries although they are out of true.

> There is one man and I believe one man alone who thoroughly understood Syria and "knew how to cope with it": it was Colonel Catroux. That is why he has gone.

It is an odd reasoning that both criticizes indirect administration and praises the man who symbolized just this kind of policy, Catroux. In de Gaulle there is always to be seen this contradiction between reflex (the authoritarian reflex) and reflection. The synthesis often arises from the "circumstances", which may take the form of a man. In this case Catroux.

During the summer the major settled his family in the hills above Beirut, at Aley, where everyone found it easier to bear a climate that was said to be "really distressing". When he wrote about this to his father, he was thinking chiefly of little Anne; many of the major's fellow-officers who were in this hill-village speak of how very kindly she was treated. Having found this healthy retreat for his children, he accompanied General du Granrut on a journey northwards, to the River Tigris.

A few months later Charles de Gaulle and his wife travelled to Palestine for a fortnight with two friends. The de Gaulles, staying with the Jesuits of Notre-Dame-de-France, went to see the Holy Sepulchre and the Holy Places, Bethlehem and Nazareth. When he came back, the Constable spoke of his impressions of these two weeks – the ludicrous rivalry between religious orders, the ruinous condition of buildings, the negligences of British political and military authorities. Were they not carrying this "worst system", that of indirect administration, to the point of caricature?

After he had spent a year in the Levant, Major de Gaulle summed it up for his friends in Paris in these words:

> The Levant is still quiet, if one can so describe the eastern minds' state of perpetual excitement when there are no immediate violent consequences. Here are to be found peoples who have never been satisfied by anything nor by anyone but who bow to the will of the strongest if only that will is expressed, and a mandatory power that has not yet really discovered how to set about exercising its mandate. This leads to a chronic uncertainty – an uncertainty, furthermore, that is to be found throughout the East.[8]

Unexpected circumstances gave him the opportunity, on 13 July 1931,* of making the appearance that set the most lasting mark on his stay in the Levant. Every year the Jesuits of the St Joseph University in Beirut asked an outstanding figure to preside over the prize-giving and to make a speech. The High Commissioner, being unable to attend, asked to be represented by an officer belonging to the General Staff. As those of the higher ranks declined "the lot fell on the youngest": besides, was not de Gaulle a pupil of the Jesuits? Gabriel Bounoure,** then professor at the Ecole des Lettres in Beirut, tells the tale:

*The date is uncertain. This is that of the official chronology. (Plon, 1973, p. 17).
**This master of poetry, having become inspector-general of Education in the Levant, was one of the first to join de Gaulle in 1940.

> It was at the annual prize-giving. I saw a tall major stand up and take two paces towards the audience; he was dressed entirely in white, he carried a long sword, and we expected nothing from him other than profound boredom. He began to speak and all at once the dullness vanished. We heard new and uncommon ideas continuously.
>
> The apparatus of speech, handled by him, rose above contingency and artifice, dealing broadly with the field of free-will and of that human energy which is capable of affecting the enormous power of history.[9]

What did he say that was so striking? Among other things, this, which certainly made him lean rather in Colonel Catroux' direction than in that of the blockheads who took the mandate for a title-deed:

> Devotion to the common good, that is what is called for, now that the time has come for rebuilding. And for you especially, the young people of the Lebanon, this great duty assumes an immediate and imperative meaning, for it is a mother-country that you have to build up. On this wonderful soil, steeped in history, supported by the rampart of your mountains, connected by the sea with the activities of the West, and helped by the wisdom and strength of France, you have the task of building a State. Not merely of sharing in its functions or of exercising its powers, but of giving it that life of its own, that inner strength, without which there are only empty institutions. You will have to create and nourish a public spirit, that is to say that willing subordination of each to the common good which is the essential condition for the authority of those who govern, for true justice in the law-courts, for order in the streets, and for the conscientiousness of the civil servants. There is no State without sacrifices: furthermore, it is quite certainly from sacrifices that this state of the Lebanon has arisen.

Here was a programme of government, and it may be asked whether any High Commissioner at that time ever uttered such a bold one. It might have been Lyautey speaking to the Moroccans, or quite simply General de Gaulle, thirty years later, addressing the Africans. Gabriel Bounoure's wondering astonishment was justified: this was the voice of a master, and a man who at last defined a policy and did so as a responsible person. It needs an effort of memory to recall that the speaker was only an officer on the staff of the army of the Levant.

Not all his pieces of those days are of the same stamp. It needs his signature next to that of Major Yvon, his colleague on the staff at Beirut, to tell one that *L'Histoire des troupes du Levant*, published in August 1931, was written in part by him. Yet re-read with care, this rather flat account of the military operations carried out between 1916 and 1930 by the French forces in the Levant – from the fighting in which the French detachment in Palestine under Allenby's orders were concerned to the occupation of the territories (Syria – Lebanon – Cilicia) which the Sykes-Picot agreement of 1917 placed under French influence, and General Gamelin's suppression of the 1925–26 rising in the Jebel Druse – is found to have an admirable clarity. But it does not bear the mark of de Gaulle's hand.

And what of the present? It was eighteen months that he had been far from the "centre of decision". His posting to the Levant had been meant to last two years, bringing him back to France in November 1931. But what should he do on his return. Once again he wrote to Marshal Pétain: was there really nothing for him at the Ecole de Guerre?[10] Colonel Audet wrote to tell him that the Marshal, who was in fact thinking of "a post as professor of history at the Ecole de Guerre" for him, "had asked for information about these lectures". And Audet ended, "I believe that you would occupy the chair brilliantly."

But the Marshal, who had just celebrated his seventy-fifth birthday, was no longer quite what he had been; his intellectual powers may have been unaffected but his influence was certainly much diminished. In February 1931 he had been obliged to hand over his really important powers to General Weygand, retaining only the vague functions of inspector of air defence. He nevertheless remained a substantial ally.

What de Gaulle was asking for, however, was a post in which he should teach strategy and the "conduct of war". And since it turned out that the Ecole de Guerre would not have him, he aimed at nothing less than the setting up of a new centre of instruction in which he would at last be able to express himself.

On 20 April 1931, in an interval between the reading or writing of reports for the Beirut staff, he wrote the last words of a document that is to some degree reminiscent of his plan for the reform of the Ecole de Guerre, written three years earlier at the Invalides. It was a question of,

> the talented presentation of the constant factors in the problem of the "conduct of war". In this way there will be laid down the bases of a doctrine of national defence among those who by their duties outside the army or in it are capable of spreading it or of being called upon to apply it.*

Specifying that this kind of teaching should be aimed at both a civilian (Ecole Normale Supérieure, civil servants in the ministries of Foreign Affairs, the Colonies and the Treasury) and a military audience (Ecole de Guerre, Centre des Hautes Etudes Militaires), Major de Gaulle concluded:

> In order to confer the necessary standing upon the person who is entrusted [with his teaching] the encouragement and the patronage of Marshal Pétain will be required, he being so eminently qualified by his fame, the part he has played, his present functions and the two seats he occupies at the Institute.

The structures of the state, economic organization, scientific research, coordination of diplomatic activities – it was upon these things that the outcome of tomorrow's war would depend. This little document is presumptuous in its form, but it is striking in that it already contains the strategic thought that was to be set in motion after June 1940.

*This was a foreshadowing of the Institut des Hautes Etudes de Défense Nationale.

It is scarcely surprising that in spite of the compliments that adorned the hook, the Marshal did not bite. Circumspection was a structural part of Pétain and it outweighed his vanity, which was circumstantial. But one is never cautious enough; for this old man's evasion led him to put forward an idea which, when it was carried into practice, did a great deal towards giving Charles de Gaulle stature as a statesman and to set him against Pétain nine years later:

> I should be happy to see you posted to the secretariat-general of the Conseil Supérieur de la Défense Nationale. There you would be employed on work of a general but concrete nature, which could not fail to help ripen your ideas and make them more exact. My advice is that you should send in a request for the posting I speak of. I shall exert myself to see that it succeeds.

Major de Gaulle, bearing up bravely against ill-fortune, but too intelligent not to see the judicious nature of the Marshal's advice and the fruitfulness of the new posting, therefore left the shores of the Levant in November 1931 in response to the summons of the 3rd Section of the Secretariat-General of the Défense Nationale. It did not take him long to realize that it was advantageous for him, before teaching others how "to conduct war" to learn about the complex mechanisms upon which war was based.

But the Constable did not leave Beirut without receiving a tribute from the chief under whom he had served. In his report at the end of the posting, General de Bigaud du Granrut wrote of Major de Gaulle:

> During the two years in which I have been enabled to appreciate his execution of his duties, I have never ceased to feel an esteem mixed with admiration for the intellectual and psychological qualities that he possesses.
>
> I particularly dwell upon the unrivalled merits of this soldier who is also a thinker, a man who is aware of his value and who by steady work increases those qualities he knows are his. What is more he knows how to make them appreciated discreetly, maintaining in all circumstances a reserved attitude marked by a wholly military correctness.
>
> He will make a fine leader, and for the good of his branch of the service and of the army as a whole it would be advantageous to move him rapidly to the high posts in which he will give of his full measure and in which he will cause no disappointment.[11]

After this who can say that until 1940 de Gaulle was never understood and that in his profession he never had dealings with any but fools?

On two occasions he had taken Germany's pulse. From the observation-post of Poland he had gauged the extent to which the Soviet Revolution weighed upon the future of Europe. And now he had gained experience in the Levant. Although he still had no knowledge of service whatsoever in Africa* he could return to the General Staff and the highways to command and he could play that role of thinker and of leader for which he was sharpening his wits and armouring himself – the

*Which cost him dear in 1940.

role towards which his gait of an upright dinosaur was leading him, with a breath-taking simplicity.

One must be prudent about what formed the substance of *Le Fil de l'épée.* People often say or write that it was just the three 1927 lectures embellished with a short preface. This is not so. In the foreword to his book published in 1944, Lucien Nachin, who was well informed, states that "these pages were written in 1930". This is not quite the case either. In the definitive text of *Le Fil de l'épée** we find long sections of the 1927 lectures, used again in the articles of 1928 to 1931. The perfectionist Charles de Gaulle, proud of a work that he looked upon as a kind of personal manifesto, never stopped working over these pages until just before the war years: the edge of this particular sword was sharpened with unflagging passion.

And one cannot resist quoting the most famous page of *Le fil de l'épée.*

> But in action, no more criticism! Wishes and hopes turn towards the leader as iron towards the magnet. When the crisis comes, it is he who is followed, it is he who raises the burden with his own arms, though they may break in doing so, and carries it on his shoulders though they may crack under it. The ordinary run of events is not favourable to him, with regard to his superiors. He is confident of his judgment and aware of his strength, and he never sacrifices anything to the desire to please. He is often far removed from passive obedience by the fact that he derives his firmness and power of decision from himself and by no means from any order. He desires that he should be allotted a task and left to carry it out by himself, a requirement found unbearable by many leaders who, for want of seeing things as a whole, take great care of details and nourish themselves on formalities. "Vain and undisciplined" say the mediocre minds, treating the soft-mouthed thorough-bred as though it were an ass that will not go forward, they being totally unaware of the fact that asperity is the failing of powerful characters, that support is to be gained only from that which stands firm, and that strong, unaccommodating hearts are preferable to easy-going, yielding minds. But as soon as matters grow serious and the danger urgent, as soon as the general safety requires immediate initiative, a taste for risk, and firmness, the whole viewpoint changes and justice comes into its own. A kind of tidal wave sweeps the man of character to the forefront.[12]

No comment is called for, unless it takes the form of a question: was this a retrospective view of Pétain in 1916 or was it a startling personal anticipation?

It was not only by the tone and the more thorough-going treatment of its themes that *Le Fil de l'épée* differed from the lectures sponsored by Pétain five years earlier. It was also because the author provided the book with a short preface which amounts to a challenge to the military world's "melancholy", a summons:

> It is time that the military élite should become aware of its pre-eminent role

*The Plon edition of 1971.

> once more, that it should concentrate upon its object, which is war, purely and simply, and that it should raise its head and look towards the heights. To give the sword back its edge, it is time that this élite should re-establish the philosophy proper to its condition.

Lastly it is because he added a new version of his 1925 article against the a priori and above all a new chapter called *Le politique et le soldat*, which, though perhaps less brilliant than the first three is nevertheless the most interesting from the historical point of view. Indeed, the position upheld in this chapter is (as in *La Discorde chez l'ennemi*) that of the two partners concerned in the "conduct of war", the politician and the soldier, the first is no less indispensable than the second.

> It could be imagined that a far-sighted state might wish to prepare a political, administrative and military élite by means of studies carried out in common, in order to direct the nation's warlike effort, should the need arise. As well as the greater likelihood of agreement between the various powers in the event of a conflict, an institution of such a kind would without doubt have the advantage in time of peace of throwing light upon the arguments and laws that have to do with the country's military strength.[13]

Not only did the major thus take the initiative of appealing to public opinion over the head of the old leader who had not agreed with him, but this time he was mischievous enough to refer to the other Marshal. Some lines further on he affirmed that "nothing great was ever done without great men"; he then chose this example: "In the lectures of Foch there could be seen the generalissimo."[14] All that the man of Verdun had to do was to take the hint.

But the man who emerges from the book's last dazzling page is quite certainly neither Foch nor Pétain!

> Let such a fervour haunt those ambitious men of the first order who see no other reason for living than that of stamping their mark on the events of their time and who from the shore upon which commonplace times retain them, dream only of History.[15]

Le Fil de l'épée has brilliance and a voice of its own which confirms the existence of a writer but above all reveals a character. The man who wrote it obviously took himself for what he hoped to become. In 1927 he may not have been quite sure whether his model was the old Imperator or himself. In 1932 (and whatever gestures, dedications and compliments he may have added in the style of those approaching Versailles or departing from it) he no longer deceived himself. The division between the historian and the character had already begun, the division between the observing "I" and the acting "him", between clear awareness and the "surge of History's sea" that carried him away. Charles was preparing to speak about General de Gaulle.

CHAPTER EIGHT

Family, I Love You

On 3 May 1932 M. Henri de Gaulle died at Sainte-Adresse, that high-perched seaward part of Le Havre in which he and his wife had been welcomed some ten years earlier by their Marie-Agnès and her husband Alfred Cailliau. He was nearly eighty-three.

The old gentleman, although kindly and studious, remained deeply attached to the calling that had been his life-long passion, and he had acted as private tutor to his grandchildren; and as one of them, Michel Cailliau, told me, he brought tireless patience and good nature to the task.[1] The comfortable cottage next to the house in which their daughter had settled the elderly pair was always open to the children. Henri de Gaulle kept abreast of everything that was published and, above all, of everything his son Charles was writing.

What is more, Captain de Gaulle asked for his help in several of his historical works. When for example he agreed to undertake the writing of *Le Soldat*, Charles de Gaulle asked his father to act as second to the ghost that he had temporarily become: thereupon he re-read Thiers and wrote very careful entries about military leaders, freely used by his son. With regard to those texts that his son showed him before showing them to the Marshal, on various occasions Henri de Gaulle made observations of a purely political nature. If there were any doubts as to the shades of meaning that separated the old schoolmaster from his second son, studying the manuscript of *Le Soldat* and of Henri de Gaulle's remarks upon it would do away with them at once.

But in any event it is clear that for the author of *La Discorde chez l'ennemi* his eighty-year-old father was still an unrivalled counsellor – a fairly uncommon relationship, and one that says a great deal about this family and the atmosphere in which it lived.

To use an expression typical of that Catholic middle class from which he came and in which he spent a large part of his life, Charles de Gaulle was *très famille.* This nonconformist crackling with sarcasm, this man of breaks and challenges, this revolutionary (sometimes in spite of himself and sometimes on purpose), appears to have been the most classic of husbands and fathers, of sons and brothers, of grandfathers and of brothers-in-law. Jacques Vendroux, who was one of them, thinks it useful to state, "My brother-in-law always took care that the circumstances should not overstretch the family links." And this is without any doubt an understatement.[2]

Whatever he might think of the intellectual relevance of agility of this relation or that, Charles de Gaulle was *très famille* to an exemplary degree, as one can be only if one belongs to a many-rooted community, tossed about by history and by cruel trials, fed on tradition, and held up and held in by uncompromising religious and patriotic convictions, a community of which each generation finds at least one tutelary character to act as a breakwater and rallying-point – and this has been doubly the case for more than a century, both with the Maillots and the de Gaulles.

It was a family united to an unimaginable degree, united even in the great dramas that divided the nation so deeply for a hundred years – a family that could not be shaken by the different views that could be taken on the Dreyfus Case. Nor was the tragedy of 1940–44 to split them apart, though in the end a crevice did appear during the Algerian troubles, when one of de Gaulle's nephews, Michel Cailliau, spoke against the policy that was to lead to the independence of Algeria.

It was a family that was all the more united because, like the Trappists, it was ruled by the law of silence. There were things that were not spoken about, and in the first place "us". A principle that Bernard de Gaulle, the general's nephew, sums up amusingly in the phrase "Silence in the ranks!"[3]

This principle must not be reduced to a kind of closing-in upon some family secret. Among the de Gaulles there have scarcely ever been any. Anne's handicap was lived with in complete openness: which would not have been the case with all families. No. The "silence of the de Gaulles" is a much more traditional attitude and one that is connected both with certain great subjects "which are not spoken of" and with a refusal to mix the family as a whole with public matters. One of these "great subjects" was Religion. God was not a subject that one spoke about. He was not even a subject at all. He was an obvious fact.

The de Gaulles were bound by a law of extreme reticence that was both a pride and a desire not to allow the pure order of the family to interact with the impure order of public life; and their sense of relative values led to the extraordinary silence at the time of the General's death. He died at about seven in the evening of 9 November 1970, and it was not until about nine in the morning of the next day that his intimate collaborator for so many years, Georges Pompidou, the President, was told. Indeed, the de Gaulles observed an exemplary silence throughout the general's extraordinary career: from London to the Elysée and from Algiers to Colombey, "nothing showed". At one point his son, Philippe, publicly stated that he thought his father's concern about reserve "almost excessive".

Another factor in this very great family solidarity was the relatively moderate incomes of both the branches that made up the tribe. To be sure, the Maillots, who had been rich, still possessed a fine house in Lille and the Vendroux had several places in the country, and La Ligerie, after all, was no hovel. But the de Gaulles were people who did not scatter in holiday-time and part of the reason was a desire not to spend too much. They went to houses that belonged to the family. When they rented a villa on the coast, at Wissant or Wimereux, they did so several households together, and they crammed everybody in.

Strict hierarchy, the use of *vous* to one's parents, a nineteenth-century attitude towards marriage, extreme reticence about money, prudishness about morals and a stubborn bigotry with regard to anything that concerned the rites: the de Gaulles seemed to have emerged from a novel by their grandmother Josephine Maillot. But if one can discover one field in this gently anachronistic society that brings them closer to the ordinary run of mortals, one may mention the cooking: Charles was not the only one of the de Gaulles to like the "vulgar dishes" – ragoûts, offal, sauces and stews – which brought them back to the level of the populace.

The Charles de Gaulle with whom we are concerned at this point had been married for ten years. He had three children and probably a brilliant future. He was a field-officer, he had been promoted lieutenant-colonel in December 1932, posted to Paris, where there was no question of a special allowance, and he received no more than a modest pay which only just enabled him to keep up his position. He ordered a suit only every other year and his wife went to the sales in the big shops – and he was not above going with her, if only to urge her not to deny herself everything.

On their return from the Lebanon they did not go back to the flat in the square Desaix where they had been neighbours with their friends the Dittes, but took quite a handsome six-room apartment on the second floor of 110 boulevard Raspail, a few yards from the Notre-Dame-des-Champs and the Collège Stanislas, where Philippe went to school. It was an excellent strategic position: the Invalides were at little more than a quarter of an hour's walk, which the colonel performed every morning and the windows looked on to the fine trees of the boulevard. The shops at the carrefour Vavin were well supplied and Yvonne had the Bon Marché only a few minutes away.

Georges Loustaunau-Lacau describes various military households in his *Mémoires d'un français rebelle*, among them that of his comrade de Gaulle, whom he had met again at the beginning of the thirties, "Virtue reigns [in these households] as it has never reigned before. The colonels' wives rule the French army. These exemplary couples, these sober-minded bachelors who marry on leaving school, provide a model of middle-class life for all the servants of the State. And abroad they say that France is a vicious country!"[4]

How can one absolutely guarantee the marital faithfulness of a person as fascinating as de Gaulle, particularly during his stay in Beirut, when, towards 1930, French officers were no less kindly treated than they had been in Warsaw ten years earlier? There is no venturing upon any such thing; yet it must be added that the few witnesses questioned on the matter either by the writer or by others only repeat exceedingly vague and not particularly credible anecdotes, without any real psychological significance. The fact is that Major de Gaulle, returning to Paris at the very end of 1931, gave no cause for any rumours of that kind.

Charles liked reading his pieces to Yvonne, setting great store on her common sense. In conversation he rarely gave her a chance to shine – which she rarely sought – but he did let her put in her word, not about ideas but about the people who were connected with their life or his own public contacts.

The boulevard Raspail flat was quite a welcoming place. One Saturday every month the de Gaulles sent out invitations ("black tie") which assembled the Auburtins, the Georges-Picots, the Nachins, the Dittes, the Pironneaus and Palewski. It is stated that the food was good.[5]

One word sums up the feelings between Yvonne and Charles: tenderness. The few letters (from him to her) that have been published begin and end with forms that go beyond what is usual in such circumstances. The most frequent is *Ma chère petite femme chérie*, which goes far beyond many of his contemporaries and colleagues: how many colonels in the French army did not confine themselves to *Ma chère amie*, *Ma chère femme*, or, more boldly, to *Ma chérie*? Yet it is a curious fact that between the de Gaulles – at least from Charles to Yvonne – the use of the familiar *tu* and the more formal *vous* should have been so interchangeable, even in the same letter. Although it has its charm, this vacillation in a man with so firm a character, so steeped in principles, is surprising. Was it the application in another form of the "doctrine of circumstances"?

A model pair? They were, in any event, united to have been able to confront a great and deeply personal trial with unfailing courage and for this to have brought them to a deeper mutual understanding, she drawing it from the depth of her faith and he by adding some degree of stoicism.

Anne de Gaulle was born on 1 January 1928 at Trèves. The delivery was very difficult. Quite soon it became apparent that the child was handicapped. By 6 January 1929, a year after the birth of this second daughter, Yvonne de Gaulle was already sufficiently aware of its gravity to write to a friend: "Good health to you all. It is the most important thing to wish; we ourselves would give up everything in the way of ambition, fortune, etc., if that could improve our little Anne's health."

At the time the child was treated with ultra-violet rays. But the physicians told the de Gaulles not to expect any miracle. So when the major heard of his posting to the Lebanon he did not think it absolutely necessary for the child's health to insist upon his remaining in France or to leave her behind. It was decided to take her to a country where treatment and remedies were less available than they would be in a French garrison-town; from now on it was clear that the only treatment the child needed was tenderness.

A few days after settling in Beirut, Major de Gaulle told his father about "a certain amount of progress" that "little Anne" had made. This did not seem very much apart from the fact that a strange companionship had already come into being between the father and the sick child. She, who could never manage "mama", felt a kind of joy in saying "papa". The handicapped child was closely associated with the life of the pair and with that of her brothers and sisters. The wife of one of Charles de Gaulle's colleagues, visiting Yvonne, was much struck by the trial the parents had laid upon themselves.

For the decision was taken once and for all: Anne was to live among her own people. No question of entrusting her to a specialized institution or of isolating her or of lightening the burden. If there was one chance in a thousand of the child's lot being made happier, it was by the care and affection that would surround her. From that time forward the de Gaulles, nomads like all officers' families, definitely made the terrible handicap of a mongoloid child a part of their lives.

During the summer of 1931 Yvonne and her children, who came back from the Lebanon a few months before Charles de Gaulle, spent some time at Wissant, on the North Sea. "It was during this stay," says Jacques Vendroux, Yvonne de Gaulle's brother, "that the handicap became apparent to the least experienced eyes. There was no hope of any real improvement." And he states that his mother, who was particularly afflicted by her grand-daughter's condition, discovered an explanation for it – a violent emotion that Yvonne had felt at Trèves.

To look after the sick child the de Gaulles engaged the services of Marguerite Potel, who never left them and became one of the family. But Anne's parents knew that the duty of bringing anything that could be likened to joy in her life was in the first place theirs. I leave the word to André Frossard, who as a friend of the de Gaulles and a Christian can speak of the tragedy that was at the very heart of Charles de Gaulle's life far better than I could do: "Anne was to be one of those children without whom there would no doubt be less love in the world, and upon whose faces anxiety watches in vain for the first light of a dawn that never rises. Anne was to say a few words and manage a few phrases, always the phrases of a child. Gentle, close and yet remote, she followed her parents' wandering life." (It was with her in mind that the de Gaulles, on the credit of books yet to be written, bought the estate of Milon-la-Chapelle, where the Fondation Anne de Gaulle, maintained by the General's royalties, opened in 1948.)

Frossard continues:

> It is not true that the foundation was set up for her, since her parents never thought of being separated from her, nor did they suppose that the family would not take their place if they were to disappear; but it is true that it was set up by her and by her mother's love and her father's love. It was at her side that the general wished to be buried. She had been his suffering, his subject of humility – his hope; and that, as Christians know, was his joy.[6]

There is a deeply moving photograph which shows Charles de Gaulle on a beach in the Nord, wearing a severe grey suit and a black hat, sitting in a deck-chair; and on his knees there is the handicapped child, dressed in white with a summer hat of the kind that all little girls wore at the time. The father's and the daughter's hands are intertwined as though in a game. The little girl's round eyes gaze passionately at her father who looks down at her with a look of infinite gentleness.

Others have described the child, still on her father's knee, endlessly playing with the object that she found more amusing and more beautiful than any other, the oak-leaved képi peculiar to generals. All these witnesses emphasize the length of these interludes and above all Charles de Gaulle's constant efforts to be there when the little girl expected him, the important meetings often broken off because of her, and the long drives in the middle of the night by the colonel in command of the 507th Tank Regiment at Metz to come back from the neighbourhood of Rheims, where he was taking part in manoeuvres, and to leave again at dawn, having rocked the little girl in his arms.

Anne died when she was twenty, in 1948, at Colombey. When the funeral was over Yvonne and Charles de Gaulle stood for a long while before the newly-covered grave. Then the general took his wife's arm and led her gently away, saying, "Come. Now she is like everybody else."

One of the de Gaulle's physicians affirms that he heard him say, "Without Anne, perhaps I should not have done all that I have done. She made me understand so many things. She gave me so much heart and spirit." Should this merely be understood as a need to sublimate a great trial? In a life given over to every kind of challenge, this was by no means the least of them. Without the presence and the memory of Anne, did not de Gaulle run the risk of increasing the cynicism that was already beginning to show in the 1927 lectures?

Whatever conclusion one reaches, Charles de Gaulle was the man who, in the evening of his life, asked to write a few words in a copy of his *Mémoires de guerre*, quoted two proverbs, one Greek and the other mediaeval, both meaning "It is by suffering that we learn."

Anne's infirmity and the way he lived through it certainly made Charles a far from ordinary father. But with regard to his two other children, Philippe and Elizabeth, the Constable was more like the millions of his contemporaries who had chosen to be what Péguy called "those great adventurers of the modern world, the fathers of a family". A tumultuous, nomadic life, the challenges of those years, a meagre pay, great schemes, a very hierarchic notion of fatherhood and family solidarity, and, as has been said, a horror of mixing public and private life.

Strangely enough it was from Hegel that he borrowed one of his favourite axioms on the subject, and it is copied down in his notebook as early as 1927: "He who is not a father is not a man." The reason that he wished to marry as soon as his military future was assured, was clearly to found a family. Two children in three years, three in seven. From the days when he was teaching history at Saint-Cyr until he left for Trèves, as a father he paid great attention to the deeds and exploits of his two older children.

Philippe de Gaulle was frequently questioned about his father's supposedly severe bringing up; but he did not appear to have retained a particularly disagreeable memory of it. Far less in any case than countless boys of that intellectual middle class confronted with a father who expects nothing but displays of genius and glory.

Although Charles de Gaulle spent much less time than his own father on duties of this kind, he paid attention to his son's marks at school, but without any fuss or showing-off. It does not appear that he inflicted any obsession with being first on Philippe. Yet Jacques Vendroux, describing the family holidays at Septfontaines, says that "Charles with exemplary conscientiousness and patience but not without a certain strictness, was checking his son's holiday task."

And there are the letters, written when the war was at its height, in which the leader of Free France asked about his son's way of life, his studies* and his service postings, or told him about his own state with a calm, straightforward affection. In the two books about his relations with the de Gaulles[7] Jacques Vendroux, Yvonne's elder brother, describes "my brother-in-law" as the faithful member of a

*The General seems to have wanted his son to go to the Ecole des Sciences Politiques: many letters show this. But when Philippe decided to become a sailor he agreed without arguing.

most exclusive family club, eager, once August had come round, to return to cousin Raymond and uncle Émile, croquet, the pear-harvest, mushrooms at dawn and parlour games like "the country marriage" in which the future general, without any urging, took the part of the Swiss with his halberd.

There can be no doubt about Charles de Gaulle's pleasure in seeing a lot of the family whose values were so close to his own, the family of the woman with whom he had chosen to share his life. Yet part of this pleasure surely arose from the de Gaulles' splendid summer visits to the beautiful demesne of Septfontaines, a former abbey, a place after his own heart, heavy with legendary poetry and full of the marks of former days.

One would give a great deal to rediscover the films which one or another of the Ardennes cousins took of Charles de Gaulle playing long games of badminton with Jacques Vendroux "in shirtsleeves on the sunlit terrace". One would also like to look at the photographs which show de Gaulle setting off for a shoot. "Charles standing motionless in the autumn-golden ride, his tall outline recognizable from his fawn gaiters and grey felt hat, doing without his perpetual cigarette out of discipline and scrupulously obeying the orders given to the guns. At this opening beat he killed his first hare outright but let two or three others go by without firing."[8]

Yet after all the symbolic place where this private man expressed himself most fully was surely Colombey. Although he did not send down his roots there until he was well over forty it was certainly at Colombey that he lived the most independent, authentic life, if indeed Charles ever took precedence over de Gaulle, a point very much doubted by André Malraux, who knew the latter well but the former scarcely at all.

In the spring of 1934 Yvonne and Charles de Gaulle – he was then on duty in Paris, at the Secretariat-General of the Défense Nationale – set about looking for a house in the country where Anne could have an open-air life and where they could escape from their political, professional and social obligations. In the *Echo de Paris* they found an advertisement of a house for sale in the little village of Colombey-les-Deux-Eglises in the Haute-Marne, not far from Chaumont, on the road to the north-eastern frontier but not too near it and only four hours from Paris in the Citroen B14 which the colonel then possessed. It was attractive. And the "two churches" could not fail to go straight to Yvonne's heart, though when they came to check, they found there was only one.

La Brasserie, so called because it had belonged to a *brasseur*, a brewer, had once been a posting-house: there were two horse's heads over the gateway. It had been given the grander name of La Boisserie by the owner, Mme Bombal. She asked 50000 francs, which was far beyond what the de Gaulles could afford, but she agreed to allow the greater part to be paid in life annuities. Charles and Yvonne de Gaulle were charmed and they signed the deed of sale on 9 June 1934. Their new property was described as a "dwelling of fourteen rooms with pleasure-garden, spinneys, orchard, kitchen-garden and pastures".

For five years on end, before the occupying Germans despoiled La Boisserie over a long period, the de Gaulles came to Colombey for the summer holidays and for stays at Easter and in the autumn: but in those days the house had neither running water nor central heating, and Anne's health was terribly frail.

Yet even so, it was there more than anywhere else that the lark sang for him.

II

THE QUEST

CHAPTER NINE

The Brotherhood

Can a man work out a system of thought entirely on his own? Since he was neither Heraclitus nor Descartes nor yet Hegel but a French officer deeply imbued with the conviction that sooner or later he was to render his country "some conspicious service", Charles de Gaulle never supposed that he could dispense with the views of other men and the kind of information and discussion that might carry him forward in his investigations. Yet for a long while he pursued his course alone. No particular friendship marked his childhood; no prophet enthralled his adolescence; no superior officer impressed him very deeply – we have seen how quickly Pétain's ascendancy dwindled into an uneven, ambiguous relationship – and it was only very late that eventually he found the collective framework which allowed his powerful imagination to spread and grow in a fertile soil.

The mid-twenties however saw the first beginnings of a group in which Charles de Gaulle could at last give full play to his social gifts and his talent for companionability, indeed for friendship. It was at the time when the "Pétain establishment" formed the setting for his official life that gradually there came into being a band made up of Étienne Répessé, André Fleury, the intendant* Ley, Major Rouget, Jean Auburtin, and above all of Captain Nachin and Lieutenant-Colonel Mayer – the first "compagnons" that the author of *Le Fil de l'épée* gathered together, before those of the Liberation.

De Gaulle was not liked in the world of the army; he still looked upon politics with suspicion; and he had no means of access to the republic of letters, which did not care for those who wore uniform. It was therefore this mixed brotherhood, where civilians fascinated by arms sat with very civilian soldiers, that de Gaulle found the most favourable environment for the ripening of his basic ideas.

Lucien Nachin, the son of a gendarme in the Pas-de-Calais, was five years older than Charles de Gaulle. He went to Saint-Maixent, where non-commissioned officers were trained for higher rank. When he was twenty-three he was made an officer and posted to an infantry regiment at Lille. In September 1914 he was wounded after a month's fighting then promoted captain at twenty-eight and taken prisoner on 18 September 1915. He spent almost the whole of the war in captivity. He ended his active military career in the directorate of infantry at the war ministry. In 1923 he joined the Paris transport system, where he did very well on

*A senior administrative officer on the quartermaster-general's staff. (trs.)

the staff-management side. Although he was not on the active list he was promoted major in 1928 and lieutenant-colonel in 1938.

Nachin was to prove a partner and a confidential friend for de Gaulle all the more valuable because he had had the good fortune to find his mentor very early – Lieutenant-Colonel Mayer.

Emile Mayer was born in 1851 at Nancy, in a poor middle-class Jewish environment. His secondary education began at Angoulême, where his father, an engineer belonging to the department of Mines, was in charge of the powder-factory, and continued in Paris, at the advanced mathematics class of the Lycée Charlemagne, where one of his fellow-pupils was the future Marshal Joffre. Mayer decided upon a military career, entering upon it by way of the Ecole Polytechnique, where the future Marshal Foch belonged to the same year. Indeed, they were friends, Foch being grateful to him for stepping in to prevent the persecution inflicted upon young practising Catholics in that very free-thinking atmosphere.

What career could be more ordinary than that of this artillery officer, shifted from garrison to garrison: Fontainebleau, Toul, Versailles, Douai. A curious one however because of its slowness: here was an obviously talented officer, one who had been entrusted with a class in ballistics – fundamental in gunnery – but who, though promoted captain at twenty-eight, had to wait seventeen years for his next step. Mayer wrote, often without asking his superiors' permission, in such periodicals as *La Revue scientifique* and his doctrines were unquestionably heretical.

As early as 1889 he maintained in this same publication that "the tactics of the future" could not be the "attack at all costs". He boldly proclaimed that sooner or later "immobile warfare" would take the place of the classic war of movement. And this was twenty-five years before Champagne, Artois and Verdun!

There was no doubt about it: the man was too gifted altogether. He no longer published in France. In May 1902 he turned to the *Revue militaire suisse*, sending it his most important essay. Under the title "Quelques idées françaises sur la guerre de l'avenir" he described a fixed, dug-in war, clamped to the ground, the "impossible battle" set against an empty horizon. The article was so new, so original and so "eccentric" that it passed unnoticed or was overlaid.

The Dreyfus affair had some unpleasant consequences for him. *Le Gaulois* denounced him as a Jewish officer sabotaging the country's defence. A right-wing deputy went so far as to speak against him in parliament because he had suggested that the military legal system should be reformed. The minister, a man named Krantz, took fright; by official decision Major Mayer was placed on the inactive list "with deprivation of office".

Major Mayer remained on friendly terms with the great leaders of the time, above all with Foch, of whom Mayer said, "He has every form of courage except that of doubting". However that may be, the future marshal gave a proof of his "courage" and of his friendship by offering Mayer the command of the Centre des Hautes Etudes Militaires that he had just set up and which was already being called "the school for marshals". But like everything else that had to do with Mayer's career the idea came to nothing. Foch's plan must have met with too much opposition.

During the war he had the modest command of the artillery of the western zone of the inner defences of Paris. His moment of glory came in 1915 when *Le Temps* reprinted his *Revue militaire suisse* article of 1902; it then circulated as an offprint and "aroused intense emotion and a great wave of curiosity. The author of these prophetic opinions at once became famous. People were deeply moved by the author's extraordinary clarity [but] also by the fantastic gap between the official doctrine [and the] facts so brilliantly put forward by Emile Mayer."[1]

There was one proposition that the old officer preferred to all others: the absurdity of war and of large-scale armament.

> In a lecture I gave at the Collège Libre des Sciences Sociales – and I expanded the theme in a pamphlet called *Plus d'armées, plus de guerres* which La Griffe published at the same time – I maintained, as I still maintain, and more strongly than ever, that the age of wars is over. That does not mean that they will not be waged. I only think that they ought no longer to be waged and if one does wage war one is committing a fault. War, as we shall soon see, has become a positive luxury, and one that we can really no longer afford. So it will vanish from our way of life just as duelling, for example, has vanished.

A remark of a kind scarcely calculated to enhance Emile Mayer's reputation with the General Staff.

The faithful Lucien Nachin, asked by his friend's family to make the funeral oration at a ceremony in 1938, tried to give some idea of the "secret of the mysterious attraction that Emile Mayer exerted on hundreds of people throughout the world" by drawing this portrait of the dead man:

> The dominant feature, evident at once, was an integrity of mind that forbade him to be satisfied with approximations and that refused to take shelter in the safety of a formula. Regardless of the consequences of his frankness he openly acknowledged the worth of his opponents, just as he spoke out against the deficiencies of his friends. He admitted his own ignorance without embarrassment. He loathed injustice, intolerance, laxity of conduct, and want of courage.

In 1930, after his wife's death, he went to live with his daughter Cécile Grunebaum-Ballin, Léon Blum's great friend, and her husband, Paul. Between them, and with the help of their cousin, the historian Jules Isaac, they meant to write a book on Grégoire, the liberator of the French Jews. The Grunebaum-Ballin's drawing-room at 21 boulevard Beauséjour, became the "Colonel Mayer Club". All sorts of people met with the utmost freedom: publishers like Étienne Répessé, barristers like Jean Auburtin, writers like Denise Van Moppès or Emile Hoog, medical men like Professor Soula, the elderly pacifist Joseph Montheilhet, and finally soldiers like Nachin or de Gaulle (when he came back from the Levant in 1932). Emile Mayer was interested in countless subjects; he was sparkling and full of spirits, but he was gentle and easy-going and no one could equal him in keeping an argument in motion, showing each of his guests to advantage. Under the attentive eye of Lucien Nachin, de Gaulle talked to the old gentleman as an equal, though not without deference.

Their connection went back to 1925, for it was then that Mayer dated his first letter to de Gaulle, a letter about *La Discorde chez l'ennemi*: "Allow me to send you my heartiest congratulations on your [book], of which I have just read three chapters with keen, unflagging interest."[2] And from that time onwards each of the two writers sent the other his works. The older man's were nearly always inscribed "for my comrade de Gaulle, to refresh his memory". "Comrade de Gaulle"?

The bond that tied de Gaulle to Mayer was clearly marked by the disciple. This is made evident by a glance at the dedications that Charles de Gaulle wrote in the copies of the articles or pamphlets that he presented to the old colonel. The one in *L'Action de guerre et le Chef*, which was to become the first chapter in *Le Fil de l'épée*, runs "For Colonel Emile Mayer, the respectful and grateful tribute of a disciple, Charles de Gaulle".

How can the intensity of relations of this kind be measured? Let us recall the words of Olivier Guichard, one of the steadiest of General de Gaulle's confidential friends during the last years of his life: he says, "Emile Mayer's name was the only one from that era which I heard the General utter with some degree of emotion."[3] Shortly before her death at the end of 1982* Cécile Grunebaum-Ballin told the present writer how much the monumental colonel, appearing in the boulevard Beauséjour drawing-room almost every Sunday between 1932 and 1937, had occupied her father's thoughts: less, it may be added, because of the ideas he maintained than because of his strength of character and the fierce independence of his mind.

If their total agreement on the subject of "circumstances" and on the necessity for a continual rediscovery of warfare, on the absurdity of the Maginot Line, on the supremacy of the political sphere over that of the military, on the basic intellectual apathy of the High Command, their low opinion of generals, and finally their agreement on the idea that the defence of the nation amounted to very much more than the "national defence" of the officials – if these things are counted as secondary, then their ideas did in fact differ widely.

What is surprising is that although he had listened to such a brilliant and enthusiastic mentor de Gaulle did not make the air force more unreservedly and more boldly a part of the strategy outlined in *Vers l'armée de métier*, Mayer being a strong advocate of the role of the air force in future wars**.

But the subject upon which they differed most widely was probably that of the professional army. Mayer was too old a republican, he had been too close to Jaurès and he was still too much attached to Léon Blum to be converted to a programme that might to some degree separate the army from the nation. Furthermore he had sound personal reasons for doubting the democratic spirit of a military organization that had been granted a relative autonomy with regard to the political "deciders".

*She was just about to celebrate her one hundred-and-first birthday, and she died three months later.

**See p. 134 below. Yet it will be remarked that although Charles de Gaulle was cautious about the part that the air force was to play in the future, he took care not to neglect it.

De Gaulle would undoubtedly have been de Gaulle if he had not known Emile Mayer. But perhaps he would not have been quite the same. It should not be forgotten that their relations, which to begin with were mostly carried on by letter, only became really close when the Constable published *Le Fil de l'épée* in 1932 and when he was most in danger of letting himself be carried away by the mystique of the leader and deviating from republican legality.

In March 1933 the Nazis arrived at the chancellery of the Reich. Charles de Gaulle's reaction to this event could not have been other than it was – a total rejection. Yet the views and the knowledge of such a man as Emile Mayer, better acquainted with the wickedness of the Nazis through his connections, friends and relations than the majority of "well-informed people" of the time, civil or military, could not but sharpen the clear-sightedness of de Gaulle.

As the decisive days came nearer Mayer tended to acknowledge the operational worth of his disciple's plans more and more. Many of his articles in *La Lumière* (the periodical run by Georges Boris, Léon Blum's close associate and later one of the very first "Free French" in London at the side of General de Gaulle) did justice to de Gaulle's doctrines. The last article he published, at the very end of his life, in the same weekly, emphasized the urgent need for creating powerful armoured columns. So, giving his "pupil's" arguments precedence over his own, the old mentor showed outstanding openness of mind. Having obliged de Gaulle to sharpen his creative imagination against his own, Mayer now gave him full credit: circumstances had pushed theory into the background. Under the "pressure of necessity" he came round to the ruling idea of the man whom he "had shod".

A little less than three months earlier the democracies had surrendered at Munich. Emile Mayer was in his eighty-eighth year and on 25 November 1938 he had just finished reading his friend's latest book, *La France et son armée*, whose proofs he had corrected with characteristic obsessive accuracy six months before, when he felt an uneasiness, a malaise. In the notebook he always had with him and in which he put down everything that happened in his life he wrote with an unmoved hand, "Today, my death." That evening he died.

Colonel de Gaulle, then in command of the 507th tank regiment, was on manoeuvres. He was unable to get away for his old friend's farewell ceremony. But no one can doubt the sorrow that he shared with all the relatives and close friends of Emile Mayer.

CHAPTER TEN

SGDN: The Constable's Cradle

One spring morning in 1932 Major de Gaulle, the author of *Le Fil de l'épée*, was hurrying along a Paris street. By way of the rue Notre-Dame-des-Champs – and in passing he glanced at the severe façade of the Collège Stanislas, where, twenty-four years after him, his son was at his lessons – then the rue de Vaugirard and the boulevard des Invalides, he reached the Secretariat-General of the Conseil Supérieur de la Défense Nationale (the SGDN), to which he had been posted on his return from the Lebanon. Now that his leave was over, and now that he had hit upon somewhere to live and had settled his wife there, arranged schools for his children and found his friends once more, he had taken up his appointment in this temple where the country was prepared for battle.

However much Pétain differed from him in essentials, the Marshal had not given bad advice to de Gaulle to join the Secretariat-General in 1931. In guiding his former subordinate towards the centre of reflection and preparation – "the centre where decisions [will be] made" – the older chief had shown excellent judgment.

In one of the early pages of his *Mémoires de guerre* Charles de Gaulle describes this stage of his life:

> Germany was bursting with menace. Hitler was drawing nearer to power. At this juncture I was posted to the Secretariat-General, a permanent body at the disposal of the prime minister for the preparation of war. From 1932 to 1937, and under fourteen administrations, I was concerned on the planning level with every aspect of political, technical and administrative activity that had to do with the country's defence.

De Gaulle, recalling how he had taken part in the drawing up of the plans for security and for the limitation of armaments laid before the League of Nations in 1932, and how in 1934 he had provided Doumergue's government (whose war minister was Pétain) with the bases on which to make a decision after the Nazis came to power, emphasized "the Penelope's web of the draft bill for the organization of the country in time of war" that he then helped to weave. And he ended: "The work I had to do, the discussions at which I was present, and the contacts I made, showed me the extent of our resources, but also the weakness of the State."

What is significant here is not the conclusions of this officer, then wholly powerless to alter the course of events, but rather these "discussions", these "contacts", the training that would enable him to undertake more important tasks.

Those who have written about de Gaulle have not paid nearly enough attention to these essential years of apprenticeship, from the months that preceded Hitler's arrival at the chancellery of the Reich to those that made ready for Munich. Charles de Gaulle was connected with all the plans, proceedings and debates aimed at placing the country, all unawares, on a war footing. What better preparation could he have dreamed of for the great matters that he was abruptly called upon to deal with from June 1940 onwards, on either side of the Channel?

If the extraordinary comprehension of problems to do with the whole world that the leader of Free France at once displayed in June 1940, as though he had spent his whole life getting ready to impress Churchill, persuade Reynaud, warn Noguès, enlighten Eden or rouse Weygand, seems surprising, one should remember what a school for the handling of files and documents if not of men his "course" at the SGDN amounted to – a course in which for six years on end he was continually in touch with the most important figures and dealing with the least strictly military questions: the broadest problems to do with the economy, with diplomacy, and with research.

The SGDN had been set up in January 1922 and was designed to prepare the country's transition from peace to war. Its task was to study all measures for economic and administrative mobilization and to draw up plans to this end for the consideration of the Conseil Supérieur, which included all the marshals and was headed by Pétain.

What was unusual about this organization was that to begin with it was not subordinate to the ministry of War but to the Prime Minister's Under-Secretary: it was therefore directly answerable to the *political* nucleus of power. Thus during the fourteen years from 1922 to 1936 this body drew up forty "Prime Minister's directives" referring to every aspect of the nation's activity in time of war.

Yet in 1936 the SGDN was moved to the ministry of Defence and placed at the disposal of the chief of the General Staff as a kind of "brains trust" for the purpose of a more concentrated preparation of the country for the war-effort and of a systematic study of cooperation with its allies.

Charles de Gaulle joined the SGDN, which was at the Invalides, as a "drafting officer" at the beginning of 1932. He was promoted lieutenant-colonel at the end of the next year* and he then became head of the 3rd Section of the SGDN, the most important, which was particularly entrusted with the perfecting of the law in time of war – law that had been in the making for the last ten years and that the Assembly, especially the Senate, had put together and torn apart in the most shameless manner.

It is important to have a general idea of the political and military scene developing on either side of the Rhine in the early thirties and of French military doctrines. The asperity, the vehemence of the arguments in which de Gaulle took part can be explained only by the very great anxiety that was necessarily felt by those who, with the evidence before them, reflected upon the security of France and its future: this was the time when, faced with the reappearance of German militarism in its most savage form, Briand's policy of pacifism and the solemn conservatism

*25 December 1933.

and resistance to progress of which Pétain had become the symbol hampered all attempts at a long-term recovery.

The increasing power of the German military instrument, on which the Nazis were to graft their fundamental unreasoning aggressiveness after 1933, dated from the summer of 1919, when the little army of 100 000 men that the Treaty of Versailles allowed Germany to maintain was taken in hand by General von Seeckt. He turned this body into the professional force that had been advocated by Emile Mayer and by Charles de Gaulle in France. He tried out prototypes of weapons such as tanks and aeroplanes that were supposedly forbidden to Berlin, doing so abroad (particularly in the USSR) and in ten years he made the Reichswehr an army-laboratory which bore within itself that force which Hitler was to hurl against the Europe of Versailles.

Confronted with this spear-head that lacked only its shaft and the arm that could give it strength, the French military establishment (at whose head Maxime Weygand had succeeded Pétain in 1931) droned on in endless discussions about the form and the extent of a wholly defensive strategy. The principle of a continuous fortified line (opposed by Joffre and Foch) had been adopted in 1930. The only issue that seemed to occupy the minds of the men at the highest level in the French army came down to a question of earth-shifting: should they cover the whole north-eastern frontier, together with that of the north from Belfort to Dunkirk, including the border skirting Belgium, as Weygand wished; or should they be content with protecting the eastern border alone, as Pétain advised: who would be mad enough, asked that reasonable man, to attempt the crossing of those impregnable natural barriers, the Ardennes and the Meuse?

Pétain's argument carried the day: they were a better fit for the requirements of a French economy in desperate straits. The cheapest solution was chosen. Since it was agreed that plain defence was enough, the important thing was to reduce the expense as far as possible. A short-sighted economy that resulted in a paradoxical situation: several of the war-ministers of this period, including Pétain in 1934, did not succeed in using all the money voted to them by parliament.

As though to emphasize the backward-looking nature of this strategy, the Conséil Supérieur de la Défence National shortened even those fortifications so that they protected Alsace and Lorraine alone. Alsace and Lorraine, after all, would be the sole aim of any enemy who might arise on the far side of the Rhine. Who could suppose that Germany might have ideas other than the recovery of the prey that Clemenceau's republic had wrested from the Kaiser's Empire in 1918? A doctrinaire defence; an ultra-conservative, unmoving defence; a diminished, curtailed defence. It is easy to conceive what the young officers of the SGDN thought of this strategy laid down by the victors of 1918, obviously incapable of imagining any other kind of war.

At the same time there appeared to be little concern for a system of alliances that might have contributed to France's security. It is true that Pierre Laval went to Moscow in May 1935 and that he there signed the Franco-Russian pact designed to act as a counterweight to the threats of the Teutonic neighbour. But until 1939 nobody thought of injecting any life into this agreement, whose French signatory seems to have regarded it primarily as a means of inducing Stalin to denounce the

French Communist Party's antimilitarist policy. In short the position was this: resistance to progress, eyes fixed on the past, and short-sighted tactics taking the place of long-term strategy. At the SGDN however, enthusiasm was reserved for other subjects.

De Gaulle, preceded by his reputation of being a powerful thinker and a brilliant stylist, had no sooner taken possession of his new office in the Invalides than he was entrusted with a task that seemed to be of a very high order. It was a question of drafting a document for a meeting of the research committee of the Conseil Supérieur de la Defense Nationale to show the necessity for a plan of national defence. The committee was not to meet until the beginning of 1933.

The paper that de Gaulle wrote called upon the military intelligentsia to undertake a work of synthesis in order that "the direction of the war" might be unified, thus avoiding the improvisation that hampered the collective effort from 1914 to 1918. In the SGDN it aroused if not a general protest then at least acrimonious criticism that showed the kind of psychological atmosphere in which de Gaulle would have to work – this officer who not only took it upon himself to play the author but who was not much concerned with preserving the basic autonomy of the military realm with regard to the political, maintaining like a famous predecessor that on the contrary war was only the prolongation of politics by other means.

The corrections that General Chabert, the head of the SGDN, made on the major's paper did not amount to a great deal, since they arose only from the Pétainesque desire to "keep it flat". Yet one of them is highly significant. De Gaulle had said that the clarity of the leaders' intentions conditioned "the trust and the attachment of the people": the general crossed out the last two words and for "the people" he put "those who carry out orders".

Charles de Gaulle's colleagues, particularly Lieutenant-Colonel Hennequin, head of the 1st (research) Section of the SGDN, and Rear-Admiral Blétry, General Chabert's second-in-command, were less restrained. Their notes contain all the venom that poisoned the relations between the eloquent Constable and the service for twenty years on end.

When de Gaulle wrote that the men "responsible for directing the warlike action of France" should find "the necessary suggestions ready at hand in time of need" and that the wished-for "comprehensive plan" would guarantee that the responsible statesmen should have a solid basis for their decisions, Hennequin could not restrain himself: "Not at all. The technicians' plan [that of the soldiers] is the consequence of the statesmen's decisions, if there are any. If there are not, the technicians do what they can, so that in spite of their failure to do their duty the statesmen will at least find something prepared."

Perhaps the richest of these comments is the anonymous note that goes far on the subject of the drafting of a comprehensive plan to be worked out by a government organization containing both political and military members: "Committing the preparation of decisions to the same organization, that is to say to a necessarily ponderous and extensive organization, means heading straight for vinous, after-dinner solutions and making sure that secrets of the utmost importance are given away." War is too serious a matter to be entrusted even in the slightest degree to civilians, from whom only "vinous solutions" can be expected at the best, and in any event a levity that ends in objective treason.

The unquestioned spokesman of this extraordinary state of mind was General Maxime Weygand, who refused to have "arguments of a political nature used in the discussion" at a meeting of the Conseil Supérieur de la Guerre, because "the reasoned opinions expected of us were technical opinions, and those political considerations that might influence the members of the council were provided by the minister". And ten years later, before the parliamentary commission of enquiry, Weygand said: "My command was nothing but a struggle against the inevitable, that is to say against all these international questions that arose, whittling our army down and bringing about its decay."[1]

It must not be supposed, however, that Charles de Gaulle did not also take a claw-like pen and lacerate a paper written by a rival at the SGDN, especially if it bore an important signature: contending with his superiors never ceased to delight him.

But he did not waste these years in office-quarrels with his immediate neighbours. He also wrote pieces that may or may not have been commented upon by his equals but that were in any event published in unspecialized magazines and were thus made available to a more receptive audience. And he did the research and worked out the reasoned sequence of what in the first place took the form of an article called "Vers une armée de métier" which was published in the *Revue politique et parlementaire* in May 1933, an article that a year later was expanded into a book which turned de Gaulle, already a debated character, into a kind of living challenge.

Before dealing with the great concern of the professional army, a subject that extended beyond the framework of the Constable's occupations at the SGDN* in all directions, we must pay close attention to two documents that provide an excellent summary of his work during that period: the one has to do with the "comprehensive plan", which occupied most of his time during his first two years at the Invalides, while the other refers to those foreign experiences in preparation for war that he became acquainted with from 1935 onwards.

At the beginning of March 1933, at the very moment when Hitler was setting up his apparatus for repression and for waging war, the *Revue bleue*, a magazine then trying to establish itself by getting "new men" to write on important subjects, published an article entitled *Pour une politique de défense nationale* in which Charles de Gaulle returned to most of the ideas touched upon in his paper on the "comprehensive plan" written at the end of the previous year for General Chabert.

Yet it is not the ideas we already know, nor even their version for the general public, that form the most striking aspect of this article in the *Revue bleue*.[2] It is the conclusion that Charles de Gaulle draws therefrom. "This great work, to be built in silence, offers the master who undertakes it little in the way of immediate gain:

*See the next chapter.

but eventually, what immortal fame! Here a statesman is required." A "master", a "statesman"? One does not write such things, intended for the public at large, without having something or someone in mind. Although it is likely that de Gaulle had already marked the role of this "Louvois that the Republic needs" for himself in the future, the year was then only 1932: he was no more than a major and the "harness" he wore offered him no short-term prospects.

Was he thinking of Paul Reynaud, already a leading politician? Or was it Joseph Paul-Boncour? And then there was André Tardieu, who was deeply concerned with military affairs and formerly one of Clemenceau's closest collaborators.

Paul Reynaud, Paul-Boncour, Tardieu? The "statesman" was not, at short or medium term, unfindable.

But after December 1933 Lt-Col. de Gaulle's mission was not confined to France. The 3rd Section of the SGDN also studied the experiments and the evolution of foreign armies and the concepts that lay behind these changes. Thus in the second half of 1933 he gathered the material for an essay that was published in the *Revue militaire française* on 1 January 1934 under the title of *Mobilisation économique à l'étranger*.

In his search for examples to cite in order to advance the idea of an eventual economic mobilization in France, Charles de Gaulle chose three countries, the United States, Italy and Belgium. Since 1920 all three had taken steps for the organization of the country in time of war and yet they represented three markedly different cases: a great economic power provided with a democratic system, a medium power stimulated by its totalitarian régime and a minor power of the "free world" but subject to heavy economic dependence on foreign countries in spite of its colonial resources. A good range for an investigator; and he took care to set the enquiry into the dictatorship between two analyses contrasting its achievements with those of the democratic system.

De Gaulle has sometimes been criticized for having praised Mussolini's régime in this respect, particularly for having written that although Italy was poor in raw materials "the fascist system allows the authorities to extract all that the existing sources can provide, without reserve or consideration for other interests". And he strongly emphasized his point:

> The imperative subordination of private interests to those of the State, the universal discipline required and obtained, the coordination of the various departments insisted upon by the Duce's personal intervention, and lastly that kind of underlying exaltation concerning everything to do with the country's greatness that fascism maintains among the people – all these favour measures of national defence to the utmost.

Here de Gaulle is describing a society that is understood to be civil and at peace until further notice. And again and again it has been pointed out how much he distrusted any confusion between the political and military spheres, and how strongly he was attached to the due precedence of the one over the other.

It does not follow that his description of the American example was therefore that of a model to be imitated. But recalling the decisive part in the victory of 1918 played by the American intervention, he observes that this outcome would have been still more rapid and decisive if at that time the United States had set their vast industrial machine in motion as they now seemed determined to do in case of war. De Gaulle reminded his readers that:

> The Armistice was signed without a single gun, a single aeroplane or a single tank made in America having appeared on any battlefield.* Afterwards an unorganized production piled up enormous stocks which subsequently had to be disposed of in disastrous conditions.

Hence the 1920 National Defence Act, which organized the United States' economic mobilization.

What could one expect of that formidable power which fifteen years earlier had decisively pressed upon the scales of Fate without even having engaged its vast industrial resources? What one might not expect when it had disciplined its economic capacities with a view to warlike action? The chief interest of this paper of 1934 lies in reflections of this kind, coming from a man who up until then had scarcely ventured upon the field.

Charles de Gaulle did not wish to end his plea for economic mobilization in France without touching upon an example that could more easily be contrasted with the attitude of the French authorities. By turning to a highly-detailed article published a few months earlier in the *Bulletin belge des sciences militaires* he was able to give a full account of "the efforts made in a free country" – the expression obviously being used in opposition to a "totalitarian state".

With increasing frequency the Constable, planner, pamphleteer and economist, carried on with his experiments and his probing. One of his most significant articles of this period, exactly contemporary with the *Mobilisation économique* and published in the Jesuits' review *Etudes*, was called *Métier militaire*. It is a document that forms a pivot between the various kinds of research that he carried out at this time as a member of the SGDN and the crusade in favour of the "professional army" into which he was soon to fling himself heart and soul.

The reconciliation between the "military calling" and the "trend of the times", according to de Gaulle, is to be explained by the evolution of living-conditions, customs, and indeed of those laws that would soon bring back to the group, to duty and authority that favour which had until recently gone to the individual, his rights and his independence. And his argument became more urgent, almost provocative:

> A society that joins unions, if not fasces,** which accepts "full powers" on the part of the government, which works on mass-production according to set scales and set models, and which wants clothes, prices and schools all of the same kind, no longer has anything that is inconsistent with the general

*This remark will be seen again in the polemics with Roosevelt during 1943.

**Mussolini's bands were called *fasci*. (trs.)

> body of soldiers, the exactness of rank and file, the orders and the uniform. When one sees industry straitjacketed, the economy directed, public opinion organized, and when one observes that all over the world nothing pleases the young more than joining themselves into bands, undergoing harsh discipline and marching in step, one tends to suppose that the military type of organization is becoming the symbol of our new times.

Does not de Gaulle go very far this time? It is as well to love one's condition and to see that it is in harmony with the present-day mood. But does he not move on from a plea in favour of his own kind to a sort of militaristic dream? When in an exulting tone he says that "the military type of organization is becoming the symbol of our new times", and when he brings forward "the full powers" and groups "formed in fasces" he is running a very grave risk. It might be said that de Gaulle proposed the "military calling" as an alternative to the totalitarian "order". This is one interpretation, easier to conceive in the eighties than it would have been in the thirties.

But in his haste was he not forgetting the essential task that had been entrusted to him and the Secretariat-General of the Conseil Supérieur de Défense Nationale – the perfecting of the draft law on the organization of the country in time of war? One draft had been drawn up shortly after the war by the first SGDN team led by General Serrigny* and it was brought before parliament by Paul-Boncour in 1927. The deputies passed it but the next year it was completely changed by the senators. Since the beginning of the thirties General Chabert's team had worked upon the draft without a pause, each new War Minister – Maginot, Tardieu, Daladier, Paul-Boncour, Pétain – wishing to have a hand in it and to leave his mark on the bill, discouraging from the point of view of efficacity but most instructive for an apprentice statesman.

It was not until the first months of 1936, when General Maurin was war minister in Sarraut's administration (that which saw Hitler militarize the Rhineland without anything but verbal protests), that the chamber of deputies passed the new bill (of which de Gaulle was the chief draftsman) – a bill that failed in the senate, but this time because of lack of discussion. Daladier, War Minister in the popular front Cabinet, did his utmost to have it adopted by both chambers in October 1936.

It was Blum's second administration, formed in March 1938 just after the Anschluss,** which succeeded in making the Assembly approve the bill. De Gaulle had had time to present his "baby", the draft bill on the organization of the country in time of war, to an audience at the Centre des Hautes Études Militaires (CHEM) on 22 October 1936, just when Daladier was trying to have it blessed by parliament. It would be tedious to summarize the five headings of this austere and highly-detailed paper. But let us mention a few points that de Gaulle himself particularly emphasized in this lecture.

The CHEM audience learnt that mobilization would no longer take place only in the event of war but also in that of "exterior tension" (the rearmament of the

*For a long while one of Philippe Pétain's colleagues.

**The union between Germany and Austria, which Hitler carried out by force.

Third Reich most obviously); that "negotiated agreement between the State and the contractor" had been preferred to the downright requisition of property in time of war; that in the light of the 1917–18 experience parliamentary control of the war would be diminished; and that in the particularly sensitive field of relations between the government and the High Command the first would certainly retain the "direction of the war".

Taking into account the personality of the chief draftsman, which we now know reasonably well, what arises from these fundamental passages is the refusal of any rigid codification of the relations between the government and the High Command, the first having in principle precedence over the second. In order to explain the flexibility of his drafting in this respect to his CHEM listeners, de Gaulle emphasized how very much these relations depended upon personality and circumstance.

The talk was given before the officers who were taking a course and to whom the Constable had been appointed lecturer in April 1936,[3] (he carried on with his work at the SGDN at the same time). This appointment, which he owed to General Maurin in spite of their differences of opinion on the subject of armoured divisions, gave him the revenge over the masters of French military teaching that he had been waiting for so long.

The doors of the Ecole de Guerre had slammed behind him in 1924, then in 1929 they slammed in his face and they were never to open for him again. But giving a course at the CHEM was of even higher standing: was it not "the school for marshals"? The few lectures he gave in 1936 and 1937 and the studies in which he took part earned him, late in 1937, this report by General Bineau,* the head of the CHEM.

> Natural gifts of unusual quality and especially a very fine talent for setting out an argument; an upright and energetic character; very wide general and military culture. But most of the time all this is hidden by a cold and lofty attitude which seems primarily a refuge. Quite mistrustful; indeed, does not put himself forward and is only very rarely unreserved.
>
> When he has more confidence in those around him and when he has thrown off this artificial attitude which hides his real aspect, he will then be seen to be an unusually gifted, strong and original character who should be pushed on to High Command. To be kept in view.

Charles de Gaulle, in rather less than ten years, had studied almost all the problems of the High Command and it would require him to solve them in the future. But we have also seen that he had made enemies as well as friends.

If he had taken more care to deal tactfully with those around him and if in both the written and the spoken word he had adopted a less abrupt tone in his relations with the people of the SGDN, would he have made them like him? No. The mere fact of having launched a public crusade for the autonomy of tanks as early as 1933 would have been enough to set two thirds of the military intelligentsia against him.

*General Bineau had already reported on de Gaulle at Saint-Cyr thirty years earlier.

Being abrupt, being right and publishing books might all have been accepted. But to bring a "military" question before the general public, to be so bold as to appeal to the clear-mindedness and common sense of civilians against the obstinacy of the military, was *not* acceptable. As we shall now see.

How did the forty-five-year-old lieutenant-colonel react to the various tragedies unfolding in Europe: the coming of Nazi power in 1933, the riots of 6 February 1934 in Paris, Mussolini's invasion of Abyssinia, the reoccupation of the Rhineland by the Third Reich, the war in Spain and the Anschluss?

There are scarcely any contemporary documents concerning these different events that can be directly ascribed to Charles de Gaulle. Very few letters to his mother can be consulted. Writing to his friends he speaks chiefly of "his" problem, the professional army. But of course we know the essential, which has just been more or less outlined: that in the great argument between democracy and dictatorship, in which the history of France and of Europe if not of the whole world during the thirties is concentrated, Charles de Gaulle never hesitated about which side to take.

However much he may have disliked a weak and garrulous Republic and however much he may have been irritated by its slowness and its blindness (which never equalled the slowness and blindness of the High Command) he never questioned the fact that the values to which he was most deeply attached – national independence, stability of the State, respect for human beings, freedom of expression, and perhaps even moral order – were more strongly associated with the democracies than with the Axis and its surrogates.

Would the author of *Le Fil de l'épée* have yielded to totalitarianism? As we have seen, he looked upon Italian fascism, though less murderous and threatening, with great reserve, however much it had been praised by authors he admired. As early as the first months of 1933, and in any case before what he called "the hostile act" of 7 March 1936 (Hitler's reoccupation of the Rhineland), he saw nothing in Nazism but war-mongering and gross violence.

Would he have judged the supporters of totalitarianism less severely if their shirts had been neither brown nor black but tricoloured? There is nothing that allows such a supposition. Neither General Dusseigneur's Cagoule nor even his good friend Loustaunau-Lacau, who was then setting up the "Corvignolles"* network to counter the "progress of Bolshevism" in France, tried to recruit this outstanding officer, the author of *Le Fil de l'épée*, that breviary for leaders.

His reputation and his words must indeed have been devoid of the least hint of sympathy for fascism for him to have remained so markedly apart from the swarms of paramilitary "leagues", legal or dissolved (mostly dissolved) that were then to be seen everywhere in the French society of the second half of the thirties, precursors of the shifty fascism that was to be one of the ingredients of Vichy.

*The Cagoule, the sobriquet for Comité secret d'action revolutionnaire, and the Corvignolles were two organizations created in the 1930s to stem the socialist tide. The former was the more extreme. (trs.)

A faultless democrat? In any event let us call him a determined opponent of fascism, giving as proof this letter to his mother, she being the one person in the world to whom he was least likely to pretend, about the Franco-Soviet pact signed by Stalin and Laval in 1935, which must have horrified the good lady:

> What do I think of the Franco-Russian pact? My answer is very simple. We are hurrying towards war with Germany, and if ever things go badly for us, Italy will not fail to give us a kick behind.* It is a question of surviving; all the rest is mere words. We do not possess the means to refuse Russian help, however much we may loathe their regime. It is the story of François I allying himself with the Moslems against Charles V.
>
> I know perfectly well that Hitler's untiring, very clever propaganda has succeeded in making many worthy people in France believe that he wishes us no ill and that to buy peace we only have to let him conquer central Europe and the Ukraine. One must be brave enough to look things in the face. At this moment everything must be subordinated to one single plan: to align as a group against Germany all those who are opposed to her.[4]

*A very rare expression even in those days. (The French has the wholly untranslatable *coup de pied de l'âne* – trs.)

CHAPTER ELEVEN

The Manifesto

Charles de Gaulle did not invent tanks any more than Vauban invented fortifications, Murat cavalry charges* or Pétain gunpowder. Nor did he make the least claim to have done so. "I had naturally taken advantage of the lines of thought set in motion all over the world by the appearance of the fighting internal-combustion engine."[1] And he quoted Estienne, Fuller, von Seeckt and a few others. Often, when he inscribed copies of his book on tanks, he wrote that it was not at all a question "of new but rather of renewed ideas".[2]

In the twentieth century the engine brought a new factor: speed. The armour's mobility diminished its vulnerability. The few minutes during which Murat's cavalrymen had to make a break-through could be turned into hours by mechanical horsepower. From this there arose the problem of rendering such a shock-force independent of other military units; a problem that had arisen ever since armies had faster, heavily armoured and more resistant units at their disposal.

The honour of being the first to put a relatively independent unit of the armoured weapon-carrying machines they baptized "tanks" into the field belongs to the British. They were sailors at heart, and they looked upon their tanks as substitutes for ships of the line. And it was not by mere chance that the name of Winston Churchill, then First Lord of the Admiralty, was linked with this decision. The Royal Tank Corps, set up at the beginning of 1916, went into action on 15 September 1916 at Flers in the Somme and then in March 1917 before Cambrai with relative success – enough at all events to build up a theory of the tank as master of the battle.

All the more so since among the French there was progress on the field. On 16 April 1917, before Corbény and then on 18 July 1918 at Villers-Cotterêts an artillery officer, Colonel Estienne, who was trying to put fire-power in motion – what he called "shock artillery" – launched the first movements of tanks in advance of the infantry; previously those who used armoured vehicles, forgetting their original function of *chars d'assaut* – attacking tanks – had only given them the task of accompanying and protecting the infantry.

These pioneers insisted upon rapid improvement. Although the tanks' break-through at Corbény had not been decisive, the attack at Villers-Cotterêts, where three hundred Renault FTs were thrown into the heat of the battle, broke so deeply into the German front that Ludendorff – who had not dared launch Germany into this kind of weapon – spoke that evening of a "day of mourning for

*Murat was one of Napoleon's marshals and commanded the cavalry on the Russian campaign in 1812. (trs.)

the German army", and on 8 October 1918, addressing the Reichstag, he said that "the use of massed tanks is our most formidable enemy".

On 12 February 1920 General Estienne gave a lecture at the Conservatorie des Arts et Métiers:

> Consider, gentlemen, the immense strategical and tactical advantage taken over the heavily-laden armies of the most recent past by a hundred thousand men capable of travelling fifty miles in a night with arms and baggage, in any direction and at any moment. The retreating enemy, with the tanks at his heels, cannot rally and make a stand: he is hopelessly beaten, as in the evening of Cannae or Jena.

This innovator was too audacious: he was sent off to command a division at Nice, where he would grow calmer. But there was nothing to be done: the tank was in fashion. Thus in the middle twenties General Flavigny, the director of cavalry, proposed nothing less than the substitution of the motor for the horse. In 1921 even Weygand advocated their systematic use. But when he reached the highest responsibilities ten years later he did his utmost to reduce tanks to their former accompanying and supporting role.

But in Germany, which for once had let itself be left behind in military affairs, the idea moved faster in the framework of the Reichswehr, which von Seeckt had turned into a laboratory of modern war. There, men like Rundstedt, Brauchitsch, Kleist, Bock and Guderian, studying everything that was written on the subject in England, Austria and France, prepared the Panzer divisions of the future. They worked so fast that the first three were established in 1934, one year after Adolf Hitler came to power.

The flowering rather than the germination of the idea in de Gaulle's mind may be placed in 1932. Lucien Nachin has given a very good account of the manner in which this "enlightenment" took place.[3] In November 1932 the *Journal des anciens enfants de troupe* published Nachin's very appreciative review of *Le Fil de l'épée*; he naturally gave his friend a copy. In the same issue de Gaulle read another article called "Réflexions d'un amateur" which was concerned with the upheavals that the "motorization and armour-plating of vehicles" was surely going to cause in the army.

This well-informed "amateur" foresaw that there would be a revival of armour, which had been laid aside for four centuries because it had become too expensive.

Did de Gaulle know or guess that Nachin was the author? The fact is that the letter he wrote after having read the article makes no reference to its origin. In his account of the matter, Lucien Nachin says with a disarming modesty, "De Gaulle was sufficiently struck by these somewhat utopian views to write, in November 1932, that this article, 'with its oblique, but original manner, [treated] certain general conceptions to do with military evolution that are from now onwards my own. Furthermore, in my spare time I am at present expanding them into a new work.' "

Before 1933 none of the Constable's writings show any interest in this weapon; nor does he ever seem to have so much as got into a tank; so what led him suddenly to devote himself to this crusade? He asserts that Nachin's article touched upon "conceptions" that were already his own. Did he derive them from the files he was working on at the SGDN? From the plan for disarmament on which he was collaborating under the direction of Tardieu and even more of Paul-Boncour, a plan that foresaw the setting-up of a mobile, heavily-armoured international force to be placed at the disposal of the League of Nations? This was held out to the international community as the miraculous solution: so why not give it to France first?

No one has spoken about the effect on Charles de Gaulle of his short course in a motorized unit at Satory in 1921 before going to the Ecole de Guerre and in his writings on the Polish campaign he does little more than allude to the raids by armoured units. But J.-F. Perrette, in his book on General Delestraint,* says that in 1925, at one of the meetings of the association of former tank officers under the chairmanship of Estienne,

> though nobody knew who had invited him to make his way into our very exclusive circle there appeared a huge, long, thin infantry captain whom I had known at the Hotel Bristol in Warsaw. His presence was little appreciated as soon as we saw that he was monopolizing "our general" whose plump, short person was half-buried in a deep armchair.[4]

So seven years before taking the field in 1932, Charles de Gaulle had set off on his quest, directly making his way into the circle and without hesitation "monopolizing" the prophet from whom, in this domain, came the truth.

From that time onwards the friends in Emile Mayer's circle were seized by a single passion: fighting engine. One afternoon at the end of November 1932, says Nachin, de Gaulle laid before his companions the themes, close to those of the "amateur" in the *Journal des anciens enfants de troupe*, from which he had formed a doctrine.

Emile Mayer disagreed with his friend about tanks, stressing the priority which he wished to give to the air force, but he was delighted by the overall idea and he encouraged de Gaulle to start a campaign, promising to open him the doors of a great non-specialized magazine. In March, as soon as he had de Gaulle's manuscript – a dozen pages – Mayer took it to *La Revue politique et parlementaire*, which published it on 10 May 1933 under the title "Vers l'armée de métier". (Towards the professional army.)[5]

De Gaulle, in his *Mémoires de guerre* written twenty years later, said: "As no one proposed anything that would deal with the situation,** I felt myself required to appeal to public opinion. I had to expect that one day the searchlights of public life would be directed upon me. It was disagreeable for me to make up my mind to this, after twenty-five years lived according to military standards."

*A disciple of Estienne and de Gaulle's future chief in Lorraine before becoming his military delegate in the Resistance. (trs.)

**The Nazi ascendency in Germany.

In any case "the searchlights of public life" were pointed at him, now and forever after. But at the end of the spring in 1933, they were not so bright as to blind him. Lucien Nachin says that the publication of the *Revue politique et parlementaire* article "caused a sensation, a lively controversy began at once, both in the parliamentary world and in military circles". This is going rather far: newspapers of the time reveal that they did not take a great deal of notice of the article.

Besides, it must be stated that although the article of May 1933 contained the embryo of some of the ideas in the book that came out a year later, it was still no more than a draft in which de Gaulle applied himself less to the description of a future war (which was to give his book such brilliance) than to advocating a reorganization of the French military structure. This foreword, more technical than the book and less lyrical, was too temperate to disturb civilians and too imprecise to win the support of the specialists.

Here and there minds began to work. In October 1933 André Lecomte and Philippe Serre, the most active members of the Jeune République, the lay tendency of Christian Democracy,* asked Major de Gaulle to draw up the plan and the questionnaire for an enquiry conducted by their newspaper, *L'Aube*, under the title of "Armed nation or professional army?" Although de Gaulle's relations with Christian Democracy were affected by the contemptuous mockery that the *L'Action française* (which he still read, with an admiring irritation) lavished upon Marc Sangnier and his friends, he did not refuse. Not only did he help them to formulate their questions, but he induced Nachin to provide them with a reply. The enquiry, which was published in November 1933, ended with an unsigned paragraph, obviously written by de Gaulle:

> Since our frontier is what it is and since our neighbours are what they are, since we possess the empire that you are acquainted with and since whether we like it or not we are bound to other, equally determined, nations, I believe that at present the regime of the armed nation is indispensable, but that is not enough for us.

Hitler's Reich, having thrown off the limitations imposed upon its armaments, now insisted upon equality with France. Paris, in response to the requests of its friends the British and of the League of Nations, wished to reduce the number of men called up for service in order to check the Germans' progress. How could this be done without at the same time building up an efficient strike-force? De Gaulle's plan was most timely. But the High Command vetoed any reduction in numbers.

Were the threats to the republican regime in February 1934 to give de Gaulle a chance to act more freely on the centre of decision? In the government of "public safety" assembled by the former president Gaston Doumergue, it was Marshal Pétain who was minister of War. De Gaulle knew that although the Marshal might happen to speak of "making the utmost use of modern machines" and of the "combination of their action", he disapproved of his proposals and above all of his campaign to bring them into effect.

*In the sense of not clerical.

Lucien Nachin states that Pétain thought of making Charles de Gaulle his principal private secretary, but that "clever manoeuvres" brought about "a most dignified abstention" on the part of the author of *Le Fil de l'épée.* General Conquet (the Imperator's new confidential assistant), on the other hand, says that de Gaulle wrote a "perfectly discreet note" to the Marshal to the effect that he would be "happy to serve under him" but that General Laure, the minister's cabinet director, let it be known that rather than see de Gaulle make part of the team "he would resign".[6]

Vers l'armée de métier came out on 5 May 1934* and was dedicated "to the French army, for the service of its faith, its strength and its glory". As in the case of his earlier books – though the subject this time was more serious de Gaulle did not ask his superiors for permission of any kind. And he simply signed himself, Charles de Gaulle.

Let us recall the general arrangement and the major themes of *Vers l'armée de métier*, whose publication was the most important event in Charles de Gaulle's life before he joined the Reynaud Government in June 1940.

The book is made up of two parts, "Why?" and "How?", each of which contains three chapters: "Protection", "Technique" and "Politics" for the first and "Composition", "Use" and "Command" for the second. The whole, put together somewhat formally, and written in an oratorical style yet without heaviness, is carried along by a movement all the more stirring since it is a plea for mobility.

The first theme is that France is doomed to be invaded because of its geography. However useful fortifications and strong-points may be, the country can be "covered", that is to say protected, only by manoeuvre; and this in the present day should be carried out only by machines handled by experts, that is to say professionals. Hence the decisive conclusion of the first section: "No French protection is possible without a professional army."

The second theme is that while the machine has become part of life, this is not the case in the military system, which is still completely impregnated with the idea of the "nation in arms" and with the imperative requirement of "quantity". Yet the military order also aspires to technical modernity, being aware of the disparity between its mission and the instrument at its disposal. "By sea and in the air, the professional army has been created," observes de Gaulle, whereas on land its elements are "few and scattered among the crowd".

The third theme is politics. Here de Gaulle is at his best, eloquently showing that "the world's tendencies, the conditions of an international organization for peace and in any event our own duty to help the weak and to maintain order in the empire, come together and require us to create professional troops". All the more so in France, which, though it is no longer the most populous nation in Europe, here has an historical opportunity to shine in the first rank; the outcome of battles no longer depends on numbers but on the "quality" of the most advanced industry and skill; what country, he asks, could make a better figure in the coming war than that which produces "French quality"?

**The Army of the Future*, first published in Britain in 1940. (trs.)

Moving on from the "why" to the "how" de Gaulle is not afraid of details, knowing that ideas, however fascinating they may be, convince only if their application can be believed in. In order to provide France with that "repressive and deterrent structure" which is called for both by the mood of the time and the spirit of the nation and which will be given the "fierce unexpectedness" required to "produce the outcome", he says that it is necessary to set up six divisions. Each will be composed of one powerfully armoured brigade comprising two regiments, one of heavy tanks and one of medium, with fast vehicles for reconnoitring; one brigade of motorized infantry; and two regiments of artillery. The equipment of each of these great units in guns and various specialized services from reconnaissance to camouflage is carefully specified.

To set up this formidable machine "of impact and speed" would call for 100 000 men; it would be easy to recruit them, since modern life gives experts, specialists and technicians such high standing: "One has but to bring the fiery eagerness of the sporting spirit to it, the immense expenditure of energy and pride that our century willingly devotes to physical effort and competition."

Having reached this stage in his argument, de Gaulle does not refrain from a kind of lyrical emotion. It can be seen that his own dream is almost too much for him when he describes these "Messieurs les maîtres", "well dressed, well fed supermen, carefree bachelors, envied for all the steering-wheels, cylinders, aerials and range-finders they will have to handle, traversing the countryside from April to November, making their tour of France as they carry out their manoeuvres". They will continually be summoned to broad-based military gatherings, by branch of service or by region, and vast masses of people will be filled with enthusiasm by these soldierly olympians, which will carry "Messieurs les maîtres" *esprit de corps* to its highest possible pitch.

When he comes to the "employment" of these phalanxes of champions, the mission the author gives them is no longer the "slow attrition" of the last war but "the great cavalry operations of former times". He does not even try to conceal that "Messieurs les maîtres'" first tasks on the outbreak of war or even as a "deterrent intervention" would be "to seize a token objective". This would make them "leap in one bound from peace into war" and it might allow "anxiety to be hurled beyond the frontiers". Then once the battle was joined, "the professional army" combining its movements with those of the air force, "will thrust into the zone of trophies. Exploitation, a dream in the last war, will be seen to become a reality".

De Gaulle in no way neglected the part to be played by aircraft in this strategy of attack, surprise and break-through. Although it is true that his views were far behind those of his friend Mayer and that his least successful forecast of the shattering events of 1940 concerned the role of the air forces, *Vers l'Armée de métier* contains some illuminating passages on combined operations of tanks and aircraft. "The air squadrons, capable of operating at a distance, endowed with astonishing speed, manoeuvring in the three dimensions and striking vertical blows – the most disturbing of all – must play a capital part in the war of the future."[7]

Charles de Gaulle did not attempt to minimize the breadth of the proposed reform, which would change "the spirit of the institution as it would change the policy and the technique of war". But it so happens that by nature the army is unwilling to accept change. Only a ruthless will can deal with its reluctance.

> A master has to make his appearance, a master whose judgment is independent, whose orders cannot be challenged – a man upheld by public opinion. The servant of the State alone, devoid of prejudice, scornful of dependents and followers, an agent wholly given up to his task, his mind filled with long-term plans, well acquainted with the people and the things in his province; at one with the army, devoted to those he commands, greedy for responsibility; a man strong enough to compel recognition, clever enough to charm, great enough for a great undertaking – such will be the minister, soldier or politician, to whom the country will owe the management of its strength.

An astonishing piece of writing, as astonishing as that quoted in the first lines of this book, written by a Charles de Gaulle of fifteen for whom France was one day to owe its salvation to "General de Gaulle". Now that he was in his forties his sense of predestination had merely grown more specific. At this point who but de Gaulle could be the "master" he spoke of here, to the combination of soldier and politician that he alone could embody?

Indeed, *Vers l'armée de métier* was not limited to the statement of this great technical and strategical plan and to the declaration of this lofty candidature for a place in history. The last page goes farther still: it is a programme of government (or of regime), the manifesto for a new Consulate:

> There is no assembly, no party, no consul that does not invoke reform, a new order, and authority. No doubt the action of the institutions, following the change in needs, will quite soon open the field to resolute men.
>
> If this national reorganization were to begin with the army, it would be wholly conformable with the natural order of things. Not only because strength is more necessary than ever for those nations that wish to live, but also for the reason that the military body is the most complete expression of a society's spirit. In the laborious work that is to rejuvenate France, the new army will act as a recourse and as a ferment. For the sword is the axis of the world and greatness cannot be divided.

This "field open to resolute men", this offer of "recourse and ferment" based upon "the sword, the axis of the word", made somewhat uneasy reading at a time when the Action Française and the Jeunesses Patriotiques ruled the street, when Déat and Doriot were beginning their drift from socialism and communism towards fascism, and when some of the most brilliant young men of the period, Bertrand de Jouvenel, Drieu La Rochelle and Paul Marion, were listening to calls from the old French anti-democratic depths.

Did it depend only upon an article by Léon Daudet in *L'Action française* hailing the appearance of a Constable worthy of "our forty kings", or upon an accolade from Lyautey for the author of *Vers l'armée de métier* to be drawn towards other paths? The explosives that he handled here, with this plan splendid in its imagination and its promises, were formidable.

Yet enlightened as we are by his later conduct we shall take care not to carry the hypothesis further. In *Vers l'Armée de métier* it is clearly stated that the "renewal" would take place by means of the "action of the institutions" and not by their overthrow. Let us also remember that none of those who were then defying the Republic even attempted to get in touch with this Master of the "Masters".

With de Gaulle one must always bear in mind that itch to challenge, that temptation to clash with his superiors (whether they were internal hierarchies or States) which perpetually goaded him. He knew that he had predecessors in the technical field and that Estienne, Flavigny and Doumenc had said practically everything there was to say. He could not confine himself to improving his forerunners' fortunate discoveries or setting them forth in the style of Corneille. If he wanted to open a deeper breach, it was not only on the subject of the use of armour that he could do so: it was also that of radical reorganization of the army's structures.

In the French army's present state of torpor (he went so far as to borrow the epigraph for his last chapter, "To wash your sleep away", from such a poor writer as Jean Richepin; but it was to show that he would use any kind of bugle whatsoever to wake the barrack-room) only a scandal could be effective. He made up his mind to it, not without something of the delight of a great beast of prey.

The de Gaulle of the thirties had glimpsed the horizons; but he was still the man who supposed that it was to the coat-tails of the army that sooner or later the country, in its confusion and distress, would cling. And this military corps was not only that by which everything would be rebuilt or preserved; it was also that which was invested with the indefinable "mission" that Péguy and Psichari had faintly perceived.

Evidence for this can be seen in the following extract from a letter de Gaulle wrote to Colonel de Ruffray, who had just published a little book called *Le Silence de Douaumont*:

> The tumult of our times and the torrential levelling of the "armed nation" only make that spiritual and moral role which is the essence of our calling the more necessary. As Psichari says, "We are pure metal or we are nothing." The reason I have launched the conception you know about into the realm of ideas and presently into that of facts was not solely that I was concerned with matters of pure technique. The army must possess within itself at least one model section whose effulgence reaches all the rest.[8]

CHAPTER TWELVE

The Crusade

The campaign that *Vers l'armée de métier* set-off must first be placed in the atmosphere of the time, in the sequence of events that hurried on from the Nazis' seizure of Germany (January 1933) to the beginning of the war in Abyssinia (October 1935), the remilitarization of the Rhineland (March 1936) and the Spanish Civil War (June 1936).

These years witnessed the liquidation of the system of European balance built up at Versailles: totalitarianism rose up, all masks thrown aside. No man who thought, wrote or spoke at that time could think of anything but that. Charles de Gaulle's arguments, considered at the end of the twentieth-century, may seem marked with nationalistic, technocratic and militaristic boastfulness. But anyone who thinks back to 1934–1935 cannot but wonder how it came about that this cry of a Cassandra was so little or so poorly attended to by those responsible for the country's safety.

"With difficulty seven hundred copies were sold," says Lucien Nachin, adding that in Germany the translation "was snapped up by the thousand" (something of an exaggeration). Yet the press was favourable. De Gaulle overlooked nothing on this point either. Already aware that no efforts to improve journalists' competence are excessive, he allied himself, as he says in his *Mémoires*, with one of the most influential of them, André Pironneau, the editor of the *Echo de Paris*, then a nationalist paper of well thought of in military circles.* Playing this connection for all it was worth, Colonel de Gaulle provided him with all the necessary information, and during the four following years this leader-writer for one of the Paris papers most read in influential circles, pleaded some forty times in favour of a motorized and professionalized army.

Praise too in the *Journal des débats*, from the pen of General Duval; praise in *L'Action française*, thanks to Colonel Larpent; and in *L'Aube* from André Lecomte. This was already a fairly good sample of the press from the extreme right to left centre and *Le Temps*, the most influential of all; only the militant left wing stood aside. De Gaulle had won his battle of the press; though for all that he did not stir public opinion. But his struggle with the world of the army was to be even more disappointing than he had foreseen.

At the time of the book's publication, the three key men of the situation, the Minister of War, the vice-president of the Conseil Supérieur de la Guerre, and the chief of the General Staff were Pétain, Maxime Weygand and Maurice Gamelin. As for Pétain, his response was indifferent; he was now more and more closely

*At that time the communist press called it "the General Staff's sheet".

surrounded by men whose polite warnings to de Gaulle in 1926–1927 had given way to active animosity: de Gaulle had left the Imperator's field of vision. His opinions were of no importance if he did not bring them forward under the old leader's aegis.

A year went by before Pétain broke his silence. An article in the *Revue des deux mondes* (March 1935) which bore his mark dealt with the relations between the traditional army and a mechanized force with apparent objectivity, but it ended with an unequivocal assertion of the excellence of the present system and of the necessity for the utmost caution in reforming the French defensive structure. This was the period when, at the end of a sitting of the Conseil Supérieur de la Guerre at the Elysée, in which he had seen to the secretarial side, de Gaulle heard General Maurin, the minister of War (he had recently taken over from Pétain), address him thus: "Good-bye, de Gaulle! Wherever I am, there will be no room for you!" And speaking to his neighbours the general said, "I'll send him to Corsica."*

But at the same time, beyond the frontiers, the arguments of the author of *Vers l'armée de métier* were attentively studied, particularly in Germany. Philippe Barrès** recounts that when he was visiting Germany in April 1934 he heard first von Ribbentrop and then Ruhenlein, the chief of the SA armoured corps, praise Charles de Gaulle's writings. "How is my great French colleague getting on?" asked Huhenlein, speaking to Barrès, who did not even know de Gaulle's name.[1]

In the Soviet Union *Vers l'armée de métier* did not escape the notice of Mikhail Tukhachevsky, once the Constable's fellow-prisoner. In the meantime he had become chief of staff of the Red Army and he had the book rapidly translated and five thousand copies printed. He presented one to Colonel de Gaulle three years later during an official visit to Paris, the last before his trial and execution.

In Britain the author of *Vers l'armée de métier* was highly thought of in the years before the war; this is shown by the tribute paid him in the House of Commons on 10 November 1970*** by the Conservative member Robert Hugh Turton:

> The first time I heard of General de Gaulle was when I was serving under General Martell who was then the greatest specialist on armour in Great Britain. He used to talk about "this Charles de Gaulle", to whom he often wrote and who in his opinion was the greatest theoretician on the tactics of armoured formations who then existed in Europe.

Yet when de Gaulle, in command of the 4th Cavalry Division in May 1940, had the British 5th Armoured Division placed under his orders, not one of the officers of that great unit had ever heard of him, as I was told by M. Hettier de Boislambert, then liaison officer between the two motorized corps.[2]

Paul Reynaud was a small man, as lean as a vine-shoot, with an oriental face and

*Later Charles de Gaulle was on excellent terms with the two sons of the minister, both of them generals. The second, Philippe, was a member of his staff at the Elysée.

**The son of Maurice Barrès. (trs.)

***The day after de Gaulle's death. (trs.)

puckered and creased eyes – the countenance of a samurai educated at Cambridge. His small head was set between his shoulders as though the Creator had given it one hammer-blow too many and he had a sharp, nasal, metallic voice, and something mechanical in his bearing, gestures and even in the presentation of arguments. His unadorned, highly-documented eloquence had established his reputation at the Paris Bar all the sooner because he had married the daughter of the leading barrister of the time, Maître Henri-Robert.

He was Deputy for the Basses-Alpes in 1919 and for Paris in 1928. He had been a minister three times since 1930 and now, at fifty-six, he was one of the three or four outstanding men in parliament, and he was said to be the Chamber's expert on economics and finance (not that that meant a great deal at the time). In 1934 his name was linked with the idea of devaluation: he was a most eloquent advocate of the measure.

This politician, who sat on the right in the Assembly, had taken up a clear position in favour of a pact with Moscow and against any concession to Hitler and to fascism. These positions were nearer those of de Gaulle than to those of his political friends. Every time Reynaud spoke there was silence on the right-wing benches, where only his old friend Joseph Laniel* supported him.[3] But he seemed to take no notice of this isolation among his colleagues. He had an independent mind, was an outstanding speaker and nobody had ever doubted his courage.

De Gaulle was looking for a man capable of taking "the bold initiative" of reorganizing the French military structure from top to bottom in order to make it operational against the totalitarian threat; and as he told his friends he had come to the conclusion that "Paul Reynaud will be that man. Although he is well known, Reynaud seems to have his future before him."

Jean Auburtin, a friend of both, set the dialogue in motion by taking Reynaud a dedicated copy of *Vers l'armée de métier*.

A week had not gone by before Paul Reynaud "telephoned to tell me of his enthusiasm" says Auburtin, and of his wish to meet de Gaulle.[4] They made an appointment for 5 December 1934 at Paul Reynaud's home in the rue Brémontier. As Auburtin was unable to go, no detailed account of this decisive conversation has been published. On page thirteen of his *Mémoires* de Gaulle confines himself to this Caesar-like summary: "I saw him, convinced him, and from then onwards worked with him."

Paul Reynaud is a little more prolix. He speaks of "a tall lieutenant-colonel of light infantry, quietly self-confident" coming into his office. "He spoke in an even tone, his voice surprisingly gentle in that great body of his, leaning his face forward. One felt that he was imbued with an irresistibly evident truth."[5]

It was now that there appeared a key figure who was not to leave the stage again and who until the last days was to remain the most steadfast and perhaps the most efficacious of the companions of de Gaulle: Gaston Palewski. He had been one of Marshal Lyautey's circle in Morocco, and at thirty-three he had become one of Reynaud's closest collaborators. He speaks of the episode in this way:

*Who was to be a member of the Conseil national de la Résistance in 1943 and prime minister in 1953.

> The antichamber to Paul Reynaud's office was a mezzanine, and there I found myself face to face with an officer so tall that his head almost touched the ceiling. As Reynaud was busy he told me to start by talking to his guest. The conversation began between the two of us, went on with the three, and only came to an end several hours later, after de Gaulle had taken me to lunch at a bad restaurant he had chosen. By the end of that afternoon I had made up my mind that from now on I should place everything I might possess in the way of influence or connections at the service of this man's scheme.
>
> However remarkable the men I had already worked for – beginning with Lyautey in Morocco – may have been, he seemed to me above the others. There have been three outstanding characters I have straight away wanted to serve under or at any rate to help: de Gaulle, Jean Monnet and Eirik Labonne.* But de Gaulle was quite apart. Everything he said had an incomparable originality and strength. During one of our first conversations I had the fleeting thought that if men like that would devote themselves to politics, what would the parliamentary professionals amount to in comparison?
>
> He was then wholly given up to one perfectly specific plan from which nothing could distract him, neither his career nor the obstacles in his way. The friendship that then arose between us came from the fact that I wholly agreed with his "crusade". We never talked of politics, except for the aspect that interested him – that of possible support for his campaign.

Twelve days after his first interview with Paul Reynaud de Gaulle sent him the first of a long series of letters, of which sixty-two between 1934 and 1939 were to be devoted to the crusade now common to both of them.[6]

In his second letter, dated 14 January 1935, de Gaulle gives his correspondent the composition of the three first Panzer divisions that had already been set up by the Third Reich whereas in France "their creation had not been seriously begun". He observes that "it is the Reich that is playing this card" and ends by speaking of "the pain felt by an officer who, having found a plan of salvation for his country, sees that plan wholly and completely brought into effect by a potential enemy."[7]

And on 14 March the Constable went farther, pointing out that interest in the new weapons in parliament was becoming evident in increasingly varied ways and solemnly calling upon Reynaud in these terms: "With support both from the left and the right, a statesman of your authority and your future now has a magnificent opportunity for stepping in and providing the country with this new military policy (whose technical form, moreover, has been entirely worked out)."[8] In thus sending his new ally to assault the conservative citadel, de Gaulle was for once not ahead of the event: Paul Reynaud had already put his name down for the great debate on general policy in which the problems of national defence were to be discussed, particularly by Léon Blum. When Reynaud went up to the tribune – de Gaulle was

*A diplomat: Resident-General in Morocco 1945–1947 and discoverer of the Sahara oil. He marked everyone who came into contact with him and perhaps he was the only man in France of his generation who could be compared to de Gaulle, whom he joined in 1940.

sitting in the public gallery – the great majority of the deputies thought he was going to approach the question of defence from the financial side. But after a rather commonplace homily in favour of peace and disarmament, Reynaud came to the heart of the matter:

> Hitler's Germany is raising up a younger generation that has been rendered fanatical and over-excited by all the means of modern publicity, a youth that has been taught that although there is no longer any hope in peace, there may still be hope in war. Can our military organization suffice for the needs of a Europe that has been totally transformed? No, gentlemen. Why not? Because war is a duel in which the attacker alone chooses his weapons.
>
> The French problem, from the military point of view, is the creation of a specialized corps capable of delivering a return blow as shattering as the attack; for if the assaulted does not possess a riposte as rapid as the assailant's, all is lost. Furthermore, our foreign policy absolutely requires us to have this striking force. *One must have the army of one's policy.* Have we by any chance abandoned the policy of assistance and pacts? Do we wish to change our policy – which we have a right to do – and let Hitler walk about Europe as he chooses?

The Constable was delighted. The next day he wrote to the man who was already being called "de Gaulle's gramophone" at the General Staff: "I did not fail to go and listen to you yesterday evening and I was filled with enthusiasm by your speech, which obviously made a deep impression."[9]

Here we must interrupt this de Gaulle–Reynaud correspondence for a moment, because it faces the reader with a fundamental question, that of the relations de Gaulle maintained with those in some sort of power. The various expressions used by de Gaulle in his letters to the Marshal (*dévouements*, *respects* and *fidélités*) had nothing about them that was not traditional, and the very wording of his dedications, such as those in *Le Fil de l'épée*, followed established convention. With Paul Reynaud it was different.

He was a man of the first rank and one to whom de Gaulle owed much, as Palewski emphasizes. Reynaud's commitment to the "crusade" was useful to his parliamentary career and it matched his convictions, but it entailed dangers, and he accepted them with courage and talent. Yet did this mean that the Constable was required to make these salutations worthy of the park at Versailles in Louvois' time? "There is not the least doubt that the near future will provide your policy and your personality with a triumph in proportion to their worth and their courage." (2 December 1935) "Great minds, said Vauvenargues, must expect success only from great ideas, great actions and nothing else. You are the living and dazzling proof of this motto." (3 December 1935)

We are often very close to obsequiousness. De Gaulle was that man "possessed" by a single idea who has already been described by Palewski and Auburtin. If a few bows were to bring about the triumph of views that would open the way to the nation's salvation, what did they amount to, directed towards a man whose vanity he had perceived at the same time as his value? Cynicism? Maybe.

De Gaulle thought it "right that the tune should be played on various instruments".[10] Since Reynaud was looked upon as belonging to the right, de Gaulle wanted to bring the left into action and the left wing's fundamental distrust of a professional army might yield before the arguments of the "crusaders" for collective security and a reduction in the number of men called up. But Léon Blum, the most outstanding left-wing parliamentarian, procrastinated. He had recently published a series of articles in *Le Populaire*, "Professional soldiers and a professional army", "Towards the professional army" and "Down with the professional army". For Blum, as for his master Jaurès, creating a professional army meant taking the risk of setting up a praetorian force, an army that might carry out a *coup d'état*.

Blum listened to Reynaud, whom he admired, with the most intense interest. He speaks of these moments in his *Mémoires*: "Paul Reynaud addressed the most urgent, emphatic passage in his speech to me, the passage in which he asserted that the divisions advocated by Colonel de Gaulle were pre-eminently the tool of collective security." But Blum only let himself be persuaded by de Gaulle too late, in January 1940.

Editorial offices, literary associations, clubs – nor did Lieutenant-Colonel de Gaulle neglect the drawing-rooms, at least those in which he might have a chance of talking about his "professional army". In his book on de Gaulle, Robert Aron speaks of an evening party at Daniel Halévy's, one of those famous Saturdays at the quai de l'Horloge where among others were to be seen the members and friends of Ordre Nouveau.*

> A tall man was standing there, isolated from the other guests. Taking no part in the talk, remote from the hypotheses about the future of our country that were exchanged in this gathering of intellectuals. He stood like the statue of the Commendatore, unmoved, marmoreal, monolithic, foretelling punishment and still trying to point out the only way to salvation.[11]

On 7 March 1936 Hitler reoccupied the Rhineland without striking a blow. He carried out that "seizing of a symbolic objective" which the Constable had made one of the professional army's specific tasks. This most strikingly confirmed the "crusaders'" arguments – the strategy of fortifications doomed France to impotence. The only defence against aggression was counter-attack and movement.

Was it not all perfectly inevitable and was not Hitler certain of impunity so long as he did not launch a direct attack, since on the fifteenth of the preceding March the French government, speaking through its minister of war, General Maurin, had declared, "When we have devoted so much effort to the building of a fortified barrier, is it to be supposed that we should be mad enough to go outside that barrier, in pursuit of who knows what adventure?"

De Gaulle took care not to thunder in the press. His reaction is known only from a letter to Jean Auburtin in which he simply states:

*A collection of modernist and progressive tendencies contemporary with *Esprit* (founded by Mounier in 1932).

> The "hostile act" of 7 March has shown what methods strength is going to use to carry out its aims: surprise, suddenness, speed. A nation that wishes to live must therefore not only obtain guarantees of help from others (mutual assistance) but must also organize its own strength in such a way that its reaction takes place in the same conditions as the aggressor's action. But we do not possess the means of doing so.[12]

The means! Those responsible did not even attempt to assert that they were going to try to make up for lost time so as not to be caught unawares any more. On 7 March Albert Sarraut, the head of the government, having declared that "France would not leave Strasburg exposed to the fire of German guns",* felt that his duty was done and left it at that. The passiveness of public opinion, the pusillanimity of most of the ministers, and London's indifference soon led to a general renunciation – and this at a time when, as we now know, a rapid counter-stroke would have brought about the collapse of the Third Reich.

It was now obvious that the man who in three years had tamed Germany by letting racist terror loose in the country, by cutting the throats of his earliest followers and by filling the prisons and the camps, was getting ready to inflict the same treatment on the whole of Europe: and that France, gone to ground behind its wall, would do nothing but wait for its eastern allies to be crushed before undergoing the final assault. Was one to be obliged to resign oneself to this once and for all?

During a sitting of the Conseil Supérieur de la Guerre, General Gamelin, who never had wavered in his rejection of de Gaulle's arguments at last uttered a plea for the creation of an armoured force: "We need armoured units," he said. "Hitler now has three Panzer Divisions. From now on we need something better than Panzers to win." But the majority of the members of the council were against an effort of this kind.

Two months later came the victory of the Popular Front, the electoral alliance between radicals, socialists and communists. Apart from a few allusions there is nothing in Charles de Gaulle's correspondence published in *Lettres, Notes et Carnets* that tells us his reaction to his event, any more than to the Spanish Civil War. A short letter to Paul Reynaud on 3 May congratulates the "gramophone" on his personal victory in Paris, but it contains no comments on what has just happened elsewhere. A letter to a familiar friend seems to show that he was not profoundly moved by the defeat of a right wing he knew well – for some years past he had been able to measure what had become of their patriotism and clarity of mind – and that he saw no reason to be alarmed by the left wing's success.

But from the point of view of his plan it did not make the prospects any clearer. Léon Blum had moved into the Hôtel Matignon,** and Blum had declared his hostility; Daladier was Minister for War, and he was scarcely any more favourable. And his best of allies, Paul Reynaud, was thrown into an opposition, which (however "constructive" it might be) did not add to his efficacity in parliament. It

*Words which were written by René Massigli and which, as he understood them, implied an action that only two ministers, Paul-Boncour and Mandel, called for.

**The French prime minister's official residence. (trs.)

had been intelligent of de Gaulle to cover himself on the left. But none of the allies he had thought of was available; neither Paul-Boncour nor Déat formed part of the government. Léo Lagrange was confined to the Ministry of Sports and Philippe Serre had to wait months before being admitted.

Yet it so happened that the Popular Front was the first government that tried to adapt French military policy to the most pressing needs of the situation. It did so quite simply because most of its leaders, beginning with Léon Blum, had begun to realize the gravity of the danger and the inescapable nature of the trial of strength that Hitler was forcing upon Europe.

For the men who came to power in May 1936 the question was not whether one day they would have to fight but just when the fighting would begin. This explains the contemptible policy of "non-intervention" in Spain, which was aimed only at gaining time so as to make up a little of the ground lost to Hitler, and at not wasting the weapons that would soon be so badly needed.

The plan for rearmament launched in the summer of 1936, which was called the "fourteen milliard programme", went 40 per cent beyond the General Staff's requirements. It was soon completed by ship-building that brought the financial effort up to twenty milliard. These plans as a whole – in principle to be spread over four years – were to double the French potentialities of defence between 1936 and 1940 (it was in the spring of 1940 that Léon Blum placed the probable opening of the Axis offensive). These figures, produced before the court at Riom in 1942, led to the breaking-off of the proceedings brought against Blum and Daladier by Vichy.

Lieutenant-Colonel de Gaulle, at his observation-post of the SGDN, was a privileged witness of this armament policy's development. He observed that the "fourteen milliard programme" (he had estimated the cost of "his" plan at two milliard) provided for the manufacture of 3000 tanks (enough to equip fifty battalions of light tanks and twelve of heavy tanks) between the present and April 1940 (he had only asked a third of that to form his armoured corps). But he also observed that the expected use had not changed: the new "Instructions for the tactical use of large units" still placed the tanks under the authority of the infantry division commanders. These trump cards, when scattered about among the units, would lose their offensive value. The new government's impressive effort deserved better treatment by the "specialists".

Léon Blum, the eloquent opponent of a professional army in December 1934, had seemed shaken by some of Paul Reynaud's arguments in March 1935. Had he not now grown so conscious of the danger that he might perhaps be persuaded to change the use of armour? Emil Mayer, whose son-in-law Paul Grunebaum-Ballin was one of Blum's intimate friends, arranged an interview for his friend with the Prime Minister. So here was Charles de Gaulle coming to the Hôtel Matignon on 14 October 1936 for a confrontation that gave rise to accounts on either side that are the more interesting for their differences. We begin with a passage from Léon Blum's *Mémoires*:

> I saw a man whose height, breadth and bulk had something gigantic about them; he walked in with an easy, even a placid calmness. Straight away one

> felt that he was "all of a piece". He was so in his physical being, and all his gestures seemed to move his body as a whole, without friction. He was so in his psychological behaviour. It was perfectly clear that the man who appeared in this way, who gazed at me so calmly and who spoke to me in this slow and measured voice of his could entertain only one idea, one belief at a time; but then he would give himself up to it entirely, without anything else coming into the scales. Clemenceau was the extreme type of those temperaments that nothing can turn aside from acting because for them action is a vital necessity.[13]

Charles de Gaulle, whose *Mémoires* came out in 1954, four years after Blum's death, gives quite a different version of the matter. In the first place he takes care to point out that the interview took place on the very day that the King of the Belgians had proclaimed his decision to revert to neutrality, basing himself upon this argument: "In any event, given the potentialities of modern mechanized forces, we should be alone." "Léon Blum warmly assured me of his interest in my ideas." " 'Yet,' said I, 'you opposed them.' 'One's view-point changes when one becomes head of the government', he replied. First we spoke about what would happen if, as it was to be foreseen, Hitler marched on Vienna, Prague and Warsaw."

For de Gaulle there was no doubt about the matter: France would watch the subjection of Europe without stirring.

Blum asked if an expeditionary force should be sent to eastern Europe. De Gaulle replied that the objective should not be the Vistula but the Rhine! "Yet," he said with bitter emphasis, "our present system forbids us to move. The Armoured Corps, on the contrary, would decide us upon it. Is it not true that a government may find a certain relief in having its plans decided in advance?"* Léon Blum agreed, but he objected that Hitler would do nothing until he had defeated France. And he pressed the point: "Our system, ill-suited for attack, is however very good for defence."

The Constable denied it strongly: "We are going to spend as much money as would be needed for a mechanized army," he said, "and we shall not have that army." And when Léon Blum objected that the government's choices were those that the military specialists had put forward, Charles de Gaulle made this severe and intensely Gaullian retort: "You must allow me to think that national defence is the responsibility of the government."[14]

His plea was in vain. The Constable was to learn that "the Prime Minister will not bring down the pillars of the temple": the agreed plan would be carried into effect without delay, before that fundamental redirection that would at last have given France the power of dissuasion or at least of delivering a counter-stroke.

Was there still another chance? A great debate on the questions of defence was arranged for January 1937. On the twenty-seventh Paul Reynaud once more argued in favour of an armoured corps. De Gaulle wrote to him the next day, saying "Magnificent! Everybody is talking about it!" (De Gaulle had written the

*A slight drift in the direction of the a priori doctrine.

speech.) But this time it was not the "gramophone" who held the Chamber's attention; it was a young deputy from the eastern frontiers, Philippe Serre, a member of the little group called the Jeune République. Fifty years later he was still struck by his first meeting with de Gaulle in 1936.

> I was immediately subjugated by what I shall call his Olympian side, by an authority, a command and an eloquence that compelled recognition straight away. He spoke with a kind of majesty, like someone who feels that he is invested with a lofty mission. As soon as he began on "his" subject he was irresistible. He was a man of one single idea. We often met. He never talked to me about anything except his "great plan". He was literally possessed by it.[15]

Serre at once offered himself as an advocate for the arguments of *Vers l'armée de métier* "from the left wing's point of view" and his remarkable speech renewed the Gaullian reasoning in a most ingenious manner.

France, said Serre, had to be "protected by two ramparts: a rigid line of concrete and a supple line of steel."

> If ever the first should yield at one point under irresistible pressure, the second would instantly come and adapt itself to the first, filling the gap. Why should France, defended by a double professional army – that of the fortifications and that of the armoured divisions – not be able to give the nation as a whole the military structure that Jaurès called for? I beg the left wing to turn this problem over. Under the shelter of the professional army *l'Armée nouvelle* can soon become a reality; without a professional army it will always remain a yearning and a dream.

Philippe Serre was a partisan of collective security, and naturally he did not forget to emphasize those aspects that had to do with respect for treaties:

> Since on the one hand France must, for its very life, help to maintain Europe's territorial status, and since on the other our people will no longer consent to throw an army of its sons, husbands and brothers into the battlefields of the world – the army that is the nation's blood, the nation's flesh and blood – to resolve this intensely painful contradiction it is necessary to give the country an army that will become the army of its international policy. This army, you see as clearly as I do, can only be an army by calling, a professional army.

Philippe Serre's speech made so strong an impression on de Gaulle that the next day he wrote to congratulate him on this "magnificant oration".[16] The Constable's feelings were so strong that in the ending of his letter he called him "Monsieur le Ministre", thus anticipating by six months a promotion that was then no more than a probability. But it is known that Charles de Gaulle had always been disposed to prophesy.

Three months later the preacher of the "crusade" began a fresh operation: the publication of *Le Problème militaire français*, with a preface by Paul Reynaud, in which were collected all the arguments proposed by de Gaulle and his companions in articles and speeches for the last three years. "This work owes more to de Gaulle than to me," said Reynaud in his *Mémoires*,[17] with a modesty unusual in him, though the work was not a success.

Even so, some progress had been made. In a letter to Paul Reynaud of 7 October 1936 the Constable, speaking of "the Chamber's underlying but ignorant good will"[18] told him that the first armoured division was to be set up in the spring of 1937.

It was from Pétain himself that there came the final counter-blast. In 1938 General Chauvineau, once professor of fortification at the Ecole de Guerre (where he had given de Gaulle good marks), published a book called *Une invasion est-elle encore possible?* in which this military leader asserted that "the failure of the tanks was startlingly obvious", that "against a continuous front a motorized attack would bite the dust", and that "the great armoured units belong to the realm of dreams".*

The Marshal thought it worthy of his reputation and useful for the country's defence to grant this ridiculous pamphlet the support of a preface signed with his name. He wrote:

> There exists a mortal barrier to the passage of tanks; it consists of mines combined with the fire of anti-tank weapons. What would become of an attack by armoured divisions if it were to run into divisions that were of the same nature but that had taken up their positions and spent a few hours in establishing an anti-tank fire-plan combined with natural obstacles and reinforced by mine-fields, and all this on a battlefield of their own choice?

The Marshal went further in a reply to an observer who was worried about the way the Maginot Line broke off west of the Ardennes. Was this not a breach in the system, a gap through which the enemy might pour? "The Ardennes forest is impenetrable; and if the Germans were imprudent enough to get entangled in it, we should seize them as they came out!"

The Imperator's decisive counter-blow to the crusaders of *Vers l'armée de métier* very nearly affected Lieutenant-Colonel de Gaulle's career. In the Autumn of 1936 he observed with fury that his name was not on the promotion roster, although his abilities and the reports on him should have placed it there. Yet however strikingly able he was, this officer had been openly opposing the General Staff's official propositions for the last three years. It is not very surprising that he should have had to suffer for it.

De Gaulle would not submit to this. He shamelessly asked for the intervention of his friend Reynaud, who spoke to Daladier on the subject. The War Minister's reply echoed his staff's observations: "De Gaulle was perhaps very able, but his

*The Third Reich had already set up four which had recently astonished the spectators at the last great Berlin parade.

service-record did not amount to enough for him to be promoted colonel at this age." (He was forty-seven.)

His service-record! Smarting with indignation de Gaulle instantly sent his reports to Reynaud, who went back to see Daladier with them: three wounds, five escapes, the risks run from Dinant to Warsaw and from Verdun to the outposts of the sanjak of Alexandretta. "I had not been told about that," said Daladier, much embarrassed. His cabinet director, General Bourret, took it upon himself to write de Gaulle's name on the roster.

Charles de Gaulle was not the kind of man who would let himself be pushed off the royal road because of good nature or contempt for intrigue like his old friend Emile Mayer. He believed so whole-heartedly in the mission he had taken upon himself that he did not scorn practices of this kind. The "crusade" had already cost him a great deal in the way of trouble, affronts, snubs and ill-will; to find that it was also a hindrance to his career would be really too much.

CHAPTER THIRTEEN

The Regiment

"I shall never forget the sight: eighty tanks coming at full speed and with a thunderous roar to the place d'Armes at Metz, headed by the tank *Austerlitz*, from which there emerged Colonel de Gaulle. The crowd, at first stupefied, burst into applause."[1]

Thirty years later Jean Auburtin was still quivering with emotion; and he added that at the time nothing could have raised his enthusiasm as Colonel de Gaulle's confidential friend and supporter to a higher pitch than the monumental sourness that seeped from the nearby staff. Poised on the Metz dais were Lieutenant-General Henri Giraud, military governor of the town and a little thickset man at his side, looking out of humour with his hat pulled down over his eyes, Edouard Daladier, the Minister of War.

This motorized psychodrama was played out on 24 November 1937 in a town that symbolized the military destiny of France, a town that focused the anxieties of the national community better than any other. Confronting the officers who had done everything they could to block his way and facing the minister who had continually wavered between a doctrine that he could not but think sound and the pressure-groups against whom he dared not use the power he possessed, Charles de Gaulle launched a rattling, thundering challenge. But although it fully satisfied his taste for glamour, his clarity of mind had long since warned him that this amounted to no more than caperings and flourishes, tolerated by those with real power because it was they and not he who had won the game.

To reach even this outward appearance of triumph, how many set-backs had been there! The placing of his name on the promotion-roster in autumn 1937, which he had obtained with such a struggle, was understood to open the way to the command of a regiment in the branch of which he had, for the last four years, been the most vehement advocate. But tanks were still under the directorate of infantry.

The real obstacle to the Constable's appointment was Lieutenant-Colonel Perré, a long-established specialist who had taken part in the first armoured operations in 1917–1918 and who entirely supported the official doctrine.

As though to stoke the fire of their hostile feelings, de Gaulle and Perré were both simultaneously promoted colonel in December 1937. Only one tank regiment was available: the 507th, based at Metz. Placed where he was, Perré seemed sure of having the command; it was given to de Gaulle. Nobody has ever explained why or after what negotiations (with Reynaud?) Daladier and Gamelin gave precedence to the heretic not to the orthodox believer. Was this to lock de Gaulle up in an existent structure, thus giving him an opportunity of measuring both his own limits and those of his ideas? Or because as they saw it the real future belonged to the regiment that was entrusted to Perré, the 8th Zouaves,* which had little armour as yet but which was being prepared and equipped in secret at Mourmelon, with the idea of making it the nucleus of an experimental armoured division?[2]

In short, Charles de Gaulle was appointed to the temporary command of the 507th Tank Regiment (RCC) on 13 July 1937. He assumed effective command at the beginning of September and on 24 December was promoted to full colonel. In the meantime he had made preliminary contacts with armoured weapons, having a unit of light tanks shown to him at Satory and then going for a course with the 501st Armoured Regiment and the school of tanks at Versailles. So at last the prophet had begun to tackle reality.

Speaking to Georges Buis, who became his ADC in the Levant in 1941, General Catroux said that when he was in command of the Army Corps at Nancy and given the task of organizing the great manoeuvres of 1937, he had a company of B tanks to test, the first modern heavy machines, which at the time put France well ahead technologically. He asked the staff to tell him what doctrine governed the use of these monsters. And the reply was that there was none, that "these tanks were practically useless and that they only existed to satisfy public opinion and a certain trend of ideas in the army".[3]

De Gaulle knew that very well, just as well as he knew about the astonishing progress of the panzers that the Third Reich was fitting out and exhibiting without reserve or discretion. It was therefore a man without illusions who, on 5 September 1937, got out of the train at Metz station, where the German genius for building was so powerfully expressed. He settled in a comfortable flat in rue de la Vacquinière and at once started to grapple with this command that he had so ardently desired.

The 507th RCC was made up of two battalions, one of light tanks – twelve-ton Renault R35s suitably armoured, equipped with a 37 millimetre canon and a machine-gun, but possessing no great power to get over difficult terrain – the other of medium tanks, twenty-ton D2s (also made by Renault), heavily armoured (40 millimetres of rolled steel), armed with a 47 millimetre canon and two machine-guns and much better at crossing obstacles; they carried a crew of three. In all they amounted to about a hundred "fighting engines", an honourable proportion of that armoured mass of 3000 tanks which for the last four years he had wanted to make the spearhead of French strategy.

We have most eloquent letters that speak of his feelings as he handled this embryo of the *Vers l'armée de métier* at last; they were sent to the men he most liked talking with, Reynaud, Auburtin and Mayer, during the first months of his stay in Lorraine.

To Paul Reynaud, 15 October 1937:

> Since I am making direct use of this equipment and the personnel that operates it, and since I am in a garrison where there are continual opportuni-

*An infantry regiment raised in Algeria in 1830. (trs.)

> ties for manoeuvre I am in a position to study from below exactly those problems which, Monsieur le Ministre, we so often pondered over from above at your house. From this very different viewpoint I come to exactly the same conclusions as those we then reached. At present, seeing things from below, I state: the modern trank is an enormous achievement. *One has to see it manoeuvre, fire, overwhelm and crush, among people who are on foot or on horseback or in cars to understand that its coming is a revolution in the form and the art of war.*[4]

To Emile Mayer, at the end of the year:

> After a few detailed experiments, I am more than ever convinced of the soundness of the ideas which I have tried to disseminate and which alas have hitherto been accepted much more willingly by the Germans than by my fellow-countrymen. Manoeuvre and attack on land can no longer be required of anything but tanks. What remains is to acknowledge this and then to reorganize the French army accordingly by setting up an instrument for manoeuvre and assault based on tanks, that is to say an "armoured corps".[5]

However passionately he devoted himself to his role as commander, Charles de Gaulle was not a prisoner in Metz. He was still quite often to be seen in Paris, where he kept in touch with Reynaud and Palewski and with Mayer and Nachin, Jean Auburtin providing the liaison between the two teams. Although the "cause" made little progress, the Constable's personal reputation increased. An important publisher asked him for a book: it was no longer he who came as an author asking to be published.*

It was during one of these stays in Paris that he met an old acquaintance once again, Mikhail Tukhachevsky, now chief of staff of the Red Army. At a dinner for "the old boys of Fort IX" the colonel sat next to the marshal, who congratulated him on his works on tanks.[6] The visitor told his hosts that the Soviet army was keeping a close watch on him.[7] Six months later he was shot.

He also entertained at Metz, much more than he had done at Trèves, inviting to the rue de la Vacquinière those he thought worthy of being mobilized for the "cause" – civil servants, parliamentarians, journalists, friends from Paris. And La Boisserie was not far away: Yvonne de Gaulle escaped there when she could, taking little Anne as often as possible. In 1938 he wrote many letters to his wife, organizing the comings and goings of the family group between Paris (where Philippe and Elizabeth were at school) Colombey and Metz. In one of these letters the colonel, speaking of the children, writes "the Babies", an anglicism that rings strangely, coming from him.[8]

In those days he was called "Colonel Motor". General Huard, speaking of the idea

*See the next chapter.

one had of life in the 507th at Metz in those days, sums it up by the motto the new colonel had given the regiment: "Always more!"[9] De Gaulle himself suggested the intensity of this activity in his letter to Reynaud of 15 October, when he spoke of this "garrison where there are continual opportunities for manoeuvres".

The colonel was everywhere, summoning one to his presence, hauling another over the coals, starting off a thunderous exercise at dawn, inspecting motors and breeches, making his R35s roar and assigning his D2s, heavier and therefore more suitable for the devastating mission. Every day he was seen to appear on the manoeuvring-ground: more than one lieutenant had a tendency to move off rapidly. But he would instantly be pinned to the ground by the commander's cry, "Since when do people flee when their colonel arrives?"[10] And all the tank-commanders would be made to plunge into the turrets of their R35s for a charge across the shockingly uneven exercise-field.

A curious figure, this Colonel Motor. He had not given up his white gloves, and they stood out with a greater contrast against the black uniform worn by these gold-laced mechanics, the tank-officers; his wife and his batman, each in turn, watched over these white gloves, they being so notoriously useful when the wearer is in touch with oily grease and various parts of an engine, fighting or not. He was a newcomer to tanks, and as though to give himself a more professional look he wore the little helmet with a leather peak that his more seasoned colleagues scarcely used at all. The regimental badge, it must be added, showed the profile of a warrior thus helmeted standing out against the turret of a tank.

His differences with the best-known of his service superiors, General Giraud, have often been described. It is necessary to return to them, less for the pleasure of the anecdote than because of the psycho-political consequences that gave this antagonism an historic dimension after 1942. General Renauld, who was then a captain, kept the notes he made during an exercise that took place at Metz at the end of September 1937, when the relations between the military governor and the colonel had not yet grown sour.[11] The theme of the exercise was that of an attack by an army corps sent to break the Maginot line at one of its weak points between Metz and Saint-Arvold. When the first phase of the exercise was over, it was agreed that in view of the attackers' greater strength the fortifications in question had fallen. Giraud then called upon de Gaulle, who had an armoured brigade at his disposal: "Your move." In the majestic tone he adopted on such occasions, the colonel began his statement by a description of his unit's deployment and progress. Giraud interrupted him. "What is your objective for the evening?" "Pont-à-Mousson." "Pont-à-Mousson? But that's fifty miles away! No, de Gaulle, so long as I command this region, you will keep your tanks to the pace of the infantry."

On one occasion Giraud assured Philippe Serre, the deputy for the neighbouring constituency, that "Colonel de Gaulle's ideas may be brilliant, but they are of the kind that may make us lose the next war".[12] And it was one of his close friends who told the members of a parliamentary commission visiting Metz that "Colonel de Gaulle was the stupidest officer in the French army".

Yet it was during this period of command in Lorraine that Charles de Gaulle met intelligent, open-minded chiefs who even agreed with his opinions – chiefs against whom his powerful and easily offended character did not revolt. Not only was there General de La Porte du Theil who, although an infantryman, had dared take de Gaulle's side against Giraud, but also and above all René Martin and Charles Delestraint.

General Martin had been appointed inspector-general of tanks at the time when de Gaulle was sent to Metz. As inspector-general he had set up a kind of study-group at Nancy, to act as something like a model for the staff of the first of those great armoured divisions described by de Gaulle in his book. During his first inspection at Metz he had been very much impressed by the 507th's conduct and activity, and he had marked down de Gaulle as one of the members of the Nancy "proto-staff".

In a letter to André Frossard General Martin emphasized Colonel de Gaulle's exceptional role in the work of the group at Nancy, a role "based on his earlier studies".[13] He therefore often entrusted the direction of manoeuvres to de Gaulle, thereby implicitly pointing him out for the command of one of the great armoured divisions of the future. Several of Charles de Gaulle's letters bear witness to the harmony between the inspector-general and himself, particularly this one, dated 27 December 1938:

> For the tanks, 1939 will be a year of prime importance, because for the first time a great armoured unit will be seen in the field and under your orders. I know with what clarity of mind and firmness of resolution you welcome and organize this immense transformation of our military art.[14]

But the real companion of those days, the one with whom Colonel Motor's thoughts and wishes were most perfectly in tune, was General Delestraint. He was a senior specialist in the armoured branch, one of General Estienne's disciples, a former commander of the Versailles tank-school and he had recently been given the command of the 3rd Tank Brigade, which included the 507th RCC. Over two years the alliance between the little general with a cat's moustache and the tall white-gloved colonel grew steadily stronger. Delestraint told J.-F. Perrette (who was later to write his life) that every day, when the morning's work was done, de Gaulle used to telephone the chief of the brigade before coming to see him so that they could both look into technical problems and questions to do with the philosophy of command. We know that this alliance, made even stronger by the fighting in 1940, survived the catastrophe. In London, in 1942, the head of the Free French entrusted his former chief with the command of the secret army in France. Delestraint, arrested by the Gestapo and deported, was murdered by his gaolers at Dachau in 1944.

The ideas that these two men and some others tried furiously to carry into practice continued to be looked upon as heretical but all around them manoeuvres and exercises on the subject of the vulnerability of the Maginot Line increased in number: it was supposed that the attacker succeeded in piercing it. Would the line at least give France a breathing-space long enough to prepare for the real assaults and time for the allies to come to the rescue? General Blanquefort, then an officer in the 507th, tells how at every one of these conferences Colonel de Gaulle stepped in with great heat, going so far as to tell the pundits of the General Staff that unless there was a decision to back the armoured weapons up to the hilt, "the Germans would advance from the Ardennes to Bayonne in three weeks".

Yet however lively they may be and however much they may foretell great things, Charles de Gaulle's disagreements with his military superiors were not the most important conflicts during these troubled days. In June 1937 the Popular Front government was overthrown, its place being taken by a Chautemps ministry that could not be said to symbolize the springtide.*

We have few details of de Gaulle's disapproval of the stages in this slow descent to the abyss, but his reaction to Munich is very well known indeed. Among a dozen let us choose the document in which he expresses himself most spontaneously – it consists of three letters to his wife, dated September and October 1938:

> Without a fight we are surrendering to the insolent demands of the Germans and we are handing our allies the Czechs over to the common enemy. German and Italian money has been flooding into the French papers these last days, particularly those that are called "nationalist" (*Le Jour*, *Gringoire*, *Le Journal*, *Le Matin*, etc.), to persuade our poor people that we have to give up. The French, like fools, utter cries of joy, while the German troops march triumphantly into the territory of a state that we built up ourselves. Little by little we are growing accustomed to withdrawal and humiliation, so much so that it is becoming second nature to us. We shall drink the cup to its dregs.

Five days later he states, "France has ceased to be a great nation."[15]

A few lines sent to Paul Reynaud on 24 September, just before Munich, should be added:

> With no surprise I see the coming of the greatest events in the history of France and I am convinced that you are marked out to play a leading part in them. Let me tell you that in any event – short of being dead – I am determined to serve you if that should be your pleasure.[16]

For him this immense collective set-back was combined with a deep personal sorrow, the death of his old friend Emile Mayer ("his death is an infinite affliction to me," he wrote to Auburtin), and with the bitterness that accompanied the ruin of the last traces of his relations with Marshal Pétain.** For these reasons the miscarriage of his great plan and his efforts' lack of progress produced a kind of down-heartedness in him.

Although Paul Reynaud joined the government in April 1939 he did so as Minister of Justice; and ministerial solidarity being what it was, he was from now onwards lost for the cause with which de Gaulle had managed to associate him. In

*Camille Chautemps, who had also formed a government in 1932, was to become one of Vichy's first ministers. (trs.)
**See the next chapter.

the same range of public opinion nothing was to be heard but repudiations and calls for surrender: *l'Action française*, in particular, went farther and farther every day in its denunciation of "war-mongers" like him. But did not the aggravation of the Nazi threat at least help to bring de Gaulle and his left-wing allies closer together? He was obliged to observe that in the name of pacifism Marcel Déat had made a choice even worse than the general inertia – that of de facto solidarity with the aggressors. To be sure, Léo Lagrange had taken another path, founding the anti-Munich group "Agir", together with some of his friends, including Pierre Brossolette; but his party, the Section Française de l'Internationale Ouvrière, in which pacifism, despite Léon Blum, seemed to feed on Hitler's provocations, warned him against any action in favour of *Vers l'armée de métier.*

There remained Philippe Serre. The deputy for Briey made frequent stays at Metz; he always paid great attention to de Gaulle's ideas and to de Gaulle as a person, and often asked him to lunch. Serre had only one notion in his head: de Gaulle must become a member of the Government. It was there and there only that he could make his salutary views prevail at last. Besides, there was talk of a ministry under Paul-Boncour, whose relations with de Gaulle were excellent. But a plain colonel could not be Minister of Defence and compel the respect of the General Staff; he needed someone of very high standing as a cover.

"What we want is Pétain," Serre maintained. "There is no doubt about his republican convictions; and he has incomparable authority. Your ideas are not the same, but you will manage to make him adopt yours. And thanks to his backing we shall reach the goal." Serre had thought he was sure of the colonel's approval: he ran into a wall of ice.

"Pétain?" said de Gaulle. "Whatever you may suppose, he has not given up a single one of his old ambitions. And he is a very untrustworthy character. Take care of him!"[17]

De Gaulle knew perfectly well that he had just lost the first great battle of his life. The crusade launched in 1933 in favour of the "fighting engine" and of the professional army, the creation of that tool absolutely necessary for the country's defence and the respect of its alliances, and that organization of "masters" which would have given the army back its predominant role in the national community's recovery – all this had come up against a conservatism that was all the more heartbreaking because it was the act of an army he had revered for thirty years. It was the leaders of this army, described by him as "one of the greatest things in the world", who had just slammed the door on hope.

If only it had been the fault of the politicians, the "politicards" of his childhood, of that body of men his whole bringing-up had led him to despise! But not at all. It was in parliament far more than on the General Staff that he had found what few chances of salvation had come his way. In de Gaulle's mind it was the whole, or almost the whole military institution that was on trial (with some exceptions, for example, Delestraint). It is scarcely surprising that a man so wounded should allow a certain distress to show.

This disillusionment was not caused by personal disappointments alone. Its chief source was the intense anxiety brought about by the continual study of the ratio of strength between the Third Reich and the Republic. In 1939 Hitler possessed five Panzer Divisions fully equipped and prepared, which they had proved by covering the Austrian roads in one unbroken journey between 8 and 12 March 1938 at the time of the Anschluss. And three more of these great units – organized according to de Gaulle's model – were being formed in Berlin.

On the French side, in the summer of 1939, when Charles de Gaulle was preparing to leave the command of the 507th RCC, no single armoured division was yet operational. The 1st DCR (Armoured Division), under the command of General Bruneau, was raised only after the beginning of the war; the 2nd and 3rd DCR in the spring of 1940; and lastly the 4th, which Colonel de Gaulle was called upon to lead in May 1940, was then no more than an odd collection of scattered elements.

The army establishment might boast of having destroyed the undertaking of this solitary reformer who had tried to make them submit by appealing to public opinion, using books and parliament to do so.

CHAPTER FOURTEEN

The Break

Snubbed as a prophet, doubted as an officer, filled with anguish as a citizen; how was Charles de Gaulle prospering as a writer? Since *Le Fil de l'épée*, he had only published a small number of articles and the thunderbolt of a tract *Vers l'armée de métier*. That was not much. We know he was very busy making his motors roar on the manoeuvring-grounds of Metz and keeping the flame of military ambition alive in Paul Reynaud's mind. But a literary spirit of such strength could not lie fallow. Presently someone took notice of the fact.

Henri Petiot, known as Daniel-Rops, was a master at the Lycée Pasteur. He was already the well-known author of two or three novels and a study called *Le Monde sans âme* (The Soulless World) that caused much discussion. Daniel-Rops had first met Colonel de Gaulle with Emile Mayer in 1935 at one of those famous Sunday morning gatherings, to which he had been taken by Jean Auburtin. He was at once captivated by the man and as soon as he had read *Le Fil de l'épée* he was captivated by the writer.

Daniel-Rops' publishers, Plon, had just commissioned him to launch a series of books that should reflect the spirit of the time, books touching upon literature, philosophy, economics and politics. He first asked the man who at that time was the embodiment of technical ability, the engineer Raoul Dautry.* Soon after, Daniel-Rops wrote to Charles de Gaulle; he wished him to write a book on the military calling.

The colonel, who had not yet been given his appointment at Metz, accepted Daniel-Rops' proposal and chose *L'Homme sous les armes* as a title for the promised book.

Seven months later Charles de Gaulle, who had scarcely written anything in the meantime, was at Metz, and he very soon found that the command of a regiment (as he understood it, at all events) left little room for literary pursuits. During a stay in Paris at the end of the year he lunched with Daniel-Rops and confessed that his professional obligations made it hardly possible for him to fulfil the contract. But among his papers he had preserved a manuscript that might, when revised, interest him. It was a kind of history of the French army written some time ago at the request of Marshal Pétain, who had refused to have it published; but the colonel undertook to have the prohibition removed.

The reader will have recognized the famous *Le Soldat*. But however deep in the safe Pétain had shut away his pen-officer's manuscript, de Gaulle had kept a copy, and from time to time he worked on it. Now, at the beginning of 1938, the time of

*Who was to become Minister of Industry in the War Cabinet. (trs.)

his conversation with Daniel-Rops, the colonel believed he was certainly in a position to induce the Marshal to lift his embargo of ten years before; he thought their relations had returned to "set fair". In reply to his New Year's wishes he had just received a particularly cordial letter from Pétain, in which his former chief said that he was following de Gaulle's career "with much interest", hoped that "he would not be disappointed", suggested that de Gaulle should come and see him, and ended by sending his *sentiments affectueux*, a phrase which came very rarely from the Marshal's pen.

The manuscript reached Plon in April 1938. A publisher's reader named Blanchard was asked to give the verdict. His report was not enthusiastic and he thought the first chapters "superficial", but observed that the book "improved steadily as it went on". The style was "well managed", the literary value "adequate" and the commercial value "only a possibility". But the same sheet has a note in Rops' hand saying that he is "much more favourable" and that he is accepting the book for the series which he had called *Présences*.[1] On 8 May 1939 Colonel de Gaulle signed the contract with Maurice Bourdel, Plon's director, who asked him to "shorten and condense the first chapters", but spoke highly of the last, dealing with the Great War.

The business was therefore thoroughly under way. Had Marshal Pétain – who as de Gaulle knew, still retained the first copy of the manuscript as his own property – even been told about it? There is no correspondence between the colonel and the Marshal that allows this to be clearly established. Yet it was only on 2 August 1938, when the proofs of the book were being corrected that de Gaulle decided to tell the Marshal. However, late it may have been, and perhaps because it was so late, this piece of Gaullian diplomacy deserves to be quoted in full.

> Monsieur le Maréchal,
>
> I have the honour of informing you of the forthcoming publication of your humble servant's book *La France et son armée*. In it I have done my best to carry out the synthesis that you entrusted to me some time ago and that General Weygand, for his part, has attempted in his recent book.[2] In former times, Monsieur le Maréchal, I looked forward to a more brilliant fate for this survey. But the passage of twelve years has caused me to abandon that hope. In any case the attitude of unmoved reserve that you have adopted with regard to the Great War made the accomplishment for the former plan impossible.
>
> The fact remains, Monsieur le Maréchal, that this work was undertaken at your instance. Perhaps you would agree to this being said, for example in the form of a preface: I take the liberty of enclosing a draft for your approval.*
>
> I beg that you will be so good, Monsieur le Maréchal, as to accept the expression of my utmost respect.

Did the Marshal already know that there was something fishy going on? His reaction came with a lightning rapidity, rare in him. Whether the draftsman was

*The text is not attached to the letter published in *Lettres, Notes . . .*, II, p. 470.

General Laure or not (only Pétain's manuscript letters can be attributed to the Marshal) the broadside was fired on 4 August. It could not have been more deadly:

> My dear de Gaulle,
> You tell me of the forthcoming publication of a book entitled *La France et son armée*. If I understand rightly you intend to use the survey with which I formerly entrusted you in this publication. This I find perfectly astonishing. My surprise can surely not seem unexpected.

And the Marshal or his mouthpiece went on to recall the vicissitudes of the undertaking, particularly emphasizing the "office hours" side and the "staff work" (which, the letter states specifically, "belongs to me since I ordered it to be carried out and directed the writing of it"). And holding it against de Gaulle not only that he should use this work under his own signature but that he should do so, says the writer of the letter, "giving a mere account, without submitting your draft to me and without even asking for my authorization"; the person who wrote this "Philippic" ends thus:

> It is my opinion that this work belongs personally and exclusively to me. I therefore reserve the right to make use of it as I may think fit. I also reserve the right to oppose its publication now and in the future. In the event of your disregarding this legitimate wish to dispose of the work as I think proper, I make all reservations as to the manner in which I shall act. I find your attitude most distressing.

This was a declaration of war with a vengeance. De Gaulle took his time, and a fortnight later, on 18 August 1938, he sent the Imperator a reply in the best Gaullian style.

Having declared that out of the 600 pages of his book (which is putting it rather high, since Plon had scarcely received half that) 480 had been written well after his time at the Invalides, and that the 120 remaining pages had since then been entirely altered from the versions "read and corrected" by Pétain, de Gaulle told the Marshal that "there no longer remains anything in these chapters of which it cannot be said with certainty 'This is by de Gaulle'." It was easy enough to show that his book was in no way related to staff work; both its aim and the "extremely personal" turn of its thought and style made it clear that it belonged to him. He brilliantly summed up this idea with the words, "It is not 'drafted', it is 'written'."

> Furthermore, Monsieur le Maréchal, and without finding fault with the reasons that caused you to put an end to my collaboration eleven years ago, it has certainly not escaped your notice that during these eleven years the factors of this matter have changed: I was thirty-seven; I am forty-eight. Morally, I have received wounds – even from you, Monsieur le Maréchal – lost illusions, abandoned ambitions. From the point of view of ideas and style, I was ignored; I have now begun to be so no longer. In short, henceforward I lack both the pliability and the "incognito" necessary for me to allow what talent I ~~may possess~~ in literature and history to be attributed to another.

Once he had made this proud statement of the case, de Gaulle admitted that the Marshal was "at the origin" of a book upon which his "influence" had been exerted, and he offered to write a preface unequivocally acknowledging the "initiative" Pétain had taken, his role in the drawing up of the "plan" and the importance of his "directives and observations", so that the public should know that he, the "great man in the background" had been capable of "protecting a talent and by no means appropriating it".[3]

Clearly, de Gaulle had learnt a great deal in the political and diplomatic as well as military field. His letter of 2 August had moved with a creaking lurch from hypocrisy to want of deference; this one is splendid in its clarity, cleverness, and even warmth. It is no longer the letter of a subordinate eager to throw off the yoke at the smallest cost, but one written by a former disciple big enough to overlook the constraints of rank without forgetting what his talent owed to the man who had encouraged its flowering.

What can the "wounds" received from the old leader have been? Was the Constable referring to the "burial" of the first version? Or to the Marshal's refusal to back his candidature for a chair at the Ecole de Guerre? Or to the Imperator's openly expressed scorn for the arguments put forward in *Vers l'armée de métier*? If "wounds" there were, it was rather the old man who should have spoken of them.

> My dear de Gaulle,
> If, instead of confronting me with a fait accompli or what was about to be a fait accompli, you had taken the trouble to tell me about your plan, as you do today, no doubt I should not have answered your last letter with such a categoric refusal.
>
> In my own mind I always thought that the work carried out during 1925 and 1926 should only be looked upon as a series of studies to be used for a later and more extensive work. The book that you are preparing shows that you are of my opinion.
>
> If you admit that some of my suggestions were sometimes useful to you, then you should acknowledge it by entrusting your book to me for a few days; this will allow me to judge what share in the production of the work could be attributed to me.

At the end of this letter, which reminds one how much Pétain's former inflexibility had with age changed into an instinct for conciliation and a spirit of withdrawal, the old leader suggested a meeting in Paris at the end of the month. The appointment was fixed for Sunday 28 August at the Marshal's house. Apart from two or three fleeting encounters this was to be the last that brought the two men together.

Thirty years later Charles de Gaulle told Marcel Jullian[4] about this meeting, and he added some further details in an interview with Michel Droit in March 1969. This is the first version:

> He had chosen a Sunday when he was sure of being at home by himself. His wife was away; so was everybody else. He did not want there to be any

> witness of our conversation. He opened the door to me himself. And he said to me, "I see no objection to your bringing out this book, *La France et son armée*; but I should like the part I took in it when you were on my staff to be known." I replied, "Monsieur le Maréchal, I ask nothing better than to state exactly how much I followed your line of thought and to say that it was to you that I owed certain initial directives." When we parted, we were in agreement.

In the second version, General de Gaulle says that at a given moment in their talk the Marshal asked him to leave the proofs of the book (in accordance with the terms of his letter of August 22). The visitor refused. "De Gaulle," said the Marshal, "I order you to give me back those proofs." "Monsieur le Maréchal," retorted de Gaulle, "you can give me orders in military matters, but not on the literary level." And he withdrew, saluting the Marshal and carrying the proofs with him.

De Gaulle's refusal to yield to the old man's requirements in this case was probably well judged. The same can not be said of his uncompromising attitude over the dedication which renewed difficulties in this troublesome business and which the Imperator had after all treated benevolently.

A week after the lively conversation of 28 August Philippe Pétain sent his former collaborator the draft-dedication, asking him for his "opinion" or his "acceptance". "To M. le Maréchal Pétain – who, during the years 1925–1927, was so kind as to help me with his advice for the preparation of chapters II to V of this volume ["Ancien Régime", "Revolution", "Napoleon", "From One Disaster to Another"] – I address the tribute of my gratitude."

De Gaulle took no notice of this very flat-footed draft. Having thought of something better, he did not even tell the old gentleman, but sent Plon these words which were to constitute the epigraph: To Monsieur le Maréchal Pétain, Who wished this book to be written, Whose advice guided the writing of the first five chapters, And thanks to whom the last two are the history of our victory." And it was thus adorned that the book appeared on 27 September 1938, the very day of the tragic Munich rendezvous.

This account of a tolerably sour-tasting quarrel cannot come to an end without an attempt at finding out why in this case Pétain yielded. We have already had occasion to suggest the strangeness of the ratio of strength established between the illustrious Marshal, supported by a staff overflowing with titles and ambition, and this solitary officer (though in certain circumstances he was backed up by his political allies).

Every time they confronted one another in open country, away from the dark undergrowth of the promotion-roster or appointments, de Gaulle always seemed to possess a greater gravity than the Marshal. What defines an ascendancy, a dominant influence? When he was dealing with prestige de Gaulle analyzed it only on the collective level, which is perhaps no more than a multiplication of the same relationship experienced between man and man.

With regard to the man he must secretly have chosen as his heir or disciple in 1925 and whose disapproval and estrangement if not contempt he must have felt from the end of the twenties and particularly after the beginning of the crusade for the fundamental renewal of French strategy, Pétain was continually on the defensive. Thirty years before relations of this kind became commonplace, Pétain, the object of general adulation, was no longer living with the ambitious young officer except in a state of apprehensive guilt, perpetually lashed by the other's vital energy and creative power. The tragedy of 1940 only sublimated, on the national level and for reasons of another order of importance, a connexion intimately experienced by the ageing Imperator and the Constable on the point of becoming himself.

Yet it would not be just if one did not see in Marshal Pétain a true benevolence as well as what may be called an old man's sense of inferiority in relation to the younger man. It was not because the Marshal ever gave many signs of a thoroughgoing hardness of heart but that we should not fail in this instance to appreciate what was not only pusillanimity but also forbearance and – let it be said at last – generosity. This "man of character" amused himself by grumbling about the stiff-necked rebel and his protesting spirit and his audacity, even when it was exercised at his expense. Even at Vichy, even at the Montrouge fort, even on the Ile d'Yeu, there were to be heard the murmured echoes of this wounded sympathy, mysterious but irrepressible.

La France et son armée was not only a quarrel between discipline and individuality, between hierarchy and talent. It was also a piece of writing whose history follows that which has just been related step by step. Two considerable sections of the manuscript, the part that deals with the Revolution and that which is devoted to the Great War, have been or may be analyzed in their various states, in which de Gaulle can be seen corrected by Pétain, and Pétain revised by de Gaulle.

In the pages of the manuscript of *Le Soldat* devoted to the Great War, where Philippe Pétain's influence was obviously exercised with its greatest vigour, de Gaulle kept so few lines that if he had submitted the manuscript the Marshal would never for a moment have presumed to maintain the claim he made in his letter of 4 August 1938.

In front of me I have this manuscript,[5] slashed with twin annotations by Colonel Laure (in ink) and Marshal Pétain (in pencil). Next to it I have placed the book published by Plon, the 1971 edition, that scarcely differs from that of 1938 except that the dedication to the Marshal has been removed. The manuscript is a positive hecatomb. In 1937–38, when Charles de Gaulle re-read the manuscript written in 1925–26, he kept few of the paragraphs corrected and sometimes rewritten by Pétain and Laure.

As he recalled in one of his letters to the Marshal, between the draftsman of 1926 and the one of 1938, there lay many years of life, three great experiences of command, a broadened culture, a strengthened style, and a reputation acquired. The de Gaulle of the late thirties was much less given to treatises on the collective psychology of nations ("The Frenchman, born shrewd and knowing"). He now paid more attention to the data of the birth-rate, of electoral sociology, of production and exchange.

If one looks for elements of comparison between the two versions where the upheaval leaves a few similar pieces and a few data more or less common to both, one may say that the writer of 1938 replaces a reference to the "lamentable judicial business" of the end of the nineteenth century by a good account of the Dreyfus affair in which the "likelihood of a judicial error" is openly pointed out. Then again a rather vague description of the measures that were taken to deal with the "moral crisis" in the French army during 1917 is replaced by a fine portrait of the victor of Verdun:

> The day on which there had to be a choice between ruin and reason, Pétain appeared. Excellent at grasping the essential, the practical in everything, his mind dominated his task. More than this, his character set its mark upon it. Confidence took the side of a master of whom it was known that he had scorned making his fortune as a humble follower. The glamour of secrecy, brought about by a deliberate remoteness, a vigilant irony and even by the pride in which this solitude was wrapped.

De Gaulle could see another mark of the "pride" that he speaks of in his personal, definitive version of the book in a note the Marshal added to the 1926 text dealing with the victory. From his pen-officer's description there arose the impression that the decision of 1918 was won by vast amorphous movements in which the nations' weariness played a primordial part: commenting upon this the Marshal wrote firmly: "As for the High Command, the soldier must be convinced that all his actions have been determined by a plan." Though he did not go so far as to take over the words written by Colonel Laure at the end of his own criticism of the same passage: "The knowledge and the character of the leaders guarantees the men's success and happiness."[6]

La France et son armée was not only a battlefield upon which an officer gifted with a high degree of talent crossed swords with a Marshal of France. It was also a book written, placed, published, sold and read like so many others. The author, subjected by his publisher to the traditional questionnaire about his personal details, his publications, his intentions and the meaning of his book, sent his reply to Daniel-Rops at the beginning of August 1938: it is significant in more than one respect. Although he thought it proper to provide Daniel-Rops with his address, a list of the books he had published and of the reviews to which he had contributed (it may be observed that they began with the civilian magazines that had published his articles, the service reviews being left to the end), he rather disdainfully referred Daniel-Rops to Lucien Nachin for everything that had to do with his biography.

In dealing with the book's contents, he states that he had wished "to consider one thousand years of French history and from it to extract the visage and the spirit of our army as it has been formed at various periods by the national temperament, the climate of the time, politics and the State". When he was asked to describe himself he replied "I think I seem to be a man who stirs up ideas". And on the subject of what was then called puffing the book he said, "I have nothing particular to recommend apart from this: make the most of what 'living' quality there may be in the way the subject is treated and in the style."

It is interesting, this way in which Colonel de Gaulle saw himself. Still more interesting is the blurb that he wrote at Daniel-Rops' request.

> This book is a biography. Its subject is France, suffering, fighting, and triumphing. But since we love only what moves us, *La France et son armée* does its best to bring out all that is moving in the fate of a nation that rises and falls at the same time as its military strength. Since great menaces are hanging over the mother-country once more, may this book be of humble use to her. The moment has come to recall that of all the swords from Brennus down to Foch, no sword has weighed heavier than ours.

The public and the press received the book well; it had a better reception than *Le Fil de l'épée* or *Vers l'armée de métier*. It is true that the circumstances were favourable; furthermore Colonel de Gaulle had become that "stirrer of ideas" whose book could not fail to attract, for good or evil, some hundreds of readers straight away.

Plon had taken a risk in printing 4000 copies, then very shortly after, 3700 more. At the end of December the author asked the publisher how sales were going, and Maurice Bourdel told him that "out of 7700 copies, we still have about 1600. The sale is rather slow, but the book is well received."

In fact the reviews were favourable. In *Paris-Midi*, a daily paper with a very wide circulation, Roger Giron wrote that, "Nobody is better qualified than Colonel de Gaulle to write the history of the French army. Charles de Gaulle, a military writer, is a true writer, a writer without any restriction." And at this point Giron called Michelet to mind. *Gringoire*, whose zealously pro-Munich temper was scarcely compatible with that of de Gaulle, paid him a tribute by means of the pen of Pierre Devaux: "Colonel de Gaulle manages to make the military life of our country immensely living and immediate."

None of this was calculated to soothe the Marshal's temper. Something that happened at the beginning of October 1938 gives a good idea of what the old chief, who had been compelled by his unbending opponent to make a tolerably humiliating withdrawal, thought of de Gaulle at that time. Roger Seydoux,* the director of the Ecole Libre des Sciences Politiques, had been struck, throughout the Munich crisis, by the extraordinary indifference to military matters on the part of French public opinion as a whole, particularly the young. He had therefore decided to institute a course on the subject in the framework of the school under his care, which then trained most of the State's higher civil servants.

He decided to consult Marshal Pétain, a member of the school's administrative council, and ask for his advice and suggestions. The Imperator received Seydoux and at once approved of the idea of a course on national defence. But who was to take charge of it? The director of Sciences-Po** observed that he had just read a

*Who was later (under General de Gaulle's presidency) to become Ambassador to Morocco, the United Nations and (under M. Pompidou's) to Moscow.

**The usual way of referring to the Ecole Libre des Sciences Politiques. (trs.)

book by Colonel de Gaulle, who seemed to him very well qualified for teaching such a subject. "I know Colonel de Gaulle well," interrupted the Marshal.

> He is an ambitious man, and very ill-bred. To a large extent I was the moving spirit behind his last book. He wrote it without consulting me and then did no more than send me a copy by post. I myself shall direct the course you mean to start, helped by officers of my staff. But I shall give the opening lecture in person, as soon as term begins.

"The Marshal," adds Roger Seydoux, "kept his promise a month later. The rue Saint-Guillaume was densely crowded. More than 800 students cheered him in the school's great amphitheatre. He gave an excellent lecture on the history of the Great War, during which neither the name of Joffre nor that of Foch was uttered."[7]

An eloquent reaction. No less eloquent is the description of Philippe Pétain that Colonel de Gaulle roughed out in his notebooks at the time. It is a series of short notes, broken phrases, sharp strokes, and sighs only just restrained – one of those sketches which are more beautiful than finished works and by which the great portraitists show themselves at their best:

> Covers the wretchedness of his solitude with pride
> Very sensitive, but only to what moves him
> He has never undertaken anything that did not end profitably
>
> The setbacks in his career had entirely preserved that critical spirit which favour and success often takes away from those who rise very high.
>
> Too sure of himself ever to give up
> too ambitious to aim at unscrupulous success
> too self-centred to despise others
> too prudent not to take risks
>
> His philosophy consists in adjustment
>
> Inscrutable
> and even a hint of irony which he uses as a protection for his thoughts and his peace
> By nature and by reflexion possessed of a taste for long-considered and prepared action in which method comes into its own
>
> More greatness than virtue[8]

Such was the Pétain whom de Gaulle had in his mind's eye between the literary quarrel of 1938 and the great challenge of June 1940. Here are not the traces of any remaining bitterness as the fact that he had grasped the measure of his opponent. When he rose up, a rebel once more, he did not forget that he had succeeded in exploring the old man in depth, determining his characteristics, that is to say his limits, and then in making him yield.

CHAPTER FIFTEEN

Cassandra's Memorandum

Charles de Gaulle had a clear idea not only of France but also of Western Civilization and in 1939 he was never in any doubt as to his duty to confront the challenge thrown down by totalitarianism. There are no documents that show his reactions at the beginning of September but various passages in his *Mémoires*, various letters written during the weeks and months before or after, and various allusions in his later speeches and messages give a fairly good picture of his state of mind at the moment when the great ordeal began.

And who better than he could appreciate the arguments of those who maintained that France and its British ally were in a position of inferiority. For the last six years he had been mapping the road to safety with the most strenuous eagerness – a road that was stubbornly ignored; and he knew that Hitler had just established his sixth armoured division (in conformity with the pattern that de Gaulle had traced five years earlier for France, where the 1st DCR was still in the process of formation). He also knew that Hitler had created an attacking air force, reported by all observers in Spain to be shockingly efficacious, and that he had carried out an unexampled economic mobilization. He knew all this and to what extent those very people who put themselves forward as the advocates of a merciless battle were affected by ambiguous ideas and influences, and how much resistance to Hitlerism and fascism were weakening within the governing teams, however "republican" they might be said to be.

With increasing anxiety he had watched the campaign for a rapprochement with Italian fascism, the withering away of the British alliance and the reconsideration of the guarantees given by France to its allies in Eastern Europe and on the Danube, led by men such as Pierre Laval and Georges Bonnet together with papers like *Le Jour*, *Le Matin* and *L'Action française* – with the Marshal's discreet backing. Indeed, Pétain lost no opportunity of telling his associates that in view of the ratio of power war should be avoided at all costs. And with a kind of eagerness he had just agreed to go and represent France in Franco's Spain.

Although he had come to Paris from Metz on 2 September to receive notification of a new command, de Gaulle was unable to be present at the heart-breaking session during which the Assembly was asked to vote military supplies; but he at once heard echoes of the attempt, prompted by Gaston Bergery, to postpone France's commitment so that Georges Bonnet, the foreign minister, might appeal to Mussolini for his mediation – an attempt parallel with that of Laval in the Senate. The Italian dictator would be satisfied with a few strips of Africa from Djibouti to Tunisia in exchange for his good offices. The two Chambers refused this, but they voted the military supplies only on condition of being reminded that "mobilization is not war". Daladier, head of the government, had therefore been obliged to assume the sole responsibility for declaring that France, together with England, would respect its promise to Poland.

On 3 September 1939 therefore, Colonel de Gaulle was not one of those who were wondering about the expediency of "dying for Danzig". Although he was thoroughly aware of the unprepared condition of the army and the nation, to the very end he was afraid that the degrading humiliation of Munich would be repeated and made even worse. As a specialist engaged in a close comparison of the efforts made on either side of the Rhine he knew better than others that the "gain" of every week might very well prove to be an advantage given to the enemy and the loss of an ally.

Just before this General Colson (later a Vichy minister: at that time the army's chief of staff) was told by one of his colleagues that "never had France undertaken a war in such unfavourable conditions". With a sigh he replied "My poor friend, we know that. But we are caught in the political toils. Besides, if we were to let Poland be crushed today, a few weeks later we should be in an even worse position, and even more alone."[1]

De Gaulle, for his part, was not given to separating military problems and "political toils" and he had not waited for Munich to know that the question was not *whether* Hitler's war-machine should be confronted with armed force but *when* and with what means and what allies. Although in March 1939, immediately before Hitler's entry into Prague, he had for a while believed in a bluff on the part of the Axis, he now knew that the worst was certain. Above all since Stalin, deceived at Munich, had seen fit to make a pact with Hitler on 23 August, taking his revenge on London and Paris by throwing the Third Reich against the "western plutocracies" and Poland, preferring "to share its prey than to be its prey".[2] There was no man in France which the war took less by surprise, no man who hesitated less about the imperative necessity for action, and no man who committed himself to it with fewer illusions.

Unlike the British and French staffs, he did not over-estimate the Polish ally's power to resist the German attack. But however slight the losses inflicted on the Third Reich by the Polish army, whose courage he admired, any fresh desertion and any additional humiliation would only make the shame worse and increase the isolation, seeing that Stalin had seen fit to become Hitler's accomplice rather than the ally French strategy needed in the east. Deserting the Poles by breaking with Britain would be making the disaster of Munich ten times worse in a single stroke.

If he had no illusions about the ratio of strength or the allies' capabilities, he had none about the French High Command. The author of *Le Fil de l'épée*, who for years on end had tried to persuade Gamelin, Weygand, Dufieux, Prételat, Giraud and so many others, knew very well what the heirs of Foch and Joffre were worth, faced with the problems of modern warfare; and *a fortiori* Marshal Pétain. As for Daladier, the man who was entrusted with the "conduct of the war", de Gaulle had seen him tamely submitting to the pressure of the "specialists" at the Ministry of Defence.

Yes, on 3 September 1939 Charles de Gaulle was a man without illusions.

According to his *Mémoires*, he was then convinced that the government hoped that "in spite of the state of war, we would not fight all out".[3] He had more reason than many others to be doubtful about the outcome of the conflict. Yet even so the worst had been avoided – the fatal consent, the betrayal of alliances, the breaking of France's word, the withdrawal into disastrous isolation, and the Nazis' insolent triumph, gained without striking a blow.

Here we should dwell for a while on the evolution of Charles de Gaulle's political thought at the time when the great ordeal was beginning. He may have despised certain customs and practices – the impotence of some and the demagogy of others – but he had also learnt to appreciate individuals. For him the political world was not an amorphous seething of dishonest schemes and sordid self-interest that most of his fellow-soldiers saw when they spoke of the parliamentary Republic. In short, if he ever was a royalist, he now set himself up as a republican. For him, being part of even the last and frailest Third Republic government was an honour; and throughout the crisis he was the closest ally of those who championed the Jacobin spirit against the "great military chiefs", who found the defeat less heart-breaking if it could be represented as being that of the democratic regime.

Certainly it was not an ideology that he was defending – and in London he displayed strong prejudice against certain figures who were symbolic of parliamentary government – but rather a state of mind that was at the basis of a strategy. At that time his sole criterion was the spirit of opposition to the Third Reich. It mattered little to him whether someone belonged to the right wing or to the left; it was by their attitude to the proceedings of the Nazis that he judged them. He had admired Tardieu, but he broke with him as soon as he joined those who were in favour of compromise with the Axis. He had scorned Blum, but he became his ally as soon as the socialist leader entered the ranks of the "warmongers".

We must go even farther. This man who had declared himself the enemy of all doctrines, of Maurras' "integral nationalism" just as much as of all left-wing ideology, came to associate himself with a group which, without playing the least parliamentary role or even becoming a political body, represented something rather more than a mood opposed to both fascism and social conservatism: the group was called The Friends of *Temps présent*, the Christian Democrats' paper. Neither *Temps présent* nor its Friends were neutral. The newspaper had been founded by "advanced" Dominicans. Under the guidance of Stanislas Fumet and the banner of François Mauriac it had put itself forward as an unorthodox paper, discreetly rebellious against a docile Vatican. In its columns Mauriac, Henri Guillemin, Claude Bourdet and Maurice Schumann thundered against Franco and Hitler. To proclaim oneself a Friend of *Temps présent*, particularly for an officer, was to be marked, and Charles de Gaulle knew it.[4]

Left wing? No serious study of Charles de Gaulle's career allows one to venture upon any such statement. But joining the Friends of *Temps présent* he moved towards that current of Christian anti-fascism from which the Resistance drew so many members. It was a fairly recent movement, judging by a letter to Jean Auburtin in June 1937.

> It has always seemed to me that in our social struggles, self-interest has been much less of a motive than jealousy. Among the "little people" this jealousy becomes envy. Among the "big men" it takes the form of pride: *Noli me tangere*! The question of money (wages, profits, holidays, etc.) would be very soon settled if something could bring the antagonists together psychologically. It must be admitted that fascism has found this something; Hitlerism too; yet how can one accept a social balance whose price is the death of freedom? What is the solution? Christianity, we agree, had its own. But who will discover the answer that will be valid for our time?

In any case, as a Friend of *Temps présent*, Colonel de Gaulle was a great way off from the followers of Maurras and the extreme right wing, against whom Emile Mayer, the only man who had had any influence over him since his father's death, had long since warned him. At the moment of plunging into the "rough sea" of history, de Gaulle certainly felt himself called upon to play the part of "a Louvois for the Republic", a French republic that from now on could survive only by beating the Nazis. Even before the miserable collusions of Bordeaux, Vichy and Sigmaringen,* and even before finding himself at the head of a kind of Popular Front, he had realized (without joy) that the fate of French independence was now indissolubly linked with that of the republican regime.

On 2 September, immediately before the declaration of war, de Gaulle was appointed to the command of the tanks of the 5th Army, which, under the shelter of the Maginot Line, covered Alsace, and whose staff had established itself at Wangenbourg, to the south of Saverne. This was a promotion. But it was also still another proof that his crusade had failed. The tanks he was called upon to command did not form one of those great units that he had continually been fighting for: it consisted of five scattered battalions equipped with R35 tanks – the 1st, 2nd, 19th, 21st and 24th BCC. It was a perfect example of that "sprinkling" that he had been crying out against for years. But what of it? He was a professional soldier, on active service, and he obeyed.

The 5th Army was commanded by General Bourret, whom he knew well: as chief of Daladier's military staff he had often spoken to the minister in favour of de Gaulle, particularly at the time of his promotion to colonel in 1937. He was a sound, straightforward man and an avowed republican; he liked people to call him Corporal Bourret, a reminder that he had risen from the ranks. His chief of staff was a certain Colonel de Lattre de Tassigny, of whom we shall hear more.

On 12 September 1939, the 24th BCC, one of the five battalions under de Gaulle's command, was engaged in an attack upon Schweix, a German frontier-post near the camp at Bitche, in front of the Maginot Line. This demonstration, a simple raid at the level of one or two companies, began with the deployment of important material, including a few of de Gaulle's tanks, under the eyes of a group of French generals gathered with their field-glasses on a nearby hill. Two months later on 11 November he sent General Gamelin, the commander-in-chief, a "note

*Sigmaringen, on the Danube, is where Pétain and the Vichy government took refuge between 1944 and 1945. (trs.)

on the use of tanks" drawn up, as he stated, in the light of the lessons drawn from the actions of "the great armoured units that the enemy has recently brought into play in Poland". This note did not even receive an answer. Had de Gaulle expected one? He was therefore to make the most of the fragmented, scattered implements that he had been granted. At Blamont he set up a centre for the instruction of the 5th Army tanks.

There were a great many visitors at the 5th Army headquarters and along the whole of this north-east front, well protected by the Maginot Line. On 23 October, President Lebrun reviewed the 19th BCC on the shores of the Moselle, the tanks being presented by de Gaulle helmeted in steel and leather. The President of the Republic, a former Polytechnician* and a lover of machinery, said to him in the friendliest manner, "I am acquainted with your ideas; but it seems to me much too late to apply them." A few days later the editor of *Le Figaro*, Pierre Brisson, was entertained by the 5th Army at Wangenbourg. Charles de Gaulle told him how much he regretted seeing our forces confined to a passive role. To this the intelligent journalist replied in a most definitive voice, "But don't you see that we have already won a bloodless Marne?"[5]

It was at this time that he wrote his first war-letter to Paul Reynaud, then Minister of Finance. At the beginning of October Reynaud had asked what military posting he could ask for (an uncommon request on the part of a member of the government) and de Gaulle, having suggested that Reynaud should have himself appointed to the staff of the 5th Army's tanks, which would have brought about an amusing inversion of rank between them, moved on to a higher level:

> Now as I see it the enemy will not attack us for a considerable time. It is in his interest to let our mobilized and passive army "stew in its own juice", while at the same time he is busy elsewhere. Then, when he thinks that we are weary, confused and dissatisfied with our own inertia, he will, finally, take the offensive against us, possessing completely different cards in the psychological and material line from those he holds at present.[6]

A few weeks later the 2nd Bureau of the General Staff circulated a small number of copies of a secret report drawing the lessons from the Wehrmacht's extraordinarily rapid and overwhelming victory in Poland. On the subject of armour the report particularly stated that "in the break-through operations the tanks have always been used in a body, on a front of from 1000 to 2000 metres for each regiment, the tanks' advance always being supported by planes attacking with bomb or machine-gun."

The specialists on the General Staff drew this conclusion alone: "The fighting methods employed by the German army in Poland corresponded to a particular situation. On the western front operations will no doubt assume a different aspect", but "the knowledge [of these methods] should allow appropriate counter-measures to be prepared in good time".[7]

Counter-measures? It was only at the beginning of 1940 that the staff made the formation of the two first armoured divisions official, while the B1 *bis* tanks, the

*A pupil of the Ecole de Polytechnique. (trs.)

best armoured vehicles then in service, only came out in dribs and drabs (no more than 60 out of the 460 ordered were then available) and the light R35s were not only equipped with most inadequate weapons (one 37 mm gun) but also deprived of the radios Colonel de Gaulle called for, so that orders from one tank to another had to be communicated by flag-signals or runners.

It is hardly surprising that at this period the Constable, receiving a delegation of British parliamentarians, should have seen fit to produce a shock. In his hunting-horn voice, he addressed his visitors in these terms: "Gentlemen, this war is lost (a long, very long silence: bowler hats and umbrellas wavering in stupefaction). So we must prepare and win another one: with machines!"

On 3 January 1940 Paul Reynaud, who had now abandoned his military aspirations, accepted Colonel de Gaulle's invitation and, in his turn, came to Wangenbourg. General Bourret took advantage of this to invite him to a meal. Reynaud opened the fire: "Soldiers, it is your turn now. When are you going to set about it?" The Constable spoke eagerly in favour of an offensive. The general and his chief of staff firmly objected that beginning an attack as early as the spring would be a mistake. The argument grew heated, so heated that the placid Bourret took offence: "That minister's self-conceit," he relates, "irritated me so much that I said to him, 'If there is an attack in spring, both the minister who decided upon it and the general who carried it out will be hanged!' "[8]

Two weeks later it was de Gaulle who was the minister's guest in Paris. Léon Blum, who was becoming more and more closely connected with Reynaud, was also at the dinner. "What is your forecast?" he asked de Gaulle, who replied without any diffidence, "The problem is knowing whether, in the spring, the Germans will strike westwards to take Paris or eastwards to reach Moscow." "Do you think so?" cried Blum in astonishment. "The Germans strike *eastwards*? But what could they do against the Maginot line?"[9]

In his *Mémoires* Léon Blum speaks of this second meeting with de Gaulle. He tells how the colonel, walking back with him to the quai de Bourbon after dinner, said with strong emotion:

> I am playing my part in a horrible deception. The few dozen light tanks attached to my command are no more than trifles. I am afraid that the lesson of Poland, clear though it was, has been rejected as so much prejudice. Believe me, on our side everything is yet to be done. If we do not act in time we shall lose this war most wretchedly. We shall lose it by our own fault. If you are in a position to work in conjunction with Paul Reynaud, I implore you to do so!

Before leaving Blum, de Gaulle told him he was sending a memorandum that he had just written and that he had called "L'Avènement de la force mécanique"*. And a few days later the Socialist leader received de Gaulle's paper, which he read at one sitting. "It was then," he says, "that I learnt and understood everything. At all costs and without any delay a mechanized army had to be formed."[10]

Léon Blum did not possess a great number of friendly contacts in military

*"The coming of the mechanized army". (trs.)

circles; but there were still enough of them for the paper to be shown to General Georges, number two in the military hierarchy, and to a few others. His influence was weaker in the political realm: Daladier, the highest authority as far as the direction of the war was concerned, did not think the memorandum worth his notice.

What then was this paper that removed the scales from the eyes of the very intelligent Léon Blum? It cannot be said that the 1940 memorandum made any deep change in the propositions advanced in *Vers l'armée de métier* but what did give it more strength than the manifesto of 1934 was the way the triumph of the Nazi armoured divisions in Poland verified its arguments. Nothing is more eloquent than the voice of facts.

About eighty copies of this most important document were made and sent to important civil and military figures by de Gaulle on 26 January 1940: we only have the much-reduced version published by Nachin in his book of 1944.[11]

"L'Avènement de la force mécanique" is in the first place a hymn to the "fighting engine" which:

> restores and increases the qualities that always have been and always will be at the base of the offensive. Acting in all three dimensions, moving faster than any living creature, and capable of carrying enormous weights in the form of arms or armour, from now onwards it holds a rank of prime importance in the scale of warlike values, and it stands there ready to renew the faltering art of attack.
>
> In relation to other forms of armament, the mechanized weapon is specifically endowed with a literally incomparable power, mobility and protection; it therefore constitutes the essential element in manoeuvre, surprise and attack. In modern warfare there is no longer any active operation possible except by means of mechanized force and according to its capacities.

The Germans, by grouping large numbers of attacking planes and several great armoured units, had come nearer to the rational solution; and in Poland they had drawn great advantage from doing so. Yet, asserts de Gaulle, their planes were insufficient in number and their tanks of a kind insufficient in weight to think of breaking the obstacles of the Maginot Line. Were not the Germans now regretting the extreme caution they had observed in the transformation of their army? And he thinks it right to add: "No one can reasonably doubt that if, on 1 September last, the Germans had had only twice as many planes, a thousand hundred-ton tanks, and three thousand of fifty or thirty tons and six thousand of twenty or ten, they would have overwhelmed France."

Dug in behind our fortifications, he continues, we are leaving the enemy every facility to seize upon Europe's resources: "In the present conflict, as in those that have gone before it, being inert means being beaten." To justify keeping thousands of men under arms, he asks, did one therefore "have to feel obliged to set about hopeless undertakings"?*

*He was writing in January 1940 when Paris was feverishly preparing for the landing at Petsamo, Finland.

At this point de Gaulle adds fresh material to his argument: can the continuation of hostilities even be conceived in a country when all economic life is suspended and while the enormous cost of war calls for increased industrial and commercial activity and agricultural production raised to its highest possible point? It is impossible both to export and mobilize; impossible to manufacture essential war-material and keep the technicians in the army. "In former times," he says emphatically, "the war of nations in arms required the mass of the people to be at the battle-front. Today total war requires the mass of the people to be at work."

According to de Gaulle the only way of reconciling these contradictory requirements was to possess the military organization that produced the greatest possible strength with the smallest possible number of men. The adoption of mechanical power necessarily brought about changes in military organization, in the extent and the rhythm of construction, and in the very character of war itself. And while a huge programme of manufacture was being carried out with the help of Britain and America, the men who were to fight the war would be indoctrinated with the sporting spirit, because "the great victories of our time will doubtless be won by champions and by engines".

> The basis of every autonomous undertaking is the great unit. In the air, divisions capable of winning local control of the sky during the battle and thence of attacking the enemy on the land or at sea, as well as long-range divisions intended for the destruction of economically important targets. The union of these great units in terrestrial or aerial formations would allow the break-throughs on a wide front, the far-reaching manoeuvres and the exploitation in depth that form the tactics of mechanized bodies, provided that they are concentrated. There is no doubt that this extension of the force's field of action will bring about an intense increase in the theatres of operations and, as a consequence, profound alterations in the political conduct of the war.

And here the Constable eagerly and with great ability adopted the part and the voice of Cassandra:

> Sooner or later the present conflict will be characterized by movement, surprise, incursion and pursuit whose scale and speed will go infinitely beyond the most shattering events of the past. Let us not deceive ourselves! The war that has begun may well be the most widespread, the most complex and the most violent of all those that have devastated the world. The political, economic, social and moral crisis from which it arose has such a depth and is so ubiquitous that it must necessarily end in a complete upheaval of the condition of nations and the structure of states. Now the obscure harmony of things provides this revolution with a military instrument – the army of machines – that is in exact proportion to its colossal dimensions. It is high time for France to draw the necessary conclusions from this fact.

"L'Avènement de la force méchanique" was therefore a manifesto in which there also appeared some appreciations of the forces that Hitler already possessed together with ingenious suggestions for keeping the productive forces active in wartime and some truly prophetic views on the events that were about to occur, the "surprises, incursions and pursuits" of spring 1940.

But it can also be seen as the most daring, the most original and the most meaningful action that de Gaulle had yet performed. For here was an officer in command of important forces at the front who, in wartime, took it upon himself to denounce the General Staff's conduct of the war and openly to recommend a different line altogether – his recommendation being addressed not only to military leaders but also to dozens of parliamentarians, especially socialists, who were called to the rescue. An "undisciplined act" is too weak: "mutiny" is nearer the mark.

Up until this time, from the Ecole de Guerre to the clash with Marshal Pétain over his last book, Charles de Gaulle had not been much of a conformist; but never yet had the rebel in him been displayed in such a spectacular manner. This leads one to ask why the chiefs whose negligence, inertness and want of imagination were once again denounced in this scathing memorandum, treated him so mildly.

"My memorandum produced no shock," is de Gaulle's melancholy observation in his *Mémoires*. If a staff did not even dare call a heretic to order, how could it have summoned up the energy to set about such an upheaval of ideas and structures at his request? In high places they chose rather to neglect the troublesome fellow. As we have seen, Daladier refrained from looking at his paper. General Georges observed, "Interesting, but the reconstruction is not up to the criticism." A staff-colonel to whom Jean Auburtin showed the memorandum on 26 January wrote this rich comment across the first page: "A colour-blind man who is talking about various tints." Only General Billotte, commanding the northern army group of the Nord, let de Gaulle know of his approval.[12]

As though to put the last seal on the decree of divorce between the heads of the French army as a whole and himself, there was the encounter at Blamont, where, carrying out an exercise with tanks moving as an autonomous body in the presence of General Prételat,* the commander of the eastern army group, he was told, "It's a fine merry-go-round. But the regulations stick to the accompaniment of infantry!"[13]

The letters he wrote to his usual correspondents at this time bear the mark of these personal and collective disappointments. To Paul Reynaud on 21 February:

> Although it is true that we took up arms to prevent the Germans from establishing their hegemony in central, Balkan, Scandinavian and eastern Europe, we have not succeeded at all; furthermore, we have not even tried. It may therefore be said that this war is lost. But there is still time to win another. This other war may undo what the enemy has just accomplished.

The defeat of Finland (Helsinki had to make peace with Moscow on 12 March)

*The only member of the Conseil Supérieur de la Guerre who had dared to speak plainly against going to war on 3 September 1939.

precipitated the collapse of Daladier's government and it was overthrown on the nineteenth. President Lebrun called upon Paul Reynaud to succeed Daladier, thus fully gratifying the wishes of Colonel De Gaulle, whose friend (then only Minister of Finance) had told him three weeks earlier of his coming appointment to the head of an armoured division.

Reynaud, Reynaud at last, was entrusted with the supreme direction of the war. Fate was displaying itself with a disturbing brilliance, perhaps earlier than de Gaulle had supposed. Whether it was among the associates of the new Prime Minister, who had made him his military guide these five years and more, or whether it was at the head of one of those great armoured units of which he was the prophet, everything caused him to foresee that at last he was going to provide the "outstanding service" that he had glimpsed in his youth and that his whole existence called for.

Two courses were therefore open to him, both extremely stirring. It is very probably the first that he wished for: he had always set the political side above everything else, that is to say the centre of decision above the executive organ. At a date that cannot be exactly fixed but that must be at the beginning of 1940, Charles de Gaulle sent Reynaud a perfectly explicit memorandum in which he frankly stated that he was a candidate for a post with responsibilities of this kind:

> 1. The Committee for the direction of the war lays down the war-plan and takes the necessary decisions in this order of ideas as events require them.
> 2. If it is desired that the sittings of the Committee should be prepared for, a secretariat that will assemble the files on each subject, study the questions and take minutes of the proceedings is necessary.
> 3. Colonel de G. might be Secretary-General for the conduct of the war.[14]

Everything foretold that Charles de Gaulle would be called upon as one of the new premier's very close associates: it was he that Paul Reynaud asked to draw up his ministerial declaration. But the short and powerful statement that he produced and that was read by Reynaud at the tribune of the Palais-Bourbon scarcely appears to have touched an Assemblée filled with prejudice and undermined by defeatism.

The atmosphere was bad, particularly on the right wing who resented Reynaud for opening his government to six Socialists (it is "a Blum government without Blum" they cried, "a cocktail of the *Marseillaise* and the *Internationale*"), and who forgave him least of all for what they called his "warmongering". It was with a mixture of fury and sorrow that Charles de Gaulle listened to the proceedings on 22 March at that sitting which he later described as horrifying – a description with which all witnesses and historians agree – a sitting in full wartime during which a deliquescent, frightened Assemblée settled its score with those of its members who stood out as the most determined to fight.

"Only Léon Blum spoke with elevation of mind," wrote de Gaulle, pointing out that it was to the Socialist leader that Reynaud owed his majority, which was of a single vote. Indeed, some time later and in the presence of de Gaulle, Herriot, the president of the Chamber of Deputies, went so far as to question whether

Reynaud had really obtained that meagre advantage. The fact is that the president of the Chamber had prolonged the sitting beyond the usual limit in order to allow Georges Mandel, the strongest of Reynaud's supporters, to "make the rounds of the corridors". Did he wish to spare himself the historic disgrace of being at the head of a right-wing government that proposed a "bloodless peace" with Hitler and wished to cover their undertaking with republican legitimacy?

The business began all the more badly since Daladier insisted upon keeping the Ministry of Defence, a requirement based upon his control of the powerful Radical Party, the hinge of parliamentary majorities. From this there arose an unfortunate double command in the conduct of the war. Daladier, clinging to his post in the rue Saint-Dominique, received a messenger from the new prime minister who had come to suggest the appointment of Colonel de Gaulle as Secretary-General of the War Committee, whose creation had been decided upon. Daladier's reply: "If de Gaulle comes here, I shall leave this office, walk down the stairs and telephone Paul Reynaud, telling him to put de Gaulle in my place." That, at all events, is the version of the scene given by de Gaulle.[15]

This being so, Reynaud made a surprising choice: on 30 March he gave the appointment intended for de Gaulle to one of the most outstanding figures in the pacifist group, Paul Baudouin, formerly head of the Bank of Indochina and now the new Under-Secretary of State in the Prime Minister's office; Baudouin was thus provided with a doubly decisive position in the middle of the spider's web woven round Paul Reynaud. Two other men were already there, playing a most important part in the same direction: Yves Bouthillier, an inspector of Finance who was passionately opposed to the régime and to the war – a man who was later to be found in the front rank of the Vichy ministers – and Lieutenant-Colonel de Villelume, who was in charge of the liaisons between the Quai d'Orsay and the General Staff.

Reynaud had the idea of making this highly talented officer the head of his personal diplomatic staff: Villelume, together with Jean de Lattre de Tassigny, was perhaps the only one of the young leaders of the army who could at that time match de Gaulle – whom he most heartily disliked. Since Villelume, throughout this period, was the most brilliant and the best informed supporter of the argument in favour of immediate peace, it is easy to imagine what the atmosphere in the circle round Reynaud would have been like if de Gaulle had had the post he longed for.

Reynaud's choice of Baudouin after Villelume is all the more disconcerting* since only two days before, during a session of the Supreme Inter-Allied Command Council in London, he had addressed the British in favour of a document drawn up at the Quai d'Orsay (he was Foreign Minister as well as premier) according to which the two partners both undertook not to make a separate peace with the Reich. London at once agreed to this proposition. The adoption of so "Gaullist" an attitude before the letter, and the choice, for carrying this policy into

*It was due to the increasingly pervasive influence of Hélène de Portes, whose feelings for Reynaud did not go so far as sharing his determination to oppose the enemy. She was the Egeria of the "bloodless peace" group, and she found places for her friends with Reynaud. The next chapter will return to this.

practice, of men who thought only of compromise, is one of the paradoxes that made up the conduct of the new head of government.

So here was de Gaulle brought back to his military vocation and obliged to return to Wangenbourg. He wrote to his mother:

> I have come back to the front. The political atmosphere in Paris was too bad and the relations between Paul Reynaud and Daladier too tense for me to be able to work usefully. I therefore asked the prime minister to let me return to my tanks until the situation should become clear. He agreed, though at the same time he told me that he would soon bring me back: so I am waiting without impatience.[16]

To make the waiting more bearable, the Constable was given a certain number of compensations. General Gamelin summoned him to the chateau of Vincennes, which he used as his retreat, to tell him that he meant to increase the number of armoured divisions at the French army's disposal from two to four, and to confirm what Reynaud had given him cause to hope for in February: his appointment to the command of the 4th DCR, which, it was hoped, might be formed by 15 May. For the friar preaching the "fighting engine" crusade it was an astonishing tribute. Charles de Gaulle spoke to his host of his "pride", though not without telling him of his anxiety about the proportion between the "mechanized strengths" on either side of the Rhine.

Gamelin, who gave de Gaulle the impression of a "scientist thinking out the effects of his strategy in a laboratory", told him that there was shortly going to be a German offensive through Belgium and the Low Countries and he said he was certain and even "impatient" to break it. Was not this Commander-in-Chief who had thus "laid down once and for all the definitive plan he meant to follow" the very type of mind which the author of *Le Fil de l'Epée* had so fought against? De Gaulle does not say so, but in this state of affairs one can see the origin of the "uneasiness" which the visitor felt on leaving the great leader.[17]

During the interval before he could take command of his division, which was still in the making, Colonel de Gaulle could not but be the witness of the increase in the peripheral strategy by which Paul Reynaud claimed to show his eagerness to "wage war". At the beginning of April the head of the government decided to revive a scheme put forward months before by Winston Churchill, then First Lord of the Admiralty, which consisted of first laying mines and then of landing on the coast of Norway, which was then neutral, to prevent supplies of Swedish iron-ore from reaching the Third Reich. It was the application of the often repeated slogan "The iron route will be cut", thanks to which Reynaud hoped to give himself the image of a man of action. But the moment the Royal Navy began the operation on 8 April, the German staff – which had been preparing its own northern attack since December – forestalled the Allies, landing forces which seized all the Norwegian ports in three days, while the Wehrmacht occupied Denmark in a few hours.

In what Reynaud called the race against time in Scandinavia, the French and British had let the enemy get away first. Hitler had managed to protect his "iron route" and keep the initiative. So now, looking for action at any cost, people talked about operations in Belgium, laying mines in the Rhine or bombing Baku. Colonel de Gaulle, who in a letter to his wife wrote, "No doubt the outcome of the Norwegian affair will create difficulties for Paul Reynaud, although he had nothing to do with it."[17] And to Jean Auburtin, "The Norwegian business is another victory to the credit of mechanized force. Alas, once again the victory is German. We shall win only when we have understood."[18]

On 3 May Reynaud received a fresh letter from Colonel de Gaulle, urging him once more to carry out the reorganization of the military system at last. He stressed that action was possible only if the premier took "the whole body of military organizations under his own direct and personal authority". On the ninth, during a cabinet meeting at the Quai d'Orsay, Reynaud staked everything on one throw: he uttered a violent indictment of Gamelin, whom Daladier defended with great acrimony. The head of the government, observing the totally divergent views held by himself and the Minister of Defence, thought the occasion favourable; he stated that the government was resigning and he went to inform the chief of state of the fact – asking him not to make the resignation public until after the formation of the "new" ministry.[19] In Reynaud's view, it could only be a question of a reorganization of the government and of the defensive system, without Daladier and under his own personal authority.

But on the dawn of the following day, 10 May 1940, Hitler's armoured divisions, driving upon Sedan, put an abrupt end to this process, which might have changed history; and they overturned it in another manner. The onward rush of the Nazis not only kept Daladier and Gamelin in office (for about ten days) but it did the same for Paul Reynaud and (over a much longer period) for Charles de Gaulle.

CHAPTER SIXTEEN

Face to Face with Disaster

Early in the morning of 10 May 1940 General Maurice Gamelin, in his Vincennes "monastery", was humming a cheerful tune: he had just learnt that the Germans had launched their offensive in Belgium and Holland. And this man who had believed in the superiority of the German army for five years was suddenly filled with a kind of euphoria because he had foreseen this attack and because nothing was more important to him than intellectual clarity.

"He's happy now; he has his own particular battle," said Reynaud confidentially to those around him. For his own part the head of the government did not conceal his underlying anxiety at Gamelin's immediate decision to send three French armies hurrying into Belgium; and he said that "he was surprised to find an officer he had confidence in, Colonel de Gaulle, entirely in agreement with Gamelin on the subject of going into Belgium, although de Gaulle was opposed to the general."[1]

A few hours later Charles de Gaulle wrote to his wife:

> So the war, the real war, has begun. Yet I should be quite surprised if the present operations in Holland and Belgium really prove to be the great Franco–German battle. In my opinion that will come somewhat later. In any case I should like the fourth armoured division to be ready as early as possible.[2]

It was on that Meuse which Charles de Gaulle knew so well, having received his baptism of fire and his first wound there on 15 August 1914, that the Führer, persuaded by General von Manstein to neglect the advice of his most outstanding generals (who wished the German war-machine to bring all its weight to bear on Holland, Belgium and the mouth of the Somme), flung his shock-troops, seven armoured divisions, the famous Panzers that had sprung fully armed if not from the brain of the author of *Vers l'armée de métier* then at least from those who had drawn their inspiration from de Gaulle.

In three days the two armoured groups of Kleist and Guderian swept through the Ardennes forest, which Pétain had said would be enough to stop them and they crushed the scanty forces posted to defend that vital pivot between the Maginot Line and the northern army group. As early as 13 May their motor-cyclists were in sight of Sedan.

Guderian was already aiming for Rethel on the Aisne and Montcornet on the Serre, with Abbeville and the Somme to come next: and thus the vast manoeuvre to encircle the armies that Gamelin had risked in the north took shape. By the evening of 13 May, the most clear-sighted perceived that the outcome of the battle of France was decided. The Panzers, supported by the Luftwaffe, had fulfilled Charles de Gaulle's prophecies. When General Georges, the Commander-in-Chief of the north-east front, received the news that night he told Captain Beaufre that "the front was utterly broken", and burst into tears.

As early as 7 May the staff had told Colonel de Gaulle to be ready to take the 4th DCR in hand, and in the calm of Wangenbourg he had begun to recruit a few assistants. But it was in a state of feverish tension that on the eleventh he received the order to take over his command, which was stationed at Le Vésinet. He arrived on the twelfth and took up his quarters in a villa called Beaulieu on the route de la Croix. At the moment of assuming command he was noticed for the very great attention he paid to the personality and the career of each man, by his exactness, his authority and the distance he assumed (loftiness, secrecy, brevity), entirely in agreement with the portrait of the leader he had drawn in *Le Fil de l'épée.* Among those about de Gaulle there were already ardent admirers and men who could not bear him. He very soon learnt to draw the utmost from the first and to do without the others. Even if it meant breaking some, who deserved better.

On the fifteenth de Gaulle – who had only been able to bring together three tank battalions, less than a third of his armoured strength and less than half his officers – was summoned to general headquarters to be informed of the nature of his mission. General Doumenc who, almost ten years before de Gaulle, had been the supporter of the "fighting engine", told him that in order to defend the Aisne, that is to say the road to Paris, against Kleist's and Guderian's armour, General Touchon's 6th Army had been hastily withdrawn from the shelter of the Maginot Line: the 4th DCR was expected to "gain time" to allow Touchon take up his positions. Then it was General Georges, "obviously overwhelmed", who received him. "Come, de Gaulle," said this old opponent of armoured corps, "you who have so long had the ideas the enemy is now applying, here's the chance to act."[3]

De Gaulle, taking notice of the fact that the staff was "making haste" to send some of the forces meant for him to the Aisne, but that it was "foundering" and that "hope was fading",[4] hurried away to Laon, setting up his headquarters in the nearby village of Bruyères. On the way he picked up some cavalry and artillery units, which were retreating in disorder and were somewhat astonished to hear the words, "You are under my orders."

That evening he wrote to Yvonne de Gaulle:

> Here I am in the middle of the fight. Called upon yesterday post haste to form a division. From that point of view, all's well. They have given me everything they could give me. We shall soon see how things turn out. What is happening is *very* grave.

And he suggested precautions to be taken for the family, as "anything may be expected".[5]

It was on the next day, 16 May, when he was in the country round Laon in search of information – it seemed to him that the enemy was not driving towards the south and Paris, but towards the west, Saint-Quentin and the Somme – that

Charles de Gaulle saw the routed soldiers: it was like a blow in the face, the sight of the collapse of

> these troops that the Panzers' attack had put to disorderly flight in the course of the preceding days. As they fled they were overtaken by the enemy's mechanized detachments, which ordered them to throw away their rifles and hurry off southwards so as not to block the roads. "We have no time to take you prisoner," the Germans shouted to them.

Turning over these very painful memories thirteen years later, Charles de Gaulle could not prevent himself from reopening the wound:

> The war was beginning unspeakably badly. So now it would have to go on. There was plenty of room in the world for that. If I lived, I should fight wherever it was necessary and as long as it was necessary until the enemy was beaten and the nation's stain washed away. What I have been able to do since then was resolved upon that day.[6]

So without waiting to receive all the elements he had been promised, and thinking that battle alone could weld his men into a coherent group, he decided that the next day he would set about the delaying mission (the sacrificial mission?) on the Serre that he had been given. He fixed upon a target, Montcornet, a large village twelve miles west of Laon, the meeting-point of the roads to Saint-Quentin (thought to be Guderian's goal), Laon and Rheims. If he could get well into it and hold on, he could make it into a block that would do the enemy a great deal of damage.

In the middle of the afternoon of the sixteenth, having privately told one of his officers that as they did not know whether the Germans were really at Montcornet or not, "the best thing to do was to go and see", he dictated "Order of the day, number one" which called for the tanks to be deployed on either side of the main road from Laon to Montcornet, which ran through the forest of Samoussy over a countryside that was fairly level and suitable for manoeuvre. Their aim was the Serre.

In the meantime de Gaulle had received an important reinforcement: Colonel Sudre's armoured half-brigade, which included a battalion of tanks in part made up of B1 *bis*, heavy and slow but massively armoured and carrying a 75 mm gun. The unit was under the command of Major Bescond, the foremost specialist in the use of the weapon. During the night and a little before the operation began, de Gaulle summoned this officer: "I must have Montcornet. You are the champion of the B tanks: it is up to you to show what they are worth. Go and win your fifth stripe at Montcornet!"[7] Coming back to his officers, Bescond said to them, "This will be my Reichshoffen."*

At 4.30 a.m. the 4th DCR, numbering at least a hundred tanks, got under way. Opposite them, on the right bank of the Serre, the German armour had halted on

*The French cavalry's Balaclava; it happened in 1870. (trs.)

Hitler's orders; he thought his spearhead Panzers were dangerously far forward: Guderian would gladly have ignored the order but his companion in the attack, Kleist, who was higher in rank, insisted on obeying it. The German armour was much superior in numbers. But by noon the first French tanks had reached Montcornet, in spite of the violent attacks of the Luftwaffe. General Delestraint, who had come to see his friend de Gaulle at the Bruyères headquarters, told him with great emotion that they were now having their "revenge upon official aberration".

The 1st Panzer Division's lines of communication were well and truly threatened, but the intervention of the 10th during the afternoon allowed it to break free of the 4th DCR's grip; and the DCR, after the death of Major Bescond, was compelled to fall back on Laon. In his *Mémoires* de Gaulle says, "We were a forlorn hope nearly twenty miles beyond the Aisne; and we had to put an end to a situation that was perilous, to say the least."[8]

The Constable's balance-sheet at the end of this first day of what he called an "offensive reconnaissance" was positive in that the operation had showed that the French armoured units and their equipment could hold their own against the enemy's best front-line troops. In a later report General Touchon spoke of a "vigorous blow" that "had slowed down the Panzers". The loss in men was comparatively slight: 25 killed or wounded. But the embryonic DCR had lost more than a quarter of its armoured vehicles (23 out of 90) to mines, anti-tank weapons or Stukas.

Colonel d'Ornano summed up this day of 17 May by saying that the operation, conceived and carried out on the commander of the 4th DCR's sole initiative, helped to "pay off the psychological mortgage of May 10".

On the eighteenth de Gaulle had received the reinforcement of two fresh regiments of motorized cavalry, the 3rd Cuirassiers under Colonel François and the 10th under Colonel de Ham. Taking the losses of May 17 into account, he now had at his disposal 150 "fighting machines", an improvised and increasingly uneven force, but one from which, he wrote, "there emanated a feeling of general eagerness and enthusiasm". At dawn on May 19 came the attack.

Crécy and Pouilly, north of Laon, whose bridges commanded the passage of the Serre, were the objectives of the 4th DCR. Once more it was a matter of delaying the advance of the two armoured corps, particularly Guderian's Panzers, which were moving along the north bank of the Serre towards Saint-Quentin, an important assembly-point in the enemy offensive. But even more cruelly than on the seventeenth, the Stukas dominated the battle, decimating Colonel de Gaulle's armour at the approaches to the bridges across the Serre.

From his observation-post on the top of a wooded hill called le Mont-Fendu, de Gaulle, after five hours of fruitless attempts, was obliged to see that the enemy's command of the air and the almost complete absence of artillery on the French side made it impossible for him to take up the positions on the far side of the Serre that he had wished to establish. In the early afternoon he disregarded an order from General Georges telling him to withdraw, and at night he had himself driven to the command-post of the 6th Army, where in a long and dramatic interview he tried to persuade General Touchon to give him two other divisions so that he might try to link up with the northern armies, cut off by the German manoeuvre. He was wasting his time: Touchon was not the kind of man who would take initiatives of such importance.

In any case this plan was chimerical. In the midst of battle and on the proposition of a divisional commander (a mere colonel), the overturning of the plans of the General Staff, however deliquescent the staff might be and however much the proposition might try to seize the last chance of re-establishing the situation, was even more improbable than defying Pétain, publishing *Vers l'armée de métier* and sending out the January 1940 memorandum. It was pure "Gaullist" behaviour at a time before the collapse of all structures allowed the rebel to manifest himself.

He was obliged to obey. The day of the twentieth was that of the withdrawal beyond the Aisne through the woods of Festieux, between Rheims and Soissons, by the Chemin des Dames and that village of Corbény where the first tank-battle had been fought under Estienne in 1917. De Gaulle had taken it upon himself to delay this very costly movement of retreat by a day.

Paul Huard was one of the chief actors in this operation; and studying it thirty years later he states that a withdrawal carried out on the nineteenth would have made the traffic-jams on the Aisne bridges even worse and increased the casualties, and that a hasty retreat would have turned what had hitherto been a technical and psychological success into a moral defeat, at a moment when "in the dark future that was closing in upon the French army, honour had to be put first, and paid for at the price required".[9]

The next day, May 21, there happened an event now quite forgotten that was to have long and well-known repercussions: an officer of the GHQ propaganda services asked Colonel de Gaulle to give a talk on the radio by way of reaction against the wave of defeatism that the Panzers' shatteringly rapid advance set off among the people. Major Faivre and Captain Viard were present at this "appeal of 21 May", recorded in the garden of the house in the little village of Savigny where the colonel's command-post was installed; they remember observations about the 4th DCR's recent engagements which de Gaulle gave as examples, and the speaker's tone, which was "energetic" (according to the one) and "solemn" (according to the other). A rehearsal for de Gaulle's next and more famous "performance", that of 18 June.

On 22 May, he was given a fresh mission, westwards by way of Soissons, Compiègne and Beauvais towards the Somme. It was during this long march, on 24 May, that he wrote to Yvonne de Gaulle:

> The fighting continues. But as far as I am concerned, things are not going badly. I have a sort of feeling that we have got over our surprise and that we are moving towards a recovery. But it *has* cost us a great deal and it *will* cost us a great deal. I am a general since yesterday.* I was told of it in a letter from Paul Reynaud [who] signed my promotion at the instance of General Weygand.

*"With temporary rank", as we know. He was forty-nine years and six months old.

Sometimes Charles de Gaulle found it difficult to distinguish between what was happening to him and what was felt by the people as a whole. Certainly, becoming one of the three youngest generals in the French army, even if only with temporary rank, and to owe this promotion to a feat of arms that sets you apart in the general humiliation thanks to a weapon of which you have been the prophet for years, is enough, in a moment of intimate unreserve, to make you think well of your own fate and to persist in a belief that is already denied by the facts.

For the second of the battles in which the new general took part, let us follow the account of General Nérot,[10] then a captain and liaison officer with the commander of the 4th DCR, whom he never left during these three days:

> By 28 May we had travelled about two hundred kilometres in six days. With about 140 tanks, six battalions of infantry and six groups of artillery, we were to attempt the reduction of the twelve kilometre pocket south of the Somme in front of Abbeville: it was the last chance of preventing the northern armies from being cut off and surrounded.
>
> General de Gaulle decided to attack towards Mont-de-Caubert at 5 p.m. The tanks were slow in coming together, and then it seemed to me that they were too close together. The enemy had a great many very well placed anti-tank weapons and they inflicted heavy losses upon us. But by the evening we had taken Huppy and there we were at Mont-de-Limeux, from which the Germans had fled in disorder, leaving their supper in their travelling kitchens. We took 400 prisoners!
>
> At 4 a.m. the general launched the second attack: the sky was overcast, the enemy planes less effective, and our artillery had been reinforced. We made our way into Huchenneville; some of our tanks reached Mont-de-Caubert; we received a signal that enemy columns were hurriedly crossing back over the Somme. Abbeville was within our reach. But the enemy counter-attacked in the Villers wood. The villages we had taken, Bienfait for example, were heavily shelled. General de Gaulle went up to the firing-line and summoned his colonels: "Colonel de Ham, you are at Bienfait; you will hold the village until tomorrow: Colonel François, you are at Mesnil-trois-Foetus; you will hold out until tomorrow morning."
>
> We spent a short night at the château of Huppy, where the wounded were being tended and which the enemy shelled. At dawn a messenger came to tell de Gaulle that Colonel François had been killed. The general's only reaction was: "Who's replacing him?" And the attack on Mont-de-Caubert began again that same day. But the division could not take Abbeville; it had reached the limit of its powers and on the thirty-first it was relieved by a large British unit commanded by General Fortune.

These were the conclusions that the Constable drew from the operation for the benefit of Yvonne de Gaulle: "The second important engagement that I carried out with my division has ended with a great success near Abbeville. You must have heard something of it in the communiqué (400 prisoners, much equipment taken). I have just been mentioned in Despatches for this business." But this news of victory did not end without Charles de Gaulle advising his wife to take refuge in the Charente, the Dordogne or Brittany.

Let us recall General Georges' testimony, given six years later before the Commission of Enquiry into the events that occurred between 1933 and 1945:

> The 4th DCR was improvised on the battlefield. Yet it was the only one that disorganized the German columns to a considerable extent when it was thrown against their flanks. So true is it that the DCRs must of necessity be commanded by bold, dynamic leaders who have reflected at length upon the potentialities of these special units in battle. Such was then the case with Colonel de Gaulle.

The point of view of those on the other side cannot fail to be interesting. Although Kleist says nothing about the Constable's role in May 1940, Heinz Guderian, on the other hand, does have something to say about it. Fate had done well in opposing the author of *Achtung Panzer*! to that of *Vers l'armée de métier*, as though it were an echo of those medieval encounters between Saracen princes and crusading kings. Guderian was too clearly aware of his superiority of arms to utter any paean of victory; he temperately says,

> We were told of the presence of Colonel de Gaulle's fourth armoured division, which had been making itself felt since the sixteenth. De Gaulle kept the appointment on the following days, and on the nineteenth, with a few isolated tanks, he succeeded in coming as close as two kilometres from my advanced command-post. I experienced some hours of uncertainty until these unwelcome visitors turned back.[11]

De Gaulle did not fail to rebuke any officer who came with news of a set-back or a delay in a contemptuous and sometimes humiliating tone. On the knoll of Mont-Fendu he called out to the officers around him who threw themselves flat on being machine-gunned by Stukas, "Come, gentlemen, behave yourselves!" (as he had done in Champagne in 1916). When on 21 May a very young lieutenant paraded his detachment in haphazard order, de Gaulle uttered the Jovian cry "Come to life, Jourdain!"*

A major who reached the command post the same day in working uniform, under fire, received this telling-off, "You come to this staff-meeting as though it were a fishing-party. I am sending you back to Tours!" And finally, when a liaison-officer explained his business at too slow a rate for de Gaulle's liking, he growled, "Do you think you are in 1970? What do you do in civil life?" "I am a curé." "That suits you very well."

It might be asked whether a character of such size and with so evident an intellectual superiority needed methods of this kind to compel recognition. In *Le Fil de l'épée* it is high standing or prestige that is dealt with, not this sarcastic

*The original is "Existez, Jourdain!" which is perhaps rather more like Jupiter. (trs.)

badgering that was certainly inflicted on a good many of those whom it was his business to incite to higher things rather than to horse-whip.

The best thing to do here is to quote the man who was present during these dramatic days, who watched the commanding officer of the 4th DCR with the utmost acuity, and whose words are based on an admiration that criticism could not shake – the future general, Paul Huard.

> A leader impressive by his physical size, by a distinction "that inspired respect", and by his faultless uniform, which was sometimes emphasized in the field by white gloves. This chief, who was exacting in all circumstances, kept his officers six yards off, creating a void all round himself, in the middle of which he stood out; unless he preferred being visible from far off, standing on a slope or even on a heap of stones, waiting for the officer – a shorter man – whom he wished to impress. He would receive an account without a word, or sting a subordinate's pride by a harsh and sometimes undeserved remark.
>
> De Gaulle exercised an independent, exclusive, authoritarian and egocentric command, based on his conviction that in all circumstances his judgment was the best if not the only valid one. This made him doubt information which, though sound, did not agree with his current ideas of the enemy. All decisions came from him alone. He accepted no opinion and still less any direct suggestion, even though in his own time he might profit by what he had seemed not to hear.

A severe portrait, but one that rings true and calls for this simple reminder: not one of the officers whom Charles de Gaulle had under his orders during these engagements saw fit to join him in London. Some, like Captain Nérot, fought courageously in the Resistance. But the reserve shown towards de Gaulle by his officers who had been able to admire his determination and energy under fire gives a somewhat negative impression of his methods of command.

Did the war-leader ever equal the politician in de Gaulle, the carrying on of the struggle in the field giving him his chance? However striking this short experience may have been, it does not allow one to assert that such was the case. Charles de Gaulle possessed a physical courage proved by a score of incidents, an almost inhuman coolness, a proverbial energy, and an intelligence and culture that are no handicaps in the military art; yet in the field he does not seem to have displayed that feeling for places, men, and moments, that hunter's instinct, that almost animal flair which mean that if one is at the head of six thousand men or of a million one is Luxembourg, Masséna or Leclerc.*

Yet though they may have been of little importance in the final reckoning, the two incidents of Laon and Abbeville were enough to number de Gaulle. In any case it was not on the military level that these days had their prime importance but

*Three outstanding French marshals. The first served under Louis XIV, the second under Napoleon (who nicknamed him the "dearest child of victory") and the third was to command the French forces that took part in the Normandy landings and the liberation of Paris (see chapters 22 and 40). (trs.)

in the private dialogue between de Gaulle and himself. These proofs that he had given in the field brought the rebellion that had been slowly developing in him to maturity. Had he been so sure of himself before? After the enormous rage that had filled him on 16 May in the very midst of the collapse, this assertion of his value as a fighting-man and of the soundness of his intuitions on the armoured corps, would help to make the decision of June more likely. His having been "different" in the field would make him more ready to accept that he was "different" in terms of destiny.

On 1 June Colonel de Gaulle was summoned to Paris by General Weygand, the commander-in-chief, who during a session of the Supreme Inter-Allied Command Council in Paris the day before had obtained Churchill's agreement that the Dunkirk bridgehead should be held long enough for the French troops to be evacuated. The recovery that de Gaulle had been hoping for since 20 May now seemed to be ruled out. The head-on battle had been lost.

At dawn on 1 June, leaving the various elements of the 4th DCR to reassemble at Marseille-en-Beauvaisis, General de Gaulle set out for Paris, accompanied by Captain Nérot. His first visit, at eight in the morning, was to his tailor (what is a general without a uniform?). Then he went to see Reynaud at his office in the ministry of War in the rue Saint-Dominique. Captain Nérot gathered that it was during this interview that for the first time de Gaulle was offered a political post in Reynaud's administration and that he accepted in principle.

The third visit was to Weygand who had set up his headquarters at Montry. Nérot was present at the meeting and he states that Weygand (who as we know had not hitherto displayed much liking for de Gaulle) came towards the new general, took him by the shoulders and kissed him on both cheeks, saying "I congratulate you. You have saved our honour".[12] Then he asked the Constable what more could be done to increase the productivity of these armoured units that had just shown their worth in the field. To this the visitor replied with a few suggestions, saying that he meant to include them in a memorandum at the earliest possible moment.

This memorandum, dated 2 June and sent to General Weygand is essentially made up of four points: firstly the armoured division, a *Garde* (de Gaulle is obviously alluding to Napoleon's Garde), should be kept at the disposal of the commander-in-chief alone; secondly, taking the losses into account, it would be better to reconstitute only three complete DCRs rather than four weakened ones; thirdly, these three units should be grouped in one single "armoured corps" which, says de Gaulle, would be "our hammer" in the next battle; and fourthly, "I propose myself as the commander of this corps".[13]

Concurrently, Charles de Gaulle made the same offer of his services to Paul Reynaud in a note dated the day before (1 June). Was this to provide himself with an alternative to the Prime Minister's offer of giving him more political responsibilities? However that may be, both texts, that to Weygand and that addressed to Reynaud, have a tone of certainty and of ambition and one might almost say of optimism, surprising at this period of collapse. To Reynaud he speaks of a possible "reversal", because "the German mechanized forces (planes and tanks) are temporarily worn out".[14]

This strange optimism – and once again we see that in him an increase of self-confidence tends to overshadow his usually very sure feeling for the general situation – did not last. As early as 3 June he wrote Reynaud another letter:[15] it is an extraordinary document:

> Monsieur le Président,*
> We are on the edge of the abyss and you are bearing France on your shoulders. I beg you to consider these points:
>
> 1. Our first defeat arose from the enemy's application of ideas conceived by me and from our High Command's refusal to apply the same conceptions.
> 2. After this terrible lesson you, who are the only person to have followed me, have become the master, partly because you followed me and because this was known.
> 3. But now that you have become the master you are abandoning us to the men of former times.** I am not unmindful of their past glory nor of their merits in days gone by. But I do say that these men of former times – if they are allowed to – will lose this new war.
> 4. The men of former times are afraid of me because they know I am right and that I have the dynamism to force their hand. So today, as they did yesterday, they are doing everything – and perhaps in perfectly good faith – to prevent me from reaching the post in which I could act with you.
> 5. The country feels the urgent need of our renewal. Its hopes would greet the coming of a new man, the man of the new kind of war.
> 6. Break away from conformism, from "established" positions, from academic influence. Be a Carnot, or we perish. Carnot appointed Hoche, Marceau, Moreau.***
> 7. Come to you as a person *without responsibilities*? Principal private secretary? Head of a research department? No! I mean to act with you, but by myself. Or else there is no point in it and I prefer a command!
> 8. If you give up the idea of taking me as Under-Secretary of State, at least make me the head – not only of one of your four armoured divisions – but of the armoured corps grouping all these elements. Allow me to say without modesty, but after twenty days of experience under fire, that I alone am capable of commanding this corps, which will be our supreme resort. Having invented it, I claim to lead it.[16]

After this who can still speak of the "miracle" of 18 June? Even before total disaster had beaten down all the walls around him, all conventions and rivalities, he was rearing, neighing, and laying down the law. He felt that he belonged to another species, this "new man whose coming" the country "would greet with hope", as he said. All at once this Reynaud, whom he both belaboured and pleaded with, no longer counted for anything.

*In France the Prime Minister is president of the Council of Ministers. (trs.)
**Pétain, vice-president of the Council, and Weygand, the Commander-in-Chief.
***Lazare Carnot, who organized the armies of the Revolution: Hoche, Marceau and Moreau were three generals he appointed.

CHAPTER SEVENTEEN

Ruling the Abyss

The last phase of the German assault began on 5 June, after the battle of Dunkirk.[1] At first the defenders seemed to hold their own on the Aisne, the Oise and the Somme. "I have a hope," wrote Charles de Gaulle to his wife that day, "that the enemy's new effort will be less unfortunate for us than the first." But he advised her to look for somewhere to stay in the countryside of Brittany.*

At dawn the next day, 6 June, the friendly voice of General Delestraint woke de Gaulle at Marseille-en-Beauvaisis: "The radio says you are to join the government." Was de Gaulle surprised? His last contacts with Reynaud, their conversation of 1 June and the letter he had sent him on the third might have let him foresee this outcome. He had himself advised it.

Half an hour later a call from Paris confirmed the news: Reynaud told him to come without the least delay. At 11 a.m. Reynaud was waiting for him at the War Ministry in the rue Saint-Dominique, where Charles de Gaulle was to settle in with him, making one of the dreams of his life come true in the worst possible circumstances.

Here he was in the office of the little man he knew so well and whom he found "as usual, confident, lively, incisive, ready to listen, quick in judgment". The new Under-Secretary of State at once took the offensive: in a government brought together "to wage war", what was the point of including Marshal Pétain, who talked of nothing but immediate peace and who acted as a screen for those in favour of giving up? "Better have him in than out," observed Reynaud.

De Gaulle peppered him with arguments to the contrary and denounced the spread of defeatism, which "might engulf everything". (Everyone knew that a good third of the members of the government and half the Prime Minister's immediate associates had been wholly won over to the notion of a rapid end to hostilities.) Although de Gaulle admitted that "the war was lost" in metropolitan France, he did so only to go on that the struggle must be continued "in the empire". That at least is the summary of his words to Reynaud which he gives in his *Mémoires de guerre*, forgetting to speak of the "Breton redoubt", an idea of which he was if not the inventor then at least an ardent supporter until about the middle of June.

What was its nature? The plan, which was conceived during the darkest days of May (about the twenty-fifth), aimed at gathering forces on the rivers Vilaine and Rance in Brittany that would be capable of holding a redoubt there, from which it would be possible to "join hands with Britain and the United States", thus

*Some days later Yvonne de Gaulle and her daughters moved to Carantec, north of Morlaix (Finistère).

preserving if not the possibility of a prolonged resistance then at any rate the means of direct contact with London and of an orderly embarkment of the state machinery and of important forces for the United Kingdom or Africa. A prefabricated Dunkirk.

A futile idea? It has often been so called. Dominique Leca, who of all Reynaud's associates was to give Charles de Gaulle credit for his historic imagination in the fairest manner says:

> The plan had an unquestionable symbolic value. [But] The Breton lure continually perturbed people's minds and behaviour in the most unbelievable way between 31 May and 13 June. Reynaud was often forced to see how at certain times the Brittany solution and its futility in practice discredited the spirit of resistance.[2]

During the afternoon of 6 June the premier gathered the new ministers and those who had changed office – the only sensation provided by the reshuffle being Daladier's elimination – for the traditional photograph on the official steps. Behind a squad of grey-headed Radicals and of prominent men whose faces were stupefied by the tragedy all around them,[3] might be seen a strange character, a tall lone wolf, morose, two stars* on his képi, dark-eyed, wearing a scornful pout and carrying a pair of white gloves in his hand: the Constable had become an Under-Secretary of State.

But not without causing a stir once more. "His appointment," says Reynaud in his *Mémoires*, "displeased Pétain, who told me a story about a book written in collaboration with him. It displeased Weygand even more. 'What do you have against him?' – 'He's a mere child.' " The two old leaders were not just displeased at the sight of de Gaulle becoming a member of the government, but exasperated.

Pétain did not confine himself to obstructing de Gaulle in the government. He poured his bile into the willing ear of a foreigner who was already playing a role of the first importance, Sir Edward Spears, whom Churchill had appointed his personal representative with the French government. Spears had been a liaison-officer in Pétain's headquarters during 1917; he had been present at the great days of Verdun and the Marshal therefore treated him with particular favour. "De Gaulle's appointment," he confided to this foreign observer, "is not going to help matters. His vanity leads him to think the art of war has no secrets for him. He might have invented it. Not only is he vain, he is ungrateful. He has few friends in the army."[4]

He had not many among the premier's associates, either. The passage that Paul de Villelume devotes to this event ought to be read:

> De Gaulle came into my office. The first thing he did was to tell me how happy he was to have me under his orders. I instantly told him that I was in no way subordinate to him. To Paul Reynaud, Baudouin and I painted the liveliest, most disturbing picture of his new colleague's boundless ambition.

*The mark of a *général de brigade*, the most junior. (trs.)

"But what more can he want?" "Your place, Monsieur le Président." An enigmatic smile told us we had failed. It now appeared that we should find it hard to diminish the effects of this appointment, which was a downright catastrophe. (Roland de) Margerie* was obviously largely responsible for it. He was a supporter of fighting to the bitter end and he had wanted to find an ally against Baudouin and me, to whom the necessity of asking for an armistice seemed more urgent every day.[5]

Leca tells how, on 7 June, he walked into the office that had just been allotted to de Gaulle; he did not find him there, but looking into the garden he saw him having himself photographed by the press. This was Leca's illuminating comment:

In 1940 he knew that France would have a vital need for a resurrection myth that was the essential thing. That everything else – the exodus and the lost battles – amounted only to details, of no account in comparison with the future rising-up out of the moral abyss into which everything appeared to be sinking.[6]

De Gaulle had not waited for the disaster and his own rise to the heights to bring the press into play, and the press returned the compliment handsomely. During the following days, from *L'Action française* to *Le Populaire*, there were nothing but respectful marks of interest and tributes of admiration for the new Under-Secretary of State, whose name, the day before, had been unknown to more than one journalist in a hundred. On the Right *Le Matin* wrote: "General de Gaulle is not only one of the shining lights of the army; he is that very light which illuminates the darkest ways. Never had a more truly prophetic voice called in the wilderness." On the Left, *Le Populaire* said: "M. de Gaulle is a thinker at the same time as a soldier; it may even be said that he is a systematic theoretician. But it so happens that in these last nine months events have provided his theories with a cruel and glaring confirmation."

What Under-Secretary of State joining a government has ever raised such a chorus of praise? For his entry into the circles of political power it may be said that from the very beginning Charles de Gaulle had the advantage of a brass band which from that moment on, and whatever the tune, never diminished it's volume except to draw breath.

But the most remarkable comment on the Constable's joining the government was quite certainly that of *The Times* for 8 June:

From the military point of view, M. Paul Reynaud's most interesting innovation is the appointment of General de Gaulle, who attracted the attention of the army world by his books. Rather aggressively "right-wing", a powerful theoretician, and an almost fanatical advocate of the massive use of tanks, he is a man with an enlightened and penetrating mind, a man of action and at the same time of dreams and abstraction.

*Reynaud's principal private secretary for diplomatic affairs.

A striking comment, and one that contains the seed of many of the arguments to be used in future days.

There he was in position, with the limelight full upon him. He hastily built up a team whose smallness, it must be admitted, is surprising. This man who had been familiar with the corridors of power and who knew the military intelligentsia from the inside did not bring together the group that the circumstances seem to have called for. Did he meet with refusals from those who thought the position too disastrous to launch into the adventure, or with snubs from comrades vexed at the idea of playing second fiddle to him?

Of all those whom one would have expected to find, the only men present were his faithful friend Jean Auburtin and the journalist Charles Giron, who had been under his orders at Metz: the head of his military staff was a Colonel Humbert, who vanished from the story almost at once, and of his civil staff Jean Laurent, the Director-General of the Bank of Indo-China, recommended by Palewski.

But there was also a young cavalry lieutenant by the name of Geoffroy Chaudron de Courcel. He had been a secretary in the Athens embassy and in September 1939 he was mobilized at Beirut; then happening to be on leave in Paris at the beginning of May 1940 he was posted by General Weygand, his former chief in the Levant to the new secretary of state's office: De Gaulle had particularly asked the staff to provide him with "an English-speaking diplomat" as an ADC.[7] It so happened that Courcel answered this description, that he was an ardent advocate of fighting to the end, and that he had read *Vers l'armée de métier*. From now on he became part of this long tale.

Here is Jean Auburtin's account of the Under-Secretary of State entering upon his duties:

> On 7 June I took up my post in the rue Saint-Dominique, which was in a state of the wildest turmoil, crowded with officers, journalists and members of the ministerial staffs – those belonging to Reynaud, whose office as War Minister was on the first floor, and those belonging to de Gaulle, on the ground floor. Though voices were kept low, there was passionate discussion of the disastrous news. All at once there was a silence: a tall form appeared in the doorway and de Gaulle strode towards a wall-map upon which was shown, like so many arrows thrust into the country's flesh, the shattering advance of the Panzers across the Somme and towards the Seine. He made a short commentary, speaking with an almost unbelievable composure that restored a little calm.[8]

Charles de Gaulle's mission, defined on 6 June, was on the one hand to organize the rear in close collaboration with Robert Schuman,* his opposite number in charge of refugees, and on the other to ensure coordination with London for the continuation of the war, wherever it might be. "On 26 and 31 May I may have

*Who was to head three governments and become a founder of the European Community. (trs.)

given [our allies] the impression that we did not exclude the possibility of an armistice," Reynaud told him, "But now, on the contrary, it is a matter of convincing the British that we shall hold out, whatever happens, even overseas if necessary. You will see Churchill."[9]

Before leaving for London, de Gaulle had to speak to the two men who at that time were seen by public opinion as the embodiment of all France's warlike activity, Pétain and Weygand. The appointment with the Marshal at the Invalides for 8 June was cancelled because of a mishap. But on the same day the Under-Secretary of State for War was received by General Weygand at the Commander-in-Chief's forward command-post, the Château de Montry. De Gaulle described the meeting in his *Mémoires*:

> I found the Commander-in-Chief calm and self-contained. But a few minutes of conversation were enough to make me understand that he had resigned himself to defeat and that he was resolved upon an armistice.
>
> "A few days ago* I told you the Germans would attack on the Somme on 6 June. And indeed they are attacking. At this moment they are crossing the river. I am unable to prevent them."
>
> "Very well. They are crossing the Somme. What then?"
>
> "What then? The Seine and the Marne."
>
> "Yes. And what then?"
>
> "Then? But that's the end!"
>
> "What do you mean, the end? What about the rest of the world? What about the empire?"
>
> General Weygand broke into a despairing laugh. "The empire? But that's childishness! As for the rest of the world, once I've been beaten here, Britain won't wait a week before negotiating with the Reich." The Commander-in-Chief looked me straight in the eye and added: "Ah! If only I could be sure the Germans would leave me enough men to maintain order."[10]

General Weygand's comment on this account of their meeting was strongly worded:

> I deny the authenticity of this dialogue aping Corneille – "*A moi, comte, deux mots.*"** I should never have borne the indecency of it. Furthermore, during this interview there was at no time any question of England's attitude or of negotiations with the Germans. As for my laugh, if it seemed desperate, that was because I was unable to bring a man back to the requirements of the present moment when he was breaking away from them by talking of other things."[11]

The context and many accounts of the attitudes and the words of the two men during the first fortnight of June tend to substantiate Charles de Gaulle's account

*On 1 June: see p. 187.

**These are Rodrigue's peremptory words to his fiancée's father in Corneille's *Le Cid.* (trs.)

if not his way of phrasing it. As for the subjects touched upon and the attitudes adopted ("childishness", English defeat, maintenance of order), there may have been, ten or twelve years later, a too artistic reconstruction on the part of the author of *Mémoires de guerre*. But in all this where can one find any trace of the "indecency" that Foch's former lieutenant would have been unable to hear? De Gaulle did sometimes maltreat illustrious men most improperly when he was talking to them. But not here, where Weygand maltreats himself quite unaided.

Before leaving for London, de Gaulle studied the possibilities of a very large-scale withdrawal to North Africa. The services put the number of men who could be transported at about half a million, provided that the navy moved quickly, that bomber command gathered all its means together, and that the British fleet helped with the operation. Quite certainly nothing more could be undertaken without the agreement and the support of the allies on the other side of the Channel. It was in this frame of mind that General de Gaulle took off for his first journey to London on 9 June, together with his ADC, Courcel, and Roland de Margerie, the head of Reynaud's diplomatic staff.

It is from this diplomat – who, according to Villelume, as we have seen, was a prime mover in the raising of Charles de Gaulle to great political responsibilities, and who, in the following weeks, was to play a most important role in the party of those who wanted to fight to the end – that the account of the expedition will be taken in the first place. The travellers left Le Bourget in a special Air France plane, reached London, lunched at the Embassy, and were received by the Prime Minister at 10 Downing Street:[12] "Churchill rose at once and began to walk up and down, his hands behind his back, literally fuming, talking an extraordinary language, half French, half English. Our heads turned from right to left, left to right and I really had the feeling of being at a tennis match."

At last de Gaulle was able to speak and he passionately urged Churchill to throw the RAF into the Battle of France immediately. To this the Prime Minister objected that the front was moving away from Britain and that fighting close to the British coast "paid better dividends": for one plane shot down far from here, he said, our airmen bring down five in the approaches to our island.

Upon this de Gaulle took his leave, conscious of having failed in his short-term mission, which was to obtain an increase in the British forces, above all the RAF, engaged in the defence of France. Everything leads one to suppose that the eloquence of the man who, in the House of Commons five days later, stated that Britain would fight to the end, "on the beaches and in the hills", convinced him.

Was it that day, as he left Downing Street, that he said to Churchill, "It is you who are right!" or was it on 16 June, when he returned to Bordeaux? Spears gives 9 June as the date, which provides one with a higher notion of Charles de Gaulle's capacity for adapting himself to the requirements of reality, whatever General Weygand might say. In these hours of anguish, for such an uncomprising nationalist to understand that the defence of the still free British Isles was of more importance to the final and collective victory than a respite granted to a collapsing France, was to display a far from ordinary clear-sightedness. A clear-sightedness that was all the more worthy of praise in that the visitor had not failed to be irritated – his *Mémoires* show it[13] – by London's look "of tranquillity, almost of indifference" (he was seeing the capital for the first time, and it was a Sunday), contrasted with the tragic upheaval of the towns in France. "It was clear that in the opinion of the British the Channel was still wide."

Churchill and de Gaulle parted well pleased with one another. The Prime Minister, who for three weeks past had been terribly disappointed by the French High Command, had at last met this "general with an attacking spirit" that Reynaud had promised to find him. As for the visitor, his impression of the British war-leader can be seen in the admirable portrait in the *Mémoires de guerre*, a portrait that he chose to place as early as their first meeting, as though Churchill had at once appeared to him in his entirety and all his grandeur, indivisible and formidable – and one is tempted to say incorrigible:

> Churchill seemed to me equal to dealing with the most arduous task, so long as it was also grandiose. His character fitted him for action, for running risks, for playing his part whole-heartedly and without scruple. I thought him perfectly at ease in his post of guide and leader. From the beginning to the end of the drama, Winston Churchill appeared to me as the great champion of a great undertaking and the great actor in a great History.[14]

Before returning to France, Paul Reynaud's envoys saw Anthony Eden, the Minister of War, the other chiefs of the British military effort, and then Jean Monnet, who presided over the Franco-British committee for the purchase of war material. They had no sooner landed at Le Bourget – the airfield was littered with unexploded bombs – when in the dead of night (the night of 9–10 June) de Gaulle was urgently summoned by the head of the government: advanced parties of the enemy had reached the Seine, the Champagne front was collapsing, Paris was immediately threatened and Italy was going to enter the war.

Did de Gaulle speak of the Breton redoubt again at this point? Perhaps so. But in his *Mémoires* there is no question of anything but a withdrawal to Africa: he urged the premier to decide upon it. He could derive no hope of a solution in metropolitan France from his visits that day to some of the chief personages of the state, beginning with President Lebrun. And as he always or almost always did, he summed up what had been a long and confused series of harsh political and strategic arguments in one striking phrase: "A repetition of the recovery on the Marne was possible, but only on the Mediterranean."

"Day of extreme anguish," he wrote of 10 June, a day which after Mussolini's entry into the war and before the government's exodus (a movement which may have been decided by those at the top or which may have been carried out like a call of nature: no one knew) was marked by a fresh conflict between Weygand and himself: once more they gave contradictory accounts. The Constable, who speaks of only one meeting, whereas there were two that day, one being at the defence committee, describes Weygand walking unceremoniously into Paul Reynaud's office and in de Gaulle's presence handing him a memorandum designed "at clearly establishing the responsibilities of each person" and advising that an armistice should rapidly be sought. "There are other prospects," said de Gaulle. To this the Commander-in-Chief replied "in a scoffing tone, 'Have you anything to suggest?' – 'The government,' I answered, 'has not suggestions to make but orders to give. I rely upon it to give them.' "[15]

It was at about 11 p.m. on 10 June, and after the departure of the majority of the members of the government and outstanding politicians, that Paul Reynaud and Charles de Gaulle left Paris, which had been declared an open city, against the advice of the Under-Secretary of State, who would have liked to see it stubbornly defended by General de Lattre. They reached Orleans and then steered for Tours, which was to be the provisional centre of a constellation of châteaux taken over as refuges: le Muguet, near Briare, which received Weygand; Cangé, where Lebrun settled in; Chissay, Reynaud's camping-place; Beauvais, where de Gaulle took up his inn; Villandry and la Châtaignerie, which were turned into asylums for the Quai d'Orsay. At the prefecture of Tours, the centre of this arrangement, Georges Mandel was trying to reorganize the means of action that in principle belonged to a minister of the interior.

Among a thousand other problems, all tragic, two of the first priority faced the Reynaud–de Gaulle team: that of the Supreme Command and that of the government's subsequent destination – the Loire was obviously not a line upon which a stand could be made.

The country's future for months if not for years depended on whether the government retained as Commander-in-Chief a man who, like many others, thought defeat inevitable and who seemed less anxious to mitigate its effects than to throw the responsibility for it on to a political world that he despised, and on whether it decided to go to Bordeaux (where there hovered the shadow of 1870*) or Brest, a bridgehead for the open sea.

De Gaulle was intensely eager to settle the first question before anything else by replacing Weygand with General Huntzinger, Commander of the central group of armies. While Reynaud was driving towards Briare, where a meeting with Winston Churchill had been fixed for 5 p.m., the Under-Secretary of State hurried off to Arcis-sur-Aube, Huntziger's headquarters. De Gaulle, confirmed in his views by the coolness that the general displayed in the midst of disaster, offered him Weygand's place straight away; and, he says in his *Mémoires*, it was accepted immediately. The move never transpired, for in the increasing confusion Reynaud would not carry it through.

Furthermore, Huntziger gave a completely different version of the matter. According to the *Mémoires* of Henri Massis the commander of the central armies talked about this visit, laughing as he did so. It had seemed to him above all "amusing", not because of the promotion offered but because of the mission that was to be carried out: it was a question of regrouping our forces "in the Cotentin, or failing that, in the Brittany peninsula." Ironically, Huntziger was the man who signed the Armistice two weeks later and became Pétain's War Minister.

* * *

*The French government evacuated to Bordeaux during the Franco-German War.

From the Aube to the Loire, the Constable once more travelled across a world of horror: troops "without a shepherd", as he put it. On the encumbered roads one could get along only by passing through wretchedness and affliction. He reached Briare by the end of the afternoon. As he made his way into the château du Muguet he met Pétain, whom he had not seen for two years. "You are a general," said the old leader. "I don't congratulate you. What's the use of rank during a defeat?" "But, Marshal, it was during the retreat of 1914 that you yourself were given your first stars." "No comparison," growled Pétain. The Constable's comment: "On this point, he was right."[16]

Here he was, sitting at the end of the table during the meeting, at 7 p.m. on 11 June 1940, in the Château du Muguet, of the Supreme Inter-Allied Command.* On the British side, Winston Churchill, Anthony Eden, General Sir John Dill, Chief of the Imperial General Staff, General Ismay, of the War Cabinet secretariat, and General Spears, Churchill's personal envoy. On the French side, Reynaud, Pétain, Weygand, General Georges (invited at the request of Churchill, who had confidence in him), Villelume and Margerie. (De Gaulle was present only at the first part of the session, that on the evening of the eleventh. When it began again the next morning, he had already left for Rennes.)

What appears most clearly from the various accounts of this supremely important meeting is the progress of the alliance's dissolution. General Weygand's report – much less defeatist, when one reads the text, than de Gaulle describes it, although it does speak of a "last quarter of an hour" which could not refer to the enemy – was heavy with half-expressed accusations about the isolation in which his army was fighting, deprived of its allies' support. Pétain brought the tension to its height by saying, in reply to a remark of Churchill's about the brotherhood of arms in 1918, that he had then come to the help of General Gough with forty divisions: "Now it is we who are being cut to pieces, where are *your* forty divisions?" And when Churchill suggested resorting to guerrilla warfare, the Marshal roughly interrupted "That would be the destruction of the country."

The British Prime Minister did not speak only of guerrilla warfare. Having called to mind the "nightmare question" of the future of the French fleet, again and again he urged the setting up of "a bridgehead on the Atlantic"; this was a revival of the Breton redoubt, and General de Gaulle was charged with looking into it the next day. Throughout this meeting de Gaulle made a deep impression on the visitors, although his observations had only been of a technical nature. Spears sums it up thus:

> He was calm, self-contained, absolutely unflustered. The British civilians and soldiers were delighted to see that Reynaud had the support of this vigorous character. The Frenchmen's faces were pale, their eyes fixed on the table. They really looked like prisoners who had been brought out of their cells to hear the inevitable verdict. Looking around for a less discouraging

*De Gaulle maintains that it was Weygand who took the initiative of "summoning" the British Prime Minister. From Reynaud's and Churchill's memoirs it appears that the proposal came from London.

> sight, I turned towards de Gaulle. He was the only one of his compatriots to show a coolness that might be compared to that of the British.*

And Spears adds, "The Prime Minister, who seemed to be searching for something in the Frenchmen's faces, looked at de Gaulle several times, and there he appeared to have found what he was looking for at last."

For his part, Churchill, who was able to talk to de Gaulle during dinner as Reynaud placed him on his left, says, "General de Gaulle, who had attended the conference, was in favour of carrying on a guerrilla warfare. He was young and energetic and had made a very favourable impression on me. I thought it probable that if the present line collapsed Reynaud would turn to him to take command." A matching comment from Charles de Gaulle: "Our conversation strengthened the confidence that I had in his will-power. He no doubt gathered from it that de Gaulle, though deprived of means, was no less resolute."[17]

At dawn next day de Gaulle left before the session began again, travelling to Rennes, where, with General René Altmeyer, he presided over a conference dealing with the possible setting up of the Breton redoubt. Although he very carefully describes the events that made up these days of cardinal importance – the eleven days during which he was a member of the government, from 6 to 16 June – he does not mention this incident in Brittany, as though the recollection of anything to do with that wild fancy embarrassed him. At all events, on the military level the Rennes conference came to an abrupt end: a simple calculation of the remaining means was enough to decide the matter.

General de Gaulle went to the Château de Chissay, after his conversations at Rennes. Waiting for him was Reynaud, who had just presided over a cabinet meeting at Cangé, the residence of the head of state – a meeting at which Pétain and Weygand had at last clearly expressed their wish for an armistice without delay.

But at this point the most urgent question was that of the government's next destination: Quimper or Bordeaux? "I was in favour of Quimper, of course," says de Gaulle. "Not that I had any illusions about the possibility of holding out in Brittany [but because] sooner or later the government would have no solution but taking to the sea. Quimper was a stage towards energetic decisions."[18] They left for Bordeaux. Reynaud wrote Weygand a message, inspired by de Gaulle, calling upon him to hold out as long as possible "in the Massif Central and in Brittany" until "the struggle could be organized in the empire".

On 13 June, the general had a telephone-call from Roland de Margerie warning him of an Inter-Allied command meeting in the afternoon at Tours.

It is easy to imagine how de Gaulle hurried; but it was in vain – he was almost an hour late at the Tours meeting, where Reynaud was accompanied only by Baudouin and Margerie, while Churchill had with him Lord Halifax, the Foreign Secretary, Lord Beaverbrook, General Ismay, Spears and Sir Alexander Cadogan,

*The highest possible praise.

the Permanent Secretary of the Foreign Office, not counting Sir Ronald Campbell, the Ambassador. It was a meeting of the first importance, but one of which de Gaulle missed the essence, which greatly diminishes the value of his account.*

Reynaud told his astonished visitors that at yesterday's cabinet meeting General Weygand had said it was "necessary" to ask for an armistice. In consequence of this he asked his allies whether they would agree to release France from the undertaking of 28 March (the Reynaud-Chamberlain agreement forbidding any separate peace).

The British Prime Minister, who spoke in pidgin-French that disconcerted everyone, reacted vehemently: "We must fight, we shall fight, and that is why we must ask our friends to carry on with the struggle!" To this his French opposite number pointed out that he had not asked what Britain would do, which he knew perfectly well, but what the British cabinet would say if a French government ("to which I should not belong", as he wished to make quite clear) were to ask for a separate peace. Would it have to give up Great Britain's friendship and the future solidarity between the two countries?

Churchill's main reply which he made in French was this:

> I understand that you are going to ask for an armistice.** We shall not waste our time in recriminations. The French cause will always be dear to us and if we win the war we shall re-establish France in all her power and glory. But Great Britain cannot be asked to give up the solemn undertaking that binds the two countries.

Having said this, the Prime Minister, with tears in his eyes, asked to withdraw with his friends to consult them on a decision he did not wish to adopt by himself.

It was during this pause, and after the essential part of the encounter was over, that de Gaulle came into the room. This did not prevent him from saying in his *Mémoires* that Churchill, confronted with the prospect of an armistice, instead of "exploding" displayed a "compassionate understanding" and let it be understood that he might come to terms about the 28 March engagement in exchange for very solemn guarantees concerning the French fleet, that "nightmare question".[19]

For once the Constable had let himself be deceived by Paul Baudouin who, at the beginning of the adjournment suggested by the visitors, circulated a statement that the prime minister's words "I understand that you are going to ask for an armistice" should be interpreted as meaning "I understand that you should ask for an armistice".***

When a little later Churchill was asked by his special envoy about Baudouin's "translation", he did explode: "When I say *je comprends* that means 'I understand, I grasp;' it does not mean that I approve of what you are doing. The one time I use the right word in their language. Tell them my French is not as bad as all that."

It is strange that General de Gaulle should have seen fit to maintain a version in

*Here those of Churchill, Margerie and Spears have been used in preference to de Gaulle's.
**The French is *Je comprends que vous allez demander l'armistice.* (trs.)
***Baudouin's French is *Je comprends que vous demandiez l'armistice.* (trs.)

his *Mémoires*, that of "compassionate understanding", which the man who uttered the words denied straight away – a version which, sanctioned by Baudouin, was to be taken up for years on end by Vichy's spokesmen, according to whom it seemed that France had never been false to its promise, seeing that at Tours Churchill had shown his "comprehension".[20]

It was when he was leaving this conference that Churchill saw de Gaulle standing "solid and expressionless" at the doorway, and "said to him in a low tone, in French, *L'homme du destin*. He remained impassive". Did the general even hear these prophetic words? Had he "understood" the prime minister's statements an hour earlier better than Baudouin? Asked about this point a quarter of a century later, General de Gaulle replied, "I did not hear. What is true is that we took to one another right away, first in London, then at Briare and then at Tours."[21]

"Destiny" or not, it was that same evening, at a cabinet meeting held at Cangé, and before Reynaud had sent Roosevelt a hopeless appeal on Churchill's advice, that Marshal Pétain had to come to the rescue of Weygand, who had argued once again in favour of an armistice; and this Pétain did by standing up and reading a solemn proclamation which contained the whole of Vichy's ideology in embryo.

> The question that arises is not whether the government will ask for an armistice but whether it will agree to leave the soil of metropolitan France. I shall stay among the French people to share their sorrows and afflictions. As I see it an armistice is necessary for France's future existence. Suffering [must be] accepted. The rebirth of France will be the fruit of that suffering.

This time it was the old man, his fame and glory still apparently intact, the upholder of an argument calculated to appeal to a shipwrecked nation, who was throwing his entire weight into the scales. An irreparable defeat for those in favour of carrying on with the fight.

Already Charles de Gaulle had felt his confidence in the two men on whom everything then depended crumbling away: Churchill "compassionate" and Reynaud (momentarily) transformed into the spokesman of those who wanted an armistice. De Gaulle at once reproached him with it: "Is it possible that you should conceive of France asking for an armistice?" To which Reynaud meanly replied that he had only intended "to shock the British, in order to get more help from them". This was not only a most important psychological mistake (it did not tighten a bond: it did ruin confidence): it also brought a fundamental problem down to the level of mere expedients.

How could the Constable remain a member of a government that, at so crucial a time, was subject to such vacillations? He was preparing to write his letter of resignation to Paul Reynaud when Jean Laurent, his principal private secretary, who had hurriedly warned Georges Mandel, told him that the Minister of the Interior wished to see him.

In a tone "whose gravity and resolution impressed me", says the author of *Mémoires de guerre*, Mandel persuaded him not to resign: "In any case, we are only at the beginning of the world war. You will have great duties to perform, General! But you will perform them with the advantage of being the one man among us all, a man with an unblemished reputation. It may emerge that your present position will make things easier for you."[22]

At the time when the Minister of the Interior was persuading Charles de Gaulle to stay with Reynaud, "the wolves made their way into Paris": and they did so before the government got under way, leaving the Touraine at dawn on 14 June and travelling towards Bordeaux through a tide of jolting, sleepy people, pain-racked and lost – the refugees, civil and military. It was a sickening odyssey, and one that wholly confirmed the worst forebodings of de Gaulle for "national defence".

Arriving in Bordeaux, the Constable turned to Reynaud and said to him: "For three days now I have seen how fast we are moving towards capitulation. I have given you my modest help, but it was to make war. I refuse to submit to an armistice. If you stay here you are going to be overwhelmed by the defeat. You must reach Algiers as soon as possible. Are you determined to do so, yes or no?"[23] Stung by these threatening words, Reynaud replied by acknowledging that his colleague's most urgent task was to go to London as quickly as possible, there to secure the cooperation of the British in the huge transportation that would be required. "We shall meet again in Algiers!" he cried.

De Gaulle called on Admiral Darlan, whom the prime minister wanted to see the next day to speak about the fleet (from now on at the centre of the question, if only from the point of view of the passage to Africa), and whose attitude told him nothing worthwhile with regard to his will to resist; then he dined at the Hotel Splendide, where Paris and the Republic, society and the court, the press and what was then authority crowded together in a limitless gabble of rancour and intrigue, pain and resentment. Pétain was dining at a nearby table. In silence de Gaulle walked over to pay his respects. "He shook my hand, without a word. I was never to see him again, never."[24]

So at Reynaud's request he was to leave for London once more. "On the morning of the fourteenth," says Geoffroy de Courcel,

> We set about looking for a plane and a pilot. We did not find a single available machine in the hopelessly disorganized town. So the general decided to travel by road, which would allow him to get into contact with those responsible for the western defences at Rennes and to go and see his mother, who was very ill, at Paimpont. We drove all night, not saying a word. At Rennes we saw General René Altmeyer and the prefect. From there we went on to Paimpont, where the general saw his mother, who was obviously near her end; then, driving without a pause, on to Carantec, where Mme de Gaulle and her daughters had taken refuge. Brest at last, and there we went aboard the *Milan* for Plymouth, which we reached at dawn on 16 June.[25]

At Carantec de Gaulle had said to his wife, "Things are very bad. I am on my way to London; perhaps we are going to carry on the fight in Africa, but I think it more likely that everything is about to collapse. I am warning you so that you will be ready to leave at the first sign."[26]

Aboard the *Milan* he suddenly asked the captain, "Would you be prepared to fight under the British flag?" On reaching London a few hours later, he gave orders that the *Pasteur*, carrying a great cargo of weapons (including more than a thousand 75 mm guns) from the United States to France, should be diverted to a British port. He had already stopped thinking in "regional" terms: he had risen to the plane of world-strategy.*

In this field he was very soon to take a still more important and conspicuous step. On the morning of 16 June, while he was dressing in his room at the Hyde Park Hotel, almost next door to the French Embassy in London, Jean Monnet and Charles Corbin were announced: the first was the head of the Franco-British purchasing committee, the key man in Inter-Allied relations, the second the French ambassador. They were the bearers of a plan "capable of completely reversing the situation" which they asked him to get Reynaud to accept.

This was the well-known scheme for Anglo-French Union drawn up in the course of the previous week by that expert in multiple convergences Jean Monnet, in collaboration with his British friend Arthur Salter and with his assistant René Pleven. It had been worked over again with Desmond Morton and Horace Wilson, confidential colleagues of Churchill and Chamberlain, while on Saturday, the day before de Gaulle's arrival in London, it was submitted to high-ranking Englishmen such as Lord Halifax and Sir Robert Vansittart.[27]

Anglo-French Union would be a federation that would gather institutions common to both – parliament, Ministries of Foreign Affairs, Defence and Economy – in one "Union" under the direction of a single government, and that would group French and English in one common citizenship. Jean Monnet tells how Winston Churchill, reading his document on 15 June, "gave a start". He does not say whether Charles de Gaulle, in his hotel bedroom, did the same.

His two visitors stressed the point that the spirit of surrender was making rapid progress in Bordeaux and that the Cabinet meeting to be held in the course of the day would be "decisive". The right thing to do, therefore, was to bring about a dramatic event that would change the atmosphere and "strengthen Reynaud". Having said this they read him the Monnet plan. "I saw at once," says de Gaulle,

> that in any event the [document's] grandiose aspect did away with any quick translation into facts. It was obvious that a mere exchange of notes could not weld England and France into a single unit even supposing that it were desirable. But [it was] a demonstration of solidarity to bring Reynaud a strengthening element and, with regard to his ministers, an argument for holding out. I therefore agreed to try to induce Churchill to take it up.[28]

Ten years later, General de Gaulle summed up his feelings about the "grandiose" plan by saying, "It was a myth, made up like other myths, by Jean Monnet. Neither Churchill nor I had the least illusion."[29]

Illusion or not, the two men quickly met for luncheon at the Carlton Club with Corbin. Having assured Churchill that whatever happened the French fleet would

*When they heard of this decision, several members of Reynaud's government called for de Gaulle to be brought to trial.

not be handed over to Germany, Charles de Gaulle broached Monnet's plan. "It's a huge mouthful," growled Churchill. But the prime minister was too magnanimous to resist his visitor's arguments, prejudiced as he already was in favour of the union by Halifax, Vansittart, and his confidential adviser Major Morton.

Churchill therefore called an urgent cabinet-meeting at 10 Downing Street for 3 p.m. that Sunday 16 June, not without word being sent to Ambassador Campbell telling him to withdraw the note he had handed to Reynaud the day before, authorizing the French government to negotiate an armistice on condition that the French fleet should be removed "out of the enemy's reach".

Here the chief hand in the operation, Jean Monnet, must be allowed to speak:

> Vansittart had passed a copy [of the plan] to Lord Halifax, who asked him to give the document the necessary form for its production in the cabinet that afternoon. That was not the least of our difficulties that day. For the Cabinet to be able to discuss a scheme in a regular manner, it has to be produced in covers known as "red binding". But the Foreign Office was closed on Sunday and the civil servants on duty were absent. After a long search we found a "red binding" that answered, in spite of it being white.
>
> Churchill was perfectly fair; he did not hide his own objections from his colleagues but he nevertheless urged them to make this gesture, which would strike people's minds. "In a time as grave as this," he told me, "it shall not be said that we lacked imagination." I can see him now, in a grey suit with pink stripes, a cigar in his mouth, coming out of the cabinet to talk to us, treating this whole business with a negligent air. This was his way of being superior.[30]

De Gaulle, who was waiting in a room next to the Cabinet, saw the doors open and Churchill came towards him,* beaming: "We agree!" (According to the account of his secretary, Sir John Colville.) The Prime Minister is also said to have added, speaking to de Gaulle, "If you like, you shall be our Commander-in-Chief!"

In the Cabinet room, filled with Churchill's ministers and assistants, Charles de Gaulle telephoned Bordeaux. Roland de Margerie took the call: "Tell Reynaud that if he wishes he can be Prime Minister of France and Great Britain combined!" Reynaud, puzzled, said "What can he possibly mean?" They were cut off.

A few minutes later, while he was receiving Ambassador Campbell and General Spears, Reynaud picked up the telephone again. Again it was de Gaulle in London, who read him a document so astonishing that he feverishly took notes: "From now on, France and Great Britain will no longer be two nations but one single Franco-Britannic Union." He interrupted: "What you are telling me now, is it you who says it or is it Churchill?" A few seconds passed and Churchill came on the line, for Reynaud was heard saying "Good evening, Prime Minister," to the speaker on the far side of the sea, who said, "It is de Gaulle who is right! Our

*Here one should note the extraordinary and so typically Gaullian way of putting it in *Mémoires de Guerre*. Describing Churchill and his ministers leaving the Cabinet room, de Gaulle says, "They all came in". A prodigious manifestation of egocentricity.

proposal may have very important consequences. It is essential to hold out!" And Churchill confirmed the appointment that had already been arranged for a Supreme Inter-Allied command meeting (henceforward a Home Affairs matter?) the next day at Concarneau.

"Reynaud was transfigured!" says Spears, who was present at the scene. He called a Cabinet meeting at once. The sitting, which began a little after 5 p.m. brought together twenty-four ministers, who were to be faced with the most important choice in the country's modern history. For the Union or the Armistice? Reynaud lost no time in reading the notes he had taken during his conversation with de Gaulle in London, notes summing up the offer of a Franco-British Union, which had been ratified by the British government.

The premier's feelings in the next few minutes indeed received a "stunning blow". He had scarcely finished reading this document before he heard Marshal Pétain utter the words, "It's a marriage with a corpse!" And at the same time there rose excalamations such as, "We do not want to be a British dominion!"

Are we to believe in the observation attributed to Jean Ybarnegaray by Churchill in his memoirs? Spears (a hearsay witness in any case) was his source for the statement that the minister said, "Better be a Nazi province. At least we know what that means." To which Reynaud is said to have replied, "I prefer to collaborate with my allies rather than with my enemies."

Thus, on 16 June 1940, on the brink of the abyss, two dozen French ministers rejected the outstretched hand. Who can be surprised that Reynaud, so powerfully stimulated a few moments before, should have lost heart to the point of handing the head of the state his resignation? The blow was so cruel, so unexpected.

But the Cabinet did not confine itself to a scornful rejection of London's offer; they meant to dwell with greater emphasis upon a suggestion put forward the day before by Camille Chautemps, the vice-premier. According to this the government might properly ask the enemy the terms upon which an armistice would be granted, it being understood of course that if the requirements were so harsh that they could only be rejected then the State as a whole should move to North Africa. Nothing could have weakened the spirit of resistance more insidiously. So Monnet's splendid plan was wholly thrust into the background by the Chautemps proposal, the cunning stroke of an unscrupulous tactician and one better calculated for the capacities of the actors in a tragedy that was turning into a melodrama.

There was no vote. This, it was observed, was not according to custom. For in this breakdown of a state and a society custom still lived on. In the last forty years innumerable calculations have been made to find what majority would have resulted had each man given his decision in turn at Bordeaux. In that late afternoon of 16 June the cabinet was divided into three groups: those who were for resistance, those who hesitated, those who were for giving up. The first "third" amounted to some ten members (including Reynaud, Mandel and Campinchi), whereas the open supporters of an armistice were scarcely more than seven. There remained about eight who were undecided; and each hour brought them closer to surrender.

What is evident is that Reynaud thought himself placed in a minority, if only because his two vice-premiers, Pétain and Chautemps, were on the other side. He handed his resignation to the President of the Republic at the end of the first part of the cabinet-meeting, at about 8 p.m., and confirmed it at 9.30 p.m. during the adjournment of the sitting. This time Lebrun, who had refused his resignation three days earlier, accepted it, though not without hesitation. He too was an advocate of the move to North Africa.

To tell the truth, the little man was exhausted. He had reached the limits of his resistance, a resistance perpetually undermined not only by the enormous tragedy but also by sour private theatricals – the incessant assaults upon his will to fight mounted by the woman who shared every moment of his life, Hélène de Portes. A score of witnesses have spoken of the guerrilla warfare that she waged against the man she loved and admired in order to oblige him to forswear himself by bringing the fight to an end.

In these circumstances, General de Gaulle pays very noble homage in his *Mémoires de guerre* to the premier who could not keep the promises made to him and many others: "a man of great worth," he writes, "unjustly crushed by events beyond measure". It would have been less generous but fairer to add that a man charged with such immense responsibilities and assailed by trials that perhaps no one could have resisted, fell short of the duties of his office by allowing Madame de Portes to add such numbers of determined opponents of his policy to his staff, men whom he knew to be opposed to it, from Bouthillier to Baudouin and from Villelume to Prouvost.

Charles de Gaulle left London for France at 6.30 p.m. (two hours after speaking with Reynaud) on board a plane that Churchill placed at his disposal. Did he already have a third voyage to England in mind? Yes, since he believed in the adoption of the Anglo-French plan, which would make London, together with Algiers, one of the pivots of the joint war-effort. He does not specifically make this point in his *Mémoires*. Later he said that in his view, as in Churchill's, this return to London was "taken for granted".[31]

However that may be, Churchill did not let the Frenchman go without adding a fresh touch to the portrait of Charles de Gaulle that he painted with its lights and its shadows throughout his own memoirs: "Under an impassive, imperturbable demeanour he seemed to me to have a remarkable capacity for feeling pain. I preserved the impression, in contact with this very tall, phlegmatic man: 'Here is the Constable of France.' "

How did this well-known nickname come to be written by the British Prime Minister? Was it Monnet or Spears, Margerie or Darlan who had prompted him? Was it only the recollection of a man familiar with Shakespeare, whose scenes of battle and negotiation crackle with the military titles of the days of Henry V and the roses of York and Lancaster? The fact of the matter is the two men had taken to one another.

When the General's plane took off from London the Bordeaux Cabinet had already rejected the plan for the union and had confirmed their approval of Chautemps' scheme; France was going to ask Hitler on what terms the Third

Reich would grant an armistice. It was while de Gaulle was flying over the Atlantic coast that Paul Reynaud's government came to the end of its existence. But the other capital decision, the nomination of Pétain as head of the government, had not yet taken place.

As soon as President Lebrun had received the resignation of Reynaud, who felt that he could not reverse his opinions to the pitch of being the man who turned to the Führer to beg him to be so kind as to stop the fighting, he sent for the presidents of the two Chambers, the dual incarnation of the sovereign parliament,* Jeanneney and Herriot, to consult them on the name of his successor. The two most distinguished men of the republic at once replied, "Paul Reynaud". That meant completely blocking the Chautemps movement – and any other more evident motion – towards an armistice. And yet it was Pétain that the President summoned immediately after.

During Pétain's trial in 1945 Albert Lebrun pleaded that, "struck by the majority which had formed in the cabinet", he had done no more in calling upon Pétain than "give a decision according to the vote that had just been taken". Now we know that there had been no vote, that the majority was doubtful. Yet people who lived through those hours, above all at Bordeaux,** cannot but acknowledge that a kind of silent plebiscite compelled Albert Lebrun to make the choice he did – a choice that seems to have caused him little difficulty, fascinated as he was by the glory of the victor of Verdun, even though that legendary character was now speaking with the utmost clarity in favour of accepting defeat and against the carrying on of the war in North Africa which Lebrun supported, as did the three other presidents, Jeanneney, Herriot and Reynaud.***

What forced Pétain upon the weakness of Lebrun's nature and his constitutional position was the vast murmur to be heard throughout the town and the countryside, the lamentation that rose from the enormous torn and scattered herd that was then the French nation, turning towards the tutelary figure of the Marshal of Verdun as towards a reprieve. Apart from well-informed people, everyone, by the intermediary of the old man, merged the former victory and the present defeat. If he accepted it, that meant it was only an illusion. If he covered it so entirely, that meant France was not beaten but only submerged. There would be an appeal and the sentence would be reconsidered.

That evening, on the roads and in the attics and cellars where families were camping, as on the town's pavements crowded with refugees and in the fine houses whose silver might vanish with the coming of an enemy who was said to be behaving correctly at present but who would certainly be exasperated if the conquered would not help him in his task, one single unanimous outcry pointed to the Marshal. So Albert Lebrun, the archetypal "average" Frenchman, acted more like an average Frenchman than he had ever done in his life. It was to be Pétain, therefore.

*Which none of the chief authorities had dared summon at Bordeaux, for fear of making "too wretched an exhibition". The third president of parliament was Reynaud, the Prime Minister.

**This was the case with the present writer.

***None of them, it may be added – except for Jules Jeanneney – appears to have made any categorical objection to Lebrun's choice.

* * *

When Charles de Gaulle landed at the Mérignac airport at 10 p.m. on 16 June he was met by Colonel Humbert, who until then had been the chief of his military staff and who told him of Paul Reynaud's resignation: he was therefore no longer a member of the government.

At 10.30 p.m. the Marshal, on being appointed by the head of the State, at once brought the list of his ministers out of his pocket, a list that included the best-known supporters of an immediate armistice: Laval for Foreign Affairs,* Weygand for Defence, Darlan for the Navy, Bouthillier for Finances – an action that plunged Lebrun into simple-minded delight: this was quite certainly the easiest ministerial crisis that he had ever been called upon to resolve!**

Later that night, just before his visit to Paul Reynaud, de Gaulle learnt of the appointment of Philippe Pétain, the meaning of which he perfectly understood. "It was certain capitulation," he says in his *Mémoires*. "I made my decision at once. I should leave the next morning."[32]

*But Weygand, who despised him even more than the other "politicians", insisted upon his removal; which was temporary.

**Since then the former President has made it clear that the reason he resigned himself to calling Pétain was that he had been told that the Marshal had a team ready.

CHAPTER EIGHTEEN

The Decision

The breach between de Gaulle and the men of the night of 16 June can be broken down into dissidence, followed by revolt and crowned by the proclamation of an alternative legitimacy. The first phase is negative. It is the refusal of any political or military agreement with the conquering and occupying Hitler. De Gaulle, eliminated politically, deprived of any army posting and the holder of a doubtful rank, said "No" and went into exile – a symbolic reaction to the intolerable. At that time he was still wondering about the extent and the meaning of his act. It was only gradually that the mission he had assumed took shape. A shape that was determined by wills other than his own: he did not know who would come to join him, or take up a position superior to his.

This first phase of the decision, that of Bordeaux, the negative phase, the refusal to compromise, was itself spread over several days. On 9 June, when he saw Churchill and was able to weigh the Prime Minister's strong determination against the collapsing morale of those about Reynaud, and when he acknowledged that Churchill was right to keep the RAF's planes for the defence of Britain and not give them to de Gaulle and for the defence of France, he had already entered into spiritual dissidence.

Thus, on the evening of 17 June, he said to Jean Monnet, with whom he was staying in London, "There is no longer anything to be done in France. It is here that we shall work." And when Mme Monnet asked him what mission he was engaged upon, he replied, "I have not been sent on any mission, Madame. I am here to save the honour of France." But on 18 June the "irrevocable words" were still limited to the military sphere. On the nineteenth, it is true, the second radio speech began the great denial of the Bordeaux government's legitimacy. It was on 26 June, the day after the Armistice, when he sent Churchill a memorandum calling for the recognition of a French committee that was already a counter-government, that the decision was really taken and formal legality defied: one destroys only that which one supersedes.

The fact remains that by taking off from Bordeaux for London at 9 a.m. on 17 June Charles de Gaulle had, for all that matters, burnt his boats and defied the "order" on the capitulation that had been laid down. From that moment, as the forerunner of a movement or the leader of a rising, he had broken with formal legality, rejected the hierarchy and opened the case against the policy based on an armistice that was now and henceforth accepted by the Marshal. It was that moment of the decision which counted more than any of the rest. His hegira dates from the morning of 17 June.

* * *

Charles de Gaulle was in Bordeaux. An isolated figure who had just learnt that power had escaped from his friend Reynaud's hands and therefore from his own, and that the country's future had been handed over to a leader, henceforward all-powerful not only because of his glory of former days but even more because of his present humility. A power handed over not for action but for submission. De Gaulle had lost the game for the time being – for a long time being, and so, he thought, had France.

He had to see Paul Reynaud, who, now that he had handed President Lebrun his resignation, had withdrawn to his present solitude, while not far away Marshal Pétain, the new head of the government, presented his request for an armistice to his ministers; in twenty minutes they had approved it and that same night it was drawn up by Baudouin and sent to Madrid to be transmitted to Adolf Hitler.

"I found him without any illusions about what the Marshal's coming to power would entail and on the other hand he looked as though he had been relieved of an unbearable load. He gave me the impression of a man who had reached the limits of hope."[1] Perhaps a mistaken impression. Other people who were present at the time certainly thought Reynaud was exhausted, but as they saw it he had not quite given up looking upon himself as a resource, sure as he was of the confidence of Jeanneney, Herriot and France's allies – and with the certainty that Hitler's requirements would be unacceptable, so that Pétain's move was doomed to failure.

When he refused Spears' offer to take him back to London, Reynaud did so not only out of weariness or despair but because of the possibility of a recall, the prelude to a departure for North Africa.* In short, de Gaulle seeing him at the very moment he had just laid down his burden, saw in him no more than a broken man. But not broken to the point of not wishing to carry on with the fight.

Reynaud approved of his companion's decision to go to London, where perhaps he might join him one day. Churchill's plane was there. From that point of view everything was clear. Yet still there were certain problems that had to be solved. Should he leave? Yes. But when? With what means? With whom? By virtue of what "mission"?

When? It was essential to leave tomorrow morning. Because the German army would be at the gates of Bordeaux in the next two or three days. Because London's immense disappointment at the rejection of the offer of union, by Reynaud's resignation and the cancellation of the Concarneau meeting must as a matter of urgency by counterbalanced by a striking mark of solidarity, if the alliance was to be saved. Lastly, because General de Gaulle's personal position was far from secure.

Reynaud at once assured him that since he had the secret funds at his disposal until the handing-over of power the next day, he would allot a sum that would deal with de Gaulle's immediate expenses. Roland de Margerie was told to deal with the matter straight away – and also, at the general's request, to obtain passports for Yvonne de Gaulle and her daughters who were sheltering in Brittany, that would allow them to enter Great Britain: they received them the next day.

*A possibility that did not prevent him, some days later, from provisionally accepting Pétain's offer of the Washington embassy.

To leave with whom? A little later that night de Gaulle gathered some of his people, less with the intention of getting them to go with him than of informing them of his decision. Two showed a certain inclination to leave: Jean Laurent promised to join him very soon in London, and gave him the keys of his Mayfair flat; Major Chomel, posted to his department after having been his Chief of Staff in the 4th DCR for a fortnight, was persuaded not to go by the general himself, who reminded him of his duties towards his numerous family.[2] The others seem to have been reserved, including the faithful Auburtin, whose conduct the general did not resent in the least. "I did not want to take a whole tribe along," said de Gaulle at a later date.

As for the "mission" that de Gaulle was supposed to accomplish in Great Britain, it has been said that on 16 June Paul Reynaud was still charged with "carrying on current business" and he took it upon himself to draw an order meant for the traveller. This document has never been produced, either by de Gaulle, or by Reynaud, or by the diplomatic archives. Although the first letter de Gaulle sent from London on 17 June had, as we shall see, the tone of an official telegram, it will be assumed that the general left for London without any *ordre de mission*.

Since it was a question of London and of a British plane, it was important to have at least the approbation of those who represented Britain on the spot. The general's conversation with Paul Reynaud took place a little after 11 p.m. At about midnight Charles de Gaulle called at the Hotel Montré, at which wine-importers had stayed for many years past: it was here that Ambassador Campbell and General Spears had taken up their quarters.

Edward Spears was seven years older than Charles de Gaulle; he belonged to the upper-middle class and was a regular soldier. He had been a liaison-officer with the French General Staff in 1917; this had brought him into contact with Pétain, for whom he conceived a very great admiration. He was elected to parliament as a Conservative at the end of the twenties and he became much attached to Churchill, to whom he was devoted. Like Churchill, he was well known as a francophile, speaking French excellently and knowing everyone worth knowing in Paris and Nice.

It has uncharitably been said that he "loved France as one loves foie gras". This is unfair. He appreciated the art of living as it is understood in France; he moved about among the "right people"; he admired the romanesque churches and the landscapes of the Midi. He loathed the left wing, trade unions and "Gallic anarchism".

He conveyed de Gaulle to London and he thought that this gave him a right to the unalterable gratitude of Free France, which, for almost a year, he supported by his influence with Churchill, in a most devoted and efficacious manner. He never understood that the status thus acquired – and fully justified – did not give him all rights over those whom he had obliged.

But the bitterness that these incidents left in the minds of Sir Edward and his wife, the American novelist Mary Borden, led them to express opinions on de Gaulle and Free France even more acid than those on Spears with which the Gaullist legend overflows.

Churchill's special envoy, in his book, *The Fall of France*, gives an account of the dramatic night in Bordeaux before General de Gaulle's departure for London that is much more like an after-dinner conversation at the Reform Club, scented with cigar-smoke, than a piece of history. From this brilliant collection of anecdotes it appears that de Gaulle, lost in the night, overwhelmed by his country's defeat and the unworthiness of its leaders, and fleeing from arrest by Weygand's myrmidons, was taken in like a waif by the energetic, clear-minded and generous Sir Edward, who, having found him alone and horror-struck in the dim light of an ante-chamber, "behind a marble column", comforted him, restored his spirits and, having offered to put him up for the night in a British ship, persuaded him to leave for London – though not without having to hoist him aboard the plane, which he scarcely dared get into. In this role of a St Bernard rescuing de Gaulle General Spears is not convincing. It would have been enough for Churchill's envoy to record the facts, which were considerable, and which gave him a most important role in the history of the Liberation of France.

Towards midnight, then, Charles de Gaulle was received at the hôtel Montré by Campbell and Spears, whom he told of his intention to reach England as soon as possible, using the plane that the prime minister had put at his disposal the day before. They made an appointment to meet at 7.30 a.m. in the hall of the Hotel Normandy, where de Gaulle had at last found a room.

Meanwhile Spears made a last attempt at persuading Mandel to go to Britain too. The now ex-minister of the interior refused, saying that in time of national disaster a Jew, more than anyone, was required to stay on the country's soil: it was with the Algerian departments as a base that he wanted to carry on with the war.*

The next morning, then, a little after seven o'clock, de Gaulle and Spears met outside the Hotel Normandy; Jean Laurent was also waiting there, with the money Paul Reynaud had promised – 100 000 francs, Free France's first credit. Courcel also London-bound was present as well; de Gaulle, now more than ever before, needed an associate who was a diplomat and who spoke English.

They drove on to Mérignac in two cars, the one for the three travellers, the other for the baggage. The airfield was the scene of one of the most extraordinary states of disorder and confusion in this disintegrating war, an indescribable mass of people, something between a scrap-metal fair and a gypsy encampment. If de Gaulle had been afraid that military security would seize him just as he was about to take off, the sight that met the three travellers' eyes must have comforted him. The chaos was so great they could be sure of escaping in the little four-seater biplane with the RAF colours, in which the British pilot had slept.

Three passengers? Very well. But what about the luggage? One bag for Spears, two for de Gaulle, two for Courcel. The ADC had to run to a hangar to find a rope to tie on these bulky objects.

In his *Mémoires* de Gaulle says "the departure took place without romanticism or difficulty". Geoffroy de Courcel confirms this with the utmost clarity: "The

*Three days later, together with about thirty other parliamentarians, he went aboard the *Massilia*, bound for Morocco; and there he was forced to see that at that shameful time a Jew did not even have the right to leave metropolitan France for the empire. He was arrested at Casablanca before being handed over to the Nazis, who first deported him and then delivered him to the Milice.

General, lost in his thoughts, seemed scarcely to be concerned with the immediate present, still less with a possible arrest, but rather with what was awaiting him over there."[3]

"We flew over La Rochelle and Rochefort," says the author of the *Mémoires de guerre*. "In these ports were burning ships set on fire by German planes. We passed over Paimpont, where my very sick mother was living. The forest was filled with smoke from the stores of munitions that were burning there."[4] Then they made a stop at Jersey, where Sir Edward Spears' pen became more acute than it had been at Bordeaux: "I asked de Gaulle if he wanted anything, and he said he would like a cup of coffee. I handed it to him, whereupon taking a sip, he said that this was tea. It was his first introduction to the tepid liquid which, in England, passes for either one or the other. His martyrdom had begun."

Let us return to de Gaulle: "We reached London at the beginning of the afternoon. While I was taking up my quarters and Courcel, telephoning the embassy and the missions, was finding them already on their guard, I saw myself as alone and wholly unprovided, like a man on the shore of an ocean who maintains that he will cross it by swimming."[5] What the confused, feverish, contradictory and controverted events in that nocturnal Bordeaux which amidst the general collapse saw the birth of a "national revolution" do not tell us about is Charles de Gaulle's break with the legality of that collapse. As for the revolution, which was hardly to be national at all though openly anti-revolutionary, it came into being in that plashing of half-hearted acquiescence and that general post of furtive desertions and already conquering greed in which the Republic and even society was being engulfed. As for the break, seen in the context of its spirit and purpose, it was an action that has scarcely any precedent since the appearance of Sovereign States. Clausewitz going to Russia after Jena amounts to no more than an individual act; Rossel, who went over to the Commune in March 1871 in order to carry on with the fight, was after all only a subaltern, and he never claimed to embody legitimacy. Charles de Gaulle says little about it in his *Mémoires*, except where he speaks of himself delivering the appeal of 18 June: "As the irrevocable words took flight, I felt within myself the ending of a life, the life I had led in the framework of a solid France and an indivisible army. At forty-nine, I was entering upon adventure, like a man whom fate had thrown out of all regular patterns."[6] This text should be worked over almost word by word, but first it is proper to give the decision taken by Charles de Gaulle at Bordeaux on the night of 17 June 1940 its moral and psychological dimension.

André Malraux remained a novelist even though he affected to despise psychology, and when, ten years later, the general read him the first chapters of his recently-finished *Mémoires de guerre*, he pointed out to the author that these fine pages had scarcely anything to say about the inner arguments that must have torn him on 17 June, about that "storm within a skull". At this de Gaulle, taking his hands, said in his deepest voice, spacing out the syllables, "Oh Malraux, it was appalling."[7]

How could the youngest general in the French army have failed to bleed from his very depths at breaking with the rules, the affections and the principles of a life devoted, at least in appearance, to "the prime strength of armies", which is, as everyone knows, discipline? And how could this man in the prime of life and already marked out for the highest rank in the field have failed to suffer by breaking with the mangled body of the French army in the midst of a most horrible collapse, quitting the dismasted ship at the height of the storm? However harsh he may have been on the subject of Marshal Pétain's words and behaviour during those June days of 1940, he was also well aware that the demonstration of strict solidarity with the bewildered nation and the broken army and the determination to remain at their side had its grandeur and its necessity. It was not easy to renounce the bitterest task, that which also had to be accomplished on the soil of France.

"Appalling", therefore. Uprooting, exile, misunderstanding, scandal: his action contained countless cruel or dangerous implications and it might turn essential friendships and allegiances from him. Was it so obvious that his mother, told as early as the evening of 18 June of the appeal by the priest of Paimpont, would react by answering, "That is just like Charles. He has done what he ought to have done."[8]

But a man rarely does the contrary of what he is. So who then was the man who the next day would claim that Rome was no longer at Rome but wherever he was, in its entirety? Before certain words made him part of history he was, as we have seen, a man of *histoires*, of troubles and difficulties. In this turbulent career, the 18 June was neither a miracle nor a revolution. It was a paroxysm.

Maurice Schumann, basing himself on a number of conversations in London with his leader, observes that if Charles de Gaulle had remained within the framework of the army he would never have presumed to cross the Rubicon, and that it was his moving over into the political world on 6 June 1940 as a member of Reynaud's government that freed him from his last bonds and gave him the courage to disobey.[9] Is not opposition in the nature of the political calling?

But whatever he might say about it, on 18 June 1940 Charles de Gaulle was not "ending a life . . . lived in the framework of a solid France and of an indivisible army". For if ever there was a life led on the fringe of the routine activities and even of the prescribed practices, in a country whose fragility he continually denounced, and in the bosom of an army that was divided (by him in person, among others), then that life was his.

Let us go back to a few of the significant stages in this continual state of rebellion:

1912. Lieutenant de Gaulle, posted to the Arras regiment commanded by Colonel Pétain, a well-known theoretician of the superiority of fire-power over offensive – a thesis that proved prophetic in 1914 – fills his notebooks with praise of movement and attack, they alone being decisive in war. He is in complete intellectual dissidence with regard to this exceptional chief that fate had provided for him.

1917. At Ingolstadt, Captain de Gaulle, giving several lectures in the presence of field officers, does not hesitate to point out the strategic and tactical mistakes of the High Command from Charleroi to the trench-warfare in Champagne, as well as the murderous stupidity of the strategy of "gnawing away".

1924. At the Ecole de Guerre, Captain de Gaulle arrogantly maintains arguments in favour of tactics based upon circumstances, as opposed to the official teaching, and particularly against that of Colonel Moyrand, the professor of General Tactics and a theoretician of the a priori use of the terrain. He is the only person surprised by the low marks that this defiant attitude earns him. He proves to be not only a heretic but a relapsed heretic, since in an article published soon after he lashes the a priori doctrine, a dogma at the Ecole de Guerre.

1927. He returns to the Ecole de Guerre at the insistence of Marshal Pétain, who compels the teaching body to invite him to give three lectures on command. This "praise of character" in a "factory for turning out officers" can scarcely be taken as an incitement to discipline, since the "hero's" lofty form already possesses features that belong to him rather than to his official model, the old Marshal.

1928. He is called by Philippe Pétain to write a "history of the French soldier throughout the ages" which is meant to bear the august signature of the conqueror of Verdun; yet he claims not to "draft" but to "write" this document and to proclaim that he is at least in part the author. An unprecedented scandal with regard to a hierarchy in which subordination applies to "pen officers" as much as it does to Chiefs of Staff or orderlies.

1934. Lieutenant-Colonel de Gaulle, without asking his superiors for authorization, publishes *Vers l'armée de métier*, a work that boldly contradicts official doctrine; and not content with this he maintains and prolongs the dispute with the army chiefs, Pétain, Weygand, Maurin, Gamelin (and Daladier, the minister) by laying siege to the General Staff's conservatism with the help of non-conformist parliamentarians such as Paul Reynaud, left-wing deputies such as Philippe Serre, Marcel Déat and Léo Lagrange, "heretical" officers like Colonel Mayer, and journalists like Pironneau: a Fronde against the military establishment.*

1938. An important publisher having asked him to write a book on the army, he presumes to resuscitate the piece on the "Soldier" drafted twelve years before at the request of Pétain and buried by the old leader after their disagreement over its paternity. There is no doubt that de Gaulle is the author of the book (particularly in its revised form) that he calls *La France et son armée*. But at this point he treats his former chief, a legendary, untouchable character, offhandedly and he clashes with the ways and customs of the intelligentsia of the army. Since when has a vassal insisted that his lord should give him his due? He, de Gaulle, does so, thus breaking for good with his old leader, who up until then had treated him with unbounded good will.

January 1940. In the midst of the war this colonel sends the country's most distinguished men a tract denouncing the General Staff's incapacity and blindness. He calls upon these men to step in as soon as possible to compel the High Command to adopt a strategy contrary to that which it has laid down. De Gaulle is the officer who, in the presence of the enemy, cries "Your leaders are inept, and you are disarmed!"

24 May 1940. This time the battle is raging, and at the head of the 4th Armoured Division Colonel de Gaulle has just proved, in the neighbourhood of

*The Fronde (1648–52), the aristocratic rebellion against the unpopular government of Cardinal Mazarin. (trs.)

Laon, that the French army, equipped with the "fighting engine" and using it in large numbers, can hold its own against Adolf Hitler's Panzers. But he is not satisfied with letting facts speak for themselves. He hurries to his superior officer, General Touchon, the commander of the 6th Army, and asks to be given two or three other divisions to try to link up the armies of the centre and those of the north, a complete disruption of the battle-plan that Weygand is setting up in place of Gamelin's.

16 June 1940. In London, at the beginning of his last mission as a member of the government, he presumes, without referring to the Prime Minister, to divert the *Pasteur*, a ship bound for France with a large quantity of arms bought in the States, to Britain.

One could not imagine a more perfect career for an insurgent, nor one that foretells a more flamboyant rebel. Charles de Gaulle seems to have done his very best to be a rebel. In him the man of character seems to be able to find expression only in challenge and refusal.

On 17 June 1940 fate did not strike Charles de Gaulle with a thunderbolt and hurl him into an opposite course. On the collective and mythical level he bore a character that he had been shaping, armouring and sharpening for more than twenty years – the character of the superior man who is aware of his superiority, who does not hamper himself with any hierarchies but who on the contrary flies out against them. A character who believes himself to be so profoundly in tune with the national interest that he finds a justification for each one of his actions and who does not consider any proceedings unworthy if they are of such a kind as to ensure the triumph of his arguments – the arguments being legitimate since he himself was legitimacy.

A highly sensitive nationalist, a fighting patriot, a repressed theoretician, everything led him to refuse to admit the defeat and to do so with the mocking serenity that the old Marshal brought to it ("I told you so!").

For Charles de Gaulle, June 1940 was less the relevation of the army's bankruptcy – he had long since weighed it up and in its collapse he saw nothing but a consequence – than the deliquescence of the State. The sight of Reynaud reduced to impotence, to dubious shifts and to a resignation in favour of his worst opponents, was, for de Gaulle, a most striking symbol of the downfall not of a man who retained his esteem but of the State itself. It was not only because those of Bordeaux had adopted a policy contrary to what he believed right for the honour and the interests of France that the Constable removed himself; it was also because he felt his life's ideal gradually crumbling away beneath his feet, that is to say a State which expressed and which by the most varied paths and ideologies served the unchangeable, incorruptible French nation. Yet on a humbler level there was also this reply to one of his first companions in Britain, who asked him whether his refusal had been based more upon a feeling of honour or upon common sense: "Much simpler than that; I had the sight of treason there before my eyes, and in my heart a disgusted refusal to acknowledge its victory. That's all."

* * *

The passenger in Winston Churchill's little biplane that was coming down over a London airfield that 17 June was a rebel, an insurgent in essence and constitution. But it was circumstances that were about to give this rebellion the meaning of a new legitimacy. Charles de Gaulle was to use the challenges and refusals that had permeated his career in the French state and the army to people his world and, for four years on end, to form the basis for a strategy of myths and words.

Like Chateaubriand he knew that it was advisable "to lead the French by dreams". Like Bonaparte he was to learn "to make his plans out of the visions of his sleeping soldiers". For four years the words coming from London were to be the night-voice of the imaginary – that spiritual rebellion against reality which may also be reality's prefiguration.

1. Charles, aged five, with curls.
2. Charles, aged ten, and already wearing a stiff collar.
3. Charles, aged fifteen, already thinking about General de Gaulle.

4. Henri de Gaulle, “man of culture, thought, and tradition”.
5. Jeanne Maillot-de Gaulle: of ice and fire.
6. Philippe de Gaulle: a family air.
7. Pierre de Gaulle, the last of the brothers.

8. 1914: a lieutenant squaring up to a shooting war.
9. 1917: Captain de Gaulle between two escape attempts.

10. Emile Mayer.
11. Lucien Nachin.
12. Paul Reynaud.

13. In the absence of armoured divisions, a microphone is a weapon.

14. At Carlton Gardens, a "certain idea of France" took shape.

15. Jean Moulin.
16. Pierre Brossolette.
17. General Delestraint.
18. Emmanuel d'Astier.

19. The admiral and the general: profoundly incompatible temperaments.
20. En route for Dakar: France in adversity.
21. Mme de Gaulle and her husband pose for the English press.

22. With George VI, faithful friend through thick and thin.
23. In the Levant, with the "Tcherkesses de Collet".
24. As portrayed by Nazi propaganda.

25. In Algiers, the president of CFLN next to Henri Frenay (behind them, Tixier, Jacquinot, René Mayer, Henri Bonnet).
26. Between Giraud and Catroux.
27. Somewhere at sea . . .

28. In Brazzaville, beside Félix Eboué.
29. In what light did he see Winston Churchill?
30. Eisenhower, without whom . . .
31. France has come back to Paris. De Gaulle to Leclerc: "You're in luck."

32. De Gaulle and military discipline. An unpublished letter to his friend André Lecomte; 1936.

22/10/36. Paris, 110 Bd Raspail VI.

Cher ami,

On dit parfois que l'armée de métier pourrait menacer, demain, les institutions. Mais c'est avec une armée de métier (Garde Mobile), sans [illegible] Mobiles, qu'on maintient aujourd'hui l'ordre public, même sur le Pont de la Concorde le 6 février. Quant aux troupes du contingent, on n'oserait pas les y employer...

Au fond, l'"ordre établi" n'a jamais rien à craindre de ses propres troupes, quand il mérite le suffrage du pays.

Bien au contraire, dans ce cas, c'est sur les éléments les plus "militaires", c'est à dire, par définition, les plus disciplinés et décidés, qu'il peut s'appuyer [...]

Mais, du jour où le consentement général est du côté du bouleversement de l'ordre établi, alors la forme de l'organisation militaire n'influera en rien sur la chute. Militaires ou prétoriens n'empêcheront pas le destin de s'accomplir. Les régimes se perdent par leurs fautes, pas du tout par leurs soldats.

Bien cordialement à vous.

C. de Gaulle.

III

FIRE OVER THE EARTH

CHAPTER NINETEEN

"I, General de Gaulle . . ."

When they landed at the sunlit London airfield of Heston at a little after 12.30 p.m. on 17 June, de Gaulle, Spears and Courcel naturally had no notion of the message that Marshal Pétain was broadcasting from Bordeaux at the same time: "It is with a heavy heart that today I tell you we must stop the fighting."

His first action on British soil did not tend to deepen the breach between "the men of Bordeaux" and himself but on the contrary it seemed to be directed at preserving (as a measure of precaution?) the possibilities or the myth of a political complementarity. For this surprising telegram addressed by de Gaulle to General Colson,* Minister of War in the Pétain government, is dated from London on the same 17 June:

> Am in London. Yesterday on M. Paul Reynaud's instruction negotiated with British War Minister on subject of war materials delivered to Allies by government of United States [and] of the German prisoners now in France [who] will be handed to British military authorities at Bordeaux. Am now without power. Should I continue negotiation? Await your orders through the embassy.[1]

This document might have been written by a sleepwalker, by a de Gaulle who had not been in Bordeaux the day before. It says a great deal about the complexity of his decision and the bitterness of his uprooting. In the same way great heretics still turn their eyes towards the Church they have cursed. Can this final telegram be seen as a kind of *ruse de guerre* meant to conceal his tracks or to keep a few contacts? Rather as a sort of last Mass, on the eve of excommunication.

After looking in at the flat in Seamore Grove, General de Gaulle's first London home, Spears took his two companions to lunch at the Royal Automobile Club. Then, at about 3 p.m., he brought them to 10 Downing Street, where Winston Churchill was waiting for them.

Two days before this, during the evening, the Prime Minister, with a few violent phrases roared down the telephone, had tried to prevent Marshal Pétain from asking for an armistice. It was quite in vain, even if he spoke of the shame of breaking one's given word. What had happened to that France he admired and whose leaders of 1918 he had placed so high, almost as high as Nelson and Wellington? Now, his calm brought back by the very magnitude of the task awaiting him, he was resting in the garden. When de Gaulle came across the lawn

*With whom, six days earlier, de Gaulle had conferred about the withdrawal to North Africa.

towards him he stood up and his mastiff-like smile, according to that attentive observer Spears, had "the warmth of friendship".

Of course the Prime Minister would rather have welcomed Reynaud, Mandel or Herriot, Darlan, Georges or Weygand. This messenger from an indomitable (and still invisible) France had as yet no fame, no party, no troops, no evident legitimacy. What Spears had brought back was a temporary brigadier-general, an Under-Secretary of State in an out-going government, a military thinker neglected by his own people – he did not amount to big game. But Churchill knew him, and his great predator's eye had recognized "l'homme du destin" and the Constable of France in this hitherto taciturn giant: "Here, my lords, is a man worth talking to."

Let it not be forgotten that although Churchill was one of those Englishmen, more numerous than might be supposed, who have a consuming and at the same time slightly condescending passion for France, in which are mingled the recollections of Agincourt and the stake at Rouen, of Trafalgar and Rethondes, the taste of Périgourdine sauces and the colours of water-lilies, Charles de Gaulle was not, when he landed at London, in the least danger of any anglomania whatsoever.

Indeed, in June 1940 the Constable might be considered an anglophobe: and this was because of family tradition, for his childhood had been marked by the sound of the word Fashoda, uttered around him; because he spoke not English but German; because he had not thought much of the conduct of the British during the 1914–1918 war and because he was accustomed to a right-wing press – including *L'Action française* – in which all the misfortunes of French diplomacy had for the last twenty years been put down to the intrigues of perfidious Albion, which the French radicals or socialists "followed like a dead dog going down the stream"; because he blamed Lord Runciman and Chamberlain for the withdrawal at Munich; and lastly because he thought that Britain's military support of France during the last ten months had been derisory.

It is true that since 9 June he had found warm and effectual allies in Churchill, Eden and Spears. But Churchill was, as de Gaulle knew, an Englishman who would do anything to prevent the first invasion of Britain since Hastings.

De Gaulle also knew what he wanted. Perhaps he had not yet defined the bases of his action as clearly as he was to do some ten years later in his *Mémoires de guerre*. Yet is is here that this great document must be quoted, since from now onwards everything was to flow from it. Anachronism? With de Gaulle one can never be sure.

> Carry on with the war? Yes, indeed! But to what end and within what limits? The help given by a handful of Frenchmen to a British Empire still standing and still fighting? Never for a moment did I look upon the attempt in that light. For me what had to be served and to be saved was the nation and the State.
>
> For I thought that the country's honour, unity and independence would come to an end if it were to be admitted that in this World War France alone had capitulated and had let the matter rest there. For in that event, whatever the result of the war might be, the disgust that the country would feel for itself and that others would feel for it would poison its soul and its life for

> generations on end. As for the present moment, what was the point of supplying another power with auxiliaries? For the effort to be worth while it must result in bringing back into the war not only some Frenchmen, but France itself.[2]

As for de Gaulle himself, engaged on this truly national task, whose spiritual dimensions he did not hesitate to point out (it was a question of France's "soul"), how was he to act?

> I was nothing to begin with. But this very destitution pointed out my line of conduct. It was by taking up the cause of national salvation, without troubling about anything else at all, that I might acquire authority. It was by acting as the unbending champion of the nation and the State that it might be possible for me to gather agreement and even enthusiastic support among the French, and to obtain respect and esteem from foreigners. In short, although I was so restricted and alone, and indeed because I *was* so restricted and alone, I had to reach the heights and never come down again.[3]

This says everything. And if everything had not been said as early as that conversation in the sunny garden of Downing Street, it may be supposed that the Constable's words and behaviour during that afternoon of 17 June were of such a kind that Churchill immediately grasped the magnitude of the plan and of the trials that it would inflict upon him.

Charles de Gaulle, therefore, came before the host who from now onwards assumed the crushing responsibility of defending the world's freedom against Hitler, as a proud beggar: "Cast away on the shores of England from the general desolation, what should I have been able to do without his help?" He at once explained his intentions to the Prime Minister; in the first place it was a matter of "hoisting the colours" by speaking to the French nation, using the British radio to do so. As soon as this help was asked for, Churchill granted it without the slightest hesitation: the BBC's microphones were placed at his disposal. But not before the Bordeaux government had asked for an armistice.

At this point a certain amount of imagination is required to grasp the ambiguity of the situation. For although it was now past 3 p.m. and Pétain had finished speaking more than two hours earlier, neither Churchill nor de Gaulle yet knew what Pétain had said: Geoffroy de Courcel is categorical on this point.[4] De Gaulle and his host therefore agreed to delay his first speech until the moment Pétain had begun the process of negotiation. Neither had any illusions; but a sudden reaction of French pride should be given every chance.

It was only after the visitors had left Downing Street that the words of Pétain's broadcast were known: they went much farther than Churchill or de Gaulle had foreseen. " . . . the fighting must stop. I applied to the enemy tonight."

Stop the fighting at no matter what price? For years the conqueror of Verdun had held Foch up to public obloquy for not persuading Clemenceau, his troops and the Allies to carry on with the war in November 1918 to impose, on German soil, a harsher treaty upon the beaten side. Even before knowing the conditions that Hitler would insist upon, Pétain now said that France must lay down its arms and submit to the enemy's rule without the slightest guarantee – he was crying "every man for himself" at the very moment that Weygand, his Minister of National Defence, was calling upon his last sound troops for a final effort.

It may certainly be said that the vast majority of French people, fleeing on the roads, machine-gunned at pleasure, bewildered and maddened by seeing the rape of the civil and military State, were longing for that moment and those words. During those days of panic, shame had been swallowed like water from a spring; all sense of it had gone. Yet the reaction of a distracted, unguided horde to despair and to the old cry of "we have been betrayed" is one thing; the decision of those who govern and whose very duty lies in not echoing but checking this reaction, is another. Pétain's popularity at this time of collapse arose from the fact that he spoke like the most wretched of refugees, crouching in a ditch under the fire of the stukas. Since he, the Marshal, said it, that means I am not a coward.

The cabinet gave Paul Baudouin, the new Foreign Minister, the task of at least asking the enemy's conditions,* and he gave the press strict instructions to rectify the deeply irresponsible and ruinous text of Pétain's speech so that it should read "we must *try* to stop the fighting".

But in the meantime Nazi propaganda had got hold of the original and had turned it into a pamphlet distributed in hundreds of thousands of copies to be read by the French soldiers, called upon by the Marshal to cease fighting at once. For their part, the evening papers in Britain had as their headline, *France Surrenders*.

And that same evening of 17 June, after dining at Jean Monnet's where he did not hesitate to denounce the "treason" of Marshal Pétain,[5] whose appeal to "cease fighting" he had read in the interval, Charles de Gaulle set about drafting his first proclamation to the people of France. Geoffroy de Courcel had already telephoned Elisabeth de Miribel, a childhood friend now working in the Economic Mission at the Embassy, to ask her to be ready to type "an important document" tomorrow.

But this was reckoning without the cares and objections of British diplomacy. However great he was, Winston Churchill was only the first among His Majesty's ministers. Even if France for him was a companion in arms who must be brought back to life with all the powers of speech and imagination, for most of his colleagues and particularly for those of the Foreign Office, France was in the first place a State, still allied to the United Kingdom and endowed with a government whose legality could not be put in doubt, however bitter it might be. So long as there remained any way of persuading that government to take care of British interests and security, it was of great consequence not to throw it into the enemy camp. A speech on the BBC by this truant solider could not but be ill received at Bordeaux. Was it really wise to take this additional risk?

Among the exiles there were confident preparations for the "hoisting of the colours" arranged for that evening at the BBC; but at the same time an unusual argument was taking place. The War Cabinet met at 10 Downing Street on 18

*A considerable number of ministers, including Lebrun, hoped the terms would be so unbearable that the war would have to continue even if it was from North Africa.

June at 12.30 p.m. (but in the absence of Churchill, who was himself taken up with drafting the great speech the Commons were to hear that afternoon) presided over by Neville Chamberlain; those present included Lord Halifax, Clement Attlee, Anthony Eden and Alfred Duff Cooper, the Minister of Information. Relations with France were at the heart of the discussion, pending news of the terms of the armistice Hitler had been asked to grant.

The chief anxiety was the future of the French fleet, upon which the security of Britain might depend. It was therefore decided that Victor Alexander, the First Lord of the Admiralty, who had already left for Bordeaux, should carry on with his approaches to the Pétain government. Everything must be done to dissuade Darlan and his colleagues from letting Hitler get his hands on the French fleet (the most modern in the world, and the third in tonnage) and the overseas ports.

It was then that Duff Cooper intervened to say that "General de Gaulle had passed him the text of a speech* that he wished to broadcast, stating that France was not beaten and asking all French soldiers to join him". The War Cabinet reacted to this by observing that "although there was nothing to object to in these words, it was undesirable that General de Gaulle, who was *persona non grata* with the present French government, should speak on the wireless so long as it was possible that the French government might act in conformity with the interests of the alliance."

Yet this remarkable document[6] is followed by a brief hand-written note to this effect: "The members of the War Cabinet, consulted one by one on this question later, agreed that General de Gaulle should be authorized to speak on the wireless, which he did that same evening."

For it so happened that Duff Cooper, who was one of the English leaders most favourable to de Gaulle, left the Cabinet and at once warned Spears, who was in Churchill's office. The Prime Minister had dozed off after his great speech in the Commons (that of the "finest hour"), and being scarcely awake he confined himself to telling Spears to go and plead with each member of the Cabinet in favour of de Gaulle. Sir Edward persuaded them one by one, and at the end of the afternoon he was able to bring the Minister of Information the green light he was waiting for.

What is so remarkable about this very British affair is that de Gaulle knew nothing about the disagreements he had aroused. Duff Cooper, who had asked him to lunch that day after the Cabinet was over, did not utter so much as a word. And it was without the least suspicion of the danger of a veto which was still hanging over his speech that the Constable, in his flat in Seamore Grove, wrote and re-wrote the text that was to make him part of history. He had spent the greater part of that morning on it, smoking cigarette after cigarette, while Courcel, to whom he handed the pages, read them first to Elisabeth de Miribel, who was so little accustomed to the work that she later asked an orderly to help and in her turn read out the almost illegible words to him.[7]

At 3 p.m. the general went back to Seamore Grove, re-read the speech, had it

*De Gaulle often denied having shown his text to the British. Almost all witnesses contradict him.

typed again and made further corrrections. This took until 6 p.m. The General called a cab to take him to Oxford Circus, dropping Elisabeth de Miribel at Brompton Square, where she lived, at the very moment Spears and Duff Cooper finally persuaded the Foreign Office that the dissident's speech was of such a kind that it would gain more support for allied resistance than it would cause displeasure at Bordeaux – where, it may be added, anglophobia, helped on by Laval, was continually increasing among Pétain's associates.

The studio in which the broadcast was to take place was on the fourth floor. There Stephen Tallents, the head of the BBC's news department, received de Gaulle and Courcel.[8] With him were two of his colleagues, Leonard Miall and Elizabeth Barker, who saw the General as "a huge man with highly-polished boots, who walked with long strides, talking in a very deep voice".

They reached studio 4B (subsequently destroyed by bombs) where the two announcers of the current programme, Maurice Thierry and Gibson Parker,[9] were waiting for them. What time was it? In his *Mémoires* de Gaulle places the event at 6 p.m. The official history of the BBC[10] states that the message was announced at 8.15 p.m. and that it went on the air at 10 p.m. This is a surprising difference in the timetables.

According to Elizabeth Barker and Gibson Parker, Maurice Thierry was reading the news when the general came into the studio; he broke off for a moment and then finished his reading. The General was then asked to make a voice-trial. He said no more than *la France* in a tone that seemed to be satisfactory. And the broadcast could begin.

To the surprise of the professionals around him, de Gaulle merely gave a rapid glance at the two much-corrected sheets that he had brought and that were set on a kind of lectern. He was pale; his brown forelock was stuck to his forehead; "he stared at the microphone as though it were France and as though he wanted to hypnotize it. His voice was clear, firm and rather loud, the voice of a man speaking to his troops before a battle. He did not seem nervous but extremely tense, as though he were concentrating all his power in one single moment."[11]

Very well known though it may be, how can one refrain from quoting the whole appeal of 18 June at this point?

> The leaders who have been at the head of the French armies for many years have formed a government.
>
> This government, alleging the defeat of our armies, has entered into communication with the enemy to stop the fighting.
>
> To be sure, we have been submerged, we are submerged, by the enemy's mechanized forces, on land and in the air.
>
> It is the Germans' tanks, planes and tactics that have made us fall back, infinitely more than their numbers. It is the Germans' tanks, planes and tactics that have so taken our leaders by surprise as to bring them to the point they have reached today.
>
> But has the last word been said? Must hope vanish? Is the defeat final? No!
>
> Believe me, for I know what I am talking about and I tell you that nothing is lost for France. The same means that beat us may one day bring victory.

For France is not alone. She is not alone! She is not alone! She has an immense Empire behind her. She can unite with the British Empire, which commands the sea and which is carrying on with the struggle. Like England, she can make an unlimited use of the vast industries of the United States.

This war is not confined to the unhappy territory of our country. This war has not been decided by the Battle of France. This war is a worldwide war. All the faults, all the delays, all the sufferings do not do away with the fact that in the world there are all the means for one day crushing our enemies. Today we are struck down by mechanized force; in the future we can conquer by greater mechanized force. The fate of the world lies there.

I, General de Gaulle, now in London, call upon the French officers and soldiers who are on British soil or who may be on it, with their arms or without them, I call upon the engineers and the specialized workers in the armaments industry who are or who may be on British soil, to get into contact with me.

Whatever happens, the flame of French resistance must not and shall not go out.

Tomorrow, as I have done today, I shall speak again from London.

Charles de Gaulle was to make more accomplished speeches, but he had immediately struck an oratorical tone in which the most classical tradition was enriched by the possibilities of the microphone, while at the same time he produced some phrases that, pending the utterance of others still more splendid, were to last in his hearers' memories. He also showed political judgment, not yet concerning himself with bringing down the government but calling upon his comrades to carry on with the fight.

Few people heard the appeal: that has been said countless times. The very people to whom it was chiefly addressed, the tens of thousands of French soliders that the operations in Norway and at Dunkirk had brought to England, had little notion of listening to the BBC. As for the British, only one voice mattered that day – the voice of Winston Churchill proclaiming, first in the Commons and then on the waves of this same BBC, from nine to ten o'clock, that the British were about to live their "finest hour".

Although the appeal had very few hearers, it was much more widely read. A few French papers published extracts from it, particularly *Le Progrès de Lyon* which on 19 June gave three of the paragraphs: not the denunciation of the military leaders but the assertion of the conflict's worldwide nature. And *Le Petit Provençal* of Marseilles reproduced almost half the text, especially the triple affirmation "France is not alone!" Nothing appeared in the Bordeaux press.

The new rulers were informed of de Gaulle's speech: the Ministry of the Interior's listening service gave an account (in the most neutral tone) of an English broadcast which stated that General de Gaulle had spoken on the London radio, saying that the French government had asked the conditions of an armistice "in dignity and independence", adding that this was a worldwide war, that France had not finally lost the war, and appealing to all the officers and other ranks on British soil. So the version of the appeal given by the British services (and only at 11 p.m.)

gave a very soothing and even a false idea of the original. Was this at the instance of the Foreign Office?

On page three of *The Times*, the page given over to the main political news, the London daily carried a seventeen-line heading summing up the chief events of the day before – and there were plenty on 18 June 1940: four for the Hitler-Mussolini meeting at Munich, seven for de Gaulle's speech, and six for Churchill's in the Commons. And under this heading the Prime Minister's speech was published in two columns; the General's – the whole of it – in one, with the headline *France is not lost*!

Yet there had been a hitch, and it had brought about the first difficulty between the exile and his hosts. As soon as his speech was finished on the evening of 18 June the General left to dine, in silence, with Courcel at a nearby hotel.

By announcing that he would speak "tomorrow" he had irritated the BBC, who were unaware of having invited him. But "General de Gaulle was already a law unto himself" as Leonard Miall acidly observed in a BBC talk given thirty years later. The next day, when he appeared at the end of the afternoon, Frederick Ogilvie, the Director of the BBC, said he should like to see him for a drink after his broadcast. When the second appeal had been sent out, Miss Barker and Leonard Miall took the General to Ogilvie. De Gaulle asked where the record of his yesterday's speech was, Miall was obliged to say that for want of means none had been made; Churchill had spoken to the world the day before and this had required all the BBC's technical resources. "I then became," says Leonard Miall, "the first Englishman to feel the effects of the General's well-known temper."

So there is no recording of the appeal of 18 June. But the text was re-read by the announcers four times during the next twenty-four hours, making part of the BBC's French news bulletin. De Gaulle, who was very anxious to prevent any fraudulent version, often referred to this deficiency, particularly in his *Mémoires*. In 1955 he even asked a colleague to circulate a memorandum to this effect.

Few though they may have been, there were still some Frenchmen in London who heard the appeal and who came up to the rebel's expectations. Geoffroy de Courcel recalls that the first to appear at Seamore Grove the next morning was a mechanic who wrote his name (since forgotten) on the first page of a register intended for the purpose. Later came the members of a delegation from the French Institute, and after them two young men, Pierre Maillaud and Robert Mengin, the first the Havas news agency correspondent in London and the second the press attaché at the Embassy.

Maillaud, who acquired a well-earned fame as Pierre Bourdan, one of the chief men of the BBC's French service, has written a very fine account of those days when, for many people, de Gaulle changed a judicious despair into a wild hope:

> In London on 18 June 1940 the light was grey. We were Frenchmen and we walked about the streets of that London like so many broken toys, useless and shamefaced spectators on the rocks of a beach being covered by an irresistible tide. There was a collapse of all standards, the ground giving way under one's feet, the unspeakable bitterness of the present, the incoherence of the imagined future.

It was in this state of extreme moral distress that Maillaud heard the appeal: at about nine o'clock the next day he, together with his friend Robert Mengin, went to introduce himself to de Gaulle whom he had never seen but whom he must now become acquainted with. They reached 8 Seamore Grove,*, a quiet little square in Mayfair; and here, on the first floor, during the morning of 19 June, the General received his first visitors, most of them civilians.**

> For my part, I felt an intense, nervous curiosity – a comforting sensation, I may add, after the moral chaos of the day before. A tall, thin, clear-eyed, large-nosed, well-mannered cavalry lieutenant asked our names, told us his – de Courcel – and without any other formalities showed us into a spacious office, comfortably furnished and as impersonal as the rest of the flat. Here stood General de Gaulle.
>
> I saw a man of another age.
>
> He was very tall; he wore uniform and leggings; and he stood exceedingly straight. Yet this straightness, emphasized by the way his head was thrown back and his arms kept close to his chest and hips, seemed a natural and easy posture for him. It gave his immobile body no stiffness although on the contrary there was stiffness conveyed by his movements and gestures – the way he carried his head, inexpressibly remote, and by the expression of his face. His features at once brought a mediaeval drawing to mind. One would have liked to frame them in a helmet and a chain-mail chin-piece.[12]

Soon other volunteers arrived: Henri de Kérillis in the uniform of an Air Force captain; Emile Delavenay, of the BBC French Service, who as such was very useful to General de Gaulle during the coming weeks; Denis Saurat, head of the French Institute in London; Henry Hauck, social attaché at the French Embassy; and André Weil-Curiel, a lawyer and an active member of a left-wing current in the SFIO,*** and attached to one of the French missions in London. He had been overjoyed by the appeal of 18 June and at once saw de Gaulle as the man for the situation "because he did not belong to the political world and would not be the prisoner of any faction".[13]

Let us also hear Georges Boris' testimony as he was to become one of the General's faithful followers.

> Towards evening, the general came back, accompanied by a single officer. I was struck by his calmness. Almost at once he asked me to go into the drawing-room with him. After the exchange of a few words and arising from a remark I had made, he began to explain England's chances. The crossing of the Channel and the landing would be attempted under the shelter of an attack from the air; if this attack were repulsed – and this was possible – the position would first be stabilized and then subsequently reversed thanks

*This is now Curzon Place.

**Apart from General Rozoy, who did not come to join but to warn the rebels (see page 309–10).

***The Section Française de l'Internationale Ouvrière. (trs.)

> to the resources of the American arsenal. We should end by winning the war.
>
> Once again I can see that room lost in the vastness of London in which a page of French history was written. Through the window, and under the implacable blue of that June 1940 sky, the greenery of Hyde Park stretched far away. The noises of the street reached us much diminished. I listened to this lucid French lesson, made up of logic and coolness, resolution and honour, spoken slowly, with very gentle modulations. General de Gaulle spared the time to give this lesson of reason and faith to a non-commissioned officer who, like himself, was a refugee in an allied but a foreign land.[14]

On 19 June, Charles de Gaulle, back at the microphone at 8 p.m., spoke much more strongly; and he did so to such a degree that this time the Foreign Office protested to the Prime Minister.

> In the name of France, I formally make the following declaration:
>
> All Frenchmen still under arms have the absolute duty of continuing the resistance. In the Africa of Clauzel, Bugeaud, Lyautey and Noguès, all honourable men have the strict duty of refusing to carry out the enemy conditions.
>
> It would be unbearable if the panic of Bordeaux were to cross the sea.
>
> Soldiers of France, wherever you are, rise up!

This time the Bordeaux government, which had been waiting for the armistice conditions for the last fifty hours, was denounced, impugned, stated to be "in liquefaction" and "fallen under enemy bondage". From now on the break was complete.

This is a question that will often be asked in connection with Charles de Gaulle: had he set his sights too high? For on 19 June he had at least three reasons for not distancing himself too far from the emerging Vichy government. In the first place he knew that the English did not wish him to, and what if Churchill, provoked beyond measure, were suddenly to drop him?

He also knew that the Marshal's government was about to receive Hitler's conditions; and however much he might despise the Baudouins and Weygands, perhaps it might be better not to disparage them too violently at the moment the ogre was about to be faced. The future of the fleet was at stake, together with that of the empire and the size of the zone in which there might still subsist some shreds of freedom and that "resistance" which his appeal of the day before had been meant to arouse.

Lastly, Charles de Gaulle was ill-advised to humiliate and caricature the authority of Bordeaux when he was attempting to win over the proconsuls of the empire. From Rabat to Saigon they would be all the less inclined to pay attention to his incitement to continue the war the more he appeared to be an unbalanced rebel opposed to Pétain whose personal prestige remained intact even in the eyes of those who had thoughts of going on with the struggle – but without moving over into dissidence.

Raising these questions obviously means asking oneself about the Constable's sincerity between 19 and 25 June, when he was sending out repeated messages to the various French proconsuls to try to persuade them to carry on the war.

We have seen how Charles de Gaulle, in his speech of 19 June, brought in the name of General Noguès as a guarantor for his policy of refusal to capitulate. Indeed, he knew on 17 June that Noguès, Resident-General in Morocco and who also controlled the whole of the French forces in North Africa from Algiers, had no sooner heard Marshal Pétain's call to stop fighting than he telegraphed these words to Bordeaux – words that ring almost as boldly as de Gaulle's appeal: "The whole of North Africa is appalled. The troops beg to continue the struggle. If the government has no objection, I am ready to take responsibility for this attitude with all the risks that it entails." General Noguès was asking Pétain and Weygand for permission to disobey, or rather to look upon him as only on the fringe of the negotiations that were about to open, though he might influence them as one of the essential assets that France still possessed.

De Gaulle, in London, sent a telegram to Noguès on the nineteenth: "Am in London in informal and direct contact with British government. Am at your disposal either to fight under your orders or for any approach you may think useful."[15]

To this appeal, which throws an interesting light upon de Gaulle's idea of his mission at that time, the Commander-in-Chief of the forces in North Africa replied with contemptuous silence. He forebade the press under his control, from Casablanca to Tunis, to publish the text of the appeal of 18 June, which, as we have seen, certain metropolitan papers had given; he even told the British liaison officer at Algiers that General de Gaulle's attitude was "unseemly".[16]

However pointless re-writing history may be, there are few questions so fascinating – even if it were only from the point of view of Charles de Gaulle's subsequent career – as that which may be put in three words: "What if Noguès . . . ?" Situated as he was, opposite Gibraltar, controlling a large part of the southern Mediterranean coast and with considerable forces under his command (in a telegram to Weygand on 22 June he stated that he could resist any attack launched through Spain and that he could even envisage mounting a preventative attack through Spanish Morocco), he might be seen by Churchill, and presently by Roosevelt, as the ideal ally. His early telegrams being taken into consideration, it may well be asked why a leader with such inclinations yielded to Weygand's directions, and after five days of hesitation, decided to give in on 22 June.

On 20 June, Gaston Palewski, who had crossed to Africa with his squadron, tried to persuade Marcel Peyrouton, the resident-general in Tunisia, to continue the struggle. "Come," said Peyrouton, "how simple you are: the English are already negotiating with Hitler." Palewski hurried round to the British Consul for a denial, which was instantly given to him. "All right," said Peyrouton, "persuade Noguès: he is the one everything depends on." On 22 June Palewski was in Algiers, and there the Commander-in-Chief told him, "Darlan refuses to let me have the fleet. All my hypotheses of resistance were based upon it." Nothing remained for Palewski but to reply to a very short telegram that he received in Tunisia on 28 June: "Come and join me at once." It was signed de Gaulle.[17]

General Noguès had finally yielded under the pressure brought to bear on him by General Koeltz, Weygard's representative: but he did not do so without sending Weygand this telegram:

> [The government] has not realized the psychological factor and the element of strength represented by North Africa, which, with its navy and air force could hold out against the enemy to the point of attrition. The government will regret it bitterly. For my part I shall stay at my post to fulfill a sacrificial mission that covers me with shame.[18]

De Gaulle did not confine himself to appealing to Noguès. He turned to all those in possession of power or command outside metropolitan France and who were doomed to direct or indirect occupation.

Between 18 and 25 June, while the cruel drama of the armistice ran its course, reaching its epilogue on the twenty-second, a copious stream of communications flowed between London, Bordeaux, Rabat, Algiers, Tunis, Beirut, Djibouti, Dakar, Brazzaville, Antananarivo and Saigon. Whether Charles de Gaulle, in his heart of hearts, really wanted, at the cost of being under their orders, to draw into the struggle men he had long since ceased to respect, like Weygand, or to whom he gave the benefit of the doubt, like Noguès, or in whose favour he was prejudiced, like Catroux and Puaux, the fact is that during those days when intense solitude gripped him in London he urged the French civil and military leaders who were outside the enemy's grasp to come back into the war.

On 20 June a telegram to the Bordeaux Minister of National Defence – transmitted quite legally by General Lelong, the French military attaché in London – conjured him "to go to overseas France and there continue the war", a telegram in which de Gaulle stated that he was ready to "serve under the authority" of Weygand or "of any other distinguished Frenchman determined to resist". Pétain's minister confined himself to returning this message to the sender, adorned with the note "General Weygand declines to receive this 'personal' letter; if the retired Colonel de Gaulle* thinks proper to address him, he will do so in the official manner."

None of the people who were close to Charles de Gaulle at the end of June 1940 have questioned the exile's sincere desire for the support of well-known men, even if they should for the time being thrust his exceedingly bold personal venture into the background. But sincerity does not exclude clear-sightedness. It is possible to wish for that which one believes to be unattainable.

De Gaulle, who was almost fifty, felt the "horrifying" side of breaking with the framework of life. He had felt it so very strongly that he could understand what such an action would be for a Noguès or a Peyrouton. He probably did not believe that he would win any of them over; they were men in their sixties or seventies, encased in honours and tradition.

Catroux, to be sure, had crossed the Rubicon; but meanwhile the men in power

*De Gaulle had had the temporary rank of general since 25 May. This rank was taken from him on 25 June and at the same time he was put on the retired list.

at Bordeaux had dismissed him from his post – as they had done for de Gaulle a fortnight earlier: insubordination is natural to those who have nothing to lose.

Is it because he had too much to lose that François Darlan remains the archetypal man of failed destiny, the man whose historic defection more than any other opened the gates of history to Charles de Gaulle? No analysis, no speech for the defence, no indictment has yet given the key to the conduct of this talented man, apparently faithful to the Republic, the holder of the only valid trump that France then possessed, who at the beginning of June seemed determined to play it for the greater good of the country, the State, the alliance and his own fame, but who confined himself to the most wretched beaten track, leading from impotence to collaboration, and from meetings at which he shook hands with Hitler to the bullets of 24 December 1942.*

Yet Admiral Darlan was the man who, on 3 June, said to Jules Moch, "If some day an armistice is asked for, I shall end my career with an act of splendid mutiny. I shall take command of the fleet and we shall sail for England."[19] And to Major d'Astier de La Vigerie, "We shall fight to the end, and if necessary I shall place the fleet under English colours."[20] Even on 15 June he spoke of his indignation at the request for an armistice that Pétain and Weygand were said to be preparing, and asserted that for his part he should carry on with the war.

Yet on 16 June, Jules Moch was stupefied at hearing him say that resistance was impossible in France and that England would be invaded, that Hitler was getting ready to conquer North Africa, passing through Spain, and that the fleet, cut off from its arsenals and bases, would be of no use. "I reminded Darlan," says Moch, "of his statement of 3 June, his 'act of splendid mutiny'. I thought him moved; he reflected for a moment and answered, 'Too late; in the next few weeks England will be done for. And then, you see, in the country's misfortune, one has no right to separate the fleet from the homeland." '[21]

In Moch's opinion, the only way of accounting for this volte-face was the offer of a ministry that Pétain was said to have made him. A rather over-simple explanation. But in any case from that time on, Darlan was the man who never did a thing nor uttered a word against the capitulation, and who, rather than be the organizer of the great exodus to Algiers, hurried to Vichy to act as second in command to an old man whose mind worked only a few hours a day.

"If Darlan had chosen to fight in June 1940, he would have been a de Gaulle raised to the tenth power," said Churchill. No doubt. And the relations between the two men and the future of the Constable (whom Darlan loathed from before 18 June 1940) are a matter that belongs to the realm of imaginative literature. It was inconceivable that the admiral should be subordinate to the general. The reverse was unworkable.

While these appeals, rejections, exhortations and counter-appeals echoed from one longitude to another, a tragedy was taking place on French soil: it had two aspects – the occupation of the territory as a whole and the Armistice that Pétain

*See pages 409–12.

was openly praying for – and with him 99 per cent of the citizens of France, dumbfounded and downhearted.*

On the morning of 19 June Hitler announced that he was prepared to make "his" conditions for an armistice known, and he asked the Bordeaux government to appoint its plenipotentiaries. This was done at once: those accredited were General Huntziger (the man de Gaulle had wanted to make Commander-in-Chief twelve days earlier), the Ambassador Léon Noël (who was representing France in Poland immediately before the disaster), Admiral Le Luc, the navy's Chief of Staff, General Bergeret (he who had said he would seize the USSR in a pincers movement between Finland and the Black Sea in December 1939) and General Parisot. These five men, accompanied by some fifteen civil servants, left Bordeaux early in the afternoon of the twentieth, reaching Rethondes in the forest of Compiègne on the twenty-first: here they were confronted with the railway-carriage in which Foch had received Erzberger and the German plenipotentiaries in 1918.

The conquerors seem to have done all they could to justify the opponents of the Armistice: the Führer had organized an aggressive ceremony of "reparation" in which everything, from his own presence and that of several Nazi leaders to Marshal Keitel's violent speech and the swastika flags blowing in the wind, to demonstrate the humbling of France and the solemn triumph of the Third Reich. Hitler had seen fit to make the railway-carriage of November 1918, formerly exhibited at the Invalides, the theatre of a psychodrama based on French humiliation.

But beyond this cruel stage-setting there was a line of strategic thought. On 17 June, Adolf Hitler had drawn up a plan, founded on three basic ideas which, in this maniac, show a diplomatic genius equal to that instinctive discernment in war. The first idea was to separate France and Britain as widely as possible by making the conquered French proposals of such a nature that "an understanding with Germany would seem to them more profitable than the British alliance". Secondly: avoid at all costs any movement of the French fleet and colonies into the British camp – and to this end to insist upon nothing "unbearable" from the Bordeaux delegates. Thirdly: to forgo the occupation of the whole of the French territory, thus allowing the setting up or the retention of a "sovereign" French government, whose authority could cover the policy implied by the Armistice. In this respect, said Hitler to his associates, "the Pétain government seems to offer favourable prospects. With this aim, its authority is valid."[22]

Given the state of liquefaction to which the French nation was reduced, what the Führer was about to propose was more in keeping with the idea of him entertained by the Marshal and his clique at Bordeaux than that held by Reynaud (who readily compared him with Genghis Khan), Mandel, de Gaulle and the responsible observers. In this case the Nazi leader, the torturer and executioner of the Jews, the conqueror of Prague, the slaughterer of the Poles, was behaving like a plebeian Metternich.

With a disturbing keenness of view Hitler had perceived how far the collapse

*Including the present writer.

had slackened the Frenchmen's sense of honour and solidarity, to what degree they would put up with the worst, how much the Dunkirk withdrawal had shaken the Franco-British alliance, and the extent to which the paternal figure of the Marshal had obscured the nation's critical sense and awareness of its responsibilities. On the basis of this analysis of what had become "bearable", he was about to win on all counts: to neutralize the fleet, strengthen Pétain and set France against Great Britain (with which he had never ceased to hope for a settlement or a compromise; he was now making tentative approaches to that effect by means of the Swedes).

The plan built up on these three basic ideas by the General Staff and the Ministry for Foreign Affairs and forced by Hitler upon Mussolini's* grotesque voracity during a tolerably stormy interview at Munich on 18 June, took the form of an armistice agreement in twenty-three points. Adolf Hitler, sitting in the Rethondes carriage opposite Huntziger, Noël, Le Luc and Bergeret, handed it to them without a word.

The three first articles dealt with the stopping of the fighting (which would not be broken off until the conclusion of the two Armistices, German and Italian) and the definition of the zone of occupation to be imposed until the peace-treaty – the whole of the Atlantic coast, Paris, the west, the north, the north-east, the richest provinces, almost two thirds of the country. Articles four to seven covered the fate of the French armaments and article eight that of the fleet: apart from those that France needed for the defence of its colonial empire, the warships would be put out of commission and laid up in their peace-time home ports: Brest, Toulon, Cherbourg, Rochefort and Lorient (apart from Toulon, all these were in the occupied zone), the victors solemnly "undertaking not to make use of these ships and not to claim them at the time of the peace-treaty".

The other articles would have been less important (ascription of the cost of keeping the occupation troops, setting up a mixed Armistice Commission, liberation of German prisoners, the Third Reich's right to denounce the agreement if France did not fulfil its obligations) if it had not been stated that the French prisoners were to remain in captivity until the peace-treaty – which amounted to a massive legalization of the taking of hostages – and if article 19 had not laid down that those of German nationality who had taken refuge in France should be handed over to the Nazis.

At last the French plenipotentiaries were allowed to communicate with Bordeaux – once on the evening of 21 June and once the next morning – and they transmitted the German conditions to Weygand and the Pétain government. There were two Cabinet meetings, one during the night of the twenty-first, the other at 8 a.m.: a memorandum was drawn up, asking the conquerors to make a few alterations: the non-occupation of Paris, the neutralization of the Air Force, the sending of the fleet to North Africa, and the deletion of the clause about handing over German refugees ("which would dishonour us").

In the meanwhile Paul Baudouin, the Foreign Minister, had told Sir Ronald Campbell the broad lines of the German diktat, bringing upon himself the most

*At which the Duce, in the absence of a victory, wanted to insist upon Nice, Corsica and Tunisia.

stinging protest: gathering the fleet in its home ports was a long way from the "putting out of the enemy's reach" that London insisted upon as a condition of authorizing France to break the agreement of 28 March.

Baudouin pointed out to his angry visitor that these arrangements would not necessarily be carried out, and that Hitler would find it difficult to compel French ships anchored in the Mediterranean to return to Brest or Cherbourg. This was forgetting that Hitler had brought such terrifying pressure on his French interlocutors that he had imposed the diktat of Rethondes upon them, together with the clauses considered "dishonourable", even before talks had begun, and that according to the terms of the armistice itself he could at any moment allege a breach on the part of France to cancel the agreement and tighten the screw a little farther, either from the point of view of territory or otherwise. Furthermore what confidence could Sir Ronald have in a man who promised him to cheat Hitler after broken France had broken its promise to its allies?

The Franco-German interview began again late in the morning of 22 June at Rethondes. Keitel would allow only a single amendment: the planes were not to be handed over. As far as the German subjects were concerned, he gave the verbal assurance that France would only be required to hand over those who had "fomented the war" (which, in a Nazi's mind, meant all the Jews, by definition).*

At 6 p.m. Keitel gave the French delegates an ultimatum: the last moment for signing the Armistice was fixed at 7.30 p.m.: after this they were allowed to communicate with Bordeaux once more. At six thirty Weygand gave Huntziger direct orders and in obedience to them he, together with Keitel, signed the armistice agreement a little before seven o'clock on 22 June 1940: apart from a few slight differences the document was as Hitler had dictated it five days earlier. The text was broadcast by the Berlin radio that evening. It was then that the British Ambassador left Bordeaux. Thus diplomatic relations had been unilaterally broken; Pétain's government had preferred the neutralization of France.

This is no place for a thorough-going discussion of the 22 June 1940 Armistice. The simplifications of Charles de Gaulle's analysis has been pointed out: in the position he had taken up, which took for granted that the men of Bordeaux had betrayed the country's fundamental interests and aspersed its honour, there could, for the exile of London, be no question of expressing the delicate shades of an historian.

A disaster has no outcome that is not wretched. The question that cannot be got round is this: was an alternative policy conceivable? It depended entirely upon the possibility of carrying on the struggle from North Africa, with the fleet associated with the Royal Navy and Noguès' forces combined with those of Wavell, the British Commander-in-Chief in the Near East, and inflicting irreparable damage on the Third Reich's Italian allies and thereby undermining the power of the Axis. This was assuming that the Wehrmacht would not nip these plans in the bud by marching on Morocco through Spain.

*But according to Léon Noël he did not seem to "attach very great importance to this requirement. It would have been possible to scatter the refugees in question or bring about their escape. Vichy, on the contrary, did everything to hand them over."

As we have seen, on 19 June Noguès asserted that he was in a position to resist an operation of this kind. Furthermore, it is unlikely that Spain would have taken the decision to break off all connections with Britain, the commander of the seas, and still less with the United States, the source of loans and supplies. Everything that emerges from the talks between Franco and Hitler at Hendaye and between Franco and Pétain at Montpellier points in the same direction. And those who were in Hitler's confidence readily emphasize how much he distrusted any undertaking based on the Mediterranean theatre.

The defenders of the Armistice always quote the evidence brought forward at Pétain's trial by General Georges, who stated that at Marrakesh, in January 1944, Winston Churchill had told him confidentially that in his opinion "the June 1940 armistice had been useful to Great Britain and that Hitler had been wrong in granting it rather than carrying on the war in North Africa". Is this belated support for the Pétain-Weygand strategy coming from the Prime Minister to be considered his innermost opinion? It is true that General Georges was his friend. But Churchill maintained the contrary view so often and with such vehemence that the confidential remark of Marrakesh can be looked upon only as one of the significant but ambiguous turns in the great Armistice trial – a subject upon which Charles de Gaulle for his part never moved an inch.

As the Constable saw it, the Armistice, which entailed the forsaking of an ally, the timorous refusal to play all the cards that France possessed, the absurdity of signing a pact that bound the nation to a person such as the Führer and the consecration of a disaster in the form of the Armistice was the inaugural act of a system of treason.

CHAPTER TWENTY

Charles-all-alone

Even before he saw the text that was signed at Rethondes, General de Gaulle, basing what he had to say on scraps of information gathered during the last three days in London, returned to the BBC's microphone at 8 p.m. on 22 June to denounce not only the "capitulation" but also the country's "reduction to bondage".

It was therefore upon inexact information[1] that the man of London then levelled an indictment affirming that "many Frenchmen reject servitude for reasons that are called honour, common sense, and the country's greater good, [reasons which] require all free Frenchmen to carry on with the fight, wherever they are and however they can."

A subsequent reading of the full text of the Armistice agreements signed on 22 June, from which it appeared that the fleet had not really been "handed over" and that France was only half occupied, did not make de Gaulle modify a single one of his statements. It was laid down once and for all, from the Gaullian view, that Pétain, Weygand and Darlan had delivered the country, the Empire and the fleet to the enemy. This being so, the exile was still more vehement and categorical on 24 June:

> This evening I shall simply say, since someone must say it, how much shame and how much revulsion is rising in the hearts of good Frenchmen. France and the French, tied hand and foot, handed over to the enemy. France is like a boxer who has been knocked down by a terrible blow. She is lying on the ground. But she knows, she feels, that she is still alive, living still with a deep and powerful life. She knows, she feels, that she is deserving of much more than the bondage accepted by the Bordeaux government. She knows, she feels, that in her empire powerful forces of resistance are afoot to save her honour. The will to continue the war has already asserted itself in many parts of the French overseas territories. One day, I promise you, the mechanized army, navy and air force, together with our allies, will give freedom back to the world and greatness back to our country.

The reason that the Constable's tone continued to rise, to grow firmer, was that the day before, 23 June, his cause had made its most important gains since he arrived in London. For that very day the British government simultaneously published two declarations that corresponded exactly with General de Gaulle's wishes – except that the document alluding to him did not specifically mention his name.

In the first declaration, which was an unprecedented affront to the Pétain ministry, Winston Churchill's government proclaimed that:

> The Armistice that has just been signed, in violation of the agreements solemnly concluded between the allied governments, places the Bordeaux government in a state of total subjection to the enemy, depriving it of all freedom and of any right to represent free French citizens. Consequently His Majesty's government no longer considers the government of Bordeaux as that of an independent country.

In its second declaration the British government said that it had "taken note" of the "plan for the formation of a provisional French National Committee" (CNF) representing the "independent French elements resolved to fulfil the international obligations contracted by France", that it "would recognize" this committee and "discuss with it all matters connected with the prosecution of the war."[2]

The "French National Committee" – here was the idea launched, and ratified by Churchill. It is possible that the Prime Minister's resentment on being confronted with the terms of an Armistice which deprived him of an ally and which might put an enemy in that ally's place, played an important part in this decisive choice. But in any event here was de Gaulle placed in orbit – an orbit that has not finished yet. From the seven lines of this proclamation and from the eight that His Majesty's government devoted to denouncing the Bordeaux ministry de Gaulle was to draw towards consequences that were then unimaginable, even by him.

Yet as early as this first evening, which was that of his first victory, a shadow came over the picture: this was the refusal of the "London strategy" by the man who then appeared the most useful French ally and the most fortunate complement of the de Gaulle phenomenon – Jean Monnet, the originator of the plan for Franco-British Union.

The rejection of surrender proclaimed by the General was an immense symbolic gesture: it had as its preface that other symbolic gesture, the exaltation of Allied solidarity in disaster. Monnet's attempt was comparable on the historical plane; it was as imposing as de Gaulle's and still richer in the realm of the imagination. In short, between the soldier out of an epic and the clever brandy-exporter who had been made manager of the Inter-Allied war-effort, there had begun one of the most promising convergences in contemporary history.

But on the evening of 23 June the alliance fell apart. Jean Monnet thought Charles de Gaulle's *démarche* "too dramatic" and "too personal", and he sent a messenger with a letter that contained a very clear warning: "At the moment London is not the place to launch a resurrection. The French would see it as a movement protected by Britain and prompted by British interests. It would therefore be condemned to failure and would make later attempts at recovery even more difficult."

Nothing could be clearer; nothing could have given the Gaullist approach a stronger check. All the more so, since Monnet stated that he had warned Cadogan, Vansittart and Spears. The Constable's reaction was remarkably mild: "My dear friend, at a moment like this, it would be absurd for us to thwart one another, since fundamentally we desire the same thing and since between us we can perhaps do a great deal. Come and see me, wherever you like. We shall certainly agree." Jean Monnet's comment: "We did indeed see one another again several times. But our good personal relations were no longer enough to overcome our disagreement. In the end he respected my decision, just as I admired his determination."[3]

Jean Monnet informed Pétain and Churchill of his resignation as President of the Inter-Allied Committee, which the collapsed alliance had deprived of life, and a few days later he left for the United States, where, having much influence with Roosevelt and those around him, he continued to play a decisive role in the war-effort of the democracies against Nazism.

"Charles-all-alone"? It is true that the recruits did not come in at a great pace and that although the English who had dealings with him were polite enough not to show their disappointment, they did not fail to wonder about the future of the French National Committee, which neither the proconsuls of the French empire nor the outstanding representatives of French political life seemed in any hurry to join.

Elisabeth de Miribel was, as it has been said, the first of the Gaullist women in London, and a remark of hers sums up this phase of the movement quite well: "In June 1940 London was not a town where you arrived but one from which you left."[4] So does this other, even more striking, observation, made a little later by Charles de Gaulle himself to Gaston Palewski who, having just joined him, asked about recruitment and desertion: "The London French, my dear fellow, fall into two groups, those who are in the United States and those who are getting ready to leave."[5]

And indeed for many people London was no more than a halt on the way to safer shores: thus three writers who were then very well known moved off – Jules Romains, Henry Bernstein* and André Maurois. The whole work of the last had seemed to be devoted to exalting Franco-British friendship, and his departure for the United States made Winston Churchill say, "We took him for a friend; he was only a hanger-on." Geoffroy de Courcel tried to persuade him to stay in London, but Maurois replied, "I am a Jew; my family is in France; they are manufacturers – I cannot ruin them."[6]

As for the two French public figures most looked for in London, Paul Reynaud and Georges Mandel, they were soon to fall into the hands of the Vichy police. The former Prime Minister (who accepted the post of Ambassador in Washington offered to him by Pétain though Albert Lebrun refused to confirm it, thinking that he would thus prevent Reynaud, whom he respected, from making a blunder) was getting ready to leave France (probably by way of Marseilles) for the United States, when on 26 June, the car that he was driving, with Mme de Portes at his side, was involved in an accident in which she was killed. Reynaud, who was injured, was arrested in early September. As for Mandel, he went aboard the *Massilia* bound for Morocco on 20 June; on 26 June he was prevented from contacting Churchill's

*Who became a zealous convert to Gaullism in the States.

two messengers, arrested at Casablanca by order of General Noguès, transferred to France and interned before being deported and murdered.

Of all those who left or who refused to join, the most notorious was the Ambassador, Charles Corbin: he had devoted his professional life to the Franco-British alliance and he had given his total support to the 16 June plan for Union. He resigned from the Foreign Office the evening the Armistice was signed, but he declined to give the Gaullist enterprise the backing of his prestige and left Britain to retire in South America. His closest colleague, Roger Cambon, the son and nephew of the two French architects of the Entente Cordiale, also resigned; yet though he was just as much in disagreement with de Gaulle's *démarche*, he remained in London to share the trials of the British nation. As for Paul Morand, a great writer whose judgment was unreliable, although he left his post as head of the French Economic Mission in London, he later became an Ambassador under Vichy.

General de Gaulle was no luckier with the two most outstanding diplomats in the service, the leader of the "old school", Alexis Léger, who was Secretary-General at the Quai d'Orsay for several years and who had been removed from the post a month earlier by Paul Reynaud (whom he never forgave for this unexplained action), and the leader of the "young school", Roland de Margerie, one of the steadiest and most eloquent opponents of the Armistice among Reynaud's advisers. The first reached London on 20 June; on 22 June he went to see de Gaulle, but left for the United States, where he had a considerable influence (mostly hostile to de Gaulle) on Roosevelt's associates.

The second, who had forged what seemed to be very strong links with de Gaulle during their joint struggle for the continuation of the war, nevertheless recoiled before the prospects opened by the Constable. Margerie, from a family of successful civil servants, had to choose "between discipline and dissidence". Although some young diplomats who admired him wished to stay in London they were influenced by his decision to stay in France and returned to see ravaged France once more and their scattered if not decimated families.

Who can tell what was the effect of the cancellation of a dinner early in July, at which de Gaulle was to entertain several of these young diplomats. Would not a direct contact with the Constable have made up his mind?[7]

But not everyone left. Some came. Where did they come to? As soon as the idea of the French National Committee was accepted on 23 June, Charles de Gaulle was allotted premises at St Stephen's House, a large, rather dilapidated commercial building, since destroyed, that stood on the Victoria Embankment, on the bank of the Thames, close to the House of Commons. Sir Edward Spears had his offices there, and he placed the third floor at the disposal of the Free French, as the Committee came to be called. The Constable moved into a triangular room that looked on to the river; it was hastily provided with a white-wood table, a telephone and four chairs. He pinned a map of France to the wall, another of the world, and set to work.

Those who joined him first settled in the neighbouring rooms; Geoffroy de Courcel; Elisabeth de Miribel (who typed the letters in the corridor, on a typewriter that stood on a box); Claude Hettier de Boislambert, the first principal private secretary, who was soon to be sent to Africa, where he had spent the greater part of his life; René Pleven, a deserter from the "Monnet establishment" who was very soon to become the General's closest adviser; and his assistant Pierre Denis, known as Rauzan, who was in charge of Free France's trifling finances.

Then came those who, gathering round these pioneers, formed the first nucleus of Free France: Lieutenant Christian Fouchet, with six companions who left Mérignac on 17 June (where without knowing it they had passed the Constable) formed the first draft of recruits; Captains Tissier and Dewavrin, who had come from Norway with the French Expeditionary Force; Claude Bouchinet-Serreulles, from Morocco; Pierre-Olivier Lapie, an officer in the Foreign Legion and recently republican-socialist Deputy for the Meurthe-et-Moselle; André Weil-Curie; Georges Boris, formerly editor of *La Lumière* and Léon Blum's principal private secretary; Professor Cassin the jurist, augur of the League of Nations at Geneva and president of the *Union internationale des Anciens Combattants*; André Diethelm, formerly Georges Mandel's principle private secretary; the journalist Maurice Schumann; then Gaston Palewski.

Some of these arrivals were perfectly calculated to encourage the creator of the Free French, hard hit by the departure of men of such value as Monnet, Morand or Margerie.* Let us take three examples: René Cassin, Maurice Schumann and Gaston Palewski. The first, getting aboard an English ship at Saint-Jean-de-Luz, reached London on 28 June. The next day he introduced himself to de Gaulle: "In what way can an old jurist like me be useful to you?" – "You come at exactly the right moment! It is a matter of preparing a treaty of alliance between a government, Mr Churchill's government, and a single man, myself." Cassin acknowledged that the case was unprecedented, but he would study the question. On what basis? "In this draft of an agreement, I take it that we are not a legion but allies re-forming the French army?" "The French army? We are France itself!"[8]

The next day it was Maurice Schumann, who had also come by way of the Basque country. Schumann found a man he was already acquainted with. As a diplomatic journalist in the Havas news agency and a writer in the Catholic papers under the name of André Sidobre, he had followed the career of the author of *Le Fil de l'épée*, and had seen him in the offices of *L'Aube* and particularly in the company of Philippe Serre, André Lecomte and the Friends of *Temps présent*. He too was an enemy of Fascism and an active opponent of Munich. As soon as he knew of the words of 18 June, Schumann had sought out their common friend Daniel-Rops in Bordeaux who, though he himself had little wish to break with legality, gave him a letter of introduction to the author of *La France et son armée*.

It was to Schumann, at 11 o'clock on 30 June, that de Gaulle made this observation whose obvious authenticity cannot be diminished by the fervour of its recorder:

> I think Russia will come into the war before America, but that both the one and the other will come in. Have you read *Mein Kampf*? Hitler is thinking of

*General de Gaulle felt lasting resentment only in the case of the second, who belonged to the "great writer" species, which for him was sacred.

> the Ukraine. He will not resist against his longing to deal with Russia, and that will be the beginning of the end for him. If Hitler had been going to reach London at all, he would have been here by now. At present the Battle of Britain will be fought only in the air, and I hope that some French pilots will take part. In short, the war is a terrible problem, but it is one that has been solved. What remains is to bring the whole of France back to the right side.[9]

Who, hearing him speak like this, would not have become a Gaullist straight away, even though one's devotion might diminish later?

Gaston Palewski joined the Free French. De Gaulle had summoned him in the most imperative tone on 27 June from Tunisia, after he had tried to persuade the various North African proconsuls to stay in the war. Palewski made haste. When, a few weeks later, he reached London and rejoined the man whose career he had been so closely following for the last six years, he took over the direction of Free France's political affairs, qualified by his friendships in England, his previous service with Reynaud and his ability as a tactician, which made him a match for the subtleties of Spears.

"There is no France without a sword," recalled the author of the *Mémoires de guerre*. For the moment this "sword" was a vague collection of battalions thrown on to English soil by the bitter adventure of Dunkirk or a chance putting into port on the way back from the Norwegian escapade. There was one light division of alpine troops, a half-brigade of the Foreign Legion, the sailors from three small ships that had sailed to English ports, about a hundred airmen and five to six hundred volunteers who were assembled at Olympia. An odd-looking sword.

It so happened that the commander of the division coming back from Norway was a contemporary of de Gaulle's at Saint-Cyr, General Béthouart. They met again. The encounter was friendly and the action of 18 June was spoken of with sympathy. Yet Béthouart was not so in favour with his comrade's undertaking that he wished to join immediately. The visitor was one of those men who had long since acknowledged the existence of something in de Gaulle that went beyond rank and seniority. But in those around him he observed a good deal of reserve and he thought himself too ill-informed about the general situation to make so important a decision, committing so many men, without having seen his chiefs: he therefore decided to return to France first. De Gaulle said, "You'll see: they are a gang of old pricked balloons. And they won't let you leave again." (Béthouart had himself posted to Morocco, where he played a decisive part for Free France in November 1942.)

Since the general was not to be persuaded, they would have to try recruiting some of the men: Béthouart made it possible for de Gaulle to see them unit by unit. The rebel General went to Trentham Park, where he made contact with some of the officers of the 13th half-brigade of the Foreign Legion and of the light division of alpine troops, enrolling about a thousand men at one stroke, they being led by Colonel Magrin-Verneret, known as Montclar, and Captain Koenig, the future general. And this he did in spite of the hostility shown by most of the British officers, who pointed out to their French comrades that if they served under de Gaulle they would be "rebels against their own government".

Let us take the case of one of these "rebels" who, having disregarded the warnings of most of his companions, received Béthouart's approval. He was called André Dewavrin, and presently he took the pseudonym of Passy. He was not at Trentham Park when de Gaulle went there. But he heard of his visit and he knew his arguments. Letting his unit go back to France alone (not without some difficulty) he tried to reach London, losing his way because all the signposts had been camouflaged or altered to deceive the expected invaders; at last he was told that de Gaulle was based at St Stephen's House. Here he met his comrade Captain Tissier, whom the Constable had just made his Chief of Staff. Courcel took him to the General.

> I walked into a spacious, well-lit room. Two large windows opened on to the Thames. The huge form unwound and stood up to greet me. [The General] made me repeat my name and then asked me a series of short questions in a clear, incisive, rather harsh tone:
>
> "Are you on the active list or the reserve?"
>
> "Active, sir."
>
> "Passed staff college?"
>
> "No."
>
> "Where were you?"
>
> "The Ecole Polytechnique."
>
> "What were you doing before the mobilization?"
>
> "Professor of Fortification at the Ecole Spéciale Militaire de Saint-Cyr."
>
> "Have you any other qualifications? Do you speak English?"
>
> "I have a degree in law and I speak English fluently, sir."
>
> "Where were you during the war?"
>
> "With the expeditionary corps in Norway."
>
> "Then you knew Tissier. Are you senior to him?"
>
> "No, sir."
>
> "Very well. You will be head of the second and third bureau on my staff. Good day. I shall see you again soon."
>
> The conversation was over. I saluted and went out. The reception had been glacial.[10]

Although in de Gaulle's mind there was no question of playing Garibaldi's part and forming a legion for the common cause, although the undertaking was nothing less than the creation of a counter-state that from dissident legitimacy would gradually swing over to total sovereignty and although he intended to set up the luminous symbol of an abstract and worldwide France most powerfully against the peasant strokes of cunning conceived by the Vichy horse-copers, he had to arrange a cohabitation with his hosts – one that would provide him with a base from which to operate and with the means of action. And in the first place he had to have himself recognized. The Pétain system had been accepted by Hitler, because as he said himself, it offered "advantageous prospects". De Gaulle's movement, which had been welcomed straight away by Churchill, must also be clearly recognized by him.

Even before the arrival of René Cassin in London, Charles de Gaulle had set himself to obtaining the first outline of a legal status. As early as 23 June he had simultaneously registered London's statement of the "non-independent" nature of the Pétain government and its promise of recognizing a "provisional French National Committee". On 26 June Churchill heard that his envoys had not been allowed to make the slightest contact in Morocco. He therefore turned to de Gaulle,* summoned him to Downing Street on 27 June and said, "You are all alone? Well, then, I recognize you all alone!"[11] Charles-all-Alone, in every sense of the word, solitary and ill-provided but also unique and of the first importance.

And the next day the British government issued a communiqué according to which it "recognized General de Gaulle as leader of all the Free French, wherever they may be, who join him for the defence of the Allied cause". This document aroused strong criticism in the Prime Minister's immediate circle, at the Foreign Office – above all from Halifax and Cadogan – and at the War Office; Charles de Gaulle however welcomed it with what seems to have been ill-concealed eagerness. That same evening he spoke on the radio and proclaimed "I take under my authority all the French who are now living in British territory or who may arrive later."[12]

Certainly, this was war-time, when authority tends to magnify and concentrate itself. Certainly, the Gaullist movement was still too small not to over-do things, and the general too much "alone" not to strain for supremacy. But in this proclamation there was something hurried, ill-considered and over-eager, something of a kind to awake a suspicion, both in the French exiles and in British circles, that continually increased, in certain cases, until it became an obsessive distrust. The Constable would have been well advised to draw less immediate and imperious conclusions from the British communiqué which, though so gratifying to him, was after all more cautious: "I take under my authority." These five words were to cause a great many prejudices and misunderstandings.

Each day, de Gaulle received some insult from Vichy. On 19 June he was ordered to return to France. As early as the twenty-second his temporary rank of general was cancelled. On the twenty-third he was "compulsorily retired" as a disciplinary measure. On 28 June, through the French Embassy in London, he received a message from Paul Baudouin requiring him "to place himself in a state of arrest at the Saint-Michel prison in Toulouse within the next five days" in order to be judged by a military court for "the misdemeanour of inciting soldiers to disobedience" (to which he replied, by the same channel, "In my view this communication is devoid of interest"). On 4 July the trial ended with the military tribunal of the seventeenth region (that of Toulouse) condemning him to four years imprisonment and a fine of 100 francs.

But the Vichy authorities did not stop there. In view of the judges' "blameworthy indulgence" an appeal led to fresh proceedings. This time it was the

*Who had just sent him a memorandum proposing the recognition of Free France.

Clermont-Ferrand tribunal (thirteenth region, commanded by General de Lattre de Tassigny) that was entrusted with judging and condemning the exile, who in the meantime had been deprived of his French nationality.

The military judges of Clermont-Ferrand would not accept the accusation of treason against de Gaulle; but they agreed that he had deserted and had entered the service of a foreign power and they therefore, by five votes against two, condemned him to death, with confiscation of all his property and dismissal from the army. It was a sentence *in absentia* which Marshal Pétain ratified, though not without saying that he would see to it that the death-sentence was not carried out.

Today it is easy to give decisions of this kind their relative importance. Seen from London, these Vichy tribunals scarcely mattered at all: the exile let it be known that he considered the sentence "null and void" and that he would discuss it "with the people of Vichy after the war".

The government and the system which Philippe Pétain endowed with a prestige that neither the surrender of 17 June nor the ignominious clauses of the Armistice nor the violation of the treaty that united his country to Britain had yet been able to tarnish, was taking on a greater appearance of legitimacy every day. This regime hastily installed at a watering-place, that brought together defeated soldiers, admirals without a ship and embittered civil servants, this artless operetta-setting for an ill-written tragedy, was beginning to take form and solidity.[13]

At the time when Charles de Gaulle, in his office at St Stephen's House, was fighting to obtain a word from Spears, the transfer of three airmen to Free France and the conversion of the New Hebrides to his cause, Vichy was receiving the Papal Nuncio, Bogomolov, the Soviet ambassador, and presently Admiral Leahy, President Roosevelt's personal representative.

In his roomy office on the Embankment, Charles de Gaulle, ex-Under-Secretary of state, ex-temporary General, cashiered, denationalized, condemned to death, supported only by an elderly jurist, three colonels, a dozen captains, an unskilful secretary, a few journalists, three battalions of legionaries and the confidence of a Prime Minister with a brilliant genius but changeable moods, claimed to be the incarnation of a country that knew him only as a nocturnal voice with strange intonations and apparently uncontrolled outbursts.

At the end of June 1940* it was perfectly reasonable to count on the defeat of the Axis and on the Final victory of the Anglo-Saxons. Yet no serious observer could then have supposed that the visionary of St Stephen's House and his meagre, openly disparaged organization would emerge from this enormous upheaval of history and from the Allied victory. Indeed some of the men who joined him at that time privately say that Charles de Gaulle was perhaps the only one of the June rebels to believe in success. The greater number of the active members who made up this first phalanx thought they were fighting a hopeless battle, fighting for personal and collective honour.

But let us read what the author of the *Mémoires de guerre*, recalling those days of loneliness ten years later, has to say:

*Above all after the defeat of the Luftwaffe in the sky over south-east England in September 1940.

Among the French, as among other nations, the huge convergence of fear, self-interest, and despair brought about a universal abandonment of France. There was not a qualified man in the world who behaved as though he still believed in her independence, her pride and her grandeur. When I was faced with the horrifying emptiness of this general desertion, my mission appeared to me in a single flash clear and terrible. At that moment, the worst in her history, it was for me to assume the country's fate, to take France upon myself.[15]

CHAPTER TWENTY-ONE

*Charles Lackland**

By the beginning of July Charles de Gaulle thought he had learnt all about this "universal abandonment". Almost everyone had gone. Almost nobody had come. Sitting there in his triangular office in St Stephen's House, was he a dissident, a rebel, or merely an exile? Still, he had been joined by a few forlorn hopes; he had acquired a microphone. And had he not won the friendship of Winston Churchill? Though he still had to learn the limits of this friendship.

On 9 June, when the Prime Minister refused his request to transfer part of the Royal Air Force to France, de Gaulle had never doubted that Churchill saw himself above everything else as the guardian of Britain, however broad his strategic views might be and however strong his friendship for France.

Now the signing of the Franco-German and Franco-Italian Armistices on 22 and 26 June had rung like a tocsin in the ears of Churchill, so preoccupied he was by the fate of the French fleet. It is true that Darlan's ships had not been handed over to Hitler, nor to Mussolini. But there were clauses requiring them to return to their peace-time bases, and this was an arrangement that caused the British the most intense anxiety. It is true that at the Italians' suggestion the Armistice commissions had provisionally modified this state of affairs, the ships for the time being allowed to go to a North African port, far from the German army, if not from the Italian. Was this not a respite provided for Mr Churchill and his admirals?

But this "respite" did not satisfy them. Even before the Bordeaux government had accepted the Führer's diktat, and even before Admiral Darlan had, at Bordeaux on 18 June, given his word of honour to Sir Dudley Pound, his English opposite number, that his fleet should never "in any event" fall into the hands of what was then still their common enemy, the British Admiralty had prepared Operation Catapult, which was aimed at nothing less than the destruction of the greater part of the French fleet.

Whether this plan was drawn up on 14, 15 or 16 June is of little importance. What is certain is that London perceived a link between France's surrender and the necessary destruction of the country's fleet. The modifications that the documents of 22 and 26 June and the Armistice commission brought to the handing over to the Axis of a force that made the threat of an invasion of the British Isles even greater were not of such a kind as to make Churchill hold back: in his opinion Operation Catapult was still necessary.

"This was a hateful decision, the most unnatural and painful in which I have

*The French is Charles-sans-terre, Jean-sans-terre being the French for King John of England, sometimes known as John Lackland. (trs.)

ever been concerned," wrote the Prime Minister in his history of the war. Among the motives that made him take the responsibility for the slaughter upon himself, and which he recalls in this book, was a tragic echo of the French revolutionaries in 1793 (for Churchill was a most ardent reader of history): Danton and Robespierre, as they hurled the King's head at the feet of Europe, proclaimed the implacable nature of their resolution and so burnt their boats.

It was the other side's boats that Churchill preferred to burn. But by striking yesterday's ally in this way, he too launched a manifesto of extremism. In launching Catapult, Churchill struck both at the inclinations for a settlement that had survived the disappointments of Munich in London and at the men who had just surrendered at Bordeaux. In asserting himself as Churchill the Terrible, the Prime Minister was flinging down an irrevocable challenge to Hitler.

To anyone who, forty years later, carefully examines the words and actions spoken or carried out on 3 July 1940 in Mers-el-Kebir, the naval port of Oran, and during the preceding days, it does not appear at all obvious that the French fleet could in no case have escaped this massive destruction. Coincidences; disinformation; silences full of mental reservations: from beginning to end, Mers-el-Kebir was also a tragedy of non-communication.

The first area of darkness dates from a week before the tragedy: the Germans' acceptance of the Italians' proposal, that the ships should be gathered at Toulon and in North Africa, was never communicated to Admiral Odend'hal, the French naval attaché, who was still in London and who, had he been told, would have informed the British. Although this measure only turned the danger of capture by the Germans into that of seizure by the Italians, it was still of a character to relieve the minds of those in London.

It was on 27 June, immediately after the failure of Duff Cooper's mission to Casablanca, when it appeared that Darlan was thoroughly resigned to seeing the fleet either paralysed or sunk that the British Admiralty mustered Force H, intended for Operation Catapult, at Gibraltar: it was under the command of Admiral Somerville, a man of little breadth of understanding, unsuited for any enterprise or negotiation. On the French side nothing at all was suspected. Certainly, on 24 June Admiral Gensoul, commanding the fleet moored at Mers-el-Kebir, had been visited by an English fellow-sailor, Admiral North, who had told him about his government's apprehensions. Is it possible that the visitor was not precise enough? Gensoul does not seem to have understood the warning.

On the evening of 2 July Winston Churchill took the "hateful decision" and gave orders to act the next day. At 7 a.m. on 3 July, Somerville sent Gensoul an ultimatum, giving the French admiral the choice between five possibilities: joining the Royal Navy to carry on with the war; sailing to English ports; going to the United States; steering for the West Indies; or scuttling the fleet. If none of these courses was taken, then at 5.30 p.m. Force H would open fire in what could only be a massacre, not a battle, for the port was mined and the French ships, whose laying-up had begun, could not manoeuvre.

Admiral Gensoul tried to warn Vichy, where the government had settled the day before. But he told his superiors of only two of the solutions: internment in an English port or "battle". As it was impossible to get into contact with Darlan,* it was his colleague Admiral Le Luc** who took the responsibility of rejecting any alternative but the second, and in order to deal with the situation he tried to send the Toulon and Algiers squadrons as reinforcements. Admiral Somerville was told of this move, and it could not fail to make him hurry things on. Gensoul having rejected the ultimatum as a whole, Force H opened fire before 5.30 p.m. In sixteen minutes everything was over. Three of the finest ships had been sunk, 1380 sailors killed, 370 wounded. Only the battle-cruiser *Strasbourg* managed to slip away and sail to Toulon.

Some of Churchill's reasons have been given. Those that induced Admiral Gensoul to conceal from his government the greater number of the possibilities offered him are not known. It may be that in the atmosphere of those days the attackers had few illusions about seeing any of the middle terms accepted. Furthermore, both sailing for the United States and the West Indies would have breached the terms of the Armistice.

The cannonade of Mers-el-Kebir was not an isolated action. On the same day, all the French men-of-war anchored at Portsmouth or Plymouth were forcibly seized by sailors of the Royal Navy, and their crews, who even the night before had been fraternizing with their British hosts, were interned. And five days later the most modern of the great French battleships, the *Richelieu*, was attacked in Dakar by English planes. It was more than a savage warning: it was an attempt at the total destruction of the French navy.

Charles de Gaulle heard of the action at Mers-el-Kebir during the evening of 3 July. According to those witnesses who were able to see him that evening – Courcel, Passy and Pleven – he reacted very violently, both as a Frenchman united in feeling with the massacred sailors and as the leader of a movement backed by the English – a movement that seemed to be condemned to failure by a slaughter of this kind. What recruitment would be possible now, above all in the navy? And indeed, although Operation Catapult made many enemies, it may be true that de Gaulle and his venture were the most obvious casualty.

There is one author who actually throws the responsibility for Mers-el-Kebir on to the man of 18 June: Yves Bouthillier, Marshal Pétain's Minister of Finance, and he carries malignance so far as to attribute the accusation to someone else:

> The Marshal always suspected General de Gaulle of being behind this extraordinary attack. There seemed to be something in it. The movement that [de Gaulle] had just launched in London appeared to us an undertaking directed more against Marshal Pétain's France than against Hitler's Germany. The greatest danger for this nascent Gaullism was the establishment of trustful relations between London and Vichy. The master-card in the game that he was to play for four years was the feeling that the Marshal had betrayed Britain. Will one ever know the exact part the General played? For neither Mr Churchill nor the British Admiralty will yield up their secret.[1]

*During these tragic days, the Minister of the Navy had retired to his house at Nérac in Gascony.
**A member of the delegation that had received the diktat at Rethondes.

Others, like Robert Mengin,[2] take notice of General de Gaulle's erroneous words about the "handing over" of the French fleet to the Germans (particularly in his broadcast of 26 June), and they say that "if a Frenchman, a patriot and an officer, is rapidly convinced that other French soldiers and sailors are capable of handing over their ships, why should Mr Churchill not be equally convinced?" According to this, the General, by thoughtlessly expressing so agonizing a possibility, had part of the responsibility for the tragic decision of the British.

Yet it is the case that Admiral Darlan, in the name of almost all these sailors, did accept and confirm the conditions imposed by Hitler at Rethondes, that is to say the gathering of the French men-of-war in four ports controlled by the occupants. Are ships not seized from the shore? When one knows how the French ships anchored at Plymouth and Portsmouth were taken over by the Royal Navy on 3 July, and when one considered the daring and the skill of the SS commandos, can the doubts about the behaviour of the fleet in the summer of 1940 be looked upon as insulting? And what happened to Admiral Derrien's ships moored in the port of Bizerta in November 1942? They fell into the hands of the Axis. The fleet was not "handed over" in June 1940, but it was not put out of reach of the Reich. Yes, a danger of capture did exist, whether or not one calls it a "mortal" danger which is the word used by Churchill himself.

Charles de Gaulle was hit very hard by the "terrible axe-blow" of Mers-el-Kebir. When Spears came to see him on 5 July, expecting the worst, he found him "astonishingly objective", acknowledging that perhaps the operation was "inevitable" from the British angle but looking upon it as so disastrous from his own perspective that he thought of "withdrawing to Canada and living there as a private individual"; in any case he said he would give himself a day or two before making his decision and explaining his point of view on the radio. Sir Edward hurried to Churchill and told him that as far as this aspect was concerned the worst had been avoided and that de Gaulle was showing "a splendid dignity".[3]

It was only on 8 July that de Gaulle expressed his opinion of what Winston Churchill himself, addressing the cheering Commons, had called "this mournful episode". Did the Constable ever face a more dreadful trial? His enterprise still rested upon the support of a single man; and he had to condemn that man. He was about to do so, and in doing it he strengthened the alliance. This was his first diplomatic feat, the herald of more to come:

> There is not a Frenchman who has not heard with pain and anger that ships of the French fleet have been sunk by our Allies. This pain and anger come from our very depths. There is no reason to come to terms with them. That hateful tragedy was not a glorious battle.
>
> From the only point of view that matters in the end, that is to say from the point of view of victory and liberation the government that was at Bordeaux had agreed to place our ships at the enemy's discretion. Out of principle and out of necessity, one day the enemy would have used them either against England or against our own empire. Well, I say without hesitation that it is better they should have been destroyed.
>
> Though seeing this tragedy as what it is, I mean as lamentable and hateful,

> Frenchmen worthy of the name cannot be unaware that the defeat of England would confirm their bondage for ever. Our two ancient nations, our two great nations remain bound to one another. They will either go down both together or both together they will win.[4]

If, among the many reasons he had for staining his hands with the blood of the sailors at Mers-el-Kebir, Churchill had also seen it as a decisive trial of his alliance with de Gaulle, one may say that the episode proved its strength both to Churchill and the War Cabinet. The alliance held firm. But how many recruits did not this operation cost Free France, that realm without any territory whose only future seemed to be on the seas and beyond?

At this period Charles de Gaulle had two bases for his being: the one British and inevitable. The other French and indispensable. On the British side things were reasonably clear and they did not change much until those summer days of 1941 when the interests of Free France in the Levant clashed head-on with those of Great Britain, and some of these English friends – on occasion for serious reasons – changed into opponents. Charles de Gaulle, since 28 June recognized as "leader of the Free French", could count above all on the Prime Minister's friendship and trust – both strengthened by the trial of Mers-el-Kebir – and on that of his immediate circle: Desmond Morton, Edward Spears, General Ismay, Harold Nicolson and Lord Tyrell. In the Cabinet he could reckon on three or four equally staunch friends: Anthony Eden, who was at the War Office, Leo Amery, and Duff Cooper. And very soon the royal family showed an evident liking for him, which was widely reported in the papers.

But there was obvious reserve at the Foreign Office and above all at the War Office: Among the diplomats; Lord Halifax, the head of the house and who had been the architect of Munich, was sceptical. His closest colleague, Sir Alexander Cadogan, was hostile: among his notes there are to be found remarks such as "that c. . . of a fellow de Gaulle"; whereas the Under-Secretary of State, Sir Robert Vansittart, was rather in favour, as was the former minister in Paris, Oliver Harvey (both of them more Francophile than Gaullist). Among the soldiers, where there was little liking for rebels, de Gaulle and Gaullism were held in low esteem, as they were in most branches of the Intelligence Service – some were even frankly hostile.

As for the press, it naturally varied. It cannot be reduced to its most famous member, *The Times*. Yet taking into account the tradition of pluralism that is respected from one column to another in the greatest British daily, an attentive reading of the pages of *The Times* in 1940 and 1941 shows a thoughtful sympathy for the cause and for most of the undertakings of this exiled general.

The paper's interest in the General's activities never failed. On 25 June, the day Hitler declared that the war in the west was over, *The Times*, with a headline in larger letters, devoted three columns to "the immense interest" aroused by the appeal of 18 June. On 27 June, under the heading "A Soldier Speaks", it quoted the whole of the exile's reply to Marshal Pétain's defence of the armistice.

When one reflects upon the real strength then at de Gaulle's disposal and upon his actual influence on the progress of the war; when one knows the great English papers' obligatory worship of facts, one is almost tempted to say that *The Times* was excessively sympathetic.

As far as facts are concerned, at that time de Gaulle amounted to almost nothing; yet this paper (like the *Daily Telegraph* too) spoke of him as a factor of great importance in the war.

But the sympathy of most of the British Press could not fully satisfy the Free French: such an organization had to have its own means of expression. Certainly from the very beginning there was the particular voice of General de Gaulle. But it was not raised without awakening countless reserves in the bosom of the War Cabinet and the Foreign Office. However carefully Spears and Duff Cooper smoothed the corners, every speech was the pretext for a diplomatic guerilla.

On 26 June, for example, the vehement words that de Gaulle addressed to Pétain aroused extreme agitation in the Foreign Office. Cadogan sent one of his assistants, Gladwyn Jebb, in pursuit of the general, to suggest certain modifications in the direction of mildness. Forty-two years later, Cadogan's messenger, now Lord Gladwyn, told the story in the course of a Franco-British meeting in London:*

> I found him at the Hotel Rubens. He stared at me: "Who are you?" I agreed that my rank was not very high, still I did propose a few slight alterations. "Give me that!" He read the paper and cried, "I think them ridiculous, perfectly ridiculous." I told him that if he did not accept these trifling changes he would not be allowed to broadcast. My ultimatum was effective. Like an elephant, he trampled the forest, but not the baobabs. "Well, I accept. It's ridiculous, but I accept."

After 8 July and the speech on Mers-el-Kebir (a speech that he had spontaneously submitted to his hosts – his targets – and that nobody had thought of asking him to alter) the supervision grew less. In October 1940, following an informal agreement between the Foreign Office and Louis Rougier,** an envoy from Vichy, de Gaulle was asked to spare the person of Philippe Pétain a little. The result was scarcely noticeable. It was still a matter of "unworthy leaders who have broken France's sword", of the "court of the sultan of Vichy", and of "those responsible for the capitulation [who] are collapsing in shame and panic fear". De Gaulle spoke on an average three times a month, in an implacable combat tone.

But one voice was not enough. During the summer of 1940 a most complex organization was set up around the French Service of the BBC. In this framework five minutes (later ten) a day were reserved for Free France, which in August, at the General's personal request, was given a spokesman in the person of Maurice Schumann.

"In three years," states Schumann, "I did not receive a single directive from the General. But I did hear two or three postwar criticisms for excessive indulgence with regard to Vichy!"[5] Quite apart from an eloquence that soon became famous, an unfailing loyalty and perfect English, Schumann could take advantage of count-

*November 1984.
**See pp. 285–6.

less friendships in London: before the war he had often accompanied Eden on his diplomatic journeys; he was a friend of Duff Cooper and even more of one of the BBC's stars, the great critic Raymond Mortimer, a specialist in French literature and for many years the London correspondent of *Les Nouvelles littéraires*.

Then came the creation of the programme called *Les Français parlent aux Français*, which played an important part in the evenings of people in the occupied countries for nearly four years. It was under the direction of Michel Saint-Denis, known as Jacques Duchêne, the head of a French theatrical company established in London, and it was run by Yves Morvan, known as Jean Marin, a Breton sailor who had become the main script-writer for the programme, in which he eloquently represented the current opinion most in agreement with the General's views. There was also Pierre Maillaud, known as Bourdan, the Havas correspondent in London, whom we saw joining General de Gaulle as early as the morning of 19 June; later he assumed an important part in this programme, and one that was characterized by a quite unusual spirit of criticism. Afterwards he became the head of an agency connected with Reuters which he called first LEF (*Liberté Egalité Fraternité*) and then AFI (*Agence française indépendante*); and this he did not without taking his distance from Gaullism – increasing distances that were sometimes very obvious.

Georges Gombault and his son Charles were socialists, friends of Léon Blum, and reached London on 28 June. There they soon found their friends Louis Lévy of *Le Populaire*, Pierre Comert, who was one of the founders of the League of Nations and who then ran the press service at the Quai d'Orsay until Georges Bonnet got rid of him for "warmongering", and after them Marcel Hoden and Gustave Moutet, the son of a popular front minister. Comert persuaded the group to found a newspaper: he interested Duff Cooper in the plan, and on 21 August 1940 Duff Cooper tried to win Churchill over. "If these Frenchmen have anything in them," interrupted the Prime Minister, "their paper will come out next Monday. After that, I've no further interest in it."[6]

France, established in the Reuter offices, appeared on 26 August, with a leader by Charles de Gaulle: "Everything that serves to strike the enemy is useful and beneficial. This applies to *France*, whose aim is to encourage the fight." The General had appointed a personal representative with the paper, André Rabache, who was one of the two editors. But the day after the first issue had come out, Charles Gombault, the other editor, had a telephone-call from "an officer in the General's headquarters" who handed on his chief's congratulations and added "We should be obliged if you would suppress the words *Liberté Egalité Fraternité* under the title." "But they are the motto of the Republic!" "No doubt, but in the present circumstances they might tend to divide the French people." Gombault states that the motto was retained.[7]

If *France* showed a degree of reserve that created a great deal of irritation among Charles de Gaulle's immediate associates, what is to be said about *France libre*, founded by André Labarthe, a brilliant physicist who had been the General's adviser upon weapons before he turned to journalism, collaborating with Raymond Aron, who reached London in July 1940? But their relations soon grew sour. Labarthe had a wonderfully fertile and inventive mind and he had seen this publication as a stepping-stone to activities from which the General stubbornly kept him at a distance: his personal ambitions had a good deal to do with this sourness, but so did the nature of the review which was "more concerned with analysis than with propaganda" as it was put by Raymond Aron who, speaking of the General's authority, goes so far as to conjure up the ghost of Bonapartism.

These quarrels between the émigrés in London concerned not only the supporters and the opponents of General de Gaulle but also the various kinds of Gaullist (Robert Mengin subdivides them into "fighters", "Carltonians"* and "humbugs") not to mention those who had been enrolled by the English (above all in the Intelligence Service and the RAF). To give some notion of their virulence and their gravity, a few English testimonies will be quoted together with some particularly significant examples of anger aroused by the man of 18 June.

It is quite certain that nothing predisposed the intellectuals of the Labour Party to rally to the Gaullist banner – apart from their common hatred for Fascism. Yet when one of the members of the Jean-Jaurès Club brought him an article attacking the leader of the Free French in an unusually acrimonious tone, Kingsley Martin, the editor of *The New Statesman and Nation*, reacted strongly: "No! De Gaulle has his faults, but he does represent something very great, much more than these people with their pinpricks. If we were to attack him, we should give Hitler and Vichy too much pleasure."[8]

Lady Astor's son, David Astor, later the editor of *The Observer*, had much to do with these concerns. He was a Liberal, in tune with the members of the Jean-Jaurès Club, and he subsequently became General Koenig's liaison-officer. Few Englishmen knew as much about the inner life of Free France. When I asked him what idea the English public had formed of Charles de Gaulle during the war, he replied:

> The English people admired de Gaulle, their companion of the darkest days, and they respected his courage. In political circles it was neither his ideas nor his character that was criticized but rather the want of sympathy that he showed for Great Britain. That was the only thing against him. As an ally and a guest we found him pretty cantankerous.
>
> Yet the most surprising aspect of the relations between de Gaulle and other people was the attitude of the French. We were constantly being surprised by the ill-will of all those who could have been called intellectuals, of almost all the politicians, and of many soldiers. This distrust that he aroused among the most outstanding members of the French community in London could not fail to strike us. In our country it was not with the British but chiefly with the French that he had trouble. And the reason these quarrels did not become more public is the pressure brought to bear by the British to restore calm.[9]

Some points in this recollection might be questioned, but not the fact that (except

*The bureaucrats in Carlton Gardens where the Free French moved to on 22 July.

at the time of the Levant Affair in summer 1941 and on the eve of the Allied landing in North Africa in November 1942) the harshest criticism that the Constable had to undergo in London came from the French.

However politically ambiguous Charles de Gaulle may have been during those years, his immediate circle was even more so. One often hears or reads that in London the Constable was surrounded by right-wing extremists, by the Camelots du roi and the cagoulards.[10]* But anyone who tries to examine, one by one, the group that gathered round the leader of the Free French at the end of summer 1940, will be astonished by simplifications of this kind.

Let us take what was thought to be the most cankered or ill-affected organization, the 2nd Bureau, that then became the SR, then the BCRAM and finally the BCRA,** set up and headed by Captain Dewavrin, "Passy". Little is known about the political ideas of this officer. It seems that in his early days in London, Passy looked upon the Republic and the democratic system with much the same unenthusiastic and authoritarian eye as his chief. Yet although in his recollections he speaks very openly about the way two of his closest and most effective assistants, Captain Fourcaud and Lieutenant Duclos, belonged to the Cagoule, he explains the origin of the legend that made him too a cagoulard so ironically that one is inclined to believe him.***

In any case when the 2nd Bureau, then the SR, became the BCRA, the organization's members included such men as Pierre-Bloch, Louis Vallon and Stéphane Hessel, who could scarcely be numbered among the right-wing. Declared left-wing militants like Philip, Moulin and Brossolette do not seem to have had any scruples about working with or in this "nest of cagoulards". But on the level of basic ideology the diagnosis must be expressed with carefully graded shades of meaning.

Leaving these debatable services to one side, who were the first associates of the man of 18 June? Geoffroy de Courcel, a diplomat coming from a conservative background, would probably have voted to the right before the war. But from 18 June onwards nobody ever heard him utter what could truly be called a political opinion. He was defined only by his loyalty. What of his successors as ADC to the General? Before the war Claude Bouchinet-Serreulles was a reader of *La Flèche*, an organ of the intellectual left win, and François Coulet was above all an unorthdox "mal-pensant" who hated the conservatives. Hettier de Boislambert? It is true that in 1983 he spoke about "order" and "authority" in such a way as to make it seem possible that in 1940 he was not one of thoese who wished to bring the Popular Front back to power.

But what can be said of René Pleven, they key man in this team, except that as a Breton belonging to the republican tradition (those that are called the Blues) he was and remained a liberal in the full meaning of the word? Who could claim to

*The Camelots du roi advocated a return to monarchy. The Cagoulards wanted to ensure a France without communism. (trs.)

**Bureau central de renseignement et d'action: see pp. 497–8.

***During a conversation in May 1984 Colonel Dewavrin-Passy told me that when he was teaching at Saint-Cyr he was strongly in favour of the Spanish Republic and against Munich.

belong to the left wing more than René Cassin,* the archetype of the anti-fascist democrat? When he reached London, Pierre-Olivier Lapie was a socialist deputy (or more exactly a "republican-socialist"), which, in the eyes of his electors in Lorraine set him far to the left. And what of Georges Boris, who had been Léon Blum's Cabinet director? Or Maurice Schumann, that vehement anti-Fascist? Or Admiral Muselier, whom the whole service called the Red Sailor? Or General Petit, a contemporary at Saint-Cyr whom de Gaulle appointed as his Chief of Staff and who was later to be seen as a senator allied to the Communists?

The Free French gathered round de Gaulle were ideologically incoherent; and if anything they gravitated to the left. It was more a microcosm of France – or at least of that part of the nation which had decided against resignation.

Yet an excellent witness tells a different story. André Weil-Curiel, a Gaullist from the beginning, was astonished to find that he was kept at a distance. Why? René Pleven led him to understand that both his Jewish origins and the past militancy of his socialist views had "however unfair it might be" saddled him with the reputation of a "terror" at St Stephen's House; and this was confirmed by René Cassin, a Jew himself, who in a fatherly way advised him to keep rather quiet.[11] Weil-Curiel states that in the event de Gaulle intervened in his favour, as he did for his other Jewish collaborators (but the fact that he had to do so is none the less sinister); yet Weil-Curiel thought this atmosphere so murky that he had but one wish – to be sent to occupied France: and indeed he went very soon, knowing the risks he was running.

An outside event helped to clarify the attitudes of the Free French. On 19 July, the parliament at Vichy, elected in 1936, offered Pétain powers more extensive than those enjoyed by Mussolini and, to Maurras' joy, a crown heavier than any worn by a French sovereign. Only eighty deputies and senators** were to be found who showed their respect for the mandate granted them four years earlier by remaining faithful to the Republic.

Once Vichy had turned itself in a Versailles of the defeat, the new émigrés found themselves invested, whether they liked it or not, with a contrary mission. They, together with the interior resistance, still in its very early stages, were the Republic, pending the time when they should be the France of which de Gaulle, at the cost of an intellectual operation that substituted symbol for reality, claimed to be the immediate incarnation: the Republic, which has not always found expeditive or authoritarian forms of conduct distasteful.***

Was Charles de Gaulle at once aware of the importance of public opinion in occupied France (half or wholly occupied) and of the enterprises that arose from it, based on his appeals of June (and even more on Pétain's just before)? The American political expert Professor Nicholas Wahl maintains that it was de

*A little before his death René Cassin said to Emile Delavenay, "You see I was right: I succeeded in turning de Gaulle towards democracy!"

**The Communists having been excluded in 1939.

***Jacques de Sieyès, the general's representative in New York, often showed a letter from de Gaulle pointing out that he more often spoke of "republic" than of "democracy".

Gaulle's quick perception of a spirit of resistance emerging in France that gave Free France its importance, efficacity and high standing. If de Gaulle had neglected this essential dimension of the struggle, confining himself only to the strengthening of his links with Churchill and to his proceedings in the empire, he would have been swept away by the after-effects of his failures at Dakar or his half-success in the Levant.[12]

Others say on the contrary that it was only much later – at the time of Jean Moulin's visit to London in autumn 1941 – that the General became aware of the importance of the Resistance, both in itself and for him, and that he really applied himself to the task of encouraging and organizing it only after the Algiers landings in November 1942, when he had to prove his legitimacy to Roosevelt. This is the opinion of men as highly qualified as Henri Frenay, the founder of the Resistance movement Combat, and Stéphane Hessel, who worked closely with Passy.

Taking into account de Gaulle's egocentricity, the monopoly that he tended to assume for himself, and the certainty he often expressed up until the end of 1941 that "without me, everything would fall to pieces, and indeed nothing would have existed", the links that were very quickly formed between London and the Resistance show the importance the General attached to this aspect from the very beginning. By means of Passy and his agents in France, de Gaulle, by the end of 1940, had been able to see that inner France was beginning to stir, and that once the first tremors of resistance had taken place the humiliated and occupied nation ceased to be a terrain that had to be reconquered and was gradually changing itself into the very instrument of its own liberation.

De Gaulle, in his *Mémoires*, speaks of a photograph taken on 14 June 1940 in front of the tomb of the Unknown Warrior in Paris and showing a crowd overwhelmed with despair: it was sent to him in London as early as 19 June with these words: "De Gaulle, we heard you. Now we shall wait for you!" He also speaks of the mass of anonymous flowers that covered the grave of his mother, who died on 16 July at Paimport. Was this the birth of home Gaullism?

As early as 17 June three very different men – Charles Tillon, a Communist deputy,* General Cochet, who had commanded the planes of the 5th Army,** and Jean Moulin, the prefect of the Eure-et-Loir – carried out an act of resistance in their own manner. Tillon, in hiding since October 1939 had no sooner heard Pétain's appeal than at 3 p.m. on 17 June 1940 he wrote a tract which was put in circulation that evening: "Now they are surrendering France. Having surrendered the armies of the north and the east, having surrendered Paris with its factories and its workers, they think that with Hitler's help they can surrender the whole country to Fascism. But the French people will not bear slavery. They have the numbers. United, they will have the strength!"[13]

General Cochet, a former military attaché in Berlin gathered his officers in the region of the Puy-de-Dôme and in the afternoon of 17 June gave them instructions to resist those who wished to impose an armistice on the country. As for Jean Moulin, there have been many accounts of how he began the long march that was

*Expelled by the Assembly.
**In which de Gaulle commanded the tanks.

to make him the supreme head of the Resistance, and of his exemplary martyrdom, refusing to sign a tract which the occupiers wanted him to endorse and trying to kill himself that same night, so that he would not run the risk of yielding under torture.

These forerunners were very soon followed by other pioneers: the film-producer Gilbert Renault, who became "Roulier", "Raymond" and then "Rémy"; Henri Frenay, a captain who founded the Mouvement de libération nationale, Combat's precursor, soon joined by Claude Bourdet, a journalist very close to Temps présent (but who had not known de Gaulle there), the trade-unionist Christian Pineau, Emmanuel d'Astier de La Vigerie, who later set up Libération, and Jean-Pierre Lévy, founder of Franc-Tireur – both these being resistance movements.

A month after the 2nd Bureau had been established at St Stephen's House, Passy sent three agents to France, "loaded with questionnaires"; their task was to provide preliminary reports, if not on the first stirrings of the Resistance then at least on the state of public opinion with regard to the Armistice, to Vichy and to the movement in London. These agents were successively Jacques Mansion, known as Jack, Moreau and Gilbert Renault, whose pseudonym was then Raymond. In spite of improvisation, rivalries and serious blunders, by the middle of the summer of 1940 links had been formed between the *émigrés* and the occupied nation, between two of the "fragments of the sword" that de Gaulle asserted he would "gather together".

Free France left St Stephen's House and the banks of the Thames on 22 July for Carlton Gardens, a charming shaded terrace looking on to the Mall, on the edge of St James's Park, where number four, a large, quite elegant four-storeyed house had been placed at his disposal. Lord Palmerston, one of the most steadily anti-French English statesmen of the nineteenth century, had lived there: Charles de Gaulle must have found this a cause for sarcastic observations. He himself settled in the corner office on the first floor, a spacious, light-filled, well-furnished room over those occupied by the information services, which were headed by Jean Massip and which included Georges Boris and Maurice Schumann among others.

From this time onwards Carlton Gardens acted as the symbol and nerve-centre for the whole of Free France's civil and military organizations, the Constable's corner-room being the central point for activities, arrivals and meetings. But as Gaullism became more popular, so a kind of devolution came about, the navy moving off to the former French Institute, Colonel Passy's section to 10, Duke Street, and the "interior" organizations to Hill Street, almost all these places being in the fashionable and political centre of London, from Mayfair to Belgravia.

On 19 June de Gaulle's family arrived. Yvonne de Gaulle, having left Carantec with her children, had been able, thanks to the British consul, to go aboard an English merchantman on the eighteenth. "There were not many ships left in the port. Two were about to leave, an English vessel and a Pole: it was the Pole that was sunk." said the General gravely.[14] It was the next day that he heard from Pleven that his family had landed in England. An hour later Yvonne rang him up.

"Oh, it's you. I'm in London. I shall be waiting for you."

As the Seamore Grove flat was too small to accommodate the five newcomers (one was Mlle Marguerite Potel, who never left Anne), even after Philippe had left for a naval cadets' school, they therefore moved into the Hotel Rubens,* opposite Buckingham Palace Mews, until they could find a permanent home. In less than a week Mme de Gaulle chose a mock-Tudor villa in Petts Wood, Kent, in the south-east suburbs of London. They settled in. The General went by train to Victoria or was driven by Etienne Bellanger, the manager of Cartier's in London, one of the very few important members of the French colony to have joined him.

The de Gaulles quite liked living at Petts Wood. But at the beginning of August the Blitz began. Two weeks later Mme de Gaulle told Mrs Plummel, the owner, that she would have to leave: "The nights are too noisy; my little Anne is terrified". She began searching for a quieter refuge, and she found one at Ellesmere, in Shropshire, between Birmingham and Liverpool, not far from the Ladies of Sion convent at Shrewsbury, where Elizabeth went to school. Gadlas Hall was a comfortless old building but surrounded by wonderful gardens. Here Anne had more peace, and her mother liked the place; but it was four hours from London, and the General could only come once a month.

From the end of 1941 General de Gaulle had to make up his mind to live most of the time separated from his wife and his daughter Anne, who meant so much to him. He therefore took a room at the Connaught where the other guests did their best to give the impression that he was unnoticed. In his *Mémoires* he pays tribute to the "discreet sympathy" that allowed him "to prove, to my own advantage, that in this great nation each respects the other's freedom." However strongly he might be aware of his own dignity, and however unyielding his determination not to give signs of effusive gratitude that might anywhere be interpreted as symptoms of weakness or allegiance, de Gaulle was more capable of praising his hosts' qualities than has often been said:

> The open-hearted kindness shown us by the English people everywhere cannot be imagined. There is no counting the number of people who came to offer us their services, their time, and their money. It must be said that England lived in a stirring atmosphere in those days. From one moment to the next the German attack was expected, and faced with this prospect everyone entrenched himself in an exemplary resolution. It was a truly wonderful sight to see each Englishman behaving as though the salvation of the country depended on his own conduct.[15]

Though everybody respected his privacy, the British leaders, beginning with Churchill, soon began to wish that their French ally was better known by the general public. Richmond Temple, a well-known publicity-agent of the time, was entrusted with "promoting" de Gaulle, who growled, "Churchill wants to launch me like a brand of soap," but who finally said that some photographers might come and see him at Petts Wood. The result was a set of photographs that the British

*At present nobody belonging to the hotel has the slightest recollection of these guests.

papers agreed to publish so as not to wound the Prime Minister, though at the same time they wondered whether they were not doing a disservice to this long-legged officer fellow, stiffer than a guardsman, his cantankerous eye gazing beyond a line of sight upon which there crouched his slip of a wife with a bird-like look.

Yet it goes without saying that neither Churchill nor de Gaulle based their undertaking on the image that the illustrated papers might give of it. For the Constable it was a matter of making Free France acknowledged as a political partner and as the embryo of a State, pending the time when his call should have gathered a force capable of influencing the course of the war; for Churchill, who had staked the future of his relations with France on de Gaulle (though without denying himself certain contacts elsewhere) it was a question of giving the General, whose name was from now on linked with his and with the British strategy, a basis and a standing worthy of the privileged ally of His Majesty's Prime Minister.

Charles de Gaulle, who began as an irritated guest but who gradually changed into a brother in arms moved by the calm magnanimity of this threatened nation, has among other things given a striking picture of Churchill standing like a church tower on his island, facing the Nazi terror, rather surprised that the Reich had not yet attempted an invasion and expecting things to grow much worse – the hammering of the big German bombers that had flattened Amsterdam and that might wipe out twenty British cities tomorrow:

> Many people, wishing to be rid of this unbearable tension, reached the point of openly saying that they hoped the enemy would risk the attack. Mr Churchill was one of the very first to find the waiting hard to bear. I can see him now at Chequers one August day shaking his fist at the sky and crying "Are they not coming, then?" "Are you in such a hurry to see your cities shattered?" I asked him. "Don't you understand," he replied, "that the bombing of Oxford or Coventry or Canterbury would arouse such a wave of indignation in the United States that they would come into the war?"

De Gaulle, whose mind was still charged with memories of June and Paul Reynaud's moving appeals, to which Roosevelt returned no more than evasive replies, expressed his doubt. Churchill quite rightly answered that one helped a country that was resisting rather than one that was in a state of collapse. The conclusion that de Gaulle draws from this conversation between leaders is well known and it is of a simplicity that only the "great" can allow themselves: "Mr Churchill and I modestly agreed upon this ordinary but final outcome: when all is said and done, England is an island; France the headland of a continent; America another world.[16]

The disagreements that later embittered the relations between these two gladiators ("He was born for things on an enormous scale," said de Gaulle; and Churchill, "He is a man of my own size") cannot prevent one from remembering that for a whole year, and in spite of the massacre of Mers-el-Kebir, there was what Geoffroy de Courcel, a good witness, called in my presence "a honeymoon". So much so, he added, that it irritated even such a francophile diplomat as Oliver

Harvey: "But after all who is this de Gaulle that Winston should be infatuated with him?" they asked angrily in the corridors of Whitehall. And when Gaston Palewski came from Africa on 31 August and was able to tell his innumerable British friends about the Constable, the old hands in His Majesty's service could be heard saying, "At last we have someone who knows de Gaulle! So it is not just one of Churchill's whims".[17]

In those days not a week passed but the man whose task it was to prevent Hitler from setting foot on British soil wrote some note or other to urge the Foreign Office, the War Office or some one of his subordinates to be useful to the people at Carlton Gardens. An example is the letter of 12 July 1940 to General Ismay: "An opportunity of assisting the French would be to make a great success of their function of 14 July, when they are going to lay a wreath on the Foch statue."[18]

Two or three hundred sailors and legionaries and one mechanized detachment: it was not a vast human mass that de Gaulle and Muselier reviewed in front of the statue of the former generalissimo of the Allied armies on 14 July 1940 in Grosvenor Gardens. But many British were there, moved and enthusiastic; none of those who joined in the Marseillaise they roared out will ever forget it. And it was then that the walls of London blossomed with a placard that had two little tricolours on top and below them these famous words:

> To all Frenchmen
> France has lost a battle, but France has not lost the war. Some chance-gathered authorities, giving way to panic and forgetting honour, may have surrendered, delivering the country over into bondage. Yet nothing is lost!
> That is why I call upon all Frenchmen, wherever they may be, to join me in action, in sacrifice and in hope.

There exists an anti-Gaullism so furious that it cannot and will not make the slightest concession, and therefore the authorship of the most famous of these sentences has been denied to the General. Some attribute it to Churchill, others to Duff Cooper. It so happens that in one of his first comments on the campaign in France, Duff Cooper, the Minister of Information, did undoubtedly say "France has lost a great battle, but so great a country cannot fail to rise again." There is a considerable difference between the English Minister's words and those of de Gaulle, whose intention was to strike and which succeeded in doing so.

Since Churchill had denied that Pétain's was an independent government on 23 June and had recognized de Gaulle as "leader of the Free French" on 28 June, the two were closely allied, and they wished to go farther. In any case the Frenchman did.

On 26 June 1940 Charles de Gaulle sent the British government a memorandum, urging it to recognize a French National Committee representing Free France; and after this, at the beginning of July, there began negotiations with the aim of putting the relations between the Constable and the United Kingdom on a legal footing. Sir William Strang conducted them on the British side, René

Cassin on the French. It was not a question of obtaining the recognition of a French legion fighting on the Allies' side, nor even of the reconstruction of an army; it was a question of having themselves acknowledged as France itself. And this, taking into account the realities of the time and the admitted truth that law cannot fail to take facts into consideration, seemed to belong to the realm of sheer paradox.

Cassin, by way of commentary on the scene during which de Gaulle said to him, "We are France itself", tells how he imagined that Hitler, watching them through the keyhole, exclaimed, "Here are two maniacs fit for the asylum." The British negotiators retained an unpleasant recollection of the Frenchman's "exasperating graspingness"; Cassin, entrusted with an impossible mission, deployed a passion and a virtuosity that the old Foreign Office hands were hardly accustomed to. As de Gaulle's lieutenant, he took over the General's maxim: extreme weakness absolutely requires extreme intransigence.

In these almost unprecedented circumstances where a single man was on one side of the scales, a whole empire on the other, Cassin based himself upon a treaty signed between France and the fragmented state of Czechoslovakia in October 1939, about which he had written an article in a legal review. However different the positions might be, Cassin found material in this treaty to back his assertion of the sovereignity of the embryonic movement whose advocate he was.

The difficulties came less from the jurist's professional stubbornness than from de Gaulle's state of mind. His words in the *Mémoires* tell us a great deal about that atmosphere that could be created when he intervened in the negotiation:

> Taking into consideration the possibility that the fortunes of war might induce the English to make a compromise peace, and, on the other hand, bearing in mind that the British might conceivably be tempted by one or another of our overseas possessions I insisted that Great Britain should guarantee the re-establishment of the frontiers of metropolitan France and of the French Empire.

Furthermore, the Constable, to emphasize that he was not merely a small additional power, claimed "the supreme command of the French forces", although "given the proportion between the resources" he consented to "the general directives of the British High Command". To those on the other side this seemed a very faint bow to the realities that they in their turn were obliged to acknowledge when de Gaulle, with Churchill's backing, required that the French soldiers recruited by the British Command since June should come under the control of the Free French and that "in no event should these men bear arms against France".*

The de Gaulle-Churchill agreement was signed on 7 August at 10 Downing Street.** This document strengthened the June convention, accentuating the part played by the movement's civil administration and emphasizing the fact that as

*Words that were to give rise to countless interpretations.

**De Gaulle in his *Mémoires* places the signing at Chequers, unlike all the other witnesses.

between the two parties, war expenses should be regarded only as advances repayable after the victory, thus symbolizing the treaty's egalitarian nature.

But as is often the case in diplomatic matters, the essential was not said in the treaty but by an exchange of letters. The moment he and his guest had signed the official text, Churchill handed de Gaulle a letter which stated that His Majesty's government "was resolved, when the Allied armies had gained the victory, to ensure the integral restoration of the independence and greatness of France."

This very generous message was accompanied by a more delicately-shaded secret letter in which the Prime Minister said, "The words, 'integral restoration of the independence and greatness of France' are not strictly related to the territorial frontiers. But of course we shall do our best."

Did the Constable here find a confirmation of the suspicions he had expressed during the negotiations? It was in the wariest style that, in the same manner, he replied to his partner, "I hope that one day circumstances will allow the British government to consider these matters with less reserve." A year later the two men came into head-on collision in the great argument over the Levant.

In one field the alliance between the British War Cabinet and Free France was brought into effect most agreeably – that of finance. An agreement signed in March 1941 – the origin of the Free French "central fund" set up eight months later – organized London's financial help for its allies in Carlton Gardens. Pierre Denis, known as Rauzan, who with René Pleven was in charge of Free French finances, has described these arrangements very well:

> The expenditure was carried out on the basis of a budget that we established [and] submitted to the Treasury at the beginning of each year. Every month the Treasury paid the funds required for the carrying out of this budget into General de Gaulle's account at the Bank of England. One must bear witness to the liberality and the breadth of mind with which the Treasury's supervision was carried out.[19]

Was this debt ever repaid? In a letter he wrote to me in February 1984, André Postel-Vinay, who was Pierre Denis' deputy in London, gave these particulars: "Worked out at the end of June 1943, this debt amounted to thirty million pounds sterling, which would represent about two billion francs in 1984. It was not dear! It may be said that we began to finance ourselves (by an inflation of the franc) from 1 January 1943 onwards. The repayment of Free France's debt to Britain took place very shortly after the Liberation, in the spring of 1945, according to General de Gaulle's wishes." Postel-Vinay also emphasizes "the remarkable broad-mindedness" invariably shown by the Treasury who never attempted to bring financial pressure to bear on Charles de Gaulle.

After 7 August 1940 Charles de Gaulle, though still without land, was no longer without rights. He had come by a strange legal status and he commanded an "administration" recognized by his powerful protector. The forces that had joined him did not exceed seven thousand fighting men. But those joining his cause were beginning to grow more significant. As early as 30 June there came from Gibraltar a high-ranking officer, Vice-Admiral Muselier, whose reputation was the subject of much comment in the navy but who was intelligent enough to agree – at least to begin with – to fall in under de Gaulle's banner.

Better known, very much better known, was that General Catroux whom de Gaulle had known as a prisoner of war in 1916 and whom Vichy had just dismissed from his post as Governor-General in Indo-China. Catroux had found himself in an impossible position: on 19 June the Japanese had insisted upon the closing of the frontier between Indo-China and China; the British had refused to help him; and Pétain's government had urged that he should, without the means of doing so, comply with the requirements of Tokyo. Moreover, he had not concealed his disapproval of the metropolitan armistice and had told his son René, who was then in London, to pass his congratulations on to de Gaulle. Lemery, the Minister of the Colonies in Pétain's government maintained that Vichy's punishment and Catroux's resentment of it were factors in his going over to de Gaulle, and that is quite possible: we have seen that in such circumstances those who have nothing to lose find it easier to decide than those who have too much.

The fact remains that this well-known and cultured general, a great expert in Eastern affairs, in high repute for his diplomatic skill, the recent holder of one of the highest appointments the state had to offer, and with four stars* on his képi, had the directness to place himself under the orders of the man of June. Twenty years later, he said to me, "From 18 June 1940 onwards, de Gaulle so obviously stood above rank and distinctions that my action was self-evident." When Catroux reached London on 31 August de Gaulle had left for Dakar: it was in Chad that they met again, some weeks later.

A third important recruit appeared at the beginning of September, an ethnologist already well-known for his abilities and his militant opposition to Fascism, Jacques Soustelle. In Mexico Soustelle had been working on the rich and influential French colony in that country to come over to Free France. On 13 July he received a telegram from General de Gaulle thanking him for his support, but also telling him that the Free French delegate for the Americas was Jacques de Sieyès. Soustelle therefore joined de Gaulle in London six weeks after.

When General Legentilhomme, commanding the French forces at Djibouti, joined, de Gaulle hoped it also meant the accession of this important East African strategic position. The general came alone. But he strengthened and diversified the still very small but, in its members, highly representative band, as did Colonel de Larminat, Captain de Hauteclocque (the future General Leclerc), the airmen Bécourt-Foch (Marshal Foch's grandson and of incomparable symbolic value for Charles de Gaulle) and Lionel de Marmier, and sailors like Savary, the future minister. It was not yet an army. But it was already more than a legion.

In an article written for *The Sunday Times* under the title "Our guest and sometimes friend", Susan Raven summed up the relations established between de

*The mark of a lieutenant-general. (trs.)

Gaulle and the English in these terms: "Wherever Churchill led them, the English followed." Speaking of "an unbounded public sympathy for the Free French", she particularly emphasized the part played by the establishment, urged on by the Prime Minister: "Lords, ladies and daughters of ambassadors acted as patrons for all kinds of committees. Lady Peel turned her house in Baron Square into a hotel. Lady Spears gave the Free French a hospital in the country. One of Mrs Churchill's cousins opened a restaurant for the French women recruits at Olympia. Captain Edward Molyneux distributed jackets and trousers, and Olwen Vaughan opened the famous Petit Club Français in St James's Place."

It was this last enterprise that was the most welcomed by the community of exiles in search of social contact. For years the Petit Club was an incomparable centre for meetings, for finding old friends again and for fresh encounters. Countless stories told by the Free French began, "It was at the Petit Club." From the gastronomical point of view Olwen Vaughan's venture was often criticized. But from the point of view of contact and friendship it was a complete success – although one saw none of the most intensely interesting people in the London of those days, the members of the Resistance sent from France, whom the rules of clandestiny kept away from places so much in the public eye.

According to Susan Raven, de Gaulle was looked upon in London as a "fearless diner", a man who devoted a considerable part of his day to meals eaten with the most influential British. The Constable often ate out, at the Royal Automobile Club or the Savoy, the Ritz or the Cavalry Club, at Grosvenor House or the Connaught, so eager was he to spread his ideas and plead his cause with all those who might be able to advance it. So eager to do so and so hungry for contacts that, still according to Susan Raven, some of his hosts thought him "rather sticky".

His days in London have been very well described by François Coulet, who became his ADC and principal private secretary* after Geoffroy de Courcel, who had obtained the General's leave to go and fight the Afrika Korps.

At about nine in the morning – the General used to get up rather late – they would leave for Carlton Gardens by car. Meetings, conferences, letters. At about 1 p.m. they would go to the Connaught, still by car; on ordinary days the table would be laid for three or four guests – very French menus, and in spite of rationing, substantial.

Coulet states that the General was "a gastronome, and with close friends he did not scorn to share his knowledge of the subject. 'What is the purée Soubise? The great turning-point in cookery and French supremacy in the field dates from the beginning of the nineteenth century and the discovery of the great sauces.'" The Connaught's cooking was good. "A few island novelties were praised," says the surprised ADC, "such as roast beef and Yorkshire pudding, and above all barley-broth."

> The conversation, led by the host, was always agreeable and at the same time always on a high level. To let the newcomers' shyness have time to disap-

*He uses the word *famulus: confidant* might have been nearer the mark.

> pear, de Gaulle would begin the talk with a short monologue, commenting upon the recent happenings with a kind of serenity and almost of joviality, foretelling that the Mediterranean would become a German-Italian lake, with the front running along the equator, and ending, "We shall win, you'll see!"

Cigars, coffee. Before 3 p.m. the general and his ADC would walk the mile back to the Free French headquarters, unless it was raining hard or there was an urgent appointment; they went by Berkeley Square, Piccadilly and St James's, and "the people in the streets stared at this tall figure in a foreign uniform, and many of them who recognized him, greeted him." On week-days he stayed at the office until 8 p.m. On Saturday evenings Charles de Gaulle carried files back to Petts Wood or later to Berkhampstead, where he saw his family again and put on civilian clothes.

De Gaulle conquered hundreds of faithful followers who were with him in London or engendered a state of extreme hostility in an equal number of unconquerables such as Labarthe, Comert or Mengin (who gives a detailed account how he tried to avoid signing the certificate of enlistment in the Free French Forces because it specifically referred to de Gaulle, or to avoid having to shake the General's hand if they chanced to meet in a Carlton Gardens corridor): his hosts however had a different view of the General.

Some British journalists, such as Gordon-Lennox and Darsie Gillie, admired him and described him well. But of the many accounts of de Gaulle, perhaps this savage and beautiful portrait is the best: it was written by Mary Borden, the novelist, who was often in his company, she being Sir Edward Spears' wife and then the head of a Free French field-hospital.

> He felt his country's dishonour as few men are capable of feeling anything; he had literally taken this national shame upon himself, assuming it as Christ assumed the sins of the world. In those days he was as it were flayed alive, and the slightest contact made him want to snap. The uneasiness that I felt when I was with him certainly came from the pain and the rage that were burning in him.
>
> His only relaxation, I might say his only pleasure, was hating. And he hated everybody, particularly those who tried to be his friends. He had never pretended to like the English. But coming to them as a beggar, with his country's wretchedness branded on his forehead and in his heart was unbearable. In his own eyes he literally was his country. When he spoke for France and in the name of France he was expressing a fact that he desperately yearned to have accepted as true, defying the whole world to disbelieve him.
>
> I should describe him as being inhuman in those days, if it were not for this story. It was Christmas Eve.* As he could not go and be with Mme de Gaulle in Shropshire we had asked him to come to us. After dinner he talked

*The Christmas of 1940.

> for a long while with my son Michael, who had come from Oxford to join us. He relaxed and grew gentler as he talked about my son's studies and about the young people of England. And when he left for London, Michael, though he is a very reserved young man, came and said to me, "I should like to serve under General de Gaulle's orders."[20]

It is impossible to speak about the de Gaulle of London during the summer of 1940 without recalling that those were the days of the Battle of Britain and the Blitz, and the huge aerial battles in which, as Churchill said, the freedom of the world was at stake, adding, in the inspired style of a Tacitus, "Never was so much owed by so many to so few."

Here the word must be passed to Pierre Bourdan, who has recounted the battle, splendidly:

> In August the German raids grew heavier, deeper and steadier. The waves of attack followed one another night and day. The enemy wanted to force England to throw in its whole fighter force. He could allow himself the sacrifice of as many planes as the entire RAF possessed and still have a powerful air force. He tried it.
>
> It was during one of the first afternoons in September that the first of the great air-battles over London was fought. Everything took place at a great altitude, probably something like fifteen thousand feet. With the naked eye one could see dozens and dozens of little mica crosses, brilliant in the light, that came from the four points of the compass as though on parade, invading the sky. For them it was a matter of life or death, but the calm serenity of the air gave the tense, bitter struggle the cheerful look of a tournament.
>
> One assumed that there was a headiness, an exhilaration of battle, stimulated by the light, the contest and the presence down there of nine million spectators watching the sky and the feats of their heroes in this moral joust. On the ground, every face was turned upwards. Newspaper-sellers, people out for a walk, drivers who had stopped their buses to peer out, shopkeepers at their door, street-sweepers leaning on their brooms, the whole of England watched these enigmatic evolutions whose meaning and outcome would be learnt from the evening communiqué.[21]

By the end of August 1940 the "flayed man" of London was still Charles Lackland. What was he? What did he amount to? But it is easier to know what he was, from that day in August 1940 when Richmond Temple who, at Duff Cooper's request, had attended to his public image, asked him for a kind of self-definition, a personal manifesto. This document is little known (did the British propaganda department think it too naive?) but a year later it appeared in the Cairo papers, at the time of the Constable's stormy visit to the Levant; and it is worth reading. Here is the de Gaulle of 1940 seen, and above all as he wished to be seen, by himself.

> I am a free Frenchman.
> I believe in God and in the future of my country.

I am no man's subordinate. I have one mission and one mission only, that of carrying on the struggle for my country's liberation. I solemnly declare that I am not attached to any political party, nor bound to any politician whatsoever, either of the right, the centre or the left.

I have only one aim:

To set France free.[22]

CHAPTER TWENTY-TWO

The Empire with Us!

The behaviour of the Free French leader is utterly incomprehensible unless one bears in mind that the immense responsibilities he claimed on the eve of the defeat were undertaken only with the firmest intention of safeguarding the country's inheritance – which was far greater than its national territory. However symbolic his action might be, it could not satisfy de Gaulle, that incarnation of France and of French legitimacy, if it remained merely abstract, vague and undefined. A symbol, yes: but a symbol formed within very exactly drawn limits, which were those of the Empire's frontiers as they stood on 18 June 1940.

From that moment on, he looked upon himself as the trustee for this enormous capital, morally and legally required to hand it back to the French nation, to France as a person, having made it increase in value by carrying it over to the side of those who were fighting and who were to be the conquerors. As he saw it, he was the legally-appointed guardian of this inheritance, and the violence with which he insisted upon its integrity, whether he was addressing his allies or his enemies, tells us a great deal about the nature of the unilateral contract that he had entered into with the nation as a whole. The notion of buying the right to appear among the conquerors by making any territorial concession was wholly foreign to his mind; indeed, it would have been anathema. From 1940 to 1945, just as Churchill was the guardian of the island, so de Gaulle was the guardian of the French Empire's integrity.

Empire: the word made its appearance in the first sentences of the appeal of June 18. "France is not alone. She has an immense Empire behind her!" The expression had been used instead of "colonies" since the beginning of the thirties, when the Third Republic, uneasy at the rising tide of danger, tried to revive the Jacobin, universalist patriotism represented by Reynaud and Mandel, both of them former ministers for this department.

The "Empire", that is to say the whole of those possessions in the five continents that were subject, to a greater or less degree, to French authority was now elevated to a compensatory myth for the crushed, disarmed French nation, whose very fleet had seen fit to sail out of history. Might not France live on there, where the irresistible Wehrmacht would be unable to gain a footing!

In June 1940 Charles de Gaulle had many reasons for making his hopes and his propaganda hinge upon the Empire. In the first place he wanted to take the responsibility for France upon himself, and thus ensure his legitimacy, which he could not do if he were to remain confined to a foreign country. How could he take the lead, compel recognition, even in his own opinion, if he had no "French" territory, no country in which French sovereignty was exercised?

Furthermore, this vast Empire was the object of innumerable covetous eyes. If it were left in Vichy's feeble hands it would soon fall a prey to German and Italian ambitions, unless it slid gently into "friendly" hands: there was no Empire so great that it could not become greater still, and that of His Majesty was no exception to the rule.

De Gaulle had another reason for giving the empire an essential importance, a purely strategic reason. As early as 18 June he had seen the war as a world-wide conflict, and in his view Africa was to be its epicentre. It was there, he thought, that the final battles would be fought. When he was weighing the chance of the opposing sides before an audience of friends, de Gaulle naturally foretold the defeat of the Axis. "Why?" "Because this time we have an anti-tank ditch." "The Channel?" De Gaulle shrugged his shoulders. "The Mediterranean?" Another denial: "No. The Sahara."

De Gaulle summed up his view in an address to the officers of his very first Staff at St Stephen's House, as early as 15 July 1940 and recorded by Passy:

> If we wish to put France into the war, and if we wish to represent our country's interest adequately both with regard to our allies and to the French in France and abroad whose eyes are upon us, it is of the very first importance that the seat of the French government that is carrying on the struggle should be on French soil. That is why I have decided – and the information I have tells me it is possible* – to go to Dakar and there set up the capital of the Empire at war.

As a good staff-officer Passy objected that it would be impossible to hold Dakar if North Africa remained under the control of Vichy (if not of the Axis armies). The General paid no attention to his words and told those present "to be ready to leave in four to six weeks time".[1]

However hasty and urgent these plans may have been, they would have been even more so if Charles de Gaulle had had wind of the striking interchange between Hitler and Vichy which was then going on and which remained buried in the archives for a very long while. Although the diktat of Rethondes put the fate of the Empire into his hands, the Nazi chancellor, as it has been pointed out, displayed "moderation" in this field, a moderation so extraordinary that it can only be explained by the instinct of a beast of prey: "if I frighten my quarry too soon, there is the danger that it will flee." Insisting upon the empire would have meant making it go over to the British side.

Now abruptly, on July 15, three weeks after Pétain and Weygand had agreed to practically everything except what the Germans knew they must not require of them, Keitel's Staff insisted that most of the airfields, railways and ports in North Africa should be placed at their disposal. This was calling into question the basis of the Armistice and of all that allowed Pétain and Weygand to maintain that they had not handed everything over to the conqueror. It was saying that de Gaulle was right and it was an *a posteriori* justification of all that was routine and abusive in his criticism of the "abominable Armistice".

*His source of information was then Hettier de Boislambert, a specialist on Africa.

This time Vichy decided not to agree tamely and answered Hitler with a proposal for reopening negotiations, at the same time appealing to his "chivalry as a patriotic soldier".[2] Inexplicably the Nazi Staff went no farther – a proof that it was sometimes possible to check the Führer's insatiable rapacity.

General de Gaulle – and the British too, at first – remained wholly ignorant of this turn of events that might have changed everything. If Hitler had pushed his requirements to the last extremity, Vichy might perhaps have moved to Algeria, and de Gaulle's undertaking would then have lost much of its significance. It emerges from this fruitless episode that in July Hitler realized that in choosing to favour the installation of Pétain's government rather than seizing North Africa he had perhaps made a blunder. Later, many of his faithful followers, including Abetz, expressed their regret. Hitler became aware of the conflict's African dimension later than de Gaulle.

The course was to be set for Dakar, then? Against Charles de Gaulle's wishes and forecasts it was not in Senegal nor even in Africa at all that Free France was first to succeed in establishing itself on a soil where the Tricolour flew. This happened in the Indian Ocean and the Pacific, far away from the Axis forces – though not from the Japanese navy.

The first to join Free France was Chandernagor, whose bold and picturesque administrator, Baron, responded to the London appeal as early as June 20. His superior in Pondicherry disavowed him but was to follow his example six weeks later.

On July 22 it was the turn of the New Hebrides. The fact of the matter is that in this Franco-British condominium Governor Sautot's life would have been difficult if he had not joined his associates. From then onwards General de Gaulle never ceased badgering the governors and patriotic societies in the Pacific islands, from Polynesia to New Caledonia, to induce them to imitate Sautot. In Tahiti an improvised referendum gave de Gaulle an overwhelming majority. In September Sautot, commissioned by de Gaulle on 27 July, had little difficulty in persuading the French colony in New Caledonia, which was by no means well-inclined to Vichy.

In short the Constable's action began with the farthest territories; and this was suitable for a strategist who had never taken a short-sighted view. Nevertheless it was in Africa that the decisive stages in the spread of Gaullism were to take place, and take place very soon.

On 19 June it seemed sure that French Somalia would join Free France, for General Legentilhomme, commanding the troops in the territory, had said that he intended to continue the struggle. This decision was all the more logical since Djibouti and its garrison (about 10 000 men) fitted into the British military system in the Near East. Between the mass of the British forces in Egypt and the Levant (50 000 men) and the important Italian army in Ethiopia (about 200 000 men), Djibouti, an almost impregnable bastion at the mouth of the Red Sea, was a position of great consequence in the battle for the East that was about to begin.

But whatever services Legentilhomme may have rendered Free France later on, he dithered at this critical moment. His indecision cost the Allies not only the neutralization of a most important stronghold, but also the loss of British Somalia, which the Italians could overrun with little difficulty once French Somalia had gone over to Vichy. The behaviour of the loyal but irresolute Legentilhomme in this instance gives a better notion of the boldness, natural authority and imagination shown by the other chief actors in the rallying of immense African territories to Free France. The personal activity of each man concerned played an essential part in these events.

Yet in spite of his words to the officers of his Staff on 15 July, de Gaulle decided to begin the operation in Equatorial Africa; and this was because on 17 July he had received an eloquent telegram from Fort-Lamy, the capital of Chad. The Governor of this territory was Félix Eboué, a black man from Guiana who had spent almost all his career as an administrator in French Equatorial Africa and who had been appointed to Fort-Lamy by Mandel. He was a man with a vigorous character and fresh ideas, and his deputy, Henri Laurentie, was one of the pioneers of an evolutive policy in the empire. Both thought that the time had come to prepare for its emancipation.

Eboué, Laurentie and their military assistant, Major Marchand, a nephew of the man of Fashoda, had joined de Gaulle without hesitation. Moreover, they were the only ones in direct contact with the enemy; Chad shared a border with Italian Libya and ran particular risks because of the disarmament measures laid down by the Armistices. On 17 July, then, Eboué informed de Gaulle of his intentions: Chad's rallying was only to be a matter of days.

Then, on 27 July, Charles de Gaulle called upon the territories of the Empire to join him. This appeal had a new side to it, for although it was primarily addressed to the governers and administrators, it also went much farther, expressing a kind of threat, a threat that implied a danger: "If necessary I shall call upon the people." The people? At that time of course de Gaulle had no notion of decolonization. He was thinking above all of the European elements.

In the event a group of Frenchmen in Brazzaville set the process in motion by forming a "patriotic association for freedom and honour" supported by a group of officers. London was told of it. De Gaulle hesitated no longer. On 31 July he had had Churchill's promise of British support for his African undertakings as a whole. On 6 August he decided on the immediate dispatch of a mission to Equatorial Africa, made up of Pleven, Parant and Boislambert: at the last moment another man was included, Captain Philippe de Hauteclocque.

Hauteclocque had arrived from France wounded, with his head bandaged, after two escapes. He found himself immediately changed into "Major Leclerc" and put on board the plane bound for Lagos, while Colonel de Larminat, who had escaped from Djibouti and had made his way round by the Cape, was waiting for them in Léopoldville.* He had been commissioned by de Gaulle to go from there to Brazzaville and proclaim himself Governor-General of the French Congo in the name of Free France.

From 26 to 28 August 1940 there occurred what the Gaullists called their

*Now Kinshasa, Zaire. (trs.)

Three Glorious Days: on the twenty-sixth, Chad joined; on the twenty-seventh, the Cameroon; on the twenty-eighth, the Congo. Seeing this, Ubangi-Shari, whose governor, Saint-Marc, had only been waiting for such a chance, came in too. In Libreville, Gabon, Governor Masson announced that he was following the example; but Mgr Tardy, the bishop of the town, and a naval officer were enough to halt the movement, and for a while Gabon, alone among the French Equatorial territories, remained attached to Vichy.

It was in the Cameroon that the most significant Free French operations took place. To begin with because it was based upon a wave of public opinion, initiated by a public works engineer called Mauclère; and secondly because in the Cameroon the colonial question took on a very particular aspect – Hitler's victory would there re-establish German law, suspended in 1918.* In this country therefore the conflict was, as it were, an extension of the European dispute, and de Gaulle was too profoundly conscious of modern history not to be aware of the operation's markedly Franco-German aspect. Lastly, it was carried out by the man who, after Courcel, had been one of the first to join de Gaulle, Hettier de Boislambert, and by Leclerc, who as soon as he reached London on 31 July, was seen as a favourite disciple.

The "missionaries" left London on 6 August. The Constable had told them to recruit two thousand Ivory Coast infantrymen who had earlier been sent to the Gold Coast.** But the British commanding officer so admired their bearing that he incorporated them in his own forces.

Then, disregarding the order from the general in command of the British Cameroon forces to refrain from action, Leclerc and Boislambert embarked about twenty volunteers in three canoes and steered for Duala, which they reached in the middle of the night under pouring rain. Leclerc "who had as it were become a colonel and the Governor, by magic, unostentatiously occupied the palace" and then summoned the important men and the Gaullist sympathizers, who were addressed by Boislambert ("he never stopped talking until all the women were in tears", says Larminat[3]). Two companies from the Duala garrison were put into the train for Yaoundé, the capital of the colony, and Boislambert and Leclerc had nothing left to do but telegraph the news of their success to London, though not without adding "We beg pardon for having assumed higher ranks . . . but the result was all that mattered."

The new "Colonel and Governor-General" Leclerc began the exercise of his functions and prerogatives by having a very singular proclamation posted up: it stated that "The Cameroons proclaim their political and economic independence", and that, "The country is ready to resume its place in a Free French Empire and it is determined to continue the struggle together with the Allies, under the orders of General de Gaulle." The "independence" of the proclamation referred only to independence from Vichy, and Carlton Gardens had nothing to worry about. Twenty years were to go by, and Charles de Gaulle was to return to power, before Leclerc's proclamation at last came into force in the

*Cameroon had been a German colony from 1884 to 1918. (trs.)
**Now Ghana.

Cameroons; while the same officer, whose ideas were more consistent than would appear, became the proponent, against the will of his chief in 1940, of colonial emancipation in another territory, that of Vietnam, in 1946.

This is not the place for a detailed description of all the meetings, surprise attacks, manoeuvres, proclamations and replacements in the Equatorial Africa of August 1940. What is to be retained above all is a certain style, a certain tone that is very well conveyed in a book written by one of the heroes of this immense pronunciamento: Edgard de Larminat's *Chroniques irrévérencieuses*, which is a capital summing-up of what was for many the very spirit of the Free French.

This newly-appointed general, who still signed his decrees "colonel", had just proclaimed himself Governor General of French Equatorial Africa in the name of an army consisting of two colonels, three captains and one second lieutenant; Leclerc, who never knew how many bands he should sew on his sleeve to overawe those he had to deal with, civil or military, French or English; Boislambert, who took Duala (and the rest of the Cameroons) with three canoes and one train; Pleven-the-Mild, who landed at Fort-Lamy with Major Colonna d'Ornano in the midst of troops who wrote a chapter in which Free France did not usurp its adjective.

Earlier the author of *La France et son armée* had chosen some singular companions to join the crusade for tanks. Then in London he had seen gathering around him a group of supporters who were somewhat reminiscent of the Popular Front, which did vex him a little. Now here he was unleashing a pack of young wolves on Africa, predators eager to devour the men of Vichy, always ready to attack, sometimes mistaking their quarry but never short of dash.

Even if one had left the Ecole de Guerre top of the list, as did Leclerc (happier in this respect than his leader), here in Africa one had no respect for hierarchy, etiquette or discipline. The Constable's "missionaries" were at this period irreverent in the extreme; and their wild, daring exploits (which for many ended in death) could not fail to give the incipient Gaullism a wild fantastic quality. The "flame of French resistance" lit on 18 June now leapt and danced like a torch.

By the end of August 1940, de Gaulle was no longer a squatter in London. Four African capitals, deeply rural though they may have been, had set vast expanses of "French" soil beneath his feet. Was this the great "taking off" that had been expected for the last two months?

From the beginning de Gaulle himself had marked out Dakar as the focal point for the undertaking. We have seen that as early as 15 July he gave his tiny Staff orders to prepare for the operation directed at the capital of French West Africa. By the end of that month he had spoken to Churchill about it. And it was on 6 August, during a tête-à-tête conversation between the Prime Minister and the head of the Free French, that the matter was settled.

De Gaulle did not contemplate a head-on attack against Dakar, a powerful fortess that Vichy had endowed with considerable means of defence, placing it under the command of Pierre Boisson, a man of exceptional ability and character who had come from Brazzaville at the end of June with the task of holding Africa against the Gaullists, whatever the cost.

Churchill also needed Dakar, an absolutely necessary base on the way to the Cape and one that might otherwise become a shelter for the German submarines.

The Prime Minister thus undertook "in an exceptional degree the initiation and advocacy of the Dakar expedition", and addressing a fascinated de Gaulle, he gave himself full scope. As de Gaulle was to say, it was indeed "a great actor with a great theme" who spoke, gestured and already moved his audience – at least, the man opposite him:

> Dakar wakes one morning, sad and unsure. Then as the sun rises the people observe that in the offing the sea is covered with ships. A huge fleet. An inoffensive little boat flying the white flag of truce comes into the port. Free French and British planes drop leaflets expressing friendship. The Governor feels that if he resists the ground will give way under his feet. Perhaps for honour's sake he may like to fire a few shots. But that evening he will dine with you, drinking to the final victory.

Charles de Gaulle was not easily impressed. But he was on that 6 August. Was he less moved by the "charming figures of speech" than by the "solid arguments" that Churchill produced? He says so. One cannot take one's oath upon it. The fact is that he was convinced. De Gaulle saw that the Prime Minister was so determined that if he, de Gaulle, were to abstain, his great "brother in arms" would carry on by himself and on his own account.

The "big show" set up by Churchill was called Operation Menace, and its conduct was entrusted to Admiral John Cunningham, at General de Gaulle's side, the brother of the Royal Navy's ablest leader, Admiral Andrew Cunningham (who had arranged for the neutralization of the French fleet in Alexandria with such skill and tact, the absolute antithesis of the tragedy at Mers-el-Kebir). On 19 August de Gaulle sent him a note on public opinion in Dakar, which his intelligence service led him to describe as "confused", though "many people still disapproved of the Armistice and continued to look upon the British as allies" and upon whom food supplies depended.[4] It was a very prudent message, and it does not allow responsibility for the failure to be attributed to Carlton Gardens' unreasonable optimism or mistaken forecasts.

The expedition dreamed up by Churchill and agreed to by de Gaulle left from Liverpool on 31 August. It was very far from being like the huge armada with which the Prime Minister had hoped to astonish the people of Dakar, since on the British side it contained only two old battleships, four cruisers, the aircraft-carrier *Ark Royal*, and a few destroyers, and on the French side three dispatch-vessels and two armed trawlers, while the Dutch had provided two transports, including the *Westernland*, in which de Gaulle embarked, wearing a strange Chasseur's béret – why this reminiscence of the Trèves batallion at sea? – and accompanied by Spears.

> With my little band* and my very small ships we left the port in the middle of an air-raid alert, and standing there on the deck of the *Westernland* I felt

*2160 men.

as it were crushed by the magnitude of my duty. Out on the open sea, in the black darkness and on the ocean swell, a poor little foreign vessel with no guns and all its lights out was sailing away, bearing with it the fate of France.[5]

These words have been held up to ridicule. Everything depends on one's idea of France's chance of success. In fact the testimonies that have survived the expedition speak of de Gaulle being filled with an immense melancholy. Here one can detect both the fore-knowledge of a man who rarely lacked it and the awareness, soon to be verified point by point, that this was an ill-conceived adventure, a misfortune for France.

They took seventeen days to reach Freetown, but in the meantime the expedition had already received a great setback: a French squadron, headed by three large modern cruisers, had left Toulon (with the consent of the German Armistice Commission) to bring Equatorial Africa back under Vichy's control, had traversed the Straits of Gibraltar without difficulty and was heading for Duala. Admiral Bourragué, surprised by the proximity of Cunningham's squadron, steered for Dakar: this saved Equatorial Africa, which had joined de Gaulle, but it instantly changed the balance of power between the defenders and the attackers in the capital of French West Africa.

There has been a great deal of talk about the Toulon squadron suddenly appearing in the midst of Operation Menace, some people throwing the whole blame on the incompetence of the defenders of Gibraltar, who let such a formidable enemy through the meshes of an apparently impassable net, others blaming the loose talk of the Free French, particularly in London – a matter that Churchill himself refers to in his memoirs. In fact British inefficiency seems to be due to mistakes in communication, mainly due to a bombing raid on London.

It is evident that both Vichy and the Axis were taken unawares by the expedition. It is no less evident that the Toulon squadron's change of direction for Dakar called the whole undertaking into question. Three powerful ships provided Boisson with a shield, their crews being violently anti-British ever since Mers-el-Kebir.

On September 16 Churchill reacted by suggesting to Cunningham that, having carried de Gaulle and his men to Duala, in "liberated" African territory, he should turn about and come home. De Gaulle would have nothing to do with this solution: as soon as the British fleet left them to their fate, the Free French would be at the mercy of the powerful forces sent by Vichy to reconquer French Equatorial Africa; the Constable already saw himself obliged to withdraw into the equatorial bush and the forest.[6] Admiral Cunningham took de Gaulle's side against Churchill: however uncertain it might have become, the expedition should still carry on. On 18 September the British War Cabinet gave him the green light. Meanwhile a small detachment led by Boislambert left Freetown for Senegal to prepare the people and to sabotage communications.

The operation consisted of three phases, which could be carried out successively. The first was the plan called "Happy", which aimed at bringing Dakar over without any fighting, thanks to the impression caused by the appearance of the fleet, by the leaflets dropped on the town, and the support of the people. The second was called "Sticky", which asked for "strong military pressure" going so far as a bombardment of the port by Admiral Cunningham's ships. The third was "Charles", which consisted of a landing at Rufisque in conjunction with the little band led by Boislambert, a schoolmaster named Kaouza and Lieutenant Bissagnet, among others.

At dawn on the twenty-third "Happy" was put into operation. But on that day the weather-report was on Vichy's side: a thick mist, reducing visibility to less than two miles, spread over Dakar Bay. A wretched state of affairs for what had been meant to be a great display by its producer, Winston Churchill.

A little before seven o'clock two small French planes took off from the *Ark Royal*, "fire-flies" that were to drop pamphlets signed by de Gaulle over the town, urging the defenders and people of Dakar "to show their patriotism without disorder and to welcome his soldiers heartily". A few minutes later an unarmed launch carrying Thierry d'Argenlieu and Captain Bécourt-Foch landed near the admiralty; General de Gaulle's representatives asked to be received by Governor-General Boisson so that they might give him a message; they emphasized the friendly nature of the operation and the (supposed) common wish to free the country from the invader, pointing out Boisson as one who had "a great role to play" and even asserting "Your hour has come!"

But a port officer told the envoys that Boisson had given orders for their arrest: they managed to get back into the boat. A few minutes later, with no warning, two bursts of machine-gun fire were aimed at the men bearing the white flag, wounding Thierry d'Argenlieu badly in the leg. Manifestations in favour of joining de Gaulle increased in the town; the Governor had them put down, throwing the leaders into prison. The first phase, "Happy", aimed at bringing the town over without blood-shed, had from that moment, become "Unhappy".

Towards noon General de Gaulle sent Admiral Cunningham a note to the effect that they should turn to "Sticky", that is to say that "after a few shots from your fleet directed at the *Richelieu* and at Goré,* the French small-craft should attempt to enter the port. If this should prove impossible, let 'Charles' be tried early in the afternoon."[7]

So the leader of the Free French certainly consented to a shelling of the French fleet and one of the defenders' positions by the British fleet. But the few shots fired by the British only resulted in a furious reply from the *Richelieu* and no French craft could make its way towards the quay without the utmost danger.

There remained the plan put forward by Boislambert, in connection with the steps he himself had taken on land – the plan "Charles", a landing of Gaullist troops at Rufique, a small port some twelve miles from Dakar, whose inhabitants had been won over. But just as the newcomers were landing, Second-Lieutenant Coustenoble, whom Boislambert supposed to be a supporter, seems utterly to have misunderstood what was going on and made his men open fire on the Free French: three were killed aboard the *Commandant-Duboc*. This time it was a total failure.

*A small island in Dakar Bay.

Was the right course to order a firm retreat, according to the wishes of the Free French leader, who had decided against any fighting with his own countrymen? During the day of 24 September Cunningham conferred with de Gaulle and Spears; if the operation were to be broken off, would that mean the end of the Free French movement, asked the Admiral? No, said de Gaulle. As far as Dakar was concerned, they should leave it at that; for Free France, it was only the loss of one battle.[8] The three men therefore agreed to go no farther.

But in London Churchill, much stung by the criticism of the British papers, Washington's sarcastic remarks and Vichy's howls of triumph, ordered the Admiral to bombard the town and Vichy's ships. After a day of mutual shelling in which the *Richelieu* on the one side and the *Resolution* on the other were badly damaged and about a thousand of the inhabitants of Dakar and almost as many fighting-men were killed, Cunningham, with the General's approval, decided to put an end to the adventure on his own authority.

It was a slap in the face for Free France. A slap in the face for de Gaulle. Here was a man who claimed to be the embodiment not only of the spirit of resistance but also of France herself, but his first solemn attempt, unreservedly backed by his great ally, who had made Hitler withdraw from the London sky, had been a total, unqualified failure! It was easy for Roosevelt to tell Churchill that in de Gaulle he had a most unfortunate ally who had drawn him on to his first defeat. And Vichy and Berlin rocked with laughter.

But Winston Churchill held firm. Just as de Gaulle had remained on his side at the time of Mers-el-Kebir, so the Prime Minister meant to give his ally complete support after Dakar: to take upon himself the responsibility for the disaster before the Commons, his colleagues and the press – a disaster that, as we know, originated with him. He did not criticize de Gaulle and lessen the tension that weighed upon him in the "storm of bitterness"[9] that rose on every hand. He was even capable of stating in the House of Commons that "all that has happened on this occasion has only strengthened His Majesty's government's confidence in General de Gaulle."

Yet on 26 September, Charles de Gaulle, coming to pay his first visit to the wounded d'Argenlieu, said with a sigh, "Major, if only you knew how solitary I feel!" And he asked him the question that was on all lips at that time, "Should I go on?" Let us hear the author of the *Mémoires de guerre* on the same subject:

> The days that followed were cruel for me. The ship lay in a port stifling with heat, and in my little cabin I finally came to understand what form the reactions of fear might take on, both among enemies who are taking their revenge for having felt it and among allies who are suddenly frightened by a failure.[10]

It has sometimes been said that he thought of carrying the moral crisis caused by the horrible fiasco of Dakar to its final outcome – to suicide. For it was not only a political and strategic set-back but also a moral defeat, one that had brought about the death of nearly two hundred Frenchmen (on the two sides combined) because of a move initiated or approved by him, de Gaulle. The rumour is to be found here and there, particularly in *Jamais dit*[11] by J.-R. Tournoux: "A few days after Dakar, the General was talking to M. René Pleven in Brazzaville. 'I did think of blowing my brains out.'" Some years later, M. Pleven was asked to comment on this, he instantly replied, "Never for a moment did I think that the General really meant to do such a thing. When he said that, he only wanted to make me feel the horror of the trial he had been through. It is nonsense to understand his words in any other way."[12]

The expedition's chaplain, Father Lacoin, whose good sense led him to observe that "no one has the right to assert that a man has never thought of doing away with himself", points out that the very active conduct of the de Gaulle he saw the next day "was not at all that of a man in despair."[13] As for Geoffroy de Courcel, he thought him "deeply disturbed" on the evening of the twenty-fifth, but on the twenty-sixth he saw him "having recovered all his zest for action and making plans for fresh undertakings."[14]

On 27 September Charles de Gaulle sent London this short communiqué from Freetown:

> General de Gaulle states
> France's recovery in the war is a game in several sets. The Free French have won the first by rallying twelve million men in the Empire.
> The Germans have won the second by forcing Vichy to fight at Dakar. The game continues. We shall see how it turns out.[15]

The communiqué tells one a great deal about the Free French leader's ability to take punishment. The off-hand tone and the sporting references had their positive side and they must have given pleasure in London. Speaking of twelve millions who had joined him in Equatorial Africa was flying a little high. And asserting that it was the Germans who had compelled Boisson to fire upon the newcomers because two or three Nazi observers had access to the Governor-General was not quite true. Yet perhaps what really mattered in this case was to show that "the game" was to go on and that Free France was recovering its forces after the set-back.

This too was the state of mind that informed the letter written to his wife the next day, September 28:

> My dear beloved little wife,
> As you have seen, the Dakar affair was not a success. Vichy was expecting it and took extraordinary precautions. As I did not want a pitched battle between Frenchmen, I withdrew my forces in time to prevent it. For the moment everything is upside down. But my faithful followers remain faithful and I have great hopes for the future.[16]

Even so, the return from Dakar to Freetown must be recorded as one of the darkest periods in that life already marked by trials. Maurice Schumann did not see him until two months had passed, but nevertheless he says "After Dakar he was never entirely happy again."[17]

Here we must not overlook the importance of the personal humiliation that was inflicted upon him, a humiliation made worse by that "capacity for suffering" which has already been remarked upon. Churchill spoke of the "accidents and mistakes of Dakar" to the Commons, but whatever influence they may have had, there was one conclusion that had to be drawn from the undertaking: Free France could not yet compete with the resources of Vichy. They would have to wait until the worldwide balance of power should change, until the United States and perhaps the USSR should enter the war (and as we have seen, all this had made part of de Gaulle's forecast as early as the end of June 1940) before the Free French movement, profiting from the increase thus gained by the anti-Nazi coalition, could hold its own with the power installed at Vichy.

Although Dakar and French West Africa were not yet within his possibilities, any more than Rabat or Algiers, there were the territories that had already come over, and there it was necessary to show himself and to strengthen his hold. Admiral Cunningham convoyed him as far as Duala and here de Gaulle was to transform the failure at Dakar (a failure balanced by the saving of Equatorial Africa).

He landed at Duala on 8 October from the *Commandant-Duboc*, and there he was welcomed by the crowd that did not seem in the least concerned by his recent failure and which displayed, as he said, "an extreme enthusiasm". This was Charles de Gaulle's first mingling with the crowd – his first *bain de foule* – and his first landing in "liberated" territory. Dakar was already far away. The operation against the "hostile enclave" of Gabon completed the obliteration of the failure in Senegal.

But now another great idea occurred to the Constable's fertile mind: that of marching from Chad, the first territory to join Gaullism, through the Fezzan and Italian Libya to the Mediterranean. So he headed for Fort-Lamy, where Eboué was waiting for him. The governor, "whose mind is broad enough to grasp very wide-ranging plans" agreed with his idea. But the officers before whom he laid out the scheme were unable to hide their "amazement".

It was also at Fort-Lamy that at last he met Catroux. After a stay in London, where Churchill thought it right to send him to Cairo, Catroux came to place himself at the Constable's disposal. Writing in his *Mémoires* of the "respectful friendship" that "from earliest times" he had felt for this "great leader", de Gaulle released a passage in which the whole of his character blossoms without the least restraint in a kind of splendid historical foreshadowing of what was to come. "Eboué and all those present perceived not without emotion that for Catroux, de Gaulle had henceforward left the scale of rank and that he was invested with duties that were not subject to hierarchical order. I felt that he left a greater man."[18] Who else would dare write that without bringing the curse of ridicule upon himself?

On 24 October, at Montoire, a village in the Loir-et-Cher on the demarcation line then separating the "free" zone from that occupied by the Reich, Marshal Pétain, six days after signing the infamous "Statute concerning the Jews", met Hitler, whose hand he solemnly shook, being photographed as he did so. The "collaboration" between the Vichy régime and the occupying power, which had been so desired by Laval and his clique, was from now on France's official policy.[19]

It cannot be said that it was this new step in the direction of subordination of the country to the enemy that determined de Gaulle to set up the Council for the Defence of the Empire at Brazzaville on 27 October 1940. But the meeting at Montoire and Vichy's adherence to Nazi antisemitism helped to undermine the legitimacy of the absolute power set up on 10 July 1940 and to cut that government off from a part of its popular support. A vast majority of the French, stunned by the events of June 1940, had hailed Pétain as he "made the gift of his person" to France: fewer were prepared to live according to the ideology of the Nazis.

Furthermore the reasons de Gaulle adduced for the setting-up of the Council for the Defence of the Empire were much more political than his earlier statements: references to the Republic and to the "people" appear at last in the Brazzaville manifesto, in which de Gaulle confirms that "he will not fail" in "the sacred duty" of "guiding the French effort in the war", at the same time "solemnly committing himself to account for his actions to the representatives of the French people as soon as it is possible to appoint them freely."

General de Gaulle brought into the Council for the Defence of the Empire two men who were then his most important colleagues in London, Muselier on the military side and Cassin on the civil; then came Catroux, the most famous adherent, Larminat, who was to supervise the African operations as a whole from Brazzaville, General Sicé of the medical corps, Governor Sautot (who represented Oceania on the council), and those two outstanding figures d'Argenlieu and Leclerc. Pleven was left out, so that he might be more free to carry out a wide variety of missions. Félix Eboué was appointed Governor-General of French Equatorial Africa, being replaced in Chad by P.-O. Lapie, who was summoned from London. Free France, cruelly humiliated at Dakar, was now certainly taking on shape and substance.

And on 17 November 1940 Charles de Gaulle left Africa to reach Britain by way of Lagos and Gibraltar. Thinking about the comrades who had joined him, he wrote these few lines about them – lines that lead one to suppose that the trial of Dakar was by now thoroughly overcome: "I reflected on the heart-lifting side that an adventure on a world-wide scale had been for them. However harsh the realities might be, I might overcome them, since, as Chateaubriand put it, it was possible for me 'to lead the French on by way of dreams'."[20]

The appeal of 18 June had been heard by the French of Indochina and often well received. In October the leader of the Free French could only reply to the appeals that came from Indochina by urging the senders to preserve their faith in Free France, by advising caution and by asking them to keep in touch with all those who were fighting for the same cause in Chungking and Chiang, in Singapore with the English, in the French settlements in India, and in New Caledonia. At the beginning of 1941 de Gaulle sent Eden a memorandum on the subject of Indochina. But, as he says in the *Mémoires*, he was well aware that "no one would do anything to help Indochina resist the Japanese".[21]

This explains the melancholy reserve with which he speaks of the country: "At that time, for me Indochina was like a great disabled ship that I could help only after a long process of gathering the rescue apparatus. Seeing her moving farther away in the mists, I swore to myself that one day I should bring her back."[22]

De Gaulle had not fought the 1940 Battle of Africa in vain. To be sure, North Africa was in Vichy's hands, under the supervision of the German and Italian Armistice Commissions. To be sure, Dakar had refused to yield to him, and had refused in a most resounding manner. Djibouti had not followed the example of its Governor, General Legentilhomme, in joining Free France; and Madagascar was to wait two years before passing under the authority of de Gaulle.

De Gaulle had attained only part of his aims by installing himself in Equatorial Africa. Yet even so he now possessed "his" land and his men, his own communications and his own radio: in Brazzaville he was no longer subject to the sometimes niggling objections of the Foreign Office. He could challenge anyone he liked. He existed: he set up the Council for the Defence of the Empire without even telling London; and from Chad he launched a miniature offensive towards the Mediterranean. As Larminat says, "Perched on our coconut-palms in Central Africa, we flung impudent defiance at Hitler and Vichy."

Was this at the cost of good relations between Free France and her allies? It is true that the Dakar affair turned the vague dislike that Roosevelt and his colleagues had felt from the beginning into a rancorous mistrust that was soon to have consequences in connection with the West Indes and Saint-Pierre and Miquelon. It is no less true that some of the Free French enterprises – in the Cameroon, for example – had irritated the British military leaders and that Churchill had shown his displeasure when he was faced with the *fait accompli* of the Council for the Defence of the Empire: a defence that was obviously aimed in every direction. Here and there the beginnings of future explosions were coming into existence.

Yet Washington's strong dislike and London's irritation were ill-founded. For in carving out an empire in the middle of Africa that was deliberately hostile to the Axis forces, the leader of the Free French had set up a centre of attraction and balance that the Nazi strategy had from now on to take into account by dealing tactfully with the defence of North Africa. In a way, de Gaulle in the south covered and strengthened Weygand's timid double game in Algiers. He was working not only to preserve Free France but also to make ready for the great undertakings that were to lead to the common victory.

CHAPTER TWENTY-THREE

The Shadow of Vichy

Moving from set-back to disappointment, de Gaulle increased in stature. But Vichy held its own. The General proclaimed that he was France. But without gross presumption the Marshal maintained that he was the country's embodiment. On the one hand an idea, on the other an obvious reality. Essence and actual existence. On one side, France as she ought to be; on the other, the French as they were – clinging in the storm to the raft of Vichy, to the former glory and the immediate presence of the Marshal.

The government settled in the Auvergne watering-place like a retired and gouty colonial official (at first the Marshal himself had thought the place "scarcely serious" and he would have preferred Lyons[1]). In the south zone (called "Non-Occupied", which was correct, or sometimes "free" which was nonsense when one thinks of the Armistice commissions and the terrible Nazi presence just at hand) a kind of compensatory mystique had been worked out. Its ingredients were a nostalgia for the past and for rural life, memories of Verdun, resentment of the masonic Third Republic, scraps of misquoted Péguy and the hiccups of a dyspeptic Maurras, a little corporatism, a fair amount of clericalism and a great deal of "ex-serviceman" militarism. A pot-pourri that was put forward as a "national revolution", so far from being revolutionary that its chief references were to the classics of the most florid conservatism and so un-national that it pretended to forget that three fifths of the country were in the hands of the most savage occupier known to France.

The Marshal, in his court at Vichy, was popular. The public bought twelve million portraits of him in 1941, almost one for every home. Crowds gathered to see him go by and people almost gave him their children to bless. Neither the "statute concerning the Jews", which he promulgated in October 1940, even before the Nazis had tried to force it on him, nor his shaking hands with the victorious Führer, an act which added the touch of cordial and solemn consent to the allegedly inevitable surrender, nor the accusing voice from London (which hundreds of thousands of French were listening to by the end of 1940, particularly in the occupied north zone) could spoil the image of the old druid redeemer.

General de Gaulle's slow advance in French public opinion, abruptly checked in July by Mers-el-Kebir and in September by Dakar, but improved in October by the meeting at Montoire,* was called into question once more on 13 December, when Pétain had Laval** arrested. The great majority of the Marshal's followers

*Where Hitler and Pétain met. (trs.)

**Speaking to Jean Chauvel at that time Pétain called Laval "a traitor" (to himself if not to France). See *Commentaire* vol I p. 258.

and most of those who preferred to "wait and see", saw this action as a proof that the old man was certainly opposed to collaboration with the Nazis, and they persuaded themselves that the theory which provided the mass of the people with their intellectual comfort was well founded – the theory summed up by the formula "the sword and the shield".*

Until November 1942 indeed, for many Frenchmen Pétain and de Gaulle only *seemed* to be opposed; in fact they were complementary, the one watching over the safeguard of the national home while the other, on the far side of the water, represented the continuing existence of the fighting spirit. It was the old dialectic of the two Frances, the introverted, stay-at-home Gallic France and the revolutionary, Jacobin France, the sower of ideas and principles. Many months and a great deal of evidence were required to dispel this stubborn dream. Nor can one wholly overlook the ambiguous attitude of various important Vichy officials towards de Gaulle as a person. François Lehideux, the former Minister of Industry said: "We admired the man and we respected his courage. But we hated his insults to the Marshal, and in our hearts we broke with him after Dakar and above all after the Syrian affair."[2]

But Vichy did not exist only in the eyes of the orthodox, rural and conservative French of the south zone. Its international standing, very shortly after the disaster and the submission to the Rethondes diktat, was high enough for all the great powers with the exception of Britain (with which diplomatic relations had been broken off immediately after Mers-el-Kebir) but including the USA, the USSR, the Third Reich, Italy, Japan, Spain and Canada (although it was a British dominion) to look upon it as the legitimate authority in France and to maintain their diplomatic relations with its government. In Washington the decision to make Vichy the breakwater for resistance to Nazism was taken as early as the beginning of July, less than a week after London's recognition of Charles de Gaulle as head of the Free French.

It is perhaps surprising that neither the swing towards absolute and arbitrary rule which began with the Vichy parliament's capitulation and which based legitimacy solely on a continuing plebiscite, nor the 'statute concerning the Jews', nor the setting up of a totalitarian system should have diminished the trust thus extended to Vichy, a trust so strong that in December 1940 Franklin Roosevelt sent Admiral William Leahy, a man of the highest rank and a personal friend, as Ambassador to the Marshal. And this Ambassador, as Soustelle says, was to be 'Pétain's alibi, just as Pétain was the alibi of the weak.' From then onwards the State Department made a show of ignoring the Free French.

Such an attitude increased the scepticism of those people in London who for various reasons, many of them connected with the old habits of the alliance, questioned the soundness of the movement that came into being on 18 June 1940. Many high-ranking English civil servants would have preferred maintaining their contacts with their traditional opposite numbers in the Quai d'Orsay and the Rue de Rivoli, even though they were now bogged down in the Auvergne, to wrangling with this arrogant general sprung fully armed from the fevered brow of the Prime

*The sword being de Gaulle and the shield, Pétain (trs).

Minister and the baggage of the scheming fellow Spears. That was the attitude of the most influential men in the Foreign Office, the War Office and the Admiralty, from Alexander Cadogan to Ronald Campbell, from Strang to Sargent, from Victor Alexander to Dudley Pound and from Dickens to Dill. How could they have failed to be confirmed in their prejudices when they observed that none of their former partners – Corbin, Cambon, Léger, Margerie, Morand, Monnet – had seen fit to cooperate with de Gaulle in London, and that a considerable body of their faithful friends such as Charles-Roux and Chauvel were serving the Etat Français.*

Indeed one should not under-estimate the influence of the Anglophile party in those about the Marshal, an influence that was exercised for a long while and that was particularly evident in the Foreign Ministry with Charles-Roux (who resigned at the end of November) and his friends. This current of personal and traditional attachment passing between the diplomats of Vichy and London, surviving the most tragic reverses and misunderstandings, did a great deal to make de Gaulle's position uneasy; he was continually threatened – at least until that day in December 1940 when Anthony Eden replaced Lord Halifax at the head of the Foreign Office – being short-circuited by some move originating in Vichy or even in London.

Was not Churchill mistaken when, at the end of June, he declared that the Vichy government had "ceased to be independent" and decided to stake the future of Anglo-French relations on General de Gaulle alone, to the exclusion of the Marshal? And even before Washington began to exercise pressure in order to make things easier for Vichy and to reduce de Gaulle to marginal importance, the Foreign Office had taken care to renew contacts with Pétain's government and its representative** in North Africa, General Weygand.

The turntable for this reinsurance diplomacy was Madrid. It was there that the most outstanding British ambassador resided, Sir Samuel Hoare, formerly head of the Foreign Office and recently the valued interlocutor of Mussolini and Laval; his French opposite number was Ambassador de La Baume. On 13 September (when it seemed that the Dakar expedition might be successful) the French diplomat handed his English colleague a message from his minister, Baudouin, suggesting that London should agree to a colonial status quo[3] and an easing of the British blockade, which would allow Vichy to draw supplies from its African possessions. If Hitler tried to intercept the convoys permitted by London, Baudouin believed that the Marshal could be persuaded to cross to North Africa and there resume the struggle on the side of the United Kingdom.

However strange these advances might sound, London listened – and told de Gaulle, then in Africa, about them. On 3 October the General replied that he observed, "with the utmost interest that for the first time in an official communication the Vichy government has contemplated the resumption of the war on the British side"; but he calmly added that if arrangements about supplies were concluded, they should be put down to a "request by General de Gaulle".

*The régime that succeeded the Third Republic. (trs.)
**Since September 1940.

The whole business came to nothing, for as the days went by Vichy showed progressively less zeal for fighting than appeared from Baudouin's first note. Churchill had had few illusions about these approaches, but Vichy's climbing down angered him. On 20 October, therefore, he decided to intervene directly. That night, he broadcast to France. With the accent of a Falstaff reciting Rabelais he denounced Hitler and "his little Italian accomplice who is trotting along very timidly at his side."

> They both wish to carve up France and her Empire as if it were a fowl: to one a leg, to another a wing. [If] this monstrous abortion of hatred and defeat has his way, all Europe will be reduced to one uniform Boche-land, to be exploited, pillaged, and bullied by Nazi gangsters. We shall never give in. Good night, then: sleep to gather strength for the morning. For the morning will come.[4]

The reason that Churchill warned the French against the Nazis with such fire was a rumour from Berne; a separate peace was just about to be signed and by its terms Vichy would make further concessions to Berlin – colonial and naval concessions. It was said that Hitler was to be given bases in the Mediterranean.

But Vichy had not given up trying to win London over. Two days after Winston Churchill's call for resistance Louis Rougier reached London; and the advances he made there have given rise to a variety of comments and interpretations ever since.[5] By means of the British consulate in Geneva he had sent Churchill a cable suggesting an agreement about the blockade between London and Vichy.

The reply was sufficiently encouraging for Rougier to speak to Baudouin, then to Weygand and then to Pétain, who saw him on 20 September when he offered to go to London and begin talks. The Marshal agreed. Rougier reached London on 22 October, and was received at the Foreign Office by Sir Alexander Cadogan, who proposed a meeting with Churchill.* On 25 October Rougier went to Downing Street, and there he found Churchill on the verge of apoplexy: the day before Pétain and Hitler had met at Montoire, and the British papers spoke of nothing but French ships and ports being handed over to the Third Reich. The Prime Minister, beside himself, spoke of "bombarding Vichy".

The visitor let the storm pass and found a way of putting forward his idea, that of the "third path": Laval wanted to fling Vichy into the war on Hitler's side; de Gaulle, by attacking the French colonies, would eventually bring the Nazis there; for their part, Pétain and Weygand were the only guarantees for keeping the fleet and the empire out of German hands. So it was upon them that one should rely (this was also Washington's view). The French envoy suggested a three-point agreement: the status quo for overseas territories, the easing of the blockade of unoccupied France, and a halt to the London radio attacks on Pétain.

Churchill did not say no. At the Foreign Office three days later Rougier and William Strang, Cadogan's deputy, drew up a protocol which, emphasizing the unanimous decision of the British to carry on the war until the Reich was crushed,

*De Gaulle was in Africa at the time.

recalled that England was determined to re-establish French sovereignty in its totality if France helped in the British war-effort* but would be answerable for nothing if Vichy were to hand bases over to the Axis.

This being understood, both governments undertook not to attempt to conquer the colonies controlled by Vichy on the one hand and by de Gaulle on the other; London would let the supplies from North Africa sail to the ports in Provence; Vichy would hand over neither ships nor bases to the Axis and would "bring the empire back into the war as soon as the British and their eventual allies should have demonstrated their strength".

Churchill, who took care not to sign this document, added two notes very much in his own style. In connection with the French Empire's taking part in the fight against the Axis, he wrote in the margin, "If Weygand raises the standard in North Africa he can count on our total support and a share of the United States' aid." And in connection with a possible handing-over of Mediterranean bases to the Nazis he wrote fiercely, "In that case we should do everything to bring down a government guilty of so base a betrayal!"

Furnished with this document, which only amounted to a declaration of intention, Rougier set out for Algiers with the hope of persuading Weygand, the chief target of the operation. The Commander-in-Chief in North Africa received him on 6 November, was handed a personal letter from Churchill urging him "to raise the standard of revolt". Weygand not only loathed revolt of any kind; he was also waiting for London "and its eventual allies" to display their strength. It is said that he uttered this remark: "If the British come here with four divisions, I shall fire on them. If they come with twenty, I shall embrace them."[6] Since Rougier neither brought nor promised any divisions he was abruptly dismissed.

Rougier returned to Vichy, where the Marshal saw him on 20 November. Pétain was unimpressed with the "London protocol"; so unimpressed that Rougier left for the United States, where he lived until the end of the war, carrying on a zealous campaign against de Gaulle.

Churchill was unable to resist letting de Gaulle into the secret.[7] The General's reaction was more delicately shaded than might have been expected. Although, addressing London, he held up the Council for the Defence of the Empire, which he had just created at Brazzaville**, as the sole trustee of France's honour and her future, he admitted, in a magnanimous and slightly condescending tone well calculated to infuriate the British, that "General de Gaulle and the Council for the Defence of the Empire understood the reasons that may at present induce the British government to adopt the appearance of handling the government of Vichy tactfully, so long as it cannot be proved that the latter has not made any fresh concessions to Germany or Italy."[8]

Rage in the Foreign Office. The private diary of Sir Alexander Cadogan, the leader of the anti-Gaullist trend, became a jet of bile when it dealt with de Gaulle, who, says he, had "a face like a pineapple and the shape of a woman": "He is a loser. Ridiculous telegram from that ass, who takes it upon himself to call upon

*Almost the very same words as the agreement of 28 June with de Gaulle.

**See Chapter 22.

Weygand to take sides at last: it is exactly what ought not to be done. I think the Prime Minister's confidence in de Gaulle [and in Spears] is shaken at last."[9] It was not. What Churchill says in his memoirs about de Gaulle's reactions to the dealings between London and Vichy shows that he thoroughly understood the General's point of view: "he thought we ought to be exclusively loyal to him [. . .] he also felt it to be essential [. . .] that he should maintain a proud and haughty demeanour towards us to prove to French eyes that he was not a British puppet."[10]

It was at this same period that London recognized the Council for the Defence of the Empire as a partner, a fighting organization destined to represent the French, but in no way a government. De Gaulle pointed this out in a very curt telegram (1 February 1941) to Garreau-Dombasle,* his representative in the United States, who had thought he might speak to the American press of a de facto recognition by London.

Although he was eminently Gaullist the Prime Minister nevertheless took care to seize upon any Germanophobe currents of opinion that might be perceived in Vichy, above all after 13 December 1940: was not the arrest of Laval, on Pétain's orders, proof that Vichy might swing over to the right direction? That the Marshal should have dared give Hitler this slap in the face and fill Laval's place with a politician like Pierre-Etienne Flandin, whose Anglophile past was perfectly well known,** meant that there were influences working in that direction and it was necessary to encourage them.

Was there about to be a fresh reversal of alliances? Lord Halifax, who was soon to become Ambassador in Washington, did not wish to go before he had done everything possible to restore the links with Vichy. He told his friend Jacques Chevalier, the most pro-British of Pétain's associates, to arrange for the Marshal to receive Pierre Dupuy, the Canadian chargé d'affaires. When Pétain raised the question of the French Mediterranean bases, Dupuy was told that they would be defended against any attacker. Dupuy asked for clarification: "So you will never hand them over to the Germans?" "It all depends," said Pétain. "If I am offered a satisfactory compensation, I may be obliged to do so." "But would not that amount to taking Germany's side against Britain?" "Yes, passively; but not actively." Upon this the old man affirmed that he considered a British victory "much to be desired" and that he would do nothing that might "damage the Allied cause", once more emphasizing his distinction between "active" and "passive" collaboration.

A week later Pierre Dupuys came to tell Churchill about his mission to Pétain and suggested that there should be an approach to de Gaulle to induce him to stop attacking the French who were faithful to Vichy and to set about the Italians instead. To this Churchill retorted that he "was not going to 'card' his friends and make them enemies in the hope of making them friends."[11]

That was clear enough, as were the relations between de Gaulle and Churchill at the end of 1940. The Prime Minister's position produced this particularly entertaining memorandum from Sir Edward Spears:

*Sieyès' successor.

**In spite of his congratulatory telegram to Hitler after Munich – a telegram also sent to the three other main figures at the conference.

> Our painstaking attempts to propitiate the Vichy government might, conceivably, make a dispassionate observer conjure up the picture of a well-meaning person bent on feeding a lettuce to a rabbit while it is being chased around its cage by a stoat. A waste of lettuce, at best, since if the rabbit were grateful, which would be unlikely, it will remain at the mercy of the stoat bent on its ultimate destruction.[12]

De Gaulle uttered much the same idea more energetically in an interview with the American journalist George Weller in August 1941, and although the words were officially denied they nevertheless obviously expressed his thoughts. Weller states that he asked de Gaulle why the British Cabinet had not yet recognized Free France as a government and that he was given this reply:

> Britain is afraid of the French fleet. Between Hitler and Britian there is a kind of *de facto* understanding, with Vichy acting as the intermediary. Vichy is useful to Hitler because it keeps the French nation in slavery and because it hands over scraps of the French empire to Germany. But Vichy is also useful to the British because it will not give Hitler the fleet. Like Germany, Britain makes use of Vichy. It is an exchange that is profitable to both the one and the other. Thus Vichy will survive so long as London and Berlin find it to their advantage.

In the autumn of 1940, an officer who, although he had rejected the Armistice and collaboration, had not condemned Vichy straight away, Colonel Loustaunau-Lacau,* noted that the Marshal was now speaking of de Gaulle with not so much ill humour as with nostalgia, and that he sometimes checked those who, like Admiral Darlan or General Bergeret, denounced the "traitor de Gaulle" in his presence.

Loustanau asked Pétain, "And what about our friend de Gaulle?" Pétain replied, "De Gaulle dropped us to go and play his own hand. I resent that and hold it against him. When the French know him better they will understand him less." "Yet even so, isn't it quite useful to have a contact in Britain?" "I don't need him if I want to get in touch with Churchill."[13]

But Loustaunau-Lacau was of the opinion that not all the bridges between "the sword and the shield" had been cut, and he wrote to de Gaulle to try to establish a connection between the two sides, emphasizing all that Pétain's fame still stood for. By an unstated route he received this reply from London, dated 13 January 1941:

> My dear friend,
> Neither I nor my family,** which is now the most numerous in France, accept what has happened nor what is now happening. We want duty to be done, whatever the consequences; and there is only one duty. For us all trickery, shuffling, and rough and ready compromise is detestable and to be

*De Gaulle's comrade at the Ecole de Guerre and his successor as Pétain's "pen bearer". (trs.)
**Free France, of course.

condemned. What Philippe* has been in the past makes no difference to our judgment of Philippe at present. We will help all those who wish to do what they ought. We shall drop all those who do not do what they ought (and they will fall very low).[14]

Loustaunau took the point; he had no intention of "falling very low" and he was already in the act of setting up the "Alliance" network, which in connection with the British SOE,** was to become one of the first links in the chain of internal resistance and to play a decisive part in inter-allied intelligence.

But what of de Gaulle himself? Could his attitude really be summed up in those few contemptuous remarks in his letter to Loustaunau-Lacau? All or nothing? Salvation on the one hand, perdition on the other? Some of his most private writings of this time show questionings and even hesitations on the subject of Vichy that bear witness to his sensitivity and even to his political shrewdness much better than the fiery rhetoric to be found in various broadcast speeches.

Let us take two letters to his son Philippe, then a midshipman at the Portsmouth naval school. The first is dated 18 December 1940, five days after the Marshal had dismissed Laval, "I believe that even for those born blind the Pétain-Vichy ambiguity is fading. Presently the ghosts and the dreams will have vanished and everywhere, even in Britain (!)*** it will be seen that between the real France and us, the Gaullists, there is only the enemy."[15] Here, then, it is the totally uncompromising de Gaulle who speaks, as on the radio.

But a fortnight later, as though he had heard of the palace revolution in Vichy during the interval, Charles de Gaulle writes to his son:

The people at Vichy are in the act of making a clear decision between crime and salvation. According to the information I receive, French public opinion and even Pétain's men have moved in the right direction during these last weeks. Yet I should be surprised if they were to adopt a truly national attitude and come back into the war, for I see them as fundamentally colourless beings and in any case deeply compromised by their earlier surrenders. Yet that is where the whole question lies.[16]

So although he was sceptical, he no longer excluded a sudden reaction, the choice of "a truly national attitude" on the part of these men whose surrender, whose treason, even, he had been denouncing these six months past.

On 24 February 1941, he appealed to Weygand's patriotism to bring North Africa back into the war. "There are still a few days left in which you can play a great national role. After that it will be too late." But the ending of the letter could only offend Weygand: "If your answer is yes, I am yours most respectfully."

*Obviously Pétain.
**Special Operations Executive. (trs.)
***This was the time of Pierre Dupuy's audience with the Marshal.

This insolent conditional respect displeased the general in Algiers extremely, and according to one of his associates he had a reply sent to de Gaulle stating that, (a) he ought to be shot, (b) that he, Weygand, was too old to turn rebel, and (c) that since two thirds of France was occupied by the enemy and the remainder by the navy, which was even worse, he was not free to act.

A document that reveals more clearly the ambiguity or flexibility with which de Gaulle could judge men who had at first chosen Vichy rather than himself is this telegram, sent in March 1941 to Roland de Margerie. Margerie had been the man in charge of Reynaud's personal office and as such de Gaulle's most active companion in the struggle against the Armistice but two weeks later he had seen fit to leave London for Vichy. This defection might have turned de Gaulle against him for ever. But not at all. On 29 March 1941 de Gaulle cabled him in Shanghai, where Margerie was French Consul-General: " . . . the present aspect of affairs and the re-awakened public opinion in France mean that a man of your kind can no longer stand aside. I ask you to join me in London without delay. Come, my friend."*

Thus we see de Gaulle himself wondering about Vichy and giving various Vichy supporters provisional exemption; it is true that this was when the Marshal's régime was still filled with honourable men who had not given up the idea of making this cul-de-sac a starting-point, men who were making plans and sabotaging as hard as ever they could – many of them were soon to be found at the head of intelligence networks or resistance movements.

The outlines of the Vichy nebula became quite distinct when Pétain appointed Darlan as his successor on 10 April 1941 and power was concentrated in the Admiral's hands. Did the Admiral "Dauphin" really believe as simply as the legend would have it that Germany was going to be victorious and that France had to carve herself out a position as the conqueror's brilliant assistant? François Lehidaux, who was then a member of his government, told me about a curious session in August 1941 in his office attended by a small group made up of Lucien Romier, Minister of State and one of the Marshal's intimate friends, Admiral Auphan and himself, during which Darlan said, "I think that from now on Germany has lost the war. It is no longer anything but a question of time. But meanwhile can France remain two or three years without a government?"[17] Yet for most observers, for the press and for the general public, the Admiral's new responsibilities certainly meant a move in the direction of the Third Reich.

De Gaulle had no doubt of it, and the next day he telegraphed to Larminat: "Darlan's arrival is a triumph for collaboration policy"; while Churchill said that "Darlan is worse than Laval." From this time forward there was no more questioning, and the leader of the Free French persuaded Churchill to state solemnly that Vichy had ceased to be a partner worthy of the slightest credit. No more lettuce for the rabbit chased by the stoat.

*Margerie did not respond to this call either, direct though it was.

CHAPTER TWENTY-FOUR

Near Eastern Clouds

When Charles de Gaulle contemplated the East at war, he did not do so with an uninformed eye. Ten years earlier at Beirut he had been in command of the 2nd and 3rd Bureaux of the army in the Levant. For eighteen months on end he had traversed the country from Aleppo to Saida and (after a detour to Jerusalem) from Tripoli to the Jebel Druse – a country that no man, and above all no believer, can easily forget.

When he landed in Africa he knew nothing that he had not read in books. The Peulhs and the Wolofs, marabouts and shepherds, Bamilékés or Dualas: all these were puzzles that he had to ask Boislambert to resolve for him. But when it was a question of the Alaouites and the Druses, the Kesrouan Maronites and the Shiites of south Lebanon, the problems of the Sanjak and the concerns of the Bec de Canard he knew what it was all about. Here his prodigious memory worked at full blast. And although the problems he studied in 1930 had by 1940 assumed a different breadth and far greater consequences, here he was acquainted with the chessboard, the pieces and most of the rules of the game; he knew the operational bases for the whole of French strategy in this country, the probable allies, the certain enemies, the reactions of one set and the reserves of another.

Furthermore the leader of the Free French knew that there was no field in which he had a more competent and experienced set of colleagues: Catroux, his representative, was rightly said, even in London, to be one of the greatest experts on these questions; Larminat had joined him only by abruptly leaving Mittelhauser, the Commander-in-Chief in the Levant; and when General Legentilhomme joined Free France he was in command of the forces at Djibouti. And as for the Free French representative in Palestine, he was the enlightened Captain Repiton-Preneuf.

At the beginning of 1941 Gaullism seemed better qualified than any other for dealing with the problems of the Near East. Besides, was it not the ally of the British who held the keys to the region? At that date the question was not so simple as it might seem, although even then it called for a delicately-shaded answer. Such was the background against which General de Gaulle's action was to be traced, a background that explains without always excusing the Free French leader's haughty self-assurance and the imperious virtuosity that he displayed throughout the great crisis of the Levant.

Nor should we forget the psychological climate at the time of his joining in the dispute. After the misfortunes of his strategy in West Africa from August to December 1940, the first four months of 1941 had been marked by a kind of military resurrection. Up until then the success of Gaullism had been of a psychological nature. The movement lacked the proof of fighting value. This was provided between January and April 1941 by the thrusts of Leclerc's column towards Murzuch and Kufra, by the presence of French units in the British victories of Bardia, Tobruk and Benghazi, the taking of Kub-Kub in Ethiopia and of Massaua in Erithrea, in which the 13th half-brigade of the Foreign Legion under Montclar formed part of the vanguard.

De Gaulle, as a man of war whose prime objective was to keep France in the fight, looked upon these victories as essential, however limited, symbolic or provisional they might be. Free France had ceased to be a Gaullist "lobby", a pressure group animated by a general stuck behind a microphone. Free France had now become Fighting France. During these months, and particularly in a speech he made on 5 April at the Ewart Memorial Hall in Cairo, de Gaulle's voice assumed the vibrant tone of an entirely new hope. As a soldier, he had to prove his worth on the field. On 14 March 1941, a fortnight after Leclerc had entered Kufra, it was a different de Gaulle, very far from the disaster of June 1940, very far from the failure of Dakar, who took the plane for the East.

"Towards the complex Orient, I flew with but simple ideas." Few lines in the *Mémoires de guerre* have been more often quoted, this being so typical of the General's style, both decorative and didactic, already shaped by history manuals.

Simple ideas? Yes. The first was firmly anchored in his heart: wherever the outcome of the war was being decided, France must be present and active. The second was no less familiar to him: that in the East and above all in the commercial ports of the Levant, France had a place marked out by history, by the services she had rendered, by the League of Nations mandate, and by her own interests. The third was more dependent on circumstances: the axis of the war had shifted. It had begun with a north-south direction; now it had swung to west-east. The Nazis' violent efforts on both sides of the Mediterranean, Yugoslavia and Greece in the north, Libya and Egypt in the south under Rommel, seemed to show that the Suez canal was the key to the war. So action was called for "where everything was at stake"; and de Gaulle was all the better situated since from Chad to Damascus France possessed very considerable means, either already in Free French hands or capable of coming over.

Yet it must be observed that at the time when the leader of the Free French laid down his plans, determined "to spare nothing" (which did not mean a great deal) to accomplish them, he could not possibly know that the launching of Operation Barbarossa, the Third Reich's invasion of the USSR – which he had foreseen, but at a later date – would downgrade and marginalize the Near Eastern campaign in a few weeks. The General was to use up much of his credit with his indispensable British friends for a partial, costly and finally minor success and to find himself politically isolated at the great turning-point of the war, brought about by the entry of the USSR into the field and then of the USA.

The idea of turning what had been a failure at Dakar into a success at Damascus and of making it into a kind of dress rehearsal for the great operation in North Africa which had been his major plan from the very first, went back to the autumn of 1940. As early as 25 October, from Brazzaville, de Gaulle sent Churchill a cable telling him that after a conference with Catroux he had just drawn up "the plan of action for Syria".

At the beginning of November a very discreet traveller, a "Monsieur Chartier", landed at Jerusalem, where he was politely received by the British authorities and lodged in an out of the way set of rooms in the Allenby Barracks. It was there that Captain Repiton-Preneuf, the Free French liaison-officer with the High Commissioner, Harold MacMichael, introduced himself to this slim, grey-clad gentleman who, filling his pipe with Virginia tobacco, uttered very intelligent remarks in a faint voice and a somewhat disillusioned tone: it was Catroux, who had come to make his first contacts and to survey the terrain. He did not need to convert Repiton, who had joined de Gaulle at the very beginning, and who, together with François Coulet, the head of the *Levant-France libre* radio-station at Haifa, had ensured the Gaullist presence among the British of Palestine and Transjordan. The enquiries of "Monsieur Chartier's" did not allow many illusions to be retained. All the dissidents' efforts, all their sending of personal messages to Pétain's representatives in the hope of making them "good Free Frenchmen by post" had failed and would continue to fail.[1] The eastern Dakar would not succeed without trouble, without ugly incidents.

On 31 December, de Gaulle, having received Catroux' report, warned his representative, now stationed in Cairo, that events in "our Levant" were to be foreseen in the near future and that he was therefore to have discussions with the British authorities in Egypt and Palestine to that effect. On 8 March de Gaulle informed his delegate-general that he was about to receive a large quantity of arms and ammunition for "the Middle East forces".

But for action to be taken the Free French could not count on more than the small division entrusted to General Legentilhomme in March: less than six thousand men rather poorly equipped and provided with only ten tanks and eight guns, to which two squadrons of about twelve planes each should be added. Catroux had received this warning from his sources in Beirut: "If you come in strength, there will only be a few symbolic shots fired for the honour of it. If you appear looking weak there will be severe resistance."[2] Weygand's philosophy in North Africa.

What of the British? In his *Mémoires* de Gaulle has an excellent description of Wavell, "highly gifted as far as judgment and coolness were concerned" and "not devoid of strategical intelligence", and harassed, when de Gaulle came into his Cairo office, by great numbers of "inconvenient and urgent" requests "in the tumult and the dust"; and all this while the Anglo-Greek forces were on the point of collapse in Greece and Rommel's advance east through Libya was going unchallenged. To be sure, in Ethiopia the Italians were falling back beyond Addis Ababa before the British thrust. But, says de Gaulle, Wavell, "his attention entirely taken up by three battle-fronts, had not the least intention of considering a fourth, whatever the price." From that time onwards it was clear that the Free French could only carry out their operation in Syria if a move on the part of the enemy forced the British Commander-in Chief to act or to allow action.

It was not only because they had other fish to fry in the eastern Mediterranean that the British General Staff in Cairo did not wish to go to war in the Levant. It was also because they feared that if they were to do so they would bring about the return of an active French body, ambitious if not troublesome, and exceedingly eager to "assert itself" in a region where London had always wished to be supreme and where the British had made such sacrifices that they felt they had a right to be so. Nothing could suit the British strategy in the Levant better than a drowsy, timid France, resigned to total defeat, anxious to be forgotten. In any case, when the Free French made their way into Syria they were to observe that a tacit agreement had come into existence between the Vichy forces and their British neighbours in Palestine and Transjordan, delighted with so total a lack of resistance.

Up until the day when this "lack of resistance" turned out to be the cover for treachery against them – the placing of strategic positions, and of the armaments retained by those in power in Beirut, at the disposition of the Germans and their allies – then, but only then, did the British command in the East agree to move.

On 2 May 1941 the Prime Minister of Iraq, Rashid Ali, who had been worked upon by Nazi emissaries for months, declared his opposition to the British and launched an attack on their base at Habbaniya. The Third Reich was trying to repeat the success of Colonel T. E. Lawrence's Arab Revolt against the Turks twenty-five years earlier, but this time against the British Empire. The loss of Baghdad would be a very severe blow to Wavell. But very soon Berlin was to realize that its Iraqi ally had launched into the adventure imprudently and would be crushed by the British coming from India, unless the Nazis provided the weapons they had promised with extreme urgency.

To save Rashid Ali and to widen the breach he had made on Wavell's eastern flank, German strategy needed Syria, its bases and the weapons stocked there under the supervision of the Italian Armistice commission in Beirut.

Britain's Iraqi enemies found French backers both in Beirut and Damascus. Ever since his installation in Beirut, General Dentz had certainly never ceased to repeat that he would defend the French positions "against any attacker". Yet on 5 May, Darlan, having worked out an overall plan with Abetz, designed to place the French air bases in the Levant at the disposition of the Axis, proceeded to Berchtesgaden, and there they were received by Hitler on 11 and 12 May, at a time when Rashid Ali's anti-British revolt looked as though it were losing impetus.

On the next day, 13 May, de Gaulle sent this message to Catroux:

> As a consequence of the Darlan-Hitler meeting we must expect a great rise in "collaboration". It seems to me obvious that it will take place first in the Syrian theatre and that we shall see the enemy in Damascus while Vichy says it washes its hands of the matter and no longer assumes the mandate received from a League of Nations of which it is no longer a member. We are up against the obstinacy of General Wavell [who] beforehand prevents any practical measures on our part. Since it is quite unimaginable that General Catroux should remain inactive in Palestine while the enemy is marching into Syria, it is essential and most urgent that you should leave Cairo.

* * *

This blackmail turned out to be paying. The withdrawal of the Free French representative in the East would make it evident that there were rifts in the alliance. Though Churchill admired Wavell, he was beginning to find the Commander-in-Chief over cautious; and his frame of mind, always eager for action, brought him over to de Gaulle's side as usual. The Prime Minister ordered the General Staff in Cairo to support the Free French enterprise and cabled de Gaulle on 15 May asking him "not to withdraw Catroux from Palestine [where he is] perhaps at this moment taking action?" and "cordially" inviting him to go to Cairo himself. This was London's green light for the operation in the Levant. Charles de Gaulle was so overcome with joy that for the first and last time he went so far as to write his reply to the Prime Minister in English:

1 Thank you
2 Catroux remains in Palestine
3 I shall go to Cairo soon
4 You will win the war.

Churchill badgered Wavell – who, from the middle of May, had thought of abandoning Iraq* or working out a compromise with Rashid Ali, in order to concentrate greater force on his western flank, in the Tobruk sector, facing Rommel – to make him provide the operation against the Levantine states with considerable backing, not only in the air but also on the land. Churchill did his utmost to convince Wavell that this was not a concession to the whims of the Free French leader but the defence of vital British interests in the Arab world. Wavell did indeed hurry on with the task but not without sending the Prime Minister a message on 22 May to the effect that "the Free French, who will only aggravate the situation" should be kept in the background.[3]

On 12 May it became apparent that at Berchtesgaden Darlan had yielded to Hitler's demands for the permanent use of the Syrian airfields by the Luftwaffe, sent to the help of Rashid Ali. Two days later General Dentz at Beirut received a telegram from Huntziger, the Vichy Minister for War, warning him of the Berchtesgaden concessions and asking whether there was a risk that carrying such a measure into effect might cause "trouble in the army in the Levant". To this Dentz replied that any permanent installation of German units should be avoided. Vichy interpreted his opinion in these terms: "In the event of German or Italian planes flying over the Levant, refrain from all offensive action. If any should land, welcome them. English planes on the contrary must be attacked by all available means."[4]

Meanwhile on 10 May two envoys from Vichy and Berlin had been sent to deal with Dentz: Dentz gave way, authorizing the Luftwaffe to make use of the Syrian airfields and sending the weapons to Baghdad.[5]

In any case the German airmen had not waited for the permission given on 15 May. As early as the ninth three Heinkels had landed at Aleppo; on the eleventh

*Iraq had been an independent country since 1930, but it was still under British military supervision.

Messerschmitts were seen at Rayak, north of Beirut; and from the fifteenth onwards 106 German planes were seen over Syria, some repainted with Iraqi colours.

These doings having naturally brought about reactions from the British, who bombed and above all machine-gunned the airfields thus used, from Beirut to Aleppo, General Dentz's office set about explaining that "some German planes" had "flown over" Syria, and that certain machines "had been obliged to make forced landings". At the beginning of June this version was changed to, "some foreign planes travelling from west to east broke their journey in Syria".

Dentz felt that his position was growing more unstable. On 30 May he cabled Darlan that a certain Colonel Jung had just called upon him "to collaborate on a military plan against the British". This Nazi officer was in fact aware that two days before Darlan and General von Warlimont had signed the "Paris protocols" which gave the Third Reich even more than the Syrian bases – the right to use Bizerta and Dakar, and important stocks of military supplies stored in metropolitan France. In return for this Berlin undertook to make concessions that would give Vichy "the means of justifying the possibility of armed conflict with Britain and the United States before its country's public opinion".[6]*

This was the situation with which the Allied command was faced at the end of May 1941: the French authorities in the Levant directly and actively encouraging the troops who were fighting against Britain with the support of the Luftwaffe. However disagreeable the position of Rashid Ali might be – the arms that Dentz had allowed to reach Baghdad could not save him from collapse on 31 May – the activity of the Luftwaffe based on Aleppo was not only a constant danger but also an open challenge to Britain. In short, as Churchill once more told Wavell, the action was by no means undertaken solely to advance General de Gaulle's personal plans.

At the beginning of June everything was ready for the Syrian expedition. On 6 June, Churchill sent de Gaulle an important telegram: having expressed his best wishes for what he called "our joint enterprise in the Levant" and having recalled that "everything possible is being done to provide support to the arms of Free France", he went on to speak of his hope that this action, and indeed our whole future policy in the Middle East, would be conceived in terms of mutual trust and collaboration. And the Prime Minister went on, "Our policies towards the Arabs must run on parallel lines. You know that we have sought no special advantages in the French Empire and have no intention of exploiting the tragic position of France for our own gain. But [. . .] we must both do everything possible to meet Arab aspirations." It was to become the subject of much later debate. And then Churchill, having made his thrust, ended warmly, "At this hour, when Vichy touches fresh depths of ignominy the Free French save the glory of France.[7]

All the dramas to come were already implicit in this basic message: Charles de Gaulle's reply confined itself to conveying his "deep thankfulness" and assuring Churchill that the Free French were "determined to conquer with you as faithful and resolute allies".

*Here Darlan went farther than Laval had ever dared to do, except in words.

"Faithful and resolute". Both sides probably were so in intention. But since each was acquainted with history, each knew perfectly well that the "joint enterprise" was pregnant with threats to the unity of the alliance. The terrain on to which they were moving, the one leading the other, had been mined ever since Lesseps made the Suez canal the gateway to India and above all since the two powers cynically shared the Near East between themselves in 1917, Paris making sure of Damascus, the heart, if not the capital, of the Arab world.

As we come to the description of what was, after Dakar, the second great military undertaking of Free France and one that wholly committed its leader's prestige, it is important to quote a passage that throws light on his state of mind as far as the "fratricidal" nature of the struggle is concerned. Although these words, written by de Gaulle to General Catroux on 10 May 1940, do not refer to the Levant but to Djibouti and the blockade that the Free French were asking London to impose in order to compel French Somalia to come over, they tell us a great deal about his attitude at that time:

> As for the argument that the British and we should bear the odium for prolonging the blockade of Djibouti, it seems to me almost ludicrous in the war we are engaged upon. We should be very simple-minded if we supposed we could make the omelet of French liberation without agreeing to break a few eggs.[8]

Certainly, but what "eggs"? That is where the whole or almost the whole problem lies. Killing enemies is the very essence of the act of war. But in this case who was the enemy? The Gaullism of 18 June was based upon the simple and unanswerable idea that the enemy remained the German invader and not, however disappointing he may have been, the British ally, to whom France was bound in honour and with whom, beyond rivalries and differences, it was in agreement on the heart of the matter – the value of the human being.

But was not this discussion about the nature of the enemy and the meaning of the battle going to degenerate once the person who was submitted to blockade today and who might be fired on tomorrow was French? The fact that the behaviour of some French citizens may then, out of weakness, fanaticism or caste-solidarity, have been morally worse than that of the Nazis was one thing. The fact that French weapons were to be turned against soldiers who were obeying the orders of a government that even since 10 July 1940 could assert that it was legal and covered by the authority of a legendary chief to whom they had sworn allegiance, was quite another.

Because he replied to this question "sparing nothing", in the belief that France's interests and honour required it, de Gaulle was to arouse hatred all the more implacable since what was at stake in this instance committed each man to the hilt, requiring him, as soon as he had the choice, to choose *himself*. What was always held against de Gaulle – and it rose up again in Algeria twenty years later – was not only that he had had fire directed against Frenchmen but that he had ruthlessly exposed the emptiness of certain forms of allegiance and pitilessly called the due order and priority of loyalties into question.

In spite of the legend, he was not a leader unable to feel compassion. At least at a juncture in which, for this soldier (more traditional than is often supposed) the notions of discipline, the point of honour and loyalty to the chief were all the more full of meaning in that he had had to trample them under foot a year before. After Dakar, Syria reopened the still-bleeding wound of June 1940.

We have given a brief sketch of the relations between de Gaulle and this "complex Orient". But we must deal at somewhat greater length with those between him and General Catroux. However open he might be to arguments on the other side, Catroux was not a man to let himself be checked by a leader who was younger and less well-informed about the particular questions he had been sent to resolve. In the correspondence between the leader of the Free French and his delegate-general in the East, we have only the letters of the first. They are often so sharp that it is easy to imagine how strongly-worded some of Catroux' objections must have been. Thus as early as 21 January 1941 the man of London writes to his representative in Cairo: "I am compelled to ask you to have more confidence in me. Please never suppose that I do anything to make the very difficult and praiseworthy mission you have accepted any harder."[9] But the cooperation between the two chiefs was still uneasy enough for de Gaulle to have to write one month later, on 17 February:

> Of course I refuse your resignation. There is no resignation to be accepted in war-time. If therefore you were to persist in withdrawing your services from Free France it would be desertion. Nobody ignores the importance of the help you personally bring to the service of our cause, which is not my cause but that of our country. Yet you will allow me, I who am as you know your sincere and zealous friend, to tell you that your greatness lies in the very fact of your bringing this help without conditions or over-sensitivity.[10]

The two leaders were surrounded by officers as unlike the common run as themselves: Colonel Collet, Captain Repiton-Preneuf, who continually showed the brilliant tactical imagination that five years later enabled him to turn the nationalist cavalryman Leclerc into the most intelligent of negotiators in Indo-China; François Coulet, whom de Gaulle was soon to choose as his *famulus*, his immediate assistant; Chevigné, who was not a minister until ten years later but who was already an intrepid fighter; Buis, a warrior of twenty-eight who was not yet sure if he might be a poet at thirty; who in any event preferred reading Mallarmé to the promotion list.

On the British side, let us consider the "Alexandrine quartet" made up of Wavell, whose talents, basic reservations with regard to the Free French, and reluctance to commit himself in the Levant when he had to deal with Rommel in the west have already been mentioned;* General Maitland Wilson, known as

*He was replaced at the end of June by General Auchinleck, the Commander-in-Chief in India, who had been given the task of crushing the revolt in Iraq.

"Jumbo", a sharp-eyed pachyderm whose one aim in life was to ensure British supremacy between the Sahara and Anatolia; the Minister of State Oliver Lyttelton, a personal friend of Winston Churchill's, who was to intervene sensibly and calmly from July onwards, though without being able to avoid the inevitable; and that fox, Sir Edward Spears, whose relations with de Gaulle had deteriorated to such a point that on 9 March, at Chequers, Winston Churchill was obliged to ask de Gaulle "as a personal favour" to be so good as to keep Spears with him "whatever his grievances might be".

In fact Sir Edward carried on with his bold support of the Gaullist cause until July, particularly in urging Wavell to send Maitland Wilson to Syria with the Free French. It was only later that, exasperated by his former protégé's inflexible attitude and siezed upon once again by the demons of a certain kind of imperialism, he took to working against de Gaulle with as much zeal as he had worked for him.

On 26 May, at Qastina, near Gaza and "under the same sun that had stunned the blinded Samson when he was bound to the mill-stone, the tall, upright figure of de Gaulle stood watching the first united advance of those Frenchmen from all over the world who [. . .] clinging to the idea that he personified [had] submitted their will to his."[11]

The leader of the Free French had hurriedly flown to Cairo on 25 May, having cabled Spears that "the march on Damascus was a matter of hours" since "there was a danger that the situation would deteriorate very quickly because of Vichy or the Germans or the Syrian nationalists or all of them together". And he had told Eden that "the declaration of the Levantine states' independence would be made in the name of Free France, that is to say of France, at the moment of the action, if that action took place." In this way de Gaulle made even the pro-Arab feeling of the British work in favour of the undertaking.

As soon as he reached the Levant he asked those around him the essential question: Will Vichy fight? This was why Lieutenant Georges Buis, who had left Beirut a month earlier, was summoned to Jerusalem one evening, a Jerusalem blacked out in the British fashion. Guided by Repiton, he suddenly found himself sitting in the presence of a giant dimly lit by a candle. De Gaulle, "Will they fire on us?" "Yes, without the slightest doubt." The General spoke of other sources who, particularly in Cairo, far from the scene of operations, had told him "Everybody is expecting you!" But Buis had come from a Beirut where "a Gaullist skated on thin ice", and his information coincided with that of Catroux and Repiton.[12] Colonel Collet, one of the great new recruits, backed up what Buis had said; there would be fighting and as in all civil wars the fighting would be very hard.

On 6 June de Gaulle sent Churchill a telegram that was also an undertaking:

> I shall proclaim and respect the independence of the Levantine states on condition of a treaty with them confirming French rights and interests. Any policy that seems to sacrifice these rights and interests at present would be bad and dangerous from the point of view of French public opinion [a fact

> that] does not seem to me to be always well understood locally. The more you hit Vichy, the more you must show an anxiety to spare the interests and the feelings of France. Despair is a formidable counsellor.[13]

The campaign began at dawn on 8 June 1941. The Anglo-Gaullists had at their disposal only one Australian division, one English cavalry regiment, one Indian infantry brigade, General Legentilhomme's little division, and 70 planes, 24 of which were Free French: about 20 000 fighting men, three quarters British and one quarter French. Against them, General Dentz could gather more than 30 000 men, 120 guns, 80 tanks and 90 planes.

As Operation Exporter was launched, General Catroux, who was in charge of the French, put out two proclamations. The first was addressed to Dentz's men, and leaving all political or tactical argument to one side it appealed only to the sense of honour of those who were faithful to the Marshal: "I am marching into Syria. Honour requires it. Honour forbids that the nations of the Levant should be placed under the hateful yoke of Germany. These demands of honour are my demands, and they are yours."

To this the Marshal replied with an appeal to Dentz's troops denouncing "the attack carried out, as at Dakar, by Frenchmen serving under a dissident flag."

> With the support of the British they do not hesitate to shed the blood of their brothers who are defending the Empire's unity and the sovereignty of France. Before force there was trickery: inventing an excuse for aggression, propaganda claimed that German troops were landing in great numbers. You who are there on the spot know it is all untrue. You know that the few planes that had made temporary landings in our territory have now left Syria.* You are therefore the object of an unjust attack that disgusts you. You are fighting in a righteous cause.

Catroux' second proclamation was addressed to the nations of the Levant:**

> Syrians and Lebanese, at this juncture, when the forces of Free France, together with those of its ally Great Britain, are entering your territory, I abolish the Mandate*** and I proclaim you free and independent. As soon as possible a treaty will be drawn up between your representatives and me. Meanwhile the position between us will be that of allies. The Free French forces are crossing your frontiers not to oppress your freedom but to drive out the forces of Hitler and to ensure the respect of your rights and at the same time those of France.

In any event, the diplomatic commitment was plain. The recognition of Syrian and

*Which is in direct contradiction to Darlan's telegram to Dentz quoted on p. 296.

**This is taken from the fifth of the eight versions prepared by de Gaulle and Catroux, the version that Catroux uttered and that he quotes as such in his memoirs.

***Entrusted to France by the League of Nations in 1920. Vichy had broken with the League: de Gaulle had not.

Lebanese independence was neither conditional nor suspensive (whatever de Gaulle may subsequently have maintained). It closely resembled those that London was then granting to other Arab states and it implied only the conclusion of a treaty defining the parties' "reciprocal relations" and in the meantime the status of "closely linked allies" for both: the one apparent limitation affecting this independence was the war-alliance – the only things forbidden to Syria and the Lebanon were neutrality (like that of Egypt until 1942) or hostility (like that of Rashid Ali).

The Free French leader, who was then in Cairo, moved up to Jerusalem on 13 June, nearer the fighting; and from there he regularly visited the forces engaged and the wounded. As soon as Damascus was taken he installed himself in that city; when Spears advised him not to stay he replied, "the Free French leaders themselves can best appreciate the right line of conduct as far as the Levantine states are concerned," and he added with a kind of waspish delight, "The capital of France is Paris. Until Paris is liberated, if God wills, I shall stay wherever I think it most useful for the prosecution of the war." The key-note was given.

As early as the evening of 8 June it was known that Dentz's troops were indeed fighting heartily. They were not very zealous against the British (though they were markedly superior in number – three to two – they gradually fell back) but they made the slightest advance of the Gaullists a very costly matter. Paul Repiton describes the state of mind of those faithful to the Marshal: for them the Gaullists "were the Devil incarnate, the scapegoats for all the anger, resentment and weakness which had been lurking in the dark places of their consciences for a year" and which the Vichyists at last got rid of by transferring them "like a herd of swine" to the Gaullists' "black hearts."[14]

Everywhere the Free French had flags of truce sent forward. And everywhere the bearers of the white flag were, as at Dakar, received with rifle-fire (or with shells). Major Boissoudy approached a comrade in the colonial infantry and heard him shout, "Blaze away! He's wearing a British helmet." Boissoudy lost a leg. "Both sides naturally accused each other of the worst atrocities, without in fact practising them. Among Dentz's men it was understood that the Free French massacred their prisoners. And the Free French brooded over the fate of their friends sentenced for desertion."[15]

On 18 June, when de Gaulle was addressing the French in Cairo and giving them an account of what Free France had done in the last year, Dentz requested the United States consul-general in Beirut to ask the British about armistice terms. On 19 June in Cairo, Wavell and Catroux being present, de Gaulle gave them to Sir Miles Locker Lampson, the British Ambassador: honourable treatment for the Vichy soldiers and civil servants, who might choose between being sent back to France and joining the Free French but who were not obligatorily to be sent back as a group; a guarantee on the part of London that French rights and interests should be preserved and that France should be represented in the Levant by the Free French. Since those present seemed to have approved of these ideas, it was with utter amazement that de Gaulle perceived, the next day, that the conditions handed to Dentz did not even mention Free France. He at once cabled Eden, expressing all his reserves on this document and warning him that he would adhere to what had been "agreed"* in Cairo on 19 June.

Damascus was taken on the twenty-first; Catroux was there on the twenty-second; de Gaulle on the twenty-third, and there he at once appointed his companion "Delegate-General and plenipotentiary in the Levant", specifying that he would exercise "all the powers of the High Commissioner". Yet in his letter to Churchill of 6 June the leader of the Free French had distinctly stated that Catroux would not be High Commissioner, a title from the days of the Mandate.

On 10 July Dentz let it be known that in principle he accepted the terms conveyed by the British, on condition that his delegate was not required to treat with any Gaullists. A meeting was arranged for 12 July at Acre in Palestine, where Britain was to be represented by Wilson, Vichy by General de Verdilhac, and in spite of Dentz's warnings, Free France by Catroux.

The Acre agreement was signed on 14 July. However brightly Catroux may have shone in the debate, he was not among the signatories. Fortunately! For Free France the agreement was a set-back. Against de Gaulle's directly expressed opinion, the accent had been put on the repatriation of the Vichy forces rather than on individual choice. Although, to leave the freedom of choice some sort of chance, it was laid down that until they left these forces should not be kept in their war-time order, Verdilhac had successfully argued that the embarkment should take place in ships provided by Vichy.

From the very beginning, de Gaulle had felt most pessimistic about these negotiations, in which he saw the influence of the pro-Arab lobby in Cairo, the Intelligence Service specialists, and the old Transjordanian experts like Glubb Pasha.** In his view these specialists, who were represented at Acre by "Jumbo" Wilson, wished for a ruthless minimization of Free France so that in the East nothing might be seen but a Vichy France, defeated, discredited, a prey to be devoured and a vacuum to be filled. In this he did not exaggerate a great deal. He was very strongly prejudiced, and although he knew that at this juncture Free France was well represented, he was convinced that at Acre "we should be cheated". De Gaulle says in his *Mémoires*:

> The only way in which I could limit the damage was to give myself space and height, to reach some cloud and from there to swoop upon an agreement that would not bind me and that I should tear up as far as I could. The cloud was Brazzaville. There I stayed while at Acre the document, whose content was far worse than anything I had feared, was drawn up.[16]

What de Gaulle held against the agreement of 14 July was that it did not take the rights of France into account and that it amounted to a "handing over of Syria and the Lebanon to the British". Above all, it brought about the massive departure of Dentz's men, whose change of allegiance de Gaulle had counted on, and the region emptied of its French content.

Catroux, knowing how de Gaulle had received the Acre agreement and seeing him come back from Brazzaville accompanied by General de Larminat, said to

*The word is abusive. The English had listened to him without committing themselves.
**See Chapter 28. (trs.)

Lieutenant Buis, his private secretary, "Has he brought Larminat with him to offer him my place? Do you think he would do that?" – "I do think so, sir."[17] But very soon de Gaulle gave up the idea of this surgical operation; it was enough for him to see Catroux on the spot to realize that he was irreplaceable, at least in the Levant.

Yet although he withheld his thunderbolts as far as his own people were concerned, General de Gaulle hurled them at his allies. As usual it was Spears (although he himself considered the agreement absurdly unfavourable to the Free French) who received the first. When he pointed out that all this moved in the direction of the joint struggle against Nazism, this was the retort: "Do you think I want Britain to win? No, the only thing that matters to me is a French victory." "But that's the same thing!" "Not from my point of view; not at all."

On 21 July, in Cairo, Charles de Gaulle was still boiling with anger when he encountered Captain Oliver Lyttelton, whom Churchill had just made Minister of State and the War Cabinet's representative in the Near East. This friend of the Prime Minister, like many of Churchill's immediate associates, thought favourably of the Free French. His good will was to be put to a very severe test.

"Wrapping himself up in ice", de Gaulle told the British minister that the "joint effort" could not be allowed to result in the installation of "British authority in Damascus and Beirut". Lyttleton pointed out that in wartime the military command possessed superior rights; and by the agreement of 7 August 1940 his visitor had acknowledged this. De Gaulle retorted that the authority in question was limited to the strategic field and against the common enemy. And he uttered these prophetic words: "When we land on French soil one day, will you put forward the rights of the command so that you may claim to govern France?"*

The fact remained, observed Churchill's representative, that the agreement had been signed and that it had to be applied.

"No," interrupted de Gaulle, "I have not ratified it." And driving his charge home he rapped out, "From 24 July, the Free French forces will no longer depend on the British command in Syria and the Lebanon. Furthermore I am ordering General Catroux to assume authority over the whole of this territory immediately." To make it clear that the alliance "could not be allowed to work to the disadvantage of France" the visitor said emphatically, "If the case were unfortunately to arise, we should prefer to suspend our commitments with regard to Britain."

Lyttelton's version of the interview is different where the atmosphere rather than the words is concerned.** The British minister says that he was "dumbfounded" by the coarseness of his visitor's tone and the extravagance of his observations; as to de Gaulle's proposals, Lyttelton says he told de Gaulle that he had not even "received" them. And he ends, "The discussion degenerated into what women call a scene."

But like Spears, Lyttelton was convinced that the Free French had been unfairly treated at Acre, and that same evening he offered de Gaulle an "explanatory agreement", which was in fact to be a revision of the 14 July convention: from now on the Free French were authorized to enter into contact with the Vichy troops

*All the dramas between the Allies in 1944 are contained in these few words.

**He became Lord Chandos and it was under that title that he published his memoirs.

and civil servants; the military supplies recovered would be handed over to them; and as well as this it would be specifically laid down that the authority of the British command would be exercised in the military sphere alone.

De Gaulle had won this battle. But it was a Pyrrhic victory, the price paid being the enmity of many of his best allies, beginning with Spears. From the point of view of de Gaulle and Catroux, Spears had been *persona non grata* for months. But in Spears' view the break came in these last days of July, and above all with de Gaulle's harrying of Lyttelton. A friend of Churchill's and a British minister could not be treated like that. And Spears' hostility, in this region where he was soon to become the director of the British strategy in the Levantine states, was to be a grave handicap.

"Without the Acre agreement we should never have been able to get into the fortress," observes Georges Buis. But, he adds, it had to be amended, "And only de Gaulle was capable of that."[18] The subsequent course of history seems to show that he was right. Whether it was in the Jebel Druse or in Gezireh, from which Dentz's soldiers and civil servants had taken the files and archives in order to make administration impossible and to call the British into the vacuum, Maitland Wilson's seizure of power was immediate. When the Free French under Major de Kersauzon came to take possession of the fort at Suweida, the capital of the Druze country, they found the English flag flying over it. Protests. Objections. Demands. All in vain. Two days later a note sped from General de Gaulle to Maitland Wilson: "I do not suppose I can vanquish the British Empire, but if you do not leave Suweida we shall fire."

Let us imagine that the British command had not fully realized that for the Free French these trifling matters of presence and flying the flag were questions of life or death. That being excluded after having assumed the frightful responsibility of firing upon French soldiers meant as far as they were concerned the loss of their very reason for existence. After the fratricidal battles against Vichy, fighting between the Gaullists and the British at Suweida would have been akin to suicide. But what then? It was a question of to be or not to be.

At Jezireh the Gaullist unit also found the fortress occupied, and de Gaulle and Catroux decided to deal with the matter on the spot. Georges Buis has an account of this expedition: de Gaulle emerging and haranguing the crowd that had appeared from nowhere; the transfer of power and flag that followed; the whole giving a lifelike impression of the makeshift aspect and the "Wild Western" style that the Constable's crusade had taken on. "Everywhere," says Georges Buis, "we had to get a hold again."

> At a time when the situation was still fluid, the British would have replaced us everywhere, but for this determination. In fact Syria and the Lebanon were quite certainly the one part of the world in which attempting an honest, straightforward collaboration between the British and the French was a risky business. The de Gaulle – Catroux team held on by their quality alone. With them gone, the British would have done us down in the end.[19]

It was Churchill's place to arbitrate between the Free Frenchmen's passionate desire to "be" and the local British forces' spontaneous inclination to "possess". The reason he did not do this, but allowed his specialists to display their shameless greed, was that enormous problems were confronting him: the battle in the Libyan desert, the entry of the USSR into the war on 22 June 1941, the great conferences with Roosevelt that were to result in the publication of the Atlantic Charter, and presently Pearl Harbour, which flung the United States into the war at last. De Gaulle had also treated Churchill in a hardly acceptable manner.

Was Churchill aware of the gravity of the disagreement? He certainly alluded to it in a letter to Eden of 7 July, speaking of the "hateful difficulties" with the French on the subject of Syria. But at that point he could not spend much time worrying about the emotions, justified or not, of a man who commanded only a few thousand rifles. It was at the end of August that the scandal became known and this time it broke out in the press, the medium to which a British statesman is most sensitive.

On 27 August 1941, the *Chicago Daily News*, a paper with a very wide circulation, published an interview that de Gaulle was said to have granted to an American correspondent, George Weller, during his stay in Brazzaville; an interview that has already been quoted in part* and in which the forms of collusion between London and Vichy are crudely and directly spoken of.

The *Chicago Daily News* interview was all the more likely to set off an explosion since before seeing it Churchill had been sent a summary from the United States in which he was accused of having made "a wartime deal with Hitler". He wrote to Eden, "He has clearly gone off his head. . . . This would be a very good riddance and will simplify our further course."[20]

Now it so happens that even before the American correspondent's article was published, de Gaulle had firmly denied having given any interview of any kind. And as soon as he had seen Weller's piece he disputed every word, particularly the remark about Britain's "fear" of the French fleet; and he threatened to have Weller expelled from French Africa. It is quite obvious that the journalist published words that were certainly uttered in his presence by a de Gaulle then in a violent fit of Anglophobia. But it was not, as Churchill believed it was, a question of deliberate public provocation.[21]

The Prime Minister, deeply hurt, took no notice of these restatements of the matter. And on 30 August, says Anthony Eden – Churchill's memoirs are surprisingly silent about the whole affair – the Prime Minister ordered the members of the Cabinet to cease all relations with de Gaulle, a direction that also applied to the "subordinates on both sides". It was a kind of freezing of the connection between the associates, a suspension of the agreement of 28 June 1940. But presently Churchill was speaking of nothing more than "letting de Gaulle stew in his own juice for a week".

On his way back to London, the General was told that his outbursts were having grave repercussions for his associates in Carlton Gardens and that he would land in the midst of a storm; if we are to believe his confidential associate and travelling-companion François Coulet, he seemed delighted. What did Churchill's

*See p. 288.

anger and a diplomatic cloud matter, compared with the injustice done to the Free French cause?

When he landed in London on 1 September he learnt that the microphones of the BBC were forbidden to him until further notice. Never mind: not a single Free Frenchman would take part in the British broadcasts. On 3 September, before he had a direct conversation with Winston Churchill, de Gaulle wrote to the Prime Minister, from whom he had received a message resembling a dismissal, and said that the interview at Brazzaville, the echo of "a rapid, unpremeditated talk during which Weller had not taken any notes", was nothing more than a "sensational exaggeration of what I may have said to him".

A proper apology? A prudent side-step, in any case, and one that allowed de Gaulle to tell Churchill that his "personal contact" with Oliver Lyttelton had left him with the "most agreeable impression", but that "the attitude of the British authorities" in the East, which had brought the Free French to the point of "gravest doubt" of their intentions made it essential that a settlement should be worked out between the Prime Minister and himself.[22]

These calm explanations did not soothe Churchill's anger; he fixed the appointment for 12 September. This famous interview has given rise to several accounts, the best being that of the Prime Minister's private secretary, John Colville.[23]

Churchill had told his secretary that he would not shake the General's hand, and since for once he did not choose to speak French he would need an interpreter – Colville himself. De Gaulle came in; he did not seem to notice that the Prime Minister did not offer his hand, and he waited. Churchill: "General de Gaulle, I have asked you to come." Colville translated, "*Mon général, je vous ai invité.*" Churchil angrily interrupted: "I did not say *mon* General, nor did I speak of *invitation*." Three minutes had not passed before Colville, checked and reproached by both one and the other, withdrew and called for a professional Foreign Office interpreter. Shortly afterwards the professional came out of the office, red in the face with embarrassment and, according to Courcel, who was waiting in the next door room, asserting "that it was impossible to work with these gentlemen". From then onwards they did without an interpreter, Churchill returning to his spoken Gaulish.

To begin with, the Prime Minister stated the grievances that he had taken particularly to heart, grievances concerning the General's "Anglophobia", of which he had heard a score of recent and scandalous instances. De Gaulle retorted that it was absurd to bring an accusation of enmity towards the United Kingdom against a man who had made the choice he had made and who was fighting the war that he was fighting against the common enemy. But he added that certain forms of behaviour on the part of the British in the Levant had "shaken him": if his isolation and his personal temperament had led him to make observations too diagreeable to English ears "he felt no difficulty in expressing his regret".*

Churchill admitted that "faults" had been committed on the British side, but he said that the General ought to have told him about them. To this de Gaulle replied that he had uttered all the necessary warnings from as early as 28 June; and he

*From de Gaulle's version, in which the words are more specific than in Colville's.

spoke of the "innumerable humiliations" inflicted upon his representatives and himself. Churchill said that Britain would "be ashamed" to make use of the ratio between their forces to take France's place and in no way aimed at any such end; yet the war-effort in the East required that the British command should exercise supreme authority while the relations between London and the Arabs implied that Syria should be given independence. De Gaulle replied that France had likewise made that promise to Damascus, but "the question could only really be settled when peace came."*

The Prime Minister did not seem struck by the restrictive aspect of these words and he said that "he was aware of the importance of treating Free France in Syria in such a manner that the French nation would realize that General de Gaulle is the guardian of its interests there."

Churchill moved on to the subject of the organization of Free France: would not the setting up of a "council in due form"** strengthen the movement? De Gaulle did not appear to be offended by Churchill's interfering in French internal affairs in this way, and he replied that he was thinking of creating a "National Committee", but (according to Colville's version) that in doing so there was a risk of endangering his movement's "political cohesion". In his own account the General does not mention this matter of "cohesion"; he says that he told his host about a plan for summoning a "Free French congress" in January.

More than an hour passed. Colville, in the next-door office with Courcel, was surprised at no longer hearing any outbursts. Had the irreparable been committed, perhaps an "act of violence"? He risked opening the door and looking in: the two men were sitting side by side, smiling and smoking the Prime Minister's cigars, and Churchill had recovered his most eloquent French to suggest that the next time Oliver Lyttelton came to London the three of them should meet.

Formally, the incident was closed. There was too much in common between the two men, whatever the circumstances. But an agreement on the Levant was far from reached. When he told Churchill that as he saw it the status of Syria "could only be settled when peace came", de Gaulle made the difference between the two points of view startlingly obvious. For the English, Syrian independence was a means of winning the war: for de Gaulle, it was only the end of the joint effort. There was much more than a misunderstanding here.

The Prime Minister was certainly glad to restore cordial relations with de Gaulle and to revitalize the alliance to which he had yielded nothing. Neither the outbursts of July nor the remarks of August 1941 were forgotten. Nothing, apart from a few forms, had altered Britain's determination.

When Catroux proclaimed the (conditional) independence of Syria and the Lebanon three months later, whom did Winston Churchill appoint as the first British Ambassador to the two countries? General Spears, who, as he knew, had become the man whose company de Gaulle and Catroux liked least. Catroux was to say that London had sent Sir Edward "for [their] sins".

Churchill was even to carry his grudge about the Levant still farther. He only

*From de Gaulle's version.
**Colville's version.

refers to the Free French (who amounted to a quarter of the fighting force, who suffered nearly half the casualties, and who played a vital part) to say that they "were held ten miles short of Damascus". Perfidious Albion? No. But the French are not the only people to be forgetful at times.

CHAPTER TWENTY-FIVE

An Admiral Overboard

What set Emile Muselier apart from the other admirals in the French navy during the Second World War is the fact that he elected to fight the enemies of France: he chose armed combat and at sea. Whatever one may think of the man, his character, his career, his ideas and his behaviour to General de Gaulle, there is this, and it must not be forgotten. Like Catroux he was of higher rank than de Gaulle, and he came to London at the end of June 1940 without even knowing of de Gaulle's existence; he belonged to a body that had little inclination to give its allegiance elsewhere, yet he too, for fourteen decisive months, was capable of accepting that remarkable authority *that was not subject to hierarchical order*, even though later he threw off the yoke with the extraordinary clumsiness that able men sometimes display once they are seized by anger or blinded by resentment.

Towards the end of the afternoon of 1 January 1941, General de Gaulle was relaxing with his family at Gadlas Hall in Shropshire. He was in plain clothes and he was happy to be with Yvonne and Anne again. The telephone rang: it was Anthony Eden speaking from the Foreign Office where he had taken over from Lord Halifax a fortnight earlier. In an anxious voice he asked de Gaulle to come back to London urgently.

At the same time Colonel Angenot, then the General's chief of staff, telephoned Commander Moullec, known as Moret, chief of staff to Admiral Muselier. Angenot warned Moret that the head of the Free French naval forces was threatened with arrest. Both men tried to get through to their respective chiefs, but in vain.

At 9.30 on Monday, 2 January, Muselier, who had just returned to his house from Portsmouth, was arrested by the police, driven, amazed, to Scotland Yard, and locked up before any interrogation. Two hours later de Gaulle, who had hurried back to London, was ushered in to the Foreign Secretary's office; there Eden, his face and voice much concerned, told him that the Admiral was accused of high treason: he was said to have handed over the plans for the Dakar operation to Vichy and to have arranged for the sale of the *Surcouf*, the biggest submarine in the world, to Darlan.

Eden brought out a file containing letters addressed to Vichy in August 1940 by the French air attaché in London, General Rozoy, who had since then left for France. "This can only be some huge mistake," asserted de Gaulle, who expressed "the strongest reserves" about the British security force's action, adding that this could only be a question of "some plot on the part of Vichy".

During that same afternoon the Admiral was moved to a cell in Pentonville Prison, where from then onwards he was treated as an ordinary offender; while at a Lancaster House lunch to which a few of the chief Free Frenchmen had been invited, de Gaulle, noticing Moret, called out, "I hear fine things about your Admiral!" and asked him to come and look into the question at Carlton Gardens.[1]

The General showed Muselier's chief of staff photographs of the incriminating documents: five letters from General Rozoy to the Vichy government in which, after various pieces of information on the relations between de Gaulle, his associates and the British, the preparations for the Dakar expedition were divulged, as though coming from Muselier. Moret's instant reaction was that these were crude forgeries, not even plausible. De Gaulle was impressed, but he wanted to think it over and he asked Moret to come back and see him late in the afternoon. The chief of staff could not restrain himself: "But time is going by and we are doing nothing about the Admiral's shameful treatment!"[2] To this de Gaulle replied, "Moret, get out or I shall send you to join your admiral."[3]

The next night Moret was woken by a call from the General: "Come at once." In his room at the Connaught de Gaulle was at his desk, the letters spread out in front of him. "You were right," he said. "These papers are forged, and the whole thing is a mere plot worked out by Vichy." And he asked Muselier's chief of staff to come to Carlton Gardens that same morning so that they might together draw up a formal refutation of the documents produced by the English services. This was done on the morning of 3 January. Yet it is noteworthy that according to the General himself this justificatory memorandum, which annihilated the police evidence and brought about the Admiral's liberation, was only handed to Spears by de Gaulle on 7 January, four days later.[4]

On the fourth, while Muselier had been shivering in cold and solitude for two days, the British Admiralty let it be known that it did not believe in his guilt and that there must be a mistake on the part of MI5. De Gaulle went to the Foreign Office and told Eden that since the incriminating documents were "extremely suspicious" he wished for the immediate release of his closest colleague and asked (at last) to see him. Muselier had congestion of the lungs and that same day he was moved to the infirmary in Brixton prison, where many of his friends and colleagues visited him.

On 6 January the Admiral was at last shown the incriminating papers: he stated at once that they were forgeries. Experts were called in and they said he was right: everything became clear. De Gaulle appeared, very coldly received by Muselier, and he congratulated the Admiral on the happy outcome of the affair, declaring that he had never questioned his innocence. Muselier, who had been in touch with Moret, doubted this. And another twenty-four hours had to pass before de Gaulle made up his mind to tell General Spears that any delay in the liberation of Admiral Muselier would bring about a break between Free France and the United Kingdom.[5]

By way of making reparation for this monstrous blunder, the British authorities did a great deal – apologies from Eden, an invitation to lunch with the Churchills, an audience of the King. In his *Mémoires* de Gaulle says that this change of attitude "soon looked excessive". He also states that this lamentable event was not wholly unfortunate in its consequences, since a week later it led to the signing of an agreement on jurisdiction according to which the French would from now on come before the Free French courts applying French military law.

But who had been behind the plot? As we have seen, de Gaulle was quick to detect the hand of Vichy, whose agents seemed to have concocted the plot in the offices of the French consulate in London with the intention of fomenting quarrels both between the leaders of the Free French and even more between Free France and Britain. But Muselier looked upon other men as the culprits, a certain Major Meffre, known as Howard, and his assistant Colin, who were taken on by the security services at Carlton Gardens "at the urgent request of the British during my stay in Africa," says de Gaulle, and against the advice of Passy.

Pointing out that Meffre was received by de Gaulle at Carlton Gardens on 27 December, five days before the beginning of the affair, Muselier insinuated that de Gaulle was perhaps not unaware of the plot; this was absurd, since such a scandal could only damage the Free French movement and be useful to Vichy's and even Goebbels' propaganda. Furthermore, the de Gaulle–Meffre interview of 27 December is easily explained because three days earlier the Admiral had complained to the General that this agent had come and ferretted about in his papers: de Gaulle had promised to speak severely to the man and to see about punishment. So there was nothing surprising about his being summoned. Summoned by de Gaulle once more on 5 January and required to explain himself, Meffre calmly replied, "Even if the allegations in these papers are false, at least they give us the advantage of getting rid of Muselier," an observation that gives some idea of the man.[6]

If there is anything plain in what de Gaulle calls this "melancholy tale of Intelligence",* it is that, first, an organization like Free France was open to many different kinds of penetration; secondly, the British authorities, understandably seized by a feverish sense of being beseiged, did not look upon the Gaullists as allies above all suspicion – and were not sorry to make them responsible for the blunders of yesterday at Dakar or of tomorrow at Algiers; and lastly, it took Charles de Gaulle several days and long periods of reflection before he unreservedly covered his closest colleague, the victim of an absurd accusation.** In any case, the relations between Carlton Gardens and Westminster House, where Muselier's team settled at about that time, were gravely distorted for ever after.

Can two more strongly contrasting characters be imagined? On the one hand, the tall, land-borne baron from the Nord, armoured with pride and rigidity, well placed to fly still higher, reaching the top of the steeple of Notre-Dame-la-France, a permanent crusader, filled with the greatness of his mission to the point of being obsessed by it, even more imperious by design than by nature, capable of shutting himself up in silence for days on end: and on the other the jovial Marseilles sailor (he seems to have inherited very little from his Lorraine father apart from the idea

*Meffre was expelled from the Free French and he spent the rest of the war in detention; then, set free by the British, he returned to "intelligence" in 1945.

**If the Admiral had been accused of wanting to seduce the Prime Minister's wife," observed Moullec, "I should have said 'Perhaps'. But treason?!"

of the cross that he made the emblem of Free France), talkative and quick-witted, with something Levantine about his eyes and gestures – a fine flow of speech and a great deal of charm, always in motion, never silent, just as the English imagine the French (and as the French imagine the Italians), darting from the conquest of a heart to a gallant action, always putting himself out to please except when he broke off to deal with an intruder or to defy a rival.

The most agreeable portrait of him comes from Edgar de Larminat, who was chief of staff in the Levant in 1940.

> Muselier belonged to a type, that of the eastern Mediterranean sailor who has mistaken his period. He would have made an outstanding admiral in the service of the Venetian republic. At present his talents as a sailor, a corsair and a negotiator were scarcely of any use. He was the kind of heavy-eyed, heavy-hipped Levantine one can perfectly well imagine doing a little belly-dance on the table at the end of a drinking party.[7]

At the end of June 1940, Muselier reached Britain by way of Gibraltar, the only one of the fifty French admirals to prefer carrying on the war against the Nazis. He overcame the trial of Mers-el-Kebir and the Royal Navy's forcible taking-over of the French ships stationed in English ports, and he set to work building up a fleet again, also setting up a school for cadets at which General de Gaulle's son, among others, was trained. And he began this French naval renaissance in close, friendly relations with his British counterparts, which was something of a feat.

The storm of January 1941 did not burst out of a cloudless sky. The relations between the General (fifty years old, with two "temporary" stars) and the Admiral (sixty-three, with three stars solidly sewn on) were far more difficult than those which Catroux had wished to establish with de Gaulle (though as we have seen even they were not so smooth). From the very beginning Muselier had never concealed the fact that he did not agree with the policy of the Gaullist plan and that he would have preferred to take part in a purely military operation with the British against the Nazis.

As for the General, Muselier's intense activity exasperated him. Early in December 1940, when Passy was praising Muselier's straightforwardness and efficiency, de Gaulle broke in with a harsh, "He's an insufferable meddler." The position is well summarized by Muselier's faithful friend, Héron de Villefosse: between these "two exceptional, outstanding French military characters, equally determined to wipe out the humiliation of the defeat, relations could not really be settled by the subordination of one to the other." But the permanent embitterment of the contacts between the Constable and the Corsair date from this disgraceful imprisonment, which Muselier attributed to de Gaulle, if not in its origin then at least in its prolongation.

It will be recalled that during their animated meeting of 12 September 1941 de Gaulle and Churchill spoke of the plan for setting up a Free French "council" on which the Carlton Gardens services would work alongside Muselier's team. Both the General and the Admiral claimed this perfectly natural idea for themselves – an idea that in de Gaulle arose from his wish to broaden the movement's bases and its legitimacy, while in Muselier it expressed an inclination to counter-balance the General's authority, if not to keep it in leading-strings.

In his *Mémoires* de Gaulle speaks of Muselier as being "the tool" of those groups which "rejected de Gaulle's authority" – a piece of gratuitous ill-will. The Admiral was manipulated by no one but himself; yet perhaps he really was, as the Free French leader spiritedly describes him, the possessor "of a double personality. As a naval officer he displayed powers that deserved great respect and that to a large extent were responsible for the organization of our small naval forces. But from time to time he was seized by a kind of feverish state of mind that urged him to intrigue.[8]

Intrigue is the word people use to discredit those whose activities they dislike. But there is no doubt that the Admiral was fond of political manoeuvres, and with his natural charm and an experience moulded by a career driven on in spite of every disadvantage he longed to assert himself in such a context. In short, as soon as he heard that de Gaulle was becoming resigned to something like a diversification or a broadening of the Free French directorate, his democratic blood instantly impelled him to make a large number of suggestions. But de Gaulle wished neither to allow an "outside" plan to be imposed upon him, nor to let anyone steal a march on him. Everything is said very finely in his *Mémoires de guerre*:

> The field of action was growing wider, and I had to set an adequate organization at the head of the undertaking. De Gaulle was no longer capable of directing everything. Since for all States the collegial form is that of power, our adopting it for ourselves would help in causing us to be recognized. On 24 September 1941, by ordinance, I established the National Committee.*

Muselier had done everything he could, not to be faced with a *fait accompli*. The two letters he had sent to de Gaulle on 18 and 20 September, were earnest appeals to him to endanger neither Free France's alliances by over-imperious enterprise nor democracy by too personal a policy. The General rather incorrectly sums this up by saying that in order to safeguard both the one and the other, "he suggested that I should place myself in an honorary position and that I should leave him the reality of power."

To be exact, it was only in the first of his two letters that the Admiral claimed the actual control of the working committee, with de Gaulle retaining a purely nominal superiority. In the second he gave himself no more than the vice-presidency, but to this was added the supervision of political decisions by himself together with his chief of staff, Moullec, and André Labarthe, both of them most outspoken critics of Charles de Gaulle.

Between the sending of the first and the second plan, there occurred what has been called "the Savoy Lunch",** which was given by two outstanding Englishmen, Lord Bessborough and Desmond Morton, close friends of Churchill, for

*De Gaulle, like Caesar, wrote about himself in the third person. (trs.)
**Or alternatively, the "Savoy Summit". (trs.)

Muselier, Labarthe and Dejean, political adviser to the Free French forces and a friend of Muselier's.* The Englishmen gave some kind of countenance to the "plot", though at the same time they diminished the plotters' excessive greed. Dejean did not fail to inform de Gaulle of this.

This was the kind of situation in which de Gaulle shone with all his brilliance, the brilliance of a lightning-flash. He launched his bolt at the unfortunate Muselier in the form of a letter dated 23 September 1941:

> You went beyond your rights and your duty when you informed me of your decision to separate yourself and the navy that I placed under your orders from Free France. Your action in so doing amounts to an intolerable misuse of the military command with which I entrusted you, the command of a Free French force whose officers and men joined as Free Frenchmen and are bound to my authority by a contract of enlistment. Furthermore you are damaging unity in a movement which, faced with the enemy and the present situation in France, may represent the country's one hope of salvation . . .
>
> I shall not allow you to do so.
>
> Bearing in mind your services in the past and the unfortunate influence that certain non-combatant members of the emigration may have had on you, I give you twenty-four hours in which to return to your senses and your duty.
>
> I shall wait for your reply until 4 p.m. tomorrow, 24 September. After that point I shall take the necessary steps to ensure that you can do no harm and that your behaviour is publicly known, that is to say marked with infamy.
>
> I must add that in this painful affair I have made sure of the support of the allies on whose soil we stand and who have recognized me as the head of the Free French.
>
> I send you my greetings.[9]

Muselier had thought he was big enough to challenge the Constable. He was not. His friends at the Admiralty and those at the Foreign Office exerted themselves to make his capitulation easier; and in the end he agreed to join the "Gaullist" committee, though not without having asked to turn it over in his mind until the last minute and to consult his friends. After much reflection the Admiral telephoned the General: "What you are doing is not workable; nevertheless, in the higher interests of the navy and of France, I agree."

After this brush between the leaders, the Committee was at last established. It was made up of ten men gathered round a de Gaulle whose authority had been strengthened by this crisis, by his evident ascendancy over his rival, and by the documents themselves: Pleven was Commissioner** for Finance, Economy and the Colonies; Cassin for Justice and Education; Admiral Muselier for the Navy; General Legentilhomme for War; General Vallin for Air; Diethelm for the Interior

*So much so that some Gaullists thought Dejean had joined the "Muselier clan".

**The title of minister, seeming to imply a claim to form a government, was thought premature.

and Labour; Dejean for Foreign Affairs. Thierry d'Argenlieu was Commissioner without portfolio.* The English press welcomed the French National Committee (CNF) and gave it a great deal of space; on 24 September 1941 *The Times* described it as "something in the nature of a provisional government", which from now on would share in General de Gaulle's authority.

Thus, by dint of having wanted to be "the most equal of the equals", Admiral Muselier was no more than the conqueror's hostage. Yet however bitter the fable may have seemed to Muselier, it would not be right to draw the conclusion that this battle for power, natural in any group without strong institutions, was an irreconcilable war between the "dictator" and Brutus. Alain Savary, Muselier's ADC, who throughout the dispute remained with the Admiral at Westminster House, states that although some people, like Moullec, behaved as though it was a question of open hostility between the two "masters", he and some others refused to look upon the inimical aspect as of prime importance and, until 1942, they succeeded in remaining loyal to Muselier without indulging in an anti-Gaullism that seemed to them suicidal.[10]

Saint-Pierre and Miquelon are two little islands near the Canadian coast inhabited by five or six thousand fishermen; and they, the minute remnants of a great empire, are under French sovereignty. As soon as he had looked at a map of the world the leader of the Free French thought it "scandalous that just off Newfoundland a small French archipelago, whose people asked to join us, should be kept under Vichy's rule."

All the more so since a powerful radio there was broadcasting the Marshal's propaganda and, according to certain Canadian papers, information intended for the Axis. London and Ottawa were therefore in favour of a "winning over" operation of the kind that had succeeded at Brazzaville. The United States, on the other hand, were less enthusiastic. Washington was anxious to handle Pétain's government tactfully and had begun talks with Admiral Robert, Vichy's High Commissioner for the West Indies, with a view to settling a *modus vivendi* that would neutralize the French territories in America.

Just as Admiral Muselier was about to sail for Canada to inspect the French ships there (particularly the submarine *Surcouf* that he had been accused, shortly before, of wishing to hand over to the enemy), de Gaulle learnt that Washington was on the point of signing the agreement worked out with Robert: he entrusted the commander of the Free French navy with the task of bringing the two islands over to the Free French side in the course of his journey. Here was a chance for Muselier to prove his spurs.

The Admiral had had the operation in mind for a long while and he launched into it with great enthusiasm, sure of his British friends' approval. But de Gaulle did not tell him that Churchill, cautioned by Washington, had asked the Free

*In his *Mémoires* General de Gaulle mentions Catroux as a Commissioner without portfolio. He adds that Jacques Maritain and Alexis Léger, asked to join the French National Committee, sent him "respectful but negative" answers.

French to postpone the rallying of Saint-Pierre. Had the General promised the Prime Minister to check Muselier? Had he misunderstood him? Or did he think it better not to have heard what he said?

On 24 November Muselier, accompanied by Commander de Villefosse, headed for Saint-Pierre aboard the corvette *Mimosa* in so rough a sea that he lost his cap, but not his flow of speech or his good humour. He was not wholly unaware that the undertaking ran against the wishes of the United States – which did not altogether displease the jovial corsair – but he had not been informed about the diplomatic obstacles in the way.

In the very heavy weather of the evening of 7 December the ship's radio sputtered out the enormous piece of news that seemed to settle the fate of the war: Japanese planes had shattered the American fleet at Pearl Harbour; the USA had been drawn into the conflict. This changed everything: the United States were now allies. What had been an amusing trick played on neutrals became an unfair blow when it was struck against companions in arms.

Admiral Muselier believed that he could no longer act by surprise, and when he reached Ottawa he asked for the consent of his hosts and the United States' representatives – who confirmed their hostility to the operation. "I take the entire responsibility for this operation which has become essential to preserve French possessions for her."

Muselier, convinced he was being made a fool, landed at Saint-Pierre on Christmas Eve 1941; he was welcomed by the enthusiastic inhabitants, and the referendum, which was organized at once, turned into a plebiscite in favour of Free France. Since the Three Glorious Days of 27, 28, and 29 August 1940 in Africa this was Gaullism's "cleanest" and most convincing operation.*

But the political and diplomatic price of the operation was to be even greater than Muselier had foreseen. In his *Mémoires* de Gaulle says that apart from a certain amount of "ill temper in the offices of the State Department", he had expected the Americans to confirm the move without fuss. But "a veritable storm" arose.

Roosevelt was ironical about this display of "the incorrigible and formidable Free French leader's wrath" at a time when he himself was in conference with Churchill and the Canadian Prime Minister in Quebec. But Cordell Hull, the Secretary of State, lost his temper and asserted that de Gaulle had broken a promise (which he had never explicitly given),** that the action of "the so-called Free French ships" had been executed "without the government of the United States having given its consent", and that Washington had asked Ottawa to look for means of "restoring the status quo in the islands".

A threefold blunder: a threefold incongruity. For Cordell Hull the "Free French" amounted to no more than a "so called" movement[1] – an expression used

*This popular vote was not the first to ratify a Free French operation. A referendum had been conducted at Tahiti.

**In a note sent to the American government in January, de Gaulle pointed out that on the morning of 17 December he had certainly undertaken to postpone the operation but that that same evening he had learnt that Washington had ended up by persuading the Canadians to act themselves, which changed everything, with regard to French sovereignty.

by Vichy. So to put one Frenchman in the place of another Frenchman on French territory, the "consent" of Washington was required? Was this American diplomat contemplating an expedition to restore Vichy's legality with his Canadian allies?

It may be thought that in the circumstances common sense was not on Charles de Gaulle's side: a fortnight after the United States' entry into the war, which changed the face of the world, the rallying of Saint-Pierre could wait, if it embarrassed these new and decisive allies: that was how Muselier and a good many Gaullists saw it and that is how most historians see it now. Yet however presumptuous de Gaulle may have been at this point, the reaction of Cordell Hull, showing his ignorance of the values involved, almost ended up by justifying it: that was the opinion of most of the American papers, beginning with their best-known commentator, Walter Lippmann, in the early days of January.

Would American public opinion have been so moved by this trifling affair, at a time when the Pacific was bursting into flames, when, from Pittsburgh to Seattle, the American industrial colossus was coming into motion, and when throughout the country the young men were putting on uniforms, if the news of the war had been better? Even if it made him ridiculous, Roosevelt was not sorry to divert attention from his little war against de Gaulle when Tojo's navy and his armies were increasing their successes against MacArthur.

In any case the storm was dying away. On 19 January Cordell Hull received Adrien Tixier, the new Free French representative in the United States, and he gave a calmer, more rational account of his government's line of conduct with regard to the Free French. On 22 January, in London, Churchill saw de Gaulle, and though he blamed him for having alienated Roosevelt in this business, he offered recognition of the *fait accompli* in exchange for a communiqué that would save the State Department's face.

It was a beaming, cordial de Gaulle who welcomed Muselier at Heston, congratulating him on his success and suggesting that he should set off for an even more exciting expedition – the rallying of Madagascar. But meanwhile he asked him to part with his nearest colleague, Moret-Moullec. De Gaulle had long since discovered that Moullec was his bitter enemy. But Muselier had come back in the mood of a conqueror determined to make the most of his victory, and this scarcely inclined him to make concessions.

So the Muselier who, on 3 March, went to the meeting of the French National Committee in the clock gallery at Carlton Gardens was in a victor's mood, the mood of the hero of the day. It was in the most amiable tones that General de Gaulle asked him to report on his mission. "There you have an operation that was carried out perfectly," said de Gaulle. "You see, gentlemen, that I was right to give the order for occupation in spite of the views of our Allies."

An unfortunate remark. The Admiral had only been waiting for a chance to launch his diplomatic offensive. Now he charged, flatly accusing de Gaulle of having hidden the truth from him, with regard to the promise to postpone the operation that was said to have been made to the Americans, and then with regard to the meeting between Churchill and de Gaulle on 22 January, which, according to the Foreign Office, had been so negative that the Prime Minister had even talked of revising the agreement of 7 August 1940. "Why was I not informed of this?" Dejean, the commissioner for Foreign Affairs, contradicted this version of the Downing Street interview and stated that no minute of it existed. "Here it is!" cried Muselier, plucking the minute from his brief-case. "This is the second time I have caught you out in the very act of inexactitude," went on the Admiral, eyeing Dejean but obviously directing his words at de Gaulle. Then, turning to the Free French leader he said, "In these conditions, it is no longer possible for me to continue working with this committee. I resign as national commissioner."

He could no longer provide de Gaulle with "cooperation of a political nature", but added that "the Free French naval forces will continue, as in the past, to make war side by side with our allies" and ended, "For myself, I am ready to take part in any naval operation that you may see fit to entrust to me in agreement with our allies."[11]

A strange statement which, in the middle of a war, claimed the right to set up a conditional cooperation on the part of the navy with the other arms (this was the "fief" concept that de Gaulle had detected in Darlan in June 1940), and then only in the event that the orders given should be approved by London and Washington.

De Gaulle reacted calmly, in three stages. On 4 March he wrote to the Admiral, acknowledging his resignation and expressing the hope that he would be able to "make use of [his] high qualities and [his] great experience as a naval commander". On 5 March he appointed Captain Auboyneau, promoted to Rear-Admiral, as Muselier's successor and sent Moullec to command the *Triumphant*. And on 6 March Muselier was granted thirty days leave.

It was then that Admiral Emile Muselier abandoned the line of conduct which had won him sympathy. He appealed to the British to intervene. His friend Admiral Dickens stirred up the government and the Admiralty and on 6 March General de Gaulle received the visit of the War-Cabinet's two most impressive figures, Anthony Eden, the Foreign Secretary, and Victor Alexander, the First Lord of the Admiralty; they had come to tell him that the government required the retention of Admiral Muselier at the head of the Free French navy.

If they had wanted to wreck the last chances of an agreement with Muselier, the British politicians* could not have done better. The General decided to deal with the situation by trying to bring over all the sailors who had not promised personal allegiance to the Admiral. First he wrote to Eden emphasizing his refusal to endanger the pride and hope of the Free French by giving way to the British demand. And staking everything on one throw, he asked the British authorities, by virtue of the agreement on jurisdiction signed a year before, that Admiral Muselier should be placed under close arrest.

On 18 March, not having received any sort of reply from the government and feeling that he might be on the eve of a tragic decision, de Gaulle retired to his house at Berkhamsted; but before going he gave three loyal colleagues, Pleven, Diethelm and Coulet, a "political will" in which he particularly said:

> If I am led to give up the task I have undertaken, the French nation must

*How could a man as perceptive as Anthony Eden commit such a blunder, knowing de Gaulle as he did?

know why. I have tried to keep France in the war against the invader. At present that is possible only in conjunction with the British and with their support. However this is conceivable only in a state of independence and dignity. But the British government's intervention in the ugly crisis brought about by Muselier is as intolerable as it is absurd.

France already understands by what path and in what manner I have done everything to serve her. She will understand that if I stop it is because my duty to her forbids me to go farther. She will choose her road accordingly. Men pass. France goes on.[12]

The gravity of his tone shows to what extent the man of 18 June felt himself threatened at that time. On 10 March he had gone to Westminster House to persuade the Free French naval officers that his decisions were sound, but he had come up against the Admiral, who refused to let him speak to them except in his presence; and de Gaulle had only managed to bring over the three most senior officers.

But on 19 June Muselier committed his second very important mistake: he called upon the Free French navy to observe a general strike. When he appealed to the British against de Gaulle, he isolated the navy from the Free French. Now, in calling for a strike he cut himself off from the British, who were very strict about naval discipline, and who looked upon this action as mutiny. The Admiralty therefore advised Muselier and Moullec to withdraw for a few weeks. For the Admiral, the game was lost.

CHAPTER TWENTY-SIX

The Great Turning-Point: from Barbarossa to Pearl Harbour

It was now a year since Charles de Gaulle had proclaimed that "the flame of French resistance will never be extinguished", at a time when only very small bodies of men, from London to Chartres and from Marseilles to Bordeaux, were filled with the same conviction. When, on 18 June 1941, in Cairo, the leader of the Free French recalled that "a year has passed in fighting, in pain, and in hope" (more pain than fighting, and indeed for many, more pain than hope), Free France was still no more than the third and minute zone of a France that was materially shattered but that thanks to him was associated with those who were on the side of freedom – a Free France that in "the appalling weakness" that hampered it, was doing its utmost to win its place in the sun, struggling on, gaining one man after another, one scrap of land (or sand) after another, making use of the tolerance of some and the charity of others.

The worst, the invasion of Britain, had been avoided. The island had held out and the only Nazi to have set foot on it, Rudolf Hess, Hitler's confidential friend, fallen from the skies to offer Churchill a compromise peace, had been tossed into a cell. But Hitler, held back by the anti-tank ditch that Nature had given the British and checked by their heroism in the skies of London, was advancing on all fronts where he was not obliged to save his embarrassing Italian ally from disaster. Between the beginning of March and the end of May 1941 he had subjected, occupied or overcome Bulgaria, Greece, Yugoslavia and Crete, while south of the Mediterranean, Rommel was retaking Benghazi. And his only failure, in Iraq and Syria (where he had committed no more than a few dozen pilots) nevertheless brought him in worthwhile dividends – the anti-British reaction in metropolitan France and the disagreements between Free France and its London allies.

In the Atlantic the British convoys loaded with the precious American armaments provided at bargain rates thanks to the Lend-Lease Act (March 1941) were suffering increasing losses from the attacks of Nazi submarines (100 000 tons in March, 200 000 tons in April, 300 000 tons in May) while in the Pacific the progressive engagement of the Japanese (particularly in Indo-China, where no significant resistance could yet be brought against them) foretold terrible set-backs for the British Empire as soon as Tokyo should move on from its continual encroachments to active hostilities.

Had Churchill and de Gaulle gazed at a planisphere with the ardent, imaginative attention common to both, they could very well have told themselves that a year earlier they had been at the bottom of an abyss from which they were now gradually emerging; they would also have been obliged to observe that the crushing of the Third Reich and the restoration of the two powers to their former greatness were still only working hypotheses – hypotheses for a work resembling the labours of Hercules.

On 22 June 1941 the armies of the Reich flung themselves upon a Soviet Russia in which Stalin, trusting of Adolf Hitler's word, had for weeks refused to take the slightest defensive precaution.* Sixteen hours later Churchill seized a microphone and said, "We have just reached one of the highest points of the war. We shall give Russia and the Russian people all the help we can. The cause of the Russians who are fighting for their country is the cause of all the people in the world who are fighting for their freedom."

General de Gaulle, wholly taken up with the Levant, reacted much more slowly. His first public declaration dates from no earlier than 11 July, when on the Brazzaville radio he rather strangely stated that in Russia, "this campaign that the enemy supposed would be easy and rapid was on the contrary assuming the pace of one of those Russian novels that with every chapter seems to be coming to an end, and that always starts again."

Still, as early as 24 June the General had cabled his directives to Carlton Gardens, giving the general lines of the Free French propaganda: "Without any present discussion of the vices and even the crimes of the Soviet régime, we are very decidedly with the Russians, since they are fighting the Germans. The German planes, tanks and soldiers the Russians are destroying and are to destroy will no longer be there to prevent us from liberating France."[1] And he ordered a "discreet but distinct" approach to Maisky, the Soviet Ambassador in London, with a view to the organization of "military relations" with the USSR.

René Cassin and Maurice Dejean went to see Maisky on 28 June; he gave them a friendly reception, saying that he was touched by General de Gaulle's decision, but that since his country was still maintaining relations with Vichy it would be appropriate for his contacts with the Free French to retain a private character. But six weeks later, when Pétain had broken with Moscow at the request of the Third Reich, the Soviet Ambassador in London welcomed the same visitors in quite another fashion and let it be understood that his government might fall into line with Churchill's and recognize de Gaulle as leader of all the Free French – an action that was indeed carried out on 26 September. In the terms of a letter from Maisky to de Gaulle, the USSR, like Britain before them, undertook to ensure "the restoration of France's independence and greatness" after the joint victory.

In his *Mémoires* Charles de Gaulle speaks of the profound upheaval brought about by Operation Barbarossa in these words:

> The fact that Russia now happened to be flung into the war opened up the greatest hopes for a shattered France. Unless the Reich managed to

*On this point one should consult Zhukov's memoirs.

> liquidate the Soviet army* very quickly, it would subject the enemy to a continual and terrible attrition. Obviously I had no doubt that a victory in which the Soviets had taken a very important part might, because of them, confront the world with other dangers later on. This had to be borne in mind, even when one was fighting side by side with them; but it seemed to me that before philosophizing one had to live, that is to say to win. Then again, the presence [of Russia] in the Allied camp, brought Fighting France a counterpoise with regard to the British, a factor that I certainly intended to make use of.[2]

To be sure, de Gaulle saw the opening of the Russian front as an immense opportunity offered to Western strategy and as a long-term weakening of the Reich. But just as quickly, seeing it as a matter of almost equal importance, he grasped that this strategic upheaval would for him be the beginning of a liberation or rather of a broadening of his diplomatic horizon.

He was perfectly aware that an alliance with Stalin would be held against him and that he would lose a good deal of sympathy – although at the same time he was sure that it would win him many new supporters. At this point French public opinion saw Vichy increasingly subject to Hitler's plans, made evident by the concessions that were known to have taken place in the Levant and that were expected in North Africa: this was a situation from which the man of London ought to profit. Yet his closer relations with Moscow did make many of the undecided recoil.

The Soviet Union frightened people as much as ever, particularly since the war against Finland, the partition of Poland, and the colonization of the Baltic states. For Gaullism the alliance formed in 1941 was a two-edged sword: up until then the caricatures in Paris newspapers had shown de Gaulle as an officer belonging to the extreme Right manipulated by London: now he suddenly changed into a vassal in the service of the Soviet Union. And Vichy propaganda scored a few points by showing him as a man with a knife between his teeth.

That was the price that had to be paid for the two important advantages he had just gained. The first was military: for he soon saw that until the United States came into the war, the fate of the world would be decided on the Eastern Front. The second was diplomatic, for the entry of the USSR loosened his ties with the British.

We have at our disposition an exceedingly curious document on the "new deal" and the possibilities that it opened for the leader of the Free French: this was published in a Soviet work on Franco-Russian relations during the war, and it is an account of a conversation between the USSR Ambassador to Ankara, Serge Vinogradov,** and a representative of the Free French, Géraud Jouve,*** on 10 August 1941. "General de Gaulle," said Jouve to the Soviet diplomat,

*A possibility then put forward by many Anglo-Saxon specialists, who were convinced that the USSR's setback in Finland proved the inferior quality of the Red Army.

**He will be found again as Ambassador in Paris, after the war.

***Later an ambassador.

attaches a very great importance to the establishment of direct relations between Free France and the USSR, for the two countries are both continental powers and for this reason they have specific aims that are different from those of the Anglo Saxon powers. The conquest of Germany will give rise to questions for us as a continental state that the Anglo Saxons do not ask themselves and do not understand.[3]

Here it can be seen that Charles de Gaulle did not look upon the beginning of the conflict in the east just as an opportunity to blunt Hitler's war-machine on the people and climate of Russia nor even just as a chance to set himself free from the tutelage of his British friends, but also as a chance to call the whole balance of world power into question. Once again, however, this de Gaulle who saw so far, so clearly, and with such depth, does not seem to have measured the immense dangers into which a game of this kind between "continental" powers would lead him.

From then onwards an odd connection between the Constable and the Soviet diplomats came into being. First with Bogomolov, whom Moscow calmly transferred from Vichy to London, where he represented the USSR with the various governments in exile and also with the French National Committee. The portrait of him drawn by de Gaulle lacks neither irony nor a hint of liking: "In so far as the crushing conformism that he was required to observe allowed him to show his human side he was capable of humour, even going so far as to smile." Bogomolov reports on 25 November 1941: "Since the fate of the world was now being decided in the Soviet-German war, there is nothing the General desires so much as to have Frenchmen taking part in the combat." And on 9 December: "The General told me that he was going to send a mission made up of two civilians and one soldier to the Soviet Union. He has also decided to send one of the two divisions he now disposes of in Syria to the Eastern Front. He thinks he can arrange for their transport as far as Tabriz."

The first Free France representative sent to the embattled USSR was General Petit, de Gaulle's chief of staff (and a contemporary at Saint-Cyr). The welcome he received from all (beginning with Stalin) was accompanied by such "advances" that de Gaulle wondered whether there was an ulterior motive. Some Free Frenchmen had no doubts: Captain Billotte and thirteen other officers,* who, escaping from German camps to Russia in 1940 were there interned by the Soviets in revolting conditions until they were liberated on 22 June 1941 and sent by way of Murmansk and Archangel to London, where Billotte took over from Petit at the head of the Carlton Gardens staff.

The plan for sending a division taken from the forces under Catroux' command at Beirut to the Eastern Front ran into long and acid objections on the part of the British. And on 3 May 1942 General Auchinleck, Commander-in-Chief to the Near East, flatly vetoed the departure of these troops for the Caucasus – although at the same time he refused to use them in the Western Desert battle. Cooperation with the USSR had to be confined to the air.

*Including Lieutenant de Boissieu, later to be de Gaulle's son-in-law.

On 20 January 1942, a month after Zhukov had broken the Wehrmacht's attack before Moscow, Charles de Gaulle came back to the BBC microphone, and in a style that bore the mark of his new allies he said:

> There is not a single good Frenchman who does not acclaim Russia's victory. The enemy has just suffered one of the great defeats of history. From now on liberation and revenge have become delightful probabilities for France. The death of every German soldier frozen in Russia give France another opportunity of rising up and conquering. The traitors and cowards who handed over [France] to the enemy will not fail to cry out that our victory side by side with Russia will bring about that social upheaval that they dread above everything. The French nation scorns the insult.

Thus the great alliance with the East grew from week to week. In February Roger Garreau left to head the Free French diplomatic mission to the USSR. In May 1942 Molotov himself, visiting London, saw the General. Having greeted him as the "representative of the real France", Molotov, Stalin's closest colleague, said that there was not the slightest reason for possible conflict, either political or economic, between France and Russia, and pointed out that although the USSR was allied to Great Britain and the United States, the Soviets "wished to have an independent alliance with France".[4]

In his *Mémoires* de Gaulle wrote that Molotov "had certainly concluded the German-Soviet agreement with Ribbentrop not so very long before with the same assurance". And he ends his account by saying, "I believe that in these perfectly adjusted gears of a faultless machine I recognized a complete success of the totalitarian system. I acknowledged its magnitude. Yet although what lay at the bottom of things may have been hidden from me, I felt their sadness."

During the conversation Molotov brought up the idea of sending fighting units to the Russian front; his government, he said, attached "a great importance" to this participation: de Gaulle, who had just met with the British staff's refusal, was obliged to say that for the moment the Free France "land troops" were "indispensable" in the Near East; though for once he did not blame the English. On the other hand, de Gaulle did suggest sending the Soviet Union about thirty pilots.

Another key question raised during the conversation with Molotov was that of the Eastern Front, so essentially important in the eyes of the Soviets, who wanted the Western powers to take the common enemy from behind, acting the role of the hammer while the USSR played that of the anvil.

A month later Moscow published a communiqué stating the USSR's wish to see France "take her place in the world again as a great democratic anti-Hitlerian power".[5] Everything would have been going perfectly but for the fact that the Polish question was already looming on the horizon. According to the CNF's telegram to Garreau on 21 June 1942, Sikorski's government was beginning to take offence at the increasingly close ties between Moscow and Free France.

But when the Soviets were speaking to de Gaulle they did not confine themselves to strategy alone. Sometimes they would also question him about the nature of the régime in a France freed from the occupier and from Vichy. We have two types of reply made by the Free French leader, the one interpreted by Maisky after an interview with de Gaulle in February 1942, the other drawn up by the General himself after the conversation with Molotov. The first cannot have failed to worry the Russians: their ambassador's summary described de Gaulle as predicting to him that after the victory France would be governed according to receipts mingling Italian-style fascism and modernized Bonapartism, with "a strong executive and a corporative parliament".[6] Had Maisky really been listening to de Gaulle or had he listened to Muselier's friends?

In the account that Charles de Gaulle himself wrote of his conversation with Molotov, he states that he defined his intentions in this way: "The French nation, [being] hostile to all fascism, would return to a democratic regime. But it would not return purely and simply to the parliamentary system. It would want the executive to have more strength and stability. Considerations of a social nature would play a more important part than purely political questions."[7] In short, Maisky had merely exaggerated certain equivocal opinions in which ill-wishers could detect a Gaullian version of Pétain's "national revolution".

Now, at all events, broad perspectives opened out before the leader of the Free French. From now on he was no longer Churchill's squire, he was no longer restrained by the War Office, censored by the Foreign Office or dependent on the Intelligence Service. He possessed a resource, an alternative.

He could be relied upon to remind Eden or Churchill very often that he was the only one of the Western allies to be fighting (at least symbolically) side by side with the Red Army, that it was always open to him to go and settle in Moscow, and that as far as the future of Germany was concerned, no one was better placed for uttering a judgment than a Frenchman, except perhaps a Russian.

The opening of the Eastern Front had another consequence, one of prime importance: the French Communist Party moved over to active resistance on a massive scale. Up until then, apart from a short period of collaboration symbolized by an attempt at bringing out *L'Humanité* again under German supervision, the PCF had confined itself to not disavowing the more and more frequent and daring actions carried out by the most anti-fascist of its members.[8] From this time onwards the FTP (Franc-tireurs et partisans), on the military side, and the Front National, on the political, were to make the occupiers' lives a burden to them.

Indeed, shortly before these vast possibilities opened in the east, Charles de Gaulle had made a bold approach towards the United States. Of course he was not unaware of the prejudices against him entertained by the White House and the State Department. From London to Central Africa and from Cairo to Beirut he had observed the American diplomats' and officers' extreme reserve with regard to himself. He deeply regretted the fact that Roosevelt should have sent Pétain an admiral of high standing while he, for his part, had to be content with brief encounters (friendly, it may be added) with John Winant, the US Ambassador in London. But he was convinced that these mistaken trends were based on mistaken analyses, and the course of events, changed as he would do his best to change it, would at last enlighten Roosevelt and his colleagues.

In short, on 19 May 1941, two months after the passing of the Lease-Lend Act which gave Britain immediate credit for war-supplies de Gaulle, then at

Brazzaville, sent Pleven a directive of the first importance: "In view of the almost belligerent attitude of the United States," he wrote, "the time has come for us to organize our relations with America. I intend to entrust this mission to you personally."

And the leader of the Free French, having drawn the broad lines of the Pleven mission – permanent diplomatic relations, economic exchanges, purchase of war-material, propaganda for the recruitment of "men of good will" – gave his chief confidential agent as many weeks as he needed to carry out his mission, which was to remain "discreet, particularly with regard to the British."[9]

From Cairo, a fortnight later, de Gaulle sent Mr Kirk, the United States consul-general, an even more significant memorandum in which he pointed out that in the eventuality of the United States' entry into the war, the British Isles, vulnerable to Nazi air-attack, could not be the best base for Washington's strategy, which, on the other hand, would find the most advantageous terrain in Central Africa: a strategic network, from Duala to Brazzaville and Fort-Lamy, was available, and Free France would gladly place it at the disposition of the American General Staff.

Nothing could be more obliging – nor more clear-sighted as well. Certainly, de Gaulle urged Pleven to couple these offers with the beginings of a recognition of Free France, which, limited or not, would have strong repercussions in Vichy. Yet Washington scorned all these advances, and to begin with gave Pleven a cold reception. Pleven was as adaptable and easy-going as his chief was imperious; he spoke perfect English; he was well acquainted with the American world (he had worked for ten years in London for a telephone company whose headquarters were in the States); and he was on good terms with his former London boss, Jean Monnet, who was much esteemed in Washington.

Pleven's first messages speak of his disappointment at finding that Free France was so little known, scarcely profiting at all from the diminution of Vichy's prestige. But gradually doors began to open. Although Cordell Hull and Sumner Welles (the State Department) still kept him at a distance, the General's envoy was received by Henry Morgenthau Jr, the Secretary of the Treasury (the most Gaullist of Roosevelt's ministers), Harry Hopkins (who was to FDR what Pleven was to de Gaulle), Henry Stimson, the Secretary of War, and Vice-President Wallace, while the *New York Herald Tribune* published a series of articles by Henry Bernstein against Pétain that caused a sensation.

Finally the State Department made up its mind to offer three concessions: Red Cross assistance for Free France; Pleven's participation in conversations between London and Washington, but only in the capacity of "expert"; and the sending of an American emissary to Africa, Colonel H. F. Cunningham. To these de Gaulle replied: no medicines without weapons; no participation in talks with inferior status; and welcome to Cunningham.

It was then that Roosevelt and Churchill announced the Atlantic Charter, which had been worked out at the beginning of August off the coast of Canada, a document that brought Washington even nearer to belligerence by associating the United States and Britain so closely that their "war aims" were merged. Hitler could no longer nourish the slightest illusion: he was going to have to confront the power of America, and that at a time when he was plunging deep into the vast expanses of Russia.

The Charter of August 1941 was the epitome of the Rooseveltian-Democrat anti-colonial frame of mind. Among other things it stated that the nations set free from Nazism would be able to choose their government freely and that the "united nations" that would emerge from the total victory over the Reich and its allies would not seek any "territorial aggrandizement": it was a most creditable piece of writing, but it was one that Churchill probably signed with his tongue in his cheek, feeling that the entry of the United States into the war was worth this statement of principles just as Paris had been worth a Mass.

The reaction of General de Gaulle was much less favourable. The message he sent his colleagues in London from Brazzaville is one of those documents that bring a biographer to a halt as he wonders about the relations this surprising man maintained with reality, and about the genius he had to possess in order to survive these troughs.

As he read the clauses of the Charter, Charles de Gaulle could only have reservations: how could the fate of the world be decided without a French presence? Here was an exile confined to a few buildings in London, a few huts in Africa and a few palaces in the Levant, who was up in arms because after a hypothetical victory people were prepared to refuse the France of 1940 any "aggrandizement". And he specifically stated in an internal Free French note that, "We must allow ourselves the possibility of extending our position in the Rhineland in the event of a collapse of the Reich."[10]

The Pleven mission nevertheless made progress. During a press conference on 5 September the journalists were surprised to hear Secretary of State Cordell Hull remark that "from all points of view our relations with [the Free French] are of the most cordial nature". And a few days later the General's envoy could cable London to say that his American hosts were willing to accept a Free French delegation in Washington. "This organization will not have definite diplomatic status" but its head would have "official contacts" with the State Department. Pending a decision, Pleven put forward two names: Etienne Boegner, a clergyman's son and a representative of the French Protestant upper-middle class, a useful asset in American governing circles; and Adrien Tixier, a trade-union leader and socialist, the French representative with the International Labour Organization. De Gaulle replied at once: "I choose Tixier. He has the reputation of a solid, straightforward man. The French unions are behaving very well in France. Lastly, the social aspect is the most important aspect of affairs for tomorrow."[11]

These reasons adduced are significant. The choice of a trade-unionist rather than a man of high standing; the great value attributed to the resistance inside France; the recognition of the prime importance of social problems. Yet de Gaulle, even if he had showed himself an advanced democrat, had, diplomatically, made an unfortunate choice: the worthy Tixier, blunt, hot-tempered and foul-mouthed, was as decided a failure in Washington as Pleven was a success in his brilliant execution of the Gaullist breakthrough.

No matter: while the Soviet diplomacy increased its friendly gestures towards him, the leader of the Free French gradually won ground in America. The launching of active resistance in France and the Nazi occupier's terrible reprisals, particularly those against the hostages of Châteaubriant, caused American public opinion to swing away from Vichy, which seemed to be giving itself up more and more to collaboration, and towards the France that was fighting – a France that the American press increasingly described as inspired by the London Committee and its leader.

Something that resembled an American-Gaullist cooperation was taking shape. There is no sort of doubt that the great step forward was the extension to France of the Lend Lease Act on 11 November 1941, the opening of unlimited credit for the supply of war-material – a move that six months earlier Churchill had looked upon as a decisive stage in the United States' entry into the war. Before this, on 11 September, the General had written to Pleven asking him to negotiate with the authorities in Washington about placing naval bases in the French Pacific Islands, New Caledonia, New Hebrides or Tahiti, at the disposal of the American General Staff. In spite of the storms caused by blunders on either side, the plan was carried out.

At the same period Colonel Cunningham, accompanied by Laurence Taylor, a State Department diplomat and formerly a secretary at the US Embassy in Paris, landed in Free French Africa, where, on the urgent, often repeated instructions of General de Gaulle to Brazzaville, Duala and Fort-Lamy, he was welcomed as a friend and an ally. And having thanked the Free French leader, on 5 October he received this cable from Charles de Gaulle:

> My dear Colonel,
> I am deeply touched by your message and in the name of all Free Frenchmen and of those who wish to become free again I bid you a cordial welcome to French territory, where you have come to advance the sacred cause of freedom. I am convinced that the arrival of your mission in French Africa is an important date in the history of this war. I ask you to pass on to the authorities of the United States of America the expression of our gratitude and our trustful friendship.

Cunningham's mission was so successful that Weygand, in Algiers, grew alarmed. In Washington, Hull warned Cunningham severely against any kind of publicity. The African Gaullists did their utmost to circumvent Hull, and since Cunningham did not conceal his favourable impressions, Vichy lodged a protest against this "unfriendly" course of action.

But presently Weygand was no longer in a position to protest against Cunningham's mission: on 18 November 1941 he was dismissed from his post by Pétain, who, hearing what Ambassador Leahy had to say about it the next day, could only groan "I am nothing but a prisoner."

Until this 18 November, the US, counting on Weygand's support from Vichy, had seen Algeria as a prospective landing place. But as soon as Nazi pressure had broken the essential link in this policy, surely it was time for Washington to change its positively pro-Vichy attitude? Leahy went so far as to recommend "a complete revision" of the policy which up until then he had personified. He was not required to do anything of the kind.

What is even more surprising, and what leads one to see something obsessive in the political behaviour of the United States in this field is that even the event of 7 December 1941, the entry of the US into the war, did not call this collusion into question.

Far from it: the Cunningham mission was recalled before the end of the year; the French liner *Normandie* was seized by the American authorities (for excellent military reasons, but without so much as a word to the CNF); and in the French Pacific islands, General Patch, welcomed as a friend by the Free French authorities, behaved as though he were in a conquered country.

We have two eloquent pieces of evidence that show General de Gaulle's disgust when he was confronted with Washington's stubborn contempt. The first is a telegram to Winston Churchill, who at the end of December had been struggling to make Roosevelt accept the Saint-Pierre operation, and who had just made a strongly anti-Vichy speech in Quebec accompanied by a plea in favour of Free France:

> I have every reason to fear that the State Department's present attitude with regard to the Free French and to Vichy may do a great deal of harm to the fighting spirit in France and elsewhere. I dread the unfortunate impression on public opinion that will be produced by the United States government's preference for those responsible for the surrender and who are guilty of collaboration. It does not seem to me a good thing that in war-time the prize should be awarded to the apostles of dishonour.

And de Gaulle added in the confidential tone of old warriors who have been through the same trials: "I tell *you* this because I know you feel it* and because you are the only one who can say it as it ought to be said."[12]

Even more significant is his reply on 20 January to a telegram from Adrien Tixier, who, at last accredited to Washington, had been received by Cordell Hull. The Secretary of State, speaking not without cordiality, had justified his pro-Vichy policy and his refusal to recognize the London CNF by an anxiety to avoid a situation in which Pétain, rejected by the democracies, should hand over the French fleet and Mediterranean bases to the Axis. To this de Gaulle replied in these words, asking Tixier to pass them on to Hull:

> If war were merely a game of chess, in which the pieces are soulless objects, we could understand the State Department's present attitude with regard to France. But war is a moral affair. For men to make war they have to believe that they are morally obliged to do so, and that in doing so they are morally upheld. The respect shown by the United States to those French authorities whose only reason for existence is to prevent France from fighting constitutes a very dangerous demoralizing factor for the French nation, all the more harmful in that it contrasts with the attitude, ungracious at the least, of

*This was one of the subjects of the Prime Minister's speech in Quebec.

the United States government's towards the only Frenchmen who are carrying on the war side by side with the Allies.

This is an essential document, one in which the spirit of fighting Gaullism is expressed in depth, on the twin planes of ethics and Machiavallism. War was a moral issue. It was also a game in which each player (in France and in the rest of the world) must be and will be rewarded according to his actions. Now before Pearl Harbour there had been Barbarossa: the checking of Hitler before Moscow outlined the world of tomorrow as clearly as the RAF's victory over the Luftwaffe and the prodigious American effort in producing armaments. When the French nation chose its future it would do so in virtue of what had been done – of what it had done for itself and of what had been done for it. Never before had Charles de Gaulle so clearly laid out his war-aims, which, over and above the destruction of Nazism, were directed at remaking France.

No description of the de Gaulle who was making his way into the second phase of the war could be more life-like than Colonel Passy's recollection of a December day in 1941.

It was a Sunday. The General had invited the head of his intelligence services to spend the day with his family at his little house in the country at Berkhamsted, thirty miles from London. During the drive down and then during a long walk the two men made a general survey of the situation in France, where, they felt, the Resistance was making very slow progress. De Gaulle's name was beginning to command respect, but when, on 31 October, he had called for acknowledgment on a very large scale, few people had paid any attention. Clandestine pamphlets were in greater circulation than ever before, whether they were distributed by the British, Communist or Gaullist services, and communications were improving; but the organizations that were gradually coming into existence were divided and self-contained, and few were in contact with the Free French. In short, the balance he struck was so disappointing that Passy suggested that his host should remove him from the intelligence side and post him to a fighting unit – an offer that de Gaulle rejected curtly.

> We came back from our long walk and we sat down in armchairs in the drawing-room. The General switched on the radio. The Japanese had just attacked Pearl Harbour.
>
> The General turned it off and sank into a deep meditation, which I took care not to interrupt. Hours seemed to pass by. Then the General began to speak: he said roughly this: "Now the war is certainly won! And the future has two phases for us: the first will be the salvage of Germany by the Allies; as for the second, I am afraid it may turn out to be war between the Russians and Americans and the Americans run a great risk of losing that war if they do not succeed in taking the necessary steps in time!

"This is a world-wide war!" de Gaulle had proclaimed on 18 June 1940; for he refused to interpret fate in terms of a Franco-German conflict on the metropolitan territory alone. The battle of France was lost: he insisted upon appealing from that verdict on the plane of the whole world. And now less than eighteen months later the war had become global. The prophet had been right. The strategist had still to raise it to the universal level, and in the first place to do so by asserting himself in the coalition as an active, fighting, and therefore respected, partner.

CHAPTER TWENTY-SEVEN

Charles Disowned: FDR and the Constable

Of twentieth-century Frenchmen, Charles de Gaulle was and certainly remains the most hated and the most revered – even more so than were Jaurès, Clemenceau or Léon Blum before him. Most of these hatreds and attachments were based on an action, a deed or an attitude that can be traced: resistance, liberation, the purge after the war, decolonization and so on. But whether these very strongly marked relations arose from or were maintained by the tragic nature of his career, by the times of conflict in which he spoke or by a personality given to extremes, there is one connection that strikes the observer as unforseeable, irrational and abstract, the more so for its outstanding political and strategical importance: the relations he maintained with President Roosevelt.

We have, from one crisis to another, begun a description of the relations between the General and Winston Churchill – relations that will continue to occupy us. However stormy they may have been, and often damaging to the common cause, they scarcely show any surprising aspects. The conflicts between the Prime Minister and the General reflect the extreme difficulty of harmonizing two dominant, pugnacious characters, expressing two different histories, two different national ambitions and two often antagonistic national interests (particularly in the East) in an atmosphere that emphasized the contradictions – made all the worse for de Gaulle, moreover, by the painful knowledge of being helped, supervised, and if not humiliated then at least made to feel inferior; and in that of Churchill, by astonishment at seeing his very sincere love of France and the French receive so poor a return.

It cannot be denied that between de Gaulle and Roosevelt there was a clash of dominant personalities; but since the direct contacts amounted to no more than five meetings, of which three were quite short, and to a few communications from the General that received virtually no reply, the essence of the disagreement cannot be found there. And although in the confrontation between Churchill and de Gaulle the foul blows were fairly evenly shared (the Englishman's were fewer, but better directed), in the exchanges beween the President and the General, it was above all in Roosevelt that one could observe an irrational and stubborn misconception that finally verged upon blindness.

It would certainly be a mistake to reduce the war-time intercourse between the United States and Free France to the personal relations between FDR and de Gaulle, whereas it would be a little sounder to make those between the two heroes, Churchill and de Gaulle, central to the Anglo-French connection. The strong dislike of Gaullism displayed by Washington had many sources other than the moods and even the will of the President: in the nature of things, French affairs and more especially those of Free France could not take up much room in the mind of a man who, to ensure the victory of the democracies, had first to consider the world of the Pacific, then that of the Atlantic, the USSR, the Mediterranean theatre and lastly the Channel, to say nothing of the battlefield of Washington which was not always the least important.

The relations between Roosevelt and de Gaulle were in the first place shaped by a large number of intermediaries, by the memorandums of "specialists", by confidences, reports, rumours – and from this point of view there are few records that astonish the reader more than those in the American archives devoted to the General. But the leader's role is to interpret the papers that he is supplied with. Let us state that in the case thus brought against de Gaulle, every time Roosevelt intervened he did so not as counsel, nor even as judge, but as prosecutor.

In a search for explanations, one may question two of the men best placed to answer: Alger Hiss, who was one of FDR's diplomatic advisers (particularly at Yalta) before becoming one of the most famous targets of Macarthyism, and Arthur Schlesinger Jr., his best-known biographer.

For the first, the responsibility for what he called FDR's "coldness" towards de Gaulle was to be ascribed to the "particularly reactionary" tendencies in the European section of the State Department, to the "animosity" of Churchill, exasperated by his everlasting quarrels with the General, and also to the incompatibility between the French leader's "acute and unconquerable" nationalism and the plans for the remodelling of the world worked out by Roosevelt.[1]

According to Schlesinger, this antipathy must be referred to three factors: (a) FDR's feeling that there was a disproportion beween de Gaulle's pride and the aims of the Allies; (b) the exceedingly bad name the British had given the BCRA* and Colonel Passy; and (c) the President's conviction that France no longer had its place among the great directing powers to which he wished to entrust the future of the world. The American historian added that FDR's political outlook was not a "personal eccentricity but was heartily shared by Cordell Hull and most of the State Department."[2]

It is true that a great many things separated the President of the United States from the leader of Free France. An American and a Frenchman, close on half a century ago, differed from one another far more than do their successors in the eighties. Churchill and de Gaulle, reflecting upon the course of events in 1940, decided that however unlike their two countries might be, America was "another world". One has only to read the newspapers or the minutes of the Senate to see how very far apart the two worlds were in June 1940.

Points in common could nevertheless be found between politicans on either side of the Atlantic: here a Vandenberg, a Sol Bloom or a Taft, there a Herriot, an Auriol or a Flandin. But what areas of contact could be found between the great politician Roosevelt, brought up in the seraglio of the New York State Democratic Party, and the unbending Saint-Cyrien de Gaulle? Only one: since January 1933

*The Free French intelligence service (trs.).

the President and the General had shared one great ambition: the destruction of Nazism. Their motivation might be different, their methods contradictory: their object was the same. But it so happened that when the time came to set this essential convergence in action, their paths ran in totally different directions.

Among the innumerable contradictions that set them apart when they confronted the common enemy, there was one which arose from two wholly dissimilar careers. The American was famous by the time the war began, and his career had been a royal road: he came from a patrician family that already numbered one president* and he moved effortlessly from the Senate to government and from a governorship to the presidency. The Frenchman's career bristled with challenges against establishment-thinking. They were also separated by two differing and indeed antithetical visions of the State, the one formed by the historical traditions of anti-colonialist federalism, the other by colonizing centralism. Among a score of other motives, it was the American's spontaneous federalism that led him, from 1940 onwards, to dividing up his relations with France by dealing with the "local authorities". Nothing could be more anathema to that centralizer de Gaulle.**

To these first oppositions should there be added the dislike that a civilian politician like Roosevelt may have felt for a soldier involved in public affairs? The argument has often been put forward; but FDR was the successor of presidents named Washington, Jackson and Grant. In the history of the United States generals have played a role that never drew the great Republic towards the abyss of militarism.

Can it also be said that a soldier did a great deal to turn FDR towards Marshall Pétain rather than towards Charles de Gaulle? The aged General Pershing, the leader of the American Expeditionary Force during the First World War, retained a deep affection for Pétain, who, had welcomed him as a saviour and had treated him as an equal. In Pershing's eyes, anyone who touched Pétain was an inconoclast:*** in Washington's eyes de Gaulle was primarily a man who had insulted the most pro-American of the great French leaders.

Another fundamental difference lay in their relations to history. René Pleven, who was better placed than any man in the world to gauge these disparities, said to me,

> The reason that General de Gaulle misunderstood the United States and Roosevelt is that he was a man for whom history counted more than anything else. In order to understand states and policies his natural and unvarying tendency was to resort to history. That was why he was so successful in describing and dealing with Britain, Germany or China. But where the United States were concerned he was at a loss; he found no historical keys.
>
> Not that the United States possess no history. But de Gaulle was not

*Theodore (1858–1919), 26th president of the USA (1901–09).

**"Be centripetal, not centrifugal!"

***When the old general received de Gaulle in Washington in July 1944 he at once asked him for news of Pétain.

> acquainted with it in 1940, and did not think it could be compared to that of "real" nations.[3]

This gives us a valuable clue. Confronted with Roosevelt, de Gaulle was, as one might say, short of history. But what is worse was the fact that for his part Roosevelt did not perceive to what extent history determined the General. He only thought of making fun of his historical references ("He takes himself for Joan of Arc, for Napoleon, for Clemenceau . . ."). What really mattered to de Gaulle was not some supposed reincarnation, but to be on guard against the progress of myths, symbols and references, "the imponderables" as Bismarck used to call them. For Roosevelt the past hardly existed. He aimed solely at the future. Who was this general, who had escaped from an army of beaten men, who came to talk to him about "indefeasible rights", "long-standing splendour" and "immortal France"?

No less important between the two men was the contrast in their conceptions of war, or rather of the relations between war and politics. For General de Gaulle, who had written and said countless times that "France was made by wielding the sword", an appeal to arms was no more than a moment, a spasmodic moment, in politics. On the highest level, any warlike activity could be referred to the art of governing the State. It was war that shaped nations. The Napoleonic Code from the battle of Marengo. In his opinion there was no attack against Douaumont, no dropping of parachutes over Brittany, no liberation of Avranches or Saint-Dié that did not reflect the history of yesterday and form that of tomorrow, that did not reveal the values and the horrors which make up a nation.

War was that activity by which a people expressed itself, *fortissimo*; and through which a culture was revealed. However ardently one might wish to avoid it and with whatever reluctance one was drawn into it, war was an essential moment in the great casting of history, the point at which the sculptor's chisel cut into the stone and fashioned what tomorrow was to be the likeness of a nation. Was not Charles de Gaulle the man who first, on 18 June, "kept France in the war" because he believed that it was in that terrible furnace that the country would forge its rebirth, winning its right to exist and its dignity as a partner?

Nothing could seem more ridiculous in the eyes of Franklin D. Roosevelt (who would probably have refused to see the kinship between these ideas and those of his cousin Theodore). For FDR, war should bring about what Milton Viorst, the historian of the President's relations with de Gaulle, calls a "moratorium in politics",[4] an historical parenthesis. As he saw it, war was only an immense fatigue-duty, a fight against a shameful disease – something like the cleaning of drains or an act of repression by the police. In such cases only the result and the lowest cost in human lives matters. Why should I fight for a town, even if it is Rome or Strasburg, if I can persuade the occupying forces to let me in, even if I have to share the keys with them? If a deal with Quisling allows me to spare the life of one American soldier by bringing Norway (sooner or later) over to the side of the democracies, why should I give battle?

So in this matter of the relations between war and politics, between meaning and profit and between history and tactics, we shall see Charles de Gaulle, the pupil of Machiavelli and the admirer of Clausewitz, hold up moral values against Franklin Roosevelt.

Was de Gaulle anti-American? The accusation is so commonplace, so usual, that one hesitates to raise the question. Let us not start with the man who was excluded from the great decision concerning the war, the leader who was not asked to Yalta. Let us take the man of June 1940. Here we have a French officer who in 1917 did not appreciate the contribution of the American troops at its real value – whereas Pétain, who had commanded them, was one of the few to do so. His letters as a prisoner of war show a few signs of the typical European officer's irony with regard to the Yankees. And between the wars he never failed to snipe at Washington's great European ideas, from the Dawes plan to the Kellog-Briand pact.

Yet as soon as he had made the great choice in his military career, the choice that led him to fight for armoured divisions, he is to be seen suddenly struck with a respect for industrial civilization, of which the United States, in the thirties, was the acknowledged model. An article on economic mobilization published by Major de Gaulle* in 1933 speaks very highly of the American system, and does so in a tone that few European officers would have adopted at that time. Then as a very close colleague of Paul Reynaud, himself a great and quite well-informed admirer of American ways, de Gaulle cannot have failed to be imbued with the same state of mind. And when the hour of disaster came, it was of the United States he thought, as did Reynaud; it was to them he turned – in the appeal of 18 June he explicitly spoke of the "immense industry of the United States".

To be sure, Washington's reception of Reynaud's desperate cries for help a few days earlier and the atmosphere in London around the American Embassy, overwhelmed by the defeatism of Ambassador Joseph Kennedy, if not with his pro-Germanism, was not of a kind to make Charles de Gaulle a wholly uncritical friend of the United States at the moment he launched into his great adventure.

Yet when he took these prodigious risks it was not only because he believed in the tenacity of the British and because he hoped that parts of the French Empire would soon join him; it was also because he trusted in the fellowship and sympathy of the United States to contribute to the common war-effort; in the knowledge that the outcome of the war largely depended on the American armaments industry.

No, de Gaulle was not spontaneously anti-American when he began his undertaking. The memorandum he sent to the State Department on 5 June 1941, offering to put the African airfields and bases under his control at the disposal of the American General Staff; the very great importance he attributed to Pleven's mission a month later; his reception of Colonel Cunningham in Africa – all these things show him well-disposed towards this very powerful (too powerful?) ally.

As soon as obstacles arose, at Saint-Pierre, in New Caledonia or simply in the State Department, then the observer would see him rear up, sometimes to the point of fury, and put himself thoroughly in the wrong. But although on such occasions his counterstrokes were excessive, they amounted to reactions rather than to the outward sign of personal prejudice.

*See p. 123.

Did Franklin Roosevelt confront this de Gaulle, whose anti-Americanism was less spontaneous than has been said, with feelings that were in the first place as francophile as those of Winston Churchill's? There can be no doubt that the great American President, coming from an Eastern Seaboard society imbued with European culture, was well-disposed towards France until June 1940. He had been a member of the war-government that ran the American strategy in 1918, and he had then admired the French military leaders; later he was among those who, like most American authorities, thought Clemenceau's or Foch's requirements excessive. During the march towards war in 1938 to 1939, he relied on William Bullitt, his friend and Ambassador in Paris, who was certain of French military supremacy, and he trusted the Franco-British coalition to rid Europe of the "brown plague". It was the disaster of 1940, however, that convinced him that degenerate France had disqualified itself as a world power.

Of course, like many other people all over the world, he was struck with dismay. On this point one should read the notes taken by René de Chambrun, a direct witness: Chambrun was an international lawyer, Pierre Laval's son-in-law, a personal friend of Marshal Pétain, and a liaison-officer with the British army up until Dunkirk; then, at the request of William Bullitt, Paul Reynaud sent him to the United States as a "special military attaché" on 9 June 1940. He was a descendant of Lafayette; Theodore Roosevelt's daughter, Alice Longworth, was his aunt; there was no Frenchman more *persona grata* in Washington – furthermore, he had dual nationality, French and American. On 14 June, the President invited him aboard his yacht the *Potomac.**

René de Chambrun describes this strange cruise, on which Harry Hopkins and Averell Harriman were also guests. It was tea-time. The weather was extremely hot. The President was brought a radiogram saying that the Wehrmacht had crossed the Seine and was advancing towards the Loire. "He seemed terribly depressed," says Chambrun, "and letting his arms fall down by the sides of his wheel-chair he said to me, "René, the show is over." Then he added with a sigh, "I don't think that Great Britain can hold out." To this Chambrun replied that although he was unfortunately right about France, he was mistaken about Great Britain.[5]

This Roosevelt, "terribly depressed" by the French military collapse, reached the point of losing that fundamental optimism which was one of his great qualities as a statesman. Those moments marked him for the rest of his life. He was never to forgive the France that had not only failed him but had also failed to keep its word to its London allies, and had led him personally to the edge of disaster (for the fall of Britain would be a political catastrophe). This defeated nation, which so kindly welcomed the American troops in 1917, had thoroughly deserved its fate and could now no longer play anything but a passive role.

Another essential factor in Roosevelt's politics was his anti-colonialism. Of course he did not look upon France as the only country guilty of colonial sin: as he saw it, Britain, the Netherlands and Portugal were all equally culpable. But of all colonial ill-doings those committed by France in Indo-China and North Africa

*In Moscow, at the same hour, Maurice Thorez was going aboard for a cruise on the *Moskva*.

were to the forefront of his mind. When the question of Indo-China came up at the beginning of 1944, FDR dictated a short note to do away with any return of the colonial power, because "France has milked Indo-China for a hundred years. The people of Indo-China deserve better than that." However little one may like the regime set up in Hanoi in 1884, it is unlikely that FDR would ever have allowed a comparison to be made with the Philippines, under US "protection" since 1902.

Everything has already been said about the American President's attempts to remove North Africa from the French orbit, particularly during his interview at Anfa with Mohammed Ben Youssef, then the "protected" sultan. Here again FDR laid his finger on a situation that was an unfortunate consequence of that deplorable system, and a "French" consequence too. Although he had taken such care to handle Vichy tactfully in other fields he could not refrain from thus shaking one of the bases of power on which Vichy then reposed, a base whose chief authority, General Noguès, was much esteemed by the American General Staff: as soon as he had a chance of striking a blow against the French imperial system, he could not resist his underlying impulse. In his view, France was not only the defeated nation of 1940, but also the citadel of colonialism.

FDR's thesis in those days was that "there was no France", and that the country was *res nullius* (these expressions are to be found in many of his conversations) until the French people spoke by means of an election. Yet he chose to retain links with that part of non-existent France in which the electoral principle was by definition excluded; while the other part, that of Free France, was crying out that, as soon as it possibly could, it would ask the voters for their decision. And in dealing with this openly non-democratic fraction Roosevelt provided it with considerable moral and political advantages by sending it an exceptional ambassador, William Leahy, who was widely known to represent not only those about the President but also the United States Navy. This was not merely the retention of a link, an office kept open; it was a solemn tribute to the Marshal and the Vichy admirals.

Franklin Roosevelt, contemplating a France "that did not exist", in order to further his strategic aims, his prejudices and his impulses, decided to bring one into "existence" at least on the diplomatic level, and to show the world and the French citizens that he, the most powerful man on earth and the certain victor, legitimated only those Frenchmen who were not fighting and the rulers who shook hands with Adolf Hitler two or three times a year.

How can one fail to be surprised by the arguments of that excellent American historian Arthur L. Funk[6] that FDR had no prejudices against de Gaulle and Free France whatsoever? The sole basis of American policy at that time, Funk maintains, was the anxiety,

> not to commit the same mistakes as President Wilson in 1919, when, having reached agreement with the governments at the Peace Conference, he came back to Washington to find that he could not win the support of either the American Senate or the political parties for the ratification of the treaties or of the League of Nations. Roosevelt wanted to be sure that everything he might bring to the Senate would be accepted. Consequently he did not wish

to recognize any government in an *occupied* country before the people had made their choice known. On that point he was immovable.

Immovable? Then why did he recognize an unelected Pétain in 1940? And an even less elected Bonomi in Italy in 1944?

Yet even so, a mystery veils FDR's immediate and perfectly clear decision in favour of Vichy and against de Gaulle from as early as the end of June 1940, at a time when all he knew about the general situation was that the power of France – apart from the fleet and the Empire – had been destroyed and that Ambassador Kennedy in London and a considerable number of American experts on the spot told him there was a very real danger of a British collapse.

Was it the reflex of a moralist who felt that Pétain was right in reprimanding the French, convincing them of their guilt, maintaining their feelings of sin, of wrong-doing, the cause of all the evil? The reaction of a political realist who drew up a balance, ruled a line, and came to the conclusion that France was eliminated as a power and was now destined only to serve as a platform for the reconquest of Europe? Or rather the calculation of a statesman who, with the possibility of an invasion of the British Isles in mind, wished to retain a window looking on to Europe and believed he found it in this humiliated but convenient Vichy. Why not make a kind of large-scale Switzerland out of this neutralized France under the aegis of a former hero, while her North African possessions could conveniently be transformed into an American aircraft-carrier?

Strategically, therefore, de Gaulle was merely a nuisance, continually springing up with hazy ideas, counter-charges and insistent requirements. When the last vestiges of Vichy's independence disappeared on 11 November 1942, it was too late for the President to change this "practical" point of view: Roosevelt could not have been mistaken. He had picked a side and he remained firm – firm well after the time of Darlan, the "provisional expedient". It was only from Washington that one could take a world view, from Guam to Sydney and from the Urals to Gibraltar. Provincial hopes and ambitions would have to wait their turn: ensure that France did not get in the way of the war-machine of the liberators, who would choose their time and their means for carrying out the great police-operation. Nothing more could be expected from the French than that they should play the part of onlookers when the gangsters were arrested: let them flatten themselves against the wall to let the G-men* pass when they came to restore order: "Pass along, there; pass along. There's nothing to be seen."

Let the French prepare landing-grounds, provide a little information, sabotage a few trains and produce their experts (providing they had any). In return they would be handed back a metropolitan territory not very much smaller than that of 1940 (there would be a few concessions made to Belgium, which ought to be made bigger) under the aegis of an American High Commission, which would re-educate them, and of an international police-force, which would maintain interior and exterior order in a "disarmed" France. This is not a caricature: it was the future that FDR foresaw for France, gathered from the general body of notions

*The agents of the FBI were referred to as G-men. (trs.)

expressed by the head of the American executive from 1940 to 1944 and even after the landings in Normandy.*

But the reason that the American President (unlike many of his colleagues) always seemed to believe that France was not conquered by Hitler but by the Allies and it was not a question of "liberation" therefore, but of military occupation,** was because he had never seen fit to take into consideration the Free French. Since France meant Pétan and Laval in 1944 as in 1940, how indeed could one fail to look upon it as a conquered country? FDR was consistent in his logic.

So FDR was neglectful of de Gaulle and the Free French. As we have seen, their different personalities and their different ideas about the war and the future of France only widened the gap between them. But what did they learn about their differences? And who told them? On de Gaulle's side it is quite plain. As early as 1940 he had at his disposal all the means of knowing about his famous partner – so famous that every one of his remarks was an event. Furthermore, de Gaulle was subject to little in the way of influence. And although he listened to this opinion or that – Pleven, Cassin, Palewski, and from the summer of 1941 Billotte – we can exclude any anti-American influence coming from those sources: Pleven and Billotte were openly-declared friends of the USA. For de Gaulle, until he had received repeated snubs and rebuffs, Roosevelt was above all the man who was going to turn industrial power into the weapon that would accomplish the denazification of the world.

For his part, Franklin D. Roosevelt had never even heard the name of Charles de Gaulle until June 1940 (nor had the majority of Frenchmen), and he would scarcely have taken much notice of the remark in a letter Churchill sent him on 12 June, just after the formation of the last Reynaud government, pointing out that "a young general determined to fight" was part of the team.*** It was therefore from outsiders, "expert" or not, that he gathered his notions of the man he was so often to find on his path.

One can make out four sources that went to the making of the "de Gaulle file" which from this time on was to help FDR come to his decisions. In the first place there was Churchill, whose correspondence and conversation included more and more references to de Gaulle. Then the official American dispatches from the London Embassy, the Vichy Embassy and the consulate in Algiers. Then the atmosphere brought into being around the White House by the body of the President's civil and military colleagues, and by the many French exiles who gave their opinions, asked for or not. And lastly the personal interviews between FDR and de Gaulle, which amounted to no more than two private conversations at Anfa in January 1943, to three audiences at the White House in July 1944, and to a few

*See p. 430.

**See Chapter 36.

***But a surprising fact, and one that already tells us a great deal about the quality of the 'information' concerning de Gaulle, is that a dispatch from the US Embassy in Paris at that time speaks of him as 'a protégé of Mme de Portes', Reynaud's pro-Armistice mistress.

notes or letters addressed more or less directly by the General to the President.

However favourable the information and the opinions emanating from Winston Churchill (until January 1943) may have been, they seemed to have had a negative effect on Roosevelt; not because the American neglected the advice of the Englishman, whom he admired, but because he thought him a Romantic magnificently astray in this century, whose opinions and actions were dictated by strong emotion alone.

It seemed to Roosevelt heroic and sound that this strong emotion, this passion, should be exercised against a racist tyrant such as Hitler; but that Churchill should favour a French general who, speaking in an arrogant tone, had claimed to have decided just when the United States should intervene in the war, and who publicly abused Pétain seemed to him absurd. Although the American war-effort certainly had to be linked to the strategy of that old jingo Churchill, just one of that kind was quite enough in the coalition.

Furthermore the American strategy could not blend entirely with that of the British Empire, still less depend upon it. From the moment that Churchill had a protégé and wished to centre his continental policy on him, the American leaders could not but see this protégé as a pawn on the British side, an instrument in a plan that they should treat with circumspection. Yes to the admirable British tenacity and to the sound advice of the Imperial General Staff; no to the conservative wiles of Downing Street and the Foreign Office. If Churchill had "his" Frenchman, we should have one or several of our own: Monnet, Léger, La Laurencie, Giraud, Darlan?

The history of Franco-American diplomatic relations is rich in examples of clearminded friendship: from the time of Benjamin Franklin and Thomas Jefferson to that of Myron T. Herrick and "Chip" Bohlen, the United States were often represented in France by distinguished and well-informed men. And the other way about. But during this period some evil spirit seems to have used its utmost zeal in embroiling the matter by means of people whose minds were entirely devoted to embittering relations and the general outlook.

Admittedly, Washington was not represented in Paris by a man like Joseph Kennedy, who looked upon all forms of resistance to Hitler as tantamount to suicide and in whose opinion Munich was the masterpiece of contemporary diplomacy. William Bullitt, the American Ambassador to Paris, was hostile to totalitarianism. He loved France and he had countless friends, including Léon Blum, who lived in the next-door flat.* But all the papers he wrote and that one can read might have been scribbled by a bat in a belfrey. It was not that he lacked good will, nor people to inform him. But he was not gifted with much judgment: in 1939 he thought that France was invincible and he struggled against any alliance with the East; on 13 June 1940 he thought it was his duty to remain in Paris to intimidate the Germans instead of carrying on with his mission to the government in flight and of trying, like his British counterpart Campbell, to persuade Reynaud to hold on. So he did not return to Washington trailing clouds of glory. His old friend FDR no longer took much notice of his advice – and as misfortune would

*At 25, quai Bourbon.

have it, this discredited oracle was one of those who, after 1943, spoke rather in favour of Free France.

It was much more the dispatches sent from Paris until the end of June 1941, than from London and lastly from Vichy by professional, experienced, senior diplomats that guided the President of the United States and the State Department on the subject of France and the leaders who could direct or represent the country. According to the messages sent by Maynard Barnes,* a shattered and defeated France was no longer a nation.

The first mentions of Free France in the American dispatches date from the 28 June agreement by which Churchill recognized de Gaulle as "leader of the Free French". This move aroused scarcely any interest in Washington, which received information from the London Embassay to the effect that de Gaulle was "without a strongly-marked personality" and sometimes that he was "an arrogant chief". Shortly after this the same observers asserted that "the British are tired of him". The first American comments refer to the defeat at Dakar; Roosevelt, who had been against the operation from the beginning, pinned the enterprise and its failure to the Free French. And as soon as Admiral Leahy came to Vichy, accompanied by that allegedly "great expert" on France, Freeman Matthews, the State Department no longer listened to anything about de Gaulle except for the accusations against him retailed in the Marshal's circle. So basic were the facts about the leader of the Free French that a year later when the President consulted the "de Gaulle file" all that the man in question amounted to (to sum up the least abject remarks) was "a viper the Marshal had nourished in his bosom" or an "apprentice Fascist". General Donovan, the head of the organization that became the OSS,** that in turn was to become the CIA, thought him "mad", and Hershel Johnson, counsellor at the United States Embassy in London, considered him a "provocateur".

Yet on 5 June 1941 the leader of the Free French (did he know what was being said about him in Washington?) handed the United States consul in Cairo a memorandum in which he offered to place the African bases under Free French control at the disposition of the United States, a memorandum accompanied by reasons which proved that this "madman" could think quite clearly and that this "fascist" was not exactly an enemy of the United States. The diplomatic experts looked upon this document as of no importance. But who were these "specialists" whose opinion did so much to shape the President's?

The official leader was Mr Cordell Hull, the Secretary of State, a former Southern Democrat senator who had helped Wilson break with isolationism in 1917. He was quite certainly an honest man, but he came from a little village in Tennessee and he knew nothing whatsoever about France – except that when the country was victorious it had caused the President of the United States a certain amount of trouble twenty years before, and that having been beaten it was causing his 1940 chief still more. Mr Hull was in his seventies, and he was naturally disposed in favour of the age-group reigning at Vichy. And the Saint-Pierre and Miquelon affair had deeply wounded this former judge, highly conscious of his

*In 1942, he became US consul-general at Brazzaville.
**Office of Strategic Services.

dignity and who found it very hard to bear the mockery in the American papers about his disproportionate reaction to this "fleabite". But unlike Roosevelt's, Hull's anti-Gaullism was to diminish.

Cordell Hull's assistant, the Under-Secretary of State Sumner Welles, controlled European affairs: he was said to be an expert on them because he adopted the Oxford manner, spoke a little French and had made a long tour of Europe at the beginning of the war. Let us observe that when he came back from this investigation he was of the opinion that on the old continent he had met only one single man of the first order, "Mussolini, that peasant of genius", upon whom, he thought, all endeavours for peace should be based.

Although Mr Welles was more clear-minded than his colleagues about Vichy's inability to resist Hitler's requirement, and although he took rather more notice of the Free French efforts, he never succeeded in concealing his suspicion of de Gaulle and his spokesmen. For Welles, the only worthwhile Frenchmen were those he had met in Paris at the beginning of 1940: Herriot, Daladier, Reynaud and Mandel. But he did see a great deal of Alexis Léger, who had welcomed him at the Quai d'Orsay and who had withdrawn to Washington. As we shall see, these contacts had their political importance.

Adolf Berle, the third man in the State Department, displayed rather more competence and rather less prejudice. But in the book *Navigating the Rapids**[7] he is seen to be continually obsessed by the fear of being manipulated by the Foreign Office and Churchill's wish to "canonize" de Gaulle. He speaks of himself as one of those who decided to keep Free France "out of the picture" at the time of the landings in North Africa. And the historian and journalist Max Ascoli, who wrote a preface for the book, does not think it right to make any distinction between Berle's attitude and FDR's: "In their antagonism towards Free France and de Gaulle, the President, Berle and the majority of the Washington officials went to the extreme."

For the President and the State Department the part played by their two representatives with official France, William Leahy, and Robert Murphy, was essential.

It is edifying to read the book of recollections that Leahy devoted to his stay at Vichy from December 1940 to April 1942, *I was there*: no France existed other than the France where he happened to be. And yet even when he was sickened by the dismissal of Weygand and then angered by Laval's recall to the government when he spoke of the need for "a revision of the United States' policy", he never allowed himself to accept that this was the only viable alternative. As an old service-man collaborating with a very aged leader, an admiral surrounded by the admirals who studded the court of Vichy, he seems scarcely to have asked himself any questions about the nature of the régime that he was strengthening by his own presence. In one of his reports to Roosevelt, Leahy quite seriously explains that one should make a distinction between the "degaullists", a small handful of men faithful to the General, and the "Gaullists", who were patriots, lovers of the ancient France which was called Gaul.

*Written by his wife, Beatrice, and based on his papers. (trs.)

One could have no notion of William Leahy's animosity towards the Free French movement unless one recalled that after the war he said to a man who was regretting that eastern Europe had been given over to Stalin, "Yes. But we also gave France over to the Gaullists!" This was the man whom Roosevelt called to his side after his return from Vichy to act as his personal chief of staff and his counsellor, a confidential adviser.

Robert Murphy was one of the stars of American diplomacy, and in Paris he had shown that he knew a great deal about French affairs. He was of Irish origin, a Catholic and very conservative; he liked soldiers (except de Gaulle), people of standing, duchesses and the clergy: Weygand was just his type. He was therefore sent to Algeria, where he was remarkably active in strengthening the position of Vichy's Delegate-General, since he reckoned that only the Marshal's regime had allowed him to set up a network of more than thirty real or apparent American consuls in North Africa and to bring forward anti-German officers such as Beaufre and Faye.

De Gaulle acknowledges that Murphy was "clever and determined", but he also says that he "tended to suppose that France was the people with whom he went out to dinner". A remark quite well confirmed by the diplomat's own writings and by the observations scattered through his book *Diplomat among warriors*. Murphy was intelligent, energetic, agreeable, full of worldly wisdom, moderate, and capable, at times, of making penetrating comments – even on the subject of de Gaulle.* When he was with Weygand, and perhaps even more after Weygand had been replaced by the very conformist Yves Chatel, Murphy played a decisive part in preparing for the American landing. But his activities always ran counter to those of Free France, whose young, active members he made use of, apparently without feeling any embarrassment, to open the way for the American forces who had landed at Algiers, and then letting them be imprisoned by the neo-Vichyist authorities.

Amongst the causes of President Roosevelt's anti-Gaullism were the dispatches sent to his colleagues by the American Embassy in London on the methods used by the agents belonging to Passy and Brossolette's Free French Intelligence Service (BCRA). They amounted to a Chamber of Horrors.

Freeman Matthews, a counsellor at the Embassy, who never hid his liking for Pétain, received information from observers in Scotland Yard: he devoted whole pages of his dispatches to reporting the practices of the BCRA's "torturers", conveniently likened to the Gestapo. Indeed, Matthews never hesitated to call de Gaulle an "apprentice Hitler".[8] Roosevelt had a particular liking for dispatches of this kind and he read them first. They could not but confirm his dislike for the Carlton Gardens "Nazi".

Did Roosevelt therefore have nobody but anti-Gaullists about him? Although we are very ill-informed about Felix Frankfurter's opinion of the Free French movement – he was a judge of the Supreme Court, and perhaps the man whose views the President heard with the most respect – we do know, by the writings of the one and the frequent testimonials of the others, that his chief confidant, Harry Hopkins, welcomed René Pleven as early as the summer of 1941, and sometimes

*See his remarkable analysis for the Anfa conference below.

tried to make FDR reconsider his prejudices against the man of 18 June.

The United States Ambassador in London, John Winant,* does not appear to have done the Free French any harm. The Assistant Secretary for War, John McCloy, a great New York lawyer, did his best to emphasize the joint nature of Fighting French and United States aims and interests. And as we shall see, on two or three occasions General Eisenhower made his influence felt in the same direction. Henry Morgenthau Jr, the Secretary of Treasury, frequently pleaded the cause of Free France at the White House, speaking particularly against the accusation of Fascism and even of antisemitism[9] directed against Charles de Gaulle by certain American leaders.

But with Roosevelt the arguments of Hopkins, Morgenthau and McCloy were constantly being counteracted by the opinions, advice and warnings uttered by those Frenchmen in whom he most believed. Three names come to mind at once: René de Chambrun, Jean Monnet and Alexis Léger.

We have already seen Chambrun on the deck of the *Potomac*, hearing FDR's first reactions to the news of France's collapse. The President received him again on 1 August. After a long discussion on the system that had come into operation at Vichy during the last month, concerning which he made a number of pertinent objections, FDR, observing that "he was intrigued by de Gaulle", asked his guest for some information about the head of the Free French. From Chambrun's notes it appears that he said he had only seen de Gaulle "two or three times in Marshal Pétain's antechamber at the Invalides". Which, by way of information, was rather wanting.

Did Réne de Chambrun really know so little about a character who had aroused so much controversy in the circles familiar to so social a man? It would be a fair bet that he spoke at much greater length and that what he said to FDR did little to help the President revise his impression of de Gaulle.[10]

As far as is known, Laval's son-in-law was not asked to the White House again during the years that followed.** But it is known that FDR retained his friendship for him, and that Chambrun was an established link between Pétain, who treated him as an adopted son, and the President of the United States. In any case, it can easily be imagined that whether he was confined to the wings or not, this eloquent, well-informed, half-American lawyer did not improve Charles de Gaulle's image with Roosevelt.

Nevertheless Jean Monnet was even more important, if only because of his great services to the joint war-effort; he provided the Inter-Allied Armaments Commission with an impulse which Keynes described as "decisive". No Frenchman had ever had such standing in Washington. Yet Monnet had left London and de Gaulle at the end of June 1940, being opposed (not without rational argument and elevation of spirit, as we have seen) to the "political" undertaking of the man of 18 June, who ought, in Monnet's opinion, to have confined himself to a military role.

*Who replaced Joseph Kennedy in January 1941. (trs.)

**Perhaps because he was too close to the man the Americans thought they were counteracting by their support of the Marshal and Weygand.

However unobtrusive he tried to remain after this,* doing his utmost to do de Gaulle no explicit disservice with the Americans, his mere presence in Washington was seen as a disavowal of the Gaullism that Monnet, a realistic businessman and a spontaneous internationalist, found by no means to his taste. Réne Pleven, who was Monnet's confidential colleague before being de Gaulle's, has been quoted on this subject. To read the general report on the situation in France that Monnet sent to Roosevelt at the end of 1940 one sees how remote he was from Gaullism at that time: even three months after a third of French Africa had joined the Free French, the name of de Gaulle is not even mentioned.

But by far the most important influence on the American leaders was that of Alexis Léger, who, after a short stay in London in June 1940, settled in Washington in the modest capacity of secretary in the Library of Congress, writing some of the poems that ensured the fame of Saint-John Perse.**

Charles de Gaulle had known him well in the days when Léger was Secretary-General at the Quai d'Orsay, and as we have seen he still thought him sufficiently well-disposed to Free France in September 1941 to suggest that he, together with the philosopher, Jacques Maritain, should join the National Committee. The diplomat sent the General a "respectful but negative" reply; but this did not prevent Léger, when he was talking to Adolf Berle about the Saint-Pierre and Miquelon affair three months later, from protesting against Washington's "choice of Vichy", and from strongly supporting de Gaulle's action in the context of "French sovereignty".[11]

Yet when I was talking to Walter Lippmann at the end of July 1971, he reminded me of the efforts of the former Secretary General of the Quai d'Orsay to convince his intimate friend Francis Biddle, the Attorney General, and Sumner Welles, and by means of them Roosevelt, of the dangers of "civil war" the country would run after the liberation because of Free France and above all because of Charles de Gaulle's character; "for never," maintained Léger, "would the French accept rulers coming from abroad."

Léger's transition from a coldness to active hostility towards Free France in 1942, coincided with de Gaulle's decision to make René Massigli head of Free France's diplomacy. Massigli was said to be Léger's sworn enemy; he accused him of having been behind Munich and all the decisions confirming France's downward course into decadence.

In any event, Léger played an essential part in the psychodrama of misunderstanding enacted around Roosevelt on the subject of de Gaulle. His best-known step was a letter of 31 January 1944 to Roosevelt, stating that France would be threatened with Caesarism if a Gaullist power were set up; this decisively revived Washington's prejudices against the General at a time when realities in France itself might have diminished them.

To these three French consultants, close to Roosevelt or farther off, let us add Roger Cambon, counsellor-minister at the French Embassy in Britain, who, when

*In his *Mémoires* Monnet wrote that he "saw neither one set nor the other", neither the supporters of de Gaulle or of Vichy. He says that his remarks about "European problems" carried "far more weight" than those he made about France, free or occupied.

**The name under which Léger wrote. (trs.)

relations between Vichy and London were broken off in July 1940, refused to leave that town, preferring to share its ordeals. In his exile he never ceased denouncing de Gaulle, whom he detested from the very beginning; his colleagues in the American Embassy paid great attention to what he said, and they often quoted him in their warnings against the General's authoritarian tendencies.

What must also be said is that in the United States the French colony as a whole was even more divided than that of London, including fanatical Gaullists, Free French sympathizers, anti-German followers of the Marshal, enthusiastic Vichyists, patriots without any label, discreet bet-hedgers, puppets of the Americans and left-wing or extreme left-wing democrats, categories typified by, among others, Philippe Barrès and Eve Curie, Charles Boyer and André Maurois, Camille Chautemps, Pierre Lazareff, Saint-Exupéry, Henri Laugier and Pierre Cot; and the atmosphere that reigned among them for three years running did nothing to enlighten the White House. Yet perhaps one might have expected that this perpetual variance of opinion would have led to open-mindedness in Washington.

What is so disconcerting in this painful business is not that Roosevelt should have had a few prejudices nor even that these prejudices should be based on so pessimistic a view of France that the country could be reduced to a handful of aged military men imprisoned by nostalgia and rendered incapable of movement by a fear of unleashing the apocalypse; it is that these prejudices could not be corrected or even lightened by any suggestion whatsoever, whether it came from associates who were very close to him indeed (Hopkins or Morgenthau) or from persons (Frenchmen among others) from whom FDR could expect a certain soundness of judgement and a certain reliability in their information.

The most striking of these interventions came from a man whom Roosevelt could not fail to admire, a man who, when he was in power, had maintained relations with him in which trust and esteem were evident, a man whose present state as a prisoner in Bourassol conferred an additional halo: Léon Blum. By his eloquence alone the former chief of the Popular Front government had compelled the judges at Riom to break off the action Vichy had brought against those "responsible" for the war of 1939,* and this had brought him enthusiastic praise from the American press; at General de Gaulle's request, he sent the President of the United States a message in favour of Free France. This document must be called to mind, because coming from a man who in the eyes of the world symbolized the strangled Republic, it amounts to the most impressive certificate of legitimacy that a French leader could then receive:

> In the midst of so many disasters, it is a stroke of good fortune that this man should exist. The reason that General de Gaulle embodies this unity** is that to a great degree he is its author. They are his actions and his words that have brought it into being. It is he who has gradually revived the nation's honour, its love of freedom, its patriotic and civic conscience. I am not making this profession of faith solely in my own name, personally; I know that I speak for all the socialists gathered in France, both in the occupied and

> in the "free" zone; I am convinced that I express the opinion of the mass of the republicans – middle class, working class or peasants. By helping General de Gaulle to now become leader one is doing democratic France a service.[12]

Did Roosevelt read this document? Was it thought advisable to keep it from him? Did Roosevelt think he knew France and its feelings, interests and the depths of its soul better than the Socialist leader who had done so much to strengthen the democratic spirit in his country and to open it to other free societies, beginning with that of the United States? Was it supposed at the White House that the Bourassol testimony came from an exhausted man, one whose clarity of mind had gone and whose imprisonment prevented him from gathering valid information? In that case one could have referred either to the statements of support for de Gaulle put out by the best-known representatives of the republican system or to the documents published by the French National Committee in London, thus obtaining an idea of the intentions proclaimed by de Gaulle and his companions.

Was it Blum's socialism that worried Roosevelt? If that was so, he could have based himself on the opinion of a man who embodied French democracy with just as much credibility and more "moderation": Jules Jeanneney, the president of the Senate. On 30 June 1942 de Gaulle, by means of an envoy belonging to the Resistance, sent him a request for advice on how to resolve the legal problems that had arisen from the creation of a provisional government and on electoral and representational matters; and in this message he said that "Clemenceau's former colleague" might be assured "that I and my companions will never give up maintaining a fighting France", and that "we are determined to safeguard democracy".

The chief points of Jeanneney's reply to this request, whose form was far from Caesarian, were these:

> It being established that national sovereignty could not either legally or materially be exercised by the parliament in office, the duty of assuming it falls to the nation itself. Once France is liberated, it will be for its people to settle its political destiny and by means of free elections to provide themselves with the institutions and the men of their choice. It will therefore be necessary to create a provisional government whose function will be to make this electoral consultation possible, governing the country in the meantime. A formidable task and one that will obviously bear with it the danger of exercising absolute power once again. It would not be prudent to entrust this to a single person.

In his conclusion Jeanneney suggested the creation of a Committee of National Safety for the French Republic.[13]

One is quite ready to believe that the President of the United States did not have time to read even short extracts from de Gaulle's speeches, not even that which he made on the second anniversary of 18 June 1940 in the Albert Hall in London, a speech in which the Free French leader, quoting Vice-President Henry Wallace's description of this conflict as "the war of the common man", asserted that the victory must above all be that of the "great masses of the people, who have remained the most courageous and the most faithful". De Gaulle thus set out a resolutely democratic programme:

"That the French people are the one and only master in their own country"; "that both the totalitarian system and the system of the coalition of private interests that has worked against the national interest in our country [should be] simultaneously and forever overthrown"; "that the imperative and closely-linked goals of national security against the tyranny of perpetual violation [should] be attained"; "that the age-old French ideal of liberty, equality and fraternity should from now on be put into practise among us"; that "fellowship and mutual aid between all the nations" should be established, "France occupying, in this international system, the distinguished place allotted to her by her worth and genius". Apart from the last piece, was there a single word in all this that FDR would have rejected in drawing up his own electoral platform?

Whether or not Roosevelt ever read this speech, he certainly saw a letter Charles de Gaulle wrote to him on 6 October 1942. The letter was delivered by André Philip, a Socialist deputy sent by the Resistance to de Gaulle, who appointed him Commissioner for the Interior and then chose him to make a first contact with the President of the United States in order to arrange his own visit. Philip, however, reached Washington during the agitated weeks before the North African landings, from which Washington wanted to exclude the Free French at all costs; he was therefore kept waiting and FDR did not receive him until 20 November 1942.

Adrien Tixier, who accompanied André Philip, has left an account of this interview and in it the differences between FDR's opinions and those of the General's spokesmen reached the point of caricature – all the more so since Tixier does nothing to diminish André Philip's vehement (one might almost say brutal) way of speaking. Twenty years later Philip told me about the meeting, and what he said clarified the fundamental difference that separated the great President, committed to the vast Algiers operation, from those Frenchmen who longed for an immediate restoration of a self-governing France before the battle.[14]

While Philip was speaking to Roosevelt about the aspirations of Fighting France, the President interrupted him: "As I see it, there is no longer any France, until the time elections provide the country with representatives." "But until these elections can take place, and to organize them?" replied Philip. "At present we are training a group of political and military specialists who will take care of the administration of France until democracy is re-established." "Mr President, for the French people a foreign occupier is only an occupier." "For my part," said Roosevelt, "I am not an idealist like Wilson; I am concerned above all with efficiency; I have problems to solve. Those who help me solve them are welcome. Today, Darlan gives me Algiers, and I cry *Vive Darlan*! If Quisling gives me Oslo I will cry *Vive Quisling*! Let Laval give me Paris tomorrow and I will cry *Vive Laval*!"

Remembering this interview twenty-two years later, Philip added, "After listening to him for a few minutes I muttered, 'Léon Blum has more class.' Ten minutes later I said to myself, 'No, it's more Herriot he reminds me of.' And after half an hour I ended, 'It's quite certainly Laval.'"

It was only after this interview, which finally convinced him of the Gaullists' "fanaticism", that Roosevelt was able to study the letter that André Philip had brought him from General de Gaulle. In this message the General tried to explain to the President both why he had decided to launch the resistance in June 1940 and how, since then, he had been intending "to bring France back into the fight side by side with the allied nations while at the same time watching over the country's sensitivities and its unity".

It was a finely pleaded cause:

> Yesterday no other man came forward who could have brought over a group of Frenchmen or a French territory. I was alone. Was I to remain silent? Tomorrow, after the odious experiment of personal power conducted by Pétain thanks to the Germans' complicity, who would be so absurd as to suppose that one could set up and maintain personal power in France?

But Charles de Gaulle weakened the force of his argument by assuring FDR that "no one accused [him] of aiming at a dictatorship, not even [his] enemies in Vichy", an assertion that Roosevelt could not fail to think ill-founded, since he himself had gathered nothing but accusations of this kind from the "de Gaulle file".

The fact is that Roosevelt, thus called upon to take notice of Fighting France, decided that he would not even reply to this foreign, allied, ill-provided patriot's appeal. He confined himself to writing a short note on it for internal use, stating that "if this letter had been written at the time the Gaullist movement was being organized, it would have had a positive effect on our relations; but it comes two years too late." FDR added that "de Gaulle will not admit that our information about France is as good as his," that "his blindness is all the more tragic since our collaboration with him increases every day", that "France must be saved not only by the French outside France but by the French in France," and that, "General de Gaulle seems to want to force himself upon the French nation by making use of the allied armies." All the usual themes of the disagreement, quite unchanged.

This was how Roosevelt continued to argue, even after he had seen an active member of the Resistance like Philip, who had come to speak to him in the name of those "Frenchmen of France" who were fighting against Nazism in a France which since the week before no longer possessed even a "free" zone. In 1940 the President had decided against de Gaulle and in favour of a Pétain who had considerable authority and a certain amount of room for manoeuvring. But from now on he was continuing to exclude the head of a movement which was no longer overshadowed by the myth of Vichy, and which the leaders of French democracy, from Léon Blum to Herriot and from Jules Jeanneney to Mendès France, hailed as the prime mover and unifier in the struggle of "the Frenchmen of France".

We shall often see a de Gaulle seized by an anti-American passion that did a great deal of harm to the common cause. But did he ever display a blindness as obstinate and as serene as FDR's in this case? What is so disconcerting about the anti-Gaullism of Roosevelt, a man of the greatest stature, capable (whatever André Philip might say) of rising to the heights of strategic thought, is that facts were only very minor elements in its composition.

It is true that the violence of the de Gaulle reaction against the British landing in Madagascar* without warning the CNF in London made Roosevelt describe him as "unbearable"; and it is true that de Gaulle's delaying manoeuvres just before the Anfa conference, his words at the conference, his peremptory requirements with regard to Giraud and their meetings in July 1944, reinforced Roosevelt's animosity. Yet none of these misunderstandings had any effect on the primordial, elementary, visceral antipathy I have attempted to describe; for they are subsequent to it.

Whatever de Gaulle might do or say, for good or for evil, one always has the impression that Roosevelt took no more notice than the pilgrim to Mecca does of the stones on the road or the beauty of the sunset: everything had been said and certainty had been reached, once and for all.

*See the next chapter.

CHAPTER TWENTY-EIGHT

"You Are Not France!"

Misfortune rarely helps to consolidate alliances. De Gaulle was in a position to verify this statement throughout the tragic year of 1942, which, before being the year of El Alamein, Stalingrad and the landings in North Africa, was marked by a sequence of British reverses in Asia and Africa, from Singapore to Tobruk, and on all the oceans.

The fact that Winston Churchill, at that time more eager for a victory over Nazism than ever before, was obliged to put up with being "no more than Roosevelt's lieutenant", forcing himself to fall into step with the American on all occasions, augured no great good in the relations between de Gaulle and the British Prime Minister.[1]

Humiliation and extreme anxiety are bad counsellors. In the days when he stood alone against the Nazis, Churchill had a natural tendency to increase the importance of the rare – too rare – followers that his energy had raised up and gathered together. Ever since he had acquired formidable allies and he had had to fall into line, the value of France had become relative for him. It was no longer the heroic commando that had been capable of coming to his rescue, but a lesser member of the coalition, ridiculous from the military angle; and very much in the way from that of politics; for both these reasons de Gaulle was to be kept away from all important decisions and actions, particularly those which had to do with territories then under French sovereignty, Madagascar and North Africa.

In the days when he made his own decisions, Winston Churchill formed a team with Charles de Gaulle to conquer Dakar or Damascus. Now that he was reduced to the role of brilliant second he kept de Gaulle apart from the Diégo Suarez or Algiers operations; and this he did because Roosevelt had persuaded him that the General was no more than his protégé and because he was obeying the law according to which a man rendered inferior renders others inferior in his turn. It required the Constable's furious determination and above all the arbitrament of the French nation to prevent this progressive marginalization of the Free French from going as far as the radical exclusion that Franklin Roosevelt had in mind.

De Gaulle was so clearly aware of this bitter evolution by the beginning of 1942, that he voluntarily opened his mind on the subject to a visitor destined to play an important part in this account: Pierre Mendès France. He had escaped from the Clermont-Ferrand prison into which he had been thrown by one of the most infamous of the courts of Vichy (which had plenty to spare) and on 1 March 1942 he had succeeded in reaching London, where the General received him at once. The conversation soon turned into a monologue in the Gaullian manner: "Was I right at Saint-Pierre and Miquelon? Was I right in Syria?" And even "Was I right on 18 June?"

Mendès France observes, "Of course this did not mean that he was wondering about whether he had been right in choosing between the Germans and the Allies [. . .] but he was wondering if he had been right to rely on the British."[2]

It was especially because at this period he was asking himself questions of such a kind, that Charles de Gaulle, the leader of Free France (which on 14 July 1942 became Fighting France, as though to emphasize the fact that from now on it was less a matter of being "not Vichy" but of fighting when the victory came) tried to diversify his contacts and his supporters more eagerly than ever.

With regard to Washington, the future suddenly appeared to lighten. John Winant, who represented the United States in London, allowed a tentative personal liking for de Gaulle to appear in two very important interviews with the chief of the Fighting French on 21 May and 30 June. (For his part de Gaulle increased his praise of this "good ambassador".) Winant spoke of associating de Gaulle with the direction of the Allies' general strategy; while in Washington John McCloy, the Under-Secretary of State for War, asked Colonel de Chevigné, the Fighting French military delegate in the States, about the form the collaboration might take.

All this resulted in the agreement of 9 July 1942, which marked the high point of the US-Gaullist relations. By its terms the government of the United States "recognizes General de Gaulle's contribution [to the Allied cause] and the French National Committee's efforts to keep the traditional spirit of France and of its institutions alive" and hails them as the "symbol of French resistance to the Axis powers". And although the US government continues to lay stress on its relations with the "local authorities" it stated that it was ready "to centralize discussion relating to the carrying on of the war with the CNF in London."

This was an arrangement of the very first importance, and when it was completed by the appointment of two high-ranking officers, Admiral Stark and General Bolté, as representatives with Fighting France,* it led General de Gaulle to describe the agreement as satisfying from various points of view – a reaction too rare to pass unnoticed.

Yet on the other hand signs of a distinct ebb in official British sympathies for General de Gaulle became apparent: the only echo from the Foreign Office to Washington's step forward, seemingly so much in agreement with the views of London, was a strangely guarded message from Anthony Eden to General de Gaulle.

The Foreign Office did not go as far as the American document, for it spoke not of the French National Committee, but of the "Free French National Committee" as representing the Free French (which effectively meant there had been no change since the declaration of 28 June 1940, despite two years of fighting and development); and it took particular care to point out to the General that "His Majesty's government is unable to accredit a diplomatic representative to you which would imply recognition of you as the head of a sovereign state". Thus London picked the moment when Fighting France seemed at last to have been

*And with other governments in exile in London.

admitted as a (symbolic) partner by Washington and to be receiving the increasingly obvious adherence of the interior resistance to do no more than stress the obstacles to any further British recognition.

But as a compensation the Soviets were then doing all they could to put themselves forward as the privileged partners of Fighting France. In order to realize the points set out in the communiqué issued after the de Gaulle-Molotov meeting, the Soviets were going to recognize the CNF as the "directing organ of Fighting France, the only body entitled to organize the citizens' participation in the war and to represent French interests with the USSR." But when Maurice Schumann wanted to read a commentary outlining this important Soviet initiative on the London radio he was refused the microphone.[3]

Yes, the relations between General de Gaulle and his British allies (without whom, as it must continually be recalled, Free France would never have been able to appear, survive or even quite simply exist) had already been cruelly damaged by the first quarrels in the Levant, the side-effects of the Muselier affair and the various forms of pressure exercised by the White House, but also by the socio-psychological factors that I have tried to suggest earlier, when the Madagascar crisis brought de Gaulle's indignation to the boiling-point.

For five months on end, from the beginning of May to the end of September 1942, the Franco-British connection passed through a critical stage that was to leave deep wounds behind it, in spite of the good will shown by Pleven, Dejean and Billotte on the one hand and on the other Anthony Eden, Major Morton and the excellent Charles Peake, the (non-diplomatic) Foreign Office representative at Carlton Gardens, of whom de Gaulle always speaks with friendly commiseration; for at that time Peake was the buffer between Winston Churchill and Charles de Gaulle.

The Constable gives a penetrating description and explanation of Churchill's attitude during the summer of 1942:

> Everything depended on the Prime Minister. Now in his heart he could not bring himself to acknowledge the independence of Free France. Every time we came into conflict he treated our disagreement as a personal affair. It grieved and wounded him in proportion to the friendship that bound us the one to the other. This state of mind and of feeling, together with the reception of his political tactics, threw him into fits of rage* that sometimes shook our relations seriously.

But, adds de Gaulle, "at the same time other reasons combined to make this great man irascible," and he lists the set-backs suffered by the British forces at sea, in the Far East and in Cyrenaica, sometimes in conditions wounding for the country's pride, reverses that hurt Churchill "as an Englishman and as a fighter".[4]

At three in the morning of 5 May 1942 de Gaulle was woken by a man from a press-agency who told him that British troops had landed at Diégo Suarez, the chief naval base in Madagascar: Operation Ironclad was under way. A few hours

*The reader would be much mistaken if he were to suppose that the fits of anger were one-sided.

later Charles de Gaulle's amazement and fury were increased by the publication of a note in Washington stating that "the United States and Great Britain are in agreement that Madagascar should be restored to France as soon as the occupation of the island is no longer indispensable for the common cause of the Allied nations". Restored? It had been confiscated without the slightest notice being given to their French allies by the newcomers, although de Gaulle had been carrying on conversations with the Foreign Office only the day before.

The overweening and even provocative nature of various steps or reactions on the part of the Constable has frequently been stressed; so here it is but right to acknowledge that what had been done fully justified his anger. For it was not a question of a British or American plan of which de Gaulle had not been warned, either because of negligence or at the request of the United States. The action on Madagascar had been at the heart of Anglo-Gaullist thoughts and discussions for months, and it was with full knowledge and great obstinacy that those who were equally responsible for the Dakar failure now excluded the Fighting French from an easier operation and one that would strengthen the exiles' standing by increasing the territory they held and enlarge their impact on the Allies' global strategy (was it this aspect which lay behind the exclusion?).

Let us go back six months. On 8 December 1941, receiving Major Pierre Billotte in his office at Carlton Gardens as he did every day, General de Gaulle began with a few words about the Japanese attack on Pearl Harbour and the probable first moves in the war between Japan and America, and then he asked his chief of staff, "what he thought would be the strategic consequences arising from the affair," Billotte at once replied, "The Indian Ocean becomes a major theatre of operations, and Madagascar suddenly takes on considerable strategic importance: the Japanese will try to seize it." "Excellent," said de Gaulle. "Get to work."[5]

Two days after this, on 10 December, de Gaulle and Billotte spoke about the matter to General Alan Brooke, the new chief of the British Imperial General Staff; they agreed that bringing Madagascar over was essential. Six days later de Gaulle wrote to Churchill, stating his views. And on 11 February a plan for French intervention, aimed primarily at Majunga, was submitted to the British General Staff.

On 19 February de Gaulle wrote more urgently to the Prime Minister, stating that with regard to bringing the island over, the FFL would ask their allies only for air and sea support.[6] Lastly, on 9 April, the National Committee sent the Foreign Office an urgent letter, emphasizing the pressing importance of an operation that included the FFL, in view of the danger of a Japanese intervention.*

The Franco-British conversations had gone so far that the Prime Minister himself, in a note addressed to his chiefs of staff, had weighed the arguments for or against the participation of the FFL in the Madagascar landings, observing that he would not be in a hurry to dismiss it, since he remembered that "Cameroon had

*This step was more and more widely foreseen. At Vichy, Pierre Laval kindly informed the Japanese Ambassador that Governor-General Annet had been ordered to fire at sight on any British or Gaullist attackers. If it was a question of Americans he was to parley and try to make them desist. He was in no way to hinder any Japanese units that should happen to appear.

been brought over by twelve men". He added that in any event a mixed Franco-British operation should be avoided.

So in this matter, which concerned the coalition's interests to the highest degree but more immediately those of the Fighting French, General de Gaulle was flatly presented with a *fait accompli* and told by the newspapers that an essential part of the "Empire" had been conquered by the Allies. Once his first gust of rage was over, his reaction, recorded by Pierre Billotte, is picturesque enough to be worth the telling.

The General handed his chief of staff the draft of a note to Eden, for comment. Although Billotte was used to the General lashing out, he thought this example was of "exceptional violence" and he warned his chief against the risk of thus turning the best of his British interlocutors against him. "Read on to the end," said de Gaulle with a meaning smile. And indeed the letter ended 'signed: Billotte". Billotte claimed the right to add a "personal restatement of the matter"; de Gaulle agreed, but Billotte at once felt the General's "pleasure drop by half".

The result was a protest in the Quai d'Orsay style, which brought a "wholly negative" reply in the style of the Foreign Office. "'Let this be a lesson to you,' said de Gaulle to me at that point. 'There are times when you can appear with your cup of tea in your hand and get results: they are rare. Today you ought to have brandished your sword in every line, thrusting and cutting; indeed perhaps you ought even to have had a tank to reinforce your argument.'"[7]

Charles de Gaulle waited six days before answering Eden's invitation, sent as early as 6 May, to come and talk the matter over. On 12 May the British minister candidly acknowledged that he ought to have warned de Gaulle. "But," he added, "we were afraid you would want to take part in the operation." De Gaulle did not even trouble to remind him that this was a strange kind of fear, since what was concerned was a joint project; he merely replied, "If the present conditions continue, we shall fall apart."

The British Foreign Secretary then stated that Great Britain had no designs on Madagascar and wanted the French administration to go on functioning. "Which French administration?" interrupted de Gaulle. He was told that Washington had it in mind to negotiate with the Vichy Governor-General, Annet, who would continue to administer the island; the newcomers would confine themselves to Diégo Suarez.

In consideration of this, said Mr Eden, it was the British government's wish that the Free French should exercise authority over the island. De Gaulle urged him to give official assurance of this and he obtained the publication of a communiqué which proclaimed the British government's intention of seeing "the French National Committee playing its due part in the administration of the liberated territory".

But the communiqué remained a dead letter. The British met with strong resistance at Diégo Suarez, which they took after forty-eight hours of fighting; after this they did no more than occupy the conquered base, letting Governor Annet run the island as a whole. When the French National Committee decided to send Colonel Pechkoff to Diégo Suarez to push things forward and obtain for the Free French the "due part" which had been acknowledged as theirs in May, he was quite simply forbidden to go there.

During May there came news of considerable importance for the Free French: out of the 1200 Vichy defenders of Diégo Suarez, 930 had asked to join the Free French as opposed to less than a tenth at Beirut the year before. This sign of a most significant change in people's minds was censored on the BBC.

Whatever London's "intentions" may have been, the pressure of Washington was in favour of the status quo, and six months had to pass before the power of Vichy was banished from the great island – to which one day, as we shall see, Roosevelt had the idea of sending an unexpected governor: Charles de Gaulle.

At the beginning of June 1942 it was felt that de Gaulle was at the end of his tether: this example of "Albion's perfidy" had struck him all the more grievously since he was just getting over a severe bout of malaria.* Those immediately around de Gaulle closed ranks and did everything they could to conceal the General's illness.

On 6 June, therefore, during an interview with the Soviet Ambassador Bogomolov, the General asked whether, should the occasion arise, the USSR would offer hospitality to himself, the French National Committee, and the forces at his disposal. The same day he sent five of the men who formed the framework of Free France in various parts of the world, from Beirut to Brazzaville and from Fort-Lamy to Nouméa (Catroux, Larminat, Eboué, Leclerc and d'Argenlieu), a moving telegram in which he told them not only of his reaction to the Diégo Suarez attack but also of his suspicions about Anglo-American designs on Dakar and the Niger loop, where Free France might be treated in the same manner. And he added: "If my suspicions prove to be justified I shall not resign myself to remaining associated with the Anglo-Saxon powers. It would seem to be a breach of faith to continue our direct co-operation with them". In that event, the General went on, we should have to "gather as best we can in the territories we have liberated. Hold these territories. Maintain no relations of any kind with the Anglo-Saxons, inform the French nation and world-wide public opinion. I believe that this would be the finest means of obliging imperialism to fall back, should the occasion arise."[8]

It was a curious message and one that must have made many of those to whom it was addressed wonder what was happening to their leader. It is clear that Charles de Gaulle was not quite himself: excessive emphasis in the style, vagueness in the information and the outlook, and even more surprising, blunders in the writing. When, three months before this, at the time of the Muselier affair, the "secret will" was drawn up, de Gaulle may have supposed that London was "liquidating" him. But his reaction then remained secret.

Now at the beginning of June 1942 his closest ally had just given him this *coup de Jarnac*;** but the expansion of his international connections and his increasing number of followers in France itself had so strengthened his bargaining power that the Foreign Office had been obliged to withdraw. There was the danger that this SOS might gravely disturb his most faithful and distant companions, who, in their remote posts, were less well informed: this was one of the times when the Con-

*The disease was to affect de Gaulle again in Algiers in 1944.
**Ordinarily understood as a bad blow. (trs.)

stable at war was lacking in strength. As soon as the body grows weak, the burden becomes heavy.

But all at once a brilliant stroke give him back both hope and energy: at a small fort in the desert of Cyrenaica called Bir Hakeim, a Free French brigade commanded by General Koenig (de Gaulle had managed to oblige the British to let it take part in the Eighth Army's campaign in those parts) suddenly reminded the Western world of the fighting value of those French who were carrying on with the war. For the first time since June 1940 there they were confronting the finest units of the Wehrmacht, commanded by Rommel, the greatest fighting general of his time.

General Ritchie had entrusted them with a sacrificial mission, that of holding the south of the front for a week, to save the mass of his forces from the threat of being surrounded by Rommel's immensely powerful and rapid advance. Koenig and his 3300 men held out from 27 May to 11 June against forces three times their strength, arousing a blaze of enthusiasm in the Anglo-American press. On 10 June de Gaulle cabled Koenig, who was preparing to bring three quarters of his brigade back to the British lines, "I must tell you, and you must tell your men, that the whole of France is watching you and that you are the country's pride."

It was quite another de Gaulle that Winston Churchill welcomed at Downing Street, wholly different from the de Gaulle who, four days earlier, had thought of withdrawing to the USSR (if not to Brazzaville). Churchill at once, and with great emotion, paid tribute to what Koenig's men had just accomplished at Bir Hakeim ("one of the finest feats of arms this war"), and then regretted that his guest should have been "hurt" by the procedure that had been adopted in order to meet "with less resistance", adding, as Eden had done a month before, that Britain had no designs whatever upon the island.

"I am France's friend," asserted Churchill. "I want a great France, for the peace and security of Europe." "That is so. You proved it by continuing to back France after Vichy's armistice. Our names are attached to that policy. If you give it up, it will be bad for you just as it will be bad for us."

"But you are not my only ally." "The American policy towards us is atrocious." "With Roosevelt, never try to rush things. See how I give way and then rise up again." "Because you have a solid State behind you, a united nation, a great army. For my part, I am too poor to afford bending." At this Churchill burst out, "One day we shall be in France! Perhaps next year.* In any case, we shall be there together. I shall not leave you in the lurch!"[9]

Six weeks later, before leaving for Africa and the Levant, Charles de Gaulle once more came to see the Prime Minister, who was still just as cordial. But a few pricks in the conversation foretold that clouds were gathering again. They were speaking of the Levant.

De Gaulle: "Spears is very busy there. He makes difficulties for us." Churchill (irritated): "Spears has a great many enemies. But he has one friend, and that is

*The plans that were being studied with the American General Staff did not exclude a landing in 1943.

the Prime Minister." And he added that the independence Free France had granted Syria and the Lebanon did not satisfy the inhabitants. De Gaulle in his turn retorted, "They are quite as satisfied as those in Iraq, Palestine or Egypt!"* Then he moved on to Madagascar: "If you had let us land at Majunga while you were looking after Diégo Suarez, the business would have been over long ago. But instead of that, you waste your time negotiating with the Vichy governor." Churchill: "He is a bad man, that governor." De Gaulle: "When you deal with Vichy, you deal with Hitler. Hitler is a bad man." With this the two champions parted, good friends.

But before he set out for a journey to the East General de Gaulle played the central part in a singular Franco-American comedy which made the relations between Fighting France and its allies even more difficult.

The date was 23 July 1942. Five days earlier General George Marshall, chief of staff of the American army, and Admiral King, his opposite number in the navy, had landed in London, where they found General Eisenhower, already appointed as Supreme Commander of Inter-Allied operations on the Euro-African Front. This gathering of great American chiefs made people suppose that the coming months might see tremendous events.

De Gaulle was not the last to take notice of it. Seeing that Washington had recently made a few steps towards him (Ambassador Winant's offer of associating him with the Inter-Allied strategic talks, the agreement of 9 July which named him as the "symbol" of France's presence in the battle, the appointment of Admiral Stark and General Bolté to the FFL, and the presence of these two officers and of Eisenhower at the military ceremonies on July 14 in London) he wondered about the reasons for this development.

He and Pierre Billotte, his chief of staff, convinced that a great undertaking was at hand, had just finished drawing up a plan for a landing between the Pas-de-Calais and the Cotentin** that would call for some fifty divisions, two of which would be French, and that could take place at the beginning of 1943.

The leader of the Fighting French therefore asked to see General Marshall, who suggested a meeting on 23 July. When de Gaulle came to the rendezvous, suite 429 at Claridge's, he observed that the personal conversation he had expected had been changed into a conference: de Gaulle had with him only his ADC François Coulet (who acted as interpreter), but grouped round Marshall he saw Admiral King, Eisenhower and his second, Mark Clark, Admiral Stark and General Bolté. Rarely has a meeting been more unsuccessful or even indeed unfortunate.

Certainly, the worthy General Marshall (who seems never to have shared FDR's prejudices against Charles de Gaulle) tried to create a favourable atmosphere by

*These countries were still under English "influence".

**The peninsula of Normandy. (trs.)

speaking warmly of the great deeds at Bir Hakeim and the good conduct of the French troops in action on the various fronts. Then he stopped, and fell silent. De Gaulle, who had obviously come to hear an account of the plans for opening a second front, sat there waiting. A long silence ensued. Clearly, the Americans were only there to have a look at the mysterious General de Gaulle in the flesh, and to see whether he was like an aurochs, a statue of Napoleon or a Fascist chief; and they wished to confine the interview to the ceremonial level.

De Gaulle then tried to get the "conference" in motion again. Would information on the French military situation interest the Americans? Marshall and his companions could scarcely say no. De Gaulle launched into an account filled with figures which could only seem ridiculous to his audience: 6000 men here, 10000 there, 20000 elsewhere. Eisenhower no longer counted in units but in divisions.

General de Gaulle was aware of it. He therefore passed on to a more exact statement, which seemed to surprise his listeners, of the Free French activity in France itself, both in the gathering of intelligence and in military action, and of the services that these organizations and networks could provide in support of a "concomitant action".

Another silence.

Once more de Gaulle, trying to revive this conversation that had promised so much and that was becoming a monologue, proposed that he should explain the French plans "for the opening of a second front" to the American visitors. The leader of the Free French began a description of the plan, a copy of which had been sent to General Eisenhower the day before, who said that he had already studied it. De Gaulle particularly wished to emphasize the part that the people of France would have to play in this event, and the fact that the "Allies would therefore have to adhere to certain conditions".

"Another silence" says the report written at Carlton Gardens. However naturally taciturn Marshall might be, the two Frenchmen were compelled to feel that something was amiss. Charles de Gaulle therefore broke off the session after half an hour. Why this fiasco? Simply because the Americans, who a month before had been in favour of a landing in France towards the beginning of 1943, according to a plan not dissimilar to de Gaulle's, had just learnt that their British colleagues had won acceptance for a strategy based on southern Europe and the Mediterranean.

In the event of a landing in France, Marshall and his companions looked upon cooperation with Fighting France as indispensable: hence the improvement in Gaullo-American relations during the last three months. But by postponing operations in western Europe and by deciding on the North African and the Mediterranean plan the Constable and his men were reduced to marginal importance.

The decision to abandon Operation Sledgehammer against Normandy or at least to postpone it until later, preferring Operation Gymnast in North Africa, was only taken officially at Washington the next day, 24 July. But Marshall and King knew perfectly well what to think about it; very soon after their arrival in London they perceived that for once Roosevelt had given way to Churchill and that the North African path had been accepted. This was the cause for their extreme embarrassment when they were confronted with a man who had been led to believe he was at the heart of the concern and who, as they knew, was about to be flung to the margins once more.

Marshall was a man of too great a quality not to be aware of the uneasy aspect of their respective situations. His silence was the outward expression of his troubled mind, caught as he was between the duty of operational secrecy (particularly with these talkative French, who had prattled too much before Dakar) and his fellow-feeling for this man who, whether he liked him or not, was his brother in arms.

The failure of this strange conference-monologue was so obvious that when he came to write the report (or correct Coulet's version of it) General de Gaulle thought proper to add inverted commas to the last word: "the General withdrew after half an hour of 'conversation'":[10] he had to wait nearly eight months after this interrupted monologue before the leaders of the armada saw fit to "converse" with him at last.

On 5 August 1942, then, Charles de Gaulle took off once more for the East; there he was to spend a few weeks that proved to be one long storm, although he had gathered the impression of "an enthusiastic welcome" from the inhabitants. To be sure, this flamboyant, eloquent and daring figure, the steward of a great historical and cultural tradition, could not fail to arouse the interest of the Middle-Eastern populace, who, in the unfathomable confusion of the war could only clearly make out the appearance of heroes endowed with a certain degree of charisma or likelihood of success. But the crowds spoken of in the *Mémoires de guerre*, and more discreetly in Catroux's book, to say nothing of Spears's*, had certain reasons for not letting their fervour overflow at the sight of the Free French leaders, not so much because of the hostile propaganda emanating from the local British authorities but because of the disappointment felt by the Syrians and Lebanese for the Gaullists' policy for the region.

It will be remembered that when he entered Syria on 8 June 1941 General Catroux put out a proclamation (carefully revised by de Gaulle) addressed to the peoples of the Levant and promising them independence, which was to be accompanied by a treaty of alliance. Four months later, in a document once more revised (and very closely revised) by his chief, Catroux did indeed proclaim Syria's independence; and two months later still, that of the Lebanon.

But since these events had taken place, Fighting France's policy in the Levant had been like a tango: one step forward, two steps back, if not three. It must be admitted that in the Levant, with the wounds of the short war of June 1941 scarcely healed and the country far from pacified by the contrasting decisions of Acre and Cairo, the conflicts assumed a character that was all the more difficult to understand because they were being carried on on the edge of the Egyptian-Libyan desert, the scene of the fighting between the British Eighth Army and the Afrika Korps, one of the battles in which the outcome of the war was at stake.

Much of the ill-temper with which the British tried to force their view on the Gaullists arose from the irritation caused by these side-issues, this squabbling over

**Fulfilment of a Mission.*

Syria or Beirut, at a time when not far away, at the gates of Cairo, so many men were dying barring the way to Rommel. If the German general crossed the Nile, what would there be left of the profits and losses marked up in the Levant?

From Damascus to Jerusalem, innumerable conflicts were superimposed upon one another in those days! The quarrel which brought the Arab desire for emancipation up against the English and the French colonial powers. The quarrel which opposed these two "allies", the one in Cairo, the other in Beirut, welded together by long-standing grudges and resentments. The quarrel which complicated the relations between the Foreign Office, which tried to implement the de Gaulle-Lyttelton *modus vivendi* so as not to alienate Fighting France, and the Colonial Office's specialists in eastern affairs, who were intensely eager to ensure an unrivalled *pax Britannica* in that turbulent region at last. The quarrel waged by the many remaining Vichy civil servants against Fighting France. And lastly the quarrel which brought about the exchange of angry letters between Catroux and de Gaulle, some of them particularly vivid.

In the midst of all these conflicts, the appearance of the Constable, armed with distrust and exasperated by the Madagascar affair, could not fail to produce some additional outbursts.

Charles de Gaulle hastened to give an account, in his own manner, of his grievances and alarms to the new British Minister of State in the Near East, Richard Casey, an Australian and Lyttelton's successor. Their conversation on 8 August 1942 in Cairo was like an echo of the meeting, a year before, that had brought de Gaulle and Captain Lyttelton into collision, shattering Franco-British relations before ending in a reasonable but belated agreement. The only difference between the interview of 1941 and that of 1942 was that the second did not degenerate into a "scene" as had the first, but, according to the Australian minister, "into an exchange of bellowings".

It is true that Casey had a somewhat particular notion of diplomacy. He must have been told that his visitor was not at all easy-going where the rights and responsibilities of France were concerned, but he at once declared to de Gaulle that elections would have to be organized in Syria and the Lebanon. De Gaulle (who, writing to Pleven at the same period, said he was convinced that sooner or later the Syrian and Lebanese electors would have to be consulted) reacted as though the Australian had spat in his face:

> Elections? Do you organize elections in Egypt?* Do you think the British authorities have nothing more urgent to do in the East than shape policy in the countries administered by France? Beating Rommel, for example? You are in a position to force us to leave the Levant by rousing the Arabs' xenophobia but your only gain will be an even more unstable position for yourselves there, and an ineradicable resentment on the part of the French nation!

This rough treatment of the British representative was all the more mistimed by

*In Egypt, yes. But it was a country that already had twenty years of democratic experience. There was no mention of them in Jordan or Iraq, other countries under English influence.

Charles de Gaulle since Casey was busy preparing the dismissal of Sir Edward Spears, whose activities seemed to him almost as maddening as they did to de Gaulle or Catroux. This challenge flung at his minister's head could not but fix Churchill in his stubborn determination to keep Spears.

In any case, were the Free French leaders right in seeing Sir Edward as a monomaniac plotting against them? From his own account of these extraordinary events it appears that Spears was then much concerned with removing John Bagot Glubb (whom King Abdallah of Jordan was to give the title of Pasha) from the Levant on the grounds that this officer "was rousing the natives against the representatives of France". This was a piece of information that was not then at the disposal of the ingenious General Catroux, who, dining one evening with Churchill in Cairo, suggested that to get rid of Sir Edward he should elevate him to the House of Lords. The Prime Minister was intransigent.

Anyone who wishes to understand these quarrels among allies must make at least three observations. First, that the British, bearing almost the entire burden of the war and at that time fighting a decisive battle in the Western Desert, needed Arab good-will; were there not many people (beginning with King Farouk) in Cairo, that centre of the Arab World, who reckoned on a German victory and who were ready to strew palms under the tracks of Rommel's tanks?* Beyond the rivalry between imperialists, there was therefore a wider interest, and one that the Fighting French leaders may have under-estimated.

But from a settlement in the Hauran to a village in the Chouf, de Gaulle and his men were defending something quite other than colonial positions. They were clinging to what were still absurdly small territories scattered over the world; they had very thin and widely dispersed forces; they were continually being denounced by Vichy as British agents; and they could not yield anything, above all to Britain, without making a present to Laval and his friends, without disavowing themselves as the Fighting French, and without starting a process of decline that would have destroyed their very reason for existence.

This was clear to men like Churchill and above all Eden, who were anxious to see a strong France at their side when peace came – if only to confront Stalin or even Roosevelt, both of them eager, though by different methods, to do away with the empires of the nineteenth century and to put Europe in its proper place.

Third observation: however honourable the aims of Gaullist strategy in the long term may have been, its application in the Levant was marked both by an irritating stridency and by verbal excesses that could not but offend the most valuable allies. Thus the American consul-general in Beirut, Gwynn, was so shocked by what the Constable had to say that he sent Washington a report according to which de Gaulle had spoken to him of "declaring war on Britain".

To be sure, the legal situation was complex. France had acknowledged the independence of Syria and the Lebanon; yet at the same time France still held the League of Nations mandate, and it was difficult to declare that this mandate was abolished without reference to the organization that had entrusted its exercise to

*At that time Rommel's prestige was immense. In Cairo the boys used to shout "*Yiahia R'mel, Yiahia*" meaning "Long live" and *R'mel* "sand".

the holder. Yet who, in 1942, could assert that the League still existed? De Gaulle, unlike Vichy, had refused to leave it, and he was quite ready to plead this abstract legal bond in order to claim "responsibilities" for Fighting France.

From this there arose an attitude that tended to justify the supervision that France still exercised over these "independent" states' defence, diplomacy, exchanges, currency, police and teaching; an attitude which was difficult to convince an exceptionally subtle and acute political society to accept.

In the telegrams he sent in those days to his associates on the London Committee – Pleven, Cassin, Dejean – de Gaulle varied his philippics against England with professions of faith in the political harmony between Fighting France and the Arabs. Thus on 17 August he wrote from Damascus: "never would French activity with regard to Syria and the Lebanon have been carried out more easily and more usefully, but for the interference of the British. Everyone here wishes for the active presence of France. The disturbances come only from Spears. General Catroux's authority is unquestioned." And a few days later, from Beirut, after a journey that had led him from Damascus to Soueida, Palmyra, Deir-ez-Zor, Aleppo, Homs and Latakia: "Everywhere a real and exceptional enthusiasm in favour of France was evident." On the same day, in Beirut, he drew up a memorandum which listed all his complaints about British "interference" and ended on a threatening note about these activities which "ruined the very possibility of sincere and effective collaboration with the British in the Levant", and which might well force Fighting France "to draw the necessary consequences".

And in a telegram of 2 September to Pleven and Dejean he said that he was "deeply uneasy about the future of Franco-British relations", "that it is impossible for us to accept [their strategy] without failing in our duty" because it was aimed at nothing less than establishing "a condominium" which would then lead to a "British domination".

Even more significant of these obsessions and this intense aggressivness in his telegram of 5 September to the unfortunate Dejean.

> The attitude I have adopted with regard to the British government in the Levant is the only one that corresponds to our dignity and our responsibilities. The stupid greed of our allies here is checked by one thing alone, and that thing is the fear of pushing us too far. We shall not increase in our importance by humbling ourselves. I mean to be upheld by the Commissioner for African Affairs* in what is once again a difficult task. If you do not feel able to do this, it is your duty to tell me so.[11]

Several other factors helped to inflame this quarrel. In a letter of 12 September to Pleven and Dejean, de Gaulle very subtly defined two of them: "the alarm on the one hand and the irritation of the British" arose from the fact "that we have brought the Eastern question on to the Inter-Allied diplomatic terrain. To be sure, I am sorry that Mr Churchill should have been hurt at finding that the Americans had been made aware of it through me", but "we are strangled by the mutes of the

*That is to say Dejean.

British seraglio". On the other, observed the General "what worries London is my presence in the French Empire at a time when important events, either in France or in the French Empire, are about to take place."

It was clear to the leader of the Fighting French (who was better informed than was for a long while supposed about the Allied plans aimed at North Africa) that Churchill would like to be able to keep him under control and supervise him at this critical time: ever since Roosevelt had induced the Prime Minister to keep de Gaulle in ignorance, there was no telling how he would react.

This presentiment of Churchill's anxiety gave de Gaulle an advantage over the Prime Minister, and he let him wait for a few weeks. Had Churchill asked him to come back to London as early as the beginning of September? Then he would not return until the twenty-fifth, after a long tour in French Equatorial Africa intended to emphasize that the leader of the Fighting French was not only the guest of a foreign government but also a sovereign in his own lands.

Before leaving Beirut Charles de Gaulle took care to further the quarrel with London by talking to Wendell Willkie, the Republican whom Roosevelt had beaten in the 1940 presidential elections, who had been sent on a mission round the world by the President. On his way to the USSR, Willkie stopped at Beirut, and he asked to meet this controversial French general.

The encounter between Willkie and de Gaulle was very lively and the interchange very full; de Gaulle thought the American "an agreeable, warm kind of fellow".

As the meeting took place in the office of the French High Commissioner in the Levant, furnished in the Empire style, Willkie suggested that de Gaulle took himself for Napoleon; and as he was dressed in white, which is usual in those latitudes, the American spoke of the splendours of Versailles; and when a colleague mentioned the General's "mission" Willkie thought it amusing to refer to Joan of Arc. All the clichés that the Roosevelt polemic had fed upon!

Among these observations apparently intended to show that he was well informed, Willkie, who had warned de Gaulle that their conversation would be the subject of a report to Roosevelt, asked some intelligent questions about the causes of the Anglo-French disagreement in the Levant and about what could be done to ease it. When he asked whether the British had designs upon certain French possessions, the General replied, "If they did have designs, their attitude would be in no way different." Before they parted Willkie assured de Gaulle of his sympathy and of his hostility to diplomatic relations between Washington and Vichy.

Yet London did take a decision that provided a chance of breaking the deadlock. On 9 September Anthony Eden summoned Dejean to the Foreign Office to inform him that as the negotiations with the Vichy Governor of Madagascar had been broken off, the British forces were about to seize Majunga and take complete control of the island; in consideration of this, the French National Committee would be asked to assume the administration of Madagascar at once. The English minister added that his government wished "to re-open negotiations with the General".

Was this important concession with regard to Madagascar only intended to cover either fresh encroachment in the Levant or a most significant silence about the great operations then in hand? The de Gaulle of those days, a rabid Anglophobic, was inclined to believe it; though he did tell Pleven and Dejean, "Yet for all that I cannot believe that Mr Eden's kind intentions amount to nothing more than a manoeuvre." And he decided to return to London, after a majestic circuit through his African domains.

But before landing in London he harassed his representatives with imperious demands, as though he wanted to make Churchill's reception of him as discordant as possible. From Brazzaville on 19 September, addressing Pleven and Dejean, who had told him that the British government thought of suspending the installation of the Gaullist administration in Madagascar because of some anti-British remarks made by him in Beirut, he sent off this verbal blast: "It is perfectly monstrous that Churchill and Eden should appear to be going back on their word on the pretext that I did not come when they whistled. If Britain does not carry out its engagements, we have neither the desire nor the right to remain in relations with it." And the same day he asked Tixier to halt all steps being taken to have the French National Committee recognized by Washington, exclaiming "France is not a candidate sitting an examination!" That was the Constable's state of mind when he landed in London on 25 September 1942, his hand on his sword.

He was no longer quite the flayed de Gaulle, quivering with pain and shame, "suffering for France" and wearing the defeat and the Armistice around his neck that Lady Spears described two years earlier. He had grown; he had become stronger. He was now half way up the slope, knowing that he had overcome the worst but that his position was still so dangerous that he looked around him with an anxious and therefore implacable eye.

He was no longer a man who could be easily pushed aside, either by Roosevelt or even by Churchill. Although he was coming to see the person who had allowed him to exist, it was not in order to ask his permission to survive but in order to insist that he should be given the rights that belonged to France, no longer as a daring vanguard and a historical symbol, but quite simply as a nation, until the State should be restored.

It was at half-past five in the afternoon of 30 September that Charles de Gaulle, accompanied by René Pleven, was received at 10 Downing Street by a Prime Minister already in an angry mood. Churchill had Anthony Eden and Desmond Morton with him and at first he tried to remain calm by keeping to politeness: he thanked the General for having come to London at his request.

"I received the compliment," writes de Gaulle, "with a humour equal to that which inspired it." But in the *Mémoires* the account of the interview is sprinkled with such words as "confrontation", "diatribes", and a "bitter and passionate tone" from the Prime Minister. And in a telegram to Catroux, written shortly after the visit to Downing Street, he speaks of a "very bad meeting" at which "the British ministers adopted a tone of cold and passionate anger that provoked harsh replies on our side."[12]

However informative these passages may be, in order to gauge the importance and the unprecedented violence of the interchange, the official British account, as it is published by François Kersaudy, must be consulted.[13] It is an irreplaceable document on the relations between the British and French leaders in 1942.*

Churchill, in a voice that was still restrained, opened by reproaching his visitor for not having managed to avoid "outbursts" during his stay in Syria. To this de Gaulle retorted by bringing forward examples of "unhappy Franco-British rivalry". There was "no question of rivalry" asserted Churchill: his argument was that London could not allow its military positions in the Near East to be threatened because the promises made to the Syrian people (particularly of elections) had not been kept. And he did not hesitate to speak of the possibility "of risings".

The General, whose tone was beginning to rise, replied by emphasizing the Syrian and Lebanese governments' refusal of any such steps: "they would resign if their hands were forced".** But Churchill came back to his idea of tension between the French authorities in the Levant and the "local population"; and from this he cruelly argued that his government was in no hurry "to open the way for similar difficulties in other important theatres of the war, as for example, Madagascar".

The challenge was open and direct. De Gaulle took it up violently, giving an historical account of the *fait accompli* in Madagascar – a region where he was on sounder ground than he was where public opinion in Syria was concerned – and observing that Britain, which on 13 May 1942 had promised to entrust the island's administration to Free France, was now trying to evade its given word. "This," said he, "is a very serious situation, and one that calls the co-operation between France and England into question."

Churchill interrupted, "Between General de Gaulle and Britain." Here we must move from the British account to the General's, which gives a better notion of the "fury" which seized the Prime Minister: for at this point he went on "You claim you are France! You are not France! I do not recognize you as France! Where is France?"

> "Why do you discuss these questions with me, if I am not France?"
>
> "All that has been put down in writing. You are not France. You are Fighting France."
>
> "I am acting in France's name. I am fighting on the same side as England but not for England. I speak in the name of France and I am responsible to France. The French nation is convinced that I speak for France and will uphold me as long as that belief continues."
>
> "I am still trying to get a clear idea of what France is. There are other sections and other aspects of France that may take on greater importance. I had hoped that we could fight side by side. But my hopes have been disappointed because you are so aggressive that not content with struggling against Germany, Italy and Japan, you want to take on Britain and America."
>
> "I take that as a joke, but it is not in the best taste. If there is any man the British have nothing to complain of, he is certainly myself."

*The following account refers to these sources.

**Certainly: the men appointed by fighting France had no desire to be brought into question by the electorate.

"In fact you are your own worst enemy. We are bearing a very heavy burden because of France. Things cannot go on like this."

"I have made mistakes. Everyone makes mistakes. Unfortunately, you have isolated me and kept me in the background."

"It is very difficult indeed for us to work with you. Wherever you have been you have sown disorder. The situation is now critical. This saddens me, because I have a great admiration for your personality and for what you have done in the past. But I cannot look upon you as a comrade or a friend."

"The French in France would be very much surprised if they could hear that. I owe my reputation in France to the fact that I wanted to carry on the struggle side by side with you. But it is for that very reason that we must give the French people the feeling that Fighting France is being treated as a genuine ally and not as a tool of the English."

"I think you made a grave mistake in rejecting the friendship we offered and in breaking off a collaboration that would have been very useful to you . . . You have absolutely not helped us at all. Instead of making war on Germany you have made war on England and you have been the chief obstacle to an effective collaboration with Great Britain and the United States."

"I shall draw the necessary conclusions."

When the visitors had gone, Churchill said to Eden that he was "sorry for the man, he was such a fool." And for his part Eden told one of his colleagues, "I have never seen anything like it in the way of rudeness since Ribbentrop."[14]

Yet whatever one may think of the various attitudes of those concerned, the "cold anger" of the British or the "coarseness" of General de Gaulle, the interview tells us a great deal. It is usually said that among the "Great" very little is spoken. In this hand-to-hand encounter at Downing Street, passions, trickery, resentment and nostalgia were all present as they might be in the works of the great political playwrights (but even so one is not required to venture upon the traditional reference to Shakespeare).

In any case, everything has been said. And however unshakeable de Gaulle might be, having heard Winston Churchill say that "there are other sections and other aspects of France that may take on greater importance", when he left 10 Downing Street he obviously had to make an effort to walk at René Pleven's side with the same assured pace as before. Had Roosevelt succeeded in forcing a different French policy upon Churchill, a policy based on an "anti-German Vichy"?

When he presided over the meeting of the National Committee the next day ("the most moving of those I attended," as Jacques Soustelle recalls[15]) he told his colleagues that he would hand in his resignation, if his removal "would serve the interests of France". There was an overwhelming refusal. He was to persevere.

The danger, on the eve of what was obviously being planned, was none the less great. Was it not possible that the Allies would take over the responsibility for France, entirely disregarding Fighting France? Charles de Gaulle was only too aware of this danger.

CHAPTER TWENTY-NINE

But What is the Resistance?

It was not because he uttered the word as early as 18 June 1940 that Charles de Gaulle had grasped what the "resistance" was or could be. For this tank-officer, a gifted strategist who had not needed much time to master political problems, the ideas of secret war, of guerilla and the maquis were not very plain.

The Constable was not a man to neglect the "psychological forces" that his master Ardant du Picq placed at the centre of the action of war.* He was intensely aware of the "political" dimensions of war and he had come to understand how much warlike nationalism there might be in a revolution, from the soldiers of the Year II to the Commune. But as he saw it, this resistance which he wished to set ablaze was in the first place to be that of a shattered, scattered military body, which, gathered together and given heart again, would reveal the permanence of the French nation, ensuring its presence among the conquerors and its right to rebuild Europe and the world.

As we have seen, neither he nor André Dewavrin (Passy), to whom he had straight away entrusted the Free French "special services", wasted much time before they attended to the home front. Yet even so, for nearly eighteen months and in spite of the feats of "Rémy" and "Saint-Jacques", of Estienne d'Orves' sacrifice and the missions of André Weil-Curiel they remained poorly informed about what was happening in France and the first Resistance envoys to London, especially Christian Pineau, were surprised (in March 1942) by the inadequacy of their information. It was not until André Philip was appointed Commissioner of the Interior in July 1942 that the symbiosis began to function. A real exchange of intelligence and services was organized between the staff in London and those who were carrying on the struggle against the occupiers in its various forms.

Charles de Gaulle had reasons for looking upon "interior affairs" with a certain mistrust. The first was that he was not very well acquainted with the terrain, having spent little time on it. His service had been chiefly in Paris and abroad. During the two years he was in command at Metz he had paid more attention to engines and tank-tracks than to the working-class or local elections. And it cannot be said that the six years in Paris allowed him to feel the heart-beat of French society. For an officer he had an uncommon amount of information about the more obscure sides of parliamentary life, acquired during his stormy campaign for armoured divisions. But although he had formed an opinion on political leaders he knew little about their electors, those who were now facing the occupying forces.

*Charles Ardant du Picq, the nineteenth-century military writer who had such an influence over the High Command in 1914. (trs.)

Furthermore, until 1942 in any case, the Resistance was a world whose motions generally escaped him, and whose mechanisms were almost entirely foreign to him. He knew how to tell Catroux, Larminat, Leclerc or even Pleven to move or not to move, just as he knew by intuition how to deal with Churchill or Molotov. But how was he to handle men whose names, faces, field and means of action were unknown to him, and whose motives were often so different from his if not in the long term antagonistic – these men who, risking their life at every moment, had reasons for doing so only as they saw fit?

And then there were those British (and later American) "interferences" which as he saw it confused the issue. He already found Spears' interventions in Syrian affairs impossible to bear; so what of these British agents whom he perpetually felt to be so active on the very soil of France itself? Even worse: they were active with the help of a very great many French citizens who, for reasons that he refused to consider noble or disinterested – or by mere chance – had preferred to work against the occupant with the more efficient, smoother-running services of His Majesty. These unwarrantable interferences in what he considered a national task drove him to distraction.

When one is considering the French Resistance, one must carefully distinguish its constituent parts; otherwise one falls into confusion and there is a danger of failing to appreciate the role of Charles de Gaulle and of those, from Passy to Moulin, from Rémy to Brossolette, from Bingen to Serreulles and from Manuel to Vallon, who formed the framework of the Gaullist resistance.

First, one needs to distinguish between the interior and the exterior. Until the summer of 1942 (when André Philip, coming from France, replaced André Diethelm at the head of what were called the "interior" services) the links between Carlton Gardens (later Hill Street)* and the Resistance were still weak. People were feeling their way, trying to make one another out; and there was not much in common between those who escaped the Vichy police in the alleys of Lyons or the Gestapo in the neighbourhood of Massy-Palaiseau, and the gentlemen in Mayfair.

Secondly, between the civil and the military. It is here one sees the remains of the General Staff conservatism that de Gaulle's mind had retained. For de Gaulle there could be no confusion between the duties entrusted to an officer like himself and civilian tasks in which politics, propaganda and deception mingle; the first being carried on in Duke Street, the others in Hill Street. But de Gaulle was too intelligent a man not to confess one day that he was mistaken; towards the end of 1942 the whole of the services centred upon the national territory were at last, after a great loss of time, rearranged, the BCRAM (*Bureau central de renseignement et d'action militaires*) becoming the BCRA, endowed with an NM (*non militaire*) section.

It is not only military traditions that separate "intelligence" from "action". And it is true that the search for information and the execution of action rarely call for the same qualities and therefore the same men.

*The address of the Commissariat for the Interior.

As for information, we have already mentioned the discussion in 1940 between British experts and French beginners haphazardly recruited in London. The British suggested training "specialists"; Passy held the opposite view that men remaining in their family, social and professional context would provide more reliable intelligence than agents who were professionals and who were therefore cut off from their sources. Passy had his way, thus helping to strengthen the body of the Resistance in relation to its brain in London and also to establish a purely French element as opposed to the British means and techniques.

The tensions between the networks of the British and those belonging to Passy first became apparent in de Gaulle's mind and then in everyday reality. They were all the more obvious since Major Buckmaster ultimately controlled many French agents and he did his best to divert them from Free France and enlist them in his own service, doing so without much delicacy: he behaved in this way to Jean Moulin. Although the Confrérie Notre-Dame (CND) network founded by Gilbert Renault, alias Raymond, alias Roulier, alias Jean-Luc, alias Rémy, was pre-eminently that of Free France, the Alliance network, which was founded in October 1940 and with which one associates the names of Loustaunau-Lacau and Marie-Madeleine Méric (Fourcade) was primarily connected with the Intelligence Service and the Special Operations Executive (SOE). Which was the most effective? The fact is that every time the relations between Churchill and de Gaulle became strained, the communications between Passy's services and the continent became obstructed.

A distinction between "networks" and "movements" is no less necessary. The prime function of the first was the gathering and transmission of intelligence with a view to action and possibly to the action itself. They existed chiefly in the north zone, where the occupying forces, the target for Allied action, were stationed; they were strictly organized and divided into separate cells, and by their very nature they were connected with London, the point from which (whether it was a question of the British SOE or the French BCRA) the blows against the occupier and his allies were to be launched. The movements were less sharply defined, more political; they aimed at reanimating and invigorating public opinion as much as providing information or carrying out actions; yet some – Combat, Libération – possessed their "action" branch.

It is important to avoid confusion between networks and movements, but one must also distinguish between movements on the one hand and political parties and trade unions on the other: these began to revive from 1941 onwards* under the aegis of some one or other of the movements (Libération-Nord gathered socialist trade-unionists for the most part; Libération-Sud an increasing proportion of Communists), while others did so under a variety of shapes, masks or sets of initials. Although the CAS (Comité d'action socialiste) blended with the SFIO, the FTP (Francs-tireurs et partisans français) were not merely the military expression of the Communist Party, nor the Front National its political outward appearance: a considerable number of the clergy were to be found in it.

Here we must make another distinction, and one of the first importance: that

*The first activities, those of 1940, took place without reference to the parties.

between the south zone (called "free" or "unoccupied") and the north zone (or occupied), where the enemy was not the Vichy police but the Wehrmacht or the Gestapo. It is obvious that under the Vichy régime both networks and movements had greater scope for development and action than under that of the Nazis.

This is the basis for the theory put out by the supporters of Vichy, by the Americans, and twenty years later by Rémy himself, according to which Marshal Pétain was supposed to have been the first member of the Resistance in France, the signature of the Armistice having allowed a part of the country to be preserved from occupation, forming a territory from which the Resistance could be launched and the reconquest begun. Undoubtedly the two situations were different, if only because of the helpers found in Vichy: most of the official intelligence and counter-espionage networks there were anti-Nazi. Their first chiefs, Colonel Heurteaux, Colonel Rivet and Colonel Groussard, protected and then supplied the Allied networks before joining them, as did Colonel Paillole.

One of Hitler's guiding ideas in June 1940 had been to divide the French by imposing a different status on each zone. On 11 November 1942 the "private preserves" of Vichy were abolished (together with the illusions of the Marshal's followers): there were now only those who were undergoing the occupation and those who were carrying it out (accompanied by their agents). In this process the Resistance lost many of its members (beginning with Jean Moulin) but it gained an essential cohesion. It also slackened the police chain here and there in the north zone (neither the Wehrmacht nor the Gestapo could be stretched indefinitely, and more men were now needed to supervise the whole of France).

The fact remains that although history has been chiefly concerned with describing the figures and the movements of the south zone, perhaps because they were more colourful, the greater part of what the Resistance contributed to the cause of the liberation was accomplished in the north zone. The repression was more terrible in the north, but the spontaneous resistance was more determined and more zealous: direct occupation arouses greater heroism than masked oppression. It was above all in the north that there took place that general rising, that *levée en masse*, of the ordinary people which according to Christian Pineau gave the Resistance its true aspect.[1]

One should also note that observed from London the differences between north and south were not so radical as might be supposed: although it is true that there the Resistance was seen through its envoys, we must remember that of the four pioneer architects of the complex whole, Moulin, Pineau, Brossolette and Philip, two came from the north and two from the south. And that although Jean Moulin was appointed to unify the southern Resistance, he very soon concerned himself with the affairs of the north. This did not take place without irritating Passy. Even though the BCRA was partly demilitarized, it was chiefly directed at gathering intelligence about the army of occupation: therefore it worked mainly in the north. Moulin's activities in that direction caused disturbance.

This having been said, history cannot fail to record important differences: human relations, organizations, and ideology. Everything was more clear-cut in the north, more complex in the south, where tactics, ideas, connections and plans were infinitely varied.

Finally, from the moment the Third Reich unleashed its invasion of Soviet Russia on 22 June 1941, a considerable force in France was set free for action – that of the Communist Party, which was to play a vital role part.

For the French Communist party these were the days of the slogan "Neither Britain's soldiers with de Gaulle nor Germany's soldiers with Pétain!" It was then that Pierre Villon, who was to become the leader of the Front National, wrote in his notebooks:

> The pro-British must be thinking that it is dangerous to count on Hitler to safeguard their privileges [and that] they must have de Gaulle in reserve as a future dictator. What still seems to me lacking is a "substantial" weakening of England and America. But it is not absolutely necessary for the sovietization of Europe. As for Gaullism, it will be swept away and it will be useful to us if we give the country freedom, peace and bread (with butter on it) before Britain arrives to do so. And I cannot see Britain capable of managing a landing in France to liberate the country before the Germans rise up in revolt. In that case we shall not wait for de Gaulle to set up soviets.[2]

For six months the official leadership of the French Communist Party had gone so far as to make an attempt at collaboration with the occupying power, particularly in trying to induce the Nazis to authorize the publication of *L'Humanité* in Paris under their control. At the time of the great miners' strike in May and June 1941, which revealed the vitality of the workers' movement, Communist pamphlets denounced the Gestapo, the Gaullist engineers, the employers, the Princes of the Church and even the "Gaullist workers" without distinction. And until 22 June 1941 Jacques Duclos, the head of the party on the national level, confined himself to letting some of the party officials and several of the active members take action against Vichy to begin with and then against the occupying forces.

The most conspicuous of the undertakings were of course those of Charles Tillon, the party's delegate for the south-west, who, as early as June 1940, basing himself first on Le Bouscat in the suburbs of Bordeaux and then on Palaiseau on the outskirts of Paris, set about forming a double network of propaganda by means of tracts and of direct action: without referring to Jacques Duclos. He trained "TP" (*Travaux particuliers*) teams; then he founded the weekly *France nouvelle* (September 1941); and lastly – this time in collaboration with the other party leaders – he set up the FTP (Francs-tireurs et partisans français).

Speaking today, Tillon says that it was by reflecting on the tactics of his fellow-countryman du Guesclin in the forest of Brocéliande that he rediscovered a guerilla warfare based on the idea of the "ball of quicksilver that your fingers seize but never manage to hold". De Gaulle? "I listened to him, but I looked after my own particular community. Later I did acknowledge him as my leader, but I never obeyed his order not to kill Germans."[3]

"Not to kill Germans." What does this mean? The London radio, over which Charles de Gaulle spoke about twice a month,* was not the Chanticleer that woke

*Sixty-seven times from 1940 to 1944.

the energies of France. Many of those who had not heard the appeal of 18 June or subsequent broadcasts, were nevertheless active members of the Resistance. Yet it would be impossible to speak of what was done against the occupation or the neutralization of the national territory without recalling what these historic broadcasts amounted to.

It has already been said that installed on the fourth floor of the BBC were a team of Frenchmen whose leading member was Maurice Schumann, the "spokesman of Fighting France", who during the five minutes of *Honneur et Patrie* was supposed to express the General's own views: in 1943 his place was occasionally taken by Pierre Brossolette or Pierre-Olivier Lapie.

The BBC then set aside half an hour for Fighting France, including the programme *Les Français parlent aux Français*, supervised by the easy-going Darsie Gillie, the head of the English service and formerly the *Manchester Guardian*'s Paris correspondent, and under the direction of Michel Saint-Denis, known as Jacques Duchesne. The team included the former naval officer Yves Morvan, known as Jean Marin, the journalist Pierre Maillaud, alias Bourdan, the poet Jacques Brunius, alias Borel, Jean Oberlé and Maurice Van Moppès, a draughtsman with a very lively turn of speech, and somewhat later André Gillois and Pierre Dac.

Not all these men were ardent Gaullists: far from it. But they all took part, one with lyricism, another with irony and a third with passion, in the preservation of hope for occupied France that month by month grew into certainty. They all helped to maintain a bond between those who felt free and those who were subjugated. They thus played their part in the Resistance, as did other more occasional contributors – Georges Boris, René Cassin, Henry Hauck, Myriam Cendrars – and two great writers whose messages were broadcast: Jacques Maritain and Georges Bernanos.*

But the aim of this daily programme was not only to keep up morale. It was the basis for propaganda campaigns; it broadcast the watchword for joining in demonstrations in France, particularly on 1 May and then on 14 July 1942. In a confidential report dated July 1942 to the head of the Vichy government (then Pierre Laval) the regional prefect of Marseilles pointed out that "it is no longer possible to put up posters with directions contrary to those of the agitators in London."[4]

Better still, the programme played an increasingly direct part in the movements and the activities of the Resistance when, from June 1941 onwards, it carried those famous "personal messages" which meant either an order was to be carried out, or a summons to London, or a parachute-drop in the Corrèze. One man, hearing "the dandelions do not like the sardine", would know that his radio-operator had reached London safe and sound; for another "Father Christmas is dressed in pink" meant that Morandat or Bingen was on his way to a landing-ground in the neighbourhood of Valence; and a third, hearing "Louis XIV greets Vercingetorix", knew that a given network had been disrupted and that it was no longer to be relied upon.

*The first was living in the United States, the second in Brazil.

This fire-ship with a crew of patriotic journalists and song-writers that was lit in June 1940 soon developed into a great psychological-war service, particularly after the non-military section of Passy's BCRA had been strengthened and increased in numbers, and after the Commissariat of the Interior had been entrusted to so active and ebullient a leader as André Philip. The programme's importance grew continually, in proportion to the intelligence gathered by these organizations, which was centralized and then circulated by Jean-Louis Crémieux-Brilhac's archive section.

From the first messages brought from France at the beginning of 1941 by Rémy to those carried by Jean Moulin, Brossolette, d'Astier or Frenay in 1942, the nature of the harvest changed. It was no longer a question of information about a given piece of sabotage to be carried out (sometimes decisive, like the destruction in February 1942 of the Bruneval radio-transmitter, opposite the British coast) or about the state of morale in Rennes or Grenoble, but of very important political or strategic intelligence on the handing over of Syrian airfields to the Reich, the annexation of Alsace or the surrender of German political refugees to Hitler in 1942: the French service of the BBC had become a turn-table for world-wide information and a launching-pad for psychological action against the Nazi occupier.

All these activities did not proceed without conflict with the British authorities, who had their own propaganda-weapons designed for France, especially the excellent *Courrier de l'air*, dropped by parachute over France in hundreds of thousands of copies.

When the first serious clashes between Churchill and de Gaulle occurred, communications with the continent – the BBC French programme's chief source – were cut off for almost a fortnight. After the very stormy encounter of 30 September 1942, the leader of Fighting France was forbidden the microphone; and the exclusion was more categorical and lasting after the Allied landing in North Africa, when de Gaulle and his companions wished to denounce the scandal of collaboration with Admiral Darlan, installed by those who claimed to be liberating France from that "treason" which he personified.

The texts of Charles de Gaulle's speeches on the BBC without the voice that uttered them, grave, sarcastic and curiously stressed, rising from the darkness and the radio-jamming, are not enough to tell what his presence amounted to in the daily (nightly) life of the French, arousing enthusiasm and irritation, anger or hope. An important presence in any event, for the Vichy statistics put the number of regular listeners of his broadcasts at 300 000 at the beginning of 1941 and multiplied that figure by ten the next year – a progress that was to continue until 1944.

There is no doubt that General de Gaulle's broadcasts mobilized public opinion; but at least on one occasion the voice from London disconcerted many of his listeners, and some of the most ardent among them: this was on 23 October 1941, when de Gaulle gave the watchword "do not kill Germans". To appreciate this order, uttered with great emphasis, at its true value, we must first recall the context in which it was given.

On 27 June 1941 a young workman named Colette fired at Pierre Laval and

Marcel Déat, both symbols of collaboration with the Reich. On 29 June, Lieutenant-Commander d'Estienne d'Orves, one of Free France's first envoys to the home country, arrested six months earlier, was shot by a firing-squad. On 21 August, the militant Communist Fabian shot a German officer stepping out of a métro carriage in Paris. In September the attacks increased in number, and they were followed by the execution of hostages at Lille. A first warning came from London on 20 September, put out by Pierre Bourdan: "Do not launch yourselves into a fruitless revolt now. What our cause needs is allies, not men who have already given their lives!"

But on 20 October the Feldkommandant of Nantes was killed, and on 21 October, at Bordeaux, it was the turn of a high Nazi official. On the twenty-second, forty-seven hostages (almost all Communists) were shot at Châteaubriant, near Nantes, and fifty at the Souges camp, near Bordeaux. On October 23, therefore, General de Gaulle spoke on the London radio:

> In this terrible phase of the struggle against the enemy, the French people must be given a watchword. This watchword I am about to pronounce. It comes from the French National Committee which is guiding the nation in its resistance. Here it is! That Germans should be killed by Frenchmen is absolutely normal and absolutely justified. If the Germans did not want to receive death at our hands, they had only to stay in their own country. Now at present the watchword I give for the occupied territory is not to kill* Germans there. This is for a single but very good reason, which is that for the moment it is too easy for the enemy to reply by the massacring of our fighting-men, temporarily disarmed. As soon as we are in a position to move over to the attack, all together, from the outside and at home, you will be given the necessary orders. Until then, patience, preparation, resolution.[5]

The General's appeal aroused some reservations. In his *Histoire de la Résistance en France*[6] Henri Noguères criticizes it in two respects. First because the General "made it known to the fighters of inside France that he looked upon himself as their leader [here indulging in] one of those sanguine anticipations of which he alone had the secret." And then "because he recommended a form of tactics that the Resistance were shortly to label *l'attentisme*, wait-and-see-ism."

Colonel Passy, in his *Mémoires*, states that although in this period the General had great standing in the eyes of the Resistance "he did not yet influence their actions". Charles Tillon, who, in his *FTP* and his *On chantait rouge*,[7] rejected that "lofty order" and said that "duty required one to disobey the General".

Did de Gaulle, Passy, Diethelm, Boris and their companions distrust the Resistance at that time? Were they afraid that it would escape from their control and above all that it would develop into a revolutionary war that would turn the Resistance and the liberation in a direction other than that which Charles de

*In the *Mémoires de guerre* Vol.II p. 228 we read "openly kill". This word does not appear in the documents of the time: what does it mean? Was it simply a warning against individual killings but not against acts of sabotage that might cause death?

Gaulle intended for it? This is a most serious question; and the documents of the time give only glimpses of the answer to it.

It has been observed that in the text of the 23 October broadcast itself the General gives "exterior" action priority over that of the "interior": chronological priority, in any case. Was his idea to limit the activity of the French interior Resistance or was it rather to supervise it, which is not quite the same thing? Let us look at what was written by Henri Frenay*:

> As the Resistance expanded and got into working order it became aware of itself and of its strength. London realized this too. It is probable that de Gaulle reflected upon the danger of being faced by a firmly seated Resistance claiming to represent France and, for public opinion, possessing the great prestige of never having ceased to live and fight on the soil of France itself.[8]

De Gaulle and his team were so clearly far from the fascism that they were accused of that to head the organization of their political action in France they chose men all of whom, with the exception of Passy, came from the Popular Front, starting with Jean Moulin and André Philip and going on to Brossolette, Vallon, Boris and Pierre-Bloch. But for all that they realized that the entry of the USSR into the war in the east and of the PCF into the struggle in France strengthened one particular design – a design which, at least in the long term, was not what they were fighting for.

Clearly, there could be no question of refusing any alliance or cooperation whatsoever, and very soon (February 1942) links were formed with the FTP, the Front National and the PCF. But an immense problem arose. De Gaulle was the man who as early as 1935 had campaigned for a Franco-Soviet pact; who, at the beginning of July 1941 had hailed the Soviet war-effort and who had increased his contacts with fighting Russia.

From the moment the USSR entered the war, France was pregnant with a revolution.* From the moment the United States entered the war, the country was subject to an invasion. For de Gaulle, even more than for his great allies, one of the essential strategic problems was to know which of these two would have the priority (and therefore the pre-eminence?). Whatever his grounds for complaint with regard to the American leaders and whatever his differences with Churchill, de Gaulle's scheme would give priority to the revolution only if the Anglo-Saxon undertaking assumed the appearance of an immense police-operation on the Rooseveltian theme: "There no longer is a France".

*Frenay founded and led the Resistance movement Combat. (trs.)

*In *Résistant de la première heure* (p. 68), Pierre Villon gives this account of his first conversation with Rémy in October 1942: "I met Rémy at the house of Dr Descombe (of the Front National des médecins), who was sheltering him. And there two conceptions of the Resistance appeared in clear contrast. The London wait-and-see attitude: one must halt all armed action and wait so as to be perfectly ready at hour H and D day. De Gaulle will be there and we shall need everybody to occupy town-halls and prefectures before the arrival of the Allies, in order to proclaim the general Chief of State [. . .] To be sure, in this argument I saw the reflection of the disagreements between de Gaulle and the Allies. But also and above all a general fear, not only of the Communists but of the people, the dread of a popular rising."

As Charles de Gaulle saw it, the liberation of France would originate in a landing (which he already placed between Dunkirk and Cherbourg) that would involve a large French contingent and that would expand with the support of the home Resistance. The landing would automatically bring "France and the French back into the war" in conformity with the first of his aims in June 1940; and the participation of French military units and then of the Resistance forces would set a truly national seal upon it.

But we must take care not to limit the debate about the "lofty order" of 23 October 1941 to strictly professional, political and strategic arguments. When they spoke of these "sacrifices" and these "massacres", neither Bourdan nor de Gaulle were reasoning as mere strategists or detached observers. They were also expressing the compassion of French citizens confronted with the horrors of Châteaubriant and Souges, horrors all the more unbearable in that they did not really serve the cause to which they were dedicated but rather that of a revolution which, in some of its extensions, they dreaded.

The discussion on the watchword of 23 October is not concerned only with the justification of attacks on Nazis but also on the limits of the authority then exercised by Charles de Gaulle over the Resistance. Here Henri Noguères, who speaks as an insider, and as a witness with expert knowledge, cannot be disputed. He is perfectly sound in calling this authority into question. His scepticism is not countered but indeed confirmed by the observation that these days at the end of October and the beginning of November 1941 are those in which, apart from the comings and goings of agents such as Rémy, Saint-Jacques or Julitte, the first important contacts between Free France and the Resistance were made.

On 18 October, at Montpellier, two envoys from Passy made contact with Pierre-Henri Teitgen, a professor of law whose nom de guerre was Tristan; he was a founder of the movement Liberté, which was presently to combine with Frenay's Libération française to form the movement Combat. Two days later Jean Moulin landed at Bournemouth. And a fortnight after this an active young Christian trade-unionist, named Léon Morandat, was dropped by parachute over the Toulouse region. Under the pseudonym of Yvon, this emissary, speaking in the name of de Gaulle, passed on to those who received his instructions to gather the various movements and organizations together. And this watchword he delivered to such men as André Philip, Robert Lacoste and Georges Bidault.

The year that marked the welding together of the London Committee and the home Resistance was 1942. One name symbolizes this broad operation which, among many other reciprocal consequences and advantages, provided General de Gaulle with the political and psychological bases that allowed him to survive the ostracism inflicted by the Allies upon him at the time of the North African landings and then to assert himself as the head of the Fighting French as a whole in 1944: Jean Moulin, "Rex".

One cannot and one must not focus this immense symbiotic operation upon Rex alone. After the pioneers of 1940 and the envoys of 1941, many people and many organizations took part in this great gathering: Christian Pineau was in London in

March, Pierre Brossolette in April, André Philip in July, Emmanuel d'Astier and Henri Frenay in September. Yet even so it was upon the former prefect that the whole action turned.

When he was faced with the immense "unknown quantity" of the Resistance and when he decided to turn it into a unified army, why did General de Gaulle pick upon the former principal private secretary to Pierre Cot, the same Pierre Cot whose help he had refused eighteen months before, thinking him too strongly identified with the left, to carry out this exceedingly important task? Moulin was in no way different from his former chief politically and there were always people such as Henri Frenay to be found who denounced him as a crypto-Communist.

For various reasons, de Gaulle did not see Jean Moulin until the end of November 1941 when he had been in London for a month. The first had to do with the visitor's former office. However little respect he had shown for hierarchies, Charles de Gaulle had such an almost religious notion of the State that in his eyes being a prefect was a virtue, like belonging to the Conseil d'Etat or the Inspection des Finances. It was not by mere chance that all the men he delegated to the most important offices in France (Moulin, Bollaert, Parodi, Chaban) belonged to these great bodies. In Jean Moulin de Gaulle primarily saw the representative of the State and of the Republic: it was upon this principle that he wished to organize the Resistance.

Jean Moulin's second virtue in de Gaulle's eyes was the speed with which he had joined the struggle. When the General was proclaiming the absolute necessity for resistance from London, Moulin was opposing the invader on the spot, cutting his throat to avoid signing the document that was required of him. What more worthy representative could the General have than this pioneer who had signed his own appeal with his blood?

But Jean Moulin's conduct also delighted him for another reason: his refusal to accept the occupation. When he was removed from office and dismissed by Vichy, he concealed his first contacts under pretence of being a picture-dealer on the Côte-d'Azur: he had only one thought in his mind – Free France. Others set up a movement or printed pamphlets. Jean Moulin, in spite of the snub inflicted upon his friend Cot, to whom he remained perfectly faithful, had only a single rallying-point: London. How could de Gaulle faii to be struck by this response to his magnetism?

All these reasons had come into play by the time the two men met. But what they then said to one another made their almost spontaneous agreement even firmer. Here again there was an irresistible convergence of ideas. Moulin might have talked about enthusiasm, boldness, or efficiency and de Gaulle would have praised him. But of his own accord Moulin stressed that point which had the strongest claim on the Free French leader's attention: the gathering together of this host of movements, organizations, parties and trade-unions. Even if he is de Gaulle, a soldier likes plain situations: let all these people be mustered into a single body!

Was de Gaulle as convinced as Moulin of the popular character of the Resistance and of the necessity for preserving its "republican" flavour? To begin with what mattered was coordinating the activities of those who were fighting and inducing them to move towards unity. Pluralism? That was for another stage. At all events, Moulin thought it essential that the General should be seen as the rallying-point and the chief for the duration of the war.

At two in the morning on 1 January 1942, Jean Moulin, known as Rex, was dropped by parachute with two companions, one of them a radio-operator, over the region of the Alpilles where he had spent his childhood and where he owned a shepherd's house and barn between Arles and Eygalières. He had with him a commission on microfilm hidden in a matchbox: it was signed by General De Gaulle: "I appoint M. Jean Moulin, prefect, as my representative and as delegate of the French National Committee for the south zone. M. Moulin's mission is, in that zone, to bring about a unity of action on the part of all those who are resisting the enemy and his collaborators."*

As early as the next day he was in Marseilles, and there he met two of the chief leaders of Combat, Henri Frenay and Chevance-Bertin. Then came other trusted members of the same movement, Edmond Michelet, Teitgen, François de Menthon . . . And at the end of January the leaders of other organizations: Emmanuel d'Astier and Aubrac for Libération, Antoine Avinin and then Jean-Pierre Lévy for the FTP. The news of his coming had spread faster than had been expected.

They all, or almost all, hesitated before accepting, if not what Rex said to them then in any case his function. The General's delegate offered means (500 000 francs, of which he handed over half straight away to the principal movement, Combat), liaisons and a radio-transmitter to begin with: he also offered a principle, that of unification. But as they listened to this slim, dark young man, radiating strength and assurance, whose authority echoed the General's in an entirely different but no less evident tone, all those present clearly saw that it was a question of a man in command.

Since he was the most powerful and the only one who could at a pinch retain his autonomy – he had founded the first paramilitary groups, being himself a former officer, and he was increasing his contacts in all directions – Frenay, known as Charvet, hung back. Although he did gradually come to agree to give his allegiance, he did so without ever allowing himself to become politically subordinate. His failure to do so led to increasing resentment by Moulin, and later by General de Gaulle.

Rex's intervention did not bring about a rapid coming together of the movements. But it did bring a grave crisis between the various Resistance groups to an end, even if it was not forgotten. Shortly after Moulin was dropped in France, a wave of arrests struck Frenay's organization, causing very great losses: Frenay, with the agreement of his directing committee, set off for Vichy, where he hoped to have the prisoners set free. On 28 January he was seen by Pierre Pucheu, the Minister of the Interior whom the Resistance held responsible for the execution of the hostages at Châteaubriant. A strange confrontation between the two Frances.

Frenay induced Pucheu to promise that no other comrades of his should be arrested. He gave nothing in exchange. But his step aroused violent reactions on

*The terms of this commission are important. Moulin's field of action was limited to the south zone, which was under the Commissariat of the Interior. The north zone came under Passy's BCRA. When, by the force of circumstances, Rex worked in the north zone, there were protests.

the part of the other organizations. Emmanuel d'Astier, alias Bernard, accused Frenay of making a "very serious error" against the spirit of the Resistance. Was "operation unity" beginning badly? Rex's support of the leader of Combat avoided the worst.

The idea of unification nevertheless made progress, sometimes independently of Rex's activities. At the end of 1941 Rémy entered into contact with Colonel Beaufils, the man in charge of the Communist resistance groups from which Tillon was forming the Francs-tireurs et partisans français (FTP) and which took that name in January 1942. In February Tillon's assistant, François Faure (known as Paco: he was Elie Faure's son), with London's direct agreement, met Beaufils now spokesman for the FTP, and then Marcel Prenant, later Tillon's deputy, with a view to military cooperation.[9] This cooperation came into effect with the formation of the Armée Secrète at the end of 1942 under the aegis of General de Gaulle: yet it did not do so without continual complaints on the Communist side of being forgotten when weapons were dropped by parachute.

By the end of April, Moulin was able to tell London that three bodies had been created to coordinate certain forms of Resistance activity and to prepare for the future within the framework of vertical organizations: the Armée Secrète (AS), the Bureau d'information et de presse (BIP) and the Comité général d'études (CGE).

To begin with, the function of the AS was not to compete with the FTP and other partisans of immediate action and the harassing of the occupying army. It was primarily directed, according to the plan outlined by General de Gaulle on 23 October 1941, towards the clandestine organization of the forces intended to come into action on D Day. Hence the sarcastic remarks uttered over a long period by the activists and Communists, accusing the AS of wait-and-see-ism.

The Bureau d'information et de presse was naturally entrusted to the best-known of the journalists engaged in active resistance, Georges Bidault, who was very close to Combat. As for the Comité général d'études, whose function was both to prepare the institutions that might be suggested to the French nation after liberation and the peace-conditions that should be proposed to the Allies, it included the legal experts who had joined the first resistance movements at the very beginning, the Christian democrats François de Menthon and Pierre-Henri Teitgen, the Radical Paul Bastid, Alexandre Parodi, Michel Debré* and the trade-unionist Robert Lacoste.

Although the progress of Gaullism in France itself tended to be seen mostly throught the activities of Jean Moulin, other links were established from the beginning of 1942, and they increased in number. The most important was the arrival in London of Christian Pineau, the head of Libération-Nord. He was the first of the Resistance leaders who could tell de Gaulle face to face about life in occupied France and what the Resistance was doing there. Until that time this information had come only from agents who were continually on the move or from a man like Jean Moulin who had not really carried out resistance among the inhabitants and who was confined to the south zone.

In February 1942, just before he left for London, Christian Pineau travelled

*A future Prime Minister (1959–62). (trs.)

down to the unoccupied zone to consult with the leaders of the southern Resistance. There he met André Philip, d'Astier and Henri Frenay, and they stressed the necessity for inducing the General to adopt a clearer attitude in favour of democracy, one that would open prospects for the future totally opposed to those of Vichy. "What you ought to bring back," said Philip, "is a manifesto addressed to our movements. If it corresponds to our idea, we could make it our charter, and by doing so unify the spirit of the Resistance."

At the time of Pineau's arrival in London, what did the General amount to for him? He sums it up in a few sentences: "He was not our leader. We had taken our first steps without him; we would have taken them in any event, even if he had not spoken on 18 June. He was not living in the national territory and so he was not sharing our dangers. Nevertheless most of us were prepared to recognize his authority. For we needed a flag, if not a guide."[10]

Christian Pineau had three interviews with de Gaulle. This is how he speaks of the first: "Without saying a word, he [de Gaulle] led me to an armchair. Then, looking me straight in the eye, he uttered his first words, 'Now tell me about France.'"

When in his turn the General spoke, Pineau observed that, most unexpectedly, what he said was not a reply to his own remarks: the General spoke about the troops in Africa, who for him represented the French Resistance, and about relations with the Allies. "He was at one and the same time filled with pride and bitterness."

As for the Resistance, he agreed that he knew almost nothing about it. He did not seem particularly moved by Pineau's account of the very specific dangers run by those who defied the Gestapo. On the subject of the message to be addressed to the Resistance, he was guarded. To set himself apart from the Marshal? "He accepted defeat: I did not! When France is liberated, we shall restore the Republic; the French themselves will say what they want."

A few days later he saw de Gaulle again. The General had drawn up a document that the visitor thought superb but that did not correspond to what he had hoped.

"The condemnation of the Third Republic is so severe," observed Pineau, "that without naming any single one, it affects all those men who were in control. Yet there are some among them who are ready to join Free France but who would find it very hard to bear being judged with the same harshness as those who support collaboration."

The General burst out, "Since I am asked for a message, I shall send it without hiding what I think. Is it I, de Gaulle, or is it you who is addressing the French?" He would have nothing to do with any emendation. And when Pineau, taking leave, asked whether he had no communication for the trade unionists, de Gaulle gave a smiling reply that chilled his visitor to the heart: "Just tell these brave people that I shall not betray them."[11]

It was only just as Pineau was about to step into the plane that was taking him back to France that a motorcyclist brought him an envelope from de Gaulle. It contained a new version of the message, including some of the changes that had been asked for. The condemnation of Vichy was more political: "Another [regime] arising from a criminal surrender, attains the height of personal power." Furthermore, there was a tribute to "the age-old French ideal of liberty, equality and fraternity". Pineau had won his case. But he had also gauged the strength of the General's character, his ruthlessness as a negotiator, his resentment against the Third Republic and his distrust of what he was later to call "the regime of parties". Although the Resistance had found a very rough leader, it did have its charter,* which, without quite coming up to André Philip's expectations, nevertheless induced him to come to London three months later.

Before this, the General and Passy saw the arrival of a man of exceptional quality and most striking influence: Pierre Brossolette. He had great standing as a socialist journalist and leader of opinion. He landed in London on 26 April 1942, coming in the plane that had just taken Christian Pineau back to France (the BBC told his comrades the news in the words "the autocycle has got rid of its squirrel"[12]), and as soon as he arrived he was recognized as being a link between the interior and London comparable to Jean Moulin, and more evident, because Brossolette expressed himself in public and because he did so brilliantly, speaking in favour of a total commitment to what may already be called ideological Gaullism.

Straight away he and Passy conceived an enthusiastic, brotherly friendship for one another – Passy, whose liking for so many other "metropolitans" was negative. And very soon he saw de Gaulle. Speaking of the General to Gilberte, his wife, during his first return to France, he said, "The man is up to the job. He listens; he has shown a deep desire to understand and to identify himself with occupied France. And also to broaden the bases and the extent of its representation in London."

Brossolette and Moulin complemented one another; for while the latter caused the various forces of resistance in the national territory to converge, the former worked to bring together the various organizations in London. More than anyone, Brossolette helped to do away with the discrimination and the barriers between civilians and service people, between "men of the interior" and "men of the exterior", and those concerned with action and those concerned with intelligence. Obviously his friendship with Passy was an advantage in this; so was the General's appreciation of the observations and suggestions of this intellectual.

The great quarrel between Jean Moulin and Pierre Brossolette arose primarily from their differing ideas about the role of political parties, an issue that was to divide the Resistance. Frenay, Passy and Brossolette on the one side and Moulin, d'Astier, the Socialists and Communists on the other, came into conflict on the question of replacing the parties by powerfully structured organizations, going beyond the rivalries of the past and expressing the new spirit of the Resistance. De Gaulle decided in favour of Moulin and those who supported him.

It was in London, at the very height of the crisis that opposed Charles de Gaulle to his British hosts and allies (autumn 1942), that the most important conference in the history of the Resistance to date took place. It brought together the leaders of the two chief metropolitan movements, Henri Frenay for Combat and Emmanuel d'Astier** for Libération, the "third great man", Jean Pierre Lévy, of Franc-

*It is the document from which extracts are given in Chapter 27.

**Who had already stayed in London, in May, before carrying out a mission to the USA. (trs.)

Tireur, having, like Jean Moulin, been prevented from coming to London by a series of mishaps; and Philip, Soustelle,* Passy, Brossolette, Vallon, and the General himself.

Frenay and d'Astier had sailed from the En-vau creek near Marseilles in a little cutter with a Polish crew on 1 September and they had reached London on the seventeenth. The talks, delayed by the prolongation of the General's stay in Africa, lasted from the third to the fifteenth of October. Two important measures were decided upon: the appointment of the chief of the Armée Secrète and the coordination of the great movements that Jean Moulin had been preparing for the last nine months.

It very soon became apparent to the "Londoners" that the only point upon which Frenay and d'Astier agreed was their shared opposition to Moulin, whose authority seemed to them exaggerated and meddlesome. But Philip and (however unlike his opinions theirs might be) Passy and Brossolette firmly defended Moulin, the king-pin of the whole structure. On the sixth day, de Gaulle, set free from his difficulties with Downing Street, joined in personally, unreservedly covering his delegate in France. Moulin remained at his post, stronger than before.

For Frenay, as for d'Astier, Moulin raised a personal problem; Frenay was compelled to yield on that point, but he fought very vigorously against the idea of which Rex, in the Constable's name, was the main supporter – unifying the organizations and the parties in a single common structure.

> "The structure of which we are speaking will look upon itself as representative, and because of that very fact it will feel itself capable of taking up an attitude on all questions. Now inevitably the points of view in France and here are different, as are the conditions of life. Is it not to be feared that these differences will lead to opposition and perhaps even to conflict?"
>
> "Well," said de Gaulle, "we shall try to understand one another."
>
> "And if we do not succeed, that will mean dead-lock."
>
> "No, because I shall give orders."

Frenay held his breath. "Now we are at the heart of the problem – the nature of the relations between de Gaulle and the Resistance." There was utter silence round the table. "General," the leader of Combat continued:

> The activity that we are carrying out in France has two aspects that cannot be separated but that are different in nature. On the one hand, in the Armée Secrète and the Groupes-France we are soldiers, and as such, parts of an organized whole. Our tasks at the time of the landing will be set by the Inter-Allied General Staff and yourself and it goes without saying that we shall obey. In other respects we are citizens free to think and act as we like. We cannot part with that freedom of judgment, which means that in this sphere we shall either obey or not obey your orders.

*The Commissioner for Information, but more and more concerned with action of this kind.

The General remained silent for a few moments. "Well, Charvet, France will choose between you and me."[13]

Yet even so, agreement was reached upon one principle, that of a simple "coordination" between the various groups – Frenay hoping thus to retain his autonomy and d'Astier glad that he would not now be absorbed by Combat, too powerful a movement for him to be a very close associate. Furthermore, Frenay irritated de Gaulle, but the General was delighted by d'Astier's spirit and somewhat anarchistic charm. It was d'Astier he had chosen for a mission to the United States, where valuable contacts had been made.

Lastly, the visitors and their host managed to come to an understanding on one important point: the appointment of the head of the Armée Secrète, whose creation Moulin and Frenay had decided upon six months before. Charvet did not conceal from his hosts the fact that he was a candidate for this command. But he was soon isolated: d'Astier was not particularly keen on seeing his rival promoted; the "Londoners" thought him too stubborn and inclined to disobedience; and the conference as a whole preferred the appointment of a general (Frenay, in June 1940, was only a captain*). During the meeting de Gaulle said curtly to Frenay, "I have generals to find places for, now that there are generals who want to fight."[14]

It was Frenay and not de Gaulle who produced the name of General Delestraint in the course of the discussion. It will not have been forgotten that this officer had had very close ties with the Constable between 1936 and 1939 during the crusade for tanks, of which Delestraint was one of the best French specialists. Unanimity on his name was soon reached. And on 23 October, having received Delestraint's acceptance, Charles de Gaulle at once wrote to him, "No one was better qualified than you to undertake this. And now is the moment! I embrace you, General: we shall remake the French army."[15]

In short, despite the absence of Jean Moulin and Jean-Pierre Lévy, there was progress at the conference of October 1942 – at least in the ascendancy of London over the interior. The General drew the conclusions when, on 22 October 1942, he sent Jean Moulin this message, which was a solemn confirmation of his powers:

> The simultaneous presence of [d'Astier and Frenay] in London has allowed the establishment of an understanding between their two resistance movements and the settling of the conditions of their activity under the authority of the National Committee. The arrangements that have been drawn up will facilitate the carrying out of the mission with which you have been entrusted. You will be required to preside over the coordinating committee, in which will be represented the three chief resistance movements: Combat, Franc-Tireur and Libération. All the [other] resistance organizations must be requested to affiliate their members to one of these movements and to transfer their action-groups to units of the Armée Secrète now being set up. I particularly wish to repeat that you have my entire confidence, and I send you my very kind wishes.[16]

*So was Leclerc, who was soon to be promoted general.

Charles de Gaulle made his "authority" ring out, an authority which for a year, since the time of the "lofty order" of 23 October 1941 (so little obeyed by those it was intended to persuade), had not merely grown: it had, in the course of one year, become established.

After Moulin returned to France, de Gaulle had formed powerful and organic links with the interior; he had gathered round him a team forged by the terrible trials of clandestine warfare; he had signed a manifesto that was already much the same as a charter for the fighting-men; he had entered into contact with the Communists by means of Rémy and he had thrust aside the various agents and tools of the Anglo-Saxon policies.

And while the Wehrmacht was failing in its prodigious effort to finish off the USSR in the summer of 1942, the United States, in the Pacific, was beginning to reverse the trend of the battle – an incomparable stimulus for the Resistance. Lastly, Laval's return to power in Vichy and his declaration in favour of a Nazi victory provided the Fighting French in London and their companions in France with a contrast that set them off admirably.

However much he might still be challenged as a political leader or in the person of his delegate in France, in the autumn of 1942 Charles de Gaulle could put himself forward as the man who had forged the federation of the Resistance in France. Was that not more than enough to convince Franklin Roosevelt and to win back the confidence of Winston Churchill?

IV

THE CONQUERORS

CHAPTER THIRTY

The Torch and the Ashes

From the beginning of the conflict, the most important of Charles de Gaulle's concerns had been Algiers and North Africa. In June 1940 he had tried to induce Reynaud and the Government to go there. When Catroux joined Free France, de Gaulle wrote to say that there was only one mission worthy of him: North Africa. And although in the great Anglo-American discussions on the strategy to be adopted for the second front, de Gaulle supported Marshall's plan for a direct attack upon "fortress Europe" rather than the British idea centering upon the Mediterranean, he took care not to underestimate the strategic bastion formed by North Africa, a bastion that Free France gazed upon with passionate desire from its two key bases, Brazzaville in the south and Beirut in the east.

Was Free France established in North Africa? Robert Murphy didn't think so; he had been there since 1940, first as the United States consul-general in Algiers and then as President Roosevelt's personal representative, and who guided the anticipated manoeuvre. The reports he sent the White House and the State Department declared that Gaullism did not exist in North Africa, and much more, that it would be harmful if it did: according to Murphy an alliance with this trifling force would have only one effect – that of setting the real forces, those of Vichy, against the undertaking. Moreover, the participation of the Free French in an operation carried out by the Allies in North Africa would make its failure certain.[1] And at least until June 1943 this was Washington's opinion, while London, tired of arguing, agreed with it.

Was Free France established in Algiers? "Gaullists make up less than ten per cent of this country," said Robert Murphy at the end of 1942, addressing the General's spokesman, who was there to protest against the isolation inflicted upon the Fighting French. Less than ten per cent? That was probably true.

From the beginning let us leave out the Muslims, who made up ninety per cent of the population and who were entirely excluded from political life and from decision. No enquiry into their feelings at this period was ever made: the only real "opinion poll" was the often heroic part played by the 150 000 North African soldiers in the campaigns of 1943 and 1944, from Tunisia to Italy and the landings in southern France. Although the power of individual decision in military matters may have been very slight, and although the personal factor where immediate commanders were concerned may have been very important, it does not appear that going over from Weygand to Leclerc was much of a problem for the Muslim troops, and it was under the orders of General de Monsabert, who had joined de

Gaulle even before the landing, that Ahmed Ben Bella* won the *médaille militaire* at Cassino.

There is no doubt that a pro-Pétain state of mind was predominant in Algeria's European circles. So long as Weygand was Pétain's representative in Algiers, the myth of Pétain "the father" and the mystique of the "leader" near at hand combined to cause a traditionally rather conservative population to rally round the *francisque*** and the "oath to the Marshal" – a population that in its majority was hostile to the "Jewish and free-mason" Third Republic and that was all the more attached to law and order because its survival on African soil seemed to depend on them. The 'Légion des Combattants' and the 'Service d'Ordre Légionnaire' (SOL), the vanguard of Vichyism, very soon recruited tens of thousands of members, and so did Doriot's PPF (Parti populaire français), including many from the Muslim community, where it benefitted from the complicity of a fringe of the PPA (Parti du peuple algérien).

The majority of the armed forces shared the same attitudes: the navy, because of its traditions, heightened by the painful recollection of Mers-el-Kebir; the army, because from July 1941 it had been reinforced by units evacuated from the Levant after the agreement of Acre, who were much embittered by that humiliating retreat. Yet from early days quite a large number of officers had joined the Gaullist side. As for the air force, even the American reports thought them more open to the influence of London and it was well known that such a man as General Bouscat (who later acted as intermediary between Giraud and de Gaulle) was much in favour of Free France.

In spite of the general attitude, Free France had adherents among the people of Algeria, where a long-established current of left-wing feeling had been strengthened by the arrival of many Spanish republicans in North Africa; this combined with a widespread resistance to "Marshalism", particularly strong among the Jews, whom the Vichy system had struck with great force by abolishing the Crémieux decree, which in 1870 automatically granted Algerian Jews French nationality. For a great many reasons this active body, well provided with able men, was deeply attached to the republican tradition, and it supplied Algerian Gaullism with many of its best militants, headed by the Aboulker family.

As we have seen, the decision placing the Allied landings in North Africa rather than on the European continent had been taken in July 1942. When General de Gaulle confronted the American chiefs in London on 23 July George Marshall, his main partner in conversation, knew that "Sledgehammer", the plan for a direct attack in Western Europe, had been abandoned or put off until a later date; Roosevelt had yielded, against the advice of all his military advisers, to Churchill.

The British Prime Minister's arguments had many facets. He was at that time wholly committed to the battle of Cyrenaica, where in the first week of November Britain won its greatest land victory of the war at El Alamein. Everything therefore made him turn towards the Mediterranean theatre. A great manoeuvre taking Rommel from behind and expelling the Wehrmacht from the southern front

*The future President of Algeria. (trs.)

**A Frankish battle-axe, used as a symbol by Vichy. (trs.)

seemed to him the most urgent of measures. Furthermore, the effort called for in the Western Desert did not allow him to bring together the British forces that Operation Sledgehammer would demand.

Lastly, Churchill saw the attack on the southern flank as the beginning of an enormous operation that, by way of Italy and Yugoslavia, Europe's "soft underbelly", would bring the Allies an area of immeasurable strategic importance – the Balkans, the Danube, the Carpathians – where Stalin must not be allowed to advance too far. As we have seen, General de Gaulle had made some observations about the future Russian victories to Passy in December 1941: Churchill did not fail to make similar observations to Eden or Morton.

However much the President of the United States might trust George Marshall, and however urgently he might wish to strike Hitler a mortal blow, he allowed himself to be persuaded by his eloquent partner, on condition of having the matter thoroughly under his control and of leaving the Free French out of it entirely. Churchill's arguments prevailed in the first place because Marshall was compelled to agree that in view of the immense operations General MacArthur was preparing in the Pacific he would not have sufficient means at his disposal for Sledgehammer before April 1943. And in the second place because the 200 000 men he could bring together would still not be enough to break the Wehrmacht: he would be able to set up a bridgehead in north-western France, thus creating the second front called for by the Russians, but without bringing about a decisive action.

Operation Gymnast (soon renamed Torch) was to be carried out at the end of October. The least that can be said is that the target was far from unknown. Mr Murphy and the thirty-three American consuls he had set in place from Agadir to Gabès had patiently prepared the ground: at the popular level they pointed out that the considerable quantities of cloth, tea and sugar the inhabitants received were the result of American generosity, and at the top level they did all they could to associate themselves with forceful executives and above all a French leader of great standing with the enterprise.

Robert Murphy's first choice was naturally General Weygand, who had the support of a strong anti-German, anti-Gaullist and pro-American party in the whole of North Africa. Even after Hitler had obliged Pétain to remove him from Algiers in November 1941, Weygand remained Murphy's "candidate", and in March 1942 the American sent an envoy (MacArthur's nephew) to Cannes to persuade him to serve at least as a figurehead for Operation Gymnast. "You do not turn rebel at my age," sighed the former proconsul.

So without Weygand, the Americans entered into contact with a group of men who were to play a part of the very first importance and who are conveniently called the "band of five" although they scarcely formed a group and numbered many more than five. Yet still, by straining the terms a little, one can use this figure for the somewhat incongruous team that made up Murphy's French brains trust for the manoeuvre.

First came Jacques Lemaigre-Dubreuil, an important manufacturer and a born conspirator, and close to the Cagoule, but as anti-German as he was pro-American; then his right-hand man Jean Rigault, a skilled tactician to whom he had entrusted the financial management of his paper *Le Jour-Echo de Paris*, one of the least collaborationist of the south zone press; Colonel Van Hecke, the head of the Chantiers de jeunesse;* the diplomat Tarbé de Saint-Hardouin; and lastly Lieutenant Henri d'Astier de La Vigerie, (the younger brother of the leader of the resistance movement, Libération) who was in the 2nd Bureau at Oran and who there exercised an influence quite out of proportion to his modest rank. No one of these "five" (who were sometimes three, sometimes twenty) was at that time Gaullist.** All of them were looking for a leader: Weygand had never filled the role for any of them.

Alongside the "five" there worked two teams, the one on the edge of this group, the other in direct competition with it. The first was made up of patriotic soldiers. Captain Beaufre, a member of Weygand's staff, but much less inclined than his chief to put up with Vichy's ambiguities and ultra-conservatism, was doing everything he could to gather together all Vichy's anti-German followers in Algeria in order to prepare a peaceful reception for the imminent landings; what really mattered for him – and he knew the North African world very well – was to prevent the Allies being received in Algiers as they had been at Dakar or Damascus. Colonel Faye was more deeply committed: he was the North African correspondent for Loustaunau-Lacau's network Alliance. Beaufre and Faye were in contact with General Mast and General Béthouart, who were already entirely in favour of re-entering the war. Beaufre was arrested in May 1941, but he was released in November and from then onwards he was at the centre of the operation.***

And then there was a Gaullist group, initiated by René Capitant, a professor of Law, together with his colleague Louis Joxe (who taught history at the lycée), Superintendent André Achiary (who was in charge of counter-espionage and who played an essential part in all these plots), René Moatti (a lawyer), Dr Aboulker and his son José, Louis Fradin, Roger Carcassone, who was active in Oran, Bernard Karsenty, and above all, Colonel Jousse, who, as garrison adjutant, could pull a number of strings.

The Gaullists were not looking for a leader. But the "five" and their military allies who would not hear of de Gaulle (unexportable to North Africa in Beaufre's opinion) were in search of a man, and if possible a general.

La Laurencie was not to be taken seriously; nor was Odic, who had refused to join de Gaulle a year earlier; and Juin, in command of the troops of North Africa as a whole, was a sphinx who discouraged any approach.

On 17 April 1942 General Henri Giraud, who had been taken prisoner on 19 May 1940, escaped from the German fortress of Königstein. At the beginning of the war it was thought that he was to be one of the great chiefs of the coming years. Reynaud had even thought of offering him Gamelin's succession in May 1940. People remembered his campaigns in Morocco, they praised his courage and spoke enthusiastically of his splendid bearing and many admired him for his unyielding contempt for anything even remotely connected with politics.

*These were agricultural and forestry work camps for the young during the war; they more or less corresponded to military service. (trs.)
**Two of them, Van Hecke and d'Astier, became Gaullists.
***Colonel Faye was arrested and shot by the Germans.

A blaze of enthusiasm glowed in the dreary gloom of Algiers when this "new" man appeared. His escape, greeted by an explosion of fury on the Nazi side, gave him a magical aura: Weygand had no sooner disarmed the most willing minds than there appeared on the scene a nimbler and indeed a providential hero.

Neither Murphy nor Lemaigre-Dubreuil saw any harm in the fact that Giraud should have gone to Vichy to present himself to the Marshal after he had escaped or, when Pierre Laval threatened to hand him back to Hitler, that he should have pleaded his cause with Otto Abetz, come to an understanding with Darlan, and finally agreed to sign a letter to Philippe Pétain in which he proclaimed his "fidelity" to the old leader.

It cannot be said that in signing this letter General Giraud was fated to become the champion of the nation's liberation. Yet that is what many people thought possible, both in France and abroad. Since Laval's return in April 1942 had wrecked the hopes of those who were in favour of an entente cordiale between the United States and Vichy, was it therefore necessary to turn to the impossible de Gaulle? Not at all, for all of a sudden here was the providential man, the embodiment of an anti-German Vichy, the dream of three quarters of the French bourgeoisie, and the army officers – and naturally of President Roosevelt.

Charles de Gaulle was not the only one to see the significance of Giraud's arrival: so did Admiral Darlan. A few weeks before, he had been removed from power by Laval, and had then made surprising overtures towards the Resistance and the Americans.[2] In October he visited Algiers, where his personal representative was Admiral Fenard, a sympathizer of the Allied cause. Darlan asked one of the officers with him to see Murphy and say that he would be back for an inspection next month and that he had some proposals to make. Darlan had scented something in the nature of a great Allied operation; but like most people who were thought to be well-informed, he supposed that it would be a landing on the west African coast.

Charles de Gaulle had caught wind of the landing as early as August 1942 and perhaps even earlier. During his meeting with Anthony Eden on 28 July, he raised the subject of the second front. The British minister, more downright than usual, told him that "it was scarcely to be thought of now". To this de Gaulle replied, "Great hopes are going to be disappointed," and he confirmed that he was soon to leave for Africa and the Levant. He then heard these words, which he did not fail to ruminate upon: "Come back as soon as possible. It would in fact be a good thing if you were here at the moment important decisions are made."

This hint provoked the Constable to make enquiries in the Levant, where that acute detective Catroux, who was on quite good terms with the British General Staff, told him rather more. In any case, on 27 August, tearing himself away from oriental Levantine complexities for a moment, de Gaulle cabled Pleven and Dejean in London:

> Basing myself on many clues, I am convinced that the United States have now taken the decision to land troops in French North Africa. The Americans imagine that they will obtain at least some degree of passiveness from the Vichy authorities. Without any doubt, Marshal Pétain will give orders to

> fight against the Allies in Africa. The Americans had at first supposed that it would be possible for them to open a second front in France this year. Now their plan has changed and at the same time we see them return to their reserved attitude with regard to the National Committee.[3]

It would not be possible to say more in fewer words, nor to combine a greater clear-sightedness with a more unerring foreknowledge. We have long known that the Constable was never so great as in adversity. Now he was in adversity without any doubt. At the very time he had done everything he could to embitter his relations with Churchill, often putting himself in the wrong, he found himself rejected by Washington. Everything told him that the whole business was taking shape without him, that is to say against him, and that all the gods were turning towards a third man, towards Henri Giraud.

The operation to concentrate on Giraud had been guided by three men: Lemaigre-Dubreuil, who had been attached to Giraud's staff in 1939 and who had been to see him in Lyons; Colonel Solberg (assistant to William Donovan, chief of the American OSS), who did not find it difficult to persuade the White House and General Eisenhower's staff that Giraud was the man for this situation, backed as he was by the North African population and already supported by the "resistants" of Algiers; and lastly Captain Beaufre, the escaped general's think-tank.

It was at this point that one of the most extraordinary events of the war took place. While Murphy was coming to the end of a stay in Washington, his associates in Algiers asked the "five" to arrange a meeting with "important leaders of the United States army" preparing the landing. A villa near Cherchell was chosen and the owners were asked to go away. On the night of 20 October old acquaintances were the first arrivals: on the one side Murphy and his assistant Knight, on the other three of the "five" (d'Astier, Van Hecke and Rigault), and General Mast, Commander Barjot and Colonel Jousse. Murphy announced that a submarine was bringing three members of Eisenhower's staff. But the sea was rough; the night passed without anyone coming; and the meeting broke up, having achieved nothing.

It was only the next day that three soaked Americans landed in rubber boats from a submarine. Even then an Arab servant, suspicious of the presence of so many big American cars in this remote spot, told the police, and nearly jeopardized the meeting, which had to be disguised as a party. The three were no less than General Mark Clark, Eisenhower's immediate assistant, General Lemnitzer* and Colonel Holmes, the link between the Commander-in-Chief and Robert Murphy.

No one will ever know why the American staff put several of its most important chiefs at risk for the sake of a conference at which, to be sure, questions concerning the place and means of landing were discussed but not the date of the operation. The French left Cherchell convinced that the operation would take place in March, whereas their guests knew that it was fixed for the seventh or eighth or ninth of November.

The French were particularly struck by one remark made during this meeting:

*The future Commander-in-Chief of NATO.

General Mark Clark said, "The operation will be carried out with means that go beyond imagination." And everyone dreamed of an armada carrying hundreds of thousands of men – the armada that Weygand or Noguès required for a welcoming reception. Lastly, Van Hecke and his companions thought that at Cherchell they had obtained the promise that the American forces would rapidly take over the operation to neutralize Algiers on the night of the landings.

On 19 October, just before this surprising conference, Robert Murphy sent General Giraud a letter which has sometimes been put forward as the "Giraud-Murphy agreement" – inaccurate in that it was no more than a rather vague three-point plan: that the United States looked upon France as an ally; that the re-establishment of its territorial integrity, both at home and overseas, was one of the Allied war-aims; and that "in the event of enemy intervention in a North or West African territory" the "coordination of the command" would be entrusted to General Giraud.

But this document, full of useful things and a remote echo of the Churchill – de Gaulle agreement of 7 August 1940, was to be completed by a curious exchange of letters. On 28 October, General Giraud continued the correspondence with Murphy by stating his requirement that the British and the "dissident French" (the term used by Vichy for the Free French) should be excluded from the expected landings: the American diplomat hastened to reply, quoting Giraud's observations word by word – including of course the piece about the "dissident French" – and added, "I am happy to assure you that the prospects you envisage are entirely in agreement with those of my government."[4]

In return General Giraud gave the Americans leave to interfere in French matters and to discriminate as they saw fit, taking their authority from this new arbiter of French interests.

Passy and Soustelle describe the attempts made by the London and Algiers Gaullists to coordinate their efforts and prepare counter-measures to deal with the radical exclusion of Fighting France carried out by Washington in the name of General Giraud. At the beginning of 1942 the BCRA had formed a North Africa section under Captain Semidei, known as Servais; but he ran into massive obstructions placed by the British.

In Algiers, the fighting Gaullist groups organized by José Aboulker, Guy Calvet and Captain Pillafort tried to obtain arms from the Americans; they were granted a few pistols and above all cigarettes. The two main Gaullist leaders, René Capitant and Louis Joxe, set off on a mission to France. The first had discussions with Combat and was told that the operation was planned for November; he then returned to Algiers and informed his friends of their comrades' decision: the organization was to commit itself to the hilt in the liberation of Algiers. In the same way, Louis Joxe, determined to prevent Algeria being "a dead weight in the Free French battle-order",[5] went to Lyons and there met the Martin-Chauffiers, Georges Altman, the organizer of Franc-Tireur, and Emmanuel d'Astier, the leader of Libération, who said to him, "Great things are going to happen; we must take part in them."[6]

On the morning of 5 November, Admiral Darlan took a plane from Vichy in the utmost secrecy: the evening before he had received a telegram from Admiral

Fenard, his representative in Algiers, telling him that his son Alain, who had been suffering from polio for some months, was very ill. In Algiers, Darlan at once conferred with General Juin,* who was in command of all the French forces in North Africa. The town was full of rumours. Important events were obviously about to take place. Darlan shut himself up at the Admiralty.

There have been endless questions about the true reason why the Admiral went to Algeria: his friends and those who explain his movements have always maintained that it was by mere chance and only in connection with his son's illness; others say that it was obviously linked to his talks with Noguès the month before and to the talks he had with the Americans; and to support their argument they emphasize the key part played by Admiral Fenard** in the middle of the picture.[7] But it is quite clear that Darlan had been in touch with Murphy's associates for nearly a month.

In London, around de Gaulle, there was resolute silence. Churchill says without hypocrisy in his history of the war that he was fully aware "of the gravity of the affront offered to de Gaulle,"[8] not only by excluding Fighting France from the operation but also by concealing it from the man who had come to join him at the time of disaster. The Prime Minister had certainly tried to persuade Roosevelt at least to inform de Gaulle a few days before the given date; but FDR had grown stubborn, continually quoting the precedent of Dakar. "From all the discussions preceding Torch," we read in Robert Sherwood's book, *Roosevelt and Hopkins: an Intimate History*,

> it was obvious that the eternally sore subject of de Gaulle and the Fighting French would again manifest itself. Roosevelt was obdurate on this point. He wrote, "I consider it essential that de Gaulle be kept out of the picture and be permitted to have no information whatever, regardless of how irritated and irritating he may become! [Sherwood goes on to say] This policy was directly attributable to Roosevelt himself and not to the State Department, and Churchill did not offer firm opposition to it.[9]

Churchill was the more inclined to yield to his American colleague's decision on the tactical level since he had to some degree imposed his own strategic choice – Torch and not Sledgehammer. So much the worse for de Gaulle, then. Churchill's master-plan for Europe's soft white under-belly by way of the Mediterranean were certainly worth this "insult" offered to the companion of June 1940.

Nevertheless, Fighting France made one last attempt to avoid being kept wholly out of the battle. At the end of October Passy asked his American colleague Arthur Roseborough of the OSS to come and see him, and he pointed out that there was a danger that the Giraud solution would cut the Resistance off from the Allies. The American envoy told his chief, General Donovan, and a few days later he came

*Who had warned him on 26 October, during the Admiral's short visit to Algiers, that the Americans were preparing to make a landing – information that Darlan does not seem to have taken into account.

**Who became one of the representatives of Fighting France in Washington the following year and organized de Gaulle's journey to the United States.

back to see Passy: "We should like to know what General de Gaulle's attitude towards the administrative authorities in North Africa would be if he were called upon to form the provisional government in Algiers." Passy at once handed on the question, and the General replied, "With these officials I should behave as I did in Syria. Those who had collaborated with the enemy – a dozen men – were sent off to French Equatorial Africa. The others stayed at their posts and they have served loyally." Roseborough immediately cabled this reply to Washington. Nothing more was heard of it.[10]

Yet even so, London did give the Constable a consolation-prize – on 6 November Eden came to see him to tell him that His Majesty's government, having definitively secured control of Madagascar the day before, had decided to hand the island back to Fighting France; and Eden even suggested that they should issue a joint communiqué announcing that General Legentilhomme, already appointed high commissioner, had left for Tananarive. De Gaulle quickly realized why the consolation-prize was being offered and wrote, "From this I gathered that things were about to happen in North Africa."[11]

During the evening of Saturday, 7 November, the United States radio stations broadcast this message: "Hello, Robert, Franklin is coming." Few signals of that kind in those days were as obvious: Robert was Murphy's Christian name and Franklin that of the Supreme Commander of the American forces. On that same Saturday evening the Soviet Ambassador gave a reception in London to mark the twenty-fifth anniversary of the Revolution. General de Gaulle was seen there, apparently impervious to the rumours. Around him, some people were already aware that the American fleet had been at sea since 24 October.

All at once, Jan Masaryk, the son of the founder of Czechoslovakia, took Pleven aside: "It's to be tonight!".[12] Pleven hurried to Carlton Gardens, where he was told that the General had gone home. Shortly after midnight, General Ismay, the head of Churchill's personal staff, telephoned Colonel Billotte, who carried out the same duties with de Gaulle. "The landings are to start in three hours, from Morocco to the Constantinois."*

It was only at about six o'clock on 8 November that Billotte went to see the General, sure as he was of arousing a tempest. The storm was proportionate to the event, to the methods chosen, and to the man. As he put on a dressing-gown over his white pyjamas, the Constable roared "I hope the Vichy people will fling them into the sea! You don't get France by burglary!" And for two solid hours Billotte underwent the dress rehearsal of what his chief was preparing to inflict upon Churchill at Chequers.

All that morning the General worked on a draft prepared for him by Billotte: it was the text of a speech that he was supposed to make that afternoon on the BBC. There is nothing like writing for calming one's mind. And when Charles Peake, who was the Foreign Office representative with de Gaulle, arrived a little before noon, head bowed and sure of the worst (his pitying colleagues had told him it would be dreadful), he found a serene Constable who told him that he was delighted that the lunch with Churchill was confirmed.

*The eastern coast of Algeria. (trs.)

When de Gaulle reached Chequers, where Churchill had been told by Peake that the storm was over, very little was known about the operation in progress. The Prime Minister could only tell his guest that apart from the participation of the British navy and air force the expedition was entirely American. "Somewhat embarrassed," says de Gaulle in his account, the Prime Minister made these remarks about the exclusion of Fighting France:

> We were forced to accept it. Yet you can be sure that we are not in any way renouncing our agreements with you. As the business takes on its full extension, we British are to come into action. Then we shall have our word to say. It will be to support you. You were with us during the worst moments of the war. We shall not abandon you when the horizon clears.

And as though it were a side-issue, Churchill asked his guest, "Do you know that Darlan is in Algiers?"

De Gaulle does not relate his reactions to this piece of news. He confines himself to recording his adverse criticisms of the operation: the Americans, by once more playing Vichy against Fighting France, were preparing cruel disappointments for themselves and they would not avoid bloodshed.

At five that afternoon de Gaulle, having returned to Carlton Gardens, presided over a session of the National Committee, to which he gave an account of his conversation at Chequers. He emphasized the points in common between Churchill's reactions and his own and on the Prime Minister's offer to send a delegation of the French Resistance to North Africa (Frenay and d'Astier were still in London). He also said that he had shown his host a letter of encouragement he had just received from Georges Mandel:* at this Churchill had asked him whether, in the event of a provisional government's being formed in North Africa, he would agree to include the former Minister of the Interior. De Gaulle: "Certainly. I should be happy to see such a man as Mandel in the provisional government of France."

And in a cable that was at once sent to the great proconsuls of Fighting France, de Gaulle added that Churchill had confirmed the "purely military" role entrusted to Giraud, the uncertainty as to whether his name was enough to bring over the Vichy forces, and the decisive importance of the help given to the disembarking troops by "the Gaullist elements".

All the witnesses agreed: on that day which, as some saw it, he was to receive his "ticket for oblivion", Charles de Gaulle was overflowing with confidence. Soustelle was with him in the afternoon, and he describes him thinking aloud: "His eyes shone; he walked to and fro, his hands hooked into his belt," saying that the statement of the solidarity of the British had made him more relaxed, agreeing that "Giraud was a good soldier", but repeating that what had to be avoided was "dissidence within the Resistance. No separate undertakings."

The words heard that evening by hundreds of thousands of listeners eager to hear the reactions and decisions of the leader of Fighting France were far from

*Who was then in prison.

echoing the storms of that morning. There was no longer any question of flinging the newcomers into the sea. Burglary or not, the Constable, speaking in the noblest tone, endorsed and encouraged the vast undertaking; although it put his personal fate in question, it set the gates of liberation ajar:

> The Allies of France have undertaken to draw French North Africa into the war of liberation. They are beginning to land enormous forces there. It is a question of so ordering matters that our Algeria, our Morocco and our Tunisia form the base, the starting-point for the liberation of France. Our American allies are at the head of this enterprise.
>
> The moment is very well chosen. Our British allies, seconded by the French troops, have just expelled the Germans and Italians from Egypt and they are making their way into Cyrenaica. Our Russian allies have definitively broken the enemy's supreme offensive. The French people, gathered together in resistance, are only waiting for the moment to rise up as a whole. So French leaders, soldiers, sailors, airmen, officials, colonists rise up now! Help our allies!
>
> Come! The great moment is here. This is the time for common sense and courage. Everywhere the enemy is staggering and giving way. Frenchmen of North Africa! Let us, through you, return to action from one end of the Mediterranean to the other, then the war will be won, and won thanks to France!

Up until that moment it had been possible to have many reservations about Charles de Gaulle's decisions and his statements, finding in them traces of intolerance, personal ambition and grievance or a kind of nationalism sometimes opposed to the interests of the majority, which others might have represented better, though with less brilliance or talent. But here, when one takes into account the full emphasis of the last four words, de Gaulle silences criticism. What more eloquent, more judicious and disinterested words could have been expected from this allegedly ambitious, selfish man?

Without yet knowing what was in store for him or what his place would be in this immense upheaval that was beginning, he launched himself into the fray, calling on everyone to fight for the common cause alone. Were not these American allies, for whom he was pleading with unrivalled force at this time, those very men who had just excluded him, doing so with a mean-minded attention to detail and an ill-tempered obstinacy? Although what he said seemed to advance Giraud at Free France's expense he hurried to the rescue of an enterprise that could have been his "ticket for oblivion" because the general interest was at stake.

It is true that at this point FDR cared very little for de Gaulle's thoughts on Torch; once again he was more concerned with the reactions of Pétain, whom, in the first draft of his message to Vichy, he addressed as "My dear old friend" – an expression of friendship that Churchill persuaded him to change. In this message, Roosevelt explained why he had sent his liberating armada to North Africa: "We are coming among you to thrust back the cruel invaders who wished to abolish for ever your right to govern yourselves, to have the religion of your choice and to live as you choose in peace and safety. We are coming among you solely to subjugate and defeat your enemies. Trust in our word. We do not wish to cause you any harm."

To this the Marshall retorted, not without point, "You allege pretexts that are justified by nothing. You impute to your enemies intentions that have never been transformed into acts. I have always stated that we should defend our Empire if it were attacked; you know that we shall defend it against any attacker whatsoever. You know that I shall keep my word."

Some of those who were present at the audience granted to the American chargé d'affaires Tuck on that morning of 8 November, say that having dutifully read this vigorous protest to his visitor, the "dear old friend" turned round and walked off to his own rooms, whistling to himself.

Algiers was not a stronghold that would drop into one's hand like a ripe fruit. In spite of the information gathered by Murphy and his agents, so proud of the intelligence they had been accumulating for two years, Vichyism in Algiers had not, as a whole, turned into pro-Americanism. The United States were quite popular there, but 10 000 soldiers and 20 000 armed civilians were ready to obey the Marshal's orders – to "resist any attack", *wherever* it came from.

There were three possibilities. Either these forces would join the newcomers right away; or they would fight, and taking into consideration the small number of men committed by Washington, this might lead to another Dakar; or partisans organized from within the community would nip all resistance in the bud. Although Robert Murphy had not given up hope of seeing the first proved true, he and the 'Cherchell' conspirators had made all their arrangements for the third.

During the conference on 21 October it had been agreed that shortly before the time of landing the Algerian partisans should neutralize the chief military commanders, take control of communications and occupy the buildings of the General Staff. The vanguard was made up of three hundred young men gathered and headed by General Mast; his staff included Colonel Van Hecke, Henri d'Astier, Captain Pillafort, Lieutenant Pauphilet and Superintendant Achiary. But the two key men in the operation were Colonel Jousse, the garrison major and as such the giver of missions, safe-conducts and arm-bands, and José Aboulker, the head of the improvised organization of local volunteers called VP (voluntaires de place) most of whom were very young: between eighteen and twenty-five.

The VPs' Gaullism has been called in question. Certainly the tendencies of the group spread in several directions. Let us take the case of Jean Daniel.[13] He joined the group, a few weeks before the operation, he had a conversation with Aboulker and among other questions he asked who the organization owed obedience to. José Aboulker replied, "Take care: until de Gaulle reaches Algiers, there's no question of obeying anyone at all." Gaullist inspiration, then, if not allegiance – until the General himself should make things plain.

On Saturday, 7 November, when the radio began to broadcast the message "Hello Robert, Franklin is coming", Colonel Jousse, for want of weapons (José Aboulker alone had a machine-gun, given to him by Murphy), issued the orders

("No bloodshed"), the password to be used with the landing forces ("Whisky?", the reply being "Soda"), and the tasks to be done: first seize the great military chiefs (Darlan, Juin and Koeltz), then arrest the most influential police officials, and lastly occupy the communications centre. By about two o'clock in the morning of 8 November the mission had been carried out. Admiral Darlan, taken prisoner by the VP, was talking with Murphy. Some of the conspirators had suggested liquidating him as a matter of routine – but this was contrary to Jousse's orders.

At 3 a.m. the landings commenced and were greeted by gunfire from the Admiralty forts. The first American soldiers came ashore at Sidi-Ferruch, where General Mast went to meet the officer in charge of the operation, General Ryder, whom he had to beg to hasten the manoeuvre, because all over the town the Vichy security forces, particularly the Gardes mobiles and the SOL, were being mobilized. To begin with they had been taken unawares and deceived by the misleading orders sent out by Jousse, Aboulker and Achiary, but now they had recovered their wits and they were counter-attacking.

Yet since midnight the essential moves had been taking place at the Villa des Oliviers, General Juin's residence, now controlled by the VP. It was to this place that Murphy had summoned Darlan, together with Fenard. The American diplomat, who had learnt only a few hours before that the Marshal's Dauphin was in Algiers, gave him a short account of the situation and asked him to prevent any bloodshed. Darlan refused, and reminded the Admiralty of the orders to fight that had already been given. At three in the morning, therefore, the battle began, while at the same time the Vichy authorities, stimulated by Darlan's orders and Pétain's broadcast message, calling for resistance to the Americans, organized and increased their efforts to regain control of the town.

Was everything going to end in disaster? No. The repressive machinery was checked by the activities of Jousse and the VP. Ryder's forces gradually advanced towards the centre of the town, though not without having to fight: it was in these skirmishes that Captain Pillafort and Lieutenant Dreyfus, among others, were killed.

A team from inside Algiers and under the flag of Fighting France had taken every risk to pave the way for the newcomers and had had to wait for them far longer than had been agreed at Cherchell.

But at the moment when everything was leading to an armistice in Algiers, another man burst into the discussion: Henri Giraud. Members of the Alliance network had taken him to Gibraltar in a submarine; from there he had flown to Blida, where the Americans had settled him three days earlier. Murphy had kept them as well informed as ever, and they were convinced that in Giraud they had an ace, a man who would "bring down the walls of Jericho".

In Gibraltar Giraud had come to an understanding with Eisenhower according to which he "agreed to cooperate with the American forces" on condition that he was made Commander-in-Chief where French troops were engaged, Washington undertaking to ensure the restoration of France and the French empire in their entirety. Eisenhower thought that in Giraud he had a most exceptional ally, one who would win him the cooperation of the French forces and administration. So when he landed at Algiers at the same time as Giraud at Blida and learnt that

Murphy and General Clark were offering Darlan the powers that he, with the agreement of the White House and the State Department, meant to hand over to Giraud, Eisenhower burst out "I shall never consent to that!"[14] Yet presently, like Giraud himself, he was obliged to take realities into account.

> General Giraud's cold reception by the French in Africa [says Eisenhower] was a terrible blow to our expectations: he was completely ignored. He made a broadcast, announcing assumption of leadership of French North Africa and directing French forces to cease fighting against the Allies, but his speech had no effect whatsoever. I was doubtful that it was even heard by significant numbers.[15]

On 9 November Darlan had received a message from Pétain: "I am glad that you are on the spot. You may act and keep me informed. You have my entire confidence." Did he interpret this as giving him complete freedom of decision? In the book he devotes to the Admiral, Jules Moch disputes this, stating that when, at 9.30 a.m. on the same day, Vichy offered Darlan German air support against the Americans, at 9.57 a.m. Darlan accepted.[16] Thirty-six hours after the landing, therefore, the Admiral was more than ever on the side of military collaboration with the Nazis. And at that point he called upon his colleagues in Tunis to place themselves at the disposal of the Axis.

When he saw Clark and Murphy, who read him the draft of the Armistice and gave him half an hour to sign it, Darlan refused to sign it without referring the matter to Vichy. Clark replied that if he did not sign, then it would be Giraud who did so. Darlan lost his temper. Juin stepped in as a mediator and eventually Darlan said he was "prepared to sign in the Marshal's name" at noon on 10 November. Having obtained the paper they wanted, Clark and Murphy went back to Giraud and told him that as Darlan was their prisoner it was to him that they were offering "civil and military authority in North Africa". Giraud refused.

It was not with "another Darlan" that Clark and Murphy were negotiating in this way. It was with a man who firmly cited the Marshal and the ideology of Vichy as his authority and who urged his Tunisian colleagues to fight on the Axis side yet agreed to collaborate with the US. Giraud therefore was to be satisfied with the military command offered to him by Darlan, suddenly promoted "High Commissioner for North Africa" without ceasing to hold himself out as the representative of Marshal Pétain, who from Vichy publicly denounced his "disloyalty".

Yet if we are to believe several of his colleagues of that time, particularly Admiral Auphan (at Vichy) and General Bergeret (in Algiers), on 10 November the Marshal sent Darlan a secret telegram approving of his having stopped fighting the Americans.* The situation was so very extraordinary that it prompted Winston Churchill to make his splendid remark in the Commons: "If Darlan were to have Pétain shot, he would certainly do so in the Marshal's name."[17]

De Gaulle, who had undoubtedly agreed to give way provisionally to Giraud on 8

*The text of this secret telegram has never been found.

November, would not do so to Darlan. How did they react, he and the Fighting French, to the Americans' installation of the Admiral?

On 9 November, when fighting was going on from Casablanca to Algiers, and when, with the consent of Admiral Esteva and Admiral Derrien,* the German forces landed at Tunis to take the Americans from behind, he observed "that there were long faces in Allied circles in London". When he received Admiral Stark, the United States representative with Fighting France, he noted that the American commander was completely bewildered by the course of events, so very different from what Robert Murphy had foretold during the last two years. De Gaulle asked him to send a Fighting French delegation** to Algiers made up of two men from the "exterior", Pleven and Billotte, and two from the "interior", Frenay and d'Astier, who were still in London. Stark promised to do his best, in agreement with Churchill; but the strengthening of Darlan's position in the following days turned Algiers into a southern Vichy, changing from a German to an American protectorate, and this made the planned mission unthinkable.

On 11 November, while the Wehrmacht was hurling itself upon the hitherto unoccupied zone, Fighting France gathered its members in the Albert Hall in London. The General, in his *Mémoires de guerre*, speaks of the "surge of enthusiasm" beneath which "joy and anxiety" fought for predominance in people's minds. Some reliable witnesses, like Hervé Alphand,[18] however, put more stress on the anger in their hearts. Had Fighting France chosen to continue the struggle on the side of the democracies merely to prolong Vichy in Africa and to support a man who in June 1940 had at his disposal the last weapons France possessed to oppose the Nazis, but who had seen fit to paralyse them before openly supporting Hitler's strategy in the East?

General de Gaulle made himself the spokesman for this muted rage; and as he did so he "held the door open for men of good will". He called for the help "of all", but without giving way on the essence of the matter, for his aim remained "the complete reestablishment of the laws of the Republic" – words that could not charm a Giraud who had joined Darlan and in whose eyes the Republic was anathema.

Was the movement of June 1940 fated to isolation and extinction? Was de Gaulle Charles alone once more? A few days later Hervé Alphand, in the notebook that he kept in London, wrote this: "The shade of a negotiated peace is hovering, a peace that in order to 'struggle against Bolshevism' would allow the rebuilding of a strong Germany."[19] If Washington was making use of Darlan in the one place, why not Goering in the other? But then where was the total victory over Nazism that Roosevelt and Churchill had sworn to win, a year before?

It was time for the Gaullists to react, and all the more so since the London radio had just installed an American censor who forbade any attack on Darlan or Pétain. Was not Darlan negotiating with General Clark with a view to an agreement that amounted to no more than capitulation, a Rethondes in a sunny climate according to whose terms all the real power was placed in the hands of the American

*Who handed over the Bizerta fleet to the Axis.

**In accordance with an idea put forward as we have seen by Churchill on 8 November.

command? The Admiral remained faithful to collaboration. He had simply changed overlords.

Charles de Gaulle's first reaction was addressed to the United States. On 15 November he received a message from Admiral Stark which spoke of the Darlan deal as "a stage". The General retorted: "I understand that the United States should pay for traitors' treason if that seems to them profitable, but the payment must not be drawn on the honour of France." Stark refused to accept this reply.

On 16 November Churchill and Eden invited de Gaulle to come and talk over the new turn given to the war by the retention of Darlan "in the Marshal's name" at Algiers. Churchill said that he "shared the General's feelings", but he pointed out the strategic benefits that underlay the recourse to this "expedient". To this, if we are to believe his *Mémoires*, de Gaulle replied with one of his most impressive declarations:

> You bring forward strategic reasons; but it is a strategic error to place oneself in a position that contradicts the moral nature of this war. We are no longer in the eighteenth century, when Frederick bribed people at the court of Vienna in order to be able to seize Silesia, nor in the days of the Italian Renaissance, when people made use of the Milanese sbirri or the Florentine assassins. And even then they were not set at the head of the liberated nations. At present we are making war with people's hearts, their blood, and their suffering. [And the Constable goes on] I then showed Churchill and Eden the telegrams from France that conveyed the stupefaction of public opinion . . . If one day France were to see that because of the Anglo-Saxons the country's liberation only amounted to Darlan, you would perhaps be able to win the war militarily but you would lose it morally, and in the end there would be only one conqueror – Stalin.[20]

Churchill asked de Gaulle on to lunch at Downing Street, and he continued the conversation thus: "Although the present state of circumstances is painful for you, the position is splendid. From now on Giraud is liquidated politically. In the long run Darlan will be impossible. Do not clash head-on with the Americans. They will come to you, because there is no alternative." To this the General replied by urging the Prime Minister not to let America take over the direction of the war, for, said he, "It is for you to carry it on, at least in the moral field."[21]

That same evening the French National Committee broadcast the following text from London:

> General de Gaulle and the CNF wish it to be known that they are taking no part in the negotiations now in progress in North Africa with the delegates of Vichy and that they assume no responsibility for them. If these negotiations were to end with arrangements whose effect would be to sanction the Vichy regime in North Africa it is obvious that they could not be accepted by Fighting France. The union of all the French overseas territories in the battle for freedom is possible only in conditions that are consonant with the will and the dignity of the French people.

The American authorities replied to this challenge by intensifying their bans and limitations upon the spokesman of Fighting France.

In mid-November two important travellers landed in London. The one was General François d'Astier de La Vigerie, the brother of Henri and Emmanuel, who was joining Free France.* The other was Yvon Morandat, who, having been one of Gaullism's first envoys to the home country, was now coming back with great news: almost all the Resistance organizations, political parties and trade unions** had just issued a proclamation in which they recognized General de Gaulle as head of the national Resistance and called for his installation at Algiers in the name of the French people.

Speaking on the BBC, Morandat described the stupefaction and anger that the "provisional expedient" had aroused in French public opinion. The American censor let this protest through, but not the document that, in the name of the home Resistance, recognized the leadership of General de Gaulle. And on 21 November, when the General himself tried to say, on the microphone that had broadcast his appeals for the last thirty months, that the French would have nothing to do with a "dishonoured" liberation, he was forbidden by the Foreign Office to express himself in this way unless Washington first gave its consent. Three days later Churchill apologized to de Gaulle for having had to yield to FDR's veto.

Churchill might burst out in public and above all in private against the alliance with the "traitor Darlan", but every day he was becoming more resigned to accepting Roosevelt's enterprises. He even said to Eden that "after all, Darlan has done more for us than de Gaulle".

The Anglo-Saxon press, however, exploded: "Both in Great Britain and in the United States a cry of indignation rose. This shameful horse-trading with so notorious a Quisling amounted to an unworthy betrayal of the Allies' ideal."[22] Roosevelt felt for once directly aimed at. To be sure, he was still entirely in agreement with Clark and Murphy's undertaking and he continued to sneer at the reservations expressed by Fighting France, showing his contempt for anything that might resemble a French national conscience. Writing to Churchill he said:

> In regard to de Gaulle, I have heretofore enjoyed a great satisfaction in leaving him in your hands. We must remember there is also a catfight in progress between Giraud and Darlan each claiming full military command of French forces in North and West Africa. The principal thought to be driven home to all three of these prima donnas is that the situation is today solely in the military field and that any decision by any one of them, or by all of them, is subject to review and approval by Eisenhower.[23]

But FDR, a good judge of public opinion, felt that his representatives were a threat

*With which he was already well known as a sympathizer. De Gaulle soon made him his military deputy.

**Combat, Libération, Franc-Tireur, the CGT, the CFTC (Confédération française des travâileurs chrétiens – a trade union organization founded in 1919 which adhered to Christian socialism), the CAS (Socialist), the Radical party and the Fédération républicaine.

to him: it was the public he had to speak to. On 16 November he called a press conference and told the journalists:

> The present provisional arrangement is only a temporary expedient justified solely by the stress of battle. It has accomplished two military objectives. The first was to save American and British lives, and French lives, on the other hand. The second made it possible to avoid a "mopping-up" period in Algiers and Morocco. Admiral Darlan's proclamation assisted in making "mopping-up" unnecessary. Temporary arrangements made with Admiral Darlan apply, without exception, to the current local situation only. I have requested the liberation of all persons in North Africa because they opposed the efforts of the Nazis to dominate the world, and I have asked for the abrogation of all laws and decrees inspired by Nazi governments or ideologists.[24]

The installation of Darlan a temporary expedient? During the following weeks nothing changed in Algiers. The racial laws were still applied. Portraits of the Marshal were to be seen everywhere. The political internees (Gaullist and Communist) remained in prison. As for FDR, it was a few days later, on 23 November, that he receive André Philip and Adrien Tixier and uttered the fateful words that so angered his visitors: "If Laval gives me Paris, I shall entertain Laval." And to emphasize that this was a long-term policy, at that time he told his confidential friend Leahy, when they were talking about the opposition raised by the choice of Darlan, "I am an obstinate Dutchman."*

Though Darlan may have "given Algiers" to the Allies, was he also capable of giving them his fleet, that fief, that domain which he had built up and of which he had been the sole ruler for seven years? What better way of proving his authority and winning London's good will after Washington's? In a cable to Roosevelt on 14 November Eisenhower who had come over to the "Darlan expedient" pointed out indeed that the rejection of the Admiral would be "giving up our hopes of the fleet in Toulon".[25]

On 13 November the Admiral sent Jean de Laborde, his colleague in command of this fleet, the order to proceed to Algiers. He received only an insulting refusal, punctuated, it is said, with the word "shit". Laborde's personal hatred for Darlan (whom he considered a more or less freemason schemer) was matched only by his violent Anglophobia. A few days before, Auboyneau, who had succeeded Muselier at the head of the Gaullist naval forces, sent the Toulon fleet an appeal to "join the armies of deliverance". Darlan may have brought a contemptuous reply on himself: for his part Auboyneau received no answer of any kind.

Since 11 November and the German occupation of the south zone, the anchorage of Toulon had been isolated, Hitler having agreed not to attack the fleet "out of admiration for our navy", as Admiral de Laborde asserted. Yet on 18 November this honest admirer insisted that the largest unit occupied with the defence of the fleet should be withdrawn. And presently several bodies of SS occupied the neighbouring heights. "Prepared for scuttling", seventy-five vessels

*The Roosevelts were of Dutch origin.

were blocked there, including three of the finest battleships in the world, eight cruisers and sixteen submarines. Who, apart from Admiral de Laborde, could believe that Hitler, having invaded the free zone, would wait and give them a chance of joining the Allied forces?

During the night of 26 to 27 November, the 1st SS Armoured Corps, carrying out Plan Lila, flung itself upon the port of Toulon "to prevent the fleet from joining the Judaeo-English war-criminals" as Hitler put it in his letter to Pétain. Thus caught in the trap that he had stubbornly seen fit to close round himself, Admiral de Laborde gave the order – ready since June 1940 – to sink the fleet that he had refused to use in battle. Anything rather than fight on the Allied side.

While the finest high-seas fleet that the French nation had ever given itself was being sunk in the port of Toulon under the furious eyes of the German assailants, de Gaulle, given freedom of speech this time, spoke on the London radio: he said that "no doubt deprived of any other issue,* the French sailors have with their own hands destroyed the French fleet so that at least the country should be spared the ultimate shame of seeing its men-of-war become enemy ships. A shudder of pain, of pity, and of rage has traversed the entirety of France."

In his *Mémoires* the General speaks personally of the disaster and describes himself as being "overwhelmed with anger and sorrow" (it was because of the great suicide at Toulon that he called this chapter "Tragedy") and as receiving the "nobly expressed but inwardly pleased" condolence of Winston Churchill, an unfair remark, in that the British were wholly uninvolved in this French naval misfortune.

Yet in all this we see that in his apparent isolation and from one disaster to another, General de Gaulle was from now on being carried forward by the tide; from now onwards there was no trial that did not turn out to be for his advantage. His exclusion from Operation Torch caused a scandal: here he stood, all the greater for having been banished from it. The Darlan expedient, that "dirty business", had given him, by contrast, a halo of virtue. The scuttling at Toulon, in its bloody absurdity, emphasized the blind-alley nature of the whole Vichy strategy, more or less taken over and revived in North Africa, where Giraud was cloaked with its disrepute. And in Algiers every passing day threw a darker shadow over this Vichyism with an American coating.

Darlan was deeply humiliated by the refusal of the fleet to join him, all the more so since Admiral Robert at Martinique and Admiral Godfroy at Alexandria had also rejected his order to sail to Algiers; and he had been deprived of his life's work by the scuttling. Nevertheless, he did have some successes: in the first place he was joined by the greatest of the African proconsuls, that same Governor-General Boisson who had flung de Gaulle back at Dakar two years before. The coming-over of this paragon among the Marshal's followers, with his seven territories and 80 000 men, completed the isolation of Vichy and the abasement of Pétain by broadening Darlan's basis of operations. Upon this, the Admiral proclaimed himself head of State and surrounded himself with a quasi government.

*Nevertheless five submarines did manage to get out into the open sea, one being the famous *Casabianca*.

But a month after he had been recognized by the American authorities, François Darlan saw his power dwindle by the day. The scuttling of 27 November had struck him a mortal blow. All the quibbling in the world, such as the attempt at founding his legitimacy on a mission entrusted to him by the Marshal when the old leader was free, could do nothing to revive his position: he drew the source of his authority from Vichy, which was one of the targets of the crusade in which he was concerned.

The Anglo-American press as a whole waged a furious campaign against this "stinking polecat Darlan", and every journalist knew that in their letters Eisenhower and Clark referred to him by the even more insulting initials, YBSOB (yellow-bellied son of a bitch). He certainly tried to climb back up this slope: on 13 December he summoned the international press to his residence of El Biar, but in attempting to justify his collaboration by the pressures that had been brought to bear on him, he finally did away with all remaining sympathies. "Pokerface", muttered one of the men there. "Disastrous general impression," observed René Pierre-Gosset.[26] He told Murphy that four plots were being woven round him. "You will end up by getting yourself murdered," his wife observed. And many witnesses of those December days state that he himself, who was receiving threats of death and police warnings, seemed to drift in a kind of fatalistic acquiescence.[27]

On 14 December de Gaulle told Adrien Tixier, his representative in Washington, that the Americans had agreed to take General François d'Astier de La Vigerie over to Algiers, the pioneer of the "second landing", that of the Gaullists. The head of Fighting France, who had been prevented from sending his chosen envoys, sent this outstanding soldier, brother to one of the leaders of the home Resistance and to one of the men in power in Algeria, Henri d'Astier, the key-man of the landings and secretary-general of the police. The envoy was given an information gathering mission. Guided by his brother Henri, General d'Astier saw a great many people, ranging from Lemaigre-Dubreuil to the Comte de Paris* and from Capitant to Murphy – who suggested that he should call on the Admiral, a suggestion that d'Astier, disobeying the orders of London, accepted.

He told the admiral he should withdraw "as soon as possible" in order to resolve the difficulties of a situation that had become impossible, leaving the military command in Giraud's hands. Darlan did not wish to hear another word and he insisted that the visitor should pack his bag and go back to London at once. This meant that the Fighting French envoy was able to deliver a report to his chief as early as the next day, a report that de Gaulle, in a telegram to Catroux, described as "fairly sanguine". In his *Mémoires*, de Gaulle says that according to d'Astier "Darlan, feeling the ground give way under him, was likely to leave the place quite soon."

Was this picture of a Darlan at his last gasp and already politically liquidated given here to clear the Gaullist movement of any involvement in the now imminent murder? It is true that the act committed the day after François d'Astier de La Vigerie's forced departure was so useful to the designs of the London committee that in the countless works and articles devoted to the subject the deed is often

*The pretender to the French throne (trs.).

imputed to it. Is it for that reason the author of the *Mémoires de guerre* particularly wishes it to be understood that his envoy departed from a finished man?

In fact Catroux's impression of a twilit Darlan, gathered on 10 December at Gibraltar, where the Admiral's secret messenger, Commander de Beaufort, told him of Darlan's coming retirement, is borne out by many other witnesses and by the American sources themselves. Yet it was decided that the best course would be to induce him to resign, allowing him to appoint a successor. It was thought that this would not be difficult, for Darlan had more intelligence than courage.[28]

On 20 November 1942, in a barn on Cape Matifou about twelve miles from Algiers, four young men, members of a *corps franc* made up of a dozen volunteers who trained in this remote place with the idea of joining the British army in Tunisia, listened to their twenty-four year old leader, Aspirant* Philippe Ragueneau, tell them about a great plan. They had come from Van Hecke's Chantiers de jeunesse and they had all taken part in the activities of the night of 7 to 8 November. What did Ragueneau tell them? That Darlan was a barrier between France and its liberation and that there was an urgent need for his physical elimination.

All the young men present volunteered. They therefore decided to draw lots and see who should carry it out. This was done at once. Straight away Ragueneau called out that he had the shortest straw, but the youngest there, the twenty-year-old Fernand Bonnier de La Chapelle, had no difficulty in showing that in fact his was shorter still. The decision was soon taken: while his comrades joined the British forces at Sbeitla in Tunisia as forseen, Fernand Bonnier should go to Algiers and prepare the act he had undertaken to carry out.

For a month this young man made contacts, learnt about the Admiral's habits, and asked advice. He once more found his companions of the night of 7 to 8 November (particularly Mario Faivre and Sabatier) and he saw two men whom he already knew, Henri d'Astier de La Vigerie,* whose protection, tacit or declared, was to be very useful to him, and above all Lieutenant the Reverend Father Cordier. Both were monarchists, and from this it has been inferred that Bonnier was too, though Ragueneau disputes it.[29]

In any event, the young man, who was in contact with various members of Algerian society and was received by the banker Alfred Pose who was a royalist and influential figure. It is clear that before he reached the Summer Palace of Algiers and the High Commissioner's offices, where he found himself face to face with the man he had sworn to kill, Bonnier had been spoken to and encouraged in his plan by several monarchists and Gaullists.

A little before 3 p.m. on 24 December 1942 Bonnier got out of a black Peugeot driven by his friend Mario Faivre: there were also two other comrades in it (Sabatier and Jean-Bernard d'Astier). In his pocket he had a revolver given to him by Father Cordier, together with a plan of the palace and an identity-card in the name of Morand. The orderly recognized him (he had already been there that

*In the army an aspirant is an officer who has just passed out of a military academy but who is not yet a second-lieutenant; in the navy he is roughly the equivalent of a midshipman (trs.).
*Whose son was one of his friends.

morning, when he was told that the Admiral was away but that he would be back in the afternoon) and took him into the waiting-room, where he was asked to fill out a form: the Admiral would not be long. "M. Morand" would be seen after the visitor who now had an appointment, Pierre Bourdan, one of the speakers to the French programme of the London radio.*

François Darlan, accompanied by his ADC Commander Hourcade, crossed the vestibule where Bonnier was waiting; just as he reached the door of his office and turned on hearing someone coming, Bonnier fired twice. The Admiral fell, hit in the face and the chest. He never regained consciousness and died three hours later at the Maillot hospital.

Bonnier was at once disarmed, beaten, arrested and handed over to the police; placed as he was, he had no chance of escape. He was at once interrogated by Superintendent Garidacci and sent before a court martial summoned by General Bergeret, which judged him during the night of 25 to 26 December. The trial was in camera: only the young man's lawyer was admitted to the hearing. Fernand Bonnier de La Chapelle, who evidently believed that someone would intervene in his favour, was shot at dawn on 26 December. All this hurry makes one think that the authorities in Algiers were eager to stifle** what might have been troublesome revelations. Troublesome for whom? For the Gaullists? Can it be believed that Giraud and Bergeret were likely to cover those "London people" they detested?

Everything leads one to suppose that Darlan's associates, drawn to this line of thought by the few clues the young murderer had given during his interrogation – the names of Louis Cordier and Henri d'Astier were often mentioned – at once thought of a royalist plot. This allowed General Bergeret to have Cordier and d'Astier arrested on 10 January.

However absurdly organized the crime had been, and however plausible the explanation that it was an act carried out by the representative of a little band of over-excited boy scouts, there are many enquirers and witnesses who implicate either the monarchist group faithful to the Comte de Paris, who had reached Algiers on 10 December (he lived in Morocco), and Alfred Pose, or Fighting France, or a combination of the two.

The argument that the operation had been mounted by the BCRA may not be sound. In any case, the most widespread theory is that which makes the monarchists responsible for the murder. In a television programme in 1978 Alain Decaux reproduced a statement by Mme Henri d'Astier implicating the pretender to the throne, who was in bed with a violent fever before the murder and who is alleged to have said to several of his supporters, including Henri d'Astier,

> "I am now certain that Darlan is a traitor. His being kept in power prevents any solution. I give you the order to eliminate him without loss of time. Everything must be finished by the twenty-fourth." My husband asked him what he meant by "eliminate". The Comte de Paris replied, "Make him disappear." Again Henri questioned him: "By any means? Is that what you

*Who speaks of the event in *Carnets des jours d'attente*.

**In his memoirs Giraud states that he did all he could to hasten Bonnier's execution.

> wish to say?" At this the Prince declared, "Yes, that's it: make him disappear by any means."

The denial expressed by the Comte de Paris in his memoirs has not convinced everybody.

But others prefer to incriminate General de Gaulle and the London Committee. This is naturally the case with Alfred Fabre-Luce, who bases himself both on a remark made by François d'Astier at the Hotel Aletti on 22 December after a conversation with the Comte de Paris: "Darlan is going to disappear physically",[30] and on information according to which a sum of dollars coming from London had been found on Bonnier (according to an Intelligence Service "revelation").

In an interview published in *L'Express* on 3 December 1975, Colonel Paillole, who was in charge of the case, asserts that Bonnier was found "to have $2000 on him".

> The military judge appointed to carry out the enquiries soon discovered that it came from Henri d'Astier's dwelling. Thanks to the Intelligence Service, the numbers on the notes allowed their provenance to be ascertained. These dollars had been delivered by the British to General de Gaulle's financial services in December 1942. A permit allowing them to be taken to French North Africa had been issued in the name of General François d'Astier de La Vigerie, Henri's brother.

This "proof by dollars" does not ring true. A payment for the crime? That was not Bonnier's style. Travelling money for the rest of the operation? Everything shows the young man resigned to capture – even though he might have to wait for intercession from on high. As for the part played by the Intelligence Service, it is perhaps rather surprising that an experienced specialist in the struggles between services should take as gospel this "confession" made against the head of Fighting France by these allies capable of successive or simultaneous fits of sincerity.

The most disconcerting side of the matter remains Henri d'Astier. He had an undoubted influence on Bonnier, who was also a friend of his son: that he should have allowed Bonnier to be shot without intervening at a time when he was still a high police official, a condottiere hardly to be suspected of cowardice, throws a dark shadow over the whole business. It is the Ragueneau version, nevertheless, the version of that little group inspired by Gaullism but isolated and at this juncture without any contact with the authorities of Fighting France, that remains the most convincing.

In London, during the days that followed, the reactions of the General and his associates were a mixture of formal caution and inward satisfaction. The first comment uttered by Fighting France made no moral judgment and confined itself to observing that this "event" which had not "disturbed public order in North Africa", could not "delay the return of that part of our Empire to the war."[31]

As for the General, who at first used the word "crime" when he was speaking to those close to him, he expressed himself on the subject in three ways. In a telegram of 25 December to General Legentilhomme, then in Cairo on his way to Madagascar together with Captain de Boissieu (who reproduces the telegram in a book[32]) de Gaulle informed all the Fighting French authorities that "neither he nor his fellow-workers" had anything whatsoever to do with the murder of Darlan. Then in a message on 26 December to General Catroux, he observes that although the conclusions François d'Astier had brought back from his journey to Algiers were "fairly sanguine", they were "more so after the end of Darlan". And after a few days he simply refered to Darlan's "execution". Lastly his silence about the Admiral's death when he spoke on the radio three days later: to say nothing about an event of such importance, which had completely altered the balance of power in North Africa and far beyond, was strange, and scarcely in his character.

As for the definitive version of the Darlan affair which de Gaulle made a point of giving in his *Mémoires*, it is contained in three short sections.

> No private person has the right to kill except on a battle-field. Darlan's behaviour, both as governor and as leader, was a matter for the nation's justice and not for a group or an individual.
>
> But [went on the General] the conditions of the enquiry, the judgment and the execution of the murder were a kind of challenge to the circumstances which, without justifying the tragedy, explain and to a certain degree excuse it.[33]

It is the word "excuse" that swims to the surface.*

Whatever may have been his relation to the deed performed, General de Gaulle's most important action at this juncture was the message he sent to General Giraud on 25 December, offering to meet him at once "either in Algeria or in Chad" (the second to make it quite clear that he could be the inviting power) so that they might discuss the setting up of a "provisional, central power".

Giraud was indeed to see himself, by the elimination of Darlan, invested with the supreme responsibilities in North Africa: although a secret arrangement by Darlan had appointed Noguès as his successor, and although a current was then pushing forward the Comte de Paris, who had supporters in the Council of the Empire, it was Giraud who came to the top. Thrust on by the Americans, he was appointed "civil and military Commander-in-Chief".

After four days of silence, Giraud replied curtly to de Gaulle's telegram: he thought the "atmosphere unfavourable" for a direct personal meeting, but he did not exclude the possibility of receiving an envoy from London. At this de Gaulle cabled his proconsuls: "General Giraud's dispositions with regard to us are not bad but it is to be feared that he is more or less playing the American game."[34]

Did this high degree of moderation arise from the euphoria that emanates from most of his telegrams of that time? Whether he was addressing Tixier, his representative in Washington, or Catroux or his other proconsuls in Africa and Asia, he can be seen, during these last days of 1942, possessed by the certainty of victory: no longer of the Allies' victory, of which only passing fits of discourage-

*Philippe Ragueneau, who claimed the prime responsibility for Darlan's liquidation, became an influential Gaullist figure, a spokesman for de Gaulle in 1958–59.

ment had ever made him doubt, but of his own. Why? His analyses and his observations both reached this conclusion, now that the battle of North Africa, fought without him and in the most ominous confusion, was at last opening out on to better strategic prospects.

The reason the Constable now changed into an eager candidate for power, was in the first place the unbelievable and most discreditable underhand dealings in Algiers; the collapse of Marshalism, which was no longer protected even by the fiction of a free zone, the elimination of Darlan, and Giraud's daily proof of his incapacity paved the way before him. Even the annihilation of the fleet served his cause: the whole framework of good and bad reasons that had led Washington to back Vichy (the free zone as a source of information, the fleet, the Marshal's fame, the possibility of being established in North Africa without firing a shot) had either collapsed or had already been carried out. From now on what was the use of anyone but himself?

De Gaulle was well aware that the prejudices against him were still very strong. He was well aware that the Americans were still hostile to him – as were most of the French military caste. Yet what of it? The tide had changed. For a while Giraud would be seen wandering about among the ruins of the shattered myth of Vichy. But it was he, de Gaulle, who was the solution, and the only one: every day Churchill's forecast, made as early as 16 November, proved more prophetic.

But other factors were working in the same direction. De Gaulle attached a great importance to the letters that Morandat had brought to him in London, immediately after the installation of Darlan at Algiers. The adherence and the faithfulness of the Resistance organization, the parties and the unions that these letters had told him of, had encouraged him not to give way to Darlan or to Giraud, and they had strengthened him in the conviction that he certainly had a mandate – the mandate of those who had carried out the hardest task against the occupier in order to express their absolute demand that France should not be treated as a mere landing-ground by the Allies but must be recognized as a partner in the battle. And he was to play this trump card with the utmost skill.

All the more so since Fighting France was increasing in size. For de Gaulle as a military leader, these weeks of November and December 1942 were a time of the deepest satisfaction. The motorized column from Chad, commanded by the young General Leclerc, in whom he had delighted more than in any other from the very beginning, had conquered the Italian Fezzan in less than a month and was now thrusting towards Tunisia, to join up with the glorious British Eighth Army. At the same time Legentilhomme, having accepted the adhesion of Djibouti, was installing a completely Gaullist administration in Madagascar, while in its turn La Réunion joined Fighting France – now a power to be reckoned with in the Indian Ocean.

But what made Gaullism a "moving force" was not only the dynamism of its leaders, the clear-mindedness of its Resistance fighters, and the sense of opportunity displayed by scores of administrators and officers: it was also that its legitimacy arose from a proper relation between action and ethics.

It is of course possible to make game of Charles de Gaulle's political morality, of his ideas of fairness, and, on occasion, of his comparative indifference to the feelings, the arguments and even the lives of others. But if one listens to him and watches him during this journey that was to lead him from London to Algiers and from Anfa to Paris, one beholds what one is obliged to call the advent of justice – with all the terrible aspect that judgment may possess.

The phase then beginning in January 1943 was perhaps the most significant in the Constable's life, the phase in which his character became concentrated and flowered. Not indeed because he circumvented, held up to ridicule and eliminated the unfortunate Giraud within ten months, an artichoke eaten leaf by leaf by a rival who had sharpened his teeth on opponents of quite another kind, but because he was to symbolize that irreducible share of morality and faith which forms part of any great policy. His dealings and words were still often cynical and even brutal; but he held himself like a man for whom politics is also made up of permanent values. And his awareness of the fact increased his strength tenfold.

CHAPTER THIRTY-ONE

The Anfa Quartet

Thirty months earlier, de Gaulle had refused to be no more than the head of a foreign legion, preferring to claim the whole of French legitimacy, to assert that he was the trustee of the national sovereignty, and to set out, starting from London, on the reinvention of the State. Sheer madness. At the beginning of 1943 this madness was in the process of becoming reasonable.

Pétain had been deprived of his last shreds of legitimacy by his obstinacy in clinging to the territory that he no longer even protected from total occupation; Darlan had been murdered; the majority of the Resistants had joined London; French military units were fighting on three continents: Charles de Gaulle had only to get a footing in Algiers, no longer a guest in London under obligations to Churchill, and, together with Giraud, to set up that "central power" which his allies disputed but which had never ceased to be his aim. Desire for power? Of course. But above all the realization that without this essential attribute of sovereignty, France would only be tolerated at the victory celebration and would be reshaped according to the strategic designs of the conquerors.

He therefore had to resume the offensive, both in the direction of those who held the keys of Algiers, and in that of the great powers. But his haste disturbed both the one and the other. The offer of a meeting in Algiers sent to Giraud was at first rejected. The plan of a journey to Washington, where, speaking through Philip, Roosevelt had invited him as early as November and which had first been settled for the end of December, was abruptly postponed until 10 January and then to the end of the month. So fate had to be coerced, and once again de Gaulle had to appeal to public opinion.

On 2 January 1943 the General broadcast a declaration which resembled one of those flares that the assailant sends up in the dark to shed light over his attack:

> The confusion within French North and West Africa is increasing. The reason for this confusion is that since the collapse of Vichy, French authority there has no basis, because the great national force of ardour, cohesion and experience that constitutes Fighting France and that has already brought back a great part of the Empire into the Republic and into the war, is not officially represented in those French territories. The remedy for this confusion is the setting up of a provisional and enlarged central authority, having as its basis national union, as its inspiration the spirit of war and liberation, and as its laws those of the Republic, until the nation should have made known its will.
>
> Such is the tradition of French democracy. In 1870, after the fall of the

> Empire, this was the way the men in charge of national defence provisionally took over power in the name of the Republic, to guide the nation's effort in the war. I have suggested to General Giraud that he should meet me at once on French territory. France's position and the general situation of the war allow no delay.[1]

He had unveiled his batteries and stated his aim: "provisional central authority." We knew that in spite of the emphatic references to the Republic and to democracy in his declaration, the document not only exasperated the American leaders but also irritated the British government. He did not care, being quite sure of the support of public opinion.

Had he placed the bar too high this time? From Washington, Tixier sent to tell him that the popular media, radio and provincial papers – were reacting unfavourably to his proposals, accusing him of "destroying General Eisenhower's authority and endangering the American expedition by internal disputes."[2]

Churchill was vexed by the declaration, but speaking to Eden he conceded that it was no longer possible to maintain the Rooseveltian idea of a France looked upon as *res nullius* until a remote and hypothetical national election should take place. On this point de Gaulle was right: his country could no longer be deprived of all representation. How could London reconcile French aspirations and American determination? A first step would be to bring de Gaulle, the spokesman for the one, and Giraud, encouraged by the other, closer together.

In the first days of January 1943 a plan took shape for a meeting between the British Prime Minister and the American President on African soil, to emphasize the strength of the alliance and to reassert the common war-aims. Churchill, who had loved Morocco for many years, suggested Casablanca. In spite of the opinion of his counsellors and security services, Roosevelt was enthusiastic for the plan and fixed the rendezvous for 14 January 1943.

It must not be forgotten that this meeting's main objective was to settle the great strategic decisions for the re-conquest of Europe. Yet the British Prime Minister also wished to make it the beginning of a solution of the French problem under his aegis and in his own best interests, confronting FDR (and Giraud) on the one hand and de Gaulle on the other. English statesmen have always liked playing the part of the "honest broker" – British greatness attests the fact. Winston Churchill landed at Casablanca on 13 January, determined to preside over the meeting between de Gaulle and Giraud and to make it into a British victory.

The conference was not to be held in the heart of that great city where anything might happen but in the handsome suburb of Anfa, where a large hotel and a group of luxurious villas had been requisitioned. Franklin Roosevelt, protected by formidable security and accompanied by General Marshall and General Eisenhower, Hopkins, Murphy and Harriman, and watched over by the United States Army, whose commanding officer in Morocco was General Patton, joined his British partner on 14 January in a mood that Eisenhower described in these words:

> His optimism and buoyancy, amounting almost to lightheartedness, I attributed to the atmosphere of adventure attached to the Casablanca

> expedition. Successful in shaking loose for a few days many burdens of state, he seemed to experience a tremendous uplift from the fact that he had secretly slipped away from Washington and was engaged in a historic meeting on territory that only two months before had been a battle ground. He speculated at length on the possibility of France's regaining her ancient position of prestige and power in Europe and on this point was very pessimistic. As a consequence, his mind was wrestling with the questions of methods for controlling strategic points in the French Empire which he felt that the country might no longer be able to hold.[3]

Murphy's account is more informative:

> His mood was that of a schoolboy on vacation, which accounted for his almost frivolous approach to some of the difficult problems, with which he dealt. Inside Casablanca's toy Suburbia, with its languid climate and exotic atmosphere, two world problems were discussed simultaneously . . . As for de Gaulle, it was apparent that Roosevelt had not altered in the slightest opinion. The President still deplored what he called de Gaulle's readiness, almost eagerness, to start civil wars. Roosevelt was more convinced than ever that he had been right in dealing with Vichy from 1940 through 1942. He never abandoned that attitude, although it became increasingly difficult to maintain.[4]

Both what Murphy calls frivolity and what Eisenhower describes as pessimism on the subject of France can be seen in the remark FDR made to Churchill as soon as the Prime Minister reached Anfa: "We will call Giraud the bridegroom, and I shall send for him from Algiers. On your side, you will send to London for the bride, de Gaulle, and we will arrange a shotgun wedding." It is perfectly astonishing that this great statesman should have let slip such a piece of grossness.

But the worst was not that FDR "on vacation" should have allowed himself this remark; it was that he should have found this way of speaking of France and the French in their misfortune so amusing that he perpetually reproduced his witticism in the days and months that followed.

Churchill rarely let his mind trail so low. But at this juncture the presidential humour squared with his own views and he at once cabled Eden to pass de Gaulle a message asking to join him there by the first plane available, as "I have the possibility of arranging a meeting between you and Giraud".

Churchill was well acquainted with de Gaulle's exceedingly sensitive nationalism. Could he suppose that the head of the Fighting French would welcome this summons – however advantageous it might be for him – sent out by a foreign head of State to bring two French military leaders together on "French" soil? The Constable's reaction was all the more unfavourable in that he scented some trap under the equivocal nature of the proceedings: why was the Prime Minister cutting the grass from under his feet by taking over the invitation he had already sent Giraud himself? Why was Churchill concealing the presence of Roosevelt at Casablanca from him?

Although in his reply to Churchill he confined himself to describing the Prime Minister's message as "unexpected", and although with studied politeness he thanked him for the "feeling that had prompted it", de Gaulle stated that the presence "of a high military assembly at the time of the Giraud–de Gaulle conversations" did not seem to him likely to favour "an effectual agreement" and that "simple and direct talks between French leaders" (as he had often suggested) would be preferable. And though at the same time he pointed out that "France's higher interests" in no way contradicted "those of the war and the united nations", he refused the Prime Minister's invitation.

Winston Churchill had received worse affronts from Charles de Gaulle; but this one was all the more painful in that he suffered it in the presence of his American partners, who did not fail to let a certain commiseration appear. So his *enfant terrible* was refusing to obey him? Moving on from "frivolity" to the crudest "sense of realities", FDR said to Churchill, "Who pays for de Gaulle's food?" "Well, the British do."* "Why don't you stop his food and maybe he will come."[5] And in better and better form, the President of the United States cabled his Secretary of State, Cordell Hull:

> We delivered our bridegroom, Giraud, who was most cooperative on the impending marriage, and I am sure was ready to go through with it on our terms.** However, our friends could not produce the bride, the temperamental Lady de Gaulle. She has got quite snooty about the whole idea and does not want to see either of us and is showing no intention of getting into bed with Giraud.[6]

Now the pressure on de Gaulle grew stronger. General Giraud arrived at Anfa on 17 January, accompanied by two advisers, André Poniatowski, who was deeply hostile to de Gaulle, and Lemaigre-Dubreuil, who was even more so. The second had just come back from a stay in Washington, where, in conjunction with Cordell Hull and the experts of the State Department, he had laid the foundations for an agreement according to which the United States would recognize Giraud as the sole trustee for the rights and interests of France until the end of the war. It was through the medium of Giraud (who did not fail to act as a willing bridegroom) that the threats of those who desired the shotgun wedding found their expression. During the evening of 18 January Henri Giraud was talking to Roosevelt when Churchill came in. Giraud was to write:

> I have the impression that the scenario had been prepared. He threw his hat on the sofa, and grumbling he said that General de Gaulle would have to choose between coming here and the subsidies that the English Treasury paid over to the National Committee. If he refused to come to Casablanca, the 1940 agreement between him and His Majesty's government would be set aside. Roosevelt approved of this attitude. I said nothing; nor was it for me to say anything in this discussion. It was not I who had staged the affair.

*Churchill knew very well that this had no longer been quite true since the middle of 1942.
**Although he loathed de Gaulle, FDR seems to have had little opinion of Giraud either.

> I had no objection to coming to an agreement with General de Gaulle; far from it. I thought him an excellent Frenchman, and if I had been free on 25 June 1940, there is no doubt that I too should have left France. On many points we had the same outlook. On the other hand I could not accept the people he had surrounded himself with, who were too reminiscent of the hotheads of 1936,* to whom I attributed a great part of the French catastrophe. With de Gaulle and the convinced soldiers of the very first moment, by all means, but with those who had primarily come to shelter their persons or their capital in London or America – that was quite different.[7]

Although there was no longer any question of setting aside the 7 August 1940 agreement (what a contradiction the Prime Minister would have inflicted upon himself, at the very moment when the solitary figure he had so brilliantly supported in June 1940 had become head of the French Resistance), the message Eden handed de Gaulle on 19 January was a summons.

Churchill recalled that the invitation sent on 16 January came also from the President of the United States; he told the Constable that the arrangements studied at Casablanca would be adopted whether he took part or not; that his attitude would be "almost universally censured" by public opinion if he refused this "unique opportunity"; that there could no longer be any question of being invited to the United States if President Roosevelt's invitation were rejected now; that the present attempts at union could not be carried on "so long as he, de Gaulle, remained head of the movement"; and finally that a fresh refusal would have extremely serious consequences for Fighting France.

When he came to write his memoirs, the General was to write, "After a good deal of experience, I was no longer much impressed by the threatening side of this message". His own feelings inclined him to stay away. But he consulted the French National Committee, the majority of which was in favour of his taking part in the Casablanca talks: on the evening of 20 January, therefore, he cabled Churchill that, the general situation of the war and the present provisional state of France do not allow me to refuse to meet the President of the United States and His Majesty's Prime Minister.

To accompany him, Charles de Gaulle chose two spirited negotiators, Catroux and Palewski, and two militants, d'Argenlieu and Boislambert. He landed at Fedala, Casablanca's military airfield, late in the morning of 22 January, just as the strategic conference was coming to an end – a conference in which the British military leaders' views had once more prevailed over those of the American General Staff: the Allies would, in conformity with the British plan, land in Sicily in 1943.

Although de Gaulle knew nothing of this decision, which he would certainly have contested if he had been consulted, he could not pretend not to notice the manner in which the American authorities received him: no troops to present arms, only second or third rate officials to look after him, American sentries

*The Popular Front. (trs.)

everywhere, and as he got into the car sent for him (and he could not quite resign himself to the fact that it too was American), General Wilbur, who had once been his comrade at the Ecole de Guerre and who had therefore been entrusted with receiving him in the name of the President of the United States, "dipped a rag in the mud and smeared the windows. A precaution intended to conceal the presence of General de Gaulle in Morocco."[8]

Worse still, a network of barbed wire surrounded the conference, and soldiers everywhere – always American – who even did the housework. In short, the author of the *Mémoires de guerre* thought himself on St Helena: "It was captivity," he ends. The fact that these rules were applied to him, and in addition applied to him "on soil under French sovereignty" gave him the feeling of "outrage".

This accounts for the way he spoke an hour later when he was invited to lunch by Giraud, who, seeing him for the first time since Metz, greeted him with a condescending "Bonjour, Gaulle." "Well, here's a fine state of affairs! Four times I suggested that we should see one another, and is it in this ring of barbed wire, surrounded by foreigners, that you have to meet me? From the national point of view, do you not feel the odious side of it all?"

The author of the *Mémoires de guerre* says "nevertheless the meal was cordial". Was it really? He says that his host did not refrain from telling about his "extraordinary escape from Königstein", but he forgets to add that as Giraud fell silent in a murmur of applause, he saw fit to call out, "And now, General, suppose you tell us how you came to be taken prisoner?"

The first visit he received was from Harold Macmillan, whom Churchill had just made his Minister Resident with the Mediterranean Command, and who was in favour of Fighting France. This did not mean he was uncritical of the Constable: "General de Gaulle is one of those horses which either refuses to come to the starting gate at all, or insists on careering down the course before the signal is given, or suddenly elects to run on a racecourse different from the one appointed by the Stewards of the Jockey Club."[9] Macmillan nevertheless managed to induce the General to come and see Churchill. Here they were, face to face once more. Which of them was the most tragic, the most picturesque, the most animated? In his history of the war, the Prime Minister speaks this time of "a very stony interview". De Gaulle says that he angrily challenged his interlocutor (might one say his "producer"?) about these American bayonets that surrounded him and obsessed him on "French soil". "If I had known, I should not have come!"

Meanwhile, the two champions got down to essential matters: the organization of a French authority associating Giraudism and Gaullism in order to carry on with the war; and Churchill spoke of a team made up of the present Commander-in-Chief in Algiers (who alone would exercise military powers), of General Georges, who was one of the two who had been heavily defeated in May 1940 but who was his personal friend, of the head of Fighting France, and of the great proconsuls of neo-Vichyism, Noguès, Boisson and Bergeret, to whom was to be added Pétain's former Minister of the Interior Peyrouton, recently appointed Governor-General of Algeria by Giraud.

I replied to Churchill [says de Gaulle] that at the level – the very worthy

> level, it may be added – of American sergeant-majors, this solution might seem adequate, but that I did not suppose he himself took it seriously. Apart from me and against me, the Allies had installed a system that was functioning in Algiers. Now, apparently deriving but a meagre satisfaction from this system, they were planning to sink Fighting France in it. But Fighting France would not comply. If it had to disappear, it preferred doing so with honour.[10]

Churchill could scarcely relish either this lecture on French affairs, which he could claim to understand pretty well, or this reminder of what honour required. Yet in spite of its insolence, the Constable's objection was relevant. Could he imagine de Gaulle returning to Moulin, Brossolette and d'Astier as the brilliant assistant of a neo-Vichyist committee?

Had Churchill thought so little about the nature of his guest's undertaking and the depth of these last thirty months of civil war in France that he could thus claim to mix fire and water straight away, while in occupied France the police of Vichy – which Giraud still quoted as his authority – were hunting de Gaulle's followers to death and while even in Algiers itself, under the authority of the civil and military Commander-in-Chief some of the members of Fighting France had just been arrested and accused of a comic-strip plot against Murphy, whose existence the American diplomat had at once denied?

Charles de Gaulle was now to confront Roosevelt. The appointment he had been given was late in the day: the General did not know that up until then FDR had been dining with the Sultan of Morocco, Mohammed Ben Youssef, in the presence of General Noguès, his official "protector", and that during this dinner the President had spoken to his guest in a way that was not exactly calculated to strengthen the French authority over the Cherifian Empire, if we are to believe the account given by Elliott Roosevelt, the President's son.

This was a move and these were remarks that the British looked upon with as much disfavour as de Gaulle would have done if he had been told about them. Macmillan says:

> Things were not helped by a dinner which Roosevelt gave in honour of the Sultan of Morocco on the very day de Gaulle arrived at the Anfa camp. It was a curious and impolitic manoeuvre. [Churchill] regarded the President's action as "deliberately provocative". The President talked a great deal about colonial aspirations towards independence and the approaching end of "imperialism". All this was equally embarrassing to the British as to the French. He dwelt at some length on possible economic cooperation between America and Morocco after the war. All this added fuel to the fire.[11]

In spite of the mental reservations and the bitternesses that might have made it burdensome, the first meeting between Roosevelt and de Gaulle passed off in a cordial atmosphere. According to de Gaulle, the President,

> as he did every other time I saw him, showed himself eager to make our

> thoughts coincide, using charm to convince me rather than arguments, but immovably set in the decision he had taken. We fenced gracefully, he with a very light touch drawing the same picture that Churchill had outlined for me with a heavy stroke, and gently giving me to understand that this solution was indispensable because he himself had decided upon it.[12]

However delicately-shaded the exchanges may have been, this conversation was nevertheless one of the most heavily laden with real threats of all those recorded in diplomatic history. To be persuaded of this, one has but to read the account written by Harry Hopkins, Franklin Roosevelt's closest adviser and confidential friend. He describes the arrival of the General, "cold and stern", accompanied by Boislambert, chosen because he spoke English perfectly; and he speaks of Roosevelt, who was dressed in white and who for the first few minutes kept his son Elliott by his side.

> I noticed that the whole Secret Service detail was behind the curtain and above the gallery in the living-room and at all the doors into the room and I glimpsed a tommy-gun in the hands of one. [Slipping away to learn more, he found the presidential body-guards] armed to the teeth, with, perhaps, a dozen tommy-guns among the group. I asked them what it was all about. They told me they could not take any chances on anything happening to the President. None of this hocus-pocus had gone on when Giraud met the President and it was simply an indication of the atmosphere in which de Gaulle found himself at Casablanca. To me the armed Secret Service was unbelievably funny and nothing in Gilbert and Sullivan could have beaten it. Poor General de Gaulle, who probably did not know it, was covered by guns throughout his whole visit.
>
> I attended all the meetings of the President and de Gaulle. There developed out of these meetings at Casablanca an apocryphal story which I think the President encouraged. The story was that at the first conference de Gaulle compared himself to Clemenceau, while at the next conference he indicated that Joan of Arc was perhaps more his prototype; and the President is alleged to have said to de Gaulle that he should make up his mind which one of these he was really like becuse he surely could not be like both of them. The story is pure fiction . . . although I heard the President tell the story.[13]

De Gaulle, that outlaw so formidable that he had to be kept covered when he met the President of the United States, that leader of a group of exiles whom the leader of the greatest State in the world thought fit to reduce by means of apocryphal anecdotes, withdrew, quite pleased with this conversation. He was usually cautious and severe in his judgments, but this time he muttered to Boislambert, his ADC, "Today I have met a great statesman. I believe we got on well together and understood one another."[14]

The least that can be said is that FDR saw things from another angle, and he changed his opinion of de Gaulle only so far as to note that even so farouche a man was capable of feeling his legendary charm. Speaking to his son Elliott he sighed, "De Gaulle is determined to set up his dictatorship in France. There is no man in whom I have less confidence."

It was the next day, 23 January, that there took place the direct conversation between Giraud and de Gaulle during which Churchill's bet was to be won or lost. It was Giraud who first put forward his plan, a plan very close, naturally enough, to that which had already been advanced to de Gaulle by Churchill ("with a heavy stroke") and then by Roosevelt ("with a very light touch"). A triumvirate would be set up, presided over by Giraud (who would also have all military powers including that over the French Resistance, under the authority of Eisenhower), assisted by de Gaulle, promoted full general, for the balance of ranks, and Georges, to whom Churchill was clearly much attached. The Vichy proconsuls would stay in place, although Giraud did think perhaps of letting Bergeret go and of adding Catroux (or possibly Eboué) to the body.

"Do you think," de Gaulle asked, "that you can obtain from the French people that basic approbation without which a government can only be a fiction, unless indeed it becomes the target for a revolution? With regard to the Anglo-Saxons, how will you be able to safeguard French sovereignty?"

It was all very well for Giraud to object that he had just arranged with the Americans that they would give him the means of equipping twelve divisions in the next six months, and that it would be difficult for his rival to say as much; de Gaulle brushed aside arguments of that kind and pitilessly battered Giraud with his own, which he put forward as "the common sense solution". He, de Gaulle, would form "a war-government, which, at the proper time, would become that of the Republic" in Algiers, Giraud being given command of the army of liberation. De Gaulle agreed that "if need be" they might form a "central authority", but on condition that this organization should "condemn Vichy, commit itself to the Republic and identify itself with the independence of France before the eyes of the world."

Agreement was obviously unattainable. Yet the Constable thought he saw in the other "more obstinacy than conviction". Once relations between them were established in which rank no longer played any part and in which matters would be decided by talent and energy, the man of June 1940 knew very well that he would overcome the man of April 1942; unless the Americans, with or without Churchill's help, threw all their weight into the scales. And this is what was to happen: Murphy brought a document which he said Roosevelt had approved and which provided the solution: never mind if the two generals had been unable to come to an understanding. It was the famous "Anfa Memorandum", drawn up by Jacques Lemaigre-Dubreuil after his talks in Washington with Cordell Hull and the State Department experts, a memorandum that included the pure and simple recognition of Giraud, based on the Giraud-Murphy agreement of 2 November 1942.

> France no longer possesses a government. In the interests of the French people and in order to safeguard the past, present and future of the country,

> the President of the United States and the British Prime Minister recognize that the French Commander-in-Chief, whose headquarters are at Algiers, has the right and the duty to act as director of the French military, economic and financial interests that are or shall be associated with the liberation movement at present established in North Africa and French West Africa. They undertake to help him in this task by all the means in their power until the time the French people are freely able to appoint their regular government.

From the military point of view, it was stated that "since the common interest" was to unite all the French fighting against the Germans "under one single authority, all facilities should be given to General Giraud to carry out this improvement".

Thus Roosevelt, that paragon of democracy, that "director of French interests", who so firmly maintained the thesis of France as *res nullius* against de Gaulle, solemnly handed over the authority to a man without the slightest evident popular support and recommended only by his military prestige. The strangest thing about this whole affair was that the document was to be signed by Roosevelt and Giraud without Churchill's being consulted, although he was made a party to it, and signed on the faith of the French version alone, without the President of the United States having even asked for an English translation.

The American historian Arthur Funk[15] asks why FDR ventured to sign so provocative a document, "a piece of anti-Gaullist propaganda", in this underhand way, running the risk of seriously damaging his relations with London and of arousing against him the whole of the Resistance, thus flouted or denied in the person of the man it had already recognized as its leader. Cordell Hull describes this document as "an agreement over a drink": Stimson, the Secretary of War, states that he got the President to confess that he signed it without having read it through. The whole shows how far, during this conference, what Murphy called the "frivolity" of this boy on vacation would go; and it betrays that lack of coolness which according to Funk led him to adopt this text only "to give offence to de Gaulle".[16] Macmillan, a key figure at Anfa, says that this action of FDR was "certainly a foolish as well as a reprehensible action".[17]

Churchill naturally set about correcting this paper that had been concealed from him. Striking out all references to the Murphy-Giraud agreement of 2 November, he had "France no longer possesses a government" replaced by the subtler words, "The question of the future French government does not yet admit of a definitive solution." But the recognition of Giraud as "director of French interests" was not called in question. Churchill has never explained how he reconciled this support of FDR's "over a drink" enterprise with his own engagements of August 1940 to de Gaulle and Free France.

The Anfa Memorandum was signed on the morning of 24 January in the presence of Roosevelt, Murphy and Giraud. De Gaulle, who so recently had flattered himself that the President of the United States "understood" him, and that at a moment when Roosevelt was preparing to sign a document radically excluding him from any accession to the central authority, knew no more of the memorandum than what Murphy had seen fit to tell him on the evening of the twenty-third: in the American diplomat's mind, was it a question of pressure to induce de Gaulle to sign the proposed agreement with Giraud, or of punishment for his refusal? The fact is that the Constable learnt enough about it that evening to see that he was threatened with the worst.

And although he was perfectly well aware of the strength of the movement that was thrusting him onwards and because of the popular support he enjoyed in France itself, the pressure that was being exerted upon him, the "concentration-camp" atmosphere that he felt all round him, and what he knew of the British dropping of him, threw him into one of those states of great anxiety and distress which – from just after Dakar to the Muselier affair and on other occasions – led him as it were to "appeal to history".

He now drew up what has been somewhat improperly called "the Anfa Testament"[18] which summed up his reactions to the conference, at the risk of a complete break with his allies, doing so with feeling and simplicity.

It was to a confidential agent, Major Tochon, formerly his pupil at Saint-Cyr and now in the Casablanca garrison, that he secretly sent this dramatic message by means of Boislambert: if things were to turn out badly, Tochon was to tell the public the truth about his behaviour at Anfa. Was it the machine-guns half-seen the evening before at FDR's villa, Churchill's threats, the American sentries patrolling everywhere? The fears expressed here are scarcely like him. In any case they show his troubled state of mind:

> As you suspect, I have been here since yesterday, brought by the Anglo-American assembly that has shut itself up in this enclosure. It is a question of compelling Fighting France to become subordinate to General Giraud. Until they can set it up in France, the Americans wish to establish a French authority in North Africa and if possible throughout the Empire that holds together solely thanks to them and that can therefore refuse them nothing. From this point of view the Giraud arrangement is ideal since it gives them the realities under an honourable outward show. Our negotiations did not in any way take place freely and with due dignity but in the midst of the Anglo-Saxons and under their supervision, in an atmosphere that they had created for the purpose and which was reminiscent of that of Berchtesgaden. I do not know how things will turn out in the end. It is quite possible that the blindness and anger of the Americans and the English may put me in such a situation that our activity becomes impossible. I would rather that than a capitulation. In the extreme hypothesis of a break, there is no doubt that Washington and London will account for things in their own way, that is to say by heaping blame on me. In that event I should have little in the way of means for informing France and the Empire. That is why I am writing you this letter and asking you to make it as public as possible if things go completely wrong. In particular please let Professor Capitant in Algiers know about it at once. The good Frenchmen in North Africa will thus be able to see that I have not betrayed them.[19]

A strange document, not only because of the unseemly reference to Berchtesgaden and the clumsiness of the style but also because of the dramatization of a dispute which, at the very worst could be brought to an end by the General's withdrawing to Brazzaville, where Fighting France had a reasonably powerful post. To be sure, the propaganda battle would have been unequal; but there were large sectors of the Anglo-American press that were favourable to de Gaulle, and they might have restored the balance. Strange too was this desire not to look like a "traitor" in the eyes of Capitant and his friends – a proof at all events that the opinion of the resistance movements then counted more than anything else for him.

While Charles de Gaulle was thus confiding his anxiety to the most faithful of his followers, the Anglo-Saxon intermediaries busied themselves with finding a formula that would at least save the faces of the "matchmakers". Was it to be said that the leaders of the two powerful Western empires had failed to make an arrogant exile yield?

Throughout the night of 23 January, a battle was fought in the President's villa. Murphy maintained that it was useless to go on negotiating with General de Gaulle and Roosevelt agreed with him. "I was of the opinion," says Macmillan, "that other attempts at finding a formula should be made; I was supported in this by Churchill, and, in a completely unexpected manner, by Harry Hopkins. Murphy and I therefore drafted a new formula that we had approved by our chiefs, and we spent the greater part of the next morning trying to persuade de Gaulle to sign it."

The British diplomat – without quite understanding it – explains the Constable's refusal by the fact that the draft dealt not with the French "central authority" that in his opinion the situation required with increasing urgency, but with a simple "administrative committee". He seems to have overlooked the point that the proposed document granted Giraud a structural primacy (and we know that Roosevelt and Murphy were in possession of the memorandum that reduced these discussions to mere nonsense, since it secured not just pre-eminence for Giraud but an exclusive and unlimited recognition).

It was with the agreement of his four companions, including those subtle negotiators Catroux and Palewski, that de Gaulle refused to sign the communiqué drawn up by Macmillan and Murphy stating that the two generals "in agreement on the principles of the United Nations, intend to form a joint committee to administer the Empire in the war". De Gaulle based his refusal on three reasons: this plan confined him to administrative functions; it implied an agreement on the main issue that did not exist; and lastly this definition of the French future seemed "to result from foreign intervention". "Nevertheless," he adds in a regal tone, "I agreed to see the President and the Prime Minister again."

"It was the roughest of our meetings," he said, referring to his confrontation with Winston Churchill, the British Prime Minister, the man who had allowed him to come into existence thirty months earlier and upon whom he had just inflicted the most unbearable affront.

This episode brought out the full measure of Charles de Gaulle's strength in adversity, his attractive-repulsive power, and the authority he exercised over others. Here was a man, the head of the British government, who a few weeks after El Alamein and at the moment when Hitler's disaster at Stalingrad was becoming known to its full extent, had just won a triumph at Anfa in the field that very rightly counted more than any other for him, that of the conduct of the war: he had once more induced his all-powerful American partner to yield and to adopt the peripheral strategy in the direction of Sicily, and, he thought, the Balkans. And that morning this more than happy mortal, this fighter now assured of victory, was no more than an old man distracted with anger against the opponent who had not only stolen his show, but had inflicted his own upon him.

Churchill seems to have felt so little pride about the threats he uttered that morning that he goes so far as to leave this meeting out of his history of the war. We therefore have only the account of de Gaulle, who had been subjected to a pitiless campaign in the press, on the radio, and in the Commons. "You are welcome to dishonour yourself," he is said to have replied; but although he told Soustelle[20] of the words, he took care not to reproduce them in his *Mémoires*, preferring to quote an answer more suitable to the scale of the persons concerned: "I confined myself to replying that my friendship for him and my attachment to the British alliance made me deplore the attitude he had adopted, an attitude unacceptable for France, disturbing for Europe, and regrettable for Britain."

With Roosevelt the distance was so great that the outward show of equanimity could be preserved. At heart, the President was secretly delighted with the General's uncompromising stand: did it not prove that he had always been right not to rely upon this impossible man? But doubt spread among Roosevelt's associates. Harry Hopkins once more describes de Gaulle coming into FDR's living-room, "cold and austere – he pleased me", but refusing the "joint communiqué".

On his side, de Gaulle quotes the highly significant arguments of the American President: "In human affairs, you have to give the public a drama. A joint declaration of the French leaders, even if it only covers a theoretical agreement, would give the dramatic effect that we must look for." To this the Constable made the majestic reply, "Leave it to me. There will be a communiqué, although it cannot be your version."

So nothing was lost: FDR would have his "dramatic effect". Churchill burst into the President's drawing-room, still red with anger, wagged his finger under de Gaulle's nose and roared, "General, you just cannot place obstacles in the way of winning the war!"[21] Roosevelt soothed him, and with Macmillan watching over de Gaulle, sent Murphy to fetch General Giraud. In the garden of the villa there were assembled dozens of journalists who had been flown in from Algiers that morning for a press-conference – they did not yet know that it was to be one of the most surprising of the war.

Giraud appeared. Then Franklin Roosevelt turned to de Gaulle. "Will you at least agree to being photographed with me and the British Prime Minister at the same time as General Giraud?" "Most willingly," said de Gaulle, "for I have the highest esteem for that great soldier." "Will you go so far as to shake General Giraud's hand in our presence and before the camera?" "I shall do that for you," replied the Constable in English.[22]

FDR then had himself carried into the garden, where four armchairs had been set out; he made Giraud sit on his right, de Gaulle on his left, and next to de Gaulle, Churchill, who, with his hat pushed back and his cigar, recovered something like a smile for the benefit of the band of astonished reporters.

This is how Hopkins describes it: "I must confess they were a pretty solemn group – the cameras ground out the pictures. The President suggested de Gaulle and Giraud shake hands. They stood up and obliged – some of the cameramen missed it and they did it again.[23]

Another angle, this time Churchill's: "The pictures of this event cannot be viewed even in the setting of these tragic times without a laugh."[24] Two days later, resting at his beloved Marrakesh, he said to the American consul Kenneth Pendar, who was asking him about de Gaulle, "Oh, let's don't speak of him. We'll call him Joan of Arc and we're looking for some bishops to burn him."[25]

As soon as the photographs had been taken, Giraud and de Gaulle withdrew, leaving the two heads of the coalition to tell the world of the results of the military conference, which were summed up in the well-known phrase that Roosevelt says he borrowed from his predecessor General Grant: no solution for the war other than "unconditional surrender". El Alamein, Stalingrad and Midway meant that from now onwards the Allies no longer had to mince their words.

De Gaulle did not forget that he had promised Roosevelt a communiqué that in some form or another should express a move towards an understanding. Now that the conference was over and the "foreign" mortgage therefore removed, and now that he had let Roosevelt have the pictures which would allow him "to give the public its drama" and make it believe that the "French question had found its *deus ex machina*" in FDR, de Gaulle gathered his associates and drew up the following document, which he meant to put to Giraud "without, of course, having made it known to the Allies".[26]

> At the conclusion of their first meeting in French North Africa, General de Gaulle and General Giraud jointly issue the following declaration:
> "We have seen one another. We have talked. We have noted our entire agreement on the goal to reach, which is the liberation of France and the triumph of democratic principles by the total defeat of the enemy. This goal will be attained by the union in war of all Frenchmen fighting side by side with all their allies."

When General Catroux came to submit this document to Giraud for his agreement, Giraud made no objection to the precedence his partner had assumed, nor to the so typically Gaullian tone of the second paragraph; but he did dislike one of the expressions. "Do you believe in them yourself, these 'democratic principles'"? he asked.

"Yes," said Catroux. "But if you like we could put 'human liberties'."

Giraud preferred this form, and therefore it took the place of the first in the text reproduced in the *Mémoires de guerre*.[27] When he was talking to me about this conflict of words fifteen years later, Catroux saw it as a summary of the conflict that opposed the two generals for months on end.

In a telegram sent two days later to Eboué, Leclerc and the delegates of Fighting France throughout the world, de Gaulle described the outcome of Anfa as "modest", stating that although the talks with Giraud had been cordial, the system he suggested could not be accepted, because it would result in the merging of Fighting France into "a local African system", putting the whole at the discretion of the Americans, "like Giraud himself", and furthermore because it would not be agreed to "by the French masses".

This document has one surprising aspect: it is the pleased tone that shows through when de Gaulle speaks of his relations with Roosevelt: "My conversations with Roosevelt were satisfactory. I have the feeling that he discovered what Fighting France really is. This may have great consequences for the future." It may therefore be observed that de Gaulle was capable of being deceived, even by an enemy. This message of the Constable's, and various confidences that he made at the time, go to show that although he by no means succumbed he at least appreciated the civilities lavished upon him by a man whose one idea was that of eliminating him.

But the most surprising part of the business is that General de Gaulle's conclusions after Anfa were less Gaullist than those of his partners or opponents. Whereas Macmillan said that de Gaulle emerged from these discussions "as a statesman in the great French tradition",[28] Murphy, in the ill-natured confusion of Anfa, discovered what he might have made out from the documents and reports that had been at his disposal for years, and he writes:

> Churchill and Roosevelt left Casablanca confident that they had fitted de Gaulle into a subordinate place, whereas de Gaulle actually set in motion there a series of events which soon would confound and humiliate his French enemies in Africa.
>
> The unproclaimed victory that de Gaulle won at the Casablanca Conference was a great step forward in his plan to assure France the largest possible share in the Allied conquests, including full restoration of the French Empire. The miscalculation which all of us at Casablanca made about de Gaulle was belief that winning the war had top priority with him, as it did with us. His thoughts were two jumps ahead of everybody else's. In 1943, de Gaulle correctly calculated that Allied victory was certain and that France would share in that victory regardless of what France accomplished or failed to do. This politically minded General decided that it was his function to concentrate upon restoring France as a great power. He sensed that he could exact greater concessions for France in the midst of total war than later.[29]

Charles de Gaulle had not yet left Anfa before he began to measure the effect of the resentment he had aroused by challenging Churchill and by showing Roosevelt his real character – not that of a fascist swashbuckler who could be got rid of in the name of sound democratic principles but that of a statesman whose exaggerated nationalism only stimulated his abilities to the highest point.

On leaving Morocco the General had asked his hosts to let him have a plane to go and inspect the French forces in Libya. He was met with a barely civil refusal.

Back in London he made the request again. This time the good Mr Peake sent him a confused message from which it appeared that this journey, particularly if it were to carry on to the Levant (as de Gaulle planned) "did not correspond to the interests of the united nations". And when after many weeks Churchill agreed to see the head of Fighting France once more and heard the General say to him "What? Am I your prisoner? Do you mean to send me to the Isle of Man?" he roared out "No. For you it will be the Tower of London!"

This was all the more so since the General did not hesitate to revive the dispute by stating, at a press conference held in London on 9 February, that the political crisis in North Africa resulted from the fact that "Fighting France had been kept out of the conception, the preparation and the execution of this undertaking", a state of affairs that had not failed "to astonish the French". Worse: in his address to the London journalists de Gaulle hailed Roosevelt, that "great statesman" but merely alluded to Churchill by name. A premeditated humiliation, and one that was delivered before his own public!

From now on there was no form of reprisal against his ally that the old champion did not contemplate. One day he had the idea of pressing Pierre-Etienne Flandin upon the French North African administration, knowing that raising up Pétain's former Minister of Foreign Affairs against the General would be a terrible affront to him.[30] Another day he asked the Foreign Office to prepare a document entitled "Guidance for the press and the BBC in the event of a break with General de Gaulle".[31] And when the General ostentatiously shut himself up in Hampstead to show his irritation at being confined to Britain, Churchill telephoned to Charles Peake: "I hold you personally responsible that the Hampstead Monster does not escape."[32]

In the midst of all this Anthony Eden undertook a journey to Washington, where there was a greal deal of discussion about the French question; and the Foreign Secretary realized that however anti-Gaullist he might have become, Churchill would still have the air of a BCRA agent if he were to venture into these surroundings.

During a dinner at the White House Roosevelt's genuine feelings not only about de Gaulle but about France were revealed to him. The President told him about his plan, at the time of the landings in France, for the Anglo-American forces to take over the direct administration of the liberated territories and the future of Western Europe's future as FDR saw it:

> After the war, armaments in Europe should be concentrated in the hands of Britain, the United States and Russia. The smaller powers should have nothing more dangerous than rifles. He thought that the three Powers should police Europe in general. His next anxiety was about the future of Belgium. [He recommended] [...] the creation of a new state called Wallonia. This would include the Walloon parts of Belgium with Luxembourg, Alsace-Lorraine and part of northern France.[33]

Those were the views of the head of the greatest nation in the world in March 1943. The mind boggles at what Charles de Gaulle's reaction would have been if the agreeable and friendly Foreign Secretary had then shown him the notes of his journey.

Was it because Eden's report of this presidential nonsense made Churchill more immediately aware of the danger, from the point of view of Europe's future, of giving an unreserved allegiance to Washington? On 2 April he received de Gaulle once more to remind him, among other things, that "in the interests of Europe and particularly of Britain, a strong France was needed."[34] But the Prime Minister could not refrain from venturing on to the delicate ground of French affairs, advising his visitor to come to an understanding with Noguès, Peyrouton and Boisson.

These remarks were all the less calculated to dispel the tension since Churchill also gave de Gaulle to understand that he could not leave for Algiers until this understanding should have been reached. The Constable makes the caustic observation that for Churchill, of course, this "understanding meant the acceptance of the conditions that had been communicated to me at Anfa".[35] And presently de Gaulle found that Churchill had lied when, during this conversation, he stated that it was General Eisenhower who was opposed to his coming to Algiers: in fact it was the Foreign Office which, by straining the regulations, had made the interallied commander-in-chief assume responsibility for the veto.

Thus the opportunity for renewing the splendid alliance of 1940 was missed. And Winston Churchill's estrangement was to deepen and turn into a febrile hostility against de Gaulle at the time of a voyage to the United States, where the Trident conference was held. On 5 May 1943, in Washington, Roosevelt gave him a memorandum and yet it was only an outline of the report which the President's specialists in French affairs were to deliver on 20 January 1944.

> The conduct of the Bride continues to be more and more aggravated [FDR told his guest]. De Gaulle is without question making his vicious propaganda staff stir up trouble between the various elements, including the Arabs and the Jews.* I become more and more disturbed by the continued machinations of de Gaulle. When we get into France itself, we will have to regard it as a military occupation run by British and American generals. In my opinion there should be a reorganization of the French National Committee removing some of the people we know to be impossible.
>
> I think we might talk over the formation of an entirely new French committee, subject in its membership to the approval of you and me, and could be called advisory in its functions. Giraud should be made the Commander-in-Chief and of course he would be a member of the advisory national committee. I do not know what to do with de Gaulle. Perhaps you would like to make him Governor of Madagascar![36]

In its most harrowing, wounding days, did French colonialism ever behave towards the overseas territories in as blind, more contemptuous way as this "very great

*The Gaullists in Algiers were calling for the restoration of the Crémieux decree that gave Algerian Jews French nationality.

statesman" engaged in a crusade for the world's freedom? Such was the image of France and the French conceived by Roosevelt when a lost battle had sufficed to turn him into a colonial potentate. One has to read these simplistic, arrogant documents to be able to judge the self-assertive general who presumed to turn them into mere scraps of paper – thus preserving the future of Franco-American relations, which can only be founded on mutual esteem.

On 21 May Churchill, caught up in this Gaullophobe and Gallophobe atmosphere, assailed with denunciations sometimes of de Gaulle's Anglophobia, sometimes of his fascist tendencies and sometimes of his sympathies for Communism, sent Eden a telegram which amounted to nothing less than the abandonment of the man of 18 June 1940:

> I ask my colleagues to consider urgently whether we should not now eliminate de Gaulle as a political force. The French National Committee would in this case be told that we will have no further relations with them or give them any money whatsoever so long as de Gaulle is connected with their body. I should be quite ready myself to defend this policy in Parliament and will show them and the world that the "No Surrender" in France around which the de Gaulle legend has been built up, on the one hand, and this vain and even malignant man on the other, have no common identity.[37]

But Churchill was uninformed in making his statement about the Resistance and its non-identification with de Gaulle at the very moment when this identification reached its crowning height in the formation of the National Council of the Resistance on 10 May 1943, eleven days before Churchill's telegram. Still more unfortunate: His Majesty's Prime Minister suggested, "If we could get Herriot on to the London Committee minus de Gaulle," nine days after Carlton Gardens had received a message which the last president of the Chamber of Deputies, the symbol of the French Republic, had succeeded in sending from his gaol, a message in which he offered to be a member of a government presided over by de Gaulle, "the only man capable of bringing about the union of the French."

And his colleagues in Whitehall were all the more dismayed as four days earlier, on 17 May, the head of Fighting France had received Giraud's long-awaited invitation to come to Algiers so that they might together form the much-spoken-of "central French authority" recommended by de Gaulle in his message of 2 January.

Churchill was advising the British Cabinet to abandon the ally of 1940 at the very moment when the Resistance in France was uniting itself under his aegis; when Herriot was pointing him out as the head of the next French government; and lastly when Giraud was at last acknowledging him as an equal partner.

Eden, strongly supported by the Deputy Prime Minister, Clement Attlee, caused the Cabinet to reject the Prime Minister's suggestion very firmly. In his *Memoirs* Eden writes "Cabinet meeting *re* de Gaulle and Winston's proposal to break with him now. Everyone against and very brave about it in his absence."[38] And the next day Churchill received three messages, which did honour to the democratic spirit within a British government even when it was at war.

His Majesty's ministers gave the old hero, led astray by anger and manipulated by his all-powerful allies, a lesson of equanimity and fairness, telling him that if de Gaulle were set aside, not a single one of the members of the National Committee would agree to remain a member, that the Free French forces would break away from the alliance, and that by acting as the Prime Minister suggested, the Allies would find themselves accused of untimely interference in purely French affairs and of treating France as an Anglo-American protectorate.[39] Everything was said, and with an admirable firmness.

Winston Churchill accepted it, but not without the bitter retort, "I have given you my warning of the dangers to the Anglo-American unity inherent in your championship of de Gaulle. I should be very sorry to become responsible for breaking up this harmony for the sake of a Frenchman who is a bitter foe of Britain and may well bring civil war upon France."[40]

In his history of the war, as he does every time he feels he is in a disagreeable position, Churchill deals very briefly with the episode: "It hung in the balance whether we should not break finally with this most difficult man."[41]

CHAPTER THIRTY-TWO

One Plus One Equals One

Is it worth relating the history of how Charles de Gaulle consumed Henri Giraud during the first six months of 1943? The energy of the one so obviously overcame the other and the outcome was so soon written on the wall that it would be almost trifling to give an account of its progress if it had not been the fruit of a threefold evolution from which there emerged the Liberation, the unification of the home Resistance under the Gaullist flag, and the progressive degradation of the Vichyist myth in a North Africa at war. It was the combination and the interaction of these three movements that resulted in the winning of power in Algiers by the Fighting French and that gave this period its importance, for the Liberation of France and the character of Charles de Gaulle.

During a press conference in London on 9 February 1943, shortly after his return from Casablanca, de Gaulle said that any attempt at reducing "the great national debate" to a quarrel between generals was "a bad joke".[1] Yet this side of the matter cannot be overlooked, for in effect behind these two unequally star-spangled flags two opposing Frances were to be seen, the France of tradition and the France of innovation, Vichy and London.

General Catroux took part in this argument and he has written about it: he very wisely points out that "what has been called a generals' quarrel was in fact a conflict on the moral plane". Were the Fighting French, in the immediate interests of "union" and therefore of the act of war, to make very great concessions to Giraud, a relic from Pétain's regime and an instrument for Roosevelt's plans for the future? Or should they above all be faithful to the fundamental message of Fighting France and the home Resistance, which considered de Gaulle their representative?

This was the question that confronted the American authorities on 8 November 1942: military realism or respect for principles? The President of the United States, with the cautious backing of the British Prime Minister, had chosen the "temporary expedient", the Darlan deal, for the American interest and to save human lives. The Fighting French, the men who wore the Cross of Lorraine, and who were unprovided with anything apart from the "signs" they bore, could not be satisfied with solutions of this kind.

For them, the "expedient" was a travesty of the future for France. There was the danger that a pact with Giraud (Pétain's philosophy supported by Roosevelt's armaments) might have major implications and turn a warlike measure into a structural reorientation.

* * *

Henri-Honoré Giraud might have come out of a box of tin soldiers. Tall, handsome, clear-eyed, upright and with a sabre-like moustache, he was the type of general young Frenchmen must have dreamed of becoming, from Waterloo until 14 May 1940.* The uniform absorbed his whole being, and for him a man could only be well-bred if he was dressed in these clothes, unless, of course, he wore a priest's cassock. He so utterly despised everything that had to do with politics that Daladier thought him a fascist, though this was untrue.

There was no vice in this smooth, polished man.** Ingenuity is the word one naturally associates with him. But did he not show weaknesses – on the field of battle, for example, where to his utter astonishment he suddenly found himself surrounded with enemies; or at Vichy, where he copied out and signed a letter that associated him not only with Pétain but also with Laval, whom he despised?

The military-man cum soldier (the two things do not always go together), flung in spite of himself into the field of public life, made his way there furnished with a small number of all-purpose axioms which he used by way of doctrine. The first – and this was the only point he had in common with de Gaulle – was that France, the victim of a temporary mishap, must be restored to the first rank; that whatever disappointments the French military might have experienced, it exceeded both its allies and its enemies in competence; that military requirements rule all others and that the man with a képi has precedence over a man with a hat; and lastly that France's misfortunes resulted from the country's having abandoned itself to the poisons of democracy and that the only salvation was a return to an order based on respect for hierarchies, beginning with the military hierarchy.

Giraud was a kindly, rather mild-tempered man, however, with a piping voice; he welcomed young Gaullists such as Joxe, and for a while he put up with his rival's mockery, impertinence and falseness; he was proud, but without snobbery or fanaticism, fatherly with the soldiers, sharing their lot and their dangers, quite ready to laugh at a simple subordinate's joke, forgetting wrongs as easily as promises, capable of magnanimity at times of success and of serenity at times of trial.

Jean Monnet was at that time entrusted with the task of being Henri Giraud's thinker; the task exhausted him. He describes the General as "a man with a fine bearing and clear and empty eyes,*** aware of his great standing as a heroic officer, unyielding on military problems, hesitant on others. I shall give no opinion upon his intelligence, which was that of a general long schooled in desert affairs and with a tendency to simplification."[2] There is a sting to these kind words, as there is in Macmillan's observation, "General Giraud had the charm that de Gaulle lacked; but that was all he had." Likewise, with Hervé Alphand: "No possible comparison with de Gaulle, that furious, violent, unrestrained force, that figure which breaks with the whole of the past, that explosion against mistakes, faults and betrayals."[3]

The reason fate seemed to hesitate before intervening between the two was that

*A date which was both that of the collapse and the general's capture.
**Yet I heard René Massigli, who often had dealings with him, describe him as two-faced.
***Elsewhere Monnet speaks of his "Siamese cat's eyes".

the older man was fighting on a terrain that was favourable to him – with a majority in Algeria, with an army nostalgic for Vichy and American forces entirely on his side – while the other drew his power chiefly from a force outside the argument, the Resistance, whose weight could only be exercised by means of the verbal image that Gaullism made of it, and the progressive installation of officials from London. These men, who were called the *hadjis* – they were those who had been consecrated at the prophet's side – were naturally opposed to the *moustachis*, Giraud's men. Algiers was, after all, in the Mediterranean world of prophets, sects and janissaries.

But this balance of power and of personalities cannot be discussed without taking into account the extreme asperity of the man whom the ingenuous Giraud tried to control. Speaking to that dogged opponent Girard de Charbonnières, Alexis Léger said of Charles de Gaulle, "It is not winning he likes, it is conquering."[4] Louis Joxe, unlike Léger who loathed the General, was a faithful follower of the Gaullist cause. But is his description so different? "Proud, haughty, vain, arrogant: he was certainly all these things. In such circumstances, who could blame him? Reserved, suspicious, grudge-bearing, indeed hard, wounding and sometimes vindictive. He was said to be scornful. His attitude was often indifferent and remote. His views on human nature were pessimistic; but in difficult times scorn becomes a virtue."[5]

Would Charles de Gaulle have survived the trials that his allies imposed upon him at this time if he had been less locked up in his armour of scorn, more aware of the relative side of things, less concentrated upon that national absolute which was symbolically his own being? But would this trial have been so threatening if he had not so obstinately defied, denied and threatened, if he had not so boldly resisted? Since he was weak, he preferred that everything should be a trial of strength, certain that in this way he would grow harder. But does there not come a day when the armour turns into an end in itself and finally takes the place of the man?

Nor can we evade the question continually raised at this time by the "matchmakers" of Anfa: de Gaulle's personal ambition. His hyperbolical character and his militarism, whose traces could still be seen in his complete contempt for the physical body, might have suggested authoritarian and even fascist tendencies.

Although it is true that in June 1940 the refugee in London tried to induce military or political figures, particularly Noguès and Mandel, to join his undertaking, to assert themselves as the figureheads of resistance, and although we must believe in the sincerity of these appeals, it is no less true that in 1943 he directed his formidable will-power towards a single goal: that of being recognized as the sole head of France at war.

Personal ambition? In so highly symbolic a character, how can one distinguish between a will for power and an awareness of incarnation? This insistence upon thrusting his rival aside can be seen as the expression of a feeling for the nation just as well as an eagerness to rule.

Yet it would be a mistake to suppose that it was only by his toughness, his pugnacity and his aggressivness that de Gaulle outdid his rival in those days; it was also and above all because he played every stroke with the medium or long term in view – farther ahead, at all events, than any of his partners (with the possible exception of the Communists). The notion is clearly expressed in Murphy's remarks quoted above. It is still clearer in this observation of René Massigli, who became his chief diplomatic associate at that time: "de Gaulle can see over and beyond the horizon."[6]

Whatever his relation to the democratic principles and the revolutionary doctrine being passionately debated by the men of the home Resistance and the National Committee's envoys, de Gaulle in 1943 was by virtue of all that he embodied, the heir of that great movement, from 1793 to Gambetta, from the Commune to the Popular Front's plan to rearm the Third Republic, that brought together the claims of justice and equality and the imperious requirements of patriotism.

The de Gaulle "legend" had been built by the Resistance, Churchill had said. What must be recalled here is how the Resistance was taken over by teams from London; André Philip's Commissariat of the Interior and Passy's and Brossolette's BCRA, for this was one of the driving forces behind the conquest.

Furthermore it is significant that two basic documents were issued by Carlton Gardens at almost the same time (on February 21 and 23, 1943), the one directed at occupied France (the source of de Gaulle's popular legitimacy), the other at Algeria (the target of his manoeuvre), both defining the global strategy that the General had taken care to found upon this base and this objective.

On 12 February 1943 Jean Moulin, who, in thirteen months and not without bitter conflicts, had acquired an ascendancy over the Resistance movements as a whole in the General's name, landed in England at the same time as General Delestraint, the head of the Armée Secrète. During the following weeks both of them had a great many meetings with the French National Committee and with British military leaders: on 21 February, for example, Moulin and Delestraint were received by General Alan Brooke, the Chief of the British Imperial General Staff.

General de Gaulle had had two very long talks with Jean Moulin telling him, with a most unusual warmth, of his confidence in him and decorating him with the order of the Liberation and appointed him "Commissioner on Detached Service"; and on 21 February he handed his instructions to Rex, who was to become Max for his final mission, that which was to end at Caluire on the following 21 June. These instructions of 21 February are of importance because they welded together the internal rising (reunified by the invasion of the south zone on 11 November 1942) and the exterior organization.

> Jean Moulin becomes the sole permanent representative of General de Gaulle and the National Committee for the metropolitan territory as a whole. At the earliest possible date there is to be set up a single Council of the Resistance for the whole of the metropolitan territory, presided over by Jean Moulin. This Council of the Resistance will ensure the representation of the resistance movements, the resistant political formations and the resistant workers' unions. The assembly is to be brought together on the basis of the following principles:

- Against the Germans, their allies and their accomplices, by all methods and particularly with arms in hand.
- Against all dictatorships and especially that of Vichy, whatever mask it may put on.
- With de Gaulle in the fight he leads to set the country free and to give the power of decision back to Frenchmen.
- The Council of the Resistance is a national representative body in embryo pending the arrival of General de Gaulle's political council in France.[7]

This extremely important document proclaims the supremacy of the man of London – and presently of Algiers. It imposed an almost military unity upon this constellation of self-governing organizations, under the direct orders of a man almost as authoritarian as the leader of Fighting France. It associated "political formations" (no one could yet dare write "parties") with this unification and thus gave them back their historical dignity. It took as targets "all the dictatorships and especially that of Vichy, whatever mask it may put on" – which might be aimed at Algiers and Giraudism. Sixteen months after the sending out of the order "not to kill Germans" the word was given to fight the enemy "arms in hand". Lastly, what all this defined was indeed a national representation around de Gaulle "when he arrives in France".

For months on end Roosevelt and Churchill thought proper to minimize the closer relations between the National Committee in London and the Resistance. Even in April, as we have seen, Churchill claimed that the two forces were moving away from each other. Apart from Eden and Macmillan, the Minister Resident in North Africa, and General Eisenhower, who gradually fell away from the active anti-Gaullism of the White House and the State Department, the French strategy of the heads of the Alliance was still based upon the eviction of the "very difficult man".

Churchill was so obstinate about this matter that he made a point of staying in Algiers the day before and the day after General de Gaulle's arrival in order to stimulate the zeal of Robert Murphy and the American staff against the man who was about to cease being the exile in London. Was it for that very reason, was it because de Gaulle was escaping from his hold in this way, that the old champion had taken so violently against his former protégé?

Throughout this period, Allied pressure took on the most varied forms. In March, for example, de Gaulle received the visit of Cardinal Spellman, the Archbishop of New York, who just happened to land at Algiers. The General gives an account of this episode with all the irony of an ex-pupil of the Fathers in one of the most elegant passages of his *Mémoires de guerre*: "This eminently pious prelate dealt with the problems of this world with an obvious desire to serve nothing but the cause of God. But the highest pitch of devotion cannot prevent business from being business." For this reason the Cardinal, brimming over with the advice of Roosevelt, in whose name he introduced himself, gave the General the counsels of his wisdom:

According to him, liberty, equality and charity should be the watchword that

> guided my behaviour. "Liberty" meant that I should refrain from making conditions about the union of Fighting France with General Giraud; "equality", that I should make part of the triumvirate* they had spoken to me about at Anfa; and "charity", that forgiveness for the men in office at Algiers, Rabat and Dakar was required.[8]

Finally, and displaying all the zeal of his charity, Spellman warned de Gaulle that it would be a great pity if the Americans had to do without him at the moment of his country's liberation.

Yet at the same period the leader of Fighting France had the pleasure of seeing that things other than the President's contemptuous hostility or the Archbishop's praise of resignation could come from the United States. On 3 April 1943 Major Laporte, the Fighting French liaison officer with General MacArthur, told him of a confidential conversation he had just had with the Commander-in-Chief of the Allied forces in the Pacific:

> As an American and as a soldier I am ashamed of the way some people in my country have treated your leader. The dirtiness that characterizes the sad business in French North Africa will take a long time to wipe out. I myself disapprove of Roosevelt and Churchill's attitude towards General de Gaulle. Tell him of my affection and my admiration. He has behind him the majority of the American and British people, who will not put up with an abandonment of this kind without protesting. Tell him I hope he succeeds entirely in his opposition to any agreement that would tend to lessen him or place him in a subordinate position.[9]

This is not a certificate of good behaviour; yet even so it was an encouraging sign for Charles de Gaulle in his struggle against his American-imposed isolation.

But he had other allies too, and he did not allow this to be overlooked. The Soviet Union – whatever the future reactions of the Wehrmacht might be, and they retook Kharkhov in February – had won the decisive battle of Stalingrad. From now on the National Committee's representative with Stalin, Roger Garreau, was told to increase his advances towards his hosts. "Had it not been for Soviet support," he said to Molotov on 26 March, "perhaps Fighting France might not have been able to survive the crisis in November."[10] And at the end of January the arrival in London of an official representative of the Communist Party with the National Committee, Fernand Grenier,** could not but strengthen its ties with the USSR. Although he was pursued by Roosevelt's and Churchill's ill-will, Charles de Gaulle did not begin his conquest of Algeria without some good cards in his hand.

At the end of the Anfa conference, the only agreement between Giraud and de Gaulle had dealt with a reciprocal exchange of representatives, General Catroux

*Giraud, de Gaulle, Georges.

**See the next chapter.

acting for the London general in Algiers and Colonel de Linares* acting for the Algiers general in London. Before leaving for his mission in the Levant, Catroux spent a few days in Algiers, from 15 to 18 February, and from this stay he drew the following conclusions for de Gaulle:

> Giraud had been a disappointment. The inn has remained the same, and only the sign has changed. The followers of Vichy are beginning to understand that the game is up and that the Allies are going to win the war. It is reasonable to conclude that Algeria can be reorganized and brought under control. This cannot be done without Giraud because he is in office. It is a question of leading him. It does not seem to me impossible to do so, given time and patience, if I am at his side.[11]

Even when the proverbial skill of this gentleman-general, an even more striking contrast to Giraud than de Gaulle himself, is taken into account, would this enterprise have succeeded if a providential ally had not joined Catroux? What is so strange is that the reinforcement which allowed Catroux to "lead" the Candide of the Summer Palace came to him from the United States. Indeed he came to him from Franklin Delano Roosevelt.

It was the all-powerful leader of the anti-Gaullist crusade, Henri Giraud's political guide and advisor, the man who, working in agreement with Catroux (and with Harold Macmillan's support) was to circumvent, direct and reduce the civil and military Commander-in-Chief entirely. The man's name was Jean Monnet.

It was one of those pieces of derision on the part of history so usual in de Gaulle's career that the man whom Roosevelt chose to enlighten Giraud and strengthen him against his rival (and whom the Constable, in his darker days, was not far from considering an "agent of the Anglo-Saxons") should have contributed almost as much as Catroux to the gentle shepherding of the civil and military leader. In his *Mémoires*, de Gaulle, having said a great many disagreeable things about Monnet, acknowledges that he was "the prime mover in this development". That was also the opinion of Murphy, who never forgave Monnet for having seduced General Giraud from his guidance.[12]

It was on 23 February that the London Committee told General Giraud about the course of conduct that it meant to follow in order to supplant him: "The French National Committee, deeply concerned, not with personal rivalries which must not and do not exist, but with the bringing together of the French nation and Empire in the war on the side of all the allies, is determined to make every effort in order to obtain unification." But on certain conditions: it was necessary that the "alleged armistice" concluded by a "pseudo-government" should be considered "null and void". From this there arose the impossibility of leaving "men in the chief governing positions who had assumed responsibility in the capitulation and in collaboration with the enemy". It followed that:

> In all liberated French territories the basic liberties must be restored.

*Who was to become Commander-in-Chief in Tonkin ten years later.

> Republican legality must be re-established. Until the complete liberation of the national territory is accomplished it will be useful, as soon as a central provisional authority is set up, to create a consultative council of the French Resistance attached to this authority, a council whose function will be to express French public opinion.

Henri Giraud had been warned. It was not only a rival who was furbishing his arms to make his way into the fortress over there. It was also a great body of people who, in the name of democracy, were being called upon to claim their rights. De Gaulle was confidently assuming that the plan to create the Council of the Resistance (which Moulin and Delestraint had not yet taken back to France) was going to be a success and thus deploying the plan in his tactics against Giraud.

Yet it would be unfair to attribute this feverish haste to nothing more than an intense desire to seize the reins of power. In various letters of this time, which undoubtedly reflect the information given him by Moulin and Delestraint, the General particularly stresses the people's distress in this fourth winter of the war. The spread of the occupation to the whole of the country, the growing scarcity of all resources, the requisitioning of food by the occupying forces, the setting up of the Service du travail obligatoire (STO)* and of the Milice** – all this helped to create a feeling of exasperation and to render the waiting less bearable. No one has described this feverish state better than Charles Rist, the eminent economist: "Here we are like trapped miners who can hear the hammering of the rescuers who are coming but who are still a great way off. There is only one thing that fills our minds! How long?"[13]

However little Charles de Gaulle may be suspected of sentimentality, he was struck by these reports and aware of the danger which despair might have on the population. The pressure he then exerted upon those with whom he was in contact, partners or opponents, both by the envoys he sent to France and by the notes he showered upon Catroux and Giraud one after the other, is also to be explained by his understanding of the immense, painful and dangerous impatience of France.

Monnet had reached Algiers at the end of February and met Giraud on 1 March; he had then begun preparing the "tin soldier". For General de Gaulle's sake? Monnet remained almost as reserved as he had been in June 1940 towards the General. He was bringing Giraud to the point where the leader of Free France would simply overtake him rather than destroy him.

Louis Joxe, who exercised upon Monnet much the same influence that Monnet exercised upon Giraud, said that "he very soon formed his judgment of General Giraud. He undertook to 'democratize' him, to paint him, to decorate him, and by the very act of doing so, to work upon the London Committee."[14] (Or *towards* the London Committee?) The fact is that Roosevelt's confidential adviser persuaded Giraud to make three decisive steps in the direction required by de Gaulle in a speech on 14 March: he denounced the Armistice, that is to say the legitimacy of

*The STO, created by Laval in February 1943, sent Frenchmen to Germany to support the war effort. (trs.)

**An armed pro-German organization set up by Vichy in January 1943. (trs.)

the Marshal's regime; in opposition to Roosevelt's views he stressed French sovereignty; and he paid tribute to democracy.

The supporters of Giraud had no alternative but to resign. Pierre Ordioni, who was closely associated with Giraud at that time, gives a most spirited account[15] of their reactions when they heard this "demagogic" speech; Rigault's dismay, General Chambe's anger, Lemaigre-Dubreuil's stupefaction. Giraud was astonished that they should have taken his speech seriously. "But come, I don't believe a word of what I said in it: that was only politics!" For in the mind of the man who had escaped from Königstein, "politics" were just that – deception, double-talk, mockery. Politics, treated in this way, always ends by taking its revenge.

Giraud also tried to use his speech as a way of ingratiating himself with the Fighting French and proving himself a worth-while partner. He wrote to Catroux on 15 March; "Yesterday I particularly wished to set out the principles that direct my conduct. No misunderstanding therefore remains between us. I am ready to welcome General de Gaulle in order to give the union a concrete form." To this the Constable replied by a communiqué: "In the matter of the declarations made by General Giraud, General de Gaulle has said, 'We observe with satisfaction that in many respects these declarations show a great advance in the direction of the doctrine of Fighting France as it was defined in June 1940 and has been maintained ever since.' "

This majestic comment was not without its mental reservations. Four days later, in a letter to Catroux, de Gaulle put the 14 March speech down to an American manoeuvre intended "to paint Giraud as a democrat" in order to drive him, de Gaulle, into a corner. He knew about the part played in this business by Monnet, whom he continued to look upon as a mere agent of Roosevelt's, and he ended roughly, "Union with Giraud is most desirable, but certainly not at any price."

His mind was made up in a manner all the more aggressive since an increasing number of favourable signs appeared from many directions just as Moulin and Delestraint were returning to France to strengthen the Gaullist ascendancy there. One day it was two well-known and highly-placed financial officials who, before taking up their posts in Algiers, asked to go to London in order to make it clear that they thought the union should be "headed by General de Gaulle". One of them was called Maurice Couve de Murville. A little later it was learnt that throughout the regions of south Tunisia reconquered by the Allied troops there were manifestations in support of Fighting France. And the mayor of Cayenne spoke of his intention to bring Guyana over to the same flag, in spite of Washington's open opposition. Gaullism was sailing before the wind.

All those signs did not mean that Algiers was already won over to the Cross of Lorraine. Even so, Giraud's change of course on 14 March produced changes: the Légion des combattants, that supreme example of Marshalism, was "reformed", and its vanguard the SOL was dissolved; most of the political prisoners (including the 27 Communist deputies) were set free from the camps; and the anti-semitic legal arrangements were annulled.

General Catroux, the National Committee's delegate for North Africa, reached Algiers on 25 March. From his first (and cordial) talks with Giraud, an old

Moroccan hand like himself, Catroux gathered the impression that an agreement might quickly be arranged by sharing the military and political functions between the two generals. Even before referring the matter to de Gaulle he suggested a plan according to which Giraud would be acknowledged as "constitutional head" with the title of Lieutenant-General of the Republic, looking after the command of the armies, promulgating the laws and representing Fighting France with the Allies; de Gaulle would preside over the executive and legislative organization of the Empire, the true source of authority. An "apparent primacy" being recognized in the elder man, the reality of power going to the younger.

De Gaulle appeared to forget that in the application of his basic principle, the political having precedence over the military, a system of this sort would ensure that he directed affairs. But he rejected these suggestions, which did not seem to him to answer either to the "ideal" or to the "solidarity" of Fighting France, and which amounted to placing France "under the personal authority of a man who is in no way qualified to exercise it". Here the Constable showed his limits as a politician, since the Catroux plan opened the way for de Gaulle's exercise of the real authority; and the incident makes it clear how much symbols and appearances still counted for him. "It was the future of the nation that was at stake in this dispute," says the author of the *Mémoires de guerre*, merging the nation and himself more than ever.

If Catroux's subtle views had been better received by his chief, the negotiations might have been shorter; but he was called back to London to help prepare another mission, from which the agreement over Algeria was eventually reached. The main actor in this was René Bouscat, an air force general, the representative of the Alliance resistance movement in North Africa, who, though he never joined Fighting France, did not conceal his admiration for de Gaulle. Giraud was fair-minded enough to think that this liking for his rival did not disqualify Bouscat as a mediator between London and Algiers.

On 17 April Bouscat left for London. On 20 April he saw de Gaulle, who welcomed him as a comrade and who he thought had not changed: "somewhat graver, somewhat thicker, his eyes sharp under his heavy brows." The Constable came straight to the point: either "Giraud is the great military leader and in that case he has no political power", or;

> He has an equal share with me of the responsibilities of government, and in that case he is no longer a military leader. Giraud can come before me at the council table: I cannot accept more. If agreement cannot be reached, so much the worse. The whole of France is behind me. Let Giraud take care! Even if he wins, he will be received with rifle-fire in France if he goes there without me.

As for the part that France was to play in the world, the Constable was already describing it as a balancing mission between the blocs, together with a rigorous sense of independence.[16]

The final terms were the offer of a diarchy, of a central organization with two heads, and of co-presidency, the two generals alternating. At first it appears to have been well received in Algiers and by the Allies. But Giraud objected. It has been suggested that he saw his importance inflated by the military successes of the French forces fighting in Tunisia* at that time, and, filled with republican zeal, insisted upon the application of the 1872 Trevenue Law: this law had stated that in the event of an absence of the organizations representing national sovereignty, the task of appointing the new authorities should be entrusted to the General Councils.**

But General Giraud was unlucky. No sooner had he launched his idea of appealing to these organizations than the three Algerian General Councils (which had declared in favour of the Comte de Paris at the beginning of December) now, on 18 April, uttered a resounding tribute to General de Gaulle, thus showing how firm their convictions were; it was already apparent that these groups of prominent men would support the strongest and would go along with public opinion.

It is clear that Giraud, ready to compromise on the essentials, was trying to gain time on the details. His letter of 27 April to de Gaulle was an acceptance of the diarchy. But he only wished to meet de Gaulle a great way from Algiers, at Marrakesh or Biskra. De Gaulle was exceedingly impatient, and it was a "sombre, tense man" who received Bouscat on 28 April: "Giraud wants to be both head of the government and Commander-in-Chief. I will not have it! I want to go to Algiers without delay. If I do not have a favourable answer by 3 May I shall ask Catroux to return and I shall set you free."

And he harshly reminded Catroux that "the matter is to be decided not between us and Giraud, which amounts to nothing, but between us and the government of the United States".[17]

And the Constable was even more insistent upon being received in Algiers after 1 May, Labour Day, when "an immense demonstration, in which Gaullists and Communists marched side by side like brothers, shouting 'We want de Gaulle?' showed that now times had really changed".[18]

Receiving René Bouscat, de Gaulle returned to his travelling plans. "It could be very simple. I arrive at Maison-Blanche*** by plane. I go to the Summer Palace. As I go there, the crowds cheer me.† What can be done about it? We show

*See the next chapter.

**This idea, which became a favourite with all those who wished to prevent a Gaullist dictatorship, did not provide for a slow liberation, department by department (which in fact occurred). When were these organizations to be considered sufficiently free and numerous to represent the nation? In June, when Bayeux was liberated, or in February of the next year, when the Germans were flung out of Colmar. And in the meantime how would France be governed? Furthermore, what is the "political" or even representational value of a General Council? All this simply amounted to laying the foundations for a neo-Vichyism on the cantonal scale and in the meanwhile for the American protectorate foreseen by Roosevelt. [These General Councils have a resemblance to the English County Councils. There is one for each department; their members are elected (one member for each canton) and although they become more important in this period they did little more than check the local administration of the prefect, the representative of the central authority.(trs.)]

***Maison-Blanche is the name of the airport at Algiers. (trs.)

†And yet Catroux observes that two demonstrations took place in Algiers on 8 May, the one purely military and the other Gaullist: it was the first that attracted the greater crowd.

ourselves on a balcony with Giraud. The union is accomplished; it's all over." An astonishing thing about de Gaulle is that one often has the impression that he might have written his *Mémoires* twenty years earlier than he did.

On 18 May when Bouscat saw him again he was full of spirits and confidence. He did not spare his visitor his usual diatribe against the "Anglo-Saxons" and the "trickery" of the perpetually postponed landings, but he came back to his Algerian strategy. "I am bringing Giraud everything, since I am bringing him France, and yet I agree that he should sit down before me on a footing of equality. But I do not wish to return to North Africa by the back door." His visitor suggested that there might be a compromise, as in the case of Catroux. "For France, I represent a number of ideas: the Resistance, the struggle against Vichy, the punishment of collaborators, etc. If I were to go to Algiers without it being certain that these problems would be settled, I should betray the trust that has been placed in me. I cannot betray France."

But on 21 May it was a man obviously feeling "a great satisfaction", though he tried not to show it, who received General Bouscat: in a message dated 17 May, Giraud had sent him an answer complying with his requirements, although one sentence contained the remains of disagreement on the essence. "We cannot be the government of France", Giraud reminded him. On 23 May, the National Committee meeting at Carlton Gardens heard Catroux speak about Giraud's latest proposals: they were agreed to unanimously. General de Gaulle would set off for Algiers on 30 May.

Before leaving London, General de Gaulle (who during the night of 27 May had heard that the National Council of the Resistance had held its first meeting in a flat in the rue du Four in Paris under the presidency of Jean Moulin earlier that day) wrote to King George VI: "How grateful I was to him personally, to his government and to his nation for the way in which they had received me during the tragic days of 1940 and for the hospitality which since that time they had shown to Free France and its leader."

When he asked to say good-bye to Churchill he was told that the Prime Minister had left "for an unknown destination" – which was, as everyone and above all de Gaulle knew, Algiers. They were to see one another again, for the better and for the worse, but not without de Gaulle's having written to Churchill that evening, "I am more than ever convinced that you will be the man of the glorious days as you have been the man of the worst!"[19] It was therefore Eden who received the Constable's farewells during a meeting that de Gaulle described as "friendly". For that to be the case it was enough for Mr Eden to speak without any constraint and for de Gaulle to have some recollection of their meeting: " 'What do you think of us?' asked the British minister. 'Nothing,' I said, 'is more likeable than your nation. I do not always think the same of your policy.' 'Do you know,' said Mr Eden pleasantly, 'that you have given us more difficulty than all our European allies?' 'I have no doubt of it,' I replied, smiling too. 'France is a great power.' "[20]

A little before noon on 30 May General de Gaulle, accompanied by a few faithful followers, Massigli, Philip, Palewski, Billotte, Teyssot and Charles-Roux,*

*The last two were his ADCs.

stepped out of a Lockheed with French colours at the Boufarik airfield, about twenty kilometers from Algiers. The reception at Maison-Blanche had not been granted.

On the tarmac he saw Giraud and Catroux. Charles de Gaulle came forward, his hand outstretched, smiling: "Good morning, General." Giraud took a step towards him: "Good morning, Gaulle." It was not much warmer than it had been at Anfa. "Not an exceptional welcome," observes Catroux; "hardly calculated to strike the imagination."[21] But Charbonnières, his chief assistant, a man who can scarcely be suspected of minimizing the worth of General de Gaulle's actions, says that the leader of Fighting France was received "correctly" and in accordance with a programme drawn up by Catroux himself; and he states that although Boufarik was preferred to Maison-Blanche that was because the first had been handed back to France whereas the second had been "Americanized" by the Darlan-Clark agreement.[22]

In any case, this time Giraud had come out to meet him. And de Gaulle noticed that "the representatives of the American and British missions stood behind the French", that the *Marseillaise* was played, that there were the proper honours and that the cars were French!

During the luncheon at the Summer Palace de Gaulle reflected upon the men who made up the "two teams gathered round the table, as bustling and self-assured as they had been before the tragedy". There were those, he writes, who had "everything" (army, politics, finances, administration, radio, the Allies' support) and those who had "nothing". "But," he says, "attitudes and looks already showed where the ascendancy lay. In his heart of hearts every man knew how the dispute would end."[23] He received a favourable pointer that afternoon, when he went to lay a Cross of Lorraine on the war memorial: although no official announcement had been made, a crowd gathered by the active members of Combat cheered him. "Nothing"? On the contrary. There were the political troops. Pending the arrival of the others.

At nine o'clock the next morning, 31 May, at the Lycée Fromentin, which had been requisitioned as the central seat of authority, de Gaulle confronted Giraud. He was in a strong position, if only because his party was more numerous than the other: Catroux, Massigli and Philip were with him; Giraud was accompanied by Georges and Monnet. De Gaulle therefore attacked straight away. The French National Committee could not accept any authority other than its own unless the supremacy of the political over the various forms of military power were reasserted and that no kind of subordination to foreign leaders should be incurred without the specific approval of the new French organization. Then he insisted upon the dismissal of General Noguès, Boisson and Peyrouton.

"The argument went on," says Catroux, "until the moment we saw de Gaulle close his briefcase, get up without a word and shut the door behind him with something of a bang. A cloud passed over the faces of those present. Then Giraud, obviously puzzled, brought the session to an end and we separated."[24]

The next day de Gaulle held a press conference in order to emphasize both the sovereignty of France and the necessity for the exclusion of the men who had collaborated with Vichy. He also received a letter of resignation from Marcel Peyrouton that evening.

This was a serious matter: it was known that this former Vichy Minister of the Interior had been appointed Governor of Algeria at the request of Roosevelt. And it so happened that his letter of resignation was sent to de Gaulle first of all, Giraud receiving it only the next day at the same time as the "co-president's" letter of acceptance. The press became extremely excited by this news and Giraud reacted with such violence that Harold Macmillan came to the conclusion that he had "lost his wits".

Judging by the letter he wrote his rival that evening, it is to be supposed that for once he was not prompted by the judicious Monnet but by André Labarthe. In this de Gaulle was accused of wishing "to set up a regime in France imitating Nazism and supported by the SS", and the writer called upon him to publish a declaration "disowning these schemes".[25] At the same time Giraud's associates told de Gaulle's that important military forces had been posted to prevent any attempt at subversion. Colonel Billotte, the head of the Fighting French staff, at once sent a message to all the commanding officers warning them of Giraud's plan and asking them to display their support for Fighting France.[26]

At the same time Catroux was astonished at receiving the wholly unexpected visit of Admiral Muselier, who had come to tell him that Giraud had sent for him and had entrusted him with the security of the Algiers region in order to "prevent a violent seizure of power". Arming Muselier against de Gaulle? In "informed circles" there was talk of a telegram from Roosevelt to Churchill advising him to put de Gaulle on a plane, to have him carried far away from Algiers and there to keep him a prisoner "whether Giraud feeds him or not".

However strongly he condemned the leaders of Giraud's party and the appeal to Muselier, Catroux could not approve his chief's action in accepting Peyrouton's resignation without consulting the co-president. All the more so since he had just learnt that the former governor-general's decision had been wrung from him by the very Gaullist Colonel Jousse. He went to de Gaulle and said, "You have encroached upon his rights."

"Giraud has no rights here."

"What do you mean, he has no rights?"

"No more rights than you yourself at Beirut!"

"My rights arise from the fact that I am there," ended Catroux, and he at once offered his resignation to the Constable, who nevertheless summoned him for the next sitting of the Committee.[27]

Intelligent observers sensed that during the evening of 2 June 1943 there could be a *putsch* in Algiers and that the officers around Giraud were considering the arrest of de Gaulle and a score of his associates on the grounds that the unrest they and their supporters kept up endangered "Allied communications".[28] De Gaulle was usually unconcerned about his security, but now he cabled to the London Committee that he felt caught in an ambush. In any case nobody arrested anybody else and they all met the next day at the Lycée Fromentin.

It was a document drawn up and read out by him, and adopted without discussion, that told the world of the creation of the French Committee for National Liberation (CFLN);

> the "central French authority [that] directed the French national effort in the war, exercised French sovereignty on all the territories outside the enemy's power, ensured the management and the defence of all French interests in the world. The Committee, [which] will hand over its powers to the provisional government to be set up in conformity with the laws of the Republic as soon as the whole territory is liberated, solemnly undertakes to re-establish all French liberties, the laws of the Republic and the republican regime.

In addition to this Giraud had to give in on the question of the proconsuls; Noguès also resigned followed soon after by Boisson. Catroux became Governor-General of Algeria, at the same time retaining his seat on the Committee. And two days later the victory of the men from London was completed by the broadening of the Committee: three Giraudists, René Mayer, Dr Abadie and Couve de Murville confronting four Gaullists, Pleven, Diethelm, Tixier (called back from Washington, where he was replaced by Hoppenot) and Henri Bonnet.

The Constable had his automatic majority, moderated by the middle-of-the-road and most constructive activities of the three "Gaullistically-inclined" Giraudists, Jean Monnet, Couve de Murville and René Mayer, and of the three moderate Gaullists Catroux, Massigli and Bonnet. Furthermore the Secretary-General of the CFLN, an official of the first importance in any still uncertain organization, was the Gaullist Louis Joxe (presently to be accompanied by two deputies, Edgar Faure and Raymond Offroy).

But the French match for power took place before an international crowd of spectators all eager to act as umpires. On 6 June* Churchill invited Giraud and de Gaulle to a "country luncheon". When de Gaulle, in Churchill's presence, expressed his astonishment at this step, the Prime Minister said that he was there to prevent "some too sudden shock, as for example if you had eaten Giraud up in one go".** The Constable replied: "That was not my intention at all. I meant to proceed by stages."[29]

De Gaulle still had one battle to win: the ascendancy of this political organization over all the military hierarchies – which did not mean only de Gaulle's predominance over Giraud but the CFLN's autonomy from the Allied command. Yet on this point Giraud, supported by Georges, resisted.

Upon this de Gaulle once more made use of his favourite weapon, a retreat into the wilderness in the midst of a deafening silence. "Wrapping himself about in woe", he writes, he shut himself up in his villa, Les Glycines, where he lived in Algiers, and on 9 June he stated that he would no longer take part in the CFLN debates. He did not quit his Aventine until 15 June.

A few days later Macmillan told the hermit that he was invited to lunch by "General Lyon". It was King George VI, who had come incognito to visit the British forces in North Africa. "If I am no longer in the government," asked de Gaulle, smiling, "will General Lyon wish to invite me?" The lunch was "very successful", says Churchill's minister (the King had had a great liking for de

*Churchill and Eden give 4 June for this meal.

**Churchill does not mention these words in his own memoirs.

Gaulle since 1940). The Constable, who on this 14 June was still "on strike", then asked Macmillan what he was doing that afternoon, and learning that he was going to bathe at Tipasa, asked if he might come too, alone.

> So I had three and a half hours of driving, walking in the ruins and continuous talk with this strange – attractive and yet impossible – character. We talked on every conceivable subject – politics, religion, philosophy, the Classics, history (ancient and modern) and so on. All was more or less related to the things which fill his mind.
>
> I still remember with pleasure this curious episode. I bathed naked in the sea at the far end of the Roman city; de Gaulle sat in a dignified manner on a rock, with his military cap, his uniform and belt. Then we had a nice little supper at the inn with the excited *patron*.
>
> It is very difficult to know how to handle him. I do my best and I know that he likes me and appreciates having somebody whom he trusts and with whom he can talk freely. I think I have persuaded him to stay in the Committee for the present and give the thing a chance. But I'm afraid he will always be difficult to work with. He is by nature an autocrat.[30]

The British intervention in the troubled affairs of the "government" – this was the expression de Gaulle used for the Committee set up on 3 June – was not always so convivial. The American interference in what the *New York Times*'s correspondent, Harold Callender, described as the "French farce", was to take on quite another style, inspired by what General Eisenhower called with brutal directness Roosevelt's "conqueror's" state of mind.

On 17 June Eisenhower invited Giraud and de Gaulle to a conference designed to bring their views on the French role in the future of the war into line. Ike had been ordered by FDR to inform de Gaulle that in the military field no authority on his part would be acknowledged "because the Allies did not have confidence in him". This was close to being a direct insult. But Eisenhower, because he was naturally kind and then because he was beginning to think the White House's prejudice against de Gaulle excessive, brought the subject forward somewhat more tactfully, though not without stating that the French army would not receive American supplies unless Giraud remained Commander-in-Chief.

De Gaulle said that this "foreign interference in the exercise of French authority" was unbearable, recalling that during the First World War France's American allies had fought for months with French guns and tanks without Paris thinking it had a right to make any observations about General Pershing's powers. But the Allied Commander-in-Chief would not yield. Yet he spoke with such courtesy and good nature that in his *Mémoires de guerre* de Gaulle pays homage "to this generous-hearted man" who was capable of showing "skill and flexibility", who "felt the mysterious sympathy that had brought our two countries close together for almost two centuries now" and who could not be blamed for the fact that "this time the United States were listening less to our distress than to the call of domination".*

*De Gaulle says "domination" where Eisenhower speaks of "conquest".

In his own memoirs Eisenhower is more discreet in dealing with his tough partner. It was during this stormy contact that Eisenhower found out who de Gaulle really was; and he told Macmillan that he had been impressed by his "powerful personality".

The American diktat isolated Giraud and Georges to a somewhat greater degree within the Committee: the "fourteen" refused to answer the document handed to de Gaulle by Eisenhower and once more resigned themselves to a division, Giraud retaining the command of what was called the "African" army, arising from Vichy, and de Gaulle having authority over the Fighting French forces. But de Gaulle was also made president of a "military committee" which co-ordinated the whole. This step angered Washington so much that James Dunn* who was in charge of French affairs in the State Department, told Henri Hoppenot, the CFLN's Ambassador, that it was impossible to come to an understanding with de Gaulle and that the only solution would be to give him the command of an armoured division.[31] And when Governor-General Boisson sent in his resignation some days later (to Giraud alone), Roosevelt spoke of having American troops land at Dakar, there to support Giraud. Macmillan states that warnings from Murphy were necessary to dissuade him.

Suddenly, on 2 July, and without having discussed the matter with the CFLN, Giraud left for Washington. An attempt at regaining control against de Gaulle? The American papers hastened to put this journey forward as an anti-Gaullist move, but nothing was openly and clearly done in that direction. Even the general's reception at the White House remained discreet, FDR carefully emphasizing the purely military aspect of the visit and taking advantage of the occasion to remind people of his axiom "France no longer exists". The only ministry that Giraud visited was that of War, where he made a speech to the journalists. But since he spoke of the policy of "union" at Algiers his text was censored. He obviously disappointed the Americans, who had wished to raise him up "against de Gaulle and French unity", as Macmillan puts it.

Even 14 July itself did not provide the occasion for any display that might magnify or strengthen the CFLN's co-president; whereas at the same time and in the forum of Algiers de Gaulle, before a huge and exalted crowd, was crying "We have been France for fifteen centuries!" Already the great voice of 1944 and 1958 was to be heard. And already Algiers had swung over from Vichyism to Gaullism.

Giraud had lost the game. He was reduced to a few strokes, some of which were very fine – the liberation of Corsica, for example, which was carried out in September 1943 without the knowledge of the CFLN but in great style and not without the decisive support of the local Communists. Yet since de Gaulle was clever enough to affirm, at least verbally, that he was ready to take the event for what it was, a stage in the country's liberation, and not, as some would have it, a revenge taken upon him by Giraud, the operation merely in no way altered the ratio of power henceforward established. In his memoirs Giraud states that his Corsican success brought about his expulsion from the CFLN: it would be risky to assert that this was not so.

*A future US Ambassador to France.

From now on Charles de Gaulle spoke as the sole head of the French "government". Whether he visited Tunisia in June or Morocco in August his address was that of the nation's leader. "It was the State that was seen to reappear," he said in his *Mémoires*, "and all the more markedly so since it was not anonymous. A kind of rising tide of wills and feelings consecrated that deep legitimacy which arises from the public welfare."[32]

These "great outbursts of emotion" in which he chose to see the source of the legitimacy which entrusted him with "embodying and directing the State" certainly had an immediate meaning at that juncture, when he was confronted by the American manoeuvres of neo-Vichyism and the theory of the French void that reinforced Roosevelt's and Alexis Léger's rancour with a sort of legal basis. But, writing this ten years later, did he not see what might be hidden beneath these words?

On 31 July the Constable put an end to the diarchy. Henceforward, he writes, the presidency of the CFLN "devolved upon de Gaulle alone", Giraud retaining no more than the right to sign documents drawn up in his absence. On the other hand, under the supervision of the military committee presided over by de Gaulle, he was confirmed in his office as "Commander-in-Chief of the French forces", and he declared that he was delighted at returning to what amounted to his *raison d'être*. In his memoirs Giraud draws this conclusion from the adventure into which he had been led by a few men whose prime concern was to do de Gaulle a bad turn:

> I let myself be beaten without a fight. This was certainly not to my credit. Formerly people were kind enough to say that I possessed genuine military qualities. The liberation of North Africa was not too badly carried out, and later, in Corsica, I showed that I had not lost my grasp of the situation or my dash. On the political level I was unbelievably incompetent, clumsy and weak.[33]

In the summer of 1943, therefore, the first draft of what might already be called the Gaullist State came into being, dominated by the formidable, masterful personality of Charles de Gaulle and marked by its adventurous origins and its provisional nature, but whose functioning never gave any offence to republicans as strict and particular as René Massigli, Jean Monnet, André Philip or René Mayer.[34] And even when it was joined by those embodiments of the spirit of the Third Republic, Henri Queuille, Louis Jacquinot or Pierre Mendès France no one spoke either of seizure of power or the sound of marching boots.

At last, on 26 August 1943, the French Committee of National Liberation (to which General Giraud and General Georges still belonged) was recognized: resoundingly by Moscow,* with restrictions by London,** and with more than

*Which recognized the CFLN as "representing the governmental interests of the French Republic".

**Which saw it as "an organization competent to ensure the defence of French interests".

reserve by Washington.* It was indeed that "central authority" to the creation of which he had devoted his energy for months, with the repeated and solemn approval of the Resistance movements, that Charles de Gaulle could brandish before the whole world. The formal and legal battles and those to do with protocol were only just beginning.

But to the "deep legitimacy" that he already availed himself of with such force – a legitimacy born of his action of 18 June 1940 and strengthened by the adhesion of territories, crowds and fighting men – Charles de Gaulle was now in a fair way to add the more modest but more certain guarantees of legality.

*Which considered it "the governing organization of the French overseas territories pending the free choice by the French nation of its government".

CHAPTER THIRTY-THREE

The Weight of Arms

On 3 June, as soon as he was appointed Secretary-General of the CFLN, Louis Joxe was received by de Gaulle at his villa, Les Glycines. "Where shall we begin?" asked the Constable, and without waiting for a reply he went on: "With the army."[1]

That refusal to accept the defeat as complete was the very essence of Gaullism: it implied the decision to carry on the struggle. The 18 June 1940 was not only an indictment of those who were guilty of bringing about the defeat and a promise of victory. It was also a call to arms. And the leitmotiv of the following days and months was above all a "let us fight on".

Later it expanded into claims of legitimacy opposed to Vichy, into insistence upon the preservation of territorial integrity, threatened by British colonial policy, and into assertions, directed at Washington, that it was truly representative of the nation. But Free France was in the very first place the part of France that was fighting: what was concerned was the nation's honour, respect for engagements and the dignity of man confronted with Nazism, and only by taking part in the battle would there be a right to share in the victory.

In the book he calls *De Gaulle contre le gaullisme* Emile Muselier accuses the man of 18 June of being so preoccupied with political questions that he did not send the volunteers who answered his appeal into battle. So he, Muselier, "in defence of the solemn undertakings" had to do this. These, however, are false accusations.

People (especially Muselier) can blame de Gaulle for many things – his authoritarianism, his egocentricity, his overweening conceit – but not a lack of pugnacity. On 14 July 1940 the Constable declared that he had "gathered up a fragment of the broken sword", and on 23 July, with a kind of rapture, that two days earlier the struggle between France and the Reich had begun again, several French airmen having taken part in the bombing of the Ruhr.

Defiance of undertakings? Muselier knew that the agreement between Churchill and de Gaulle of 7 August 1940 excluded any fighting on the part of the Free French "against France", not certain Frenchmen. Had not Muselier himself, agreeing to bring Saint-Pierre over to the Free French side, run the risk of a "fratricidal" combat? And were the members of the Milice and the volunteers for the LVF* to be looked upon as untouchable just because they were born in France?

No, Charles de Gaulle was certainly not guilty of delay; what he might be blamed for was haste: this might partly explain the lamentable blunder at Dakar if

*Légion de volontaires français, who fought for the Germans on the eastern front. (trs.)

not of the loss of lives in the winning over of Gabon and Syria. And although the leader of the movement never had to spur on the first Free French officers, such as Montclar, Larminat, Leclerc, Koenig or Chevigné, that was because they were already fanatical and wished to wipe from the record the failure of those regiments shut up in their barracks, of the fleets immovably at anchor and those squadrons grounded at the moment when history was being made and when the nation had a right to expect that its military men should behave like soldiers.

The return of the French forces into the war, in violation of the Armistice of June 1940 (any Frenchman bearing arms against the army of the Third Reich would be shot by firing-squad),* was carried out in three phases: the first was that of the pioneers that ended with Leclerc marching on Kufra; the second saw the rebuilding of the great units, from Koenig's formation that fought at Bir Hakeim to Larminat's two Free French divisions that fought alongside the British Eighth Army throughout 1942; the third opened with the Tunisian campaign and the first merging of Giraudists and Gaullists, blossomed out as the expeditionary force under Juin in Italy and culminated in the First French Army's landing in Provence on 15 August 1944. Four years after the Rethondes Armistice de Gaulle had given back the French forces, whether they came from Free France, the neo-Vichyism of North Africa or the home Resistance, an active role in the liberation of the country and the victory over Nazism.

General Giraud's services in the rearmament of this reborn army should not be under-estimated. In a letter to his sons, Giraud expressed the axiom upon which he thought he should base the country's military recovery: the mind is made in France, the troops in Africa, the war-material in America. As soon as he was free he tried to combine these three notions, maintaining the Vichy spirit in the African units and, from his first contacts with Murphy and Eisenhower, emphasizing the priority the United States ought to give to the rearmament of the French forces.

As early as the Anfa conference Giraud obtained the means to equip three infantry divisions and one armoured brigade together with a hundred aircraft in the next two months, as well as promises to arm eight further divisions, including three that were to be armoured, and three or four hundred planes. When he left for the United States on 2 July 1943, Giraud took with him the advice and the guarantee of Jean Monnet, who had inspired and then encouraged Roosevelt's Victory Programme of 6 January 1942 (300 000 aircraft, 100 000 tanks, 125 000 ships).

Giraud's journey to the United States may have been a failure but as far as weapons were concerned it was a success. It led to the quick delivery of American weaponry which allowed the formation of units as effective as General Leclerc's Second Armoured Division.

* * *

*After Bir Hakeim the Wehrmacht announced that the French prisoners would be executed. De Gaulle at once let it be known that his prisoners would be treated in the same way. Berlin then revised its decision.

However powerful weapons may be, their strength lies in the conviction with which they are used: in the spring of 1940 were not the French forces, at least on land, roughly equal to that of the Reich? The important means that Giraud obtained during the summer of 1943 were to point towards an end that was not solely military and were to be put into action by fighters whose eyes were not directed merely at the ridge behind which German soldiers were taking shelter.

"This war is a moral war," said de Gaulle to Churchill on 16 November 1942. A war in which, at least as far as the French forces were concerned, a Bergeret and a Bouscat, an Esteva and a d'Argenlieu were not interchangeable. The historic break of June 1940 was not of the kind that could be repaired, within a military formation, by mere alterations of command.

The Free French based their life on the great refusal to accept defeat. Let us attend to these words of Pierre Messmer, one of the first to join de Gaulle in London and at that time a lieutenant in the colonial infantry:

> A little before the Gabon operation, where we knew we should have to confront our own countrymen, some of us (including Magrin-Verneret)* spoke about their dislike for doing so (not me, though). So it was decided to vote. When Koenig was told about this curious decision he came to see us individually in order to prevent defections. The only one of the officers to ask to go as a non-combatant was our comrade de Lamaze (only for that particular operation: he was in on many others!).
>
> And it began again in Palestine, just before the Syrian operation. It was Magrin-Verneret once more, though he was damnably anti-Vichyist, who called us together in the Qastina camp and said "I'm not going along with it." So we had to find someone to lead the regiment of the Legion that I belonged to from then onwards. It was decided to appoint him by referendum. A fellow imposed upon us from above would not have been accepted: he would have been turned out. Once again de Lamaze refused. For our part we wanted Amilakvari, a saintly man.** But at that time he was only a junior major. So we fell back on Cazaux. You can imagine de Gaulle's face when he was told about these "revolutionary" machinations! He was furious, Long Charles was: furious! He wanted to give us a lesson. Then he swallowed the pill: we fought well.

Here is Leclerc (who refused to wear his third star, so as not to humiliate his fellow generals) speaking to the two kinds of officer he had in the 2nd Armoured Division in September 1943 at Temara, near Rabat: "Senior members of the Free French, you are people according to my own heart; but so as not to make my task impossible you must put aside the old man. Newcomers, you are accepted as full partners: but you have to forget being what you are in order to become what we are."

*Known as Montclar: the first field-officer to join Free France.
**Killed at El Alamein.

These quarrelsome troops did not confine themselves to intolerant words. They also displayed unusual qualities of hardiness and austerity. A little before the raid on Kufra the ration lorries were being prepared. "Where is the wine to be put?" Leclerc replied with a savage glance, "No wine!" He looked upon war not as a calling nor as a public works undertaking. It was a total engagement, a passion, the adventure of a resurrection.

In the mind of the Free French, of the men who had been at Massawa, Damascus, Bir Hakeim or Kufra there could be no question of fusion but only of naturalization – in so far as Giraudist *moustachis*, that is to say Vichyists, were up to it, and if, to use Leclerc's words, they were capable of "becoming what we are".

For men like Beaufre who for two years on end, whether he was in Weygand's group or Giraud's, had never ceased preparing for France's re-entry into the war, and who had therefore met with active hostility (and even prison) on the part of the enemy, this type of insistence was all the harder to bear since until June 1943 de Gaulle did nothing to make things less rough. Unlike those Gaullist officers such as Catroux who tried to round the corners and who warned their young comrades not to threaten the Giraudists' and take their equipment, the Constable was entirely behind those who like Leclerc felt that any blow was fair in this field – the delight of swiping a tent, a jeep, a lorry or a Piper Cub from the Vichyist unit!

Pierre-Olivier Lapie, who was successively deputy for Nancy, de Gaulle's diplomatic adviser in London and Governor of Chad, was at that time in command of a company in the Free French Legion. He gave me an amusing account of how he had to refuse recruits, less out of respect for what Catroux called "the proprieties" than because he did not possess the necessary equipment. This trade from Giraud's side to de Gaulle's was influenced by feats of arms such as that at Kufra, by the atmosphere of extraordinary freedom and also as he admitted with a laugh by "the argument of clothes". During May, in the south of Tunisia, it was better to walk about in shorts and shirt-sleeves in the English fashion rather than swathed in the cloth uniform of the old African army.[2]

Another example of the swaggering Free French is given by General de Guillebon*. When the English decided to take control of Madagascar without de Gaulle there was so violent a reaction that they literally cut him off from his territories: no more mail, no more radio, no more planes.

> Upon this, [says Guillebon] General Leclerc, my commanding officer in Brazzaville, gave me orders to prepare hostile military action against Great Britain in Chad. I decided to block the air traffic: now all war-planes being sent to the Middle East passed through Chad. Supplies, maintenance, repairs, shelter, radio and goniometres – all these were a vital necessity for the Royal Air Force of the Western Desert. As well as forbidding over-flight, I prepared the disarming and internment of several British servicemen stationed in Chad.
>
> At Fort Lamy, I summoned the officers who would have to carry out these orders, which certainly called for an explanation, and I made them counter-

*Who was one of Leclerc's closest companions from the very beginning, and later his chief of staff.

> sign the preparatory orders which I sent to Brazzaville. On his side General Leclerc sent for the British Consul-General, Mr Parr, who arrived, it seems, in a morning coat and striped trousers. General Leclerc bluntly reproached the British government for having cut off our communications with our chief and for relying on disagreement among the Free French. Then he gave him the preparatory orders to read. Next day everything was put right.[3]

After this, one can hardly be surprised that for many Englishmen the Free French, as Guillebon puts it, "bore the taint of rebellion".

So here we are in Tunisia. It is important to emphasize the essential role that this long and hard campaign – it lasted from November 1942 to May 1943 – played in the French army's return into the war. It was here that the forces which had been neutralized since the summer of 1940 renewed their acquaintance with battle. It was here that Alphonse Juin, the best professional of his generation, was brought into action again. It was here that the most uncompromising Gaullists were obliged to admit that their Vichyist comrades had not, during their time of inactivity, lost all their warlike qualities. Indeed, after the British attack upon Tunis, it was first General Barré's small forces and then the Constantine division and the Algiers army corps that allowed the Americans to reform and prepare the March counter-offensive.

The affair had opened badly. In spite of the advice of Catroux (formerly in command of the 19th Corps at Algiers) and of his British colleagues, the Allied landings had neglected Tunis and Bizerta, bases whose control would have allowed the attackers to broaden their undertaking to the Mediterranean scale but which in fact the defenders were able to use for launching their counter-attack. At Tunis, Admiral Esteva and at Bizerta, Admiral Derrien, had, on Vichy's orders, welcomed the Wehrmacht and had allowed General Nehring to set up an excellent bridgehead in this most favourable sector, giving the Axis not only a chance of holding on in North Africa but of preparing its reconquest. General Barré had nevertheless managed to withdraw his forces from the enemy's grasp, retreating westwards and to the central Tunisian highlands until the promised Algerian reinforcements should arrive.

For close on three months no important strategic move was undertaken. Then in February, Rommel, withdrawing towards the west after his defeat at El Alamein, attempted a huge operation, enveloping the Tunisian front by the south, from Gabès to Constantine. Now the fighting became extremely fierce. In March the French were thrust back at Kasserine but the Americans halted the German advance, while Juin's attack at Zaghouan caused a terrible number of casualites. But once this price was paid, the British broke through the German lines at Medjez el-Bab and at the beginning of May the Germans were giving way everywhere, from Sfax to Bizerta. And on Cape Bon General von Arnim's 250 000 soldiers surrendered to the Allied forces.

Although the Tunisian campaign thoroughly exemplified that re-entry into the war that General de Gaulle had so eagerly sought, it seemed to escape from his own grasp, being dominated, from the French angle, by Giraud and Juin. Yet from March, and even more after 30 May, Tunisia played an important part in his victory over Giraud. Not only did the Free French distinguish themselves most conspicuously, but from Gabès to Bizerta and from Sousse to Tunis their troops were continually greeted with ovations that could be understood as calls for de Gaulle.

The entry of the French forces into Sfax gave rise to such demonstrations in favour of the Cross of Lorraine that the *New York Herald* wrote: "when one reflects upon the ovations of liberated Tunisia, can one still wonder where the strength and the glory of our cause are to be found?" The plebiscite became even stronger when Tunis was won. Alan Moorehead was then a press officer with the British army, and in his *African Trilogy* he writes of the event in these words: "While our propaganda-teams put up posters showing General Giraud, the Cross of Lorraine was being chalked everywhere on the walls of the capital; it was really difficult to explain to the people of Tunis that it was not de Gaulle who had liberated them but another general called Giraud."

To this "political" referendum there was added a "military" version: on all sides there were Giraudist units asking to join the men who wore the Cross of Lorraine. At Sfax the 4th Spahis insisted that they should either "go over to Leclerc" or carry out their threat to disband; elsewhere it was the 7th Chasseurs d'Afrique, made up of young men from the Chantiers de jeunesse and recently entrusted to Colonel Van Hecke, who had arranged for the Algiers landing, that came over. And when Catroux, who had been reproached by Giraud for inciting his troops to disobey, warned Leclerc against this recruiting he received a violent put-down from de Gaulle, who on 5 May sent Leclerc a cable: "All who wish to join us are to be accepted. Foreigners' opinion is of little importance."[4]

Yet even so it was important enough for some measures to be taken against those who went too far. "I had set up an escape-line for the Giraudists in the direction of our units," says Pierre Messmer. "It worked so well that towards the end of April I was summoned by Koenig, who usually forgave me for anything. At the request of the Inter-Allied General Staff he was obliged to read me a lecture and even to send me away: I was found a convenient mission to the West Indies."[5]

But for de Gaulle the Tunisian campaign was not only an opportunity to erode Giraud's position on both the political and the military planes. It also allowed him to break away from that sectarian spirit which up until then had so strongly marked the history of Free France and to rediscover that sense of the State which, in a character like his, asked for nothing more than to grow stronger. As soon as he had obtained a footing in Algiers, already certain of his pre-eminence, he renewed his contacts with a man from whom he had been separated for the last three years. This was Alphonse Juin, who had passed out at the head of the list at Saint-Cyr when they were there together.

On 2 June 1943, when what he called the Algiers "ambush" was forming round him and the sound of marching boots was growing more emphatic, he wrote to his former comrade: "My dear Juin, I should like to see you.* I know what you have

*Here de Gaulle uses the familiar *tu* to his former school-fellow: it was very rare with him.

done since the beginning of the Tunisian campaign. I send you my hearty compliments. I should like you to know that you can rely on my esteem and my friendship."

We should not forget that Juin had been Weygand's right-hand man, then Darlan's. He had been the very symbol of that African army which had resigned itself to not fighting for these last three years – a symbol all the more striking in that he was said to be the army's best tactician.

At the end of 1942, when Charles de Gaulle mentioned Juin among the leaders from whom France might expect a great deal (just as he had done for Noguès on 19 June 1940) many of the earliest Gaullists, such as Claude Serreulles,[6] his ADC, had been shocked, for Juin was not only a Vichy official: he had also accompanied that paragon of collaboration, Benoist-Mechin, on a mission to Goering.

For Juin de Gaulle's letter was like an order of release. He answered warmly: "Your note touched me very much indeed. All my wishes are for a rapid solution at Algiers in the sense of union. People have confidence in you." This "confidence" coming from the man whom most officers in Africa thought to be the most able and the least political of their number was important. If de Gaulle, overcoming his prejudices, was capable of doing justice to this great professional because of the coming campaigns, Juin's coming-over to the Free French signalled the arrival of the most outstanding of the Giraudists.

The battle of Tunisia, therefore, did not only cause the French army as a whole* to move over into the war; it also caused the majority of these forces to join the banner of the Cross of Lorraine. It is Messmer again who tells us: "Until Tunisia we were not perpetually talking about de Gaulle. He was followed because he represented the right path, but we rarely thought about it. It was in Tunisia that we really learnt to be Gaullist against Giraudism." In short, for three years de Gaulle had been moving quicker than the pace of history: and now history caught him up. However much of a prophet he may think himself, any public man must relish moments of that kind.

When on 19 June 1943 Eisenhower summoned the two French generals, co-presidents of the CFLN, to inform them that the French forces would be supplied with American equipment only if Giraud remained at their head, he added that this requirement was intended only to secure his rear positions before the launching of an operation against the Italian coasts. For the first time the French military leaders were entrusted with the secret of an Allied plan. But they were not asked to take any part in it.

Churchill and Roosevelt, upon the point of confronting an enemy who claimed to have finished with France for good and all after the defeat of June 1940, had once more decided to keep the Free French out of it in spite of the role played by the new French army in Tunisia. For what if de Gaulle, having fought in the battle, should take it upon himself to intervene in the peace-settlements with his neigh-

*Since November 1942 only a symbolic regiment remained under arms in metropolitan France. This was the 1st régiment de France.

bours? Might he not carry impertinence so far as to make use of this at a later date in claiming to have a say in the treatment of his national affairs when the landings in France took place, and after them?

It was therefore without any help from French troops that the Allied landings on the eastern coast of Sicily took place on 10 July 1943 under the orders of the British General Harold Alexander. It took George Patton, the impetuous commander of the American Seventh Army, thirty-eight days to conquer the slopes of Etna and to enter Messina, already evacuated by the Italian and German forces. But in the meantime the Sicilian campaign had brought about a most important political event: as early as 25 July Mussolini had been disowned and dismissed by the Fascist Great Council and to succeed him the King had appointed Marshal Badoglio, who as everyone knew was as eager to carry on with the fight as his colleague Philippe Pétain in 1940.

From this moment, taking into account the exclusion of the French military forces, the question of the settlement arose. On 27 July de Gaulle, speaking on Radio-Alger, stated the problem in full:

> The fall of Mussolini is a strikingly obvious sign of the certain defeat of the Axis. At the same time it is a proof of the failure of that political, social and moral system known as totalitarianism, which claimed that it could buy grandeur at the price of freedom. For the democracies it is in the first place a justification, since it shows their ability to overcome those who have defied them, and in the second an opportunity to prove that they keep faith with themselves and are capable – as was the French Revolution not so long ago – of bringing the right and the means of practising their own principles* to all the countries reached by their arms. I also affirm that the eventual settlement of the Italian war cannot be lasting unless France has a part in it.[7]

The Allies had been warned. Five days later these views were specifically expressed in a note handed to the London and Washington governments "on the importance of French participation in the negotiations that will ratify the Italian defeat [with a view] to the protection of French interests within the framework of an Inter-Allied Commission."[8] Yet no one is more deaf than a man who does not wish to hear. On 8 September René Massigli, the head of the CFLN's diplomatic service, was called upon by Murphy and Macmillan, who had come to tell him that in consequence of contacts with Italian officers as early as 22 August a "purely military" armistice had been signed the day before by General Eisenhower and Marshal Badoglio's representatives.

Massigli observed that once again the French had been kept out of it. Mr Macmillan replied first that it was primarily a piece of bluff intended to mislead Italian public opinion on the eve of fresh landings to be attempted south of Naples; then he asserted that General Giraud had been kept informed. Upon enquiry it appeared that the Commander-in-Chief had known nothing of these negotiations.

A few days later the British government informed Algiers that the CFLN would soon be admitted, as representing France, to the Mediterranean Committee,

*Therefore no "provisional expedient" of the Algerian kind.

which was particularly empowered to discuss the fate of Italy. Was this a diplomatic approach? A consolation prize? Charles de Gaulle did not see it in this light: his nature (and his tactics) inclined him rather to dwell upon the formal insult that had been inflicted upon France than to show any delight at the presents offered to placate him, and he saw fit to tell the Allies of his "displeasure" and his "disappointment".

And in fact he now won two points. First with the admission of the CFLN to the Commission for Italy, where he was represented by a delegate of international stature, Maurice Couve de Murville (who now began his move from finance to diplomacy). Then because there was soon to be a call for French troops to play a part in the second phase of the Italian war.

Indeed, the operations in Italy were not going well. Although Montgomery's steady pressure and Patton's violent thrusts had thoroughly dislocated Kesselring's army, which was no longer supported even by the last remaining soldiers of Mussolini (who had been reinstalled for a few months by Nazi agents at the head of the phantom "Salo Republic"), General Clark's landing at Salerno on 9 September very nearly turned into a disaster, although it coincided with the announcement of Badoglio's surrender. When they reached Naples, "the Allies were nearly exhausted and they found that in this mountainous country they needed infantry more than armour. Hence the idea of turning to the French forces."[9]

It so happened that from 18 May 1943, just before de Gaulle's arrival in Algiers, Giraud had entrusted Juin with forming a "French expeditionary force" to be furnished gradually with the weapons promised to the "civil and military Commander-in-Chief" at Anfa. This force was the result of the merging, then in course, of the Free French and the Giraudists: it included two Moroccan divisions, one Algerian division and the 1st DFL, which Diego Brosset had inherited from Koenig and Larminat. All of these were armed with new equipment, American for the first three, British for the last.

On 25 November Juin and his first advanced units landed at Naples. Two weeks later they were engaged in a first offensive directed against Rome by way of Cassino. But the Anzio landing, which was to have come in on the flank of the operation, was no more than a half-success. The Wehrmacht halted the advance of the forces under Juin, who had changed the plan of the Inter-Allied staff so that Cassino should no longer be attacked head-on but encircled. This was a failure, but it was one that made it clear that the newcomers represented an essential strategic striking-force. Strangely enough this aspect of the situation did not appear of the first importance to the author of the *Mémoires de guerre*, who has much less to say about how the conduct of Juin and his men in Italy supported and strengthened his theories than the diplomatic and psychological aspects of the matter.

It was not until the following spring, between 11 May and 6 June, that the French expeditionary force – whose numbers had passed from 15 000 to 115 000 between November 1943 and May 1944 – reaped the harvest of these earlier efforts: the offensive from the Garigliano to Rome and the taking of the Belvedere, which as Clark himself observed was to remain the greatest feat of arms in the campaign. Yet from now onwards the political effects of the "return to the war" of an important unit fighting under the French flag were considerable. It was thanks to this warlike effort that the CFLN could henceforward "speak with a louder voice in the sphere of policy".

Apart from Roosevelt there was now scarcely a single person of consequence in America or Great Britain who did not acknowledge that France had now ceased to be *res nullius*. Whether it was called "government" or "committee", a central authority whose forces could affect the progress of the war in this way was now entitled to make its voice heard.

Yet General de Gaulle's strategic views could not be confined to the Mediterranean theatre. Although, since he possessed no navy, his only claim to any share in the great battles of the Pacific was that of the power governing bases as important as that of Nouméa, he paid the greatest attention to the Eastern Front and to the assertion of a French presence at the Red Army's side. Though at the same time he did not omit to make contact from 1943 onwards with those in Indo-China who refused to submit and who, with the British, were preparing for the return.

In February 1942 he had been unable to induce the British to transport the Free French first division to the Caucasus or Persia. But after his talks with Molotov in May 1942 he did succeed in sending the USSR the Normandy air force unit; they flew Soviet Yak fighters in a large number of battles* and they won a most unusual reputation among the Russians. Under the command of Colonel Pouyade they became the Normandie-Niemen regiment, the only Western force to fight on the Red Army's side on the eastern front.

As we shall see, apart from a few diplomatic gestures in favour of the CFLN, from the Teheran conference to that of Yalta, these efforts did not lead Stalin to take a more comprehensive view of French aspirations. It was summed up by the Soviet dictator's remark about the Pope: "How many divisions does he possess?" It may even be said that de Gaulle suffered few diplomatic failures more painful than Stalin's indifference, apart from some occasional decorations and tributes, to Free France's military cooperation. This confirmed him in the idea that the policy of States has certainly nothing to do with sentiment. But did he need to have this proved to him, and proved by Stalin?

The war was indeed fought on all possible fronts. Yet in this war, which was not only "moral" but also so total, few fronts were so important as that of intelligence, deception, what is more loosely called the "special services". France, subjected to a foreign army and thrust aside from the battle, was above all the scene of a battle of intelligence and influence, and of multifarious and secret activities directed at winning over minds and courageous wills until the decisive fighting should there take place.

Since there is no field in which dissension is more disastrous than that of the mind, perhaps it was where the secret war was concerned that the dualism set up

*5000 sorties, 268 Luftwaffe aircraft shot down, five pilots made Heroes of the Soviet Union.

in Algiers most adversely affected the installation and the progress of the new authority. General Giraud, more and more confined to his military activities, took great care of the intelligence department he had inherited at the time of the landings, the three heads of Vichy's Special Services, General Ronin, Colonel Rivet and Major Paillole having then come over to Algiers with neither arms nor baggage but with abilities acknowledged by their British colleagues. In fact the three men had long since transformed the double game of the first months into a more and more active collaboration with the Allies.

In Algeria, with Giraud's encouragement and the support of the heads of the Alliance network and the British Intelligence Service, Paillole set up a system competing with Passy's BCRA. A rivalry arose between the two, which embodied their respective chiefs and took on the aspect of a conflict of power and doctrine. For de Gaulle the political authority was supreme and therefore the Special Services should depend on the government – which he dominated. For Giraud the Special Services were no more than one of the advantages of the High Command – which he controlled. So here, as clearly drawn as a diagram, was the outline of a head-on collision in this crucial field.

"The struggle for power and for the predominance over the liberation of France and its political consequences was the underlying cause of distressing conflicts. It was we who were at stake," says Paillole. He adds that between May 1943 and April 1944 this disagreement went beyond "the bounds of decency".[10]

Against this his rival Jacques Soustelle brings the argument: "Rivet's and Paillole's services were cut off from the complex reality of occupied France, a fundamental defect which, added to the faults of an out-of-date organization, prevented this agency from providing the services that might have been expected of it."[11]

Was the "merging" less difficult in this domain than in others? No, although the two were complementary. Passy was the superior in attack, in finding information, while Paillole was better at defence, in counter-espionage and security. But it is easier to transfer a tank regiment from one side to another than a complex network of agents, suppliers of information and partisans bound by long-standing traditions, principles, interests and loyalties.

Was the tension between the services increased by a plan that Paillole was said to have thought up at the beginning of November 1943? Twenty years later,[12] André Philip openly stated that Paillole had meant to have de Gaulle seized by sailors from the *Richelieu* and that it was he, Philip, who had nipped the scheme in the bud by posting a number of loyal men in front of the villa Les Glycines and by talking about the very important protective measures on a telephone-line that he knew Paillole had tapped.

Nevertheless Charles de Gaulle did try to bring together the rival services under the guidance of a man whose military origins would give him standing with Rivet and Paillole and whose seniority in the Resistance would impress Passy and Brossolette: this was General Cochet. But what Paillole called his "incompetence" and Soustelle his "bitter and suspicious" mind led him to by-pass both the one and the other. After two weeks therefore Passy no longer reported to anyone but de Gaulle and Paillole only to Giraud. This led to Cochet's very early resignation.

On 27 November 1943 the "Direction Générale des Services Spéciaux" (DGSS) was set up: the organization was to rearrange the two "firms" under the direction of Jacques Soustelle, de Gaulle's most particularly trusted colleague. Giraud's protest was all the more vehement since the move coincided with a new phase in his exclusion from the Committee. On November 30 Soustelle, Passy, Rivet and Paillole met in conference. The men from London spoke as masters. It was clear from what they said that their colleagues from Vichy would be reduced to acting as technical advisers.[13]

Some weeks later de Gaulle had a friendly talk with Rivet. He seemed troubled by decisions that he appeared to think over-hasty, but he remained convinced that their long stay in Vichy had "corrupted" Rivet's men, and he maintained that the networks had "a political task which would complement their military function". Immediately after the interview Rivet told Paillole that he was surprised at "the importance that de Gaulle attached to gossip", but that he listened to what Rivet had had to say. Later Rivet was to see that his arguments had not carried conviction.

Paillole at last had his meeting with de Gaulle on 2 May 1944, who in the meanwhile had confirmed him as the head of counter-espionage. The General seemed to be chiefly interested in the doings of Colonel Malaise, who worked for Rivet in Madrid, though not without displaying an active dislike for Gaullism. But a little later the Constable paid tribute to his visitor's work, recalling that Soustelle had spoken to him about Paillole's service with the highest praise "and about the confidencē" with which the British and the Americans regarded him. "I count on you."[14]

Although Paillole, because of his competence, maintained his autonomy within the DGSS, those who worked for him, according to Rivet, were nothing more than a "Hottentot bazaar". He says that Soustelle was not good at withstanding "the pressure of a crowd of people blinded with partisan passion and out of their wits with pride. A cohort of self-styled pure of the pure, faithful of the faithful, obliged this frail construction to use methods based upon delation and tale-bearing".[15]

It is scarcely to be imagined that two rival systems should describe one another differently. The force of circumstances – that is to say the political victory of the men from London, of those who from the very beginning had believed in a total war, over those who in all sincerity had intended to wage, against the same enemy, a war like ordinary wars – carried the day. From the beginning of 1944 General de Gaulle secured the control of all the organizations working in occupied France thanks to the setting up of the Comité d'action en France: the most outstanding members of the body were the Commissioners for the Interior (Emmanuel d'Astier replacing André Philip) and for War (André Le Troquer after October 1943), Soustelle, Billotte, and, until his retirement in April 1944, General Giraud. Giraud protested against the presence of Soustelle, "this civilian": de Gaulle replied kindly, "If that worries you, we will dress him up as a general."[16]

A committee "of action"? From the Pointe du Raz to the Vercors, from the copses of the Limousin to the hills of the Ain and from the Glières plateau to the Ardennes, an army was fighting. After the early, scattered local enterprises of 1940 this slow taking up of arms was carried out in four phases: the beginning of the war between Germany and Russia on 22 June 1941 brought the Communist Party's clandestine fighting organization into action; the founding of the Armée Secrète with General Delestraint at its head in October 1942 started the amalgamation of the Groupes-Francs that many of the Resistance movements had created; the invasion of the south zone on 11 November 1942 accompanied by the disbanding of the French Armistice army gave a great impetus to the Organisation de Résistance de l'Armée (ORA); while from February 1943 the Service du Travail Obligatoire (STO) instituted by the Germans threw tens of thousands of young men into a position of illegality. This did not always happen at once and it did not always lead them on to the struggle; but they formed a pool from which the various fighting organizations against the system of occupation-collaboration could draw recruits.

It is obvious that any activity against the occupier (intelligence, deception or propaganda) in so far as it weakens, disturbs or alarms the enemy and provides the various forces working for the country's liberation with information and plans is to be reckoned as part of the war-effort. Yet since we are here concerned with the military operations that contributed to the French re-entry into the war and thus to the strengthening of Fighting France, we shall confine ourselves in the first place to those organizations that were specifically designed for action.

The activities of Charles Tillon, who from the beginning of 1941 carried out various acts of sabotage with the help of his small groups of TP (initials that as he amusingly observes might mean "travaux particuliers" just as well as "travailleurs partisans"), have already been spoken about. Henri Frenay, who provided the Combat resistance movement with action-groups, has also been mentioned; and that in October of the same year he agreed to merge these in the larger body which London persuaded him to join.

It was during 1942 that the three bodies which the Allies could look upon as their vanguard in France fell into position: the FTP, under Communist leadership; the AS, under Gaullists; and the ORA, which for a while had Giraudist persuasions. With the reorganization at the end of 1943 these gradually merged under the aegis of the National Resistance Council and its Military Action Committee (COMAC), and then in April 1944 they formed the FFI (Forces Françaises de l'Intérieur) under General Koenig.

The FTP were made up of young men who belonged to or who sympathized with the MOI's Communist party (MOI stood for main-d'oeuvre immigrée – Manouchian's immigrant worker organization), of members of the OS (organisations spéciales) and of the TP. Charles Tillon had launched an appeal for "immediate action" in the first issue of *France d'abord* in August 1941 and was its founder; then, together with Eugène Henaff, Raoul Vallet and Albert Ouzoulias, he was its leader. In both *Les FTP* and *On chantait rouge* he states that by the middle of 1943 the movement numbered 25 000 men and ten times as many on the eve of the liberation. These figures cannot be verified but it is evident that from 1942 onwards the FTP was the most active and effective paramilitary formation.

It is no less certain that as early as January 1943 the FTP was part of Fighting France: Fernand Grenier, the deputy for Saint-Denis, was received in London by de Gaulle as the representative of the French Communist Party, and he gave the

General a message from Tillon saying that the FTP "asked the great soldier that you are, not to let the fact that we too belong to fighting France remain unknown".[17] To this the General replied that the FTP's coming-over was a "demonstration of French unity".

From then onwards the Constable reckoned this revolutionary organization as part of his establishment. He took the FTP into account in his discussions with the Allies, in his relations with Moscow and at the time of the liberation: what is more he thought it quite natural to merge them with the French First Army; thus more or less successfully carrying out the laborious amalgamation between the fighting French and the Giraudists.

Although it was not de Gaulle's private property, the Armée Secrète had been founded under his aegis, and was led by General Charles Delestraint, the officer in charge of military action in France. Delestraint, using the pseudonym of Vidal, returned to France on 23 March 1943 after a stay in London during which he had met several of the chief Allied military leaders. Quite soon after this he came into conflict with the heads of the Resistance movements. During the ten weeks or so in which he was able to exercise these very dangerous responsibilities (that is to say between his return from London and his arrest on 9 June 1943) he had to face various kinds of criticism.

The task of summing them up may be left to Claude Bourdet, who before his deportation was Frenay's closest lieutenant at the head of Combat:

> The first was his difficulty, as a fifty-five year old regular soldier, of realizing just how new this war was: we members of Combat had displayed a curious militarism in choosing a general officer for this most unusual task. The second, quite like the first, was connected with what the sharper tongues among us called "jourjisme", referring to that famous jour J or D Day for which we should prepare ourselves and pile up weapons: the FTP, invoking the doctrine of "immediate action", were not the only ones to criticize this view, which was inherited from the well-known Gaullist watchword of 23 October 1941.* Lastly – and this was primarily the grievance of Tillon's friends – Delestraint was accused of aiming above all at the setting up and strengthening of permanent, immobile maquis – convenient targets for the enemy – and of depriving the FTP groups of the weapons parachuted from London in favour of these settled maquis.

Frenay told Delestraint all this without mincing his words, particularly during a conference at the beginning of May 1943. After Vidal's capture and deportation, it was once again the leaders of Combat who, following the disastrous meeting at Caluire (called by Moulin to find someone to succeed Delestraint), proposed the name of another officer – Dejussieu, known as Pontcarral. He was better prepared for this kind of struggle; he had left-wing views (he was said to be a freemason, which, in the army, placed a man) and he got on more easily with the leaders of the underground. But less than six months later Dejussieu-Pontcarral too fell into the Germans' hands. His

*"Do not kill Germans."

> successor, Malleret, whose pseudonym was Joinville, was not put forward by us but by the Communists, who had good reasons for nominating him.[18]

Charles de Gaulle governed this Secret Army, and he generally entrusted the command to soldiers: there were twelve regional military delegates, eventually headed by an interim national military delegate, Jacques Chaban-Delmas. And the General gave the organization tasks that, in his public utterances, varied a great deal. Although on 18 April 1942 he spoke of the "national insurrection" and although on 14 July of the same year he said that in the struggle "between the people and the Bastille it is always the Bastille that ends up by being in the wrong", he also emphasized the "order" in which the effort of liberation was to be carried out. Indeed, against the advice of the FTP staff and a fair number of the leaders of Combat and Libération, he quite soon came round to the strategy of the "mobilizing maquis" intended to fix and then cut up the occupying forces.

Yet it would be unfair to confine Delestraint to the role of procrastinator and the man who immobilized the Armée Secrète. A few days before his arrest on 4 June 1943, Jean Moulin wrote to London to say that having been in touch with the leaders of the FTP, Vidal had come over to the "immediate action" whose principle General de Gaulle had very clearly accepted in instructions dated 21 May, thus authorizing a movement which, spurred on by Tillon, then assumed considerable proportions.[19]

The fact remains that between November 1942 and June 1944 the AS recruited something like one hundred thousand effective fighting-men who, from the Périgord to the Alps, and from the Ain to Brittany (where they received considerable reinforcements of parachutists belonging to the 2nd RCP detached from the British forces) created zones forbidden to the enemy, blocked his transport, sabotaged the various means of communication and disrupted the Vichy administration. This force was placed under General Koenig's orders in April 1944, and before D Day it played so important a part in Inter-Allied strategy that General Eisenhower stated that in the battle for the liberation of France it had been worth "fifteen divisions".

The first leader of the ORA was General Frère (formerly at the head of the Seventh Army and then president of the Clermont-Ferrand court-martial that condemned General de Gaulle to death) with General Verneau as his assistant.* At the beginning (late 1942) it was an organization close to Giraudism, deeply suspicious of Gaullism, and very far removed from direct action. When an envoy from Delestraint got into touch with Frère at Chamalières in January 1943 he was received very coldly and told that "this was no time to launch into adventures".[20]

But soon the influence at the top of the ORA passed from General Frère to Colonel Descour who, based in Lyons, made the first contacts with the Gaullist AS, and then to Colonel Revers who committed himself to a direct policy of cooperation. Major Zeller, whom Revers sent to Algeria at the end of September 1943, saw Giraud there, but also de Gaulle. And it was at this period that the

*Frère and Verneau died while being deported.

alliance between the AS and the ORA had its spectacular origin: it was the AS that organized General de Lattre de Tassigny's escape from the prison at Riom, but it was the ORA that saw to his leaving for London.[21] From then onwards the officer corps in France, which had remained Giraudist at heart or in their feelings, swung over towards Gaullism, which, to an ever-increasing degree, appeared to be a principle of action.

In one of the lampoons on Charles de Gaulle produced by the American intelligence services, which only stopped calling him a Nazi in order to accuse him of getting his food on the black market, we find it said that the leader of Fighting France was rarely to be seen on the battlefield. Let us say nothing about the value of such an argument used against a man in whom cowardice, as the world in general knows, was scarcely the most obvious defect; but on the other hand we should pause to consider what was one of the most lasting elements in the lack of understanding between the Constable and his most powerful allies – the subordination of the act of war to political action.

It cannot be doubted that Charles de Gaulle often wished to be with Larminat, Leclerc or Koenig in the firing-line. His almost unnatural fearlessness had done wonders there. But what of it? Were there not sound specialists for those things? *De minimis non curat praetor.* He had too high a notion of his political responsibilities and of himself as the man entrusted with this mission to risk what Emmanuel d'Astier called "the Symbol" in some minor excitement.

It was his duty to summon the arms of France for the restoration of the country's national sovereignty. It was for others to make those arms speak. "General?" he said to Macmillan one day. "I am a general no longer. I have set myself above these hierarchies."

CHAPTER THIRTY-FOUR

The Stokers and the Helmsman

"If it had not been de Gaulle, it would have been someone else," maintains Claude Bourdet.[1] Is that really so? For better or for worse, de Gaulle was unique because he was both the savage embodiment of a principle – the principle of national sovereignty – and the boldest manipulator of that raw material of politics known as circumstances. In his relations with his powerful allies, with his political supporters and with the men in uniform he is continually to be seen making use of this mixture of conceptual rigour and tactical flexibility: the same applies to his more and more central and decisive relations with the Resistance, in which from May 1943 he saw the source of his legitimacy and the base of operations for his Inter-Allied strategy.

Being France? He could not make a better claim to that condition than by accepting the Resistance, without allowing it to overshadow him. The great undertaking of strategic recentering and the re-rooting of Gaullism in metropolitan France started at the beginning of 1943, when Passy and Brossolette on the one hand, and Moulin and Delestraint on the other left for France in order to set up the structures for action that had been planned in London. But from the point of view of the principles concerned and also for tactical reasons, this movement could succeed only if it were unanimous. Since de Gaulle was manning his ship with what Brossolette calls "glory's stokers" he could be the helmsman only if he called upon all those who were fighting, and particularly the most effective among them: the Communists.

When in Paris the clandestine *L'Humanité** was denouncing "de Gaulle [as] the lackey of the City bankers", the Free French radio showed the utmost reserve towards the French Communist Party, as it did with regard to the USSR. The word Communist was never pronounced. It was as though de Gaulle, certain of the conflict between Hitler and Stalin, did not wish to do anything that might hinder the return of the Communists, the "separated brothers", to the fold.[2] And from 22 June 1941 onwards there was an evident cordiality and even a convergence of opinions that assumed all (or almost all) possible forms.

It is true that there was never any reply to the suggestion made by a member of the Soviet government to Captain Billotte (the future head of de Gaulle's staff) when he was transferred from the USSR to London in September 1941: what would the General's reaction be if Maurice Thorez, the Communist Party leader who fled to Moscow in October 1939, were to ask if he could leave for London

*Clandestine because it had failed to obtain the Nazis' permission to reappear openly, a failure that saved the leaders of the PCF from ignominy.

with his "detachment" to join de Gaulle?[3] Everything leads one to suppose that the Constable thought the matter so delicate that it was better to pretend not to have heard. Yet ideas of this kind were in the air.

Ten months later, in Paris, at the beginning of May 1942, Rémy* and his deputy met Beaufils, known as Joseph or Colonel Drumont, the representative of the FTP. Relations were established, and the BCRA, informed by Rémy, tried to strengthen them, in spite of what Passy calls "this organization's shillyshallying".[4]

But the talks between Beaufils and Rémy ended in an invitation to the French Communist Party, the PCF, to send Carlton Gardens a representative. This was Fernand Grenier, the deputy for Saint-Denis, and he left for London with Rémy at the beginning of January 1943.

Fernand Grenier has given an account of his first interview with de Gaulle, whom he asked, straight away, for "increased help for the patriots who are fighting weapons in hand":

> "You will look into that with Passy," de Gaulle interrupted. De Gaulle then asked me two questions: "And what do you think of Giraud? What will happen after the liberation?" I replied that in our opinion a provisional de Gaulle–Giraud government should be set up in Algiers as soon as possible. After the liberation of France it was the French nation itself that would decide what institutions it wanted.
>
> The talk had been free and open. Yet as I left the staff of Fighting France I asked myself a question: why did the General pay so little attention to what was happening in France at present and so much to what would happen at the liberation? I had expected him to ask me a great quantity of questions about the FTP's armed struggle, the deportations, life in the prisons, etc. Nothing, nothing!" [But Grenier nevertheless adds] I trusted the General. Once he was informed, his action would be more favourable to the Resistance.[5]

At all events Charles de Gaulle seized the opportunity and about 10 February he sent the party's central committee a cordial letter:

> The coming of Fernand Grenier, the accession of the Communist party to the National Committee which he brought me in your name, the placing of the courageous formations of francs-tireurs that you have raised and trained at my disposal as Commander-in-Chief of the Fighting French forces – these are so many demonstrations of French unity.
>
> Great efforts and great sacrifices will be asked of you, after all those that the members of your party have already accepted in the service of France. It is essential that French patriots should take their share in the liberation of the national territory side by side with our Russian and Anglo-Saxon allies. I know that Fighting France can rely on the French Communist Party.

From then onwards the PCF formed part of the whole in the strategy of Fighting

*Whose extreme right-wing views had not prevented him from making this necessary alliance.

France. Relations between it and the Gaullist staff were often tense and sometimes even stormy. The Communist representatives in London – Waldeck Rochet followed Fernand Grenier – often complained of the way their broadcasts on the BBC were hampered and above all of the discrimination between the AS and the FTP in the parachuting of weapons.[6]

Now that he had made an alliance with the organization that was the hardest to fit in with his plans, it was possible for de Gaulle to develop his metropolitan strategy in three phases. The first consisted of sending Passy, and his closest adviser, Brossolette, to France. He was entrusted, among other things, with numbering and regrouping the forces on which Fighting France could rely in the north zone. The second chiefly concerned General Delestraint, who was flown back to France on 23 March with the task of mustering the whole of the Armée Secrète's effectives, asserting his authority and applying the tactics of "immediate action" already practised by the Communists. The third and the best-known had as its chief actor Jean Moulin: it concerned the setting up of the CNR, the National Council of the Resistance, according to the instructions General de Gaulle had given his national delegate on 21 February.

But this immense undertaking by which General de Gaulle assumed the control of the Resistance as a whole had been preceded by a mission whose code-name was Pallas; though outwardly more discreet it was perhaps the most decisive, and it was carried out between December 1942 and January 1943 by André Manuel, the deputy head of BCRA.

The Pallas report was circulated at the beginning of February 1943: it established, above all, the importance the political parties had retained in the country's life. This observation was based upon a very large number of contacts, but chiefly on an interview with Daniel Mayer. The Secretary-General of the Socialist Party's action-committee stated that he was ready to support "an authoritarian government with democratic principles" led by General de Gaulle "which gives the democratic guarantees that we insist upon until the choice is given back to the French nation eighteen months to two years' later." So that the General should be "supported and guaranteed by those who represent the various forms of public opinion", Daniel Mayer suggested that "the political parties and trade union movements that have resisted since June 1940 and which run from Marin to Thorez should be allowed to take part in clandestine action on the political level"; for at the liberation this would win General de Gaulle "the guarantee of French unanimity".[7]

The views put forward in Manuel's paper were all the more likely to impress the General since three months earlier he had received a letter from Léon Blum. The former leader of the Popular Front government had just done the best turn that de Gaulle could have expected of him – the letter in which, addressing Churchill and Roosevelt, he vouched for the General's democratic intentions and for the way in which he represented French aspirations.[8] Lastly Blum was then the man of the Riom trial (February to April 1942) to whom the Vichy régime had offered a public platform and who had there become the "nation's prosecuting counsel" against the occupying powers, the first great protesting voice that had been raised on the soil of France for two years.

All this gave the letter the Constable received from Blum its full impact: "There is no democratic State without parties. Their moral standards must be raised; they must be re-examined; they must not be eliminated. A democratic State is necessarily a federation of parties."

Charles de Gaulle never overcame his distrust of political parties. But he was a sufficiently able strategist to know how to decide the priorities where urgent tasks were concerned and sufficiently confident of his strength and his talents to feel capable of dealing with any challenge. The first priority in these tasks was the liberation of the national territory; then came the setting up of an authority powerful enough to cope with the terrible requirements of that liberation; and finally the restoration of a true national independence. All these were watchwords calling for every form of support, of representation and of guarantee in France and abroad. So let the political parties be mobilized!

Besides, had not the leader of Fighting France already committed himself to the Communist party by inviting their official representative to join him in London, having gauged the power of the PCF, the FTP and the Front National? He could not risk the appearance of a French "Tito" and he did not wish to do so: in order to show the world a united, independent and loyal Resistance he had to have the Communists' accession, without which the situation would be ungovernable when the country was liberated.

But in that case how were the other parties to be treated? It could certainly be maintained that the PCF, by its origins, its structure, its recent history and its methods was not a party like any other. Yet how could arguments of this kind be put to its rivals? The Communists were represented in London by Grenier; but the Socialists were scarcely less so by Gouin. And French democratic life could not be confined to the two great left-wing parties; the spirit of resistance filled other and highly varied currents of opinion beginning with the different kinds of Christian popular democracy and the different nationalist tendencies. So how was this situation to be dealt with?

De Gaulle expressed his choice in the most striking manner in his letter to Léon Blum of February 1943, written a little before the famous instructions to Jean Moulin:

> We know the part – a part of the first importance – that the Socialist Party has played in this Resistance. We see how the influence of the political leaders, together with that of the ideas they still personify, seeing they have not betrayed them, becomes an essential factor in mustering the nation for action. That is why we wish to see the setting up of a concrete organization within the country that will gather together the representatives of the political parties under the single banner of the struggle for the country and democracy.[9]

Had not everything now been said? With the Manuel report and this exchange between Blum and de Gaulle, Fighting France's political strategy in relation to the Resistance seemed settled, the decisions taken: a front consisting of the movements, the trade unions and the parties supporting a provisional government provided with a mandate until elections could take place after the liberation.

And yet the game was far from being over. This Blum–de Gaulle strategy (which Jean Moulin adopted, though not, as we shall see, without hesitation) was opposed by men such as Passy, that out-and-out Gaullist, and the Socialist intellectual, Brossolette, because they distrusted the old political parties. More Gaullist than de Gaulle?

De Gaulle was playing the part of a many-sided, flexible strategist, making the best use of circumstances, once more. But the letter to Blum was not written by another hand, nor did it contain asides addressed to those in the know. It was the result of a free decision: it may be thought heavy with tactical mental reservations, but it is one that traces a "line", the line of the "authoritarian government with democratic principles" that summed up political Gaullism for a quarter of a century.

For two days Winston Churchill tried to oppose the mission called Arquebuse-Brumaire (after the pseudonyms of the two chief actors); he felt that Passy and Brossolette possessed too many military secrets to be endangered on the soil of France; but the head of the BCRA insisted upon going because he thought it vital for the maintenance of his authority in the eyes of those who, faced with the Gestapo, were risking their lives day and night.

Pierre Brossolette (Brumaire) left on 26 January 1943; Passy (Arquebuse) on 26 February, accompanied at his own request by an SOE agent known as Shelley. They met in Paris on 27 February.

Their mission was confined to the north zone. It had three aspects: the first was to lead to a stricter separation between "intelligence" and "action" both within the movements and the networks. The second consisted of making an inventory of all forces, either Resistance movements or political, trade-union or religious organizations that were capable of playing a part in the national rising aimed at liberation. The third was the quest for those who would "direct the provisional administration at the time of the liberation".[10]

They were also given a commission authorizing them "to express and interpret General de Gaulle's directives",[11] which opened a very wide field for personal initiative – and, as we shall see, for conflicts over 'interpretation'. The second task, making contact with the "political organizations" with a view to the uprising, was to form the basis for one of the most serious disputes the Resistance had ever known, on a footing with that about the principle of immediate action which had been going on since 1941.

The word "party" did not appear in their instructions, any more than it did in those given to Jean Moulin on 21 February. But it was certainly parties that were concerned. And it was on this point that Arquebuse and even more Brumaire were to enter into conflict with Rex, who, now called Max, landed in France one month later, furnished with wide powers – powers of whose breadth neither Brossolette nor even Passy had been informed. Now since it increased Moulin's jurisdiction in both zones when Passy and Brossolette assumed they had full powers of decision in the north zone, this last document of the General's was likely to offend the first two envoys.

But the argument did not bear solely on the question of territorial jurisdiction: it also had to do with a most important political choice. In order to ensure the General's democratic legitimacy in the eyes of his opponents and his allies, was it or was it not necessary to rebuild the former political parties and make them the partners, even the equals, of the Resistance movements?

Although Brossolette and Passy were ignorant of the extent of the powers conferred on Jean Moulin after their departure and even of the increase in his territorial jurisdiction, they did know that the delegate-general was to come back to France at the end of March. And, even if it were only through their contacts with Meunier and Manhès, his lieutenants in the north zone, they wished to steal a march on him by 'interpreting' the General's thoughts.

Since October 1942, the conferences with Frenay and d'Astier and the creation of the MUR (Mouvements Unifiés de la Résistance) in January 1943, it had been clear that the General Staff at Carlton Gardens intended to coordinate if not to unify the Resistance organizations in order to present a united front to rivals, friends and allies.

Now Pierre Brossolette, a convinced Socialist and for a great while the SFIO spokesman on foreign policy as well as a member of the Jean-Jaurès club in London, had violently denounced the "old parties" of the Third Republic in an article in *La Marseillaise*. In his view they amounted to corpses expelled from the nation's life for good and all. Was he thinking of a purely Gaullist "gathering", or of other forms of representation?* He knew that Jean Moulin was much more in favour of a union including the parties than he was himself, and so he meant to try to create *faits accomplis* before Moulin's arrival.

Arquebuse and Brumaire made haste to enter into contact with the representatives of the five chief north zone Resistance organizations (Organisation Civile et Militaire (OCM), Libération, Front National, Ceux de la Résistance, Ceux de la Libération) and then to bring them together in a meeting at which they reached an agreement whose text was sent to London during the evening of 26 March: Moulin, coming by way of the south zone, was expected in Paris on 30 March. This agreement provided for the representation within the CNR of "the various shades of the French resistant spirit" (communism, socialism, free thought, Catholicism, nationalism) but rejected the "permanent executive commission" envisaged in London.

Thus, outstripping the man who had been entrusted with the task of carrying out the great unifying plan in both zones together – a plan that included the parties – Brumaire and Arquebuse effected a resolution which confined itself to mentioning the "various shades of spirit" (a check on the recognition of the parties) and excluded any "executive commission" (a check on the unification). On both the plane of the constituent elements and on that of the forms of the unification this was an uncommonly restrictive "interpretation" of the London

*In May 1984 Colonel Passy thus described Brossolette's plan for the present writer: a clarification of French political life by the dividing of its forces between a great "labour" party and a great "conservative" party. The British style.

plan; and it was made, we must repeat, when the chief envoy sent by Carlton Gardens was expected four days later.

In case of doubt one should assume that people act in good faith. The two emissaries had acted as pioneers; and however limited it may have been the agreement reached with the five resistance organizations was a step forward. For amalgamation in the north zone was the hardest of tasks.

We possess no document nor even any oral account showing Charles de Gaulle's reaction to Brumaire's and Arquebuse's enterprise. This absence of evidence leads one to suppose that he came to the prudent conclusion that Passy and Brossolette had opened the path and that this sketch of a union (whatever "shades" it may have brought to the general plan) paved the way for Jean Moulin, whose task it would be to bring the agreement to its definitive state.

But this was not at all the way in which Moulin took things. He thought himself not betrayed but cheated, and he made no bones about telling his two comrades what he felt.* Gilberte Brossolette, basing herself on her husband's recollections, uses the word "altercation" in describing the first of these two interviews, which took place in the Bois de Boulogne on 31 March, and she speaks of "complete and violent frankness".[12]

According to the account of Colonel Passy, who was both a witness and a participant, the dispute grew heated when Brossolette set about explaining to Jean Moulin the reasons why it was better that the coordinating committee should gather "the fundamental tendencies of French thought" rather than the political parties. This was a frontal attack.

Instead of dealing with the main issue at once, Max began with the preliminaries. Why had his close fellow-workers in the north zone been excluded from the negotiations? Then he spoke out against the privileged position, in this first arrangement, of the OCM which had the reputation of being reactionary and technocratic. Since the tone was growing more heated on both sides, Passy thought it right to postpone the rest of the discussion until the next day, when they would meet at the flat in the place des Ternes** where he and his comrade had been living since their arrival in Paris – a place more suitable for an open discussion than the paths of the Bois de Boulogne.

On the next day, 1 April, the dispute was fiercer still, both men accusing one another of "ambition"; and when one now reflects upon the forms that noble passion assumed in those days the accusation no longer seems a form of blame but rather a tribute. Passy says that he took particular care to make peace with Moulin, who was now calm but "filled with a cold hatred" for Brossolette; and he states

*In his essay "Jean Moulin et le CNR" (*Institut d'études du temps présent*, p. 123) Daniel Cordier, who was an intimate colleague, says on this subject that "Brossolette was preparing the transformation of the Resistance into a 'party', Moulin the rebirth of the institutions. Brossolette was a politician, Moulin a statesman."

**In a letter published after Daniel Cordier's "Jean Moulin et le CNR", Pierre Meunier, Max's deputy, says that this meeting, at which he was present, took place in the rue de Rome. He also states that as Jean Moulin was leaving Passy drew him aside and said "You have a great leader; take care of him!" But the former head of the BCRA does not remember having uttered these words (interview of May 1984).

that the best he could obtain was "an armed truce" between them – a state of affairs that nevertheless bore fruit.

The mission that had been entrusted to Max began discordantly, therefore. And yet two days later, at the general meeting summoned by Passy in the avenue des Ternes at the request of the national delegate, a sudden agreement with Jean Moulin's views became evident. Moulin played his cards with great care, avoiding anything that might sound like a permanent executive of the Resistance, and he induced all those taking part to join in a general agreement with a view to the creation of the Conseil national de la Résistance.

The CNR would be made up not only of the five north zone organizations that had already responded to Arquebuse's and Brumaire's call to combine, together with the three great south zone movements (Combat, Libération and Franc-Tireur), but also of the two main trade unions (CGT and CFTC) and six political organizations (PCF, CAS,* the Radicals, the Popular Democrats and two small right-wing parties).** Considering the caution with which he had spoken, this agreement with his views was so sudden that Moulin took care not to suggest any specific date for the setting up of the CNR: having won his game in the north zone, he was now ready to carry on the operation in the south.

This was what might be called his own country, a region that he had been working over tirelessly ever since 1 January 1942: sixteen months of advances, of conciliation and argument in order to bring about first the convergence and then the unification of the movements. We know the kind of opposition he had already had to overcome to persuade the movements and their leaders to agree to a plain coordination and after that to the foundation of the MUR, headed by a directing committee at the beginning of 1943. Organizations of this kind, arising from the heroism of a few men whose suspicions were increased by their isolation in the midst of a society at first hostile or indifferent, were very much inclined to particularism and to strictly separated units; from this it followed that they favoured the retention of autonomy in all its forms. "We were wolves," said Emmanuel d'Astier, "adventurous visionaries who did not want anyone to get a hold on us." Uniting Frenchmen is always difficult. But uniting French rebels!

Yet Moulin wanted to go farther and farther in this direction. Moving on from coordination to unity was a bold step. Bolder still was that of including in this whole the "political parties" – two words that in themselves were enough to make the founders of Combat and Libération foam at the mouth.

"We were perfectly willing to cooperate with the Communist party, whose people we saw fighting bravely," said Claude Bourdet. "At a pinch we agreed to ally ourselves with what remained of the Socialist party. But the others, those ghastly Radicals and that right wing party, oh no!"[13]

It has often been said or written that it was Moulin who revived the parties in order to broaden the CNR and give it greater consistency. No. It was General de Gaulle in person who took this decision for the reasons that have been pointed out;

*Comité d'Action Socialiste.

**The Alliance Démocratique, Paul Reynaud's party, and the Fédération Républicaine, which was that of Louis Marin.

he did so because of the influence of the Pallas report, of Léon Blum and of his Commissioner for the Interior, André Philip. Moulin was not the initiator of this strategy. He was no more than the man who carried it out, only coming round to this view at his chief's particular urging. But like many converts he overflowed with zeal in the execution of the plan; and as we have seen he did so not without skill.

But now he was to be confronted with still greater trials. Although in the south zone he was surer of his surroundings, his supports and his liaisons than he was in Paris, here he clashed with an adversary more formidable than Brossolette and his OCM friends; for all his passions, moods and prejudices Brumaire was still a faithful Gaullist, and as soon as he had understood that what Moulin was saying and doing did in fact represent the General's intentions, he loyally fell in with his opinion.

Henri Frenay, the founder of Combat and the authority for military action within the MUR, was something else again. He was the creator and the leader of the oldest and most powerful movement. He was most pre-eminently the pioneer. He was "Charvet", "the boss". His rival Emmanuel d'Astier nicknamed him *figure de chef*, but however sarcastically d'Astier might look at him during the coordination sessions it was Frenay who had the greater weight and who spoke with the louder voice, certain as he was of his historic role, his military abilities, his experience of underground warfare and of the extent of his basic support. He was the only man who dared withstand not only Max but the General himself. D'Astier was neither timid nor conformist, since he had discovered certain flaws in the statue of the man he called "the Symbol". But he was too much under the charm of the General to rise up against him.

Frenay was rougher and less subtle and his reasoning was based on relative strength and services rendered. He calmly considered that his two and a half years of being hunted, of audacious strokes and inventions, put him on an equal footing with de Gaulle. But perhaps he had not perceived that the man of London had grown, that in gaining a foothold at Algiers he had taken root, that in standing up to Roosevelt and Churchill he had acquired an international dimension, and that the accession of great military leaders – Juin, de Lattre – was continually strengthening him.

He summarized his views in a letter to Moulin; it is an indictment that cannot be read without a certain embarrassment when one knows what happened to Moulin. But it is a striking piece of evidence about the spirit of the Resistance:

> Let me tell you in a friendly but firm manner that you know only one side of the Resistance. You have only seen through the big end of the telescope. You have not had the time to look through the little end. The freedom of the movements' organization must therefore be most zealously preserved. If the united nations were to come to believe that the leaders of the Resistance were no more than the National Committee's salaried agents, these leaders' opinion would no longer have any power behind it and Gaullism would lose the vital part of its influence. Yet at this very moment we see an attempt at turning the Resistance into a body of officials. When we utter opinions that

> do not exactly coincide with those that reach us from London you are scandalized and you come very close to accusing us of disloyalty.

And at this point Charvet brought up the argument he had used against de Gaulle at the time of his visit to London in the autumn of 1942. From the military point of view the Resistance was (though not without reserves) at London's orders. From the political point of view it considered itself independent. And he defined his view in this way: we look upon ourselves as a party that supports a government without consequently being at its disposal.

Clearly this called the whole of Jean Moulin's authority in question. Charvet was replying to the man de Gaulle had made his plenipotentiary, with insubordination, supporting his refusal to obey with an ingenious and powerful argument based primarily upon the irreplaceable nature of the spontaneity of the support of the Resistance. But had he measured Moulin's development, and had he understood what powers Moulin now possessed? Had Frenay perceived, on the eve of the affirmation of the General's authority in Algiers, that he was not of sufficient importance to make such a stand?

It is true that Henri Frenay thought he could base this claim for independence on an important advantage. In Switzerland one of his lieutenants, Guillain de Benouville, had made contact with a leading member of the American OSS, who offered him unlimited assistance which was not conditional on support for Giraudism: letter-box, printing-press and considerable sums of money – all those were placed at the disposal of Combat's envoy. Benouville told the man he was speaking to that nothing could be settled without the agreement of the French National Committee. Meanwhile he reported to the MUR directing committee, which authorized him to carry on with the contacts. Could such advantages be refused?

Yes, of course, cried Jean Moulin as soon as he was told about it, yes, they must be refused. A move in that direction meant giving the American intelligence services a hold over the French Resistance and over the whole strategy of Gaullism. For the Resistance, agreeing to be financed by Roosevelt's agents was the same as giving away a part of its independence at a moment when a decisive contest with Washington was in progress: for, though Frenay and his friends could not know it, the worst anti-Gaullist campaign was now breaking out in the United States on the occasion of Churchill's visit. Could the supporters of this general who was called a Nazi in the notes that passed between London and Washington accept money from those same sources?

In an attempt at calming the dispute André Philip suggested that the American offers should be accepted on condition that they should pass through the delegate-general. In a report sent to London a month later Frenay described this as a mark of distrust directed against the MUR and himself. "The American money can be handed to Rex* but not to us. There are some insults that cannot be accepted."[14] This shows how high the tone had risen and what kind of an atmosphere reigned at the beginning of the most important phase of the Moulin mission: the setting up of the CNR with the political parties as participants.

*The pseudonym Max was not used until later.

So on 7 May, before crossing swords with his partners of the MUR, Jean Moulin, who was anxious to associate de Gaulle even more closely with the mission, sent him an exceptionally interesting message. Max's intention was not only to increase his own reputation with the General; he also had to diminish de Gaulle's idea of Charvet's influence in France. He therefore, and not without treachery, recalled his opponent's contacts with Vichy, then with the Americans; spoke of Frenay's criticisms of de Gaulle, who, according to him, acted "imprudently" in appointing Delestraint to the head of the Armée Secrète; and pointed out that de Gaulle's name had been withdrawn from certain issues of the Combat bulletin. Then, speaking directly to the General, whom he obligingly reminded that the Resistance could have no other military chief than de Gaulle, he took up the theory Charvet advanced to justify his refusal of any political subjection to the General, according to which he looked upon himself as the head of a party supporting a government without consequently being at its disposal, and he turned it about this way:

> At the present moment [May 1943] I feel that you should consider yourself much more the head of a party than the head of a government. What is in question, apart from the liberation of the country? For you it is a matter of seizing power against the Germans, against Vichy, against Giraud and perhaps against the Allies. In these conditions, those who are very rightly called Gaullists should not have and in fact do not have any more than a single political leader, and that is you. It is, moreover, striking to observe that the most zealous advocates of submission to you are now the supporters of the former political parties.

There is no trace of any observation that the Constable may have made to Max on this subject. However, we may point out that twenty months earlier, when a broadcast from Radio-Brazzaville spoke of setting up a party in France that should draw its inspiration from the Resistance and that it should be called "Libération", the General at once cabled to the station authorities, "The French party of Liberation is Free France."[15]

Yet the great de Gaulle-Moulin plan was moving forward. Max overcame the obstacles set up on his path by the easily-offended Frenay and the swaggering d'Astier, and on 7 May he was able to tell London that "agreement had finally been reached". A week later, on 15 May, Moulin (who knew to what an extent his mission was connected with the operation his chief was carrying out in Algiers), speaking as president of the CNR, sent London the Resistance "parliament's" first message which proclaimed that on the eve of General de Gaulle's departure for Algeria, "all the resistant movements and parties of the north zone and of the south zone once more send him the assurance of their total adhesion to the principles he embodies," asserting that "the people of France will never accept the subordination of General de Gaulle to General Giraud," and calling for "the rapid setting up of a provisional government in Algiers under the presidency of General de Gaulle [who] will remain the sole head of the French Resistance, whatever the result of the negotiations may be."

In later years de Gaulle said that this summons "gave me greater strength, while without any pleasure but with clear minds Washington and London gauged the full implications of the event." And as we know, two days later Giraud invited his rival to Algiers.

At the same time the leader of Fighting France sent the new-born organization a message:

> For France the present war is above all an immense revolution; it becomes immediately necessary for the nation so to arrange matters that it will emerge from the liberation with order preserved and in independence, and this implies that beforehand it should be organized in such a fashion as to be governed and administered straight away as the nation itself desires until such time as it can express itself normally by means of the citizens' vote. At the moment of the liberation itself the Council must come forward as a kind of first representation of the wishes and feelings of all those who have taken part in the struggle within the country [in order] to assert the rights and interests of France in relation to the foreign powers without delay.[16]

Everything was therefore clear. The CNR, the provisional parliament of metropolitan France at war, was not only as, Claude Bourdet puts it, "a means of drowning the PCF and Combat in an immense insipid political soup". For de Gaulle its mission was to incarnate a nation already prepared to assume the responsibilities of its liberation and the subsequent management of its own affairs. It was in the highest sense the instrument for challenging Roosevelt: no, France would not undergo the "protectorate" against which Anthony Eden had already warned his colleagues in Washington.

In any case, by creating the CNR the Constable killed three birds with one stone: as a good soldier he unified his heterogeneous troops; as a good politician he merged his two present opponents, Frenay and the PCF, in a mass that could neutralize them; and as a good diplomat he strengthened his legitimacy with regard to his contemptuous allies.

On 27 May 1943, at 48 rue du Four, the first session of the National Council of the Resistance, made up of seventeen members, took place. Moulin had particularly wished this meeting to be held in the capital. Was it because this increased its symbolic value? Was it to overcome the reservations of the north zone organizations? Was it because his chief opponent, Frenay, was less sure of himself in Paris? Neither he nor d'Astier nor J.-P. Lévy (who was in London) attended the meeting. They were represented (brilliantly) by Bourdet, Copeau and Claudius-Petit.

Max, the *ex officio* president, took care to point out that although "as General de Gaulle has said and written, the democratic process implies the existence of organized parties, the presence of representatives of the former parties in the Council must not be seen as an official approbation of the reconstitution of the said parties as they functioned before the Armistice", and that only "an intellectual effort" and "discipline" would ensure "the solidarity and stability of French public life".[17] The meeting then unanimously adopted a motion proposed by Bidault (there were already close links between him and Moulin) which, having paid a tribute to the Frenchman fighting in the war, called for a provisional government presided over by de Gaulle.

But this did not do away with Frenay's objections. The leader of Combat told the present writer that he looked upon the creation of the CNR both as a taming of the Resistance for the sole benefit of de Gaulle's prestige and as a historic chance given to the PCF to come forward as "a party like any other" before outclassing its rivals;[18] and later he said that the day the CNR was set up was "one of the saddest in his life", and that by this act Jean Moulin became "the grave-digger of the Resistance". Yet very soon Moulin had to confront emergencies even crueller than the reluctance of the founder of Combat: a fortnight after the foundation of the CNR his most important colleague, General Delestraint, was arrested in Paris together with his deputy Captain Gastaldo, at the La Muette metro station.

For the Armée Secrète General Delestraint was an asset of the first importance: he had been proposed by Frenay and supported by de Gaulle, a personal friend; he was respected by the higher ranking soldiers because of his military career; he was accepted by the Inter-Allied leaders who had met him in London in March; and he was sufficiently clear-minded to adapt himself gradually to the requirements of "immediate action". Vidal's only failing was taking too many risks and failing to camouflage himself enough: it would be hard to replace him. The question was urgent. And it was the search for an early solution that led Max to his doom.

Charles de Gaulle describes Moulin in his *Mémoires* as "having grown impressive in his conviction and authority" but "aware that his days were numbered".

On 7 May Max sent this message to de Gaulle: it has the ring of a cry for help.

> Now both Vichy and the Gestapo are after me, and thanks in some degree to the methods of certain elements in the movements they know everything about my identity and my activities. I am quite determined to hold out as long as possible, but if I were to disappear, I should not have had the time to put my successors in touch with the present state of affairs.

Here is a document that deserves very careful examination, because it calls into question the "methods of movements", because he thought his enemies knew more than they did in fact, and because he speaks of his successors.

This loneliness, which was made worse by the feeling of being hunted, was to be relieved: London promised to send him a deputy. Claude Serreulles, who had been the General's ADC for two years, volunteered for the post. Passy and Brossolette had introduced him to Max in March, during his stay in London. Serreulles, who wanted to fight, asked de Gaulle to let him join Moulin. "Impossible," growled the General. "You are beside me in too many photos: you will get yourself arrested at once." Yet in the end de Gaulle gave way to the BCRA's requests and the parachuting of Serreulles, who had adopted the *nom-de-guerre* of Sophie, was fixed for the end of April. But the plane was hit by German anti-aircraft fire; the passenger was wounded, and he had to go back to London.

> It was only on 15 June that I managed to land in the Mâcon region, where I was astonished to find that no one was there to meet me. I had to take a very

slow train to Lyons and there look for Max; in the end a liaison-agent put me in touch with him on 19 June. I felt as though I were a hair falling into the soup. Moulin said, "I was no longer counting on you. I had forgotten you", but he made me very welcome and we went for a long, two-hour walk in the Bagatelle park.

He was short of news and he very eagerly questioned me about the way the de Gaulle–Giraud dispute was developing in Algiers. Then he asked me what I wanted to do. I told him I had studied the files chiefly with the idea of being his deputy for the north zone. "No," he said. "It is on the military level that I need help, now that Delestraint has been arrested. There will be a meeting to deal with his succession very soon. You will attend it." During those hours I did not think that Jean Moulin had anything of the look of a hunted or exhausted man. He was very much master of himself, carrying out his mission to the full.[19]

Max saw Serreulles again the next day to talk about Delestraint's successor, and he gave his new colleague a rendezvous for 21 June, the day a decisive meeting was to take place. Serreulles and Moulin saw one another again on the morning of 21 June, a few hours before the ambush at Caluire: there Serreulles was introduced to Aubrac.

Why was I not at the tragic meeting at Caluire? [said Serruelles] Because I had to take the funicular railway that they call "the String" in those parts: I mistook the line, got into the wrong train and found nobody at the top. For better security only Moulin, Aubry and Lassagne knew the meeting-place, Dr Dugoujon's house. We were to gather by threes at the terminus of the funicular and go on from there to the rendez-vous. So there I was, alone and lost, desperate at the idea of what Moulin would think of his new deputy; and all this time my comrades were setting off for the ambush.[20]

Here we shall not deal with the arrest of Moulin and his companions nor of the doings of Hardy, who was brought there by Aubry and whose immediate escape has given rise to so much suspicion, since it is better to refer the reader to Henri Noguère's account, the best that has yet been written;[21] nor shall we deal with the circumstances of Max's death, so well handled by his biographers, his sister Laure, Henri Michel and Henri Calef. At this point let us consider the situation brought into being by the seizure of the president of the CNR and of Aubrac and Lassagne, whom he seems to have thought of as possible successors to Delestraint. What was the state of devastation in which he left the Resistance? Here we must pass the word to Claude:

I had an appointment with Aubrac for the evening of 21 June to discuss the results of the Caluire meeting. He did not turn up, and I had a premonition of the disaster. This was confirmed next day by Maurice, the liaison-agent. I then took the decision, required by the circumstances, to assume Moulin's succession – the interim succession, of course. I straight away telegraphed

> de Gaulle "I am carrying on". Then I made a few suggestions: Billotte might come and take over the military succession, Soustelle the political.[22]

Serreulles had the advantage of having been so close to de Gaulle for two years. The fact that he was only thirty did not set him apart from most of the Resistance chiefs. But he had only been concerned with the great mission for three days. Although he had an excellent knowledge of its history and its complex difficulties he had not yet shared in its trials. The worst was the solitude in which London left the interim-delegate, a solitude very soon noticed by the leaders of the MUR. Quite naturally Moulin's disappearance brought the desire for autonomy back to life in various quarters: once the unifier was gone, what could remain of the union?

Serreulles, treated with irony by some and with silence by others, had to face up to the situation. He was surprised to find that, perhaps because of the shock of the Caluire disaster, the south zone authorities scarcely raised any objection to his taking over.

He met with more prejudice in Paris, where he arrived on 10 July, at the very moment when the leaders of the OCM and Ceux de la Résistance, Blocq-Mascart and Vogüe, were setting up a Comité Central de la Résistance which aimed at nothing less than taking the place of the CNR. Serreulles was told that he would not be invited to attend the constitutive meeting of this organization. But since the acting delegate-general had observed that the operation set on foot by the OCM and CDLR (backed by Combat) was not followed by the other movements (Libération, Franc-Tireur and the Front National above all adhered to the structure created by Moulin), he counter-attacked, had the meeting arranged by Blocq-Mascart cancelled and summoned another for the next day, 13 July, at the Institut de Géographie in the boulevard Saint-Germain; and he found means of presiding over it. From that time onwards the Comité Central was no more than a pale reflection of the CNR. The Council Max had formed was saved – provided that a president could be found.

Georges Bidault was called for. He was a distinguished Resistance leader, a political personality and as head of the BIP (Bureau d'information et de presse) he had worked side by side with Moulin for months; it was he that Max had chosen to propose the first motion at the inaugural session of the CNR. He was likeable, clever and flexible. It was Georges Bidault who was chosen in September 1943.

Throughout this period it is striking to note the reserve, the circumspection of the teams in London and Algiers with regard to these extremely important developments. It is as though the elimination of Max had cut the umbilical cord between the great home Resistance organizations and their supporters abroad. Furthermore, all the great memoirists of Fighting France, from the General himself to Passy and Soustelle, glide swiftly over the subject, as though the succession to Jean Moulin had neither created any problems nor assumed a very great importance.

The CNR had been founded "from above"; it was a kind of roof set down on dissimilar structures; and it was built in such a way that it ran a great risk of collapsing once its architect was removed. The wonderful thing is that it did nothing of the kind, and that when Serreulles had skilfully set them in place,

Bidault and the team entrusted with taking over were capable of maintaining the course, with the more and more encumbering (or predominating) help of the various organizations of Communists or fellow-travellers.

As de Gaulle saw it, the first CNR had two outstanding virtues; through the medium of Max it was his own creation; and at a critical phase of his struggle for power, that of the "taking of Algiers", it had allowed him to play a winning trump. When that result had been obtained and when the man to whom he had entrusted that "enormous task" had vanished, the CNR certainly remained one of the pillars of his legitimacy, but soon it also took on the appearance of an outspoken parliament which no longer confined itself to applauding but also thought it could advise, claim, dispute, plan. Was this organization that had allowed him to eliminate Giraud going to become the PCF's instrument for taming him, de Gaulle?

A few days after Bidault's election as president of the CNR de Gaulle appointed Emile Bollaert as Moulin's direct successor with the title of delegate-general. Moulin, prefect of Chartres, had cut his throat rather than obey a humiliating German order; Bollaert, prefect of Lyons, refused to serve Vichy. It was always to this rebellious fraction of the State, but an expression of the State nevertheless, like himself, that the Constable turned to direct the home Resistance.

Charles de Gaulle took no notice of the objections to Bollaert. He wanted him, that high civil servant. And he was not the only one to want him. Passy and Brossolette, who did not get on well with Serreulles, the acting delegate-general, were of the same opinion; they thought that the former prefect of Lyons, more an administrator than a politician, would be primarily concerned with carrying out their decisions. Furthermore, it was Brossolette who was entrusted with getting into touch with Bollaert (known as Baudouin) to tell him what was afoot and then to take him to Algiers, where he would be enthroned by the General. Since de Gaulle had not given him the post of Moulin's successor that he must surely have wished for, Brossolette accepted the situation philosophically; he was too much of an intellectual not to find the role of prompter, of the power behind the throne, of mentor, preferable to the direct exercise of power.

In the middle of September, Brumaire left for his last mission. "One too many," said Passy gloomily to Gilberte, his wife. But Pierre Brossolette had wanted to return to action, to direct responsibilities, whatever the cost, even if they were to cause him many disappointments, give him the feeling that the machinery of underground fighting was breaking down, and bring him into frequent conflict with the Serreulles–Bingen team, which he criticized freely in his reports.[23] Six months passed; he fell into the hands of the Gestapo, and to escape the risk of talking he flung himself from the sixth floor of the building in the avenue Foch occupied by his torturers.

The "Symbol". It was Emmanuel d'Astier de La Vigerie who tried to find one word that would sum up that remote galaxy formed by de Gaulle himself, by de Gaulle alone, for the men of the Resistance. The word is admirable for its abstract quality, and it echoes that "idea of France" without which the Resistance would have found no counterpart in London but a little foreign legion and that excellent machinery of secret war which continually provided the Allies with victory.

Yet beyond that idea and that project there was a man and a strategy of liberation, perceived with very different eyes by those who came to see de Gaulle for short missions "between two moons"* or who arrived to stay for good in London or Algiers. And from these varieties of views arose adhesion or hostility, estrangement or faithfulness, that left their mark on the evolution of the Resistance and the later history of Gaullism and of France.

That the Constable should have charmed d'Astier, Brossolette or Vallon, or have clashed with Frenay, Rivet or Sermoy meant that the effectiveness of a given movement and the balance of power within the Resistance would be affected. Hence the importance of "meeting with de Gaulle", that immediate connection which is one of the central themes of Gaullist historiography.

Let us first take the case of those resistants who did not have any direct contact with the General, which was obviously the great majority. Germaine Tillion, who was one of the first to set the Musée de l'Homme network in motion before she was deported to Ravensbrück, says this:

> We were Gaullists in the sense that since 18 June 1940 we had thought of General de Gaulle as "the man who was right", or rather "the man who was of the same opinion as ourselves" – but we knew almost nothing about him. Among the "resistants" of 1940 I knew some who did not become "Gaullist" until 1942 and others who did not become Gaullist at all: they could not bear the presence of the Germans in France and they required no other motive for action. As for me, it was only in prison and therefore beyond action and even beyond life – that I came to know any living details about General de Gaulle: I received them with infinite gratitude. *We were right*, and I believe none of us doubted it – but what an immense comfort to tell oneself that so much suffering was not in vain, that somewhere it was all coordinated and made use of for a reasonable end or purpose by a clear-minded, honest and unyielding man, a man on the scale of the immense requirements of our trust.[24]

Then let us hear Claude Bourdet:

> Gaullist? I probably was by about 1942. Before that I had only thought of fighting the Nazis, without any particular reference to the Cross of Lorraine. I got into touch with a Polish network and with the British, and then I thought of leaving for London. In the north zone, under the direct pressure of the Nazis, the right wing was patriotic, and very soon the Resistance was headed by the natural leaders of the community, the higher civil servants and the heads of firms (in the OCM) and trade-unionists (in Libération-Nord). In the south zone the right wing was Vichyist. The Resistance was the anti-right wing: it needed a figure to set up against that of Pétain. It had to improvise. Referring to de Gaulle was useful. But I began to draw back if not

*The time when clear nights allowed planes to land and take off.

from Gaullism then at least from the London and then the Algiers direction in 1943, when the absurdity of the orders given to Jean Moulin became apparent – the absurdity of separating the Armée Secrète from the movements, of checking "immediate action", and reviving the parties to bring them into the CNR.[25]

The "meeting with de Gaulle". Let us now turn to a few that were particularly significant, if only because of the traces they left behind them. Such as that which, proceeding from violent disagreement to misunderstanding and then from the exercise of charm to enchantment, bound Emmanuel d'Astier to de Gaulle. The founder of Libération was in London during April 1942:

> That night I was suddenly asked to go to his place. He was weary. He kept raking over history as though these were the days of Fashoda. It did not matter that he was only the leader of a handful of men and a few remote territories; his enemies and his pride had increased him to such a size that he spoke as though he bore a thousand years of history within him or as though he were standing back for a century and seeing himself written in it. He drew a dark picture of his Calvary – that of France in person. And it suddenly occurred to me that he was giving himself up to this black fervour purely to stimulate the genius of France to recover its national and historic power, the only one he believed in.
>
> Although he was capable of drawing so much wisdom from a piece of madness, he perceived nothing but empiricism. He so thoroughly embodied the nation, he so wholly felt himself to be the nation that he forgot the people in it and the immediate present and the incoherence and the necessary Utopia and that remote future which is called mankind. How could one tell him of it? There is no arguing with a Symbol about that which he symbolizes.[26]

With all its strangeness the alliance between two atypical aristocrats, two great intellectual beasts of prey, two virtuosos of domination, came into being. And from this winning over, of d'Astier, there were to come many other acts of bewitchment – acts involving almost all those, from Aubrac to Morandat, who brought about the liberation.

By way of antithesis, here is Daniel Mayer, a typical product of French democracy, who had already found a father-figure in Léon Blum and who by definition distrusted "heroes", above all if they wore uniform. In April 1943 he came to the Constable in London as the ambassador of French Socialism, eager to demonstrate his adhesion to de Gaulle and at the same time to try to reconcile the two socialist tendencies in London, the Gaullist (Brossolette, Philip and Hauck) and the anti-Gaullist (Comert, Lévy, the Gombaults).

De Gaulle received him three days after his arrival.

> I had scarcely sat down before he launched into a violent indictment of London and its colonial encroachments. There was no way of getting him to

talk about anything else.* For someone who had just come from France, where Britain was looked upon as a friend, a model democracy and a haven for the world's freedom, this exhibition of disunion was deeply upsetting.

When I left his office I had only one wish, and that was that the plane taking me back should crash in the Channel. Anything rather than have to write a report that would make the Resistance despair. I may add that this wish for suicide was not transient; it grew more marked in the two or three following days. Then I went to the Jean-Jaurès club and there my anti-Gaullist friends gave me the advice that saved everything: one had to stand up to him!

Two days later I was summoned to Carlton Gardens again. De Gaulle began, "These Americans! You would not believe ..." "Forgive me, General, but I have not travelled from France to London to learn of your difficulties with Churchill and Roosevelt but primarily to inform you of French socialism's support for Fighting France."

Then I saw a perfectly charming de Gaulle, talking about the Resistance, about French democracy and its principal leaders "who have not come here but whose support is known to me" – and he went on to mention Louis Marin, paying a tribute to "his courage", Edouard Herriot, Léon Blum "who must have suffered a great deal", etc. He spoke of his esteem for the resistants, particularly, I thought, those who went back to France. I no longer had any wish to kill myself at all. Yet this second impression of de Gaulle did not wipe out the first, but rather corrected it.[27]

Let us stay in London. There Stephane Hessel, one of the BCRA's specialists in intelligence and political action, had succeeded in joining his friend Tony Mella in March 1942. He was the inventor of those famous personal messages on the BBC, and he worked with him. Was Hessel a Gaullist? He came from a Jewish family driven out of Germany in 1933 and he was above all an anti-Fascist.

There was no question of not joining Free France. But de Gaulle? We were possessed by a threefold suspicion. The first was ingenuous: was he working for personal glory? It was of no importance – what if he was? The second went deeper: how far and towards what was this furious struggle for independence leading? A clash with the Allies? The third and most serious: what would this formidable leader mean for French democracy tomorrow? What régime, what society was he intending to set up?

We were perfectly used to asking these questions, at least until 11 November 1942 and his speech at the Albert Hall the day after the landings in North Africa. That day, our doubts vanished. It was then, between November 1942 and his leaving for Algiers on 30 May 1943, that we came to understand the meaning of his policy and at the same time of his character, which was taking shape under our eyes. It was then that he himself defined

*April 1943 was the time of Churchill's journey to Washington and his attempt to drop de Gaulle.

> his role and his means, his aims and his limits, and the requirements of French independence within the framework of victory over Nazism.
>
> It was then that he built up his strategy of liberation and the taking over of power by basing himself above all on the home Resistance, with the consciousness of living France – which he really was, both against the occupying forces and against the American campaigns with their attempts at imposing Giraudism and their plans for treating France as a conquered country and forcing a foreign protectorate upon it. Yes, it was then that we became Gaullists.[28]

It was hard for anyone to act more continuously or more boldly from June 1940 until the Liberation than Lucie and Raymond Aubrac, whether they were together or separated by the vicissitudes of the struggle (or of prison). She was the daughter of a peasant family; she had passed the *agrégation*;* she had become a member of the Communist youth movement, but she had moved away from the party after the August 1939 pact. He was a civil engineer in the service of the State; ideologically he was not defined except in so far as the left wing provided the boundaries for his thought and anti-Nazism its driving force. By way of intelligence missions, messages and propaganda tracts they joined Libération.

> When we began the struggle we were left-wing people, anti-militarist and with anarchist sympathies. For us, de Gaulle was a general; and our first reaction was distrust. But since he was fighting the Nazis, so much the better. Our conversion came about in three or four stages. To begin with, Jean Cavaillès saw d'Astier, who gave him a quite surprising picture of de Gaulle. Then we became friends with d'Astier himself, and we changed our relation with de Gaulle into something like a love-hatred.
>
> After that [Raymond Aubrac went on] we rationalized this relationship, above all after my meeting with Jean Moulin. I was the first of the Libération leaders to get into contact with him – that was under the colonnade of the theatre in Lyons, in January 1942 – and we often saw him later. At that time our Gaullism was based on one observation and one piece of reasoning: de Gaulle being what he was, his existence provided the best protection against the development of the Resistance in the direction of a civil war according to the Yugoslav pattern – Tito against Mihailović. There was a danger that the radicalization of movements such as Libération in the south zone and the vitality of the right-wing currents, particularly in the north zone, would lead to tragic conflicts: de Gaulle and Moulin were the only men who could prevent them.[29]

We must also take into account the reaction of the philosopher Jean Cavaillès who, strongly influenced by d'Astier, went to London and there found a de Gaulle intellectually on a level with his reputation but, as Cavaillès saw it, so indifferent to

*Very roughly the equivalent of an English first-class honours degree; but the *agrégation* is competitive. (trs.)

people and so insensitive to the trials suffered by those in France, that he summed up his impressions in four words: "He is not human."[30]

Not human? The great voice of Cavaillès is not to be impugned. But at this point a message sent by de Gaulle to the leaders of the NAP* network in Paris on 23 August 1943 must be quoted: "My comrades, The honour and the grandeur of France depend upon what you are doing, upon what you are suffering in the Resistance, that is to say in the battle. The end is near. The reward is coming. Presently we shall all of us weep for joy together." Clearly these were words he never said either to Frenay or to Jean Cavaillès.[31]

But none of these "stoker to helmsman" relations were so filled with significance and complex ambiguity as that which liked Jacques Bingen and Charles de Gaulle.

Jacques Bingen had been in charge of the merchant navy in the first 1940 Comité Français before Muselier took his place; then he had been appointed to the political services of BCRA. He was parachuted into France on 16 August 1943 to share the overwhelmingly arduous task of succeeding Jean Moulin as delegate-general in the metropolitan territory with Serreuilles. At this period Bingen, a thirty-three-year-old engineer who came from a middle-class Jewish family in Paris related to the Citroëns, was seen to be one of the three or four most exceptional characters revealed by the Resistance. But he did not see the liberation: when the Gestapo arrested him in June 1944 he had time to take poison.

Here are extracts from two of Jacques Bingen's letters: the first, dated 14 August 1943, is a will written just as he was about to leave on his mission to France; the second, of 14 April 1944, is a report of sorts on the execution of that mission. In both cases Bingen speaks of Charles de Gaulle's character and responsibilities with an exactingness and nobility that have no equal.

In his will the new delegate for the south zone was anxious to explain the reasons for his choice to fight "on the home front", rejoining those who were there carrying on "a dangerous and unequal struggle" for "a sacred cause". Then, before saying good-bye to his mother and his relations, he devoted these words to de Gaulle:

> I beg that General de Gaulle may be told of the great admiration for him that I have gradually acquired. During these hard years he has been the very emanation of France. I implore him to preserve his nobility and purity but not to forget after the glorious victory that although France is a great lady, the French will be very weary. For them he will have to have not only a great deal of ambition but also a great deal of indulgent tenderness.

Eight months later, on 14 April 1944, a few weeks before falling into the hands of the Gestapo, Jacques Bingen was to add a postscript to these heart-rending farewells in the form of an even finer warning:

> I am writing these few pages this evening because for the first time I feel

*Noyautage des administrations publiques, founded by Claude Bourdet.

myself seriously threatened and because in any case the coming weeks are going to bring – no doubt to the whole country and certainly to us – blood and I hope wonderful adventure.*

Let my mother and my dearest friends know how immensely happy I have been during these eight months. No suffering can ever take away the delight in living that I have felt [during] this heavenly period of Hell. [Having proclaimed his "joy" Bingen was also bent on proclaiming his anger at the faults and shortcomings of Fighting France.]

From October to April neither the Committee** nor the Allied services*** nor the intelligence services† have fulfilled their minimum duties. I have never had a word of comfort, never a letter (or a card) of encouragement. A scandalous and inhuman failure [responsible for] the falling away of many friends and comrades. [And it was at this point that Jacques Bingen implicated the leader of Fighting France.]

Lastly, turning to Charles (who must be shown what has been written up to this point) I warn him against three serious errors that may be very costly not only to him (which is his concern) but to the France that trusts in him.

1. Charles does not think so, but the choice of men is extremely important; and this good, very careful, reviewable and patient choice is the first duty and the chief responsibility of a true leader. Any one man is not of the same value as any other man. Not all are equally contemptible. "Faithfulness" is not always a mark of devotion.

2. One cannot be an innovator, a "revolutionary", and have one's judgment clouded by official titles, which is the case with Charles. A general, a bishop, an ambassador, a high civil servant or a former minister deserves a favourable bias at the most, but that only for certain posts and not for all. Neither Stalin nor Hitler would have had even their temporary success if they had had bourgeois values rooted in their hearts, as Charles still has. Take care; this is very serious.

3. Charles should not suppose that he is awaited like the Messiah. To be sure, he will rightly be very well received here, and the hopes of millions of French men and women hang upon what he will do. But his credit is *not* unlimited, far from it. Let him be on his guard and be *human* in both home and foreign policies and in the choice of those about him. Let him beware of docile followers who are merely ambitious, worthless, cunning schemers. They may very quickly bring him down.[32]

Such was Jacques Bingen's last look at his fight, his companions and his leader. Did Charles de Gaulle read the admirable warning uttered by this fighting-man with a fearless outlook? If he did, let us be sure that it caused him less bitterness than pride. To have inspired these prophetic words!

*The landing took place seven weeks later.

**The CFLN, presided over by General de Gaulle.

***The English services.

†The Algiers DGSS, run by Jacques Soustelle.

CHAPTER THIRTY-FIVE

A Government At Last

In 1940 the capital full of admirals taking the waters at Vichy could claim that it was governing reality. London was living a great dream – but not much more than a dream. The realities survived in Vichy: formal legality, the apparatus of the State, international representation, and all this based upon a broad support among the people. By 1942 everything had swung round. The Marshal still retained something of his personal hold on the crowd,* but Vichy was merely an abandoned myth. It was at Algiers that the State was in action and that the nation was taking on a new shape.

What could look more different than that little watering-place in the Auvergne, snuggling beneath its mountains and its springs, a comfort-loving huddle of expensive hotels with carefully arranged walks, and this brilliantly-lit city of corsairs rising from an enormous port and dominating the sea? And yet what similarities there were between these two manifestations of the State – the provisional conditions in which those in authority crowded angrily into hotels in the one case, and into villas in the other: The Hôtel du Parc and the Pavillon Sévigné in Vichy and Les Glycines, Les Oliviers and the Lycée Fromentin in Algiers. But as everybody knew, it was not the same. In Vichy everything turned towards withdrawal, towards an exaltation of the past. In Algiers, with the wind blowing in from the open sea, people spread out, they were filled with ambition for the future, they made plans not merely for survival but for rebirth.

> Algiers [says Soustelle] swarmed with uniforms, jeeps and lorries. Men and vehicles were climbing up hills or going down them; the cafés were overflowing with people and one had to wait in a queue to find a seat in a restaurant. As for the hotels, which had been wholly or partly requisitioned by the Allies, only the very highest authorities, after telephoning in every direction, could find you so much as a niche. So many people literally slept in the street that I saw some puzzled members of the parliament take their revenge for their miserable quarters by blaming the head of the provisional government for having so little respect for the country's representatives.[1]

Charles de Gaulle and his family – except for his son, Philippe, who carried on with his duties in the navy – took up their abode at Les Oliviers,** the agreeable

*This was to be seen in April 1944, when he was warmly welcomed by the ordinary people in Paris.

**Now the residence of the French Ambassador to Algeria.

residence of a well-placed Turk, with just enough of the East in its forms and colours to underline the point that London had been left behind; a place that he had described to his wife as soon as he reached it, "Just the house we need". And he had his office in Les Glycines which Giraud's people had assigned to him on 30 May 1943, showing no excessive generosity, since they kept the impressive Summer Palace for their chief.

Les Glycines "was a jumble of furniture, knick-knacks, papers and typewriters," says Soustelle. "Many people were still sleeping there on camp-beds that were folded up during the day. It was rather like a headquarters during an action. On the ground floor, with great difficulty, Palewski, de Courcel and Charles-Roux maintained a little order around a small drawing-room in which the imperturbable General de Gaulle worked away in a temperature of a hundred and four degrees."[2]

"Now that the goal was coming nearer, I had the impression that I was walking on a more yielding soil and breathing a less pure air. Interests were rising up around me, rivalries were coming into existence, and every day men were growing more human."[3] A strange expression, and one that tells us a very great deal. Yes alas: that "idea of France" which had been conceived and which the apparent madness of the undertaking had preserved in its elevated purity – here it was, pitting itself against reality, against all too human human beings.

Three tasks were far more important than the rest: the rebuilding of the State; ensuring an international status for it by means of victory and negotiation; and lastly freeing a more or less reassembled nation from the civil war that was now raging with greater fury than ever in the country and in people's hearts. These were tasks that could not be separated, since France's return to the international scene depended as much on the conduct of its soldiers on the battlefields as on the reorganization of the apparatus of the State and the gradual replacement of faction and hatred by unity from top to bottom. Yet they were distinct, and the Constable set about them in a sequence that corresponded to the intellectual order that he had laid down long since (the State is to be served first), but also to circumstances.

These matters were difficult, arduous, and complex: but that was not all. De Gaulle also perceived that in Algiers he was less well placed than he had been in London – not perhaps for action, but at all events "for making himself heard" as he puts it in his *Mémoires*, for the "Algiers radio was less well known in France than that of the BBC". What is more, for the Resistance Algiers was not the ideal aircraft-carrier that London still remained. There, one or two hours were enough to travel from the battlefield to the General Staff; in Algiers the time and the effort had to be multiplied by three. The services responsible for action inside France therefore retained powerful organizations in London (Passy and Boris), while the Commissariat for the Interior (Philip and then d'Astier) and Soustelle's DGSS worked in Algiers.

The tool was unsteady in its handle. But action was called for, very rapid action: although the General tended to think his partners and those about him "too human", he too was keenly aware of the trials that were overwhelming the country and therefore of the urgent need for a solution. The author of the *Mémoires de guerre* speaks with a sombre eloquence of "this wretchedness in which the great majority of French people were wasting away"; and he recalls the tribute paid by his own family.* Writing to his son Philippe on 26 October he said, "France is becoming exhausted."[4]

To begin with, the apparatus of the State was to be rediscovered, put together and set in motion. That is to say an executive worthy of the name and a national representation capable, until the promised elections could be held, of bearing witness to the democratic spirit of the future institutions and at least to some degree of reflecting the wishes of the people.

On 17 September 1943 the decision was taken to convene a consultative assembly in Algiers so as to provide "as wide an expression of the national opinion as is possible in the present circumstances," it being understood that this body would be dissolved as soon as "the assembly entrusted with appointing the provisional government should be set up". This rough draft of a national representation was made up of forty envoys from the metropolitan Resistance (including Henry Frenay, Jacques Médéric, André Hauriou and Louis Vallon), twelve delegates from the Resistance outside France (including Henri d'Astier and René Cassin), twenty members of the Chamber of Deputies and the Senate** (such as Vincent Auriol and Pierre Cot) and twelve representatives of the General Councils (among whom, at Algiers, there was one solitary Muslim). One woman: Lucie Aubrac.

The assembley met in the Palais des Délégations, and Emmanuel d'Astier has a caustic description of the birth of this sub-parliament of "consultants" with which "de Gaulle was going to trip up his opponents".

> Since I had never set foot in an assembly, I was curious. Most of the men present were novices like myself and it only needed a few hours for them to be manoeuvred by the experienced parliamentarians, however much discredit hung about them – a discredit that had promoted them to behave with a prudence and humility which they soon threw off. The manoeuvres for the presidency*** and the vice-presidencies took place in the corridors. In the assembly-room the men sat in a circle, sleepy, inattentive or impressed ... All this only amounted to an incoherent mumbling. I tried to establish a link between the life of the French underground and this exhibition.[5]

The first session was opened on 3 November by Charles de Gaulle, who was still accompanied by General Giraud. He denounced the "abominable régime of personal power" which had "imprisoned the sovereign nation"; he paid tribute to the Resistance, the "elemental expression of the national will"; and he called for the help of the Assembly, which he defined as "a first step in the resurrection of the French representative institutions upon which the future of our democracy depends". It was not possible to be more respectful to the great principles, and both the cheers of the delegates and the comments in the Anglo-American press gave the Constable's speech an impressive resonance.

*A terrible tribute: his sister Marie-Agnès, his brother-in-law Cailliau and their son, Michel, were deported, as were his brother Pierre and his niece Geneviève. His paralysed brother, Jacques, was only just saved from the Gestapo.

**Brought to life again after their abolition on 10 July 1940.

***The "London" socialist, Félix Gouin, was chosen.

He was pleased with his parlimentary beginnings and after this he spoke on a fair number of occasions. He did so about fifteen times.

On 2 October the CFLN passed a motion stating that "it would elect its [single] president for the term of one year, and that he would be re-eligible". The "monarchy" having been re-established, all that remained for Charles de Gaulle to do was to cause his former alter ego to be eased out of the team. On 6 November he persuaded all his colleagues to resign in a body: Louis Joxe was entrusted with having this resignation countersigned both by Giraud and by Georges. The latter was stubborn at first but then complied. The former, who did not really understand what it was all about, signed straight away with a simple-mindedness so perfectly in line with his reputation that the Constable's envoy could not help feeling a certain remorse.

The exclusion of Giraud, who was still nominally Commander-in-Chief, proceeded, from title to functions, until April 1944; but henceforward de Gaulle had a free field for reshaping "his" executive, for strengthening it, and for providing this committee of important civil servants, distinguished men and soldiers with an increasingly massive proportion of home resistants and political figures. Thus between September and November 1943 the call went out to François de Menthon, the prime mover in the Comité Général d'Études that Jean Moulin had founded, to André Le Troquer, a Socialist deputy and formerly Léon Blum's barrister, to René Capitant, the leader of the Gaullists in Algiers, to Louis Jacquinot, a conservative deputy from Lorraine, and to Henri Queuille, a figure symbolic of the radicalism of the provinces and of government continuity.*

And then on 9 November General de Gaulle introduced a Comité de Libération (he said "government") that conformed to his wishes.

He offered the Ministry of the Interior to d'Astier, who accepted it. Henry Frenay for his part was entrusted with the prisoners and deportees, a role that "he did not much care for", observes Louis Joxe, who goes on to say: "The man seemed to have aged all of a sudden. And he had various other moods. In particular it seemed to him that the drift towards the left was growing stronger without any good reason, he found Communism everywhere, just as some people find arsenic in chair-legs. Like Astier he thought that the heroic period was coming to an end."[6]

But the strengthening of the CFLN was also carried out by calling upon political figures of the first rank. Before leaving for Algiers, de Gaulle saw Gaston Deferre, who advised him to appeal to Pierre Mendès France, who, as we have seen, had declined all political functions and who for some months had been fighting as a member of the Lorraine squadron. "Still another Jew," blurted out the Constable. (Commenting upon this, Mendès France said, "Anti-Semitism was foreign to him. But he was sensitive to balance and to public opinion; and above all in North Africa public opinion was less innocent than he."[7])

However that may be, on 9 November Captain Mendès France, at an English base in Hertfordshire, received a telegram from de Gaulle which ended with these imperative words, "Rely on immediate presence in Algiers, best wishes." A week

*He had already been a minister twelve times.

later he became the head of the Commissariat of Finance, where he drew up plans for the resuscitation of the French economy, plans that he was only allowed to put into action for a few months.

Broadened in this way and fortified by the presence of men of such value as Catroux, Jean Monnet, Massigli, René Mayer and Mendès France, the CFLN of November 1943 had the look of a real government of France. But as the Liberation came closer, so the threats, disagreements and exclusions mounted up.

On 25 November 1943 Charles de Gaulle, addressing the consultative assembly, thus defined what was more than ever his primary aim: "The return of a great power to its position as a great power by means of war and of effort." He still, however, had to convince the Allies, who throughout these last months of 1943 went on conferring between themselves from Moscow to Cairo and from London to Teheran without taking the least notice of Fighting France's opinions or aspirations.

Washington continued "to look upon France as fallow land and the de Gaulle government as a disagreeable accident".[8] The same applied to Field-Marshal Smuts, the Prime Minister of South Africa, who was in London in December and who declared that France, having ceased to be a great power, had no other choice but to join the Commonwealth.

Could de Gaulle rely on Soviet support to counterbalance these formidable prejudices? We have spoken of the advances made to Moscow, particularly at the time of the great crises with Churchill (September 1942, April 1943), when Stalin replied by granting the CFLN a semi-recognition, more explicit than that of the other two great powers. But when the foreign ministers (Eden, Hull and Molotov) had their conference in Moscow in October 1943, Stalin made not the least objection to the exclusion of the French, just as he agreed with Roosevelt to do the same at Yalta.

The CFLN sent Pierre Cot on a mission to Moscow some months later and there he was told that however much sympathy the Soviet Union might feel for Fighting France, the Russians' interests required them to set a greater value on their relations with Roosevelt than on those with de Gaulle.[9] This made everything plain; and almost the same words, at the same period, were uttered by Churchill.

Once the great anti-Gaullist rage that brought Churchill to the verge of a break with de Gaulle in the spring of 1943 had passed, the efforts of a team (Eden, Macmillan, Duff Cooper and Oliver Harvey) which was faithful to the entente cordiale and which did not believe that a nation struck down by a military defeat therefore ceased to be a "reality", re-established an atmosphere of alliance; and they did so all the better as on the other side the patient advances of such determined Anglophiles as René Massigli, René Pleven and Pierre Viénot,* the CFLN's "ambassador" in London, responded to their efforts. But these results were spoilt by three events, the one of an international scope – the revival of the Levantine crisis – the others apparently more commonplace, but still of such a nature as to call the principles of national sovereignty into question on one side and the other.

* * *

*Formerly Under-Secretary of State for Foreign Affairs in the Popular Front government.

"It was only possible to measure Catroux's talent after he left the Levant, when de Gaulle called him to Algiers," remarks Georges Buis. "Once he had gone, everything very soon took a turn for the worse in Beirut."[10] Indeed, less than six months after the departure of the man who had proclaimed the independence of the two States of the Levant, fire broke out again in the Lebanon.

Whether or not he was encouraged to do so by Sir Edward Spears and the British special services, on 8 November 1943 the Lebanese Prime Minister Ryad el-Sohl (and to tell the truth he was quite big enough and brave enough to undertake it on his own) caused the Assembly elected five months earlier to vote for the abrogation of the French Mandate in the Levant. To the French officials the step, taken under cover of the British presence, was a twofold challenge.

Ambassador Helleu, who had succeeded Catroux as High Commissioner at Beirut, lost his head, vetoed the assembly's decision and (without referring to Algiers) went so far as to arrest not only the Prime Minister but also the President of the Republic, Bichara el-Khoury! Demonstrations, repression: several Lebanese were killed.

De Gaulle reacted at once by sending Catroux and by cabling Helleu on 13 November, "The measures you saw fit to take were perhaps necessary. In any case I must consider them so since you took them. We shall not disavow you."[11] Yet under the pressure of the circumstances – and of the English – that was certainly what he had to come to in the end. As soon as he reached the Levant, the CFLN's envoy found himself confronted with an ultimatum from Richard Casey, the British minister in Cairo, insisting upon the immediate release of the interned President and Prime Minister, the British command in the Near East being unable to tolerate any incident whatsoever because of the state of war.

London went so far as to threaten "military intervention" to lessen the effect of any "weakening" on the part of the French authorities, a systematically humiliating procedure and form of expression that the French High Commissioner's murderous blunder did not quite justify. In a letter to Massigli, de Gaulle spoke of a plain withdrawal from the Levant to make London retreat; though at the same time he said he was convinced that the Lebanese were prepared "to put up with our energetic steps".[12]

Catroux stated that "in spite of the odious nature of the British requirements" he thought it absolutely necessary to make"the handsome gesture of reparation that the Lebanon expects of us", and de Gaulle had to yield: Bichara el-Khoury and Ryad el-Sohl were released and the first was reinstalled. But people at the Foreign Office admitted to Pierre Viénot that Churchill had handled the whole business rudely and clumsily; being convinced that it all arose from "a whim of de Gaulle's", and being vexed by the re-structuring of the CFLN and the exclusion of Giraud and Georges, he had wanted to give de Gaulle a good lesson.

This fresh outbreak of ill-feeling between France and Britain was made worse by affairs that were of minor importance but nonetheless set the Prime Minister against the General.

Maurice Dufour, an officer in the Vichy army, was recruited by the Intelligence

Service. He came to England at the beginning of 1942 and then joined Free France without revealing his earlier activities. He was suspected of continuing to work for his previous employers, was arrested, accused of unauthorized assumption of rank and desertion, and interned at Duke Street, where he was interrogated. He escaped from the Fighting French camp at Camberley, joined the British once more and in September 1943 brought an action against General de Gaulle, Colonel Passy and Captain Wybot* for false imprisonment and torture. The Foreign Office summoned Pierre Viénot and told him that in view of the total separation of powers in Britain, the law would follow its course (a solicitor having been appointed by the court to defend de Gaulle) unless a settlement were arranged between the man of 18 June and Dufour.

It is easy to imagine the reaction of the Constable (who furthermore devotes no less than four pages of his *Mémoires* to this murky business). It was easy for him to observe that according to the Churchill-de Gaulle agreement of 7 August 1940 and even more to the Eden-de Gaulle convention of 15 January 1941 (which was negotiated after the scandalous arrest of Muselier), members of the Free French forces in Great Britain were answerable only to French military law.[13] The pressure on the leader of Fighting France to submit to the criminal proceedings continued until the day his own intelligence services were able to confront London with an affair of a similar kind, a Free Frenchman by the name of Stéphane Manier being said to have "committed suicide" in an English police station.

The press, especially in America, devoted a great deal of space to Dufour versus de Gaulle, while at the same time there were lampoons and scurrilous pieces about Fighting France and its "Gestapo", particularly a memorandum from Roosevelt to Churchill in which the man of 18 June was sometimes described as an apprentice dictator.

The Dufour affair was not the only one to arouse spirited press-campaigns against the BCRA and its methods. In one report the Gestapo is mentioned and the tortures inflicted by these "French Nazis" are denounced – reports that very rightly moved Roosevelt and Churchill, until a note from the Foreign Office brought the temperature down.

According to one of the BCRA officers who carried out interrogations, apart from the case of Dufour (who was not tortured but violently knocked about and who brought this treatment to an end by his fearless attitude) there were three affairs in which the methods of the Gaullist counter-espionage could be accused. In these three cases the "pressure" brought to bear on the prisoner was of a kind to justify the strongest criticism. But nothing, according to our witness, which could be compared with the scandalized indictments of the American "observers" and the French and British anti-Gaullists.**

* * *

*The head of the counter-espionage service.

**Let us add this remark made to the author by Colonel Passy (May 1984): "People have talked about the torture-chambers in Duke Street. It was a small building, continually open to outside visitors. Who would not have heard the shrieks of the 'victims'?"

This was the time the Allies were discussing how to bring the Third Reich to its knees. In Moscow, from 19 October to 3 November there were talks between the foreign ministers of the three great Allied powers, Eden, Hull and Molotov; and if we are to believe the first they easily reached an agreement on the question of the opening of the Second Front, on the delivery of Western arms to the USSR, and on the measures to be taken for the reorganization of Europe. On their way home Cordell Hull and Anthony Eden stopped at Algiers. The American took advantage of this to have his first direct conversation with General de Gaulle, who was not, he discovered, the fascist ogre that his agents had described.

It was this that led Henri Hoppenot, the CFLN's representative in Washington, to write on 30 October that "Mr Cordell Hull is said to have spoken here of the very agreeable impression he derived from his recent talk with General de Gaulle [adding] that until now the American government seemed to have been badly informed about the General's character and his ideas."[14] It is not known what happened to the "bad informers", but the fact remains that from the time of this meeting a somewhat more favourable attitude towards the ideas of Fighting France could be observed in Washington's aged Secretary of State.

In Teheran between 28 November and 1 December the three leaders of the coalition Roosevelt, Stalin and Churchill, came together and decided that the two landings planned for in the spring of 1944 would take place on the French coast and not in Yugoslavia as the British Prime Minister had proposed.

Until then Winston Churchill had always managed to persuade Roosevelt to adopt his strategic preferences, but this time he came up against Stalin, a harder nut to crack. The Soviet dictator knew perfectly well that the British plan would tend to bar his road to the Balkans and the Danube. He therefore came to the rescue of the American strategists, who brought about the adoption of their plan "Overlord", which had been postponed a year earlier for the benefit of Torch. So France was in the limelight once more, and as a necessary consequence so was the question of the exercise of power in the liberated territories.

But the most important part of what happened at Teheran was not only the American strategy being preferred to the British and the advantage the Soviet Union derived from this state of affairs; Stalin spoke, according to the author of the *Mémoires de guerre*, "as the person to whom reports are submitted." He gave away nothing about his own plans, but he so arranged matters that his two partners revealed theirs and that he then passed judgment on them.

Looking westward, de Gaulle could not but observe that things had never been worse. Four months before the North African landings, the American military leaders had been eager to see de Gaulle. Now, as they were about to make France the next battlefield in which the fate of Europe would be decided, the two British and American leaders did not even think of consulting a French military expert or a man who could speak for the people who were going to be the background for this tragedy.

Once the decisions had been taken, neither of the two Western leaders saw fit to inform the CFLN, even in the most general way, of the talks and their outcome. If Roosevelt and Churchill had wanted to set de Gaulle against them they could not have done better.

The storm between de Gaulle and his allies was revived on 20 December 1943 by the arrest of three Vichy men with whom Churchill suddenly found he had bonds of friendship: Boisson, Peyrouton and Flandin. Had he forgotten that day of 23 September 1940 at Dakar when Governor-General Boisson ordered the British fleet to be fired on? Had he forgotten that Peyrouton was Vichy's Minister of the Interior and then, in Algiers, the most important colleague of that Darlan whom London so hated at that time? Had he forgotten that Flandin, before being Laval's successor at Vichy, had sent Hitler (and the other signatories) a telegram of congratulation the day after the Munich agreement?

The fact that the CFLN dealt severely with these men who had indirectly served the interests of the Third Reich concerned French sovereignty alone, just as the measures taken in Britain against Oswald Mosley were a matter that had to do with British authority. But the Prime Minister would not see it in that light and he thundered against the Constable.

A fortnight after having written to Roosevelt that the "lamentable excesses" committed by the French in the Levant justified "a break" with de Gaulle that "world opinion would approve of", the Prime Minister burst out again, cabling the President in words whose only purpose seemed to be to urge him on to the worst: "The Americans have more compelling obligations in this matter than us. I therefore hope you will take all measures in your power to make the French Committee understand the madness of their present step." FDR asked no better: he telegraphed Eisenhower to "order" the Committee to take no measures against the individuals concerned. Was FDR thinking of having his fleet fire on Algiers as he had thought of having it fire on Dakar at the time of Boisson's recall? The Foreign Office, and, it seems, Eisenhower, cooled things down. Yet once again the worst had been envisaged.

When he left Teheran, Churchill spent a while in North Africa, as he had done on the way there. Of course he did not see fit to inform the local authorities: was he not travelling under the name of Colonel Warden? This off-handedness on the grand scale irritated the president of the CFLN intensely. So when the Prime Minister, who was convalescing from an illness in Marrakesh, invited de Gaulle to join him there, at first he received only a very reserved reply. Macmillan, who had the task of conveying Colonel Warden's invitation, gives a most detailed account of the hesitations of the one and the impatience of the other, a subtle and violent game that the two chief actors were thoroughly used to.[15]

On 12 January de Gaulle landed at Marrakesh, where the Prime Minister and an impressive court was waiting for him. What with all the dramas that had just taken place, not only with regard to the arrest of Boisson, Peyrouton and Flandin and the Dufour business but even more the Lebanese crisis, to say nothing of these most recent hesitations, there was a great deal to be feared from this interview on Moroccan soil. Duff Cooper was most apprehensive. His is the only account that throws light on the meeting. In *Old Men Forget* he describes de Gaulle as "very harsh" and speaking "as though he were a combination of Roosevelt and Stalin": but he does observe that the two men parted "in a friendly manner". In his own memoirs Churchill speaks of the meeting more warmly, quoting a very pleasant remark he made himself: "Now that the General speaks English so well he understands my French perfectly", which, he says, caused de Gaulle "to burst out laughing". "Disarmed" from that moment on, it appears that the General listened to his remonstrances, which dealt mainly with the lot of Boisson, Peyrouton and Flandin, with no violent outbursts.

Confronted with the Prime Minister's calm interference in his affairs, Charles de Gaulle remained inflexible (this must have been the Stalin-aspect observed by Duff Cooper), pointing to the wish of the people (this the Roosevelt-aspect) which, expressed by the Algiers consultative assembly, insisted that the high collaborationist authorities should be brought to judgment. Yet Churchill gives his usual description of his guest as a "warm and picturesque" character, though without stating that when de Gaulle tried to raise the two questions which, in the Constable's opinion, were to be the main point of the meeting – the arming of the French Resistance and the CFLN's taking-over of the administration in the territories liberated after the landings – his host assumed the expression of one who has not heard. From the political point of view it was a failure. De Gaulle nevertheless ends his remarks about the Marrakesh interview by paying a tribute to this "alliance for which I had so much affection."[16]

Since this affair was concerned with play-acting as much as with history, we must quote something of the versions provided by d'Astier, whose governmental functions did not prevent him from appearing there primarily as a Resistance fighter greedy for arms.

> The Symbol gave me a short account of his talk with Churchill. He found it easier to acknowledge him as his equal now that he could pity him: "He is very weary. He is going downhill and yes, I talked to him about weapons: he agrees, but you must not count on it – what advantage would it be to them?"
>
> I did not answer. I was dealing with the Gallic cock standing on tiptoe in front of Albion's bull, and in the end the two emblems hid the two countries . . . Since England was the greater, Churchill felt a certain indulgence and a certain friendship for de Gaulle, who retained the bearing of a man superior to his fate, superior to his country's fate.

But some days later, when he reported on the talks he had with Churchill after the General's departure, d'Astier's eyes were fixed on a horizon beyond journalistic literature:

> The Prime Minister spoke of his satisfaction with his conversations with you. He praised you yourself and what you represent in a very lively fashion. In his opinion you are unquestionably "the man of France"; you have succeeded, etc. Of course he sprinkled his talk with sharp words about your "xenophobia" and the "aggressive attitude" you have shown towards him since the Syrian campaign.

The founder of Libération went on to say that Churchill had taken his request for arms for the Resistance very well, and that since he, d'Astier, had been back in London he had noticed a distinct "improvement in our relations with the British services," which were placing "greater quantities of material at the disposition of their French opposite numbers."[17]

The Soviets were persuaded that the CFLN was truly representative; the British no longer made a complete reconciliation depend on absurd conditions, such as calling off the prosecution of the Vichy men, that only reflected Churchill's personal, changing moods; American figures as important as Cordell Hull were changing their views of General de Gaulle for the better; and now everything that had to do with France's future, liberation and sovereignty came up against Roosevelt.

At this point Duff Cooper wrote, "it is unbearable that a stubborn old man should set himself against all solutions in this way". But it so happened that this "stubborn" individual was the most powerful man in the world. And at that juncture there was nothing that allowed anyone to foresee an evolution in the general, all-embracing attitude which he had adopted towards France and which François Kersaudy sums up in these words: "An unqualified opposition to General de Gaulle and his CFLN, a certain appetite for some parts of the French empire, a total disregard for French sovereignty, and a persistent sympathy for the old Marshal Pétain, all this hidden under a virtuous cloak of respect for the 'real wishes' of the French people."[18]

The CFLN had never specifically asked its allies for recognition. General de Gaulle, provided with the more or less exact assurances from Moscow, London and Washington at the end of August 1943, took the matter for granted, often saying in public or in private that all that mattered to him from now on was the decision of the French nation – a decision that he declared had already been secured.

It was not on this field of principles that he was fighting, but more cleverly, on that of the administration of the territories freed by the landings: for now, a month after the Teheran conference he could no longer be unaware of the fact that these landings would take place in France. He openly claimed the exercise of power in liberated France by right of national sovereignty, and he launched a threefold offensive to induce the Americans (the British had more or less come round to the idea) to admit that no authority other than that of the Algiers Committee could administer the French nation as and when it was liberated.

On 27 September 1943, immediately after the Italian capitulation, the CFLN sent the Allies a note stating that it had every intention of exercising authority on French territory, bearing in mind the prerogatives in the military field ordinarily attributed to the Allied High Command. In the following weeks René Massigli, having ensured that France should take part in the Control Commission for Italy,* called for the revision of the Darlan-Clark agreement of November 1942. Lastly, in December 1943 the CFLN sent Jean Monnet, a detached member of the Committee, and Hervé Alphand, Massigli's deputy for economic affairs, off to the United States on a mission that had many aspects but whose aim was very simple – the admission of France as a full partner in the Alliance.

On the first theme, that of the administration of the liberated territories, the

*On which France was represented by Maurice Couve de Murville.

negotiations began under the worst of omens. In 1942, Roosevelt had not concealed the fact that liberated France would be placed under an Anglo-American occupation. When Hervé Alphand was staying in London in September 1943 he was told by Commander Tracy Kittredge,* the American naval attaché, about the plan for temporary administration that his government was about to send to Algiers.

"It was a bomb-shell," writes Alphand. "The Allied command would take the administration upon itself and would appoint the civil servants. It would not recognize Vichy *except* as the body capable of handing over the authority!" And the mild Hervé Alphand, who was already one of the most zealous supporters of the Franco-American alliance writes firmly, "This must not be, otherwise it might result in appalling but long-lasting misunderstandings."[19]

A few weeks later, just before the Teheran Conference, Roosevelt summed up his views to Cordell Hull: "The thought that the occupation when it occurs should be wholly military is one to which I am increasingly inclined."[20] Was this because the anti-Nazi Resistance was "more and more" established, the authority of the CFLN "more and more" recognized, and Vichy "more and more"discredited, that Roosevelt thus felt "more and more" inclined to submit France to a military occupation of the kind one imposes upon one's enemies?

Obviously the French authorities remained in ignorance of this note. But they could no longer nourish the least illusion after the conversation between Henri Hoppenot and James Dunn on 2 December 1943. Dunn was in charge of French affairs at the State Department, and he began by telling his visitor that there was no question of negotiating with the CFLN, either on the bases suggested by the note of 27 September or on any others, the Allies' decisions being irrevocable. And referring to the currency, Mr Dunn stated that it would be notes printed by the Allied command.

It was in vain that Hoppenot pointed out that such behaviour would convince the French that they were being treated like an occupied nation and would lead them to compare this currency with the German military marks they had known; he pointed out that the newcomers "could hardly commit a more unfortunate blunder," but in vain: Dunn was opposed to any discussion whatsoever. It was a matter, said he, that depended solely on military authority.[21]

Thus warned of Washington's intentions, de Gaulle instructed Viénot to probe those of the Foreign Office. "Do you, in short, contemplate an AMGOT** plan for France?" asked Viénot. And when the man he was talking to, Sir Orme Sargent, protested, Viénot made things perfectly clear: "If you set up an AMGOT in France, you will do it by yourselves without the slightest cooperation from the Committee. You will have to deal with troubles that can be avoided only by the authority of the Committee, recognized as the government by virtually the whole of the nation." And Viénot ends; "My interlocutor was obviously disturbed by this outlook. They cannot do without us and they know it. We are on safe ground."[22]

Yet however safe the ground might be, the other side was playing a game whose

*Who wrote some of the most poisonous reports on Fighting France and its leaders.

**Allied Military Government for Occupied Territories.

object was to tame the CFLN. This was clear in the Darlan-Clark agreement, signed at the height of the "provisional expedient" phase by a man who was prepared to yield everything to the conqueror in order to be placed in power. The Darlan-Clark agreement was uncompromising, unfair and oppressive, if only because it placed all the North African military installations in the power of the newcomers – ports, fortifications, airfields, transport. It was a system of military occupation, of jurisdictional surrender: in short, a political protectorate – a status so humiliating that Giraud himself asked for its abrogation the day after Darlan's death.

For ten months, from August 1943 to May 1944, René Massigli unceasingly called for the rescission of a document that reduced French authority to the level of fiction. Three times Robert Murphy and then his successor Edwin Wilson replied that the matter was under consideration. Since the few improvements that Massigli obtained were at once annulled by the occupying forces, only one solution remained: on 13 May 1944 General de Gaulle took the decision purely and simply to denounce this last remnant of the "provisional expedient".

But for all that the Roosevelt plan for the Allied administration of France moved on to its preparatory phase. The AMGOT agents had already been recruited, and they were being trained at Charlottesville, in Virginia: there they were supposed to learn in two months how to become prefect of Chartres or sub-prefect of Carpentras. That was why they were called the sixty day marvels.[23]

At the same time studies were being carried out for the printing of notes to be put into circulation at the time of the landings. Roosevelt was against any possibilities that these notes should carry the least mark that might lead people to suppose that de Gaulle and the Committee would be called upon to govern France. The Secretary of the Treasury, Henry Morgenthau (who, out of all the American leaders, had been the most favourable towards the Free French) suggested that at least the words République Française might be printed on them. FDR objected "Who can tell what kind of a government we may be dealing with? Perhaps it will be an empire."[24]

Yet there still remained one hope of clarifying these Franco-American relations, poisoned by the "stubborn old man": it lay primarily with Jean Monnet, whom Charles de Gaulle had appointed *commissaire en mission* so that he should be able to devote himself entirely to the task of reconciliation with Washington – an appointment that made it quite clear that the Constable was not looking for a quarrel and that by sending Roosevelt this very kindly-disposed and friendly envoy he was determined to overlook nothing that might soothe and reassure his most powerful partner.

Less than a month after the mission had arrived in Washington, Hervé Alphand wrote in his diary: "With Jean Monnet we are moving in the right direction. Now all the agencies are convinced of the necessity of dealing with a French authority that possesses the nation's confidence."[25] And a few days after this Jean Monnet himself thought he could state in a report to de Gaulle and Massigli: "The negotiations with which I was entrusted by the Committee and which had to do with the Committee's recognition as the sole national authority in France at the time of the landings are on the point of succeeding."[26]

This hopefulness was mistaken as Monnet soon acknowledged. It had been based on the changes in what Alphand calls "the agencies": not only the State Department but above all the War Office, where the old Secretary Henry Stimson, influenced by his Under-Secretary of State John McCloy, was from now onwards convinced that an understanding with the CFLN would be in the interests of the invasion-troops: "America cannot supervise the elections of a great country like France. That would result in terrific dangers and would be likely to permanently alienate the friendship of France and the United States."[27]

But all plans, all forms of progress came to nothing when they reached the President, whose chief counsellors for French affairs were more than ever Admiral Leahy, who in this spring of 1944 continued to state as an axiom that "the only man capable of reconciling the French was Marshal Pétain", and Alexis Léger, who for some time had been steadily fuelling FDR's obsession about "a seizure of power by General de Gaulle."[28]

In Washington, all forms of advance were blocked, at least until the landings. Meanwhile de Gaulle spent his time arranging things at home, attending to the provisional institutions, to the relations between the "two Frances", and to the Empire. And in the first place he turned to the future of Africa – the Africa which was bringing Fighting France to the very gates of the metropolis.

The idea of bringing the status of Africa and the condition of the Africans into line with present circumstances had originated in the minds of the three men who were the civilian pioneers of that Africa to which de Gaulle came in search of the space, the weapons and the men needed for the liberation – Félix Eboué, Henri Laurentie and Pierre-Olivier Lapie. The first was Governor of Chad and later of French Equatorial Africa; the second was Secretary-General of l'Afrique combattante; the third, a former Socialist Deputy for Nancy, was de Gaulle's diplomatic counsellor in London and then Eboué's successor at Fort-Lamy, Chad. All three and particularly the second were favourable to solutions leading towards the emancipation of the African territories and their people.

René Pleven was the Commissioner for the Colonies. He was an intelligent man, not at all rigid, more cautious than the other three but open to their arguments – so long as General de Gaulle was not against them. In any event it was he who, speaking on the Brazzaville radio on 13 October 1943, announced that in three months time a conference would meet "to ensure the progress of the French peoples of the African continent".

Charles de Gaulle had immediately grasped the advantages of this plan. He perceived the truly disruptive nature of the war; in 1941 he thought that this "revolution may bring about a deep and wholesome transformation, revealing Africa to itself."[29] From this he drew the conclusion that the colonial powers could only emerge from this upheaval either as reformers or with their authority destroyed. He then saw a vast American enterprise taking shape, an enterprise that would call the colonial system in question and reshape it under the form of internationalization or trusteeship – if not of plain transfer of sovereignty.

Whether it was through the Federal Council of Protestant Churches, which, urged on by John Foster Dulles, denounced the "illegitimacy" of colonization[30] in 1942, whether it was by means of the press or those Congressmen who in a more down-to-earth manner simply claimed Dakar or Nouméa, or lastly whether it was through the White House, which mingled the moralizing of the first and the realism of the second, the American offensive against what was called the French "Empire" was steady and continuous.

As the Constable saw it, there could be no question of allowing the United States to carry out an undermining operation in Africa like that of the British in the Levant. They had to be forestalled: the Brazzaville Conference would show that France intended, of its own free will and in its own time, to let Africa evolve, providing its "protégés" with a better status than the segregation allotted to the blacks of Alabama or South Carolina. Furthermore the preamble to the conference stated that "France, without waiting for the Atlantic Charter, had regarded the principle of Africa for the Africans as the beginning and end of its colonial policy."

But two serious causes for anxiety had their effect on these great prospects. The first was one of those constant factors in the history of Free France. When he took possession of French "legitimacy" in 1940, General de Gaulle set himself up as the trustee for a given patrimony and he had undertaken to restore it to the country on the day of liberation. His hands were therefore tied whenever it came to dealing with the great affairs of the "Empire" in the light of circumstances, from Damascus to Dakar. And according to Gaston Palewski this explains the "timidity" of the Brazzaville decisions.[31]

There is another point that has to be taken into account. Some weeks before the opening of the conference, Lapie, who had become a member of the consultative assembly, and who was now visiting de Gaulle, suggested that he should make the Congo meeting a "colonial fourth of August night", setting the gates of federalism open wide. This brought him the remarkable answer, "Autonomy? For a variety of reasons I do not think we should be wise to grant it at present; the first and most important is this: the Europeans in North Africa would seize upon the occasion, taking advantage of it to separate Algeria from metropolitan France and to set up a segregated South Africa in Algiers. That would not be worthy of France, and we cannot take the risk."[32]

General de Gaulle travelled to the Congo by way of Morocco and Dakar (where he was welcomed with what he considered "indescribable enthusiasm" in the town where "three years before he had been received with gunfire"). He opened the conference on 30 January 1944 with a speech in which he proclaimed that:

> In French Africa there will be no progress that is progress* unless the people on their native soil do not profit by it morally and materially, if they are not able gradually to raise themselves to the level at which they will be capable of taking a share in the management of their own affairs in their own country. It is France's duty to see to it that this will be the case.[33]

But after eight days of work on the part of the eighteen governors and high civil servants (but no Africans), in the presence of nine delegates from the Algiers consultative assembly led by their president Félix Gouin and of a score of observers and experts, the conference ended with recommendations that were

*A turn of phrase typical of de Gaulle; this is one of the earliest examples.

followed by a statement to the effect that "the object of the civilizing task accomplished by France in its colonies rules out any idea of autonomy, any possibility of development outside the French bloc of the Empire; the possibility, even the remote possibility, of forming self-governments in the colonies is to be set aside."

In his *Mémoires*, which were written at the height of the colonial debate, de Gaulle affected to praise these conclusions, asserting that while "constitutional questions" could not find their answer at Brazzaville, "the path was traced out". Few episodes in the history of Gaullism are as hard to gauge as this.

Here is one reply, given by a man who never sinned by conservatism or timidity, Jacques Berque,* who came from Morocco as an observer:

> The sessions of the conference were dull, never leaving the administrative aspect. They were all stamped with that Jacobinism of well-meaning men who perpetually refuse to relinquish anything, taking it for granted that the continuation of their "presence" will do all that is required. And yet there were the crowds of blacks, both on the Belgian side of the water and on the French, who were cheering a new hope. So true it is that motions or speeches owe their value not to their explicit but to their symbolic aspect. The General alarmed and upset the colonists. Once again France was "defeated" in advance. But for my part I made a point of going to see Allal el-Fasi** in his place of exile at Mayama, and I wondered where the advance could be seen. Although it did start an immense process, the speech at Brazzaville had no intention of going beyond Brazza.***[34]

Forty years later, Governor Henri Laurentie, the king-pin and the most active member of the conference, offered this general view:

> At Brazzaville there were two conflicting tendencies: on the one hand the assimilation extolled by Governor Saller and on the other the granting of political freedom to the territories, as proposed by Eboué and Laurentie. Those belonging to the first tendency were in favour of allowing citizenship to all concerned; those belonging to the second were for evolution towards autonomy and perhaps towards independence. The General made no clear decision; according to his usual plan, he let things ripen. Pleven remained neutral. Eboué was deaf, and he found it hard to follow the debate.† The result was a series of thin proposals that made no sense.
>
> But although they were not invited to attend, the Africans‡ paid the

*Since then a professor at the Collège de France, and an Arabist.

**Moroccan nationalist leader deported by the Rabat authorities.

***Pierre Brazza, the nineteenth-century explorer, had become the symbol of "humane" colonization. (trs.)

†He died in Cairo three months later.

‡Yet reports were written by many of them, including M. Fily Dabo Sissoko, the delegate from the canton of Nyamba, who later became a member of the government of the Fourth Republic: he spoke strongly against assimilation and in favour of a particular form of development leading to association.

most passionate attention to the proceedings, convinced that evolution was under way: that was how the legend of Brazzaville came into being – a legend that was to strengthen the General after his return to France, when he gave his press conference on 25 October 1944 and spoke out in favour of a system of autonomy. The idea made its way, and fifteen years later he gave it a real existence.[35]

Contradictions in Algiers were to echo the ambiguity of Brazzaville. When de Gaulle made Catroux Governor-General of Algeria and Commissioner of State for Muslim affairs he knew that he was choosing a new policy, since this officer had always been known for his forward-looking attitude, his natural dislike of repression, and his preference for negotiated or friendly solutions.

As soon as Catroux came back from his mission in the Levant, he put the last touches to reforms that he had been working upon ever since he was appointed Governor-General of Algeria in June: this granted full political rights to certain categories of Muslims (ex-servicemen and those with secondary-education certificates), a community that the *statut personnel* had hitherto confined to the ghetto of the second electoral college, which made them second-class citizens, and numerical equality of representation in the elected councils.*

On 12 December 1943, from a platform set up in the place de la Brèche in Constantine, Charles de Gaulle publicly announced the decisions prepared by Catroux – decisions that horrified the Europeans without satisfying the spokesmen of nationalism, much stimulated by the presence of the Americans. The author of the *Mémoires de guerre* says that he saw Dr Benjelloul, the spokesman for (non-nationalist) Muslim claims, "weep with emotion" in front of the platform in the place de la Brèche. For Benjelloul, the pioneer of individual rights, this was the realization of a dream.

What did Charles de Gaulle think about Algeria's future in those days? André Philip says that after the Constantine speech he spoke to the General about the necessity for an evolution towards internal autonomy for the Algerian departments. De Gaulle told Maurice Schumann that although he did not feel that he should call the "fiction" of the departments into question for the moment, he thought that "those who imagine that after a war like this the status quo can be prolonged and that Algeria can remain the Algeria we learnt about at school are profoundly mistaken."[36]

Prophetic views, as usual; and, as usual, short-term reforms. Yet it was the then repressed Muslims who placed their hopes in de Gaulle, and it was the so carefully protected Europeans who never forgave him for his initiative at Constantine. They had thoroughly grasped the fact that the mere evocation of the idea of equality and the acknowledgment of "rights" acquired by the Muslims on the field of battle** questioned the very basis of a system founded on the power of a minority.

* * *

*Decisions dealt with by the ordonnances of 17 March 1944.

**Twenty-two years earlier, Clemenceau had wished to make this the basis for a reform; but the European minority nipped it in the bud.

But the problem of relations between communities did not affect only Muslims and Europeans. At that time it made an even crueller division between the "two nations" of the French, those who had followed the Marshal and those who had joined de Gaulle. While in metropolitan France what Henri Amoureux calls the "pitiless civil war"[37] was raging, rendered more savage month after month by the increase in the number of maquis (they multiplied by ten between January and August 1944) and by the greater ferocity of the repression carried out by Darnand's Milice, in Algiers the CFLN had now to draw the line between what was to become reconciliation and what was already repression.

If he had had a free choice, would Charles de Gaulle have raised the question of the "purge" as early as this? However that may be, on 8 August 1943 he stated that "national union cannot be accomplished and cannot be enduring unless the State can honour those who have served it well and punish the criminals."[38] One month later the CFLN decided that all those who had exercised decisive powers under Vichy should be brought before a high court. And in November it was the new commissioner for justice, François de Menthon, a respected legal authority, who stated that "justice is a weapon to help the Resistance."

It was above all the pressure of the consultative assembly that seems to have hastened the arrangements for judicial proceedings. During two passionate sessions on 12 and 13 January 1944 the representatives of the Resistance insisted upon the "rapid trial of the traitors" the new authority had been able to seize. Jacques Médéric, one of their leaders,* called for justice without delay, "otherwise the Algiers government will lose the confidence of the French". And Médéric gave four names: Pucheu, Boisson, Admiral Derrien and General Bergeret.** At that point however the debate was not concerned with the necessity of taking action but with the legal process, the majority of the assembly calling for special courts.

Did this amount to decisive pressure on de Gaulle? The next day, at Marrakesh, when Winston Churchill complained of the treatment of Boisson, Peyrouton and Flandin, the General simply showed him a newspaper with an account of the proceedings of the Algiers assembly, saying, "I wanted to democratize my authority. From now on I have to take public opinion into account." Very soon the great argument concentrated on the Pucheu case. Compared with the others, Pucheu was a different case altogether; his responsibilities had been greater, and the passions he aroused, particularly in Communist circles, were far more intense. A Boisson or a Peyrouton could plead legality or say they were acting under orders. Pucheu had often taken the initiative, and he fearlessly stood by what he had done. In its completeness his trial would be that of Vichy as a whole; it therefore began as soon as the one man who could have prevented it, General Giraud, decided not to take the risk of doing so.

Pierre Pucheu was what is called a leader. He was of humble origin, but he had been to the Ecole Normale Supérieur; he was eloquent, athletic and brave; at the

*Some weeks after this, during his last mission to France, he was arrested by the Gestapo and he killed himself.

**Respectively the former Vichy Minister of the Interior, the former Governor-General of French West Africa, the former port-admiral of Bizerta, and Darlan's former right-hand man.

age of forty he was at the head of the firm of Japy.* He was in the forefront of the politically active employers and he acted as the link between industry and Doriot's Fascist PPF, to which he belonged until 1940. At the beginning of 1941 he joined the Vichy government, becoming Minister of the Interior in July. Three months later he played a central part (we shall return to this) in the execution of forty-seven Communist hostages at Châteaubriant on 21 October 1941. In the course of January 1942 he secretly received Henri Frenay and tried to come to an agreement with him. The leader of Combat would have nothing to do with it. In the following April, Laval's return to power expelled this anti-German Fascist from Vichy: he was appointed Ambassador to Berne.

Some months later he made his way to Spain in the hope of reaching North Africa, there to fight the Nazis. On 4 February 1943 he wrote a letter explaining his position to General Giraud, who replied on the fifteenth telling him that "rightly or wrongly he had acquired a great many enemies" but that he, Giraud, was willing "to receive him and give him a post in a fighting unit" on condition that he "did not concern himself with politics".

As Pucheu saw it, this letter amounted to a safe-conduct. He arrived in Morocco, where his protector, who had been warned that he had got himself into an awkward position, told him to go and keep out of sight in the remote garrison of Ksar-es-Souk. But since June, when it became legal again, the PCF had undertaken to settle its accounts. And apart from Laval and Darnand there was none that was more unforgiveable than that with the man who was suspected of having led the Nazis to the victims of Châteaubriant.

On 15 August Pucheu was arrested at Ksar-es-Souk and imprisoned at Meknès: Giraud made no attempt to intervene. Pucheu could scarcely have had any illusions. Although he was defended by three talented barristers,** he was appearing before a special court made up of two civilian judges and three generals, with a public prosecutor strongly motivated against him, General Weiss.

The trial began in Algiers on 5 March. Pucheu at once denied the competence of the court. The chief witness for the prosecution was Fernand Grenier, the Communist Deputy for Saint-Denis and a member of the consultative assembly, who had been interned at Châteaubriant and who had succeeded in escaping before the terrible day of 21 October 1941. He called Pucheu a murderer, without bringing forward any proof that it was the minister who had drawn up the list of the hostages to be shot. Pucheu firmly denied that he had done so.

The defence expected a great deal of General Giraud, a witness the next day: he had just learnt of the death of his daughter, deported to Germany some months earlier – a painful circumstance that did the accused no good. At no time did the General utter a word to show that he understood Pucheu or felt any solidarity with him, and he ended with a call for the punishment of "bad Frenchmen". Indeed it was said in Algiers that "a passport signed by Giraud leads you straight to the scaffold."[39]

The case was virtually decided. To convince the court, General Weiss, the

*The great metal-working firm. It made tanks, heavy machinery, even typewriters. (trs.)
**In France at this time the prisoners of the Milice were not allowed any defence.

prosecutor, had only to quote the Vichy decrees which, under Pucheu's authority, set up the terrible special tribunals. It was useless for the defence to argue that since Pucheu had left France, the repression, under Laval and Darnand, had grown worse. On 11 March the judges, who had received a telegram from Jacques Bingen, the CFLN's delegate in France, stating that "any weakness on the part of the court would, at the time of liberation, lead to individuals settling their own scores", passed the death sentence.

Six days later, and in spite of an approach by Giraud, Charles de Gaulle refused to pardon Pucheu, and he was shot at dawn on 20 March in the courtyard of the Hussein-Dey prison, crying out that he was the victim of a "political murder" and himself giving the order to the firing-squad. In fact the perfunctory investigation, the hurried trial and the shabby conduct of the man who had covered Pucheu's coming to North Africa shed a sinister light on this "justice".

Speaking of the matter in his *Mémoires* ten years later de Gaulle says that in Algiers, in March 1944, "everything led one to think" that Pucheu had pointed out the hostages to the executioner. And he adds, "the proof was to be found at the Liberation".[40] This is the same as saying that Pucheu was condemned before he had been proved guilty. When Giraud learnt that the condemned man had spoken of him "in the most savage way at the moment of his execution", he confined himself to observing, in *Un seul but, la victoire*, "I refuse any responsibility for the death of Pierre Pucheu."

"State reasons required that an example should be made rapidly," writes the author of the *Mémoires de guerre*.[41] Bingen's argument had great force; so also had the reminders of the crimes then being committed by the Milice; so had the appeals for rigour uttered by the threatened members of the Resistance. But the whole affair was terribly murky, and the General remained troubled by it. The evening before the execution he asked the lawyers to let the condemned man know that he, de Gaulle, "retained his esteem" for Pucheu. And Louis Joxe says that the next day de Gaulle "his cheeks hollow with lack of sleep" told him confidentially: "If I had pardoned him, the criminals of that kind would all have made their way to Algiers. Our prisons would have been filled and their occupants would peacefully have waited for the end of the war and oblivion!"[42]

Another incident shows the Constable's anxiety on this same score. Louis Vallon was telling him that some time before the Pucheu affair the BCRA had learnt that Darnand had offered to come to London and there to denounce Pétain and his régime. What a political godsend! The possibility of receiving Darnand had been looked into. It was de Gaulle who put a very abrupt end to the matter: "What next? If Darquier de Pellepoix* has himself circumcised, am I to accept him too?"[43]

While "justice" was only at the beginning of its sudden, cruel and dubious decrees, the State fell into place, its successive members fitting into a CFLN that already looked upon itself as nothing less than a body with all the attributes of an acknowledged government. Until such time as the most powerful of the Allies should see fit to accept this reality, de Gaulle took decisions, acted and dealt out

*Vichy's Commissioner for Jewish Affairs: a professional anti-Semite.

punishment as though nobody but himself and his team were to exercise authority over the French as and when they were liberated.

Almost all the politicians of the last twenty years who had been elected to power, from Louis Marin on the right wing to the Communists on the left, with Jeanneney, Herriot, Reynaud, Mandel, Blum, Mendès France, Queuille and Paul-Boncour, had spoken out, at great risk, in favour of the "legitimacy" won by Charles de Gaulle. There was not a military leader of high standing, from Juin to de Lattre and from Sevez to Revers, who had not placed himself under the orders of the man of 18 June.

Was this enough to silence the more severe upholders of legality? It was not. But this did not make Charles de Gaulle feel vulnerable. During one of the committee's sessions, the Commissioner of State, Henri Queuille, told de Gaulle that perhaps some given provision was not quite in agreement with republican legality. To this the Constable replied in his most solemn tones, "Commissioner of State, are you aware that you are already a member of an insurrectional government?"[44]

In any case the CFLN's decisions between 10 January and 3 June 1944, which took the form of ordinances, borrowed its terminology if not indeed its inspiration from the First rather than the Third Republic. On 10 January the CFLN appointed not eighty-nine prefects but eighteen Commissioners of the Republic; and the choice of these commissioners showed very clearly that the republican State then being born was not to be a mere resurrection of the regime brought down in June 1940: although about a third of the men who were entrusted with the task of bringing the new Republic to life on the ruins of Vichy came from the traditional administration, the greater number was made up of those who would derive their authority from their great achievements in the struggle against the occupying forces.

On 14 March an ordinance informed the world that each section of liberated territory would be administered by a delegate appointed by the CFLN. In principle this resolved the problem that for months past had been exercising the minds of the American, British and French chancelleries. Washington and London had a *fait accompli* set before them, that of a wholly formed State system. Then on 21 April came the promulgation of a document recalling that "the French nation decides its future institutions in full sovereignty" and that "a National Assembly *is* summoned as soon as possible in order to proceed to regular elections". Meanwhile the municipal and departmental councils in office in 1939 would be restored. As for the consultative assembly, it would move to France and there ensure the country's representation until the election of the constituent assembly.

All that lacked in this bold construction was a government which bore that name. "What exists in fact," writes the author of the *Mémoires de guerre*, "should be expressed in words. It was time for the government to assume the name that was due to it." But before this General de Gaulle wished to do two things: to increase the dimensions of the coming "government" to those who had made the struggle possible by including representatives of the Communist party; and to make a last appeal to the Allies.

On 1 January 1944 he received a letter from the leaders of the PCF in Algiers stating their wish "to help the government", and he replied with emphatic praise of those "French Communists" who "served their country well, placing national duty before every other consideration".[45] Once this point was settled, the dialogue began.

On 18 March, de Gaulle stated his intention of "including in the government all the forces fighting for the country's liberation." Six days later a letter from the PCF delegation informed the General that the party "was ready to take part in the CFLN". On 28 March a delegation headed by Billoux, Bonte and Marty was received at Les Glycines. And on 4 April François Billoux became Commissioner of State and Fernand Grenier Commissioner for Air, while André Le Troquer was entrusted with the administration of the liberated territories – and General Giraud, deprived of his command, refused the post of Inspector-General of the Armed Forces that de Gaulle offered him and retired to the little town of Mazagran.*

Before crowning this edifice with the open proclamation of the provisional "government", General de Gaulle tried addressing his allies, so that he could not be accused of flinging what might look like a challenge at their heads. On 7 May, at Tunis, he spoke of "the moment when the armies of freedom were getting ready to carry the vicissitudes and the destruction of battle to our country" and he ended by saying: "We most fervently wish that French realities may be clearly acknowledged."

On 13 May the benches of the consultative assembly were crowded. It had been learnt that Vincent Auriol was to mount the tribune and there proclaim the solemn accession of French democracy to the "Government" – of that French democracy which he, a senior left-wing parliamentarian and an intimate friend of Léon Blum, symbolized more than any other man. The Popular Front minister spoke out clearly:

> Neither the Committee nor the Assembly has been recognized, so that the French people's future should not be judged beforehand and so that they should be left free to express their opinion. But in order that this people should vote, it is necessary that a government should summon them, prepare the electoral laws, and administer the country. What authority is capable of doing this? Not Pétain, nor Hitler, nor certain other people who are mentioned. It is therefore the *de facto* government that will undertake the task.
>
> It is this government that the people will adopt. It is this government to which arms are given, this government that all the parties, old or new, have chosen, because it is faithful to France, to its allies and to the République.
>
> When I am told that one must not encourage dictatorship, it is the workers of Ferryville who answer your cry of "Vive la République", Monsieur le Président, with the double cry of "Vive la République" and "Vive de Gaulle!" thus combining the man and the Republic he has promised them. One must take care not to wound a people's patriotism or its feelings, because the result will be bitter nationalism.

*There, an attempt was made on his life: against all likelihood he attributed it to some "Gaullist agent".

Vincent Auriol then waved a paper which he said he had read and re-read "with tears in his eyes", and which expressed the total support of the Council of the Resistance. He uttered the words with a grave, measured emphasis:

> The National Council of the Resistance, at the approach of those decisive days for which the French nation is preparing itself in a spirit of sacrifice, proclaims that the CFLN is the legitimate government of France. Without knowing the reasons for the delay, this has deeply wounded French public opinion: [it asserts that] logic, common sense and necessity will sooner or later compel this recognition.

The assembly stood up; General de Gaulle raised his hand; the speaker passed the word to him so that he might address the meeting, as he put it, "in the name of the government".[46]

On 1 June, Henri Hoppenot asked Cordell Hull whether any change could be expected from the United States; the Secretary of State replied, not without sadness, that he could say nothing, "all French affairs [being] decided by the President alone".[47]

On 3 June therefore the CFLN published this ordinance: "The French Committee of National Liberation takes the name of Provisional Government of the French Republic".

CHAPTER THIRTY-SIX

Overlord

On 30 December 1943 Eisenhower and de Gaulle met in the little drawing-room of Les Glycines which acted as the office of the president of what was still the CFLN.* The American said that this was just an impromptu visit; he had particularly wished to pay his respects before leaving North Africa for the United States and then Britain, from where he would launch the assault against the European Fortress.

De Gaulle at once expressed his pleasure at seeing such a leader take the command of operations that were, he said, "vital for my country", and he went on to speak of the growth of the French forces, of General de Lattre's plans for the landing in Provence and of the necessity for an important French unit to take part in the "northern operation". And he ended by adjuring Eisenhower not to arrive in Paris without French troops.

General Eisenhower:

> You may be sure that I have no notion of entering Paris without your troops. People have given me the reputation of being abrupt. I have the feeling that you formed your opinion of me without having made enough allowance for the problems I was confronted with in performing my mission with regard to my government. At that time it seemed to me that you did not want to put your full weight behind me. As a government you had your own very difficult problems. But it seemed to me that the carrying out of operations had absolute priority. [At present] I admit that I was unjust to you and I had to tell you so.

General de Gaulle: "You are a man."**

Having paid his visitor this tribute, de Gaulle assured him that everything would be done to help the Inter-Allied Commander-in-Chief, and begged him "if any difficulty should arise" to "rely on him" and get into contact – particularly "when he was confronted with the question of Paris in the field of action".

General Eisenhower:

> I am prepared to make a declaration stating the confidence I have derived

*Here we refer chiefly to the best version of the conversation, that which was drawn up at once by General de Gaulle's personal staff and which appears among the appendices to the *Mémoires de guerre*, II, p. 674–6.

**He said this in English.

> from our contacts, acknowledging my injustice with regard to you, and adding that you have said that you are ready to help me in my mission. For the forthcoming French campaign I shall need your support, the assistance of your civil servants, and the backing of French public opinion. I do not yet know what theoretical position my government will require me to adopt in my relations with you. But apart from principles there are facts. I must tell you that as far as facts are concerned I shall acknowledge no authority in France other than yours.*

Here was de Gaulle strengthened immediately, and the future defined in a few sentences. Certainly, it was Roosevelt who was the head of the armies, and Eisenhower was well aware that the President would do anything to prevent de Gaulle and his people from taking power in liberated France. But against this "theoretical position", which nothing would change, "there were the facts". De Gaulle, an adversary of *a priori* reasoning (the "theoretical position") and a friend of "circumstances", had found a powerful ally here. And it so happened that this ally was the man who, on the field of action, would control the arms of freedom.

Eisenhower was less ignorant of his government's "theoretical position" than he made out. During a recent stay in Washington he had not failed to learn that the White House was inflexible on two points: first, that the Inter-Allied General Staff would use the French forces put at its disposal as it saw fit; and second, that it would exercise a total authority, political as well as military, in the liberated territories as well as in the fighting-zone.

Three recent meetings on 16, 17 and 27 December, had seen the appearance of startlingly obvious contradictions between de Gaulle, Giraud and Massigli on the one hand and on the other Wilson, the American ambassador, and General Bedell Smith, Eisenhower's chief of staff. De Gaulle went so far as to say that if the CFLN did not consider the Allied staff's use of the great French units likely to "correspond to the national interest, our armies and our freedom of action" might be taken back.

But at the third conference on 27 December General Bedell Smith gave the assurance that while the greater part of the French forces were intended for the southern landings, forming part of an army that would if possible be autonomous, one French division would be set aside for the northern operation. At this de Gaulle agreed that an understanding would be possible on those bases, provided that it would be an armoured division. This was how things stood at present.

It seemed, then, that some progress had been made in bringing the Allied efforts and the French participation into line. But Roosevelt had persuaded Churchill to keep the General and the CFLN ignorant of the timetable laid down for the liberation of France.

The operation has been named Overlord. The main lines had been agreed upon in May 1943; and they were confirmed at the conference of Teheran. The operation

*It will be seen that things did not turn out to be as simple as this.

was centred on the beaches of Normandy,* and it was to be completed by a landing on the coast of Provence, which was given the code-name Anvil.

By March 1944 American forces reckoned at more than a million men were gathered in Britain for Overlord. The northern landings were to take place round about 1 June 1944, and Anvil was to follow two or three months later.

Overlord was similar to the plan that de Gaulle and Billotte had prepared in the spring of 1943, and Anvil to that which Giraud and Beaufre had suggested at about the same time; but neither the CFLN nor its leader were told anything about either except about the use of French troops. When Churchill suggested to his great ally that on the present occasion, when it was a question of French territory and an established *de facto* authority, this exclusion had something shocking about it, Roosevelt reminded the Prime Minister of the fiasco at Dakar.

De Gaulle and his colleagues nevertheless prepared to participate in the battle. Most of the French troops were in Italy, where the forces engaged in the advance on Rome under the command of Juin amounted to about 130 000 men. During his conversation with Eisenhower, de Gaulle had acknowledged that he only had 2000 men in England. But he had obtained Eisenhower's virtual promise to have an armoured division transferred to Britain – or rather the officers and other ranks of an armoured division that would be provided, on the spot, with material brought from the United States.

It was the 2nd DB, trained for battle by General Leclerc at Temara, near Rabat, that was given the task of being the great French unit without which Eisenhower "had no notion of entering Paris". It was sent to Britain at the beginning of April 1944.

On 28 March 1944 the CFLN appointed General Koenig its military delegate with the Allied High Command for the great "northern operation", and a little later Commander-in-Chief of the French forces of the interior, supervising the leader of the Armée Secrète (Dejussieu, known as Pontcarral, and then Malleret, known as Joinville). Koenig had had great personal standing in England. His appointment brought about a renewal of the British demands in Washington: FDR remained immovable.

More than that: he now persuaded the British government to forbid any coded messages between Algiers and its diplomatic and military delegations in London after 19 April because of the necessity for maintaining secrecy on the eve of the great operations. The French were to be deaf and blind. De Gaulle was not the only one to look upon this as what he called "an outrage". Koenig and Viénot were at once forbidden to maintain any relations whatsoever with their British counterparts.

Churchill and Eden were well aware of the disadvantages of this situation: Roosevelt was the head of the coalition, the distributor of power, weapons and means. But the French general was the arbiter of the situation on French territory, that is to say on the field of battle. It was no longer possible that discord between the master of fire-power and the master of the country should continue indefinitely. Could not the honest British broker manage to bring them together?

*Because of intelligence supplied to the Inter-Allied staff by the French resistance.

The points of view had rarely been so opposed. Whereas the CFLN looked upon itself as the custodian of the powers in the liberated territories that it handed over to delegates on 14 March, the next day President Roosevelt sent General Eisenhower a directive reminding him that he disposed of full authority in these same territories, but that he "might consult" the CFLN in the course of carrying out his mission, just as he might consult "other authorities". For de Gaulle, there was only one authority: his own. For Roosevelt there was another, "that of a god", which he had conferred upon Eisenhower. Two rulers in a single realm.

A few weeks later, however, Cordell Hull, by putting forward the administration of the liberated territories in France as a matter that depended on cooperation between the Inter-Allied Commander-in-Chief and the French authorities, made the President's attitude less rigid. It is clear that Jean Monnet had been to see him: the General's "missionary" gradually eroded the administration's resistance, and reported to Algiers the slight concessions on the part of the Americans. He particularly underlined the freedom of manoeuvre that both FDR's directive and Cordell Hull's speeches left to the Commander-in-Chief; for like de Gaulle, Monnet now knew that Eisenhower was no longer ignorant of who held the keys to France.

At this point London intervened: Duff Cooper, Ambassador to the CFLN, was instructed to tell de Gaulle that Churchill undertook to see that Roosevelt would receive him in Washington, providing that de Gaulle made his wish to go there known through his delegation in the United States. De Gaulle was naturally mortified at having to solicit the good will of a man from whom he had for years received nothing but rebuffs. But after a long consultation with Massigli he resigned himself to "leaving the door open but without crossing the threshold" by writing this letter to the British Ambassador: "With regard to the matter of which you did me the honour of speaking yesterday, I may tell you that I agree that the plan you mentioned should follow its course."[1]

Furnished with this lukewarm blessing, Churchill went ahead and told the American President about General de Gaulle's forthcoming advance – which would not be made unless Washington's consent was obtained beforehand. True to form, Roosevelt replied that "the question must be raised by the French representatives in Washington in a month's time". The intention of humiliating the man who asked for the meeting was so obvious that however much he might agree with the wishes of his great ally, Winston Churchill could not refrain from writing, "I had hoped you would go a little further than this."[2]

All the documents and letters of this period show a de Gaulle very much under control. At a time when London was cutting off his means of communication and when Washington was treating him like the dictator of some banana republic, he refrained from almost anything that could make the disagreement apparent to worldwide public opinion. His press conference on 21 April was an uninterrupted flow of warmth; and when Jean Monnet told him of his American interlocutors' continuing opposition to French Sovereignty, he replied that in the present circumstances he preferred to abstain from any controversy.[3]

The only outburst de Gaulle allowed himself was a speech he made on 7 May at Tunis in which he answered those who thought that as it advanced through

France, the Inter-Allied staff would confer here with a Gaullist mayor, there with a Vichyist prefect:

> Let us fix a day, not far ahead, for meeting those who imagine that when it is set free, France could return to the feudal period and be divided between several governments: let us meet them in Marseilles on the Canebière, in Lyons in the place Bellecour, at Lille in the place Nationale, at Bordeaux on the Quinconces, in Paris somewhere between the Arc de Triomphe and Notre-Dame!*

But with the landings only a few weeks away (the first week in June) was it not absurd and even suicidal not to know who was the authority to whom the Allied commander must look for support at the height of the battle? The British papers cried it out aloud, the American papers repeated it: why this delay in treating with the CFLN, whether it was recognized *de facto* or *de jure*?

In the House of Commons Anthony Eden was challenged, though everyone knew that privately he agreed with those who harassed him. In any case, replying on 19 April to a member who called upon him to answer with a yes or a no to the question, "Does this mean that the authority with which we deal in liberated France will be the CFLN?" he replied, "Yes, sir."

But all the plans for an agreement with the CFLN piled up on Roosevelt's desk and there remained buried. To get them moving again London took the initiative once more. Apart from the urgency connected with the imminence of the landings and from the pressure of British public opinion, voiced by a press so Gaullist these last few weeks that it was as though Fleet Street had moved *en masse* to Carlton Gardens, a new factor made the British move: the high reputation that Fighting France had suddenly won by means of its expeditionary force in Italy. It was on 14 May that Juin broke the German front on the Garigliano.

On 24 May, then, Churchill informed the Commons that General de Gaulle had been invited to London with a view to negotiating about the relations between the Inter-Allied command and the French authorities. He had hoped that these words would satisfy public opinion: they raised a positive storm of protest. Harold Nicholson, an even more open Francophile than Churchill, and a Conservative member, spoke vigorously, telling Churchill that his shuffling before the plain, downright recognition of the CFLN was both "grotesque" and "discourteous" in relation with an "ally which has recovered herself and regained her repute among the nations of the world."

It angered de Gaulle to see a man of Churchill's size behave with such docility to his American ally, and he replied to the invitation that Duff Cooper passed on with a curt, "The government will decide what answer to give." It was that day, well before the publication of the 3 June ordinance, that the CFLN decided to give itself the name of government.

Of course the new ministers spoke in favour of de Gaulle's journey to London, though not without making it clear that the General would not be accompanied by any member of the government, in order to emphasize the point that because of

*Six months later he kept all these appointments.

the absence of any representative of the American executive and therefore the impossibility of tripartite conversations directed at solving the problem of political responsibilities in France, there was no question of "negotiating". Furthermore, de Gaulle made his voyage conditional upon the cancelling of the British authorities' month-old ban on coded communication between London and Algiers. Duff Cooper agreed to this at once.

And so that London should have no illusions about the meaning of his visit or suppose that he was any less firm, on 25 May de Gaulle sent Viénot a telegram in which he repeated his position with a most startling firmness: "We are asking nothing. There is either ourselves or chaos. If the Western Allies bring about chaos in France, they will be responsible for it and they will be the losers."

Was it because he saw that de Gaulle was even more stubborn than he was himself and that the approach of the great event gave the Frenchman's attitude a greater weight while at the same time it weakened his own? In any case, Roosevelt took a surprising step: on 27 May, in the utmost secrecy, Admiral Fenard paid Charles de Gaulle a very secret visit: the Admiral, formerly Darlan's confidential colleague, was in charge of the CFLN's naval mission to the USA, and it was this survivor of the "provisional expedient" that Roosevelt, by way of demonstrating the continuity of his policy at the moment he changed course, had chosen as a messenger to whisper discreetly into de Gaulle's ear that although Washington did not wish to lose face by inviting him officially, it would be enough for de Gaulle to accept a visit to the United States "without its being necessary to state publicly which of the two, de Gaulle or Roosevelt, had taken the initiative".

The author of the *Mémoires de guerre* calls this to mind with a gourmet's relish: "An effusive reply was by no means suitable. I asked Admiral Fenard to make a delaying reply, one that noted the invitation Roosevelt sent me but I was about to leave for London. It would be better to get into touch again later."

So it was Roosevelt who would have to wait! And the writer adds these words, which surely came to his mind at that very moment: "The President's approach made things quite clear to me. I saw that the long, hard-fought match with the Allies for French independence was reaching the desired conclusion."

On 2 June he received a very cordial message from the Prime Minister, in the best Churchillian vein: "I beg that you will come now, with your colleagues, as soon as possible and with the utmost secrecy. I give you my personal assurance that this is in France's interest. I am sending you my own York* together with another York for yourself."

When he arrived at Carlton Gardens from Algiers two days later, accompanied by Palewski and Béthouart, he was greeted by a letter from the Prime Minister reminiscent of the happiest days of their companionship:

> My dear General de Gaulle,
> Welcome to these shores! Very great military events are about to take place and I should be glad if you could come to see me down here in my train, which is close to General Eisenhower's headquarters [who] is looking

*The Prime Minister's personal aircraft.

> forward to seeing you again and will explain to you the military position which is momentous and imminent. If you could be here by 1.30 p.m. I should be glad to give you *déjeuner*.[4]

General de Gaulle had landed in London during the morning of 4 June, the very day the Allied forces – the French among others – entered Rome. It was the greatest victory for four years in which the French troops, in very large numbers and in the front rank, had taken part. The next day de Gaulle sent Juin this telegram in the style of Bonaparte: "The French army has its great share in the splendid victory of Rome. It had to be done! You have done it! General Juin, you and the troops under your command are worthy of the country."[5]

Winston Churchill received de Gaulle, accompanied by Viénot and Béthouart, in his train, parked in a siding near Portsmouth station. "An unusual notion," remarked de Gaulle ironically. Yet he was aware that railway-carriages had played an important part in the life of strategists for a long while, and that Churchill, dressed in a variety of uniforms, was very fond of playing the soldier. Eden, once again in agreement with the Constable, observed that the Prime Minister's train had only one bath and one telephone, and that "Churchill seemed to be always in the bath and General Ismay always on the telephone. So that it was almost impossible to conduct any business".[6]

Churchill welcomed de Gaulle very heartily and, says his visitor, "came to the point at once". He first gave a striking description of the immense warlike enterprise that was on the point of setting out from the British shore, emphasizing "the essential role that the Royal Navy was about to play".

Charles de Gaulle always appreciated grandeur, even when it was the grandeur of others, and he expressed his "admiration of this plan". An admiration in which he tacitly took his own share: here was the man, here was the nation, from whom he had refused to separate the fortunes of France even at the worst point of the disaster and who were now seeing

> the policy of courage that [Churchill] had personified since the darkest hours most brilliantly justified. Although the coming events must cost France still more, the country was proud of being in the line of battle for the liberation of Europe together with the Allies in spite of everything. At this moment of history the same breath of esteem and friendship wafted over all the French and all the English who were present.[7]

All this changed as soon as they "got down to business". With his visitors, Churchill had moved to the next carriage to have lunch, and taking advantage of the emotion aroused by the circumstances and his own blazing eloquence, he thought the moment had come for "talking politics".

But just as he had charmed his visitor when he spoke of the herald of the crusade in Europe, so he now irritated him by suddenly bringing forward the idea of impromptu negotiations. Had not de Gaulle specifically told Duff Cooper that he had accepted the invitation to London "for the landings" and not with a view to negotiations?

For some little while, says Béthouart. "I had felt that de Gaulle was tense, deeply wounded at having been invited in this way as a spectator and at the last moment, without any previous discussion or understanding on the prime question of the exercise of authority in liberated France, a question that was nevertheless about to arise directly."[8] So towards the end of lunch, when Churchill proposed that they should "talk politics", those present saw de Gaulle stiffen and say in his most arrogant voice, "Politics? Why?" It took more than that to disconcert Churchill, who came back to his great plan, the rapprochement between Roosevelt and de Gaulle. Could there not first be a Franco-British agreement, a document that de Gaulle would go and submit in Washington? Even if Roosevelt were not to be in favour of it, at least the two men would have talked, and sooner or later FDR would come round to recognizing the Algiers government. At this de Gaulle exploded:

> Why do you seem to think that I am required to put myself up to Roosevelt as a candidate for power in France? The French Government exists. I have nothing to ask of the United States of America, any more than I have of Great Britain. That being understood, it is important for all the Allies that relations between the French administration and the military command should be set in order. We have been proposing this for the last nine months. Since the armies are going to land tomorrow, I quite see that you are in a hurry to have the question settled. We ourselves are ready. But for this settlement, where is the American representative? Furthermore, I observe that the Washington and London governments have taken measures to dispense with any agreement with us. The troops who are preparing to land have been furnished with a so-called French money which is absolutely unrecognized by the government of the Republic. Tomorrow General Eisenhower in agreement with you [will proclaim] that he is taking France under his authority. How do you expect us to negotiate on this basis?[9]

Churchill was not a man to let himself be outdone and he roared back:

> And what about you? How do you expect us, the British, to adopt a position separated from that of the United States? We are going to liberate Europe, but it is because the Americans are with us to do so. For get this quite clear, every time we have to decide between Europe and the open sea, it is always the open sea that we shall choose. Every time I have to decide between you and Roosevelt, I shall always choose Roosevelt.

These words have rightly remained famous. But while the great man was flinging them in his guest's face, de Gaulle watched Eden, who, "shaking his head, scarcely gave [de Gaulle] the impression of being convinced". Ernest Bevin,* spoke up and told the General that the Prime Minister was speaking "only for himself", and not "in the name of the British Cabinet".[10]

*The Minister for Labour and National Service and a member of the War Cabinet. (trs.)

His fury having died away, Winston Churchill had the magnanimity to raise his glass: "To de Gaulle, who never accepted defeat". To this the General replied, "To Britain, to victory, to Europe."[11]

At 2 p.m. the Prime Minister, wearing the blue uniform of a group-captain in the Royal Air Force (it was rather tight), took his guests to General Eisenhower's headquarters, a cabin in a nearby wood. Ike and his chief of staff, the austere Bedell Smith, took pains to make things plain to their French visitors "with great clarity and self-control" says de Gaulle: eight divisions, 10 000 aircraft and 4000 vessels were ready to attack the coasts of Normandy. "I observed that in this very hazardous and very complex affair the Anglo-Saxons' talent for what they call planning was developed to the highest degree."

Yet there was still one unknown factor: the hour of going into action. Everything had been based on an attack between 3 and 6 June, when dawn would be early and the very low tide would show the greatest number of the obstacles set up by the defenders. Yet, as Eisenhower says in his memoirs, on the morning of 4 June the news was discouraging: "low cloud, high winds, and formidable wave action were predicted." "Air support would be impossible. And even the handling of small boats would be rendered difficult. Montgomery* believed we ought to go. Tedder** disagreed. If we had persisted in attempting the operation on 5 June it would almost certainly have ended in disaster." But in that case was the assault to be postponed until another moon and delayed for several weeks?

The Commander-in-Chief had the intelligent civility to turn to General de Gaulle: "What do you think?" The visitor replied that whatever the one man responsible should decide had his unqualified approval; but he nevertheless added, "If I were in your place, bearing in mind the disadvantages of a delay of many weeks, which would prolong the psychological tension of the attacking forces and endanger secrecy, I should not put it off."

As it had just been the case with Churchill, everything began well with Ike; but with him too everything went bad. As de Gaulle and Béthouart, fully informed about the situation, were about to leave, the Commander-in-Chief, "with obvious embarrassment", handed the General a typed sheet: it was an address that Eisenhower was going to read to the people of western Europe, particularly to the French, at the moment of the attack.

He read the document, and once more he stiffened. Nothing could have been farther removed from Eisenhower's words to him at Les Glycines on 30 December. The proclamation his host was now showing him faithfully reproduced Roosevelt's ideas – though it is said that Eisenhower had toned them down a little. Whereas Ike spoke to the other nations as a soldier, the French, for their part, were required "to carry out his orders", while the administrative officials here and there were to "carry on in the exercise of their functions" until "the French themselves should choose their representatives and their government".

De Gaulle emphasizes that this "pamphlet" did not contain "a single word about the French authority which for years had been arousing and directing the

*The Commander-in-Chief of the land forces.

**Eisenhower's deputy as Supreme Commander. Both he and Montgomery were British.

war-effort of our nation, which had done Eisenhower the honour of placing a large part of the French army under his command."

The American general was too clear-minded not to see that de Gaulle was deeply wounded by his address. He amiably, but not without hypocrisy, told him that "I am ready to change it according to your remarks". That night de Gaulle hastily drew up an appeal in which, without ever naming himself or referring to his government, he confined himself to calling upon the liberated people to "comply with the orders of the qualified French authority" which, "when the oppressors had been expelled, would provide the means for you yourselves to choose your representatives and your government."[12] Nothing could have been more discreet nor more faithful to the principle of self-determination that, according to Roosevelt, inspired the United States. But the amiable Eisenhower had been trifling with Charles de Gaulle: the text the General was shown had been printed and distributed several days before he read it. What the French heard, therefore, was an appeal that denied the appeal of 18 June. It was a summons to obey a foreign general.

Everything that followed, from the evening of 4 June to the sixth, arose from this dismal play-acting. The very fact that he had been refused a horse made the General all the more eager to be a lone rider. Having settled in at the Connaught once more and returned to Carlton Gardens in the afternoon of 5 June, he received the visit of the admirable Charles Peake, who had come to tell him that as the landings had been decided for dawn the next day, it was arranged that he would speak on the radio after the rulers of Norway, the Netherlands and Luxembourg, the prime minister of Belgium and General Eisenhower. De Gaulle replied with a flat refusal. He said that he did not wish, by speaking after the Supreme Commander, to seem "to endorse what he will have said, of which I disapprove."

When Churchill arrived at the meeting of the War Cabinet summoned late that afternoon he was informed that de Gaulle refused to speak or to send the Allied units about to land in Normandy the military liaison mission that had been provided for. In the presence of his ministers he burst into such a rage that Alexander Cadogan, the least Gaullist of Eden's colleagues, wrote in his diary, "We endured the passonate anti-Gaulle harangue from PM. On this subject, we get away from politics and diplomacy and even common sense. Roosevelt, PM and – it must be admitted de Gaulle – all behave like girls approaching the age of puberty."[13] Between nine on the evening of the fifth and four in the morning of the sixth – when the vanguard of the Allied forces was landing on the Sainte-Madeleine beach – the most furious of the conflicts between Churchill and de Gaulle took place: it was only the fact that Viénot and Eden were there as interpreters that prevented the two heroes from coming to blows.

At 9 p.m. on the fifth, Eden telephoned Viénot, asking him to come and see him: the crisis arising from de Gaulle's refusal was very serious. Viénot hurried to the Foreign Office to deny that de Gaulle was refusing to speak but to confirm the refusal to send the liaison mission: Fighting France could not associate itself with an "occupation" of the national territory.

With Eden thus informed, if not comforted, Viénot went back to the Connaught, where de Gaulle greeted him with an outburst against Churchill, whom he called a gangster. "They wanted to trick me. I will not be tricked. I deny their right to know whether I shall speak to France!" Viénot, whose straight-forwardness was called in question, retorted that he had been the first to warn the Allies that "if there were to be an AMGOT, it would be without us" and that he had always told the CFLN to beware of the situation in which they were floundering at the present crucial moment. De Gaulle: The CFLN does not exist. They are people of no consequence. Viénot: If the CFLN is not responsible for the mistake, it is you, General de Gaulle, who are.

The Ambassador left, carrying the General's decision: de Gaulle would speak – at his own time and without supervision – but the military mission would not leave. Viénot went to see Eden: it was Churchill, accompanied by the Foreign Secretary, that he found, and it was Churchill that he was to hear.

> I explained the misunderstanding that had arisen on the subject of the talk on the radio. Eden was obviously relieved. Churchill broke out in curses. He no longer took notice of any facts. It was an explosion of rage, an explosion of hatred for de Gaulle, who was accused of "treason at the height of battle". Ten times he told me that this was a monstrous failure to understand the sacrifice of the young Englishmen and Americans who were about to die for France. "It is blood that has no value for you."
>
> Several times I stood up and said to him, "I cannot listen to this kind of language." At one point he said that having known de Gaulle it seemed to him that the misfortunes of France were understandable and deserved.
>
> At the end of the interview, during which I often found it difficult to retain my self-control and conceal my emotion, Churchill did not rise nor did he hold out his hand. I said to him "You have been unjust; you have said untrue and violent things that you will regret. What I wish to say to you on this historic night is that in spite of everything France thanks you."
>
> Churchill looked at me with an astonished, deeply moved expression. He stirred. I walked out.

Pierre Viénot went back to de Gaulle, whom he found calm, relaxed and serene: the General remarked that when one talked to Churchill "everything turned to violence".

> He said to me, "I will tell you my fundamental line of thought. We must talk – arrange a dinner with Eden, Duff Cooper and you. We will go to the bottom of these questions. There is a Franco-British solidarity to be brought into being. The 1940* idea is no longer possible, but something more permanent than an alliance on a basis of economics and security must be found."
>
> As for his idea of a conversation with Eden, I pointed out to him that it was more difficult today than it had been yesterday, when he had scornfully refused it. I told him of Eden's remark, "De Gaulle seems to think that

*Monnet's plan for a union which the French cabinet had rejected at once.

> Great Britain no longer exists." De Gaulle replied, "He is somewhat mistaken, though." I could see both a shade of regret at having gone too far and an arrogant satisfaction.*

But while the Frenchman was becoming reasonable once more, the Englishman was plunging deeper into rage. This de Gaulle was an enemy to Britain: there was only one thing left to be done with him – let Eisenhower "put him on a plane and send him back to Algiers, in chains if necessary. He must not be allowed to set foot in France!"[14] Arriving in an attempt to pacify his chief, Eden (says d'Astier) found him dictating a letter to de Gaulle, requiring him to leave British territory at once.

But saving the situation was no new thing for Anthony Eden: the letter expelling de Gaulle was burnt. And before the night of 5 June came to an end the General promised that he would speak during the afternoon of the sixth. But what would he say?

There were two ways in which it could have a disastrous effect. Either by letting something of the Inter-Allied dissensions appear, or by inciting the commencement of the "general rising" that the Allied services did not want. As early as the beginning of May the British SOE under Colonel Buckmaster and the CFLN's "services de l'intérieur" represented in London by Georges Boris had clashed on this subject. An agreement had been reached, laying down that the rising should be called for and set in motion only by General Koenig's direct order, and then zone by zone.[15]

But as it happened, from the evening of 5 June onwards, the messages put out both by the British and the French on the BBC initiated a far more important movement than had been foreseen. This was no longer only the sabotage of communications, as the SOE and the BCRA had arranged, but the beginning of an insurrection. It was in this context that Charles de Gaulle made his appeal of 6 June 1944.

Between two visits from Viénot, Charles de Gaulle had particularly wished to spend that night, that vigil of arms, with his son, who was ashore for a few hours. In a whisper the General let out the great secret, just as the first parachutists were landing: "It is for tonight."

He spoke on the radio early in the afternoon. The speech, which had caused his English hosts so much concern, was a call to arms; but he took care not to use the most explosive formula, that of "national insurrection":

> The supreme battle has begun. It is the battle in France and it is the battle of France. France is going to fight this battle furiously. She is going to conduct it in due order. The clear, the sacred duty of the sons of France, wherever they are and whoever they are, is to fight the enemy with all the means at their disposal.

*This account by Pierre Viénot, dictated to his friend and colleague Jacques Kayser during the morning of 6 June 1944, was published in a more complete form in *Le Monde*, 6 June 1974.

The orders given by the French government and by the French leaders it has named for that purpose [must be] obeyed exactly. The actions we carry out in the enemy's rear [must be] coordinated as closely as possible with those carried out at the same time by the Allied and French armies. Let none of those capable of action, either by arms, or by destruction, or by giving intelligence, or by refusing to do work useful to the enemy, allow themselves to be made prisoner; let them remove themselves beforehand from being seized and from being deported.

The battle of France has begun. In the nation, the Empire and the armies there is no longer anything but one single hope, the same for all. Behind the terribly heavy cloud of our blood and our tears here is the sun of our grandeur shining out once again.[16]

But although this fresh appeal addressed to the people of France had for the moment freed de Gaulle from the secondary wranglings and disagreement, it had not disarmed him. Even before returning to the famous microphone of the BBC he had, on 6 June, sent his colleagues in the Algiers government a telegram speaking of the "storm" in London, the urgent necessity for an official protest against the emission of the "spurious money" that the Allies were going to use in France, and his bitter conviction that "Churchill, in total agreement with Roosevelt, meant me to come here chiefly to cover what they were doing."[17]

The dinner he gave on 8 June at Carlton Gardens in honour of Anthony Eden was not calculated to smooth things over. He found no better subject than a denunciation of London's "dependence " on Washington.

While the great powers were needling one another in this fashion, a furious battle was being fought on the Calvados coast from Omaha Beach (Colleville) to Utah Beach (La Madeleine) and from the Pointe du Hoc to Courseulles. On the evening of the sixth it was learnt that the landings had succeeded: that is to say, in twenty hours 156 000 men had won a footing on the continent and for fifty kilometres between the Vire and the Orne the Atlantic Wall had given way. The next day, when Eisenhower visited the bridgehead, the British had taken Bayeux and the Americans Isigny; but a counter-attack by Panzers blocked the first a few kilometres from Caen, where a battle between ten divisions under Rommel and eight American divisions under Bradley together with six British and Canadian under Montgomery began on 11 June.

On 12 June, when the bridgehead had increased to a width of about a hundred kilometres and a depth of twenty, Winston Churchill visited the troops engaged near Bayeux; he saw fit to travel accompanied not by General de Gaulle but by Field-Marshal Smuts, the man who had wished France to join the Commonwealth. The British press became extremely indignant, thinking it indecent that the Prime Minister should not set foot on French soil together with the man who had come to his side four years earlier. Voices rose in the Commons, asking whether it was really true that General de Gaulle had said that he wished to go to France and had been prevented.

The pressure became all the stronger since the British intelligence services reported that "one name and one name alone is heard everywhere – de Gaulle.

The testimony was overwhelming and indeed seemingly unanimous."[18] At the same time all the governments in exile in London, with the exception of that of the Netherlands, recognized the "provisional government" of General de Gaulle, particularly that paragon of international democracy, Eduard Beneš's Czechoslovakia. Upon this, the best-known leaders of opinion on either side of the Atlantic "let it be known that the joke has lasted long enough".[19]

The Prime Minister therefore made up his mind to authorize the head of the French government to visit France. But not without reserves and restrictions. In a note to Eden, Churchill said:

> It would not be possible for de Gaulle to hold meetings there, or gather crowds in the streets. He would no doubt like to have a demonstration to show that he is the future president of the French Republic. I suggest that he should drive slowly through the town,* shake hands with a few people and then return, leaving any subsequent statement to be made here. On the other hand, everything in the way of courtesy should be done to him.[20]

Astonishing arrangements that might have been laid down by a colonial governor with regard to the movements of a dependent African dignitary. Let it be remembered that the person in question was the head of the government of a country whose armed forces were fighting in the war, whose maquisards were everywhere giving their lives to help the Allies' advance, and whose people, in many places, were being massacred by way of reprisals for the landing.

On the very eve of the journey, when General de Gaulle was at a dinner at the Foreign Office, given by Anthony Eden to celebrate his coming return to France, the Foreign Secretary received a message from the Prime Minister raising some last objections to the voyage. After a short consultation with Attlee, the deputy Prime Minister, and the three members of the War Cabinet present, Eden decided to keep to the plan already laid down.

The day before his visit to France, Charles de Gaulle appointed his former ADC François Coulet Commissioner of the Republic for the liberated part of Normandy and Colonel de Chevigné, the former military attaché in Washington, as military authority in the sector. The French State too had established its bridgehead.

*Bayeux.

CHAPTER THIRTY-SEVEN

A Plebiscite

At dawn on 14 June the destroyer *Combattante*, which had taken part in the battle of the landings under the order of Captain Patou, sailed from Portsmouth. The evening before this General de Gaulle had gone aboard, accompanied by Pierre Viénot, Béthouart, d'Argenlieu, Palewski, Billotte, Courcel, Teyssot (then his ADC) and lastly Coulet and Chevigné, who were to take up their posts in Normandy.

It is hard to believe, but as he set foot on the soil of France once more the General was filled with gloom. A party organized by the sailors the evening before had left him totally unmoved. At first light he was seen standing on the bridge, watching for the opposite coast to appear. The captain came forward to say good morning. De Gaulle stared at him: "Patou, I shall not yield." "Of course not, General," said the captain, somewhat taken aback. "On the question of bank-notes made out in francs and issued in America. It is false currency!"[1]

They landed a little after midday on a beach between Courseulles and Graye-sur-mer.* De Gaulle, muffled in an immense pilot-coat that seemed to isolate him from the world, enveloped himself in silence. One of his companions, Boislambert, came over to him and said, "Has it occurred to you, General, that it is four years ago to the very day that the Germans entered Paris?" A silence. Then de Gaulle said, "They were in the wrong, Boislambert."

After a short walk on the beach cluttered with the vehicles of a Canadian regiment that had just landed, de Gaulle got into a jeep (T8-5537365) driven by a Scots sergeant who had taken care to fasten a French flag to his windscreen. Béthouart and Viénot took the back seat. But what of the contact with the people of France? General Béthouart gives a good description of these first encounters:

> Presently our fellow-countrymen appeared. They were mostly old, the women dressed in black. They looked at us without understanding who we were, since they did not recognize the French uniforms. We stopped and talked to them. They cried out with joy. One of them, fascinated by my four stars, said to me "Is it you who are General de Gaulle?" "No. That is General de Gaulle, there, in front of me." The man gazed at the General's two stars, obviously amazed.[2]

Suddenly behind them there was the sound of a galloping horse. A priest leapt

*Subsequently there was an argument between the two municipalities about whose territory the General landed upon. Courseulles won.

from his mount: it was M. Paris, the curé of Vaux-sur-Seulles, who thus addressed de Gaulle: "General! I heard your appeal of 18 June, I have helped patriots, I have sheltered parachutists, I have been in touch with the maquis; and you have passed through my village without even shaking my hand! Well, if I had suspected it would turn out like that." Smiling, de Gaulle got out of the jeep and took the priest in his arms: "Monsieur le Curé, I do not shake your hand, I embrace you."

A little farther on the jeep met two gendarmes peacefully bicycling towards Courseulles. De Gaulle made the jeep stop and had them called. The gendarmes dismounted, stood to attention and saluted this officer* in a long coat buttoned to the neck. It was clear that they had no idea who they were talking to. The leader of Free France introduced himself. The two gendarmes, astonished and horrified, let their bicycles fall and stammered out apologies.

"My friends," said de Gaulle, "do me a kindness. I am on my way to Bayeux. Will you turn back and tell them I am coming? That will prevent anyone being caught unawares. We shall not move from here for a quarter of an hour." The gendarmes remounted their bicycles and hurried off towards Bayeux. Turning to his companions, the General declared, "Gentlemen, the reconnaissance has been carried out."[3]

They arrived at Montgomery's quarters; the British general had settled in a Louis XIII château whose owners went on living there as though nothing had happened, and he worked in a lorry converted into an office, decorated with photographs of Eisenhower and Rommel. De Gaulle describes him as combining "prudence with rigour" and "keenness with humour", adding that his operations "were following their course".

At Bayeux he was received by the mayor and by Coulet, who had assumed office an hour before. Bayeux which had been the object of the battle that had raged all round it, was almost untouched. The British soldiers had done their utmost to preserve the town so dear to the Plantagenets. The Vichy sub-prefect, who was still in place, showed his adherence to Gaullism by hurrying to the salle d'honneur and removing the photograph of Marshal Pétain, which nobody had thought of taking down for a week.

Béthouart describes this entry into Bayeux as "triumphant" and he speaks of "the cheers of an enthusiastic crowd". De Gaulle was to write that "at the sight of the General, a kind of amazement seized the inhabitants, who then burst out cheering or began to weep. I was surrounded by children. The women smiled and sobbed. The men held out their hands. Thus we went along, all together, brotherly, overwhelmed, feeling the nation's joy, pride and hope rising up once again from the bottom of the abyss." Other people who watched these scenes write in a more restrained tone, yet even so they do not deny the warmth of the reception.

In the castle square a great tricoloured streamer had been stretched out, with American, British and Canadian flags pinned to it. There was a little platform and a microphone, and here there appeared lieutenant Maurice Schumann, pale with

*Gendarmes (as opposed to the various police forces) form part of the army: they are under the command of officers. (trs.)

emotion under his great béret. Just as he used to do in London he cried "Honneur et patrie! Here is General de Gaulle!"

Standing there with Béthouart and Koenig on either side of him, the General addressed the crowd:

> This is no time to speak of feelings. What the country expects of you who are behind the front line is that you should carry on with the battle. Our cry is now as it always has been the cry of war. I promise you that we shall carry on fighting until the sovereignty of the last inch of French territory is restored. No one will prevent us from doing so. We are fighting alongside the Allies, with the Allies, as an ally.

But at Isigny, thirty kilometres farther on, there was a far more wounding picture of the horrors of the battle than there had been at Bayeux. It was not the British who had had the task of taking this little town but the Americans; it was in ruins, and the General's jeep travelled along a path that had been cleared through the débris. Here, therefore, emotion took on an entirely different force. "Bodies were still being extracted from beneath the wreckage,"[4] says de Gaulle; it was above all the halt at Isigny that marked this 14 June for him.

The General walked, awestruck, through these tragic surroundings, in the midst of an awestruck gathering. But each side was gauging the other, taking the other's measure in a mutual weighing up. De Gaulle still walked with an uncertain tread; he did not yet possess that air of an experienced champion sailing on the swell of the crowd that he was later to acquire. At that time he was in his early stages as a leader and his charisma was not yet in action.

De Gaulle's face, carriage, size (and even his two stars) surprised the children, the curés and the gendarmes of Normandy and took them aback. But his name was familiar to them all. Astonished, the people crowded round him; they grew more and more attentive, more friendly, and in the end enthusiastic. So the severe voice of the nation's public prosecutor, the exacting nocturnal voice that made its way through the fog of jamming, belonged to this giant in an earth-coloured greatcoat, walking with long strides and gazing at the ruins with a proud melancholy – the ruins of "his" country.

They went back to Courseulles and the *Combattante*. In the course of the journey the Constable greeted detachments of Allied troops making their way to the front and "a few squads of our forces of the interior", of which some, he states, "had given effective help in the landings".

The return voyage was made by night, for German planes were continually harrying the Allied ships. On board the *Combattante* the General, more talkative than on the outward journey, said to Béthouart, "You see, we had to face the Allies with a *fait accompli*. Our new authorities are there, actually installed: you will find that the Allies say nothing. Our national sovereignty is virtually assured. We can go back to Algiers!"

The conclusion to be drawn from this day was deeply significant; the author of the *Mémoires de guerre* puts it thus: "It had been proved the French people had shown whom they relied upon for the duty of leading them." This walk through the liberated ruins meant that within a few hours AMGOT had been put to death.

Here we must turn to the account of its "executioner", François Coulet:

> As he left Montgomery's headquarters, de Gaulle said to him in an offhand tone, "I am leaving Major Coulet behind me; he will look after the population." This was the only notice of my appointment that the Allies were given.
>
> In Bayeux I observed straight away that the public treasury was overflowing with money, which made the "spurious currency" put into circulation by the Allies useless: in any event the cautious Normans had refused it from the start. I was well and truly settled, provided with undisputed authority, recognized by the "population".
>
> The AMGOT and Civil Affairs people did not appear until a week later. In an exceedingly disagreeable manner they informed me that military problems had priority and that they would "tolerate me until they had instructions from their governments". Some months later Eisenhower's chief of staff, General Bedell Smith, told me that there had been a plan to seize me and send me back to England.[5]

A week after Eisenhower's appeal no authorities had appeared other than those appointed by General de Gaulle. No, Normandy was not an "occupied territory", a conquered enemy country. It was – which for the relations between France, Great Britain and the United States meant salvation – a liberated region, taken in hand by a troublesome, awkward, but determined ally of Churchill and Roosevelt.

On the afternoon of 15 June Anthony Eden, impressed by what he had been told of the Normans' reception of de Gaulle and by the papers, which, like the *Daily Mail*, hailed this "demonstration, so simple and so spontaneous", hurried to Carlton Gardens. As we know, the Foreign Secretary was not one of those who were displeased by this news, which he saw as a means of at last forcing Churchill's hand, and then that of Roosevelt: the recognition of the Gouvernement Provisoire de la République Française (GPRF) was now no more than a matter of weeks.

Of course Eden would have preferred the British government to bring about the forthcoming and inevitable rapprochement between de Gaulle and Roosevelt; and he had been working to this end. Yet he was still of the opinion that he and Viénot could work out an agreement and that all they would have to do was to show it to Washington so that there might be joint signature by the British, French and Americans. In any case, said Eden, "Roosevelt was only waiting for de Gaulle's journey to Washington to change his attitude."

De Gaulle thought these prospects "acceptable", and it seemed to him that the time had come for him to send Churchill a message that would "pour balm into his self-inflicted wounds". In his letter therefore he spoke highly of "the power of the British nation", of "its friendly feelings for France" and of the "indissoluble affection" between the two peoples; he hailed "the impregnable bastion of Europe, which was now one of its chief liberators" and said he was convinced that the United Kingdom and its Prime Minister had thus acquired "undying honour".

Churchill was recovering too slowly from the blows they had exchanged between the fourth and sixth of June to let his natural generosity have full play. He spoke of his regret at not being able to help improve the relations between the CFLN and Washington. "A sincere friend of France since 1907", he felt "great sorrow" that the visit he had "personally arranged" should not have brought about "the hoped-for understanding" and now he would confine himself to hoping that "it may not have been the last chance".[6] Churchill was perfectly well aware that his great plan was close to realization and that de Gaulle was expected in Washington. But this was not an understanding "à l'anglaise" and, confronted with the sarcastic Constable, he could not refrain from voicing his displeasure like a guardian whose charge has escaped.

General de Gaulle returned to Algiers on 16 June and on the thirtieth he received a letter from Pierre Viénot telling him of the striking results of his negotiations with Anthony Eden:

> I think I may say that we have reached that "ninety per cent success" which I said you could hope for – an agreement that in practice amounts to a positive recognition of the provisional government, a categoric assertion of French sovereignty, the disappearance of any notion of "supervision" by the Commander-in-Chief even in the forward zone, and the affirmation of the provisional government's complete equality with the Allied governments.

As Eisenhower said, "There are the facts". But to make sure that they should predominate over theories it is better to make them quite clear. Before going to Washington to remove the last burden that still weighed on French independence, the head of the provisional government went to Italy, not only to get in touch with the representatives of the new Italian government, that of Signor Bonomi, who had succeeded Marshal Badoglio after King Victor-Emmanuel's abdication.

He also intended to see the Pope. For, as he wrote fifteen years later with a serenity that he did not always possess between 1940 and 1944, "the Holy See, with its everlasting prudence, had until this point remained reserved towards Fighting France and then the Algiers government." Mgr Valerio Valeri, who was the papal nuncio in Paris in 1940, retained his office at Vichy under the Marshal.

De Gaulle gives a description of the Pope's reception of the head of the new French government in which the pupil of Catholic schools seems to outweigh the enemy of the Axis: he speaks only of "benevolence", "sensitivity" and "clear-mindedness", to say nothing of the "supernatural responsibility", the gifts of "authority", "influence" and "eloquence" with which God had endowed this pontiff. It seems that the visitor was no longer troubled by anything at all, not even the terrible silence of the successor of Pius XI about the fate of the Jews and more generally of the victims of totalitarianism. After his conversation with de Gaulle in June 1944 it appears that Pius XII became more acutely aware of this curse; for henceforward it was a question of the progress of communism.*

Yet after all the heart of the matter was the fighting between Caen and Saint-

*Alexander Werth (*De Gaulle*, p. 165) describes this portrait as "a little masterpiece of *vacherie*". (*Vaches* – cows – have an indifferent reputation in France, roughly equivalent to that of swine in England; and a *vacherie* is a dirty trick or worse. trs.)

Lô. From the French point of view the battle chiefly concerned the FFI, the French Forces of the Interior, then reckoned at close on 300 000 men, commanded since the end of March by General Koenig. But Koenig was completely under the thumb of the Inter-Allied command for everything that had to do with weapons, activities, communications and general tactics. One of the most urgent problems that arose at the time of the "battle of France" was that of connecting the FFI's rising with the Allies' offensive.

As we have seen, for three years the argument opposing "immediate action" and temporizing had raged between London and its emissaries on the one hand and on the other wide sections of the home Resistance (particularly the Communists) who protested against what they called "jourjism", postponing action until D Day. This notion, which seemed to come directly from General de Gaulle, had continued until May 1943 when the commander of the Armée Secrète came round to the principle of immediate action. And on 18 May 1944 de Gaulle, in a directive dated from Algiers, wrote: "As soon as the Allies land, the home forces should, in liaison with the Allied forces, intervene directly in the battle by actions aimed at the liberation of whole regions of the country."[7]

In April 1944 General de Gaulle sent Lucien Rachline, known as Socrate, to France for the coordination of military plans: with Alexandre Parodi (Quartus), the new delegate-general who had succeeded Bollaert, and with de Gaulle's two chief military representatives in France, Colonel Ely* and Chaban-Delmas he had signed a document according to which the national uprising would not be automatically set off by the landings but only when the Algiers government decided upon it.[8] This document had been instantly denounced by Malleret-Joinville and his Communist friends.

The argument should have been settled by the proclamations and appeals put out on 6 June, at dawn by Eisenhower and at four in the afternoon by de Gaulle. Nothing of the sort took place. Whereas the Supreme Commander said that "each one of you should carry on with his present task unless he has been given an order to do otherwise" – which might be taken as an order to temporize or at least to be cautious – the president of the provisional government (from whom Eisenhower, as he says in his memoirs, expected orders of the same kind) launched a positive call to arms: "the clear, the sacred duty is to fight the enemy with all the means at their disposal." Yet as we know he did not explicitly call for a national insurrection. In short, de Gaulle the "symbol" was calling to arms at the same moment that de Gaulle the strategist was advising the resistants to bide their time.

In any case, on 6 June there were two opposing "lines": inside France the Socrate-Quartus line (wait for orders) and that of the Communists** who, from the FFI General Staff (Joinville) to the CNR military committee (Villon) and the FTP (Tillon) governed the mass of the available forces, and who were pressing more than ever for immediate action: and outside France, Eisenhower's line and that of General de Gaulle's public proclamation. In point of fact, as early as 6 June Eisenhower's staff and the Inter-Allied special services had lit the fuses of the

*Later chief of the General Staff.
**This is of course an over-simplification.

explosives under their direct control in France, and the prudent Socrate-Quartus orders were soon made out of date by de Gaulle's 6 June appeal.

Once again it was circumstances that were in control – that perilous and dynamic combination of ungovernable happenings and of irresistible passions. The organized or partially independent mass of resistants, called upon to temporize by the military chief but to act by the political chief, while the political chief's military delegate told them to wait for orders and the military chief's special services urged them to go ahead, felt in their hearts that D Day or not, the decision was at hand.

At all events, in the departments directly involved in the battle, the Calvados, the Manche and to some degree the Orne and the Eure, the activity of some thousands of FFI was primarily concerned with the destruction of bridges, such as those of Fervacques, Vire, Vassy, Prêtreville (thus carrying out the "plan tortue"), the sabotage of railways ("plan vert"), guerrilla fighting in the wooded country ("plan rouge") and the guiding of Allied parachutists. In Brittany, and especially in the Morbihan, an exemplary operation began, carried out both by General Guillaudot's maquis, which numbered nearly 10 000 trained fighting-men, and the parachutists of the 2nd RCP under the orders of Colonel Bourgouin.

But in many places throughout the country, people following de Gaulle's "public" incitement if not his inner intention, set about undertakings that often had a tragic end. Although some attempts at seizing towns such as Tulle, Ussel or Guéret succeeded for a few hours, they could not but cause disasters, the Nazi forces being still so fresh and well coordinated.

It cannot be denied that some of these tragedies also slowed down the enemy's movements, particularly those that delayed the notorious SS division Das Reich, which Marshal von Rundstedt had summoned to Normandy from the neighbourhood of Toulouse. But the price paid in various places seems to have gone beyond any military justification: how many other lives were given in exchange for the 650 victims of Oradour?

In many sectors, particularly in the Languedoc-Roussillon, where the AS and FTP staffs coordinated their activities well and limited the scope of operations in the early days, or in that of Toulouse, which had the advantage of being directed by Ravanel, an expert war-leader, the action was "profitable" and was hailed as such by Eisenhower.

Four days after the landings the national authorities drew up a balance-sheet. On 10 June, General Koenig sent out a message saying, "Put maximum check on guerrilla activity. Impossible at present to supply you with enough arms and ammunition. As far as possible break off contact everywhere to allow reorganization. Avoid concentration of large numbers. Set up small isolated groups."[9]

It had needed four days of fighting for the authorities appointed by General de Gaulle to wage this kind of war* to issue the most elementary of directives in such circumstances. One may be sure that Tillon, the proponent of the "ball of quicksilver", had no need of advice of this sort to fight in a way that would do the enemy most harm. From Le Mont-Mouchet to the Vercors, it was too late to call out

*Koenig's staff included none of the military leaders of the home Resistance.

"Pax" to the men in field-grey. The repression had begun: what that courageous southern fighter, Henri Noguères, speaking not without anger, calls the "Koenig pause" came either too soon or too late.

It is clear that the staff of the FFI made a mistake because they had no real experience of this kind of warfare, nor, above all, any authority over the greater number of fighting-men, who obeyed the orders of the Communist party (or the FTP) rather than theirs. From this there arose the terrible muddle that in the end cost the lives of far too many men.

There is no question here of accusing General Koenig, or of denouncing the "lone rider" attitude of the PCF. Yet it must be pointed out that at the very moment he was preparing to bring off his greatest political victory, the triumph of the GPRF over AMGOT which established the country's national independence, General de Gaulle suffered a military and a human defeat: the French Forces of the Interior did not work with the Allies as he had hoped, but ebbed and flowed like an unpredictable tide.

From the military point of view, this Resistance which had ensured him his legitimacy against Vichy, Darlan, Giraud, London and Washington was not under his sway because it was divided into three branches, AS, FTP, ORA, and he could only claim the first as "his". It took him three months to bring the Resistance under control. Not until October were all the branches of the FFI made more or less part of the French army and placed at the service of the State.

Furthermore it is striking to observe the rarity of General de Gaulle's papers referring to the FFI's activities during this decisive phase that ran from 6 June to the end of July. The *Mémoires de guerre*, written years later, deal with the subject very fully. But the pieces written at the time, which are to be found in the annexe to the *Mémoires* and in the *Lettres, Notes et Carnets* are few in number – until the very last days of July, when two messages show that his diplomatic preoccupations and his journeys to Italy or the United States had not turned his mind away from the progress of the battle.

The first was written to Alexandre Parodi, his delegate-general in France. In this the president of the GPRF recalls that "no form of struggle against the enemy within the interior of France must be neglected" and that "naturally it is the fighting properly so called, that of the armed forces of the interior, that must be the heart of the matter".

The second is a letter addressed to General Eisenhower and General Maitland Wilson emphasizing the activity of the French Resistance, "an effective instrument in the fields of intelligence and of action" which deserves a greater place "in the present and future Allied operations", particularly in Brittany "whose maquis are especially bold and enterprising, and despite the successive set-backs in the Glières, the Ubaye and the Vercors where the guerrilla warfare was begun too soon".

And General de Gaulle states: "In the coming phase of the battle, the French Resistance would normally be capable of more effective operations than those which are foreseen at present; so long as the necessary support is given, it would be reasonable to hope for successes more rapid, more decisive and lastly less damaging to France in every way."

It is agreeable to see that last touch, which shows the General's anxiety to have the least possible number of trials inflicted upon his country and his people. Yet one must certainly admit that although the extraordinary diplomatic and political dividends that he was then gathering in, that can be summed up in the words "resurrection of French sovereignty", are to be put to his credit and attributed to his energy and tenacity, the conditions in which the citizens of France entered the fighting in June 1944 demanded reservations.

Since he knew just how far the resistants, in action, depended on supplies furnished by the Allies should he have called them to arms as he did on 17 May in Algiers and 6 June on the BBC? It is the text of the appeal he wanted to have read by Eisenhower which was that of a responsible leader: "No premature rising".

In June 1940 Charles de Gaulle was condemned to madness if he were not to lose all hope of France. In 1944 he was condemned to reason, in order not to bleed France white. He took up the challenge of excess better than he did that of moderation.

CHAPTER THIRTY-EIGHT

A Voyage to America

To go or not to go? When, armoured with the Norman plebiscite, de Gaulle came back to Algiers on 16 June that was the great question. Washington's discreet but repeated advances called for a reply. An opportunity was at hand. But there were great risks.

These American approaches took three forms: the first was military, the second diplomatic, the third came from the White House. The soldiers were the most impatient; it was after all they who had to solve the most urgent problems at the Bayeux bridgehead. Chevigné had been acknowledged, the French liaison-officers were arriving, the mechanism was in gear. But men as methodical as Marshall, Eisenhower and Bedell Smith needed to be better acquainted with their partners and above all to know what powers they disposed of.

The diplomatic attack was more patient and traditional: it reflected the evolution of such men as Cordell Hull and his Ambassador to Algiers, Edwin Wilson, and the influence that the charming Henri Hoppenot was acquiring in Washington. For these men, devoted to forms and documents, the position of a government that was not a government verged upon absurdity; a solution had to be found. As for Roosevelt, he was sailing very close to the wind, obsessed by the coming presidential election: on 1 November he was to ask for a fourth term of office.

FDR could not risk a close-run re-election; but a very serious candidate, Governor Thomas Dewey, was standing against him. Roosevelt therefore had to deal gently with that rapidly-growing section of public opinion which was in favour of de Gaulle while at the same time he must not seem to be admitting that he had been mistaken.

Roosevelt had not changed his mind about the Constable. He told Henry Stimson, his War Minister, that de Gaulle was "a fool"; he assured all those who cared to listen that "de Gaulle will be confounded by the progress of events", that "other parties will spring up" and that "he would become a very little figure".[1]

The American press was far from being wholly converted to the cause of Fighting France. Its best-known leaders such as Lippmann, Mowrer or the Alsop brothers spoke in favour of the General; but in June 1944, prejudices were still very much alive, and the battle of France did not improve Charles de Gaulle's standing in the eyes of all Americans.

In a telegram sent to Algiers on 16 June 1944, Henri Hoppenot reported the opening of a violent press campaign (obviously prompted by the White House and the State Department) after de Gaulle's refusal to send all the promised liaison officers to Normandy. The theme of the campaign was "Americans are being killed while the French talk politics and General de Gaulle hampers the Allied war-effort", an argument that the President himself produced at his press-conferences.

Yet the American démarches concerning a visit to Washington by de Gaulle increased in number. In London de Gaulle was visited by General Bedell Smith, who, says he, "literally adjured him to agree to the meeting with the President"; Bedell Smith was followed by Admiral Fenard who, with his unvarying discretion, repeated the invitation sent a month ago. And lastly in Algiers the American Ambassador, supported by his British colleague, pressed the point: the General was expected whenever he chose to come; let him suggest a date.

De Gaulle put the question to the GPRF. Even though Monnet and Mendès France were not there, a clear majority (including Massigli, Pleven and René Mayer) were in favour of the visit. De Gaulle thus defined the nature of his mission in a telegram to Hoppenot on 24 June:

> I should look upon this journey as a tribute paid by France at war to the President himself, as well as to the American people and the American armies which have made and which are making such efforts and such sacrifices for the liberation of Europe and Asia. Bearing in mind the present state of Franco-American relations as well as the somewhat obscure and heavily-charged atmosphere surrounding them, I do not intend to make any specific claims or requests. In particular the United States' formal recognition of the provisional government is a question in which I take little interest and which I shall not raise. The practical economy of the Franco-American connection seems to me much more important and urgent.[2]

Although his Ambassador in Washington had warned him against the manoeuvres of various people, de Gaulle made his decision at the end of June. And it was from Rome that he wrote to Massigli, stating his acceptance and making it perfectly clear that he was determined "not to undertake or agree to any negotiations on any subject".[3]

The visit, which was to last from 6 to 10 July, was not to be confined to Washington; the General would make a stop at New York and he would then return by way of Ottawa, Montreal and Quebec.

> It would be absurd for me to visit the United States without going to New York. It would be improper for me to go to New York in a clandestine manner. There is no question of arousing any demonstrations in New York from the point of view of American politics.* For the head of the French government it is a matter of testifying to the friendship of France at war with America at war in the greatest city of the United States. The thing can and must be done with dignity.[4]

But in another telegram the Constable – who had advised Hoppenot to organize

*Roosevelt's challenger, Dewey, was the governor of the State of New York, and it was the New York press that gave Gaullism the most support.

the journey "in a very, very free-handed manner" – emphatically excluded any meeting with "Alexis Léger, Labarthe, Tabouis, Kérillis, Géraud or Chautemps". An odd assembly, this band of New York anti-Gaullists, with such active opponents of Gaullism as Labarthe or Kérillis* and luke-warm people such as Tabouis or Géraud who had sometimes written very favourable articles about the General, particularly the second, whose pen-name was Pertinax, in 1941.

On 5 July Charles de Gaulle, accompanied by Palewski, Béthouart and Teyssot,** set off for Washington in a plane sent by Franklin Roosevelt. Just before this, on the fourth, it being the Americans' Independence Day, he had sent the President of the United States a cordial message: he recalled that "just as they had done twenty-five years ago, the American armed forces were now unsparing in their feats of heroic valour for the liberation of the soil of France" and he expressed "his country's gratitude towards them".

During the flight from Algiers to Washington (which took almost thirty hours) the General had a long talk with Hervé Alphand, who, appendaged to the official delegation, was going to help Jean Monnet in the negotiations on French rights and the aid, both economic and military, supplied to the country by the United States – negotiations whose aim was now to bring Franco-American relations into line with the draft agreement arranged by Eden and Viénot in London.

This conversation "greatly encouraged" Alphand, who writes, "The General was clear-sighted and he did not want to have anything to do with that France based on Maurras' ideas, xenophobic and closed in upon itself, that I must admit I had feared. Not at all: he wished above all to restore France to its place, to provide the French with the mystique of reconstruction and unite them without tyrannizing over them."[5]

As he set foot on American soil, the Constable had one of those inspirations which had already given him that virtuosity in public relations which was to reach its height fifteen years later: He uttered his first address to American public opinion in English:

> I am happy to be on American soil to meet President Roosevelt. I salute and pay tribute to all those American men and women who at home are relentlessly working for the war and, also, those brave American boys: soldiers, sailors and airmen who abroad are fighting our common enemies. The whole French people is thinking of you and salutes you, Americans, our friends.

"On the threshold of the White House Franklin Roosevelt welcomed me, all smiles and cordiality," writes the author of the *Mémoires de guerre*. There is no doubting the cordiality of the smile, which a photograph has fixed for posterity, nor the warmth of the hand-shake exchanged by the omnipotent man confined to his chair, under the attentive eye of the irreplaceable Miss Lehand, and his very tall visitor, bowing with the awkwardness of a well-bred albatross.

*The author of *De Gaulle dictateur*.

**In Washington he rejoined Pierre Mendès France, who was taking part in the Bretton Woods conference and who became one of the visiting group.

Are we to rely on the memoir-writer for this episode? According to his text he was surrounded by nothing but expressions of esteem and friendship in these circles where some looked upon him as a mountebank, others as a fascist and only a minority as the true representative of France at war.

The fact is that the atmosphere was favourable. He had his quarters at Blair House, where official guests were lodged. And he was granted three tête-à-tête conversations with the President. As we shall see, he had the feeling that Roosevelt understood him – he had the same impression at Anfa.

Tea with the President, dinner with Cordell Hull, lunch the next day at the White House ("solemn but very cordial" says the visitor again), dinner with Henry Stimson, a reception given by Hoppenot crowded with senators and diplomats – yes, this "fool's" welcome came up to the hopes of those who had been in favour of the visit. So much so that at first the British papers displayed a certain irritation and that Churchill began to think that his efforts at bringing the two men together had perhaps gone farther than he had wanted.

The visitor did not omit any of the ritual gestures expected of him, from the tomb of the Unknown Warrior at Arlington to George Washington's Mount Vernon and the military hospital where the aged General Pershing was coming to the end of his very long life. It was quite obviously without the least evil intention that the former Commander-in-Chief of the American Expeditionary Force in Europe at once asked de Gaulle for news of his "old friend Pétain". The General was sufficiently well-bred to answer gently "I believe he is quite well."

In his *Mémoires* Charles de Gaulle carries on to hand out prizes to his American hosts on a grand scale. Although Hull, the Secretary of State, is criticized because of the "summary nature of his knowledge of anything that is not America", he is immediately afterwards praised for his "magnanimity"; the Secretary of the Treasury Morgenthau is (rightly) described as a "friend to our cause", Marshall as a "bold organizer", Admiral King as "fervent and imaginative". As for Admiral Leahy, it was Charles de Gaulle's turn to show a certain "magnanimity" by saying that the Admiral "was taken aback by events that defied his conformism, astonished at seeing me there but making the best of it". And the Constable summed up his opinion of the American governing circles as a whole in one short phrase: "Because of Roosevelt's sparkling personality no one assumed more than a limited brilliance."[6]

"Roosevelt's sparkling personality." To speak in such terms of a man who by continually neglecting and humiliating him for four years had neglected and humiliated France, de Gaulle must indeed have had a great relish for grandeur. During the three interviews in which both took care not to raise immediate, urgent subjects he had time to study the man while at the same time he had the surprise of hearing his observations, in which "idealism clothed the will for power".

> It was with admiration that I saw the flow of this torrent of confidence that was carrying the American élite* along with it, and I remarked that optimism

*Not "governing circles" but "élite": an emphatic expression, particularly when it was used by a former pupil of the Jesuits.

> suits those who have the means for it. President Roosevelt had no doubt that he possessed them. I thought his conception as grandiose as it was disturbing for France and for Europe. In his view, a directorate of four powers, America, Soviet Russia, China and Great Britain, would deal with the problems of the world. A parliament of the united nations would give this authority of the four great powers a democratic appearance. The American force [would dispose] of bases distributed over all parts of the world; some would be selected in French territory.

The fact that Charles de Gaulle did not react violently to these words, and that FDR, "that artist, that enchanter [who] proceeds by subtle touches", did not provoke a vehement philippic from the Constable, who had often flung his thunderbolts for much less than this, shows the extent of the great politician's talent and his charm. The former Saint-Cyr professor did of course give Roosevelt a lecture on those trifling realities known as Europe and France; but in speaking of his own country de Gaulle took care to remind FDR that "it was, it is and always will be your ally".

"Roosevelt's great mind was open to these considerations", asserts de Gaulle, who perceived in his host "a real affection for France" which had been diminished only by the disappointment caused by "yesterday's disaster". Is loving a country only when it is victorious loving it at all? "The American president's observations finally proved to me that in relations between States, logic and feelings have little weight in comparison with the realities of power; what matters is what one seizes and what one can hold on to; and that in order to recover its place France should count only on itself." And he attributed this conclusion to Roosevelt: "It is true that by way of being useful to France, no one can replace the French people."[7]

So although he was fascinated by this striking mixture of "idealism and the will for power" it was the lesson of the second that Charles de Gaulle retained ("what matters is what one seizes and what one can hold on to"). From these few hours spent in the Oval Office of the White House, the Constable found an idea that might have come from Frederick the Great – which in any case he had discovered by himself.

Charles de Gaulle must be given merit for recounting in his *Mémoires* how struck he was at the meeting with Roosevelt in Washington. For he came to know what his host had written about him in a letter that was not meant to be published and that must therefore have been sincere.* A week after the General left, the President wrote to the congressman J.C. Baldwin, who was not however an intimate friend: "In our conversation we went deeply into the future of France, of its colonies, of peace in the world, etc. When it was a question of future problems he seemed perfectly manageable so long as France was treated on a world-wide basis. He is very touchy where the honour of France is concerned, but I think he is essentially selfish."[8]

This is another very well known remark and an essential ingredient in Gaullist historiography so long as it is completed by Charles de Gaulle's brief comment: "I

*Kindly sent to him by an anonymous hand.

shall never know whether Franklin Roosevelt thought that in matters to do with France Charles de Gaulle was selfish for France or for himself."[9] It must be confessed that the distinction is not always easy to make. In the light of his general behaviour, it seems that Roosevelt's words must have their most commonplace meaning. It may be said that until the very end, Franklin Roosevelt, though he charmed de Gaulle, failed to understand him.

Charles de Gaulle thought it right to face the press before leaving Washington for New York. As generally happens with the best American journalists, the questions went to the heart of the problems straight away. Thus one of them asked him whether "in his opinion the United States had the intention of interfering with French sovereignty". The visitor replied:

> I am convinced that neither President Roosevelt, nor the American government, nor the American people intend to annex any French territory whatsoever, and all Frenchmen are convinced of this too. But the organizing of international security, which concerns all territories and particularly French territories, may give rise to friendly discussions.

And when he was asked whether, with a view to being recognized by Washington, he contemplated organizing a plebiscite in France he answered much more sharply, "The way the French will set about the reconstruction of France is an exclusively French question."

Upon the whole he had a good, even a very good, press, considering the distance he had had to travel. According to the *Chicago Daily News*, "Here in Washington the General has brought the old friendship between France and the United States back to life. The President [has] dispelled the clouds that weighed on our relations and regularized a situation that had caused discomfort to say the least ever since the day our troops landed in North Africa." *The Nation*, a very active left-wing weekly said "Mr Roosevelt has at last retreated from an untenable position, whatever reservations he may bring forward to conceal this retreat. Let us therefore be grateful to him for having done so." But the best article was Ann MacCormick's in the *New York Times*:

> General de Gaulle, in flesh and blood, seems subtly different from his photographs. He is more human, less austere, les formidable in the French sense of the word [but] both from the point of view of behaviour and of size, he is in no way the usual kind of Frenchman.
>
> The General was certainly obliged to shout, for in those days the voice of France was so stifled and so weak! He has carried on in the same way since, making himself unbearable, so that the Allies should not forget that France is a power to be reckoned with. At present the General can speak more softly.
>
> The security of France, like our own, henceforward depends on new conceptions. The French statesman is now sure that France will be associated with the organization of the system. So long as France was dependent it had to assert its independence, but as the country recovers its freedom of

action and is treated on a footing of equality, it will be more and more inclined to accept the necessities of interdependence.

A man's behaviour and his political vision of the world could not have been analysed with more intelligent sympathy.

The attitude of the English press is interesting too: on 13 July the *Times*, which had been reserved about Gaullist views ever since the well-known night of 5 June and the landings, published a very constructive leader: "By having confidence in the men through whom France can henceforward express itself and by frankly acknowledging France's role as one of the most important belligerents, we can make the good-will displayed on the battlefields of Normandy the basis of a lasting alliance full of promise for the future of the world."

Everyone agrees that de Gaulle "was interested in everything around him", that he asked a great many questions and that he did not try to conceal France's present poverty by his legendary affectation of arrogance. Cordell Hull was happy to see him, in public and in private, so freely stress the American war-effort, which he thought "prodigious". William Bullitt* was surprised at his interest in everything that had to do with the coming presidential elections. Henry Wallace, the future Vice-President, was surprised at his simplicity; and Walter Lippman, who had given him such valuable support, was glad to see him "already talking much more about peace than war, much more about balance than revenge".[10]

This man so deeply concerned with the most traditional history, so ignorant of finance, economics and production, was immensely and instantly impressed by the sight of an America bursting with promise and with industrial creativity. Many of his companions of that period, particularly Léo Teyssot, his ADC, retain the memory of a de Gaulle who had "seldom been happier in the course of his life".[11] The success of his contacts during these days from 6 to 10 July 1944 was largely due to the eager cheerfulness which he was then feeling.

It must be acknowledged that neither the American genius nor the connection he had had with that nation until the present made this privileged relationship at all obvious. So in considering de Gaulle one should never forget this American euphoria which so brought out everything that was modernist and even futurist in this mediaeval crusader.

Must all this be brought down merely to a veneration for scale and magnitude – the Empire State Building and General Motors, the capability of building 30 000 planes a year and flinging a million men on the coasts of Europe at the same time as two million towards the islands of Asia? It was not so much the scale of the undertaking that interested him as what it revealed in the way of optimism, dynamism and creativity.

Not that this prevented de Gaulle from preserving his statesmanlike coolness and on 7 July he cabled Massigli in a more professional tone:

My stay in Washington is proceeding in an atmosphere that both sides wish

*Formerly the United States ambassador in Paris.

> to be cordial. This morning I saw the President again, just the two of us together for a long while, before lunching at the White House, and I shall see him once again tomorrow. Hopkins, Morgenthau and McCloy each make it known that they have obtained the President's approval for the wording of an agreement with us very close to Viénot's draft agreement with the British. I expect to see the paper emerge from the President's pocket tomorrow.* My reply will be that we shall study it at the government level as soon as I get back.[12]

This was the watchword he also gave Pierre Mendès France, his Minister of Finance, whom he met at Washington, coming from the Bretton Woods conference.** This letter to Mendès France is more interesting as it highlights the divide between de Gaulle's wonder and his distrust. "My dear friend, if Morgenthau approaches you, do not negotiate yourself at any price. The diplomatic path is open and it is the only one that allows business to be carried out with a proper distance and reserve and without surprises."[13]

But both by "the diplomatic path" and by those he took here (where the radio and the written press played so essential a part) the "business" of French independence moved forward with great strides. While the General was in the United States, Washington received favourable reports on the conduct of the provisional administration – civil and military – in liberated Normandy.

Every day that passed thrust AMGOT and the supposed "local authorities" somewhat farther into the void. Coulet and Chevigné had a good press. So before he left Washington de Gaulle could cable Algiers, "As to the chief problems of the future, I believe we may suppose that there will no longer be any attempt at settling them without France."

Late in the morning of 10 July, Charles de Gaulle and his team left for New York, where they had to avoid compromising the progress made in Washington: the problem consisted of "not providing the occasion for any popular demonstrations which, at three months from the presidential elections, might seem to be directed against what, until this time, had been the President's policy."[14]

The problem was solved in this way: the mayor of New York, Fiorello La Guardia, a former Republican, had come over to FDR with great enthusiasm, and he was campaigning for him. By personally taking the General's New York triumph in hand he turned it, by association, into a triumph for Roosevelt. "Overflowing with friendship," the mayor of New York received the visitor at the City Hall, where there was such a crowd that some of the old New York Free French were unable to get in.

The little Sicilian had conceived an affection for de Gaulle in which it may be that electoral considerations played only a minor part. La Guardia spoke to and administered this crowd that the General gazed upon for so long that it was with surprise that he at last came to identify himself with it. And now de Gaulle suddenly murmured to Mendès France, who was delighted by the day's very

*An expectation that remained unfulfilled, but not for long.

**Whose object was to set up a worldwide monetary organization.

popular atmosphere, "So in short my supporters are the Negroes and the Puerto Ricans, the misshapen and the cuckolds, the émigrés and the Jews?" "Yes, indeed, General," replied Mendès. "You will have to get used to it. Here you are, turned into the head of a kind of Popular Front."[15]

Was this Charles de Gaulle's first real "mingling with the crowd"? No: there had been 3 June 1943 in Algiers, for example, or the visits to Bayeux and Isigny. But until today the man of 18 June had never been able to appreciate the underlying nature of his struggle, whatever the reasons for his refusal may have been at the beginning. By taking that decision in 1940 the Constable had joined the anti-Nazism camp: a camp which the privileged, the distinguished and the powerful were not always the first to join.

For all those who were cheering him that day in the New York streets, de Gaulle was less a patriotic French general than the leader of a movement and the symbol of a refusal, the refusal with which he had confronted a power that had expelled, persecuted and harried those immigrants who had now become Guardia's and Roosevelt's electors. Perhaps it was not without astonishment that he became aware of this fellow-feeling. But taking the microphone he acknowledged it warmly, in English:

> Since the terrible days of June 1940 how often we have seen encouragement, sympathy and help coming from New York. How often have you yourself, Mr Mayor, expressed and directed this with an eloquence, a fervour and a zeal that the French will never forget! From the very first, your city, which is literally a world, perceived where the soul of France had its being . . . You have listened only to your generous ideals, your faith in the power of right and of democracy. It is up to us Frenchmen to show that we can return help for help, faithfulness for faithfulness.[16]

He also went to meet the French exiles at the headquarters of France for Ever, that association founded in 1941 by Eugène Houdry, a Philadelphia industrialist: this action had earned Houdry insults and disappointments, but he had nevertheless maintained a "Free France" current of opinion in circles where first Vichyism and then Giraudism were more in vogue. The great lawyer Henry Torrès, one of the leaders of France for Ever, welcomed de Gaulle, whose sharp eyes did not fail to recognize among those present the faces of people who not so long ago had been less inclined to support him – people who, according to his caustic words in the *Mémoires de guerre* "had been lavish with their criticisms, and even their insults". He was not a man to forget his grievances easily.

That evening he was torn away from a dinner with Mgr Spellman to be taken to Madison Square Garden, where the famous black singer Marian Anderson in her warm, bell-like voice sang the Marseillaise in his honour. He found this tribute stunning, and in the taxi that was taking them back he mumbled to his ADC, "You must send that woman some flowers."[17]

On 11 July Charles de Gaulle was in Quebec – a place that we shall have occasion to speak of again.* This visit in 1944 in no way foreshadowed that of

*See *De Gaulle: The Ruler (1945–1970)* to be published in 1991.

1967. To be sure, the author of the *Mémoires de guerre* writes that there he felt "submerged by a wave of French pride, soon drowned by one of aching pain." But although the society of Quebec received the General as a head of State in a ceremony that Mgr Vachon, the city's bishop, recalls with emotion,[18] on the whole witnesses do not speak of any waves of enthusiasm: "French Canada" was deeply permeated with the Vichy spirit.

Although he speaks warmly of his reception in Montreal the next day, it is curious to find that it was his stay in Ottawa that seems to have struck General de Gaulle most of all, at least when he was writing his memoirs. Whether it was a question of the federal government's war effort, or the research on nuclear weapons carried out in Canada with the help of French scientists such as Pierre Auger and Bertrand Goldschmidt (who, says de Gaulle, were collaborating "on this apocalyptic work with my authorization"), or the qualities of Prime Minister Mackenzie King, the virtues of Lord Athlone, the Governor-General, or those of General Vanier, who was Ottawa's representative with the GPRF, it was a steady stream of tributes to this federal Canada that later he was to speak of in quite another manner.

Charles de Gaulle landed in Algiers on 13 July and there he received the dividends arising from his journey: a declaration from Washington which certainly contained fewer words than the number of months of battle needed to extort it but which said practically everything – "The United States recognizes that the French Committee of National Liberation is competent to ensure the administration of France," Admittedly, Washington had refrained from speaking of "provisional government"; but as the General said on leaving for America, it was not so much the formal recognition that counted as the general understanding of the relations between the two countries and above all that "administration of France" for which Roosevelt and his colleagues now acknowledged that the GPRF was "competent".

The day before the publication of this decisive communiqué, which the President of the United States had discussed in a very positive manner and at considerable length at a press-conference, Henri Hoppenot cabled Algiers to say that from now on all progress in the relations between the GPRF and London would be extended to Washington and vice versa. In what had to do with the French administration of France, liaison with the Allied armies, and the issue of money for which, as it was acknowledged, the French government was the sole emitting authority, all the aims that de Gaulle had put forward when he proclaimed the GPRF had been attained.

While General de Gaulle was playing the part of a diplomatic Columbus, the negotiations carried on in London between Anthony Eden and Pierre Viénot were reaching their end and were announced by the French representative on 30 June.

But Pierre Viénot did not long survive his success: this forty-six-year-old Socialist had done wonders both as one of Lyautey's colleagues in Morocco and with Léon Blum as a member of the Popular Front government, in which he was Under-Secretary of State for Foreign Affairs; he had been condemned by Vichy and he had escaped from the same prison as Mendès France. He came to London, where, in spite of his fragile health, he took the toughest of tasks, that of being intermediary between de Gaulle and Churchill. During the last month he had been subjected to two extremely trying experiences – the terrible night of 5-6 June, when, as he hastened from the de Gaulle hurricane to the Churchill typhoon, history in its most hysterical form flowed over him; and then the return to French soil on 14 June. He had put up with being so badly treated by the two great men, but he had come back from the fabulous day of 14 June – the sands of Courseulles, the ruins of Isigny, de Gaulle making his way through the wonderstruck crowds – utterly exhausted. It had been too much.

He died of a heart-attack on 20 July 1944, having experienced all these things and having with his own hands (and the brotherly help of Anthony Eden) built up the treaty by which France recovered its independence. His thin brown face with an aquiline nose that made him look so very like the Prince of Condé and his tall bowed figure would no longer be seen in the corridors of the Foreign Office or on the stairs of Carlton Gardens. He had carried out his task. But both de Gaulle and his country were to miss him sorely.

Had his journey to Washington been a complete success? Charles de Gaulle was not so simple-minded, nor indeed so dazzled by his journey, to believe it. He had been overwhelmed by the extraordinary power of America and by the confidence that arose from it; yet when he compared all that strength and that ambition with the realities of France, even if these realities were to be immensely stimulated by an upsurge in national pride and the country's own genius, when he came back to Les Oliviers he was assailed by a kind of deep anxiety. This was what he said to Louis Joxe, a colleague who was already a friend as well: "Where is France in all this?" A pause, and then, "It is in ourselves."[19]

CHAPTER THIRTY-NINE

"Frenchmen, One More Effort"

"We were giving France back Independence, the Empire, and the Sword." The *Mémoires de guerre* are written with a masterly splendour, but they do not always disdain oversimplification.

Independence? The agreements whose negotiations Monnet and Alphand finished at the end of July 1944 in Washington were its legal expression. The Empire? If this was only Africa that would be true, but in the direction of the Near East, we know what burdens were then weighing upon the Levant:* and as for Indo-China, neither a telegram from the President of the GPRF to General Mordant, called upon to head the resistance to the Japanese there, nor the setting up of an ad hoc committee under René Pleven in Algiers could restore it to France. The Sword? It was quite certainly sharper than it had been four years earlier, when the rebel General spoke for the first time on the London radio. Yet, "How short was the sword that France could wield at the moment the Allies were launching their attack upon Europe! Never yet, in so grave a crisis, had our country been reduced to such relatively limited forces."

But what of it? They existed once more, and they were taking part in the battle. The troops that General Juin had led to victory in Italy were being regrouped in Corsica and North Africa to become General de Lattre's First Army,** which, under the command of the American, General Patch, was to march on the Rhine from the shores of Provence, having conquered Elba on 18 June by way of practice. General Leclerc's 2nd Armoured Division was the best equipped of all French units, and it landed in Normandy on 1 August in order to take part in the march on Paris.

Some of the FFI's most daring attempts had been crushed by the enemy, particularly in the Alps and the Massif Central. But in Brittany, where Bourgouin's parachutists supported Guillaudot's maquisards, the occupants withdrew entirely at the end of July 1944 – an operation of great importance, since Eisenhower had let it be known that he would not launch the great offensive in the direction of Paris so long as the peninsula in his rear had not been freed from Wehrmacht units.

At the end of July 1944 there were still three obstacles between Charles de Gaulle and his consecration: a Wehrmacht which under the command of those great

*If territories under mandate are to be reckoned as "Empire".

**Called Army B in the first place.

commanders von Rundstedt and Rommel retained its fighting spirit and strongly resisted the British and American pressure between Caen and Avranches; insurrectional movements, more or less organized by the Communist party, which might have endangered the authority of the State henceforth embodied by the man of Algiers; and a political manoeuvre on the part of Pierre Laval which, if it had been agreed to by the Germans and encouraged by the Americans, might have made de Gaulle run the risk of being, if not excluded, then at least being thrust into the background for a while or compromised.

One indication that de Gaulle did not think the game was over by the end of July is a message he sent on the thirty-first to his delegate in France, Alexandre Parodi: "an important part of the metropolitan territory will be liberated in the next seven or eight weeks. Yet a liberation of Paris in the very near future is not to be expected."[1]

By 1 August 1944, fifty-five days after the landings, only two departments* had been handed over to Coulet's administration: the Manche and the Calvados. The Allied staff's plans had been held up by the very powerful resistance of the Germans in the sectors of Saint-Lô and above all of Caen; the two battles of 11-16 June and 1-10 July were needed to take the town.

But let us hear de Gaulle speaking to the people of France on the Algiers radio on 7 August, after Leclerc's 2nd DB had joined the battle and just before the First Army's landing in Provence. How, all of a sudden, the tone had changed!

> The French battle, the battle of France, is spreading and increasing its pace. While in Normandy the enemy is retreating, in Brittany his resistance is finally collapsing. I tell you that soon, very soon, a powerful French army, equipped with the most modern material and inured to battle, will be engaged on the Inter-Allied front in France. The hour of our great revenge has come! There is not a single Frenchman who does not feel, who does not know that his plain and sacred duty is immediately to take part in the country's supreme warlike effort.[2]

In the meantime two important events had taken place, changing the outlook further: on 20 July, in East Prussia, a military plot had tried to do away with Hitler: Colonel von Stauffenberg, entrusted with the blowing up of the Nazi dictator's headquarters, failed. Hitler was safe, but the purge he began in the Wehrmacht upset the German High Command in France and presently brought Rommel, its most popular leader, to suicide. This directly undermined the determination with which the Nazis had hitherto checked the Allied advance.

It was on 31 July that there came the breakthrough that had been waited for for so long; while Montgomery's British forces round Caen held the mass of the Germans blocking the way to Paris, the American General Patton began a large-scale movement to outflank them in the south, the turning-point of the movement being what was called the "Avranches breakthrough".

Charles de Gaulle paid the utmost attention to this encircling manoeuvre. A great French unit was taking part in it, the unit with the highest standing, the unit

*Out of the 89 in the whole of France. (trs.)

dearest to his heart, General Leclerc's armoured division, which he had literally forced upon Eisenhower to symbolize the French army's share in the liberation of Paris.

Why the 2nd DB? In the first place because of all those companions who had joined de Gaulle's undertaking in the last four years, its commanding officer was the one who best personified its spirit and who most boldly defied an unkind fate; and secondly because it was under the orders of this most uncompromising Gaullist that, in an atmosphere of victory, the fusion between the two armies, that of the Free French and that which Giraud managed to raise against the Germans, had been carried out – a difficult fusion, but, as de Gaulle saw it, more necessary than any other.

It was an amalgamation of the 501 Tank Regiment, with its men wearing the traditional black beret, so obstinate where discipline was concerned that they were said to be commanded by a kind of "soviet of captains",[3] with the custom-loving blue-capped troopers of the 12th Chasseurs d'Afrique under Colonel de Langlade.

We have good evidence for Charles de Gaulle's concern about the 2nd DB's entry into the battle and its conduct. On 12 August he telegraphed to General Koenig: "I wish you to keep me continually and personally informed about [Leclerc division's] operations. I suppose you have taken the necessary steps with the Inter-Allied Command to receive Leclerc's reports without delay as well as information concerning him."[4]

Being in such close touch with the deeds of these most faithful of followers, therefore, it was with delight that de Gaulle saw them race through between Avranches and Mortain with Patton in a dizzying thrust that bore south and then slanted eastwards: Alençon, Le Mans, Chartres. Sometimes in later years General de Gaulle would be found installed before a television-set watching a rugby match in the Five Nations tournament: in 1944 did he know how very like the best rugby Montgomery's manoeuvre was, when he pinned the enemy scrum so the stand-off half, Patton, could make a gap and send that splendid wing three-quarter Leclerc through for a try? We may be confident that he had no need of this sporting metaphor to appreciate the operation as an expert.

The traditional battle on the north-west front was going well at the moment the fighting started in the south. The operation first called Anvil and then Dragoon opened on 15 August. General Patch had been recalled from the Pacific to command the manoeuvre as a whole, sending the American Eighth Army in the direction of Grenoble by the Route Napoléon while General de Lattre, who had landed on the fifteenth between le Rayol, Saint-Raphaël and Cavalaire, had as his objectives Toulon, Marseilles, the Rhône valley, Lyons and the Rhine.

The development of the movement that began with the Avranches break-through bore within it the reconquest of Paris by the American Third Army under General Patton; and the 2nd DB, which belonged to General Gerow's 15th Army Corps, was only one of the ingredients in this Third Army. But when was Paris to be taken? Eisenhower was tempted to thrust northwards to surround the Wehrmacht. Yet from the 15 August onwards the strike of the Paris police made it clear that a Parisian rising was about to try to liberate the capital on its own initiative and perhaps set up a de facto authority with which the head of the Algiers government would have to compound.

General de Gaulle's plan, which naturally aimed at having Paris liberated by the Leclerc division, could be realized only if Eisenhower and Patton agreed first to move in the direction of Paris, placing the Leclerc division in the van, and if the Parisian rising did not outstrip the 2nd DB advance – or was not crushed first, as the rising against the Nazis in Warsaw was crushed.

From this there arose a manoeuvre whose complexity was suited to Charles de Gaulle's political genius: he had both to persuade the Americans to give up their plan – the best from the tactical point of view – which consisted of by-passing Paris in the south, and to make them adopt a new, faster but more costly move; a forced march on Paris that would allow Leclerc to enter the city before the rising had entirely triumphed or had been put down.

Forty years later it is hard to form a very clear idea of what Charles de Gaulle, in August 1944, thought of this insurgent movement, of the part played in it by the Communist Party, and of the danger of such a strategy for law and order in France. The only really direct documents one can consult are the pages of the *Mémoires de guerre* concerning August 1944.[5] However penetrating they may be, however full of facts, judicious evaluations and certain elements of proof, they were if not written then at least published at a time when the relations between the General and the PCF were no longer those of the "great wartime alliance". In the meanwhile there had been fierce conflicts and a certain number of revelations had been made.

Although the General may not have been impartial, he was enough of a historian to be attended to. Yet he was so committed a historian that the present-day observer need not refrain from putting forward other interpretations of the argument.

We have spoken of the uncertainty shown in de Gaulle's directives to the leaders of the home Resistance from 6 June 1944 onwards, calling for a mass rising while at the same time wanting to make Eisenhower say that the general insurrection might be premature, letting Koenig call for "a pause" in the "immediate action" and then glorifying the sacrifice of those who had spontaneously gone into action from the tribune of the Algiers assembly on 25 July and on the radio on 7 August. But although he then spoke of the battle of "our troops of the interior" in the highest terms, on 11 August we find him writing a new and very much more cautious "directive to the resistants":

> For Paris and the great occupied cities:
> 1. Do not carry out tasks useful to the enemy; if the enemy tries to enforce them, go on strike.
> 2. If the enemy weakens, seize his employees in the factory whatever their jobs may be. Use them as hostages.
> 3. In any event, prevent the retreating enemy from taking his staff and machines with him.

4. Return to work at once and in an orderly manner as soon as the Allied forces arrive.[6]

An odd, scrupulously realistic document which shows an anxiety that the popular forces should be carefully controlled by giving them objectives that were civilian as much as military.

Three days later, in order to make the authority of Algiers even more certain, he took the double decision of appointing Alexandre Parodi delegate-general in the occupied territories and a full member of the government, as Jean Moulin had been the year before. And in a telegram he sent to Roosevelt the same day he thought it proper to assert that according to the reports he was receiving from France, "it will be possible to establish order there at the liberation without any great upheaval."[7]

It is worth noting this optimistic note, which corresponds to the greater part of the information then coming from the "liberated territories" – information confirmed three days later by André Le Troquer, who had been installed at Bayeux in the government's name on 12 August. This serene tone contrasts with that used by the General in his memoirs:

> Some political elements of the Resistance wanted to profit from the exaltation, perhaps from the state of anarchy, that the struggle would produce in the capital to seize the levers of command before I could take them over. Quite naturally this was the Communists' intention. If they succeeded in setting themselves up as the leaders of the rising and in taking control of the forces in Paris, it would be easy for them there to establish a *de facto* government in which they would play the leading part. On my arrival I should find this "popular" government functioning; it would crown me with laurels and invite me to take whatever office it might appoint; and it would pull all the strings until the day the dictatorship said to be that of the proletariat should be established.[8]

Is it accurate to set the popular rising and the State in opposition as boldly as the author of the *Mémoires de guerre* does in this place, letting it be understood that the one necessarily called the other in question, and that the FTP, the Front National and those Resistance organizations with a strong Communist element (such as the CNR and its active force the COMAC) aimed at bringing down Vichy and the Nazis only to be better prepared for blocking de Gaulle's path or for seizing power before him?

Generally speaking, at present historians tend to disparage this view. Some, like J.-B. Duroselle, quote the reports sent at that time to the General by his Ambassador in Moscow, Roger Garreau, on his frequent conversations with the Secretary-General of the PCF, Maurice Thorez, who assured him, in January and then in April 1944, that his party excluded any taking of power "at the time of the liberation [or] during the period of the country's convalescence and restoration". And Thorez said this with an insistence and a precision that did not fail to impress the diplomat.

It is even acknowledged that however exalted the leaders of the PCF in metropolitan France (headed by Duclos and Frachon) may have been by the party's astonishing progress since the beginning of 1944, with its great increase in membership, they too refused to lose their heads, and they made a clear-minded analysis of the relative strengths of a party supported by a poorly-equipped militia, and the mass of the Allied armies, which would quite certainly support the General against any form of "subversion".

Even so the question remains open about the FTP. Certainly the FTP were a movement dependent on the PCF, but they possessed a certain operational autonomy with regard to the party and they were led by men overflowing with a self-confidence won by succeeding in very perilous trials – men who were filled with a revolutionary romanticism. Might not the FTP replace "scientific" analysis with something resembling obstinacy? Were not men like Charles Tillon, their national leader, or Georges Guingouin, that Tito from Limoges, be tempted to think that power was at the rifle's end?

Tillon, whom I questioned in June 1983, denied it firmly:

> Our aim was purely anti-Fascist. We were fighting to root Fascism out of France – both its German and its French aspects. We had never thought of taking over power. We had a concrete part to play in the French battle, and it was directed only at ridding the country of the occupying forces and the Vichy authorities. Even when we had seen the Allies' distrust of anything that could look like revolutionary attitudes among us, and even when we saw that Vichy's men were often replaced by people with ideas of much the same kind, we never thought of using our weapons against anyone belonging to London or Algiers.[9]

Jacques Soustelle, who was then Director-General of the Special Services and of the Action Committee for metropolitan France, provides a large number of quotations from some of the chief authorities of the Front National and the COMAC, and he speaks of the "Communist take-over of all the military formations, that is to say of the levers of power".[10] He wrote this in *Envers et contre tout*, and he remains persuaded of it still.

One of the Resistance leaders closest to the Communists, Pascal Copeau, Emmanuel d'Astier's deputy at the head of Libération, maintains that "it might be said that in the spring of 1944 there were two authorities: the authority of the home Resistance and the authority of General de Gaulle. There were difficulties but the primacy conceded to General de Gaulle's authority was never really contested."[11] This was also the opinion of another of d'Astier's comrades and a former fellow-traveller, Raymond Aubrac. But not, as we know, of Henri Frenay.

On 20 July 1944 Emile Laffon, an important figure in the delegation attached to Parodi, sent Algiers a report in which he asserted that "there is no real Communist danger for tomorrow. They want to obtain everything by legal means. They will certainly not take the initiative of a break, either now or even in the first stages of the liberation".[12] Not only did de Gaulle confirm this point of view but he then agreed with those who were in favour of the legalization and integration of the

PCF as opposed to those who, like Roland Pré (Oronte) already had the witch-hunting reaction.

Let us leave the last word to Claude Bourdet, who, at the head of Combat, often had difficulties with the PCF and its official or disguised representatives:

> It is hard to answer with a yes or a no. In any event a distinction must be made between what we thought at the time and what we know at present. In 1943–1944, when we saw an increasing number of active members infiltrating the organizations at all levels, it was difficult for us to suppose that – to use Malraux's words about the RPF* – the Communists were advancing "to the edge of the Rubicon merely to sit there with a fishing-rod". And yet when you look at things closer, away from what was then the prevalent atmosphere, you see that they did everything a political organization ordinarily does – making sure of as many positions as possible with a view, sooner or later, to the exercise of all or part of the power. That is the essence of political action.
>
> I do not think that de Gaulle, as I knew him, believed for a moment in what he wrote ten years later in the *Mémoires de guerre* about the "Communist plot". Personally I do not think that, even at the regional level, there were one or several Communist plans aimed at taking over power in the summer of 1944. Both in the COMAC and at the head of the FTP people made serious analyses: the ratio of power was not in their favour.[13]

As we shall see in the liberation of Paris, it sometimes happens that the current of events takes little notice of deep-laid plans and intentions. And although it is true that the General's description of his relations with the Communists in August 1944 in his *Mémoires* seems a little dramatized, it is none the less true that the Parisian rising set in action forces and emotions perfectly capable of taking everybody unawares and going far beyond the plans of either Jacques Duclos or Charles de Gaulle.

Whether it really existed or not, therefore, a threat against the accession of de Gaulle was taking shape on his left. The manoeuvre that was then beginning on his right, on the other hand, was far more discernible. It had two separate aspects. The first, coming from Pétain's side if not initiated by him, tended to make the General the Marshal's legitimate heir. The second, a move on the part of Laval, was aimed at setting the barrier of the Third Republic's institutions between de Gaulle and power; in a way this was a resurrection of Alexis Léger's idea of the legal vacuum, a notion that he had elaborated in Washington and that the former Secretary-General of the Quai d'Orsay had been selling to his State Department friends since 1942.

In November 1943 the Marshal had thought of summoning the 1940 Chambers and he had appointed a directorate of seven members to ensure the transition between himself and a Gaullist regime whose advent already seemed to him inevitable. Rather than be expelled, why not come forward as a generous donor?

How could the men who in 1940 had assumed power in the name of reality and

*The Rassemblement du Peuple Français. (trs.)

material facts suppose that, contemptuously rejected by the man who had been nothing when they had almost everything, they could come to an understanding with him when they no longer amounted to anything and he was already almost everything?

It must be admitted that the old Marshal had few illusions. He said to Admiral Auphan, the best-known of the emissaries he was using at the time, "I know de Gaulle. He is too vain. In any case, you can tell him that I never meant to have him shot." And he added, "I am ready to stand aside. Do not let us break with legality; do not let us break with legitimacy, let us avoid revolution." Gabriel Auphan, once Darlan's principal private secretary, had of all the ministers been the most zealous in urging the Marshal to withdraw in November 1942: on 11 August 1944 he set out to meet de Gaulle, and on 27 August he was able to have a message given to him in Paris suggesting an amicable transfer of power in order "to avoid civil war". A suggestion that General de Gaulle refused to consider.

On 14 August, three days after Admiral Auphan had left for Paris, Henri Ingrand, who had just been appointed Commissioner of the Republic at Clermont-Ferrand, was called upon by another Vichy emissary, Captain Oliol, who said that the Marshal, fearing that the Germans or the Milice might attempt to seize him, wished to put himself under the protection of the FFI. He proposed a declaration advising the French to follow General de Gaulle; this would "ensure the continuity of legitimate authority and avoid a provisional government's being installed by the Americans".[14] A remarkable concern, coming from a man whose government had had protectors of a somewhat more compromising nature.

Ingrand and his colleagues sent this message on to Algiers, where, says Soustelle, it only arrived on 21 August, after the General had left for France. The director of the DGSS "in agreeement with d'Astier for once" was of the opinion that there was no question of having "de Gaulle enthroned by Pétain" and at once cabled Clermont-Ferrand to put an end to this attempt of "establishing a link between the Vichy usurpation and the provisional government". Vichy was not discouraged: another messenger, who used the name of Satine, appeared, and he saw fit to warn Algiers, by way of Ingrand, that the Americans had forbidden de Gaulle to set foot on French territory unless there was an agreement between Pétain and him.[15]

The plan set in motion by Pierre Laval at the same time was rather more serious. Laval did not intend to turn himself into de Gaulle's sponsor but to keep him out by resuscitating a ghostly parliament – that of the Third Republic, whose throat he himself had cut and whose body he had trampled under foot on 10 July 1940 at Vichy. Laval could only succeed in this manoeuvre with the consent of the Germans, the support of the Americans, and the collusion of some one of the outstanding figures of the Republic. As we shall see, neither the first nor the third condition was fulfilled, while the second remained in suspension. In any event it seemed in that summer of 1944 that Pierre Laval was less abhorred by Franklin Roosevelt than he was by Adolf Hitler.

The man Laval picked upon as the basis for his operation was Edouard Herriot, the president of the 1936 Chamber of Deputies. Jules Jeanneney, the president of the Senate, was even more of a symbol, but although he was still living at liberty in the region of Grenoble, everyone knew that he was in favour of de Gaulle and moreover that he was not easily managed. Herriot was scarcely less favourable to the General (Laval must have known of his letter of May 1943), but his character was not so resolute.

According to his biographer Alfred Mallet, Laval arrived in Paris on 10 August, after having tried in vain to persuade Pétain to take refuge in Eisenhower's headquarters: there he had his plan approved by an impromptu assembly of mayors of the Parisian region (appointed by Vichy). He sounded former ministers like the Radical Anatole de Monzie and the Socialist Paul Faure without success, but his friend Otto Abetz gave him the green light and he then tried to get in touch with the Americans. Enfière, a friend of Herriot's, told Allen Dulles about the plan: Dulles was the head of the American intelligence services in Europe, and he was based at Berne: the reply he had conveyed to Laval was simply: "If you have Herriot set free, Roosevelt will bear your action in mind."[16] In his *Mémoires* de Gaulle wrongly interprets this by the words, "He confirmed that Washington would look favourably on a plan that tended to give de Gaulle a superior or to set him aside."[17]

On 12 August, while Patton's armour was racing towards Chartres and de Lattre was putting the last touches to the preparations for his Provence battle, Pierre Laval travelled to Nancy to fetch Herriot, who was interned in the Mareville hospital, and bring him back to Paris – "without any conditions", he states. It was only a question of summoning the 1940 parliament. Whatever people may have said at the time, Herriot's mind was still working quite well, and he knew his Laval: he studied the map, grasped the situation, and to gain time said that he would do nothing without having consulted Jeanneney.

But the extreme collaborationists and the Führer's General Staff had already got wind of Laval's operation. Although, as de Gaulle says, "Abetz, Ribbentrop and others were of the opinion that once France was liberated it would be as well if there were an executive in Paris that would drag out the sequels of Vichy rather than a fearless and irreproachable government," the true ideologues of Nazism were angered by this expedient, which looked like a tribute rendered by the new Europe to the symbols of democracy, that abomination: on the one hand Déat, Darnand and Brinon, and on the other Hitler and Himmler put an end to the manoeuvre. Herriot was arrested on 16 August and taken to Germany the next day; he was interned near Potsdam (and liberated by the Red Army eight months later).

The Algiers government had just suffered two defeats: the one, psychological and just plainly humiliating, was the Inter-Allied staff's firm refusal of an operation in the Massif Central known as Caïman (or C) which de Gaulle was much attached to, he having thought of it and entrusted it to his close colleague and confidential friend Pierre Billotte. Carried out almost entirely by French troops, it was to have been "from the French national point of view, the final consecration of the efforts of metropolitan France to free itself from the enemy."[18] General Maitland Wilson and then Eisenhower, basing themselves on the lack of means that could be put at the disposal of the GPRF and not being at all anxious to start too many undertakings, called a halt, depriving de Gaulle both of a symbolic operation and an opportunity to station reliable troops in the Auvergne, which the late régime had made its sanctuary but in which there were very large numbers of maquis.

Yet this mortifying set-back was nothing compared with the appalling moral and human defeat of the Vercors – the fall of the Vercors. These bastions were the most important application of the strategy of the "mobilizing maquis" worked out in the days of General Delestraint, and they were intended to become the first morsels of liberated France: they brought together several thousands of maquisards, and they had been denounced as inefficient and dangerous by the best specialists in underground warfare – beginning with the FTP.

Later, Colonel Descour, the military augur of the Rhone-Alps region, denied having wanted to make the Vercors into a bastion capable of defending itself against any German counter-offensive; his wish was rather to make it a centre from which many-sided actions could radiate in various directions, and coordinating with the landings in the south.

On 6 June, when General de Gaulle had called upon the "sons of France to fight with all the means at their disposal", the maquisards of the Vercors, some three thousand men, might well believe that the moment had come for them to take up their action stations, sure that the Algiers government had made preparations to support them and that the Allied armies would very soon come up from the south. Between 28 June and 7 July the parachutings became more frequent and instructors were sent from London. But the landings began later than they had expected, while at the same time the disturbances in the mountains over Grenoble had become so evident that the occupying forces could not fail to react.

The leaders of the maquis knew from the first days of July that the tragedy was on the way. The help received from London and Algiers bore no comparison with the repressive forces mustered by the Germans. On 8 July, Dalloz came to Algiers to ask for a rapid increase in the sending of arms and munitions, if not an earlier landing in the south. Three parachute-drops were carried out from Algiers on July 11, 16, and 17 while London supplied the region with more than a thousand more containers.[19] But on 20 July the Germans launched a massive operation, their great numbers overwhelming the maquisards: 650 were killed,* while 280 civilians in the village of Vassieux were tortured and massacred by a rogue SS regiment.

In his very fine account *Le peuple impopulaire* Alain Prévost, Jean's son, maintains that the maquisards of the Vercors had been abandoned by Algiers and London, too "red" for their liking.[20] Alain Le Ray strongly disagrees with this view. In the first place he recalls that it was a spontaneous rising of dissidents which brought these excessive numbers on to the plateau and then a collective over-enthusiasm that made them break out too soon.[21]

The fall of the Vercors nevertheless brought about a violent crisis between General de Gaulle and the Communists who were members of the Algiers government, for Fernand Grenier, Commissioner for Air and a leader of the PCF told the press that the crushing of the maquisards was due to the deficiencies of the command and that the GPRF was responsible for the "abandonment" of the Vercors.

*Including the great writer, Jean Prévost.

De Gaulle's reaction was what might have been expected. Louis Joxe describes it very well:

> On the morning of 27 July the General arrived in the Moorish setting of the Summer Palace, his face expressionless and livid. No question of setting about the agenda. He addressed Grenier directly, reproaching him with having accused the government of showing a "wait and see" attitude which the Communists looked upon as a crime against the country. [De Gaulle insisted that Grenier should either apologize in writing or resign; and Grenier could have Joxe to help him in the drafting of his letter.]
>
> Everyone withdrew. Billoux* stayed with Grenier and the three of us looked at one another for a long while. Grenier wrote. Outside, the whole government gazed attentively at the gravel on the paths. The General walked to and fro. The atmosphere had never been so tense. But [Grenier and Billoux] chose the political expediency, the session began again, the General read the text put forward by Grenier: "Let us move on to the agenda. The incident is closed."

*The other Communist minister.

CHAPTER FORTY

The Consecration

What did he have in common with the man who had left France four years earlier, a half-clandestine traveller into the impossible, clinging to the raft of the vanquished, more an actor than a general, more illegal than heroic, more of a scandal than a prophet?

From failure to rejection, condemned by Vichy, made game of by the eminent, reviled by his equals, denied by Roosevelt, disowned by Churchill, he had survived and increased in size; he had mastered fate. And now, shaped for four years on end by the most dangerous "surge of history" ever faced by a man sailing the high seas in a cockle-shell, here he was, turned into himself at last by the trial.

We know that he had never doubted that he would be at the head of "French affairs". General at fifteen or lecturer at the Ecole de Guerre, author of *Le Fil de l'épée*, colonel of a tank regiment or Under-Secretary of State – these were only the manifestations of leadership in the process of formation. Gaston Palewski had a confused perception of it at their very first meeting in 1934, though he did not like to ask himself the question "What would the heads of French parliamentarianism amount to, compared with such a man?" He had never even had to confront them, they all having come over to him very soon, consenting, not without magnanimity, to his "taking over the watch".

At first he had surprised people: that mythical name coming from the remotest ages, that voice, now strident and now deep, that came with its horn and trumpet tones from the other side of the sea, making its way through fogs and jamming. Then he had moved, a pathetic watchman who, not content with standing upright, sent true reasons for hope through the darkness. He had also angered some with his conscientious presumption and his denial of an obvious collective collapse that went much farther and much deeper than the humiliations of Rethondes and the presence of field-grey uniforms on the Champs-Elysées. And lastly he had convinced them, when the few fruits of the Armistice had gone bad, when the Marshal had preferred to remain imprisoned at Vichy, and when he, the émigré, had obtained an undeniable vote from the fighting-men inside the country.

And here he was at last, marching towards his consecration through a landscape of ruins and barbed wire, in a confused noise made up of shrieks from torture-chambers and the song of the resistants, the uncompromising bearer of a hieratic legitimacy – a consecration with no Rheims cathedral, no robe studded with bees or fleurs-de-lys, no sacramental formula or lay Mass.

The Republic could not wait to be proclaimed by his voice – even though it might fear being stifled under his weight. All he had to do was to appear, spread his prodigious antennae and speak with his vibrant, crusade-preaching voice for Coutances, Rennes, Chartres and Paris.

In the first place it was the giant who struck the people's imagination. This height of rather more than six feet four inches stalking above the ordinary motions of his contemporaries attracted the attention of the most indifferent. Curious windmill motions, surprising jerks, strange lurches.

"An odd-looking fellow" is a usual description of someone out of the ordinary. No words could suit him better. Merely by walking into a room, merely by standing, high above the crowd, his arms like maypole ribbons, he was continually making people stare. If only the ground were suitable, as it was near Montcornet in May 1940 for example, he saw fit to increase his height by standing on some knob, bank or mound, thus adding more layers of air between the eyes of those addressing him and his own. Thunderbolts ought to come from on high.

Then his face. Whether or not it was crowned by that képi in the shape of an imperfect tube that the French army inflicts upon its higher ranks, it was rich in unlikely planes and above all in a nose whose Bourbonian proportions seemed all the greater for being directed at his opponent like a gun-barrel, a nose so large that it took away from the chin's asperity and made the beholder forget the forehead bordered with brown locks that seemed to have been plastered flat by some imaginary rain.

A face of a time before our ordinary and orderly epoch, a head for a helmet, a ruff or a periwig, a face like a parchment scribbled upon by Froissart or Commines, lit by the cautious gleam of little eyes, flashing like a sentinel's bayonet from the depths of their cavernous orbits.

At the walls of Jerusalem, Godefroy de Bouillon and Renaud de Châtillon must have had this heavy bearing, these vast gestures, those angry outbursts and those flashing glances that the French, after Winston Churchill, Robert Murphy and Henri Giraud, were to learn to recognize during the summer of 1944.

Did this unusual body distress him? He paid no attention to it at all, feeling neither heat nor cold and being very insensitive to pain – pain arising from wounds between 1914 and 1916 but not from illness, which he was almost always spared.

He did not mind bad weather. He had a good appetite; he ate fast, drank moderately and could do without food for long periods. This great frame in which he housed his great dream did not inconvenience him. Indeed he thought it had certain advantages: in the first place it turned him into a semaphore, giving his gestures such as the V formed by his arms, a superhuman dimension.

He was a soldier. Up until the period we have reached, August 1944, he was in no hurry to take off his uniform, even when it was a question of charming foreign political leaders or statesmen, and he wore mufti only with his family. He took pleasure in the straps, accoutrements, sword-belts, boots and leggings – everything that irks an ordinary man. It was in vain that he despised his colleagues: he found it very hard to suppress the reflexes of his caste, he loved going back to the staff-officer's style, drafting communiqués, using the barracks vocabulary and even returning to the ancient jokes of Saint-Cyr. And he devoted many pages of his *Mémoires de guerre* to talking shop.

It is true that war is never anything but the most convulsive form of politics. This he both said and wrote. And in the order of values he set the writer above the great civil servant and the great civil servant above the officer. But after all that was where his profession lay. Although he had no great esteem for military men, he valued warriors very highly indeed. He had chosen the profession of arms, he had exercised it with passion, and it was a calling that he still loved enough to keep his most savagely sarcastic remarks for it.

He was a politician. He was ambitious in his views, clever in his proceedings, relentless in execution, attentive to circumstances; his only inhibition was that "idea" he had conceived of France, as upright as a cathedral spire, an idea that gave his bearing a stiffness. A great project is of course fitting for a great politician. But even so he must know how to avoid becoming its prisoner; he must be able to cast about, to try other doors, to follow other scents.

He was an intellectual: by which I mean that he was a man whose life, decisions and acts were inspired and motivated by ideas. Of course this man of action strongly distrusted doctrines and applied himself to a proper evaluation of circumstances. As he saw it, doctrines were harmful in that they caused the free motion of ideas to coagulate into systems. This Machiavellian was an idealist who, paying great attention to the real, rendered it conceptual by a continual effort of will. In those famous words which serve as his motto for ever, "All my life, I have formed a certain idea of France", the key word seems to be "formed". Inspired by an idea, certainly; but by an idea that he had formed for himself, that he had carved according to his own image, an exacting, proud, inaccessible idea.

A realist? Undoubtedly in immediate aims and procedures, and where the strategy was long-sighted only to correct the general myopia that prevailed all round him in the government, the institutions, his colleagues, the world at large . . . But he was a realist who imagined, one who with his powerful hands manipulated, kneaded and dealt with data that his inventive spirit had already shaped.

And then again he was a man. A man whose solicitude for his family, even in the most violent times, strikes the observer – his care for Philippe's studies and then his service appointments, for Elizabeth's work, and for the welfare of Anne. Writers quote letters to his wife which show a surprising tenderness and freedom, though they never brush the weight of history aside. He did not think Yvonne unworthy of being told about his most important cares as a "symbol" and as President of the GPRF.

Many of his colleagues who had seen the pitiless roughness of his conduct and had suffered from his deviations have doubted whether so savage a fighter can have been a good Christian. It would scarcely be wise to offer a simple answer to this question. Yet it may be observed that, at the end of 1940, when a London public-relations agent asked him to give a description of himself, the second phrase in his self-portrait was "I believe in God". And we may take notice of his reply when his nephew Michel Cailliau asked him whether his great scheme was compatible with religious belief: "I am a Christian by history and geography."

Lastly he was an artist. The writer never resigned in him although he wrote with difficulty, crossing out and rephrasing his sentences. Was he looking for subjects worthy of him and of an art that would have been out of place dealing with the affairs of César Birotteau or even those of Paul Reynaud's cabinet? "De Gaulle is a man who never stops scribbling drafts of his memoirs, wherever he is," observed the Ambassador Jean Chauvel, a man who had watched him with great indulgence.

Redraw the map of the world to find material for the writing of a masterpiece in the process? Why this dichotomy, when writing may prove to be the man of action's finest weapon if not indeed the finest form of action? "I do not speak without a purpose," he used to say. And it is true that when he seized the remains of a slaughtered country with the intention of bringing it back to life and restoring at least the outward show of its greatness, he found nothing better than words.

From behind those words that he had been launching like so many bottles into the sea, these four years past, the French were to see a body and a face come into sight. But though the words were thus incarnated, it was still words that were to lead the nation, words hammered out and put together by a tragic poet who seemed to be concerned with magnifying France solely to make a tottering history suit his majestic style.

On Friday 18 August, while the American armour was racing towards Chartres, while de Lattre's vanguard was within sight of Toulon, and while in Paris the explosion was imminent, Charles de Gaulle took off for France. The issue was very close at hand: he was in a hurry to seize the controls, and to do so on the spot.

The day before, the Gestapo had taken Herriot away from Paris and Laval's manoeuvre had thus failed. Two days later the Marshal, having given up the idea of placing himself "under the protection" of the FFI ("They will murder you" he had been told by those close to him), was taken towards Belfort by a Wehrmacht unit, though not without having protested against this "forcible action which made it impossible for him to exercise his prerogatives as head of the French State".[1]

At the airfield of Maison-Blanche, the Americans insisted that de Gaulle should get into the Flying Fortress rather than his usual modest Lockheed. But for many reasons, easy to imagine when one knows the man, the simplest being that he preferred his usual pilot, Lionel de Marmier, the President of the GPRF travelled in the unarmed old Lockheed.

Having made a halt at Casablanca, he observed that his plane was ready to take off again at once, whereas the American Fortress – in which General Juin was flying – was delayed by a mechanical failure, a failure that happened again when they stopped at Gibraltar. He set off again and landed at last at eight o'clock on Sunday 20 August at the little airfield of Maupertuis in Normandy.

He was received by Koenig and Coulet and he asked them for their news. It was good. In the north-western sector Patton's drive was moving fast, following a curve that surrounded the capital. In Paris, where his two chief representatives Parodi and Chaban had agreed that the rising, fomented by the Communists for several days past, should now begin, the police, who were on strike, had seized the Prefecture; fighting had broken out almost everywhere; representatives of the GPRF were taking over the ministries; the Resistance had seized many of the suburban municipal buildings – and most observers reported weak resistance on the part of the occupying forces.

General de Gaulle, taken at once to Eisenhower's headquarters, congratulated his host on "the astonishing speed of the Allied forces' success" and then listened as the Supreme Commander, more cordial than ever (and now accompanied by General Bill Morgan, who never faltered in his support of the French cause with his chief*), explained the progress of the operations and the possibilities that were coming into view. While the Allied left wing – Montgomery's army group – was advancing towards Rouen, the right wing under Bradley was carrying out the immense manoeuvre entrusted to Patton and performed by two columns, the first with Mantes as its objective, to the north, and the other with Melun, to the south of the capital. And from there Eisenhower was getting ready to launch Patton and his armoured columns towards Lorraine.

But what about Paris? De Gaulle expressed his astonishment:

> I cannot understand why, since you cross the Seine at Melun, at Mantes and at Rouen, it is only at Paris that you do not cross. If it were a question of an ordinary place and not the capital of France, my opinion would not be binding on you, because normally the conduct of operations is your concern. But the fate of Paris is of essential consequence to the French government. For this reason I think myself obliged to intervene and to urge you to send my troops. It goes without saying that it is the French second armoured division that must be selected in the first place.[2]

If we are to believe the President of the GPRF, Eisenhower "did not conceal his embarrassment"; he spoke of the risk of destruction consequent upon an operation aimed at Paris and said that "the Resistance had begun fighting too soon". Why too soon, asked de Gaulle, when the Allies had reached the Seine at several points and were less than fifty kilometres from Paris? The Allied Supreme Commander, who gave de Gaulle the impression of inwardly agreeing with him, assured him that although he could not fix an exact date he would soon give the order to march on Paris, the 2nd DB being of course entrusted with the mission.

De Gaulle knew how much Eisenhower sympathized with what he represented, and the American's shuffling puzzled him. Also, why had the Leclerc division been moved from Patton's Third Army, always in the vanguard, to Hodges' Seventh, which was held in reserve? Was it to prevent the 2nd DB "racing towards the Eiffel Tower"?[3]

And why had the agreement settling the relations between the Allied commander and the French forces that had just been reached with Washington and London still not been signed between Eisenhower and Koenig? What did these delays and evasions really mean? And for fear that the reader should believe that his questions were prompted by some ill-will towards the President of the United States, the author of the *Mémoires de guerre* thinks it proper to say "From his contacts with the General Staff Juin drew the same conclusions as myself."[4]

Walking among the crowds in the Cotentin, the Perche and Brittany swept away these unpleasant mists: from Cherbourg to Coutances, Avranches, Fougères and

*This is pointed out particularly by Hettier de Boislambert, liaison officer with the American general staff.

Rennes, de Gaulle felt himself borne up "by a great swell of popular enthusiasm and emotion". From the capital of Brittany he sent two messages whose effects were to be felt in the next few days. The first, to Dwight Eisenhower:

> My dear General,
> The information I have received from Paris today makes me think that in view of the almost complete disappearance of the police and of the German forces in Paris and the extreme shortage of food there, serious trouble is to be expected in the capital very shortly. I believe it is necessary to have Paris occupied by the French and Allied forces as soon as possible even if it means a certain amount of fighting and a certain amount of damage within the city. If a disorderly situation were now to arise in Paris, it would be difficult to take things in hand again without serious incidents, and this might even hinder subsequent military operations. I am sending you General Koenig, who has been appointed military governor of Paris.

Once he had sent this fresh appeal to the man upon whom everything depended, the General telegraphed to his colleagues in the Algiers government:

> The people's spirit is truly magnificent. The great and urgent question is that of Paris. The Germans have left only a few military elements there. The French police have vanished. The Vichy administration is powerless. Certain elements of the population have begun pillaging the food-stocks and the shops. If the Allied forces do not occupy Paris very soon, grave disturbances may occur.[5]

On the same day de Gaulle received a letter that Leclerc had sent from his headquarters near Argentan. From this it appeared that there is no man so daring but that he may find his master: the head of the 2nd DB, having given a rapid summary of the last two weeks' operations through Normandy, announced that he, Leclerc, had just taken the decision to send a detachment towards Paris; it was commanded by Major de Guillebon, whose orders were "to make contact, to inform me, and to enter Paris if the enemy withdraws".

When one knows what the great Inter-Allied operations amounted to, the extreme care in their preparation, the complexity of the machinery set in motion, the initiative taken by Leclerc at this point, sending this armoured column across the countryside before receiving Eisenhower's orders, was quite certainly a court-martial offence.* These men really were steeped through and through with the spirit of 18 June. In any case, the next day de Gaulle telegraphed to this leader after his own heart: "I approve of your intentions. Eisenhower has promised me that you were going to be sent to Paris. I shall sleep at Le Mans tonight and shall try to meet you tomorrow."[6]

* * *

*The reaction of General Gerow, Leclerc's immediate superior, was tough. In vain. Leclerc was tougher.

The question of taking over power in Paris, which was still to occasion such stormy arguments, had been carefully worked out by the GPRF's general delegation in France. In a telegram sent to Algiers on 11 August Alexandre Parodi and his team defined the measures taken in common by the delegation, the military command, the police and the Parisian liberation committee in these words:

> The governmental sector, liberated by force, will be directly under the orders of the government. The non-governmental sector will be liberated by the FFI and placed at the disposal of the Parisian liberation committee. The liberation of the capital will be entrusted to forces that are composed of the following elements: Garde républicaine and gendarmerie as to three quarters, patriotic militia and FFI as to one quarter. Mixed detachments are provided for all buildings of a symbolic nature. The police themselves and elements of the Resistance will carry out the occupation of the Prefecture of Police.

It is easy to imagine that on reading this paper, a compromise between the State and the people's organizations, Charles de Gaulle decided that it was far better that he should be on the spot.

From this point on it was necessary to try to synchronize two lines of approach: the one, as it were eruptive, on the part of Paris to liberate itself; the other, tactical, on the part of de Gaulle to hasten the intervention of the 2nd DB and for himself to reach the centre of the position in which the fate of millions of Parisians and his own legitimacy were at stake. But any man who wished to synchronize and combine these two operations had to take into account the influences of at least six separate forces:

Firstly: the German occupant, embodied by a fairly traditional leader, General von Choltitz, an officer who was no more inclined to destroy Paris (although he had been ordered by the Führer to do so)* than he was to deal with the "terrorists" who had risen up from the Paris streets: he still had about 25 000 men, several hundred armoured vehicles and guns, and an impressive reserve of explosives.

Secondly: the representatives of the GPRF (Parodi, Chaban, Roland Pré, the prefect of police Luizet, etc.), the gendarmerie and the police – in other words the State. In general, unity prevailed, though there was a passing disagreement between Chaban (who, having information coming from the Allies, tried to check any rising, convinced that if it were left to itself it might end in an urban Vercors and infinitely more bloody) and Parodi, who did not underestimate the risks either but who was more aware of another vital factor – the unity of the Resistance. Delaying the explosion meant running the risk of turning it into an implosion and bringing about the separation of the movement into revolutionaries on the one hand (the COMAC, the Front National, the Communists) and the supporters of the State on the other. In that case civil war would loom ahead.

Thirdly: the Resistance movements, assembled in the CPL (Comité parisien de

*_Paris brûle-t-il?_ is an interesting book on the subject written by D. Lapierre and L. Collins.

la libération) whose president was the Communist André Tollet, an unusually impetuous man who had not been endowed with any subtlety of mind, and whose political head was the very intelligent Léo Hamon (who for his part was haunted by the siege of Warsaw and the massacre of the insurgent population by the SS while the Red Army remained coldly inactive).

Fourthly: the FFI, whose regional leader (for the Ile-de-France as a whole) was Colonel Tanguy, "Rol", a Communist with real military qualities, a man who had fought in Spain and who was thoroughly accustomed to street warfare: his role was all the more important in that he was wholly supported, if not urged on, by the COMAC, the CNR's military committee, whose most active members were Villon and Maurice Kriegel, alias Valrimont,* both of whom belonged to the PCF.

Fifthly: the 2nd DB that de Gaulle was so longing to commit to the battle as soon as possible – and it was known that by 22 August the division had pushed a very hazardous vanguard as far as the neighbourhood of Versailles.

Sixthly: the American army, the supreme but peripheral arbiter which would intervene only to support the blows inflicted by others but which would on a variety of occasions influence the decisions and the calculations of those concerned.

On 22 August General de Gaulle was at Le Mans. It was there that a message from Parodi told him that the truce – or rather the suspension of arms - proposed by the Swedish consul Raoul Nordling and accepted by Parodi, Chaban and Hamon during the night of 19 August but opposed by the Communists had been broken as early as the next day, though not, as its supporters emphasized, without "having gained time, thus allowing a better synchronization of the rising and the arrival of the 2nd DB".[7]

As the fighting started again – not that it had ever really stopped[8] – Charles de Gaulle learnt, on the twenty-second, that most of the public buildings in Paris were held by the Resistance, but that foreseeing the hard fighting that was going to follow the breaking of the truce, the FFI were asking for the air force to attack the German troops being called back to Paris, the dropping of Allied airborne commandos in the outskirts of the capital, and the flying-in of weapons.

Lastly, during that evening, the President of the GPRF heard the news that he had been waiting for most impatiently: Eisenhower had just opened the way to Paris for Leclerc. But the Supreme Commander had not yielded only to General de Gaulle's requests. Another factor had influenced his decision: this was the intervention of one of Rol's staff-officers, Major Cocteau, who had left Paris for Corbeil on the twentieth, hoping to persuade Patton to enter Paris to support the insurgents.* The commander of the Third Army had sent him on to the staff of his superiors, Hodges and Bradley. Moved by Cocteau's account of the risks the Parisians were running, of their determination and of the immense psychological

*His book, *La Libération*, is nothing more than a call for a "national uprising".

*This seems to contradict the argument that the Communists wished to delay the arrival of the Americans as long as possible. Unless the situation was then thought so dangerous that it was better to make sure of the victory in Paris even though the political exploitation of the success would have to be postponed.

effect that the liberation of the capital would have, Bradley's chief of staff urged Eisenhower to revise his plans and send an important unit to uphold the Paris rising.

In short, on the evening of the twenty-second Leclerc was given the order to march on Paris. March? It is rather the word rush that should be used.

Between the evening of the twenty-first and the twenty-second, three events of symbolic and real importance took place in Paris. First, barricades were erected: not only in the old revolutionary Paris from the Nation to the République and from the place d'Italie to the Père-Lachaise, but also in the rue de Rivoli, from the Hôtel de Ville to the Théâtre Français.

During the afternoon, at the Hôtel Matignon and under the chairmanship of Parodi there took place the first miniature "cabinet" of the liberation. In fact, attending Parodi, a real minister, there were only "secretaries-general" (Miné, Guignebert, Monick, Bloch-Lainé) who were there until the ministers should arrive.

> We all of us, including Parodi, came on foot, between two bursts of rifle-fire, [said François Bloch-Lainé]. A Garde Mobile major, still wearing his francisque,* saw to the reception; then suddenly he apologized: "I shall only be gone a moment, gentlemen; I just have to go to arrest my colonel."[9] But those who were present – including Yvon Morandat, who had come on his bicycle the day before to reoccupy the seat of government together with his wife Claire [appointed secretary of the session on the spur of the moment] – certainly had the feeling that they were taking part in a rebirth of the State.[10]

And it was above all in the evening that Paris beheld the appearance of newspapers that had emerged from underground and that bore – together with the old ones such as *le Figaro*, *le Populaire* and *l'Humanité* – new titles linked to three years of clandestine struggle: *Combat*, *Libération*, *Défense de la France*, *Franc-Tireur*. From that evening on, Choltitz's forces were virtually barricaded in six bases; and it was then, according to Colonel Rol, that "Paris had won its battle".[11]

On 23 August Charles de Gaulle left Le Mans for Chartres. Speaking of his strange oblique journey towards Paris, dictated by an Inter-Allied strategy whose soundness he was always ready to dispute, he particularly emphasized the popular atmosphere in which he moved: "I felt myself carried along by a kind of river of joy." Everywhere he stopped he was cheered, he was begged to speak: this he did, profusely and not without emotion. Though his whole mind was reaching out towards Paris, the risks the scantily-armed people and the State were still running there, he was capable of sharing in this emotion aroused by his name, his appearance and his legend.

It was the day before, when he arrived at Le Mans, that there happened the most amusing incident in this progress. There was an enormous crowd. A group of

*A badge of loyalty to the Marshal.

enthusiastic women blocked the way; one of them, with a bunch of flowers in her hand, cried *Vive le Maréchal*! and the next moment she was seen to be horrified by her blunder. But at this de Gaulle took Michel Debré's arm* and said, "How do you expect them to find their bearings?"[12]

At Chartres he received a message from Leclerc telling him that Guillebon had found himself confronted with "a good many Germans" in the Trappes sector, south of Paris, and that even if "the FFI have liberated inner Paris" there would have to be fighting. Conclusion: "I shall therefore begin the operation at dawn tomorrow". De Gaulle thereupon sent Leclerc these words in the manner of Bonaparte writing to Lannes:

> I have received Captain Janney and your note.
> I should like to see you today.
> I expect to be at Rambouillet this evening and to see you there.
> I embrace you.

Then he steered for Rambouillet, and having overtaken the tanks of the 2nd DB on their way to Paris all that afternoon, he settled in the château. It was there that he summoned Leclerc. The man who had been given the finest mission a French patriot could receive, that of liberating Paris, explained his plan for making his way into the city to this chief who had risen up from complete disaster four years before: at dawn the next day Colonel Pierre Billotte, General de Gaulle's closest and steadiest military colleague for the last two years, would be entrusted with the main attack** by way of Antony and the Porte de Gentilly, its final aim being the Hôtel Meurice, where von Choltitz had taken up his quarters. On his flank there would be Langlade's unit, whose axis would be Clamart and the Pont de Sèvres and he would be supported by Dio's unit, which would go by the Porte d'Italie and the Porte d'Orléans. "Then," said de Gaulle to his dearest companion, "who was already at grips with the battle and who could see a wonderful combination of well-timed circumstances opening before his courage,'You are lucky!' It also occurred to me that in war, the generals' good fortune was the government's honour."

But perhaps the most "Gaullic" of all the documents inspired by these hours of historic imminence is the brief message he sent that evening to "his" prefect of police, Charles Luizet, whose impromptu envoy, Dr Favreau, had brought a report to Rambouillet, making his way through the enemy positions to do so: "Tomorrow will be decisive in the wished-for direction. When I arrive I shall go straight to the 'centre'. We shall organize the rest at once with Quartus and you. I think General Koenig will be with me and M. Le Troquer too."[13]

All the words here are worth commenting upon separately, so much do they say about de Gaulle and the state of mind in which he approached this last phase. The "centre", the "we", which, since it is not collective (the end of the sentence makes Luizet into consideration as well) can only be regal, and the chosen order of

*Commissioner of the Republic in Algiers. (trs.)
**It would be an understatement to say that this choice caused a certain amount of jealousy among Leclerc's old companions.

precedence, with the name of the civilian minister being accompanied by a patronizing "too". But it would be best to leave the task of annotating to the memoir-writer: ten years later he analyses himself with a striking relevance:

> My intention had been to go first, not indeed to the Hôtel de Ville where the Council of the Resistance and the Parisian Committee of Liberation were sitting, but to "the centre". As I saw it, that meant the Ministry of War, the obvious place for the French government and High Command. It was not that I did not urgently wish to get into contact with the leaders of the Paris rising. But I wanted it to be established that the State, after trials that had been unable either to destroy or to subjugate it, was in the first place simply returning to its own dwelling. As I read the papers, *Combat*, *Défense de la France*, *Franc-Tireur*, I was both happy to see the fighting-spirit they expressed and strengthened in my determination not to accept any sort of investiture for my authority other than that directly given me by the voice of the crowd.[14]

Some days later de Gaulle explained to Louis Joxe his choice of the Ministry of War for the new authority's "centre" rather than Matignon or the Quai d'Orsay or the Hôtel de Lassay: "I am settling here; do you understand why? The war is not over, and in case there should be any tendency to forget this, it is necessary that the fact should be known. And then again the Ministry of War means Clemenceau. I am not using his office, though; take notice of that."[15]

Philippe Viannay, who was both the founder of the movement Défense de la France* and a major in the Seine-et-Oise FFI, was the kind of man de Gaulle wanted to have by him in times like this. Viannay was told that there were "three forces in France, the capital, the Communists and de Gaulle". "And what about the Resistance?" "The Resistance *is* de Gaulle!" And when the visitor was telling the General how his friends and he hoped to see the liberator provide himself with a strong, durable power in order to carry out a true revolution, de Gaulle interrupted, "As for dictatorship, I know the way in: I do not know the way out. France is a country that is carrying on; it is not a country that is beginning."[16]

On the same evening of August 23 the General received another visit: that of a surprising delegation led by the banker Alexandre de Saint-Phalle, Parodi's financial adviser, and consisting of Jean Laurent, once principal private secretary to de Gaulle in Reynaud's 1940 government and subsequently a director of the Banque d'Indochine, Consul Nordling's brother, and a certain Baron Poch-Pastor, Choltitz' ADC and (according to de Gaulle) "an Allied agent".

What did these envoys want? In the first place, like all those with possessions, they wanted to hasten the entry of regular troops into Paris. Then to persuade de Gaulle to summon the National Assembly in order to give the new authority legal bases. How anxious all these people were to provide de Gaulle with a legality and to set him against the power of the crowd!

It is easy to imagine the effect of these suggestions on a man who, although he

*To which the General's niece Geneviève had belonged before being deported.

would not allow what he considered "his" authority to be diminished by the patriotic insurgents who had his sympathy (and his mistrust), was even less inclined to bear the notion that the power of money and the rottenest parliamentarianism should assume to itself the least right of inspection where he was concerned. The fact that this approach was made by a delegation one member of which was a man who, having had the extraordinarily good luck of being his principal private secretary in June 1940, did not see fit to join him in London, was not calculated to increase its authority.

On 24 August the battle raged in Paris: this was probably the day when the Paris volunteers, emerging from a much disparaged "truce", showed their greatest spirit, skilfully making use of the system of barricades that allowed them to confront the attacks of the enemy armour on the main axes. On the Left Bank Choltitz's forces held not much more than two strong-points, the Luxembourg-Sénat-Odéon sector and that of the Ecole Militaire and the Invalides. On the right bank they had L'Etoile, La Défense, La Muette and Clignancourt. But they increased the number of their patrols, which caused heavy losses among the insurgents and which suffered even more themselves.

It was this morning that *Le Figaro* published the finest article devoted to Charles de Gaulle at that time: it was François Mauriac's "Le Premier des nôtres" which was like a searchlight directed upon the liberator's face. The Paris fighters' morale was all the higher since that afternoon a reconnaissance plane belonging to the 2nd DB dropped a message on the Ile de la Cité from Colonel Crépin, saying in Leclerc's name, "Hold out: we are coming!" It was at once broadcast by the insurgents' radio, which had been seized by a team under Jean Guignebert and Pierre Crenesse.[17]

The forces that Leclerc had meant to throw into the town as early as the evening of the twenty-fourth encountered powerful resistance in the sectors of Massy and la Croix-de-Berny. They suffered losses. Heavily engaged at Antony and at Fresnes, Colonel Billotte decided to halt there for the night and not to begin the attack until dawn the next day; this was something of a disappointment to Leclerc, who did not refrain from launching a raid on Paris – a raid in his own style. At nightfall Captain Dronne, an officer with a great deal of fighting experience in Africa, was sent into the heart of Paris with three vehicles. In the evening of 24 August, on the place de l'Hôtel de Ville, Dronne was able to salute the men of the Paris barricades in the name of the survivors of Chad.

Billotte's decision also gave de Gaulle the lie, since at eight o'clock on 24 August the General had telegraphed Algiers: "The Leclerc division is entering Paris today. I depend on being there myself this evening," adding for the benefit of his colleagues, "Parodi has the situation well in hand. Contrary to reports, the capital is in a good state. I ask all the members of the government to join me in Paris without delay."[18]

On the same day, the General received a telegram that moved him: King George VI, having heard the BBC announce that Paris had been freed, told him of "the deep emotion" he felt on learning that "the inhabitants of Paris have expelled the invader" and ended, "With Your Excellency I rejoice in this hour of their triumph, just as I felt close to them during their long years of suffering".[19] The Constable was never short of disobliging analyses even in triumphant moments and he used this message to point out the difference between his allies, the warmth of the English in contrast with the cold tone of the Voice of America.

On the twenty-fifth, Paris awoke to an extraordinarily brilliant day. So light-filled a sky, flecked here and there with the smoke of a burning tank or barricade, might surely belong to triumphs and tragedies. Who did not hold his breath?

By way of the Portes d'Orléans and Gentilly, by the Pont de Sèvres and Auteuil, the Shermans, the jeeps, the TD and the command-cars under Leclerc, Billotte, Guillebon, Dio, Crépin and Rouvillois made their way into the town like so many gimlets into a plank, in a stupefying atmosphere of mingled fighting and cheering, bursts of fire and shouts of welcome, an unimaginable symbiosis of battle and jubilation.

Now in these places marked by such a mixture of thankfulness and tragedy, of delight in life, of violence and happiness, men came tearing forward mounted on those steel monsters that Colonel de Gaulle had wanted to fling in the Führer's face ten years earlier – La Horie, Branet, Buis, Galley, Karcher, Franjoux, Massu, all coming from the other side of the world and of history, all mad with conquering rage. They were irresistible, these Free French armoured by their passage through the fire, these men to whom de Gaulle, meeting them during these days of euphoria, would say, "You are still here? You are lucky."

At nine o'clock Billotte appeared at the prefecture of police, Massu a little later at the Etoile, Buis on the place de la Concorde at ten; and Leclerc was already settled in the Montparnasse station, from which he directed the operations as a whole pending the arrival of de Gaulle, who was expected in the middle of the afternoon. The main point was to obtain von Choltitz' surrender.

At ten o'clock, Billotte, who for the occasion had promoted himself general, sent Choltitz an ultimatum which spoke of "total extermination" in the event of rejection. The officer in command of inner Paris having claimed that this message "had not been received", the men of the 2nd DB – La Horie, Franjoux, Karcher – attacked Choltitz' headquarters, the Hôtel Meurice, a little before half past two. They seized the German general and took him to the prefecture of police where General Leclerc was waiting for him – in his pocket Leclerc had his appointment as temporary military governor of Paris, acting until Koenig should appear.

"Sind Sie General von Choltitz? Ich bin General Leclerc."

It was now that the two leaders signed the document by which the Paris garrison surrendered; and an hour later, at Montparnasse Station, they initialled another, calling upon the troops belonging to the German garrison to cease fighting. This was countersigned, at the request of the Resistance chiefs by Colonel Rol, the commander of the Ile-de-France FFI and the moving spirit of the Paris insurrection for the last six days.

This counter-signature on the second document, which Leclerc agreed to have beside his own with a very good grace, has given rise to innumerable commentaries and observations and above all to some remarkably bitter criticism on the part of the General. De Gaulle says that when Leclerc gave him the text of the agreement bearing Rol's signature next to Choltitz' and his own, he blamed him for having allowed this association, since at that point, as military governor of Paris, he was "the highest-ranking officer, and therefore the only authority". But above all, he added, "the claim that led you to allow this signature arises from an inadmissible tendency". And he then showed Leclerc a proclamation issued that very morning by the CNR "putting itself forward as 'the French nation' and making no allusion to the government or to General de Gaulle".

This was written ten years later, after bitter conflicts with the political parties, especially the PCF. But at that point there was no serious challenge to the State's authority. Because of the General's unyielding attitude? Certainly. But in speaking of this day of happiness, why does the memoir-writer bother to fire his arrow at his "noble companion", Leclerc?

Let us go back to Charles de Gaulle on the morning of that day of days, walking up and down on the terrace of the château de Rambouillet and reflecting on the lessons and the hazards of history. That evening, Rome would be in Rome once more. So it had needed four years and two months for him to be able to dispose of one of the six great armoured divisions that he had called for in 1933. It was from "the deficiency of those in power" that all the evil arose, he observed. Hence this conclusion: "I was therefore all the more determined not to let mine be encroached upon. The mission with which I was invested seemed to me as clear as possible. As I stepped into the car to go to Paris I felt both gripped by emotion and filled with serenity."

An ordinary traveller needs an hour to go from the château de Rambouillet to the middle of Paris, so long as there is not too much traffic at the gates. On that 25 August, it took no longer for this man who had spent four years on the journey from Bordeaux to Rambouillet – by way of London, Brazzaville, Beirut, Algiers, Washington and Chartres – to reach Montparnasse Station.

This journey was a voyage through an "exulting tide", particularly after Longjumeau. The crowd grew denser by the mile. Towards the Porte d'Italie, the car had to force its way through. But the great masses of people who had gathered from Denfert-Rochereau to the Seine, particularly on the boulevard Saint-Michel – for who could doubt that he would go first to the Hôtel de Ville where the Resistance chiefs were waiting for him? – were disappointed: he turned off along the almost empty avenue du Maine for Montparnasse.

It was here that at about a quarter past four he was received by Philippe de Hauteclocque, alias Leclerc, who at once introduced his two chief companions, Colonel Rol-Tanguy and General Chaban-Delmas. There was nothing about the FFI leader that surprised de Gaulle, who had foreseen, under the black beret, this young and active strength of an armed working-man. The appearance of his "national military delegate" on the other hand so astonished him that he almost forgot to shake hands.** "Well I'm damned, well I'm damned . . ." he was heard to mutter. But he collected his wits and embraced this beardless general whose temporary rank seemed to him more evident than his own.[20]

*Delmas, alias Chaban, alias Arc, had made only one trip to London, in July. De Gaulle had not been there.

Whatever he may have said at the time to Rol-Tanguy, in his memoirs he devotes these fair-minded words to him:

> It was the action of the home forces during the preceding days that had expelled the enemy from our streets, decimated and demoralized his troops, blocked his units in their fortified retreats. In addition, since that morning groups of partisans, who had nothing but their very meagre arms, had courageously helped the regular troops in dealing with the places where the Germans held out.

There are still a few photographs of these scenes: they show the immense Constable sitting in an armchair at a table set somewhere in the hall that has now been destroyed, between Leclerc, who has a lock of hair drooping over one eye, and Rol, enveloped in his new dignity; the General, with spectacles on his nose, is studying the jointly-established plans for the last cleaning-up operations. The American, General Barton, who had entered Paris well after Leclerc, stands well to one side; and that evening he carried amiable modesty so far as to say, "You ought to have been alone today!"

A little before five o'clock, Charles de Gaulle, who had had time to embrace his son Philippe, an ensign in the 2nd DB's marine regiment, which had taken part in the fighting round the Palais-Bourbon, left the Montparnasse station for "the centre". But a burst of fire at the level of Saint-François-Xavier (his family's parish church) obliged him to take the rue Vanneau. Finally, at about five o'clock he made his entry into 14 rue Saint-Dominique, though his chief administrative officer (who in spite of the legend does sometimes get there first) had had some difficulty in persuading an FFI unit to leave, so that there should be room for him.

At this point we cannot refrain from quoting that classic passage where Charles de Gaulle speaks of his return to that place from which the disaster had expelled him four years earlier:

> France had very nearly foundered. But at the Ministry of War things retained their unchanging aspect. Not a piece of furniture, not a tapestry, not a curtain had been altered. [He even thought he recognized the attendants.] The telephone was still in the same place on the desk and exactly the same names were to be seen under the buttons. Presently I was told that it was just the same in the other buildings that formed the setting of the Republic. Nothing was lacking, apart from the State. It was my task to set about it again. So first I settled myself in.[21]

Until he should arrive the two pillars of the State were Charles Luizet, the Prefect of Police, and the delegate-general Alexandre Parodi: they came to explain the situation to him. Law and order and food supplies were their chief concern: and supported by Yvon Morandat, one of London's first political envoys to France, they also told him about "the irritation" felt by the National Resistance Council and the Paris Liberation Committee when they learnt that the General was not going directly to them as though to set the seal on the nation's unanimity. Parodi asked whether the General could not change his mind. Had not these men who had taken the most terrible of risks for years the right to be acknowledged as the heart of the nation on that day of all others? In vain. Charles de Gaulle preferred giving priority to the centre of the State.

And as though to emphasize his unyielding determination to place the structures of the State above the Resistance movements, even though he did so in the presence of Parodi and Morandat, who had so many reasons to sympathize with the men left waiting in the Hôtel de Ville, he stated that when he left the "centre" his first visit would be to the prefecture of police; only the second would be for the men of the civilian Resistance. But before these two encounters, he and his visitors settled the plan of what would be the great moment of the liberation tomorrow: the procession on the Champs-Elysées and beyond, from the Arc de Triomphe to Notre-Dame.

Parodi and Luizet said they were "filled both with enthusiasm and anxiety" by this plan. They had plenty of reasons. To risk this symbolic, essentially irreplaceable figure in the heart of a city where the enemy was still hiding, maddened by defeat, and where countless devoted followers of the vanquished régime could not but be thinking of revenge or retribution – it was madness!

So it was the prefecture of Police that received him first. Had he expressed the wish that none of the men implicated in so many sinister "maintenance of order" operations in Paris for some years past should be present? In that case surprises might have occurred. In any event at the prefecture de Gaulle chose to see none but those who ten days earlier had given the "battle-signal", thus taking their revenge for a "long humiliation".

And now here he was, setting off on foot through an enormous crowd, accompanied by Parodi, Luizet, Le Troquer and Juin, for the Hôtel de Ville: waiting for him on the steps of Etienne Marcel's House,* together with Flouret, the prefect of the Seine, stood the presidents of the CNR and the CPL, Georges Bidault and André Tollet, their "irritation" repressed. The visitor, hurrying up the steps of the great staircase, asked Flouret "How is the purge coming along? This question has to be settled in a few weeks."[22]

They reached the great hall: "In spite of the weariness on so many faces, the stress of the dangers undergone and the events experienced, I did not see a single motion, I did not hear a single word that was not wholly worthy of the occasion. The wonderful success of a meeting dreamed of for so long and paid for with so much effort, so many sorrows, so many deaths!"[23]

And in answer to the tributes then paid to him by Georges Bidault and Georges Marrane** de Gaulle gave one of his finest speeches which was, he says in his memoirs, uttered without preparation and on the spur of the moment:

> Why should we hide the feelings that fill us all, we men and women who are

*Marcel was a fourteenth-century provost of the merchants of Paris: he does not seem to have been a very estimable character (he was killed trying to hand the city over to Charles the Bad of Navarre) but his name remains linked to the Hôtel de Ville, and the rights of the people of Paris. (trs.)

**In the name of the CPL: he had been asked to speak instead of Tollet.

> here in our own city, in Paris that has risen to free itself and that has succeeded in doing so with its own hands? No! Do not let us hide this deep and sacred emotion. There are moments that go beyond each of our poor little lives. Paris! Paris outraged! Paris broken! Paris martyrized! But Paris liberated! Liberated by itself, liberated by its people with the help of the armies of France, with the support and the help of the whole of France, of France that is fighting, of France alone.

The film that was then made, or at least what is left of it, shows us the tall figure towering above faces raised as in an El Greco Ascension, his arms taking the shape of a lyre, the giant's pale face thrown back as though for a consecration. And that famous voice chanting the intensely lyrical phrases, phrases springing from this community of exaltation and awareness. Here de Gaulle truly spoke for the nation; he was the echo of the great Christian orators and of the members of the Convention calling for the mass rising.

He had no sooner uttered this cry of truth, this rallying cry, than disagreement broke out once more. Bidault, on the verge of tears, turned towards him: "General, here and in the name of resistant France, we ask you solemnly to proclaim the Republic before the people here assembled." The idea was noble and worthy of the moment these men were living through. In five scathing sentences that fell on the unhappy Bidault like so many blows from a sabre, the Constable struck him down: "The Republic has never ceased to exist. Free France, Fighting France and the French Committee of National Liberation have each in turn embodied it.* Vichy always was null and void and it remains so. I myself am the president of the government of the Republic. Why should I proclaim it?"

This was the lapidary statement of legitimacy assumed since 18 June 1940 with which he had confronted those who had then wished to make him adopt the idea at Algiers. Thirty years later Edgard Pisani, who was then Luizet's right-hand man, wrote, "Perhaps he was right. But it would have given us such pleasure!"[24] There were already some people in the CNR and the CPL who thought of taking up this "challenge" and of having their revenge for this "distance" that he continually emphasized. While de Gaulle, not satisifed with appearing at the window of the Hôtel de Ville, climbed on to the sill, a giant in its niche, causing the ovation to double in force, they, in an atmosphere of feverish bitterness, considered proclaiming this Republic that he claimed to have embodied without a pause, doing so in spite of him and in his absence.[25]

At this juncture de Gaulle was a blend of strength, diversity and ruthlessness. At the Hôtel de Ville he had just uttered one of the most fervent cries of love that a town has ever inspired; now he regained his control and resumed the direction of the matter point by point.

One would have been happier, however, if he had at once been capable of doing more justice to those who had been here for years, fighting against the Gestapo on the spot. It is not a question of comparing different forms of courage. But in this case the cold monster of the State was crushing emotions and generous impulses.

*No question of the CNR here.

Yet had his mind opened more readily to this kind of communion, would he have been there at all?

François Bloch-Lainé, an unimpeachable witness, saw that he was "ill at ease, remote", creating an atmosphere that lacked "vibrancy". But, he adds, people were "too happy to be disappointed", although "around that tall, awkward, intimidating figure there were already swarms of clever people renewing their contacts – 'Dear Palewski, what a delight to see you again!' He is an enterprising creature, he is even a brave one, your opportunist".[26]

Was it because he was already filled with contempt for this kind of attitude? An hour later, back at the rue Saint-Dominique, he received Maurice Schumann, his London spokesman, with these astonishing words, "You won't catch me at it again!"

Paris liberated! The miraculous event was known at once throughout the world, even in those places where the news could cause the deepest joy – the concentration camps. Christian Pineau tells us that at Buchenwald, where "the German news bulletin was highly responsible", they learnt it the night after de Gaulle's entry into Paris.

At Dachau, Edmond Michelet was at once summoned by the camp's three political chiefs. They announced with tears in their eyes "the greatest news since we have been here: Paris has been liberated, and Paris is unhurt!"[27] In Great Britain the enthusiasm was in proportion to the incomparable services the British had given for the liberation of France during the last four years, and that most faithful of friends Anthony Eden expressed a joy full of the ring of truth on the BBC.

But in liberated Paris itself, conflicts arose on every hand. At least in one of them de Gaulle did not begin it: this was the disagreement that opposed the Resistance and the highest Catholic authorities. On 25 August the Cardinal-Archbishop of Paris, Mgr Suhard, had been warned that because of his attitude under the occupation his presence at the ceremony arranged for the twenty-sixth was "not desired". The prelate said that he was "much distressed". The Cardinal drew up a protest, which was read in the churches on the following Sunday. And during the ceremony "one of his colleagues, Mgr Brot, addressing General de Gaulle, asked him, 'General, may I offer His Eminence your regrets for the incident?' – 'Yes,' replied the General. 'That is well said, General.' – 'Yes, my regrets.' "[28]

Conflict again – but this time more traditional: with the Allies. De Gaulle had told Leclerc to make the 2nd DB the guard of honour for the consecration the next day. But in the course of the morning of 26 August Leclerc received a note from his immediate superior, General Gerow, in command of the Fifth American Army Corps, to this effect:

> Since you are operating under my direct command you are not to take orders coming from other sources. I am told that you have been instructed by General de Gaulle to cause your troops to take part in a parade this after-

> noon at 2 p.m. You will pay no attention to this order. The troops under your command will not take part in the parade either this afternoon or at any other time except on orders signed by me personally.

Of course, both de Gaulle and Leclerc would have had to be shot to make them give up a plan whose symbolic significance seemed to them wholly irreplaceable. Gerow gained nothing but humiliation. Throughout the morning of 26 August, announced hour by hour over the radio, the ceremony took form. From the Arc de Triomphe to Notre Dame, section by section, there were posted the men of the 1st Chad Infantry Regiment, the oldest of old soldiers; the Spahis' light armoured-cars; the 501's tanks; and the tank destroyers belonging to the marines, one of whom was called Philippe de Gaulle.

And at 2 p.m. the heroes of the celebration began to gather on the place de l'Etoile, while loudspeakers broadcast this striking appeal: "General de Gaulle entrusts his safety to the people of Paris. He asks them to see to the maintenance of order themselves and to help the police and the FFI in this duty, they being worn out with five days of fighting."

De Gaulle had just laid a Cross of Lorraine made of gladioli on the tomb of the Unknown Soldier: with him there were the presidents of the CNR and the CPL, Georges Bidault and André Le Troquer; the national military delegate Chaban-Delmas, the prefect of police Luizet, the best-known members of the CNR, Daniel Mayer, Joseph Laniel; there were the generals Juin, Koenig, Vallin and Leclerc and Admiral d'Argenlieu; and then, as always happens, those who were all the more eager to be seen there because they had been seen elsewhere.

As the first line was forming with de Gaulle in the middle and Bidault and Parodi, Le Troquer and Laniel on either side of him, the General, from the height of the conning-tower that Nature had provided him with, saw a very young man with an FFI armband and a cigarette in the corner of his mouth, ready to play the Gavroche* in this celebration of insurgent Paris. What pleasanter symbol? De Gaulle beckoned; he came running, delighted – the General had noticed him and meant to use him to pay a tribute to all those young men who had just been fighting so that this moment should be possible. Three paces off, the General stopped him: "There is no smoking during a procession."[29]

Finally, at 3.18 p.m., in an enormous din and a cloud of golden dust, the procession, like a wave turning the world's most illustrious avenue into an ocean current, got under way, preceded for a few minutes by an usher with a chain about his neck. When it reached the Grand Palais, Clemenceau's statue, adorned with a tricolour scarf, seemed to join the crowd. "It was the most unusual procession that this history-loaded avenue had ever seen, the most brilliant victory Paris had known since the taking of the Bastille," wrote the *Time* magazine reporter.[30]

These pictures are famous, if only because they are like the description of them given by the author of the *Mémoires de guerre*. The procession timed its pace to that of General de Gaulle, which was not slow. But all at once, although he had carefully set himself ahead at the beginning, he felt another marcher beside him, in

*Gavroche, a ragamuffin in Victor Hugo's *Les Misérables*. (trs.)

the same line. It was Bidault, who heard a voice as harsh and cutting as it had been the day before at the Hôtel de Ville, "A little to the rear, if you please!"

And now here is the memoir-writer:

> Stretching before me, the Champs-Elysées.
>
> Ah! It was the sea! An enormous crowd packed tight on either side of the roadway. Perhaps some two million souls. The roofs too were packed with people. As far as I could see it was nothing but one living swell in the sunlight and under the tricolour. Since everyone there had in his heart chosen Charles de Gaulle as refuge from his suffering and symbol of his hope, it was important that he should see him, familiar and fraternal, and that at this sight the nation's unity should blaze out. It is true that [I] have neither the appearance nor the liking for attitudes and gestures that can please an audience. But I am sure they did not expect them.
>
> So I walked on, quiet and deeply moved in the midst of the crowd's indescribable exultation, through a storm of voices that echoed my name. At that moment there was occurring one of those miracles of national consciousness, one of those gestures on the part of France that in the course of centuries sometimes come to light in our history. And I, in the middle of this passionate outburst, I felt that I was fulfilling a function that went far, far beyond myself personally, that of acting as the instrument of fate.[31]

Did de Gaulle, forming the sum total of the national community, realize the enormous risk that he was running and that he made the nation run? Less than fifty miles away a Wehrmacht general had a direct order from the Führer in his pocket, requiring him to direct a rain of V1's and V2's on Paris, the most terrible explosives of the time. But that was not where the problem lay. To an adviser who told him of the extent of the peril he retorted, "The procession will make the nation's political unity."

The enormous wager had been accepted.

But in the very heart of the triumph, he would not have been de Gaulle, he would not have been "France", if at that moment his anxieties, his uneasiness of mind, had not been living in him like a troubled conscience:

> Nor could I forget the Communists' unyielding scheme, nor the rancour of so many outstanding men who would not forgive me for their error, nor the eager desire for agitation that was once more stirring the political parties. As I marched at the head of the procession I felt that even at this very moment I was being escorted by ambition as well as by devoted attachment.

Being de Gaulle meant that too. By dint of being an incarnation one incorporates everything and the noxious exhalations are there even at times of the greatest happiness. It is an intolerable burden to be the symbol.

With a nobility very much aware of itself, but without condescension, he walked through these wounded, ravaged people for whom his presence was like a release from prison. Let us take notice of the movement of his hands that came to him at this time – the half-opened hands held out to the deeply affected crowd. A "tapestry" gesture that might have been invented by Péguy.

Did he then say to himself, as Clemenceau said on the evening of 11 November 1918, "I should like to die now"? He was less sentimental, less personal, but even more proud; he was thinking of the history of France, of France's place in the world, and of his place in that history.

The rebellion was over; the rebel had become the ruler.

NOTES

The following books by Charles de Gaulle have been translated into English:

Vers l'armée de métier: *The Army of the Future* (Hutchinson, 1940).
L'Histoire de l'armée française: *France and her Army* (Hutchinson, 1945).
Mémoires de guerre: *War Memoirs*; Volume I, *Call to Honour, 1940–42* (Collins, 1955), Volume II, *Unity, 1942–44* (Weidenfeld and Nicolson, 1959).
Le Fil de l'épée: *The Edge of the Sword* (Faber and Faber 1960).

CHAPTER ONE

1. Charles de Gaulle, *Lettres, Notes et Carnets* 1905–1918 (Paris, Plon, 1980), Vol. I, p.7–8
2. P.-M. de La Gorce, *De Gaulle entre deux mondes* (Paris, Fayard, 1964), p.40
3. Paris, Le Seuil, 1978
4. Entretien avec Jean Mauriac, *l'Espoir*, No.39
5. *Lettres, Notes* . . ., I, p.26
6. *Articles et Ecrits* (Paris, Plon, 1982) p.24–7

CHAPTER TWO

1. *En ce temps-là* . . ., No.8, p.23
2. *Charles de Gaulle, général de France*, p.17
3. *Lettres, Notes* . . ., I. p.45
4. *Ibid.*, p.47
5. *Charles de Gaulle, général de France*, p.23
6. *Mémoires de guerre*, Vol. I, *L'Appel 1940–1942* (Paris, Plon, 1954), p.2
7. J. Pouget, *Un certain capitaine de Gaulle*, p.42
8. *Charles de Gaulle, général de France*, p.19
9. *Lettres, Notes* . . ., I, p.59–61
10. J.-R. Tournoux, *Pétain et de Gaulle (Paris, Plon, 1964), p.66.* These words seem directed at de Gaulle.
11. *Lettres, Notes* . . ., I, p.57
12. Quoted for the first time by J.-R. Tournoux in *Pétain and de Gaulle*, p.383
13. *Un certain capitaine de Gaulle*, p.49
14. *Lettres, Notes* . . ., I., p.67
15. *Ibid.*, p.67
16. Charles de Gaulle, *La France et son armée* (Paris, Plon, 1938), p.238

CHAPTER THREE

1. *Lettres, Notes* . . ., I. p.79–80
2. *Ibid.*, p.78
3. *Ibid.*, p.82
4. *La France et son armée*, p.243
5. *Lettres, Notes* . . ., I. p.106–7
6. *Ibid.*, p.130–1
7. *Ibid.*, p.143
8. *En ce temps-là* . . ., No.6 p.95
9. *Lettres, Notes* . . ., I, p.185
10. *Ibid.*, p.205
11. *Ibid.*, p.273
12. Letter to colonel Boud'hors, 8 December 1918, in *Lettres, Notes* . . ., I. p.527
13. *Un certain capitaine de Gaulle*, p.94
14. *Lettres, Notes* . . ., I. p.527

CHAPTER FOUR

1. *Lettres, Notes* . . ., p.311
2. *Ibid.*, p.317
3. *Ibid.*, p.317
4. Interview with the author, March 1964
5. *Lettres, Notes* . . ., I. p.413–7

6. *Ibid.*, p.417–18
7. *Un certain capitaine de Gaulle*, p.114
8. *Lettres, Notes . . .*, I, p.302–6
9. *Ibid.*, p.411
10. *Revue de la France libre*. See the following-up of this portrait on p.43
11. *Ibid.*, p.519–20
12. *Ibid.*, p.525
13. *Ibid.*, p.536

CHAPTER FIVE

1. *Lettres, Notes* . . . 1918–June 1940 (Paris, Plon, 1980), vol. II, p.14
2. *Ibid.*, p.16
3. *Ibid.*, p.44
4. *En ce temps là, de Gaulle* No.22, p.86
5. *Lettres, Notes . . .*, II, p.79
6. Cat-Mackiewiecz. *Les Yeux verts* (Varsovie, Editions Pax)
7. *Lettres, Notes . . .*, II. p.102
8. *Ibid.*, p.35
9. *Yvonne de Gaulle, ma soeur* (Paris, Plon, 1980)
10. *Lettres, Notes . . .*, II, p.91
11. *Mémoires d'un Français rebelle*, p.55
12. Paris, Flammarion, 1962, p.122–3
13. *Miroir de l'histoire* (1964)
14. *Mémoires d'un Français rebelle*, p.51
15. Published for the first time by J.-R. Tournoux in *Pétain et de Gaulle*
16. Paris, Berger-Levrault, 1924

CHAPTER SIX

1. *Mémoires d'un Français rebelle*, p.93
2. *Un certaine capitaine de Gaulle*, p.186
3. *Ibid.*, p.46
4. *Lettres, Notes . . .*, II. p.217–18
5. J.-R. Tournoux, *Jamais dit*, p.30
6. *Lettres, Notes . . .*, II. p.310–11 (It is this letter which is so strangely dated 3 March 1927)
7. *Jamais dit*, p.36
8. The Pétain-de Gaulle correspondence is published in *En ce temps-là . . .*, nos. 15–16
9. *Lettres, Notes . . .*, II. p.330
10. *Ibid.*, p.336–350
11. *Charles de Gaulle, général de France*, p.52

CHAPTER SEVEN

1. *Charles de Gaulle, général de France*, p.49
2. *En ce temps-là . . .*, No.29
3. Interview with the author, July 1978
4. *Journal officiel*, parliamentary debates, 17 March 1929
5. *Charles de Gaulle, général de France*, p.54–5
6. *Lettres, Notes . . .*, II. p.350–51
7. *Une histoire politique de l'armée*, p.120
8. *Charles de Gaulle, général de France*, p.57
9. Letter to the author, October 1965
10. *En ce temps-là . . .*, No.15
11. Text communicated to the author by the bâtonnier de Bigault du Granrut, nephew of the General
12. *Le Fil de l'épée* (Paris, Plon, 1971), p.64–6
13. *Ibid.*, p.200
14. *Ibid.*, p.202
15. *Ibid.*, p.202

CHAPTER EIGHT

1. Interview with author, January 1983
2. *Cette chance que j'ai eue*, Paris, Plon, 1973
3. Interview with the author, 16 November 1982
4. *Mémoires d'un Français rebelle*, p.118
5. Marcel Jullian, *Madame de Gaulle* (Paris, Stock, 1982), p.117
6. *En ce temps-là . . .*, No.30, p.117–19
7. *Cette chance que j'ai eue*, and *Yvonne de Gaulle, ma soeur*
8. *Cette chance que j'ai eue*, p.49

CHAPTER NINE

1. L. Nachin, *Paroles d'adieu*, unpublished work.
2. Catalogue of the exhibition "Charles de Gaulle, 1932", p.62
3. Guicharel, O, *Mon général*, p.59

CHAPTER TEN

1. Quoted by J. Nobécourt, *Une histoire politique de l'armée*, p.222
2. No. 3, 1932
3. *Journal officiel*, 16 April, 1936
4. *Lettres, Notes . . .*, II, p.442

CHAPTER ELEVEN

1. *Mémoires de guerre*, vol. I, p.10
2. *Une histoire politique de l'armée*, p.194

3. *Journal des anciens enfants de troupe*, p.63–70
4. *Le Général Delestraint*, Paris. Presses de la Cité, 1972, p.44
5. *La Revue politique et parlementaire*, no.462
6. E. Pognon, *De Gaulle et l'armée* (Paris, Plon, 1976) p.92
7. *Vers l'armée de métier*, p.210 (1971 edition)
8. *Lettres, Notes . . .*, II, p.420. Written in November 1936

CHAPTER TWELVE

1. *Charles de Gaulle*, by Philippe Barrès (Paris, Plon, 1944; first edition 1941), p.8
2. Interview with the author, 3 May, 1983
3. Interview with Philippe Serre. 5 May, 1983
4. *Le Colonel de Gaulle*, p.26
5. P. Reynaud *Venu de ma montagne* (Paris, Flammarion, 1960), p.430
6. Published in *Paul Reynaud mon père*, by Evelyne Demey (Paris, Plon, 1980), p.287–321 and in *Lettres, Notes . . .*, II, p.376–494
7. *Lettres, Notes . . .*, II, p.380
8. *Ibid.*, p.381
9. *Ibid.*, p.381.
10. *Mémoires de guerre*, I, p.13
11. Robert Aron, *De Gaulle* (Paris, librairie académique académique Perrin, 1972), p.42–3
12. *Le Colonel de Gaulle*, p.49
13. *Oeuvre (1940–1945)* (Paris, Albin Michel, 1972), p.14
14. *Mémoires de guerre*, I, p.19–20
15. Interview with the author, October 1983
16. Unpublished letter
17. Paris, Flammarion, 1957
18. *Lettres, Notes . . .*, II, p.43

CHAPTER THIRTEEN

1. Interview with the author, June 1965
2. J.-F. Perrette, *Le Général Delestraint*, p.64
3. G. Buis, *Les Fanfares perdues* (Paris, Le Seuil, 1975), p.38
4. *Lettres, Notes . . .*, II, p.454
5. *Charles de Gaulle, général de France*, p.86
6. This he did in his *Ecrits sur la guerre* (Paris, Plon, 1967), p.250
7. *Un certain capitaine de Gaulle*, p.127
8. *Lettres, Notes . . .*, II, p.474
9. P. Huard, *Le Colonel de Gaulle et ses blindés* (Paris, Plon, 1980), p.20
10. *Ibid.*, p.22
11. And told to Paul Huard, who published them.
12. Interview with the author, May 1983
13. *En ce temps-là . . .*, No.38, p.5
14. *Lettres, Notes . . .*, II, p.429
15. *Lettres, Notes . . .*, II. p.474–6
16. *Ibid.*, p.475
17. Interview with the author, 4 May 1983

CHAPTER FOURTEEN

1. *En ce temps-là . . .*, No.15
2. *L'Histoire de l'armée française* (Paris, Flammarion, 1938)
3. *Lettres, Notes . . .*, II, p.471–73
4. *En ce temps-là . . .*, No.15, p.2–3
5. Very kindly communicated by Jean Pouget, the author of *Un certain capitaine de Gaulle*, often quoted earlier.
6. *Lettres, Notes . . .*, II, p.424
7. Interview with the author, 4 January 1983
8. *Lettres, Notes . . .* vol. III. June 1940–July 1941 (Paris, Plon, 1981), p.429–31

CHAPTER FIFTEEN

1. *Une histoire politique de l'armée*, p.285
2. *Mémoires de guerre*, I, p.22
3. *Ibid.*, p.22
4. J.-R. Tournoux, *Jamais dit*, p.61
5. *Mémoires de guerre* I, p.23
6. *Lettres, Notes . . .*, II, p.486
7. J.-F. Perrette, *Le Général Delestraint*, p.70
8. Général Bourret, *La Tragédie de l'armée française* (Paris, La Table ronde, 1947), p.161
9. *Mémoires de guerre*, I, p.23
10. *Oeuvre* (quoted in J. Lacouture, *Léon Blum*, Paris, Le Seuil, 1977)
11. *Charles de Gaulle, général de France*, p.98–105
12. Interview with Pierre Billotte, June 1983

13. *Le Colonel de Gaulle et ses blindés*, p.40
14. *Lettres, Notes* . . ., II, p.473
15. *Mémoires de guerre*, I. p.27
16. *Lettres, Notes* . . ., II, p.491
17. *Ibid.*, p.494
18. *Ibid.*, p.492
19. P. Reynaud, *Mémoires*, p.338

CHAPTER SIXTEEN

1. Paul Baudouin, *Neuf mois au gouvernement, avril-décembre 1940* (Paris, Editions de la Table ronde 1948), p.50
2. *Lettres, Notes* . . ., II, p.495
3. *Mémoires de guerre*, I, p.30
4. *Ibid.*, p.30
5 *Lettres, Notes* . . ., II, p.502
6. *Mémoires de guerre*, I, p.31
7. *Le Colonel de Gaulle et ses blindés*, p.143
8. *Mémoires de guerre*, I, p.34
9. *Le Colonel de Gaulle et ses blindés*, p.279
10. *Ibid.*, p.285
11. H. Guderian, *Mémoires d'un soldat*
12. Interview with the author, June 1983
13. *Lettres, Notes* . . ., II. p.500
14. *Ibid.*, II, p.475–6
15. *Ibid.*, II, p.476
16. *Ibid.*, II, p.476–7

CHAPTER SEVENTEEN

1. Apart from direct information given to the author by Palewski, de Courcel, Pleven, Schumann and Massigli, this chapter, like the next, is based primarily on: *Mémoires de guerre*, vol. I, of Charles de Gaulle; *The Second World War*, Vol. II, *Their Finest Hour*, by Winston Churchill; *Assignment to Catastrophe*, Vol. II, *The Fall of France* by Edward Spears; Anthony Eden's *Memoirs Vol. II The Reckoning*; the *Mémoires* of Jean Monnet; *Un certain 18 Juin* by Maurice Schumann; *Le 18 juin* by Henri Amouroux; *Neuf Mois au gouvernement* by Paul Baudouin; *L'Abîme* by Jean-Baptiste Duroselle; *Journal politique*, by Jules Jeanneney.
2. D. Leca, *La Rupture de 1940* (Paris, Fayard, 1978), p.166–7
3. Around Reynaud are to be seen MM Frossard, Chichery, Jean Prouvost (who was to be one of the man of London's worst enemies), Février, Delbos and Pernot.
4. E. Spears, *Assignment to Catastrophe*, Vol. II. *The Fall of France* (Heinemann, 1954) p.85
5. *Journal d'une défaite*, p.393
6. *La Rupture de 1940*, p.102
7. Interview with the author, February 1983
8. Interview with the author, June, 1965
9. Geoffroy de Courcel's interview with the author, February 1983
10. *Mémoires de guerre*, I. p.44
11. M. Weygand, *En lisant les Mémoires de guerre du général de Gaulle* (Paris, Flammarion, 1955), p.36
12. *En ce temps-là* . . ., No.6, p.85
13. *Mémoires de guerre*, I, p.46
14. *Ibid.*, p.47
15. *Ibid.*, p.51
16. *Mémoires de guerre*, I, p.53
17. *Ibid.*, p.54
18. *Ibid.*, p.55
19. *Ibid.*, p.57
20. *Ibid.*, p.57
21. H. Amouroux, *Paris-Match*, 15 November 1970
22. *Mémoires de guerre*, I, p.58
23. *Ibid.*, p.59
24. *Ibid.*, p.60
25. Interview with the author, 5 February 1983
26. H. Amouroux, *Paris-Match*, 15 November 1970
27. J. Monnet, *Mémoires* (Paris, Fayard, 1976), p.20–30
28. *Mémoires de guerre*, I, p.62–3
29. H. Amouroux, *Paris-Match*, 15 November 1970
30. J. Monnet, *Mémoires*, p.167–74
31. H. Amouroux, *Paris-Match*, 15 November 1970
32. *Mémoires de guerre*, I, p.65

CHAPTER EIGHTEEN

1. *Mémoires de guerre*, I, p.65
2. Interview with G. de Courcel, February 1983
3. Interview with the author, February 1983
4. *Mémoires de guerre*, I, p.67
5. *Ibid.*, p.67

6. *Ibid.*, p.71
7. André Malraux's interview with the author, January 1973
8. Geneviève de Gaulle's interview with the author, July 1964
9. Interview with the author, May 1983

CHAPTER NINETEEN

1. *Lettres, Notes . . .*, II, p.503
2. *Mémoires de guerre*, I, p.69
3. *Ibid.*, p.70
4. Interview with the author, June 1983
5. Interview with the author, February 1983
6. Published by Maurice Schumann in *Un certain 18 juin*, Paris, Plon, 1980
7. The original document was published in *En ce temps-là . . .*, No.9.
8. Interview with the author, June 1983
9. Interview with Mr Parker, 1964
10. A. Briggs, *The History of Broadcasting in the UK* (Oxford University Press), p.242
11. E. Barker's description, *En ce temps-là*, No. 9, p.128
12. P. Bourdan *Carnets des jour d'attente* (Paris, Editions Pierre Trémois, 1945), p.9–32
13. Interview with the author, November 1983
14. *La France au combat*, No. I, August–September 1943
15. *Mémoires de guerre*, I, p.268
16. M. Schumann, *Un certain 18 juin*, p.236
17. Interview with the author, 30 May 1983
18. André Trichet, *Revue d'histoire de la Deuxième Guerre mondiale*, No.3, p.36
19. J. Moch, *Conversations avec Darlan* (Paris, Plon, 1968), p.149
20. C. Longuechaud, *L' "Abominable" Armistice de 40* (Paris, Plon, 1980)
21. *Conversations avec Darlan*, p.149
22. These views of the Führer are admirably summed up in a letter by General Böhme (published by *Le Monde*), who was then drawing up the German conditions, to Colonel Goutard, author of an excellent book on the armistice

CHAPTER TWENTY

1. In his *Mémoires* Charles de Gaulle blames the British and American press agencies, admitting (ten years later) that there was no "direct enemy seizure" of the fleet.
2. Texts published in *Mémoires de guerre*, I, p.270
3. *Ibid.*, p.172–4
4. Interview with the author, July 1977
5. Interview with the author, 5 May 1983
6. Interview with the author, February 1983
7. Interview with the author, July 1983
8. R. Cassin, *Les Hommes partis de rien* (Paris, Plon, 1974)
9. Interview with the author, June 1983
10. Colonel Passy, *Souvenirs* (Raoul Solar, 1946), p.32–3
11. *Les Hommes partis de rien*, p.76
12. *Discours et Messages* (Paris, Plon, 1970), Vol. I, p.10
13. Jean Chauvel, *Commentaire* (Paris, Fayard, 1960), Vol. I, p.137
14. *Mémoires de guerre*, I, p.73–4

CHAPTER TWENTY-ONE

1. Y. Bouthillier, *Le Drame de Vichy* (Paris, Plon, 1950), Vol. I, p.148–9
2. *De Gaulle à Londres* (Paris, La Table ronde, 1965), p.82–3
3. E. Spears, *Two Men who Saved France* (London, Eyre and Spottiswoode, 1966), p.164
4. *Mémoires de guerre*, I. p.275–6
5. Interview with the author, 16 June 1983
6. Charles Gombault, *Un journal, une aventure* (Paris, Gallimard, 1982), p.29–35
7. *Ibid.*
8. Alexander Werth, *De Gaulle,* (London, Penguin Books, 1965), p.112
9. Interview with the author, 17 June 1983
10. *Histoire de la France libre* (Paris, PUF, 1972), p.29
11. A. Weil-Curiel, *Le Jour se lève à Londres* (Editions du Myrte, 1945), Vol. I, p.331
12. Interview with the author, July 1983

13. C. Tillon, *On chantait rouge* (Paris, Laffont, 1977), p.301
14. H. Amouroux, *Paris-Match*, 15 November 1970
15. *Mémoires de guerre*, I, p.86
16. *Ibid.*, p.88
17. Interview with the author, May 1983
18. F. Kersaudy, *Churchill and de Gaulle* (New York, Athenaeum, 1981), p.88
19. *Souvenirs de la France libre* (Paris, Berger-Levrault, 1947), p.212
20. *Journey down a Blind Alley* (London, Hutchinson), p.113–15
21. *Carnets des jours d'attente – Juin 40–Juin 44*
22. *Lettres, Notes et Carnets* (June 1940–July 1941), III, p.76

CHAPTER TWENTY-TWO

1. *Souvenirs*, p.41
2. J.-B. Duroselle, *L'Abîme*, p.237
3. *Ibid.*, p.137
4. *Lettres, Notes . . .*, III, p.89
5. *Mémoires de guerre*, I, p.101
6. *Ibid.*, p.103
7. *Lettres, Notes . . .*, III, p.122
8. Interview with Claude Hettier de Boislambert, October 1983
9. *Mémoires de guerre*, I, p.109
10. *Ibid.*, p.109
11. *Jamais dit*, p.88
12. Interview with the author, March 1983
13. *En ce temps-là . . .*, No.13, p.28
14. Interview with the author, February 1983
15. *Lettres, Notes . . .*, III, p.125
16. *Ibid.*, p.127
17. Interview with the author, June 1983
18. *Mémoires de guerre*, I, p.114
19. *Chroniques irrévérencieuses*, p.173
20. *Mémoires de guerre*, I, p.120
21. *Ibid.*, p.137
22. *Ibid.*, p.137

CHAPTER TWENTY-THREE

1. *Commentaire*, Vol. I, p.80
2. Interview with the author, June 1983
3. L. L. Woodward, *British Foreign Policy in the Second World War* (London, 1970), p.410
4. *The Second World War*, Vol. II, *Their Finest Hour*, p.453
5. L. Rougier, *Mission secrète à Londres*, Montreal, Beauchemin, 1946
6. J. Soustelle, *Envers et contre tout*, p.82
7. R. Cassin, *Les Hommes partis de rien*, p.236
8. *Mémoires de guerre*, I, p.303
9. *Cadogan Diaries* (London, Cassell, 1971), p.336
10. *The Second World War*, Vol. II, p.451
11. J. L. Ralston's unpublished diary, quoted in *Churchill and de Gaulle*, p.119
12. E. Spears, *The Free French, Vichy and ourselves*, quoted in *Churchill and de Gaulle*, p.127 (note)
13. *Mémoires d'un Français rebelle*, p.203
14. *Lettres, Notes . . .*, III, p.224–5
15. *Ibid.*, p.202–3
16. *Ibid.*, p.212
17. Interview with the author, July 1983

CHAPTER TWENTY-FOUR

1. François Coulet, *Vertu des temps difficiles* (Paris, Plon, 1967), p.90
2. *Lettres, Notes . . .*, III, p.309
3. *The Second World War*, Vol. III, *The Grand Alliance*, p.290
4. H. Seyrig, *Les Allemands en Syrie sous le gouvernement de Vichy*. Pamphlet reproduced in *L'Espoir*.
5. *Ibid.*
6. J.-B. Duroselle, *L'Abîme*, p.287
7. *The Second World War*, Vol. III, p.294
8. *Lettres, Notes . . .*, III, p.318
9. *Ibid.*, p.232
10. *Ibid.*, p.259
11. P. Repiton-Preneuf, unpublished memoir communicated by G. Buis, p.59
12. Interview with the author, August 1983
13. *Lettres, Notes . . .*, III, p.355–6
14. P. Repiton-Preneuf, Unpublished memoir, p.102
15. J. Nobécourt and J. Planchais, *Une histoire politique de l'armée*, Vol. II, p.31
16. *Mémoires de guerre*, I, p.164
17. Interview with the author, August 1983
18. Interview with the author, August 1983
19. *Les Fanfares perdues*, p.78

20. *Churchill and de Gaulle*, p.151
21. *Lettres, Notes et Carnets* (July 1941–May 1943) (Paris, Plon, 1982), Vol. IV, p.32
22. *Ibid.*, p.54
23. *Footprints in Time* (London, Collins, 1976), p.113–15

CHAPTER TWENTY-FIVE

1. *De Gaulle à Londres*, p.173
2. *Ibid.*, p.173
3. *Ibid.*, p.175
4. *Mémoires de guerre*, I, p.334
5. *De Gaulle à Londres*, p.178
6. *Souvenirs*, Vol. I, p.132
7. *Chroniques irrévérencieuses*, p.325
8. *Mémoires de guerre*, I, p.220–1
9. *Lettres, Notes . . .*, IV. p.70–1
10. Interview with the author, 7 September 1983
11. *Mémoires de guerre*, I, p.656
12. *Ibid.*, p.659

CHAPTER TWENTY-SIX

1. *Mémoires de guerre*, I, p.541
2. *Ibid.*
3. *Sovietsko Frantsuskie Otnoshenyia vo Vremya* [Soviet-French relations during the war] (Moscow, 1959), p.44
4. *Mémoires de guerre*, I. p.549–50
5. *Sovietsko Frantsuskie . . .*, p.81
6. *Ibid.*, p.60
7. *Mémoires de guerre*, I, p.551
8. *On chantait rouge*, p.343
9. *Mémoires de guerre*, I, p.471
10. *Ibid.*, p.482
11. *Ibid.*, p.482
12. *Ibid.*, p.503

CHAPTER TWENTY-SEVEN

1. Letter to the author
2. Letter to the author
3. Interview with the author, 15 March 1983
4. *Les Alliés ennemis: FDR et de Gaulle* (Paris, Denoël, 1965), p.110
5. *Notes et souvenirs sur ma mission aux Etats-Unis* (M. de Chambrun kindly communicated this memoir to the author: it had not been published at the time of their conversation), p.9
6. Colloquy "La libération de la France", 1974
7. New York, 1973
8. Nerin Gun, *Les Secrets des archives américaines* (Paris, Albin Michel, 1979), Vol. I, p.373
9. The author's interview with Pierre Mendès France, March 1981
10. *Notes et Souvenirs sur ma mission aux Etats-Unis*, p.41
11. *Navigating the rapids*, p.391
12. *Oeuvre de Léon Blum*, Vol. VII
13. *Journal politique*, p.314–17
14. Interview with the author, July 1964

CHAPTER TWENTY-EIGHT

1. *Mémoires de guerre*, II, p.3
2. Interview with the author, November 1980
3. J. Soustelle, *Envers et contre tout*, p.359
4. *Mémoires de guerre*, I, p.199
5. Interview with the author, June 1983
6. *Lettres, Notes . . .*, IV, p.209
7. *Le temps des armes* (Paris, Plon, 1972), p.223–4
8. *Mémoires de guerre*, I. p.602–3
9. *Ibid.*, p.604–5 and British report in *Churchill and de Gaulle*, p.191–3
10. *Mémoires de guerre*, II. p.343–5
11. *Lettres, Notes . . .*, IV, p.363–9
12. *Mémoires de guerre*, II, p.373
13. *Churchill and de Gaulle*, p.202–9
14. *Ibid.*, p.210
15. Interview with the author, June 1983

CHAPTER TWENTY-NINE

1. Interview with the author, January 1984
2. Pierre Villon, *Résistant de la première heure* (Paris, Editions sociales, 1983), p.182–4
3. Interview with the author, June 1983
4. *Les Voix de la liberté* "Ici Londres" (Documentation française, 1975), 5 volumes
5. *Les Voix de la liberté* "Ici Londres", Vol. I, p.314–15
6. Vol. II, p.156–62
7. *Ibid.*, p.344
8. *La nuit finira* (Paris, Laffont, 1973), p.565
9. Marcel Prenant, in *Vie et Mort des Français*, 1934–45 (Paris, Hachette, 1971), p.385

10. *La Simple Vérité* (Paris, Poche-Hachette, 1969), Vol. I, p.150
11. *Ibid.*, p.168–9
12. Gilberte Brossolette, *Il s'appelait Pierre Brossolette* (Paris, Albin Michel, 1976), p.134
13. *La nuit finira*, p.256–7
14. Interview with General de Boissieu, March 1983
15. *Mémoires de guerre*, II, p.376
16. *Ibid.*, p.376

CHAPTER THIRTY

1. R. Murphy, *Diplomat among Warriors* (Collins, 1964), p.103–5
2. Renée Pierre-Gosset, *Expédients provisoires* (Paris, Fasquelle, 1945), p.148–56
3. *Mémoires de guerre*, II, p.360
4. J. Soustelle, *Envers et contre tout*, p.442
5. L. Joxe, *Victoires sur la nuit* (Paris, Flammarion, 1981), p.41
6. *Ibid.*, p.47
7. See particularly *Expédients provisoires*, p.154–60
8. *The Second World War*, Vol. IV, *The Hinge of Fate*, p.542
9. R. Sherwood, *Roosevelt and Hopkins: An Intimate History* (New York, Harper & Row, 1950), p.629
10. Passy, *10, Duke Street, Souvenirs*, Vol. II, p.352
11. *Mémoires de guerre*, II, p.35
12. Interview with the author, March 1983
13. Interview with the author, November 1983
14. *Expédients provisoires*, p.172
15. D. Eisenhower, *Crusade in Europe* (Heinemann, 1949), p.116
16. *Conversation avec Darlan*, p.171
17. *The Second World War*, Vol. IV, p.641
18. Interview with the author, November 1983
19. H. Alphand, *L'Etonnement d'être* (Paris, Fayard, 1977), p.130
20. *Lettres, Notes . . .*, IV, p.434
21. *Mémoires de guerre*, II, p.51
22. W. Langer, *Le Jeu américain à Vichy* (Paris, Plon, 1948), p.385
23. *Roosevelt and Hopkins*, p.650
24. *Ibid.*, p.653–4
25. *Ibid.*, p.654
26. *Expédients provisoires*, p.213
27. John MacVane, *Micro au poing*, p.124
28. *Le Jeu américain à Vichy*, p.394
29. Interview with the author, November 1983
30. A. Fabre-Luce, *Deux Crimes d'Alger* (Paris, Julliard, 1980), p.45
31. *Les Voix de la liberté*, "Ici, Londres" Vol. III, p.54
32. Général de Boissieu, *Pour combattre avec de Gaulle* (Paris, Plon, 1981) p.171
33. *Mémoires de guerre*, II, p.67
34. *Lettres, Notes . . .*, IV, p.476

CHAPTER THIRTY-ONE

1. *Mémoires de guerre*, II, p.432
2. *Ibid.*, p.434
3. *Crusade in Europe*, p.151–2
4. *Diplomat among warriors*, p. 208–14
5. W. Leahy, *I was there*, p.173–4
6. *Churchill and de Gaulle*, p.243
7. H. Giraud, *Un seul but: la victoire* (Paris, Julliard, 1949), p.98–9
8. *Mémoires de guerre*, II, p.76
9. H. Macmillan, *The Blast of War* (Macmillan, 1967), p.316–17
10. *Mémoires de guerre*, II, p.78
11. *The Blast of War*, p.250–1
12. *Mémoires de guerre*, II, p.79–80
13. *Roosevelt and Hopkins*, p.685–6
14. C. Hettier de Boislambert, *Les Fers de l'espoir* (Paris, Plon, 1973), p.383
15. A. Funk, "The Anfa memorandum", *Journal of Modern History*, No.XXVI, p.246–54
16. *Ibid.*, p.251
17. *The Blast of War*, p.260
18. *En ce temps-là . . .*, No.30, p.27
19. *Ibid.*, p.28–9
20. *Envers et contre tout*, Vol. II, p.124
21. *Diplomat among Warriors*, p.219
22. *Mémoires de guerre*, II, p.85
23. *Roosevelt and Hopkins*, p.693
24. *The Second World War*, Vol. IV, *The Hinge of Fate*, p.621
25. *Adventures in Diplomacy* (Cassell, 1966), p.148
26. *Mémoires de guerre*, II, p.86
27. *Ibid.*, p.440
28. *The Blast of War.*
29. *Diplomat among Warriors*, p.223–4

30. A. Eden, *Memoirs*, Vol. II, *The Reckoning*, p.367
31. *Churchill and de Gaulle*, p.261
32. *Ibid.*, p.262
33. Eden, *Memoirs*, Vol. II, p.372
34. *Churchill and de Gaulle*, p.267
35. *Mémoires de guerre*, II., p.96
36. *Churchill and de Gaulle*, p.272
37. *Ibid.*, p.275–6
38. Eden, *Memoirs*, Vol. II, p.386
39. *Churchill and de Gaulle*, p.279–80
40. *Ibid.*, p.280
41. *The Second World War*, Vol. IV, p.716

CHAPTER THIRTY-TWO

1. *Envers et contre tout*, II, p.181–2
2. J. Monnet, *Mémoires*, p.221
3. H. Alphand. *L'étonnement d'être*, p.156
4. Girard de Charbonnières, *Le Duel Giraud-de Gaulle* (Paris, Plon, 1984), p.204
5. *Victoires sur la nuit*, p.141
6. Interview with the author, October 1983
7. *Mémoires de guerre*, II. p.445
8. *Ibid.*, p.95
9. *Ibid.*, p.461–2
10. A. Werth, *De Gaulle*, p.151
11. *Mémoires de guerre*, II. p.444
12. *Diplomat among Warriors*, p.227–8
13. Charles Rist, *Une saison gâtée*, Paris, Fayard, 1983
14. *Victoires sur la nuit*, p.100
15. Pierre Ordioni, *Tout commence à Alger* (Paris, Stock, 1972), p.543
16. René Bouscat, *De Gaulle – Giraud, dossier d'une mission* (Paris, Flammarion, 1967), p.92
17. *Mémoires de guerre*, II, p.469
18. Yves M. Danan, *La Vie politique à Alger 1940–1944* (Paris, Librairie générale de droit et de jurisprudence, 1963), p.173
19. *Lettres, Notes . . .*, IV, p.600
20. *Mémoires de guerre*, II, p.102
21. *Dans la bataille de Méditerranée*, p.365
22. *Le Duel Giraud – de Gaulle*, p.199
23. *Mémoires de guerre*, II, p.366
24. *Dans la bataille de Méditerranée*, p.370
25. *Mémoires de guerre*, II, p.488
26. *La Vie politique à Alger 1940–1944*, p.188
27. *Dans la bataille de Méditerranée*, p.369
28. *La Vie politique à Alger 1940–1944*, p.188
29. *Mémoires de guerre*, II, p.110
30. *The Blast of War*, p.345–6
31. *L'Abîme*, p.442
32. *Mémoires de guerre*, II, p.123
33. *Un seul but, la victoire*, p.265
34. *L'Abîme*, p.473

CHAPTER THIRTY-THREE

1. *Victoires sur la nuit*, p.122
2. Interview with the author, May 1983
3. Général de Guillebon, *Colloque sur la libération de la France* (Paris, 1974), p.586
4. *Lettres, Notes . . .*, IV, p.583
5. Interview with the author, October 1983
6. Interview with the author, October 1983
7. *Discours et messages*, I, p.314
8. *Mémoires de guerre*, II, p.519–20
9. Général Beaufre, in *Vie et Mort des Français*, p.460
10. *Services spéciaux*, p.526
11. *Envers et contre tout*, p.286
12. Interview with the author, July 1964
13. *Services spéciaux*, p.530
14. *Ibid.*, p.539
15. *Ibid.*, p.540
16. *Envers et contre tout*, p.293
17. *On chantait rouge*, p.354–5
18. Interview with the author, November 1983
19. H. Noguères, *Histoire de la Résistance en France*, p.352
20. J.-F. Perrette, *Le Général Delestraint*, p.104–5
21. *Histoire de la Résistance en France*, p.630

CHAPTER THIRTY-FOUR

1. Interview with the author, October 1983
2. J.-L. Crémieux-Brilhac, interview with the author, June 1983
3. Pierre Billotte, interview with the author, July 1983
4. *Duke Street, Souvenirs*, Vol. II, p.309
5. F. Grenier, *C'était ainsi* (Paris, Editions sociales, 1959), p.131–3

6. J. Duclos, *Mémoires* (Paris, Fayard), Vol. II, p.300
7. *Livre blanc du BCRA*, communicated by one of the editors.
8. J. Lacouture, *Léon Blum* (Paris, Le Seuil, 1977), p.492
9. *Lettre à Léon Blum* (Archives L. Blum FNSP, February 1943)
10. Gilberte Brossolette, *Il s'appelait Pierre Brossolette*, p.193
11. *Ibid.*, p.194
12. Interview with the author, July 1983
13. Interview with the author, December 1983
14. H. Noguères, *Histoire de la Résistance en France*, p.291
15. *Revue de la France libre*, November 1983, p.10
16. *Mémoires de guerre*, II, p.474
17. Report to André Philip, quoted in H. Noguères's *Histoire de la Résistance en France*, Vol. III, p.400–2
18. Interview with the author, 1965
19. Interview with the author, June 1983
20. Interview with the author, June 1983
21. *Histoire de la Résistance en France*, III, p.438–61
22. Interview with the author, June 1983
23. *Il s'appelait Pierre Brossolette*, p.214
24. *Revue d'histoire de la Deuxième Guerre mondiale* (October 1962)
25. Interview with the author, November 1983
26. E. d'Astier de la Vigerie, *Sept Fois sept jours* (Paris, Editions de Minuit, 1947) p.80–1
27. Interview with the author, July 1983
28. Interview with the author, November 1983
29. Interview with the author, November 1983
30. Gabrielle Ferrières, *Jean Cavaillès* (Paris, Le Seuil, 1982), p.183
31. *Lettres, Notes . . .*, IV, p.64–5
32. Letters from Jacques Bingen, communicated by Jeanine Raynaud, to whom I express my sincere gratitude

CHAPTER THIRTY-FIVE

1. *Envers et contre tout*, II, p.264–5
2. *Ibid.*, p.264
3. *Mémoires de guerre*, II, p.172
4. *Lettres, Notes . . .*, IV, p.97
5. *Sept Fois sept jours*, p.138
6. *Victoires sur la nuit*, p.189
7. Interview with the author, June 1980
8. *Mémoires de guerre*, II, p.188
9. Interview with the author, 1976
10. Interview with the author, June 1983
11. *Mémoires de guerre*, II, p.598
12. *Lettres, Notes . . .*, IV, p.107
13. *Mémoires de guerre*, II, p.219
14. *Ibid.*, p.595
15. *The Blast of War*, p.446–8
16. *Mémoires de guerre*, II, p.116
17. *Ibid.*, p.616
18. *Churchill and de Gaulle*, p.318
19. H. Alphand, *L'Etonnement d'être*, p.167
20. *Churchill and de Gaulle*, p.319
21. *Mémoires de guerre*, II, p.606
22. *Ibid.*, p.608
23. The author's interview with Pierre Billotte, June 1964
24. *Morgenthau Diaries* (New York, Truffel, 1970), p.168
25. *L'étonnement d'être*, p.173
26. Quoted in J.-B. Duroselle, *L'Abîme*, p.493
27. Henry Stimson and MacGeorge Bundy, *On Active Service in Peace and War* (Hutchinson, 1949), p.312
28. *L'Etonnement d'être*, p.174
29. *Discours et Messages*, I, p.121
30. Quoted by Eric Branca, Nice Colloquy, January 1983
31. Nice Colloquy, introduction
32. Interview with the author, June 1983
33. *Discours et Messages*, I, p.373
34. Letter to the author, 9 December 1983
35. Letter to the author, 20 November 1983
36. Quoted by E. Branca, Nice Colloquy
37. H. Amouroux, *La Vie des Français sous l'occupation* (Paris, Fayard 1983) V
38. *Discours et Messages*, I, p.318
39. J.-P. Azéma, *De Munich à la Libération* (Paris, Le Seuil 1979), p.309
40. *Mémoires de guerre*, II, p.179
41. *Ibid.*, p.179
42. *Victoires sur la nuit*, p.136
43. Interview with the author, 1971
44. *Victoires sur la nuit*, p.151
45. *Lettres, Notes . . .*, IV, p.138
46. *Victoires sur la nuit*, p.179–80

47. *Mémoires de guerre*, II, p.639

CHAPTER THIRTY-SIX

1. *Mémoires de guerre*, II, p.626
2. *Churchill and de Gaulle*, p.324
3. *Lettres, Notes . . .*, IV. p.193
4. *Mémoires de guerre*, Vol. II, p.640
5. *Ibid.*, p.694
6. Eden, *Memoirs*, II, p.452
7. *Mémoires de guerre*, II, p.223
8. Béthouart, *Cinq Années d'espérance*, p.240
9. *Mémoires de guerre*, II, p.223–4
10. *Ibid.*, p.224
11. *Cinq Années d'espérance*, p.243
12. *Lettres, Notes . . .*, IV, p.229
13. *Churchill and de Gaulle*, p.346
14. André Gillois, *Histoire secrète des Français à Londres* (Paris, Le Cercle du nouveau livre, 1973), p.23
15. Colloquy on the liberation of France, J.-L. Crémieux-Brilhac, Paris, 1974, p.20
16. *Discours et Messages*, I, p.407
17. *Lettres, Notes . . .*, IV, p.233
18. *Churchill and de Gaulle*, p.354
19. *Mémoires de guerre*, II, p.228
20. *Churchill and de Gaulle*, p.352 (note)

CHAPTER THIRTY-SEVEN

1. *Victoires sur la nuit*, p.147
2. *Cinq Années d'espérance*, p.249
3. Rémy, *Dix ans avec de Gaulle* (Paris, France-Empire, 1971), p.146
4. *Mémoires de guerre*, II, p.231
5. Interview with the author, May 1984
6. *Mémoires de guerre*, II, p.231
7. *Ibid.*, p.689
8. *Envers et contre tout*, II, p.373
9. *Histoire de la Résistance en France*, p.147

CHAPTER THIRTY-EIGHT

1. *Churchill and de Gaulle*, p.361
2. *Mémoires de guerre*, II, p.648–9
3. *Ibid.*, p.651
4. *Lettres, Notes . . .*, IV, p.257–9
5. *L'Etonnement d'être*, p. 179
6. *Mémoires de guerre*, II, p.237
7. *Ibid.*, p.237–40
8. *Ibid.*, p.240
9. *Ibid.*, p.241
10. Interview with the author, 1971
11. Interview with the author, 1964
12. *Lettres, Notes . . .*, IV, p.261–2
13. J. Lacouture, *Pierre Mendès France* (Paris, Le Seuil, 1981), p.160
14. *Mémoires de guerre*, II, p.655
15. Interview with the author, June 1980
16. *Lettres, Notes . . .*, IV, p.262–3
17. Interview with Léo Teyssot, June 1964
18. Interview with the author, April 1983
19. *Victoires sur la nuit*, p.150

CHAPTER THIRTY-NINE

1. *Lettres, Notes . . .*, IV, p.275
2. *Discours et Messages*, I, p.437
3. Interview with Georges Buis (who was one of them), September 1983
4. *Mémoires de guerre*, II, p.697
5. *Ibid.*, p.291–3
6. *Lettres, Notes . . .*, IV, p.289
7. *Ibid.*, p.291–2
8. *Mémoires de guerre*, II, p.291–2
9. Interview with the author, June 1983
10. *Envers et contre tout*, II, p.423–30
11. Colloquy on the liberation of France, p.413
12. *Ibid.*
13. Interview with the author, November 1983
14. *Mémoires de guerre*, II, p.701
15. *Envers et contre tout*, II, p.483
16. *L'Abîme*, p.469
17. *Mémoires de guerre*, II, p.290
18. *Lettres, Notes . . .*, IV, p.277
19. *Envers et contre tout*, II, p.409
20. A. Prévost, *Le Peuple impopulaire*, Paris, Le Seuil, 1956
21. Interview with the author, February 1984

CHAPTER FORTY

1. *L'Abîme*, p.472
2. *Mémoires de guerre*, II, p.296
3. *Ibid.*, p.297
4. *Ibid.*, p.297
5. *Ibid.*, p.703
6. *Ibid.*, p.705
7. Interviews with Léo Hamon (March 1984) and Jacques Chaban-Delmas (September 1983)
8. Maurice Kriegel-Valrimont, *La Libération* (Paris, Editions de Minuit, 1964), p.194

9. Interview with François Bloch-Lainé, January 1984
10. Interview with Claire Morandat, November 1983
11. *Le Monde*, 25–26 August, 1969
12. Interview with Michel Debré, February 1984
13. *Mémoires de guerre*, II. p.303
14. *Ibid.*, p.303
15. *Victoires sur la nuit*, p.238
16. Interview with the author, February 1984
17. D. Lapierre and L. Collins, *Paris brûle-t-il?* (Paris, Laffont, 1964)
18. *Mémoires de guerre*, II, p.708
19. *Ibid.*, p.709
20. Interview with Jacques Chaban-Delmas, September 1983
21. *Mémoires de guerre*, II, p.306
22. Robert Aron, *Histoire de la libération de la France* (Paris, Fayard, 1959), p.441
23. *Mémoires de guerre*, II, p.308
24. E. Pisani, *Le Général indivis* (Paris, Albin Michel), p.20
25. Léo Hamon, interview with the author, March 1984
26. François Bloch-Lainé, *Profession: fonctionnaire* (Paris, Le Seuil, 1976), p.67–8
27. E. Michelet, *La querelle de la fidélité* (Paris, Fayard, 1971), p.70
28. R. Aron, *Histoire de la libération de la France*, p.57
29. Interview with Daniel Mayer, June 1983
30. 4 September 1944
31. *Mémoires de guerre*, II, p.311–12

INDEX